Debating Terrorism and Counterterrorism

Debating Terrorism and Counterterrorism

CONFLICTING PERSPECTIVES ON CAUSES, CONTEXTS, AND RESPONSES

STUART GOTTLIEB, EDITOR

Yale University

CQ PRESS

A Division of SAGE
Washington, D.C.

CQ Press
2300 N Street, NW, Suite 800
Washington, DC 20037

Phone: 202-729-1900; toll-free, 1-866-4CQ-PRESS (1-866-427-7737)

Web: www.cqpress.com

Cover design: Matthew Simmons
Cover photos: © Patrick Robert/Sygma/Corbis
Composition: C&M Digitals (P) Ltd.

♾ The paper used in this publication exceeds the requirements of the American National Standard for Information Sciences—Permanence of Paper for Printed Library Materials, ANSI Z39.48-1992.

Printed and bound in the United States of America

13   12   11   10   09   1   2   3   4   5

Library of Congress Cataloging-in-Publication Data

Debating terrorism and counterterrorism : conflicting perspectives on causes, contexts, and responses/ Stuart Gottlieb, editor.
    p. cm.
  Includes bibliographical references.
  ISBN 978-0-87289-961-2 (paperbound : alk. paper) 1. Terrorism. 2. Terrorism—Prevention. I. Gottlieb, Stuart. II. Title.

HV6431.D4335 2010
363.325—dc22

2009037174

CONTENTS

FOREWORD

FIRST . . . CORRECTLY IDENTIFY THE ENEMY . . .

The week after the historic 2008 U.S. presidential election, the French newspaper *Le Monde* featured a cartoon of Barack Obama surfing on a wave of red, white, and blue with the excited caption "Happy New Century!"

In his inaugural address, however, President Obama saw a perilous landscape in "this winter of our hardship," where "everywhere we look, there is work to be done."

Having inherited a long and difficult to-do list, President Obama called for a "change of the mindset that ignores long-term threats and engages in the sorts of actions that are not making us safe over the long term."

Obama's exhortation was certainly justified. Yet it does as much to keep open central questions about the nature of modern threats and how to react as it does to settle them.

This volume provides a timely and important overview of the central debates about one crucial item on the security agenda: the nature of terrorist threats and how to respond to them. The fact that these basic questions remain the subject of fierce disagreement inside and outside of government is suggestive of the complexity of the challenge in conceptualizing and effectively countering terrorism. This volume treats this complexity with sophistication and comprehension, capturing the variety and scope of expert and scholarly opinion as well as the intensity of disagreement.

The great military theorist, Carl von Clausewitz, offered a good starting point for analysis of all kinds of conflict, including terrorism, when he wrote: "The supreme, the most far-reaching act of judgment that the statesman and commander must make is to establish . . . the kind of war on which they are embarking; neither mistaking it for, nor trying to turn it into, something that is alien to its nature." In sum: *know your enemy*.

The hand the United States was dealt on September 11, 2001, was a difficult one, and efforts to come to terms with the new and profound threat were bound to be imperfect. Nonetheless, shortcomings in America's initial responses to al-Qaeda offer timeless lessons.

In 1941 Japan attacked the U.S. naval base at Pearl Harbor, Hawaii, killing 2,402 Americans. Less than twenty-four hours thereafter, in his address to Congress, President Franklin D. Roosevelt requested that it declare a state of war in response to what he called "the unprovoked and dastardly attack by Japan." President Roosevelt promised to defeat Imperial Japan and to "make it very certain that this form of treachery shall never again endanger us." Congress passed the war resolution. Three years and nine months after that "day of infamy," the Japanese surrendered unconditionally.

Analogies are not identical, but they can be instructive. Imagine that in the aftermath of Japan's attack on Pearl Harbor, Franklin Roosevelt declared war not only on Japan and its Nazi ally, but also on Joseph Stalin's Soviet Union. The result would almost certainly have been defeat for the United States in World War II.

In the case of the Bush administration's post-9/11 policy toward Iraq, understandable concerns about a possible nexus between state weapons of mass destruction programs and terrorist groups like al-Qaeda provided the rationale for the 2003 U.S.-led war. But in ultimately conflating the war against the terrorists who attacked the United States on 9/11 and Saddam Hussein's Iraq, President George W. Bush and key members of his administration failed to heed Clausewitz's advice. Operationally, the shift in focus from al-Qaeda to Iraq meant moving scarce resources, particularly predator drones, intelligence assets, and special operations forces with the relevant language skills, to Iraq before al-Qaeda's leadership was eliminated. Conceptually, this shift led to confusion within and between successive layers of government as they attempted to develop strategy and rationales for what were in fact two distinct and fundamentally different undertakings.

Indeed, when initially faced with the decision to define the enemy narrowly as the terrorists who attacked us on 9/11 and their affiliates, on the one hand, or as terrorism writ large, on the other, the Bush administration chose the latter. Conflating disparate threats—al-Qaeda versus Hamas, for example—into a single, undifferentiated enemy undermined efforts to devise an effective strategy for the war.

What have been the results? An April 2006 National Intelligence Estimate (NIE) on global terrorism stated that the Iraq War had become a "cause célèbre for jihadists." A subsequent NIE concluded that al-Qaeda "has regenerated key elements of its homeland attack capability including: a safe haven in Pakistan, operational lieutenants and its top leadership," and "continues to plan high-impact attacks" with "visually dramatic destruction." In the fall of 2008, the director of the Central Intelligence Agency, Michael Hayden, reiterated this assessment, stating that "al-Qaeda . . . remains the most clear and present danger to the safety of the United States," and predicting that "if there is a major strike against this country, it will bear the fingerprints of al-Qaeda." To this day, Osama bin Laden and his deputy Ayman al-Zawahiri continue to operate just hundreds of miles from their pre-9/11 headquarters, issuing scores of audio and video messages, receiving visitors, and training thousands of new terrorists.

And what of the threat of nuclear terrorism, which President Bush defined as "the single most serious threat to the national security of the United States"? In December 2008, the bipartisan Commission on the Prevention of WMD Proliferation and Terrorism offered its unambiguous assessment: "Our margin of safety is *shrinking*, not growing." As former senator Sam Nunn testified to the commission, "The threat of a successful nuclear terrorist attack today is greater than it was on 9/11."

Strategic planning in the United States starts with the president's conception of the threat and nature of the challenge. From that starting point, national and departmental strategies are developed. When initial conceptions of the enemy are flawed, the policies that follow will be similarly confused: objectives will be inflated and imprecise, resources will be misallocated, and the scope of the response, both geographic and moral, will be diffused.

None of this is to imply that terrorism is not a daunting challenge—as President Obama has no doubt discovered since becoming president. Terrorist groups have many potential motivations and goals, ranging from limited territorial gains to global millennial war, and a variety of lethal tactics that may be employed to try to achieve those goals. Successfully combating this phenomenon requires not simply effective military, law enforcement, and homeland security measures. Most important, it requires, as a necessary prerequisite, *knowing the enemy*: what makes it tick, what comprises its support base, what are its vulnerabilities. As the individual essays in this book demonstrate, there exists a range of reasonable opinions on and approaches to this phenomenon, some of which are in diametric opposition. Encouraging this debate and probing the grounds of differing opinions will make us all smarter.

Graham Allison
Douglas Dillon Professor of Government
Director, Belfer Center for Science and International Affairs
Harvard University

CONTRIBUTORS

Max Abrahms

Max Abrahms is a postdoctoral fellow at the Center for International Security and Cooperation at Stanford University and on the Empirical Studies of Conflict Project sponsored by Princeton University and the U.S. Military Academy at West Point. His research focuses on terrorist outcomes and effectiveness and counterterrorism strategy. He has published on these topics in the journals *International Security, Security Studies, Studies in Conflict and Terrorism*, and *Terrorism and Political Violence* and in several edited volumes. He has been a lecturer at Johns Hopkins University, a research associate at Harvard University's Belfer Center for Science and International Affairs, a fellow at the Moshe Dayan Center at Tel Aviv University, a fellow at the Washington Institute for Near East Policy, and a commissioned op-ed writer on terrorism for the *Los Angeles Times*.

Matthew Bunn

Matthew Bunn is an associate professor at Harvard University's John F. Kennedy School of Government, and one of the principal investigators for Harvard's Project on Managing the Atom. His research interests include nuclear theft and terrorism, nuclear proliferation and measures to control it, and the future of nuclear energy and its fuel cycle. Before coming to Harvard, he served as an adviser to the White House Office of Science and Technology Policy, as a study director at the National Academy of Sciences/National Research Council, and as editor of *Arms Control Today*. He is the author or co-author of some eighteen books or major technical reports (most recently *Securing the Bomb 2008)* and over a hundred articles in publications ranging from *Science* to the *Washington Post*.

David Cole

David Cole is a law professor at Georgetown University Law Center, the legal affairs correspondent for *The Nation*, and a frequent contributor to the *New York Review of Books*. He is author of several books, most recently *Justice at*

War: The Men and Ideas That Shaped America's "War on Terror" (2008) and *The Torture Memos: Rationalizing the Unthinkable* (2009).

Alan M. Dershowitz

Alan M. Dershowitz is Felix Frankfurter Professor of Law, Harvard Law School. One of the world's best-known criminal and civil liberties lawyers, he has published more than one hundred articles in magazines, newspapers, and journals, including the *New York Times Magazine, Washington Post, Wall Street Journal, New Republic, The Nation, Commentary, Saturday Review, Harvard Law Review,* and *Yale Law Journal.* He is the author of nearly thirty works of fiction and nonfiction, most recently *Rights from Wrong; The Case for Israel; The Case for Peace; Blasphemy: How the Religious Right Is Hijacking the Declaration of Independence; Why Terrorism Works; Preemption: A Knife That Cuts Both Ways;* and *The First Amendment in an Age of Terrorism.* He has been honored by the New York Criminal Bar Association for his "outstanding contribution as a scholar and dedicated defender of human rights."

Lindsay Fritz

Lindsay Fritz is a research associate with the Department of Defense Analysis, Naval Postgraduate School, Monterey, California. She has studied at Tulane University, the Monterey Institute for International Studies, and the University of Hamburg.

F. Gregory Gause III

F. Gregory Gause III is professor of political science at the University of Vermont. During 2009–2010, he was also the Kuwait Foundation Visiting Professor of International Politics at the John F. Kennedy School of Government, Harvard University. His most recent book is *The International Relations of the Persian Gulf* (2010).

Fawaz A. Gerges

Fawaz A. Gerges is professor of Middle Eastern politics and international relations at the London School of Economics. Formerly, he held the Christian A. Johnson Chair in Middle Eastern Studies and International Affairs at Sarah Lawrence. His articles and commentary have appeared in many venues, including *Foreign Affairs, Foreign Policy, National Interest, Democracy, Survival, New York Times, Washington Post, Los Angeles Times, Christian Science Monitor, The Independent, The Guardian, CNN, Al Jazeera,* and *Al Hayat.* He is the author of, most recently, *The Far Enemy: Why Jihad Went Global* and *Journey of the Jihadist: Inside Muslim Militancy.* He is writing a new book tentatively titled *Genealogy of Revolutionary Islamism: Sayyid Qutb and His Disciples.* He has spent several years conducting field research and interviews with dissidents, activists, clerics, and civil society leaders in the Muslim world, and recently returned from a fifteen-month sabbatical as a Carnegie Scholar in the Greater Middle East region.

Rohan Gunaratna

Rohan Gunaratna is head of the International Centre for Political Violence and Terrorism Research and professor of security studies at the S. Rajaratnam School of International Studies at Nanyang Technological University in Singapore. He has more than twenty-five years of academic, policy, and operational experience in the fields of terrorism and counterterrorism. Author of twelve books, including *Inside Al Qaeda* (2003), he serves on the editorial boards of *Terrorism and Political Violence* and *Studies in Conflict and Terrorism*, the two leading academic journals in the field. Gunaratna has debriefed detainees in Asia, the Middle East (including Iraq), Europe, Australia, and North America, and testified as the U.S. government expert in the Jose Padilla trial. He was invited to testify before the 9/11 Commission.

Ted Honderich

Ted Honderich is one of Great Britain's best-known and most prolific political philosophers. He has been the Grote Professor of the Philosophy of Mind and Logic at University College London and visiting professor at Yale University and the City University of New York, and he is now visiting professor at the University of Bath. Among many other books and dozens of articles, he is author of *How Free Are You? The Determinism Problem* (1993, 2002); *A Theory of Determinism: The Mind, Neuroscience and Life-Hopes* (1998); *The Oxford Companion to Philosophy* (2005); *Humanity, Terrorism, Terrorist War: Palestine, 9/11, Iraq, 7/7* (2006); and *Philosopher: A Kind of Life* (2001). His 2003 book *After the Terror* sparked controversy in Germany and elsewhere for its moral defense of Palestinian terrorism against Israel.

Walter Laqueur

Walter Laqueur is one of the world's foremost authorities on political violence and terrorism. Over a long and distinguished career, he has been director of the Institute of Contemporary History in London, founding editor of the *Journal of Contemporary History*, chairman of the International Research Council of the Washington-based Center for Strategic and International Studies, and founding editor of the *Washington Quarterly*. Author of countless articles, he has also written more than twenty books, including *Guerilla* (1976), *Terrorism* (1977), *The Age of Terrorism* (1987), and, most recently, *Voices of Terror* (2004), *The Last Days of Europe* (2007), and *Best of Times, Worst of Times* (2009).

Susan B. Martin

Susan B. Martin is a lecturer in the Department of War Studies at King's College London, where she is also affiliated with the Centre for Science and Security Studies. Her research focuses on a neorealist explanation of the role of chemical, biological, and nuclear weapons in international politics. She is a co-editor of *Terrorism, War or Disease: Unravelling the Use of Biological Weapons* (2008). Her work has appeared in *International Security*, *Journal of Strategic Studies*, as well as various edited volumes.

Andrew C. McCarthy

Andrew C. McCarthy is a senior fellow at the National Review Institute and a contributing editor to *National Review*. He formerly served as assistant United States attorney for the Southern District of New York, where he led the prosecution against the mastermind of the 1993 World Trade Center bombing, Sheikh Omar Abdel Rahman. McCarthy is the recipient of the U.S. Justice Department's highest honors: the Distinguished Service Award (1988) and the Attorney General's Exceptional Service Award (1996). His most recent book is *Willful Blindness: Memoir of the Jihad* (2008).

Gordon H. McCormick

Gordon H. McCormick is professor and founding chairman of the Department of Defense Analysis, Naval Postgraduate School, Monterey, California. He was formerly a senior social scientist with the RAND Corporation and has taught at the University of Pennsylvania, Johns Hopkins University, and the University of North Carolina, Chapel Hill. His interests lie in the areas of international politics, mathematics, and classical History and philosophy.

Tamar Meisels

Tamar Meisels is a senior lecturer in political theory at Tel Aviv University in Israel. Her primary research interests are liberal nationalism, territorial rights, and the philosophical perspectives on war and terrorism. She is the author of *Territorial Rights* (2005, 2009), *The Trouble with Terror* (2008), as well as various articles on related topics. During 2009–2010, she served as the visiting Goldman Professor at Georgetown University's Government Department.

John Mueller

John Mueller holds the Woody Hayes Chair of National Security Studies, Mershon Center, and is professor of political science at Ohio State University. He is currently working on terrorism, and particularly on the reactions (or overreactions) it often inspires. His book on the subject, *Overblown: How*

Politicians and the Terrorism Industry Inflate National Security Threats, and Why We Believe Them, was published in 2006, and his next book, *Atomic Obsession: Nuclear Alarmism from Hiroshima to Al Qaeda*, was published in late 2009. His book on international and civil warfare, *The Remnants of War*, was awarded the Lepgold Prize for the best book on international relations in 2004.

Brigitte L. Nacos

Brigitte L. Nacos has taught for more than fifteen years at Columbia University, following a career as a newspaper correspondent. Her research and teaching interests are the links between the media, public opinion, and decision making, and domestic and international terrorism and counterterrorism. She has published many articles and book chapters as well as eight books, among them *Terrorism and the Media* (1994, 1996), *Mass-Mediated Terrorism* (2002), and *Terrorism and Counterterrorism* (2006).

James A. Piazza

James A. Piazza is an associate professor of political science at the University of North Carolina at Charlotte. His research examines the root causes of terrorism, terrorism and human rights, terrorism and failed states, and the causes of suicide terrorism. His work has appeared in the *Journal of Politics, International Studies Quarterly, Comparative Political Studies, Terrorism and Political Violence*, and *Studies in Conflict and Terrorism*.

Michael H. Posner

Michael H. Posner is assistant secretary of state for democracy, human rights, and labor—the country's chief human rights official. Before entering government service, he was president of Human Rights First and served as its executive director from its founding in 1978 until 2006. A frequent commentator in newspapers across the country, he has testified dozens of times before Congress on a range of human rights issues and is a frequent speaker at conferences in the United States and abroad. From 1984 to 2009, he served as a lecturer at Columbia Law School, and he was Yale Law School's 2009 Bernstein Distinguished Human Rights Senior Fellow.

Eric Rosand

Eric Rosand is a senior fellow and co-director of the Center on Global Counterterrorism Cooperation and a nonresident fellow at New York University's Center on International Cooperation. Earlier, he worked for nine years at the U.S. Department of State on, among other things, multilateral counterterrorism issues. He has published numerous articles and book chapters and lectured widely on strengthening international and regional cooperation to combat terrorism. His most recent article is "Combating WMD Terrorism: The Short-Sighted US-led Multilateral Response," published in *The International Spectator* (March 2009).

Michael Rubin

Michael Rubin is a resident scholar at the American Enterprise Institute and a senior lecturer at the Naval Postgraduate School, Monterey, California, where he teaches regional issues and strategy to U.S. military units deploying to Iraq and Afghanistan. From 2004 and 2009, he edited the *Middle East Quarterly*, and from 2002 and 2004 he was an adviser for Iran and Iraq in the Office of the Secretary of Defense and at the Coalition Provisional Authority in Baghdad. He has also taught at Yale University, Hebrew University in Jerusalem, and three universities in Iraqi Kurdistan. He is author of two books about Iran and was drafter of the Bipartisan Policy Center's 2008 report *Meeting the Challenge: U.S. Policy toward Iranian Nuclear Development*. He is completing a study of engagement with rogue regimes, *Talking to the Enemy: The Promise and Perils of Engagement*.

Zachary C. Shirkey

Zachary C. Shirkey is assistant professor of political science at St. John Fisher College. His research focuses on the causes of war, deterrence and balancing, conflict resolution, and terrorism. His recent book *Is This a Private Fight or Can Anybody Join?* (2009) explores the role that revealed information plays in why and when states join ongoing wars.

Alexander Spencer

Alexander Spencer is assistant professor in global governance and public policy at the Ludwig-Maximilians University in Munich. His research centers on the potential of constructivist international relations theory for the field of terrorism research. His most recent publication, with Rainer Hülsse, is "The Metaphor of Terror: Terrorism Studies and the Constructivist Turn" which appeared in *Security Dialogue* (December 2008). His book *The Tabloid Terrorist: The Predictive Construction of "New Terrorism" in the Media* will be published in 2010.

Karin von Hippel

Karin von Hippel is co-director of the Post-Conflict Reconstruction Project and a senior fellow with the International Security Program at the Center for Strategic and International Studies in Washington, D.C. Previously, she was a senior research fellow at the Centre for Defence Studies, King's College London, and spent several years working for the United Nations and the European Union in Somalia and Kosovo. In 2002 she advised the Organisation for Economic Co-operation and Development on the role of development cooperation in discovering the root causes of terrorism. Her publications include *Democracy by Force* (2000) and the edited volume *Europe Confronts Terrorism* (2005), as well as many other works on counterterrorism and development.

Jennifer L. Windsor

Jennifer L. Windsor has served since 2001 as executive director of Freedom House, a nonpartisan, nonprofit organization that supports the expansion of freedom in the world. From 1991 to 2001, she worked at the U.S. Agency for International Development, in roles that included deputy assistant administrator and director of the Center for Democracy and Governance. Earlier, she worked on Capitol Hill on foreign policy issues with Sen. Daniel Patrick Moynihan and Rep. Ted Weiss. She has written numerous articles on democracy and governance.

John Yoo

John Yoo is professor of law at the University of California at Berkeley School of Law and a visiting scholar at the American Enterprise Institute. From 2001 to 2003, he served as a deputy assistant attorney general in the Office of Legal Counsel in the U.S. Department of Justice, where he participated in the development of counterterrorism policy in the wake of the 9/11 attacks. He has published more than seventy scholarly articles on foreign affairs, national security, and constitutional law in some of the nation's leading law journals. His work has also appeared on the editorial pages of the *Wall Street Journal, New York Times, Washington Post,* and *Los Angeles Times.* He is the author of *The Powers of War and Peace* (2005) and *War by Other Means* (2006), and is currently finishing a book on the history of presidential power.

PREFACE

In many ways this book is an outgrowth of the crash of United Airlines Flight 175 into the south tower of New York City's World Trade Center at 9:03 a.m. on September 11, 2001. Seventeen minutes earlier, American Airlines Flight 11 had crashed into the World Trade Center's north tower. Even though the initial Flight 11 crash and subsequent collapse of the north tower would alone have been the deadliest terrorist attack in world history, the vast and skilled coordination shown by the al-Qaeda organization with its follow-on airliner attacks against the south tower and the Pentagon, and the failed attack against the U.S. Capitol, instantly, radically, and perhaps permanently transformed global perceptions of terrorism and counterterrorism.

Since the events of 9/11, a tremendous amount of global activity has, of course, surrounded terrorism in terms of both terrorist incidents and government responses. The United States has been at the forefront of recent counterterrorism efforts—Washington has spent many hundreds of billions of dollars since 2001 on new Pentagon priorities, homeland security initiatives, and increased counterterrorism-related activities around the world, including two ongoing wars in Iraq and Afghanistan. But the United States is certainly not alone. Terrorism, whether ethno-religious, territorial, or ideologically based, remains a top security and policy priority from western Europe to western China; from South America to South, Central, and Southeastern Asia; and from northern and eastern Africa to the Middle East and Persian Gulf.

And yet, even though the world is currently living through what can fairly be described as an unprecedented era of terrorism, the fact is that terrorism as a form of political violence is as old as civilization itself. While much raised in its profile (and its purported lethality) by the 9/11 attacks, terrorism itself has not been transformed as a human social phenomenon. It will continue to be used by those around the world who choose violence as a means of redressing grievances and challenging established orders.

Along with the upsurge in global terrorism and counterterrorism activity since 9/11, there has been a tremendous amount of intellectual (and not-so-intellectual) discourse on the topic within and among academic, public policy, and think-tank communities, and across the spectrum of media. Whether

measured by quantities of spilt ink or decibel levels, these debates can be ener-
vating, difficult to navigate, hugely partisan, and simply overwhelming.

The purpose of this book is straightforward: to isolate, engage, and enrich
debates on the most important contemporary terrorism and counterterrorism
issues. To accomplish this goal, leading authorities from policy, academic, and
think-tank communities were invited to write timely and original essays that
juxtapose pro and con arguments on hotly contested topics of clear importance to understanding the past, present, and future of terrorism and counterterrorism.

This book's contributors benefited, as will its readers, from the evolving
hindsight of the last eight-plus years. The intense flurry of counterterrorism-
related activity that defined the months and years after 9/11 has since become
more settled, thereby giving the authors a unique opportunity to pause, reflect,
and carefully analyze what the 9/11 attacks and the al-Qaeda organization have
meant (or not meant) in the context of the broader history of terrorism and
age-old questions related to terrorism.

This book also benefited from the change in U.S. presidential administrations in 2009. The transition from Republican president George W. Bush, who
had declared "war on terrorism," to Democrat Barack Obama, who has moved
away from the hard-line rhetoric of his predecessor while maintaining most of
his hard-line counterterrorism policies, has helped to illuminate the consisten-
cies in perceptions of the present threat and the ongoing challenges facing
those who must address it.

Each of the twelve issues selected for debate in this book—six on terrorism
and six on counterterrorism—are presented as questions on which thoughtful
people differ. Few subjects in the realms of policy, academia, and public discourse evoke as much passion and emotion as terrorism and the issues that
surround it. This book does not pose straw man questions. Nor does it shy
away from any controversial topics. Instead, it addresses these thorny problems
head-on, firm in the belief that an open discussion aimed at bridging understanding of the different perspectives is the best recipe for making proper sense
of the challenges arising from terrorism and fashioning the most prudent and
effective responses.

ORGANIZATION OF THIS BOOK

The book is organized as follows. Each of the six chapters in Part 1, "Debating
Terrorism," addresses a vital question related to the threat of terrorism in a way
meant to both evoke and illuminate. The comprehensive headnote at the beginning of each chapter introduces the nature of the controversy surrounding the

topic and summarizes the two authors' forthcoming arguments. The following topics are debated in Part 1:

- the nature of terrorist organizations, looking specifically at how al-Qaeda and other contemporary groups fit into the historical evolution of terrorism
- whether poverty and socioeconomic underdevelopment are possible root causes of terrorism
- whether and how terrorist violence can ever be justified
- the role played by religion—particularly radical Islam—in the modern wave of global terrorism
- whether suicide terrorism is an effective strategy to advance political goals
- the likelihood that the nightmare of nuclear terrorism will become a reality.

The six chapters in Part 2, "Debating Counterterrorism," focus on the central counterterrorism questions of the day:

- whether diplomatic or military strategies should serve as the foundation of counterterrorism strategies
- whether promoting democracy in the Arab and Muslim world can help combat terrorism
- what role, if any, the United Nations and other international institutions can effectively play in fighting terrorism
- whether an outright ban is the best way to address the practice of torture in counterterrorism intelligence operations
- whether trade-offs with civil liberties are necessary to protect national security in an age of terrorism
- whether the threat of terrorism is being overstated, and what that may mean for the future of terrorism and counterterrorism.

Although the authors of the twenty-four essays in this volume may disagree on many things, we can all agree that terrorism will remain an important global challenge—both in terms of addressing its causes and in terms of reducing its effects—long after the 9/11 attacks fade from memory. The policy and intellectual activity of the last eight years has opened an important door to increasing our collective understanding of terrorism—not just that of yesterday and today, but also that of tomorrow. By isolating the important questions and encouraging open and rigorous debate, this book hopes to seize the moment and contribute knowledge of and insights into one of the world's most enduring, complex, and high-stakes challenges.

ACKNOWLEGMENTS

For me, this book has been a tremendous undertaking, stretching over several years. It also has been a fulfilling personal and professional achievement.

Such a project cannot possibly come together without the invaluable assistance of many special people. Brigitte L. Nacos at Columbia University and Zachary C. Shirkey at St. John Fisher College both selflessly assisted me with the initial conceptual development, as well as ideas for debate topics and prospective authors. I thank them for this, and for contributing excellent essays to the book. Erica Chenoweth at Wesleyan University provided helpful advice (and some important editing) along the way, and served as a crucial sounding board as I wrestled with the many controversial issues and topics broached in the pages ahead. Eric Lorber at Duke University assisted all along the way with research support, editing, and creative ideas. And Rachel Yemini at the U.S. Senate and Ahmed Salim at Columbia University provided valuable reviews of draft chapters and chapter headnotes. Early reviewers of the proposal for this volume provided excellent advice and criticism. My thanks to: Gardel Feurtado, The Citadel; George A. Lopez, Notre Dame; Susan Sample, University of the Pacific; and Ronald Vardy, University of Houston.

Many of our authors are busy professionals who rely heavily on outstanding assistants to manage correspondence and ensure deadlines are met. Among these, I would like to offer special thanks to Emily Stanfield, Sarah Neely, and Elizabeth Ong. The Macmillan Center for International and Area Studies at Yale University provided financial assistance, for which I am very grateful.

Finally, this book would not exist without the outstanding work of the professionals (in every sense of the word) at CQ Press. Special thanks go to Charisse Kiino, Elise Frasier, Allyson Rudolph, and freelance editor Sabra Bissette Ledent. You made this project both enriching and far more enjoyable than it had any right to be.

Debating Terrorism and Counterterrorism

is the "new terrorism" really new?

NO: The "new terrorism" of al-Qaeda is not so new
Alexander Spencer, *Ludwig-Maximilians University, Munich*

YES: Al-Qaeda is an example of a "new terrorism"
Rohan Gunaratna, *Nanyang Technological University, Singapore*

Terrorism is an age-old phenomenon, extending as far back as human records take us. Although scholars and practitioners will likely never agree on a definition of *terrorism* (including many of the authors in this volume), at its core *terrorism* is the use of violence against noncombatants for political purposes.[1]

A primary challenge to developing a firm definition of *terrorism,* aside from the inherent subjectivity of the act itself, is that the term has evolved over time. In the 1790s, Robespierre employed the first modern usage of the word *terrorism* to describe his regime's coercive efforts to protect post-revolutionary France from counterrevolutionaries.[2] Yet since the mid-nineteenth century, the term has been used most often to describe organized substate violence against established political orders—monarchies, colonial powers, national governments—for purposes ranging from national liberation (the Stern Gang in Palestine is one example), to territorial succession (the Basque separatist group ETA in Spain), to ideological revolution (the Revolutionary Armed Forces of Colombia). For many terrorism analysts, such groups and their motivations fall under the rubric of what is often called "traditional terrorism."

Beginning in the late 1960s with the hostage takings, skyjackings, and random out-of-area attacks by Palestine Liberation Organization (PLO)–affiliated groups, terrorism assumed a decidedly more international flavor. However, underlying grievances and motivations remained primarily local and territorial, and the violence utilized was often tempered by the need for groups to maintain organizational legitimacy and credibility as players in a possible future negotiated settlement. In this sense, the global terrorism sparked by the PLO had much in common with traditional terrorism.

Some terrorism experts believe that the 1990s witnessed the rise of a unique brand of terrorism—often referred to as "new terrorism."[3] This new incarnation is said to consist of groups with explicitly religious motivations, maximalist demands, and a commitment to inflicting mass casualties, potentially through the use of weapons of mass destruction. Such groups are further segregated from prior forms of terrorism by their purported ability to operate as independent global actors free from direct reliance on states.

Although the new terrorism was flagged as an emerging national security challenge years before the attacks on the United States on September 11, 2001, those attacks, and the al-Qaeda organization that perpetrated them, gave instant credibility to the notion of the coming-of-age of a new and more destructive form of terrorism. In response, the United States and other nations have recalibrated their assessments of the nature and threat of terrorism and altered their counterterrorism strategies accordingly.

But were these new assessments warranted and accurate? Do al-Qaeda and other groups often placed under the rubric of new terrorism—such as Aum Shinrikyo and the Christian Patriots—represent a truly novel form of terrorism?

Alexander Spencer believes the answer is no. He certainly agrees that al-Qaeda, the exemplar of the new terrorism, is a highly effective terrorist organization. And he understands why, in the wake of the events of September 11, some experts sought to attribute newness to a very old phenomenon. But he takes strong exception to the notion that this form of terrorism is actually new. Indeed, Spencer argues that the very same characteristics that define the terrorism of today can be identified in the terrorism of generations past. To show this, he places three core aspects of the new terrorism—motives, tactics, and organization—into conceptual and historical frameworks, and concludes there is far less "new" than meets the eye. He warns that calling the current terrorist challenge "new" may permit acceptance of overly aggressive—and possibly unnecessary—"new" countermeasures.

Rohan Gunaratna contends that an identifiably new and more dangerous form of terrorism has in fact grown out of the post–Cold War globalized era. He specifically points to the post-1989 rise in internal ethnic and religious conflicts, the free flow of migrants and refugees, the proliferation of weapons technologies, and the revolution in digital communications as contextual contributors to the emergence and evolution of the new terrorism. Although some of the core characteristics of the new terrorism may be found in older forms, features—and combinations of features—are unique to the new terrorism. Indeed, Gunaratna believes that what gives new terrorist groups such as al-Qaeda (his primary example) their strength and resilience are the creative ways in which they adopt and nurture the best of both old and new. That creativity also makes such groups extremely difficult to combat, let alone defeat; innovative countermethods are essential, he says.

The emergence of al-Qaeda and similarly inspired groups has not altered the fundamental meaning of the word *terrorism:* as noted by both authors of this chapter, terrorism as a form of political violence may change over time and contexts, but it does not break radically from its past. Yet the degree to which today's terrorism differs from prior forms remains a vital question. The world is currently experiencing one of the most challenging periods in the history of terrorism. Understanding the nuances of contemporary terrorism is necessary both to counter current groups effectively as well as to recognize the early warning signs of emerging groups that may seek to emulate the highly effective terrorism template of today.

The "new terrorism" of al-Qaeda is not so new
NO: Alexander Spencer, *Ludwig-Maximilians University, Munich*

The Myth of "New Terrorism"

Terrorism is one of the most disputed terms in the social sciences.[4] The problem of defining *terrorism* is well known and has been examined extensively.[5] Apart from the challenge of distinguishing terrorism from guerrilla warfare, crime, or mad serial killers, the well-known phrase "one man's terrorist is another man's freedom fighter" is often used to highlight the problem of implying a moral judgment when classifying a particular act as "terrorism." If one identifies with the victim of the attack, then it is considered terrorism, but if one can identify with the perpetrator, it is not.

The field of terrorism research seems to have become bored with the subject; some scholars such as Walter Laqueur have concluded that "a comprehensive definition of terrorism . . . does not exist nor will it be found in the foreseeable future."[6] Others have struggled on in their quest for the all-encompassing definition. In one of the most rigorous attempts, Alex Schmid and Albert Jongman examine 109 different definitions of terrorism and issue a lengthy consensus definition incorporating the most common elements.[7]

In a more recent study, Leonard Weinberg, Ami Pedahzur, and Sivan Hirsch-Hoefler examine seventy-three definitions of *terrorism* from fifty-five articles in three leading academic journals on the topic, and come to the conclusion that "terrorism is a politically motivated tactic involving the threat or use of force or violence in which the pursuit of publicity plays a significant role."[8]

Regardless of whether or not one believes in the importance (or possibility) of a definition, it is generally accepted that terrorism has changed since the mid-1990s into an inherently new form with new characteristics. Many academics, government officials, and politicians have articulated the concept of "new terrorism," which they assert involves different actors, motivations, aims, tactics, and actions than the "old" concept of terrorism used previously.

This essay takes issue with the notion that this supposedly "new" terrorism is actually new. The aim is not to challenge the established characteristics of terrorism today, but to question the validity of the term *new terrorism* by showing that many of the trends underlying it can be identified in terrorism years ago.

The section that follows examines the concepts of old and new terrorism and illustrates what are commonly designated as their defining features. The next section questions the presumed nearly dichotomous relationship between old and new and—through an examination of terrorist motives, tactics, and organizational structures—argues that new terrorism is not new after all. The final section offers conclusions and indicates the possible consequences of using terminology such as the "new terrorism."

THE OLD AND NEW TERRORISM

Terrorism as a form of political violence is by no means a new phenomenon. One of the earliest known groups was the Sicarii, a Zealot Jewish sect fighting against Roman rule in Palestine between AD 66 and 73. During the Middle Ages, a religious sect of Ismailis and Nizari called "Assassins" struggled against the empire of Saladin, and in the sixteenth century small "terrorist" groups in Albania and other regions resisted the armies of the Ottoman Empire. The term *terror* was first used around 1794 in association with a policy to protect the fragile government of the post-revolutionary French Republic from counter-revolutionaries. From about the mid-nineteenth century to World War I, revolutionaries and anarchists frequently used bombings and assassinations as weapons in their struggle against autocracy. After World War II, terrorism became a critical part of the anticolonial struggles. As Paul Wilkinson points out, this development has important significance as one of "the only clear instances in modern history where sub-state organizations using terror as their major weapon were able to achieve their long-term political goals, i.e., the withdrawal of the colonial power and establishment of a form of government favoured by the insurgents."[9]

Many scholars agree that the period prior to the early 1990s was marked by so-called traditional or "old terrorism," which can be roughly divided into different types such as left- and right-wing, ethno-nationalist, and separatist terrorism, as well as the "global terrorism" that emerged with the Palestinian groups after the late 1960s. Although in reality many of these "old terrorist" groups were a combination of these different types, it is argued that they all had some general common characteristics.

"Old Terrorism"

For one thing, traditional terrorist groups are classed as having predominantly secular motivations and rational political reasons for their acts of violence. For example, left-wing terrorist groups aimed to use violence to politicize the working-class masses and convince them to rise up against the capitalist system. And ethno-nationalist terrorists wanted independence for their ethnic group in the form of a separation of their territory from that of another country, the creation of their own sovereign nation-state, or the merger with another state. Whatever way, their specific demands were often rationally negotiable, such as when they demanded the release of certain jailed comrades, or payment in exchange for the release of hostages in a hijacking. Even when demands were difficult to meet, such as the reunification of a divided country, the creation of an ethno-national homeland, or the abolishment of the existing capitalist system, in many circumstances there appeared to be room for dialogue or negotiation.[10]

Related to this observation, it is believed that violence by "old terrorists" in general was "targeted and proportionate in scope and intensity to the practical political objectives being pursued."[11] Terrorists did not want to use excessive indiscriminate violence themselves because it would reduce their claim of legitimacy and alienate them from supporters, thereby reducing their access to new recruits and funding. Thus by keeping the level of casualties low, terrorists "preserved their eligibility for a place at the bargaining table and, ultimately, a role in successor governments."[12] "Old terrorism" was viewed as discriminate, with terrorist groups selecting their targets very carefully. They usually directed their precision attacks at well-defined, highly symbolic targets of the authority they opposed. These targets might include leading politicians; government officials; members of the aristocracy, military, or banking sectors; or other symbols such as government buildings. Groups tried to use their actions as a means of propaganda to increase their popular support. Terrorists sought maximum publicity for their acts, playing to an audience and spreading their ideological message. Brian Jenkins famously wrote that "terrorism is theatre" and that terrorist attacks were often choreographed for the media.[13] An attack was nearly always followed by a communiqué taking credit for the act, laying out demands, or explaining why it was carried out against that particular target. The targeted violence was generally perpetrated with conventional tactics such as hand-held guns and machine guns, as well as bombs. Terrorists showed little interest in new tactics and nonconventional weapons such as weapons of mass destruction (WMDs). In general, they tried not to kill innocent bystanders because such casualties would alienate the population and go against their aim of inciting a popular uprising. At times, they even expressed sorrow for accidental deaths in the attack.[14]

Finally, the "old terrorism" has an obvious hierarchical organization with fairly well-defined command and control structures. Although it is impossible to clearly demarcate the different layers, James Fraser argues that "old terrorism" is organized like a pyramid, with the leadership, who decide on the overall policy and plans, at the top. Underneath is a larger layer of active terrorists who carry out the attacks and are often specialized in certain activities such as bomb making, assassination, or surveillance. At the next level are the active supporters, who supply intelligence, weapons, supplies, communications, transportation, and safe houses. At the bottom are the passive supporters, who agree with the goals of the terrorist organization and spread their ideas and express their emotional support.[15]

New Terrorism

In contrast to "old terrorism," "new terrorism" is said to be characterized by a whole new range of attributes and to have begun around the early to mid-1990s. Many supporters of the "new terrorism" concept point to the prominence of religion as one of its main characteristics. Whereas old terrorism was primarily secular in its orientation and inspiration, terrorism linked to religious fanaticism is on the rise. According to Nadine Gurr and Benjamin Cole, in 1980 only two out of sixty-four identifiable international terrorist organizations could be classified as religious—a figure that rose sharply to twenty-five out of fifty-eight by 1995.[16] New terrorism is therefore often portrayed as terrorism that rejects all other ways and promotes an uncompromising view of the world in accordance with the belief of the religion. In contrast to old terrorism, new terrorism is said to lack a political agenda or precise political demands. Hoffman believes this religious motivation is the defining characteristic of the new terrorism, producing "radically different value systems, mechanisms of legitimization and justification, concepts of morality and, Manichean world view."[17]

Related to the religious motivation, many "new terrorism" supporters point to another of its main features: an increasing willingness to use excessive, indiscriminate violence. Laqueur, for example, argues that "the new terrorism is different in character, aiming not at clearly defined political demands but at the destruction of society and the elimination of large sections of the population."[18] These religious-based new terrorists see their struggle as good against evil, thereby dehumanizing their victims and considering all nonmembers of their group to be infidels or apostates. As a result, indiscriminate violence may be not only morally acceptable, but also a righteous and necessary advancement of their religious cause. Whereas "old terrorists" tended to strike only selected targets, "new terrorists" have become increasingly indiscriminate and try to produce as many casualties as possible.

Religious terrorists are often their own constituency, unconcerned about alienating their supporters with their acts of destruction, and holding themselves accountable only to God. Thus "new terrorists" do not always claim, and sometimes even deny responsibility, for their actions. They see the action itself as important and not the claim to it. They are not interested in any sort of negotiation. According to Matthew Morgan, "Today's terrorists don't want a seat at the table, they want to destroy the table and everyone sitting at it."[19] Moreover, "new terrorists" are deemed far more willing to engage in risky, complex, and seemingly irrational acts. Whereas most actions by "old terrorists" involved an escape plan, "new terrorists" are more willing to give their own lives while orchestrating a terrorist act; martyrdom is viewed as a way of reaching heaven.[20]

The threat of mass destruction is a fundamental part of the concept of "new terrorism." Many scholars believe that because "new terrorists" are motivated to use extreme violence, they are more likely to obtain and use biological, chemical, and radiological weapons, as well as nuclear WMDs. Hoffman warns that with the rise of the new terrorism "many of the constraints (both self-imposed and technical) which previously inhibited terrorist use of WMD are eroding."[21] And with the collapse of the Soviet Union, acquiring material that could be used for WMDs has become easier, and it no longer requires the cooperation of a state sponsor.

Another key characteristic of the new terrorism is precisely this inherent lack of state backers. Some academics believe that the explicit nonstate nature of new terrorism has enhanced terrorists' willingness to use extreme violence because it is virtually invulnerable to a direct backlash.[22] And the financing of new terrorism is no longer based on money received from state sponsors, but on other illegal sources such as drug trafficking, video piracy, and credit card fraud, as well as legal business investments and donations from wealthy individuals and charities.

Finally, one of the most emphasized aspects of the new terrorism is its loose network and less hierarchical organizational structure, aided by the emergence of new communications technology. As Rohan Gunaratna points out, each group within this network becomes relatively autonomous, but all are still linked by advanced communications and their common purpose. They therefore become much more flexible and can adapt and react more easily to different situations. Although members do communicate with their leadership, groups can also operate self-sufficiently.[23] Steven Simon and Daniel Benjamin refer to this as a combination of "a 'hub and spoke' structure (where nodes communicate with the centre) with a 'wheel' structure (where nodes in the network communicate with each other without reference to the centre)."[24] This type of integrated structure is much more difficult to identify and penetrate than a traditional hierarchical structure. It is far more resilient because each cell can still operate even if the leadership of the organization is lost.

To summarize, proponents of the new terrorism believe its component parts consist of a fanatical religious motivation, excessive indiscriminate violence (with the possible use of WMDs), an increasing independence from state sponsors, as well as a new ad hoc network structure aided by modern communications technology.

THE MYTH OF THE NEW TERRORISM

A more detailed examination of the individual characteristics of the new terrorism raises questions about the validity of the concept and concerns about the common practice of dichotomizing the relationship between "old terrorism" and "new terrorism." This section examines three aspects of the supposedly "new terrorism"—motives, tactics, and organization—placing them in conceptual and historical perspectives. The results call into question the concept of new terrorism.[25]

Motives

Proponents of the "new terrorism" concept argue that the motivations of terrorists have changed, pointing to the growth of religious fundamentalism. Hoffman, for example, asserts that "the religious imperative for terrorism is the most important defining characteristic of terrorist activity today."[26] But does the rise in religiously motivated terrorist groups legitimize the existence of the term *new terrorism?* Historically, religious terrorism is by no means a new phenomenon. According to David Rapoport, religiously motivated terrorism aimed at killing nonbelievers has existed for thousands of years. From the first-century Zealots to the thirteenth-century Assassins, and even up to the nineteenth century and the emergence of political motives such as nationalism, anarchism, and Marxism, "religion provided the only acceptable justification for terror."[27]

Religious motivation is not so much a new characteristic as it is a cyclic return to earlier motivations for terrorism. Audrey Kurth Cronin, for example, suggests that "the forces of history seem to be driving international terrorism back to a much earlier time, with echoes of the behavior of 'sacred' terrorists such as the Zealots-Sicarii clearly apparent in the terrorist activities of organizations such as al-Qaeda and its associated groups."[28] In addition, many "old" terrorist organizations also had close links with and were at least partly motivated by religion. The most prominent examples of this are the Irish Republican Army (IRA) with its predominantly Catholic membership, the Protestant Ulster Freedom Fighters or Ulster Volunteer Force, the primarily Muslim National Liberation Front (FLN) in Algeria, the Jewish terrorist group

Irgun, and the National Organization of Cypriote Fighters (EOKA) in Cyprus, which was influenced by the Greek Orthodox Church.

It is also important to recognize that although the actions of modern Islamist terrorist groups are religiously motivated, they still have specific political agendas. An examination of the demands and goals of al-Qaeda or other "new terrorists" associated with them reveals that many are based on clear political goals and targets—for example, the spread of political Islam, the withdrawal of foreign influence from the holy lands, the overthrow of the existing governments in Saudi Arabia and Egypt, the creation of a worldwide pan-Islamic Caliphate, and the elimination of Israel. In reality, it is often extremely difficult if not impossible to distinguish between religious and political motivations. As Chris Quillen points out, assigning religious motivations to individual terrorist attacks is subjective and open to interpretation. He cites the example of the 1995 Oklahoma City bombing, which one might interpret as an act motivated by Timothy McVeigh's devotion to the Christian Identity movement or as the reaction of a political terrorist to gun control measures and the bloody federal raids at Ruby Ridge and Waco.[29]

Tactics

In addition to the different motivations, "new terrorists" are also said to use different tactics than "old terrorists," and they use new technologies, possibly weapons of mass destruction, suicide tactics, and, most important, excessive violence to achieve their goals.

Use of Technology. The proliferation of technology and the accessibility of information useful to terrorists on the Internet are considered dangerous new trends that have contributed to the emergence and vitality of the new terrorism. However, the availability of information is arguably nothing new. Advice on bomb making and terrorist tactics has been available in newsletters and handbooks for well over a hundred years. An early example was the pamphlets published by the anarchist Johann Most at the end of the nineteenth century with "details on 'revolutionary chemistry' which included instructions on explosive devices, flammable liquid compounds, poison bullets and daggers, as well as on the best places to hide and use them."[30] Perhaps the most famous terrorist how-to guide was *The Anarchist Cookbook,* published in1971.[31]

Weapons of Mass Destruction. To consider the use of WMDs as a characteristic of the new terrorism is also problematic. The example of the 1995 sarin gas attack on the Tokyo subway by Aum Shinrikyo is frequently cited to make the connection between the new terrorism and WMDs. However, terrorists have planned and attempted to use WMDs for many decades. In 1972 members of the right-wing group "Order of the Rising Sun" were arrested and found to be in the possession of 30–40 kilograms of epidemic typhus pathogens; they were seeking to poison the water supply of Chicago, St. Louis, and other midwestern cities in order to create a new master race. In 1984 members of the Bhagwan Shree Rajneesh's group contaminated salad bars with *Salmonella typhi,* thereby poisoning 750 people in Oregon. In the 1980s, European authorities discovered botulinal toxin and considerable quantities of organophosphorous compounds, used to make nerve gas, in Red Army Faction (RAF) safe houses in France and Germany. In addition, the Kurdistan Workers' Party (PKK) and the Tamil Tigers, both examples of "old terrorists," have used chemical weapons. In 1992 the PKK poisoned water tanks of the Turkish air force near Istanbul with lethal doses of cyanide, and in 1990 the Tamil Tigers attacked a Sri Lankan military camp with chlorine gas. The PKK and Tamil attacks are significant because they clearly disprove the idea that all "traditional terrorist groups would avoid using nuclear, chemical or biological weapons under any circumstances."[32]

The threat of nuclear terrorism has also been linked to the concept of new terrorism. So far, terrorists have not undertaken any attacks with nuclear weapons. The most devastating terrorist attacks have employed bombs, conventional explosives, and, most famously, box cutters. And yet, even though no nuclear bombs have been exploded, traditional terrorists made numerous attacks on nuclear power stations in the 1970s and 1980s. One of the first occurred in 1973 when a commando from a left-wing Argentinean group entered the construction site of the Atucha atomic power station north of Buenos Aires. During the years that followed, the separatist group Basque Fatherland and Liberty (ETA) conducted several attacks against the Lemoniz nuclear power station near Bilbao, Spain. Other attacks were directed against plants near San Sebastian, Pamplona, Tafalla, Beriz, and other sites in northern Spain. In 1982 the terrorist wing of the African National Congress (ANC) sabotaged two South African nuclear power plants. Both of their reactors were substantially damaged, but because they were not in operation at the time, there was no release of radiation.[33] Although it was not proven that any of these groups were seeking to cause a nuclear explosion or contamination, these incidents prove that even "old terrorists" were clearly willing to cross the nuclear line.

Suicide Tactics. The same can be said of suicide tactics, which are often included in the description of the fanatical nature of the new terrorism in general and Islamic fundamentalism in particular. However, suicide bombing has been used extensively by the separatist Tamil Tigers in Sri Lanka since 1983. For example, Robert Pape points out that the Tamil Tigers carried out 75 of 186 suicide terrorist attacks between 1980 and 2000.[34] Even before this, during the Middle Ages the Assassins' use of daggers at close range showed their "willingness to die in pursuit of their mission,"[35] and the Anarchists of nineteenth-century Europe regularly died in the process of attacking their targets.

Use of Excessive Violence. Supporters of the "new terrorism" concept have argued that terrorists have become more lethal and willing to resort to unlimited violence to cause large numbers of casualties indiscriminately. In their view, the traditional terrorists were more restrained in their use of violence and the number of casualties they sought. However, one could argue that indiscriminate mass-casualty attacks have long been a characteristic of terrorism. Examples of the mass fatalities produced by the "old terrorists" are the simultaneous truck bombings of the U.S. and French barracks in Lebanon in 1983, which killed 367; the downing of Pan Am Flight 103 over Lockerbie, Scotland, which took the lives of 270; and the bombing of an Air India flight in 1985 by Sikh separatists with 329 fatalities. It is easy to forget that one of the most violent incidents of terrorism prior to September 11, 2001, was the 1979 attack on an Abadan movie theatre in Iran that killed about five hundred people. And as Rapoport points out, evidence indicates that the Thugs of South Asia were by far the longest-lasting and most murderous terrorist organization in history, killing around half a million people over a period of roughly four hundred years.[36]

Even if the indiscriminate targeting of innocent people, such as the children in the attack on a school in Beslan, Russia, in 2004, is considered to be a characteristic of the new terrorism, one finds examples of "old terrorists" who did the same. For example, members of the Democratic Front for the Liberation of Palestine machine-gunned children in an Israeli school in 1974, killing twenty-seven and injuring seventy. And even if one disregards the numbers and argues that the gruesome violence of the "new" terrorism, such as the beheading of the *Wall Street Journal* reporter Daniel Pearl in 2002, is more excessive than before, the "old terrorists" could be just as ruthless. For example, Martin Miller describes how in 1884 "a Viennese banker and his eleven-year-old son were hacked to death with an axe in front of his other son" by anarchists.[37]

It is true that none of these examples can be likened to the casualties caused by the 9/11 attacks. However, the term *new terrorism* appeared long before 2001. Marie Breen Smyth points out that "the scale of atrocity at the World Trade Center was unprecedented in the practice of modern terror; however, the emphasis on the scale of the attack has tended to negate the value of previous scholarship and experience of 'terrorism.'"[38] In fact, examination of the data on international terrorism incidences reveals that although the number of events has generally declined since the mid-1980s, the number of fatalities per incident has steadily increased over the same period. Considering that the new terrorism is supposed to have started in the 1990s, this increase in fatalities might not be directly linked to the phenomenon of the new terrorism. An equally plausible argument is that the increase in casualties is due at least in part to better technology. Explosives and timing and remote-control devices have substantially improved in recent decades, with a corresponding effect on the numbers of casualties. Furthermore, since the 1980s governments have adapted to terrorist techniques such as kidnapping, hostage taking, hijacking, assassination, and sabotage by increasing security at airports, securing embassies, guarding likely kidnap targets, training specialist commando troops, and sharing intelligence with other states. In response, terrorists have adjusted their tactics by placing more emphasis on coordinated bombings and hit-and-run tactics. Although it has become increasingly difficult for terrorists to get close to their traditional targets, they continue to find other ways of capturing the public's attention. The use of more spectacular coordinated violent tactics is one way of gaining greater media coverage.

Scholars such as Ray Takeyh make a compelling case that public opinion plays as vital a role in the new terrorism as in the old terrorism. One example is the 1997 Al-Gama'at al-Islamiyya attack on the Temple of Hatshepsut in Luxor, Egypt. The attack, which killed fifty-eight tourists and four Egyptians, was widely condemned not only by Western governments but also by many radical Islamists, who believed the attack damaged their cause. Takeyh points out that support for Al-Gama'at al-Islamiyya fell dramatically in Egypt as a result of the attack. Although the group remained active, its attack alienated the people to whom it most wanted to appeal, and over time this development gravely hindered the group's efforts.[39]

The importance of public opinion is particularly true when one considers terrorists' political agendas. These political goals, such as the establishment of an Islamic state, will restrain terrorists. Public support will be required for the establishment of a new state, and therefore terrorists must be careful not to alienate their supporters and sympathizers by using excessive violence. This very concern was evident in a 2005 letter from al-Qaeda's second-in-command, Ayman al-Zawahiri, to the then-leader of al-Qaeda in Iraq, Abu Musab al-Zarqawi.[40]

Finally, the use of terrorist violence as "theater" has not faded with the emergence of the new terrorism. It is hard to think of a more symbolic and dramatically theatrical set of attacks than those of September 11. Targeting the World Trade Center (a symbol of Western capitalism), the Pentagon (heart of the U.S. defense establishment), and the U.S. Capitol seems too much even for a Hollywood film. Terrorists still want a big audience, and the larger, more coordinated, and more dramatic the attack, the bigger the audience will be. Therefore, the rising level of fatalities can be viewed as an ongoing process, which does not necessarily represent a unique feature qualifying the concept of the new terrorism.

Organization

One of the main differences between the old terrorism and the new terrorism as postulated by proponents of the new terrorism is their form of organization. Whereas traditional terrorism was organized along hierarchical lines with a clear command structure, the new terrorism is a loose, stateless network that is more weakly organized and has no strong command structure. However, the network structure in the new terrorism is not a particularly new phenomenon in terrorism, and even Hoffman admits that the newness of the loose network structure associated with the new terrorism is debatable. For example, over a century ago the anarchist movement, responsible for a number of high-profile attacks against heads of state in Russia and across Europe, pursued a similar strategy of violence carried out by loosely networked, largely unconnected cells of like-minded radicals.[41]

Different forms of network structures also can be found in traditional terrorist organizations. For example, the Palestine Liberation Organization served as an umbrella group in which the dominant faction, Fatah, did not have a monopoly of power. For decades, the different factions within the PLO were fairly independent and had different policies and strategies. Hezbollah is as an umbrella organization of radical Shiite groups in which the relationship among members is unpredictable and does not follow strict lines of control. Network structures also existed in left-wing revolutionary groups such as the RAF in which second-, third-, and fourth-generation terrorists did not really form a hierarchical organization but rather a loose confederation with similar common goals.[42]

In the same way in which there are network structures in "old terrorist" groups, there are clear signs of hierarchical command structures in the "new terrorist" organizations such as al-Qaeda. They possess a clear leadership structure, operative subunits responsible for conducting attacks, as well as "specialized units directly below the top leadership level" that are responsible for certain tasks such as recruitment, finances, procurement, and public relations.[43] As Richard Shultz and Andreas Vogt note, "Below Bin Laden is the shura majlis or the consultative council. Four committees report to it. A military committee recruits fighters, runs training camps and launches terrorist operations."[44] Despite being rousted years ago from its safe haven in Afghanistan, al-Qaeda continues to operate in a highly organized and centralized fashion.[45] At the same time, today's terrorist organizations, including al-Qaeda, have many different types of members, including core members or professional terrorists, part-time terrorists, or amateurs, who also lead normal lives outside of the organization, as well as less closely associated supporters. These different types of members exist in both "old terrorism" and "new terrorism" to an equally fluctuating degree.

CONCLUSION

The emergence and effectiveness of terrorist organizations like al-Qaeda have sparked an understandable search for newness in a very old phenomenon. But as this essay has shown, there is actually far more consistency than difference between "old terrorism" and "new terrorism" in their key component parts, including motivations, tactics, and organization.

Some scholars may now ask: does it really matter what the kind of terrorism perpetrated by groups such as al-Qaeda is called? Some may argue that the predicate "new" is meaningless because it is a word devoid of any real significance. Others, me included, would disagree and argue that words matter a great deal. Calling a problem "new" forces one to automatically buy into the belief that the appropriate solutions must also be new. Although it is certainly appropriate to adjust counterterrorism measures to address the terrorism challenges of the day, one should remain wary of accepting a whole new set of hastily formed, restrictive government countermeasures without their being debated, publicly discussed, and independently monitored. Such measures may not even be necessary.

Al-Qaeda is an example of a "new terrorism"
YES: Rohan Gunaratna, *Nanyang Technological University, Singapore*

Al-Qaeda and the "New Terrorism"

Since the onset of the contemporary wave of terrorism in 1968 the world has witnessed violence conducted by five categories of nonstate threat groups: left- and right-wing (ideological), ethno-political, politico-religious, state-sponsored, and single-issue.[46] Ideological, ethno-political, and state-sponsored terrorism were the most dominant forms of violence during the Cold War. But with the collapse of the Soviet Union in 1991, the ideology of communism lost its appeal and support, and left-wing groups diminished. With the end of the Cold War, the Soviet bloc of countries ended their support for socialist governments and left-wing groups, and the Western bloc of countries ended their support for right-wing governments and groups. Although the threat posed by ethno-political groups continued, a new form of terrorism emerged and grew steadfastly into the twenty-first century. Thus even though the end of the Cold War marked the decline of traditional or "old terrorism," the post–Cold War witnessed the emergence of a new and more dangerous form of terrorism.[47]

Skeptics of the existence of a "new terrorism" debated until al-Qaeda attacked America's most iconic targets on September 11, 2001. The continuity of attacks since has made it clear that 9/11 was not an anomaly but a trend: the global threat of terrorism has only grown; it has not plateaued. Al-Qaeda and its operationally linked associates in the Muslim world as well as its ideologically affiliated cells in the West are the exemplars of this new terrorism. In addition to mobilizing thirty to forty groups in Asia, Africa, and the Middle East, al-Qaeda has successfully inspired segments of Muslims in both the territorial communities of the Middle East, Asia, and Africa, as well as the diaspora and migrant communities of the West. Despite being the world's most hunted class of terrorists, al-Qaeda, its associated groups, and its affiliated cells pose an unprecedented global threat. In the early twenty-first century, preventing and suppressing the new terrorism have become a high priority of most governments.[48]

THE CONTEXT

The rise in globalization in the 1990s transformed the thinking and behavior of politically motivated threat groups. As the conduct of terrorist groups that target civilians and guerrilla groups that target combatants changed, both academics and practitioners began identifying their actions as the new terrorism. The post–Cold War globalized era can be characterized by four features that have significantly influenced threat groups:

1. *The ease of international travel, particularly migrant workers and refugees.* Most refugees came from internal conflict zones where they experienced human suffering and internal displacement. They were also the most vulnerable to indoctrination by virulent ideologies.

2. *Accessibility to weapons, dual-use technologies, and specialist trainers.* With the downsizing of Cold War armies worldwide, militaries privatized and lethal technologies proliferated.

3. *A shift from international to internal disputes, especially ethnic and religious conflicts.* In contrast to ideological conflicts featuring left- and right-wing groups (Colombia, Philippines, Nepal, India), about 70–80 percent of contemporary conflicts worldwide are ethno-political and politico-religious.[49]

4. *The free flow of ideas, information, and technology through the proliferation of new platforms for communication, including the Internet.* Sustained propaganda disseminated through these platforms has been radicalizing both territorial and émigré Muslim communities. The territorial communities live in the Middle East, sub-Saharan Africa, Asia, the Balkans, and the Caucacus. The émigré—diaspora and migrant—communities live in North America, Europe, Australia, and New Zealand. More than the territorial Muslims, the émigré Muslims are susceptible to radicalization.

A threat group's operational environment is the single most important parameter of influence. However, little if any research has been conducted to assess the impact of the environment on the origins, evolution, and trajectories of terrorist groups. Defining characteristics of the new terrorism proposed by scholars and practitioners include: networked, not hierarchical; politico-religious, not secular; transnational, not territorial; autonomous, not state-sponsored; mass casualty, not restrained; destruction, not political goals; amateurs, not professionals (see Table 1-1).[50]

Since the attacks of September 11, scholars' understanding of threat groups and their operational milieu, especially with regard to al-Qaeda, has grown. Against the defining features of new terrorism and old terrorism, it is time to test.

Table 1-1

New Terrorism versus Traditional Terrorism

Trait	New Terrorism	Traditional Terrorism
Motivation	Religious	Secular
Organization	Networked and ad hoc	Hierarchal and organized
Sponsorship	Autonomous	State
Violence	Extreme	Restrained
Aim	Destruction	Political goal
Personnel	Amateurs	Professional
Range of operation	Transnational	Territorial

THE BACKGROUND

Terrorism is the threat or the act of politically motivated violence against non-combatants. Ideologically and operationally, terrorism is constantly evolving. Terror specialist Martha Crenshaw argues that "terrorism has changed over time, but the difference represents an evolution to the phenomenon and not a radical break between the past and the future of terrorism."[51] In every generation, the world has witnessed the emergence of groups with new intentions, capabilities, technologies, and tactics, and the range and types of threat they pose have differed. A confluence of factors—environmental, historical, intellectual, and others—create and shape new forms of terrorism.

When the contemporary wave of terrorism emerged in the Middle East in 1968, none of the identifiable international terrorist groups had a religious affiliation. However, after the Islamic revolution in Iran in 1979 and the anti-Soviet multinational mujahidin campaign in Afghanistan from 1979 to 1989, a new class of networked groups emerged. Like the groups over the previous decade, these threat groups had political aims, but they sought to use religion to justify their courses of action, which included violence.[52]

CHANGING LANDSCAPE OF THREAT

Since the end of the Cold War in 1991, the contours of the global threat have changed fundamentally. The threat of international conflict has receded, and the threat of internal conflict has advanced. With the exception of Iran and North Korea, no government currently poses a real threat to international security. At the global level, terrorism by nonstate actors has emerged as the tier-one national security threat. Despite sustained investment by the international community to reduce and manage the threat, terrorism remains the predominant challenge to the West. Ideological extremism and its vicious by-product, terrorism, have become more widespread. Existing and emerging classes of politico-religious groups, especially of the Islamist variety, dominate the global threat landscape.

Two principal operating environments are contributing to the current terrorist threat: the Global South and the Global North. Over 90 percent of threat groups—terrorist and insurgent—have emerged in the Global South. Asia, Africa, the Middle East, and Latin America, with their swathes of great poverty, illiteracy, injustice, and corruption, have witnessed the rise of economically and politically motivated violent groups. These threat groups or their representatives in migrant and diaspora communities have built state-of-the-art support networks in the Global North, where freedom of movement and protest, as well as human and minority rights, are protected by local constitutions. Because of this political liberalism, North America, Europe, Australia, and New Zealand remain ideal arenas for the operation of terrorist support networks.

Conflict zones in the Global South (Palestine, Lebanon, Afghanistan, Chechnya, Kashmir, Algeria, Iraq) are the most conducive environments for the rise of extremist ideologies and terrorist recruitment and activity. Those affected then migrate to the Global North. Some bring ethnic and religious differences from their homelands and contribute to instability in the host nation. First- and second-generation migrant and diaspora youth searching for new identities, in the absence of finding one, become susceptible to terror recruitment through the use of virulent ideologies crafted and disseminated by groups like al-Qaeda. The core of the message focuses on U.S. intervention (Afghanistan), invasion (Iraq), and occupation (Saudi Arabia) in Muslim lands, as well as support for secular dictatorships (Egypt, Libya, Jordan, Pakistan, Uzbekistan) in the Muslim world.

Terrorist groups continually adapt to changing environments. What is unique today is the globalization of communication, which has enabled terrorists to successfully penetrate ideologically the migrant and diaspora communities. As a result of this ideological penetration, terrorist groups enjoy support from both their territorial and migrant and diaspora communities. At the extreme is terrorist control of territory and popular influence: Hamas in Gaza, Hezbollah in Lebanon, Tehrek-e-Taliban in tribal Pakistan, Afghan and Pakistani Taliban in southeastern Afghanistan, and the Kurdistan Workers' Party in northeastern Turkey. As a consequence, today's governments and societies are suffering not only from traditional group-centered terrorism but also from homegrown terrorism. These self-radicalized youth seek to link up with formally structured terrorist groups for training and guidance.

The single biggest threat stems from al-Qaeda, which is led by Osama bin Laden, a former citizen of Saudi Arabia. Al-Qaeda and its conglomerate of groups and cells represent a new and increasingly dangerous form of terrorism. This Global Jihad Movement, consisting of al-Qaeda, its associated groups in

Asia, Africa, the Middle East, and the Caucacus, and the self-radicalized home-grown cells, is resilient, and the threat is enduring. In the coming years, the movement will continue to challenge mainstream Islam and both Muslim and secular states. The narrative highlighting the suffering of Muslims (actual and perceived) finds resonance among territorial, migrant, and diaspora Muslims. Correcting both the reality and ideality of the grievances among these broad communities is most necessary. Thus countering jihadi propaganda and reducing violence in conflict zones in Muslim countries will be paramount to lessening Muslim support for extremism and terrorism.

ORIGINS OF THE THREAT

The origins of the Islamist strain of the new terrorism emerged with the anti-Soviet jihad (mujahidin) in Afghanistan during the 1980s. In 1984 Abdullah Azzam, a Palestinian-Jordanian, founded Maktab al Khidmat lil Mujahidin al-Arab (MAK), known commonly as the Afghan Service Bureau, which provided the Arab mujahidin and their families with significant assistance. Bin Laden joined hands with Azzam, and, as MAK's principal financier, was considered his deputy. At the height of the foreign Arab and Muslim influx into Pakistan-Afghanistan from 1984 to 1986, Azzam recruited several thousand Arab and Muslim youths, and bin Laden channeled several million dollars in financial and material resources into the Afghan jihad. MAK operated independently of Western and Pakistani governments that assisted in the fight against the Soviets, but it tapped into the vast Muslim Brotherhood network and the resources of the Saudi government.[53]

Toward the end of the anti-Soviet Afghan campaign, Azzam and bin Laden decided to form a vanguard group—al Qaeda al Sulbah—that could unite the whole Muslim world into a single entity. Azzam was the ideological father and the intellectual leader, but gradually bin Laden took over.[54] Although bin Laden's worldview was initially shaped by Azzam, formerly of the Muslim Brothers, around the time of the Soviet withdrawal in 1988 bin Laden's relationship with Azzam deteriorated, primarily over disputes about post-Soviet Afghan leadership and the next steps for the jihad movement. Along with the Egyptian members of al-Qaeda, bin Laden wished to support terrorist action against Egypt and other Muslim secular regimes. Having lived in Egypt, Azzam knew the price of such actions and opposed them vehemently. The issue was settled by Azzam's assassination in November 1989 by the Egyptian members of al-Qaeda in Peshawar, Pakistan.

After Azzam's death, the ideological vacuum was filled by Ayman al-Zawahiri, the leader of the Egyptian Islamic Jihad. A professional medical practitioner and qualified eye surgeon, al-Zawahiri became both bin Laden's doctor and spiritual mentor. Bin Laden took over Azzam's MAK, and, using its trainers and camps, he built al-Qaeda. Al-Zawahiri became his deputy and the principal strategist of the jihad movement.

The group al-Qaeda takes its name from a concept attributed to Syed Qutb, a mid-twentieth–century Egyptian scholar who wrote *"al-qaedah al-sulbah"* (*The Solid Base*). The term *al-Qaeda* refers to the successful early Muslim generation, also known as *salafi,* who received education and guidance from the prophet Muhammad. They were companions of the Prophet, and their devotion and commitment to the Islamic struggle against Arab pagans were unmatched by later generations for whom the *salafi* became a source of inspiration and a model for Muslims to emulate. In conceptualizing al-Qaeda, Azzam had drawn from the pages of Islamic history. He defined al-Qaeda's composition, aims, and purpose in the context of the struggle of the Islamist movement after the victory over the largest land army in the world—the Soviet military. Although the concept was transformed to meet the changing landscapes, al-Qaeda was, in fact, never intended to be a terrorist organization.[55] Azzam stated in the founding charter of al-Qaeda in late 1987–early 1988 that he envisaged al-Qaeda as an organization that would channel the energies of the mujahidin into fighting on behalf of oppressed Muslims worldwide.[56] He viewed the organization as an Islamic "rapid reaction force," ready to spring to the defense of its fellow believers on short notice.[57]

Officially formed in August 1988, al-Qaeda is an organization with a global reach. Its real strength is not its membership per se, but its overarching, highly appealing ideology. In keeping with Azzam's original mandate, its principal aim is to inspire and incite Muslims worldwide to attack those who threaten Islam. Its principal strategy is to attack iconic targets in or belonging to the United States and its allies and friends in order to inspire and instigate a perpetual campaign.

Although al-Qaeda does not enjoy widespread support among Muslims worldwide, it opportunistically seeks to exploit the anger, suffering, and resentment of Muslims against the United States. America's lack of understanding of the Muslim world—for example, its unequivocal support for Israel, its assistance to secular Muslim rulers, its invasion of Iraq—has given Islamic terrorism and extremism a new lease on life. In view of the current support for the Global Jihad Movement in Asia, Africa, Middle East, and elsewhere, the campaign has been a success. Al-Qaeda averaged one major attack every year before 9/11, but since 2001 the frequency of attacks by al-Qaeda and its associated groups has grown exponentially.

A key strength of al-Qaeda has been the ability of its leadership to understand both the importance and power of modern communications. After its training and operational infrastructure was dismantled in Afghanistan in late 2001, al-Qaeda remained relevant only by periodically communicating to the outside world. Today, al-Qaeda, the most hunted terrorist group in history, has successfully mobilized Muslim communities worldwide, spawning a network of individuals forming cells and clusters of cells.

AL-QAEDA, THE GLOBAL JIHAD MOVEMENT, AND THE NEW TERRORISM

A defining feature of the new terrorism is its network. Although al-Qaeda emerged as a centralized group, it has worked with other groups and individuals to form a network. Instead of building support for the group, it seeks to reinvigorate its global capacity to strike.[58] Indeed, since the events of 9/11 al-Qaeda itself has been surpassed by the emergence of the Global Jihad Movement, consisting of al-Qaeda and other groups that advocate global jihad. The movement has three overlapping components.

The first is the initial al-Qaeda group established by bin Laden and Azzam. Also known as al-Qaeda core, al-Qaeda central, or al-Qaeda classic, the post-9/11 al-Qaeda group is operationally weak but ideologically potent, appealing to both associated groups waging local jihad in conflict zones and radicalized cells in migrant and diaspora communities in the West.

The second component is al-Qaeda's thirty to forty operationally associated groups in Asia, Africa, and the Middle East. Also known as the al-Qaeda network, these groups receive from the al-Qaeda core training, weapons, financing, and ideology. The groups hold declared or undeclared membership in the World Islamic Front for Jihad against the Jews and the Crusaders, which was formed by fatwa, or religious decree, in February 1998. Members of the World Islamic Front include the Salafi Group for Call and Combat (GSPC), Moroccan Islamic Combatant Group (GICM), Takfir Wal Hijra (TWH), Tawhid Wal Jihad (al-Qaeda of the Two Rivers), Lashkar-e-Taiba (LeT), al-Jamaah al-Islamiyah (JI), and Abu Sayyaff Group (ASG).

The third component is al-Qaeda's ideologically affiliated cells, which are operationally unconnected to al-Qaeda but driven by an ideology of global jihad articulated by it. Examples include the cell responsible for bombing the trains in Madrid on March 11, 2004, and the disrupted British cell led by Omar Khayam.[59] Both cells were self-financed and independent of al-Qaeda's operational control. The robust post-Iraq Islamist milieu in North America, Europe, and Australasia is transforming support cells into execution cells.

Today, al-Qaeda's real power is the disparate groups and cells it has trained, financed, armed, and, most important, influenced ideologically. The al-Qaeda network (al-Qaeda core plus its associated groups) and ideologically affiliated cells comprise the al-Qaeda movement. The threat is not monolithic. Members could be violent (for example, the extremist groups Laskar Jihad and Front Pembela Islam in Indonesia), or nonviolent (for example, Hizb-ut-Tahrir and al-Muhajiroun in the UK). Some of these groups have publicly criticized bin Laden and al-Qaeda, but they believe in global jihad. The groups in the Muslim territorial communities and cells in the Muslim diaspora represent a multi-dimensional threat against the United States and its allies and friends. The global jihadists challenge both the "infidel" (non-Muslim) and "apostate" (Muslims who have forsaken their faith) regimes. The threat is both ideological and kinetic.

As a result of U.S.-led global counterterrorism policies, al-Qaeda central has been severely weakened. Nevertheless, events such as the high-impact 9/11 attack, the U.S.-led coalition intervention in Afghanistan, the U.S. invasion and occupation of Iraq, and the media reporting on Abu Ghraib and Guantanamo Bay have strengthened support for likeminded associated groups and cells as well as Islamist groups unconnected to al-Qaeda. Exploiting suffering, resentment, and anger of Muslims, the terrorist and extremist groups are now able to replenish their human losses and material wastage and continue the fight. Indeed, al-Qaeda has morphed from a group of three to four thousand members in October 2001 to a movement of several tens of thousands of members, supporters, and sympathizers. Today, the Global Jihad Movement, consisting primarily of Sunni groups connected or unconnected to al-Qaeda, remains highly robust.

A MIXTURE OF OLD AND NEW TERRORISM

A closer look at al-Qaeda demonstrates that the group has features of traditional terrorism, as well as important features unique to the new terrorism. It has creatively adopted and nurtured the best of the old and the new in six ways.

First, although al-Qaeda is hierarchical, a classic feature of traditional terrorism, it is also part of a network of groups, a classic feature of the new terrorism. By organizing itself and its affiliated groups under the banner of the World Islamic Front for Jihad against the Jews and the Crusaders, al-Qaeda created a transnational network. In addition, although the central al-Qaeda members and members of affiliated groups in conflict zones are professionally trained, many operatives in diaspora communities are amateurs. In that sense, al-Qaeda is a hybrid, comprised of both professionals, a characteristic of the old terrorism, and amateurs, characteristic of the new terrorism.

Second, even though al-Qaeda operates globally through its network of groups and cells across regions and countries (classic new terrorism), most of the groups in this network are national or regional groups. These groups include Tehrek-e-Taliban, an alliance of Pakistani groups; the Islamic Movement of Uzbekistan and its splinter Islamic Jihad Movement, groups seeking to create an Islamic state in Uzbekistan; the Eastern Turkistan Islamic Movement, a Uighur Chinese group seeking to create an Islamic state in western China; and the Libyan Islamic Fighters Group, a group seeking to establish an Islamic state in Libya. Although all of these groups believe in a global jihad, the model promoted by al-Qaeda, they are all fighting to establish Islamic states in their own countries, which is in line with traditional, particularly ideological, terrorism.

Third, al-Qaeda has used multiple sources of support, including state support. For example, it received the support of Sudan (1991–1996) and Afghanistan (1996–2001). However, unlike for the state-sponsored groups characteristic of traditional terrorism, no government has leverage over al-Qaeda. Indeed, al-Qaeda functions like a modern global business and investment firm, which also penetrates global charities. And it relies on its extraordinary global multimedia production arm, al-Sahab, to generate and sustain support. In its commercial outlook, al-Qaeda functions like a modern multinational corporation investing in a range of opportunities.

Fourth, al-Qaeda's ultimate aim is to establish a global Islamic state, or caliphate, which is clearly a "new terror" aspiration. This goal, however, is not a religious one but a political one, similar to that of traditional terrorism. Political leaders in the United States have often argued that al-Qaeda has no political goals. Some proponents of the new terrorism argument would go beyond that and claim that al-Qaeda seeks to destroy the world. However, al-Qaeda's goal is to create evermore Islamic states by carrying out an armed struggle—jihad or holy war—against those who, in its view, are trying to prevent the establishment of such states. Although some proponents of the new terrorism would argue that al-Qaeda is a religiously motivated organization, an examination of the group reveals that it is a political organization that is misusing religion to legitimize its actions. It is wrong and counterproductive to blame religion.

Fifth, al-Qaeda is a highly patient organization that is promoting a multi-generational campaign. Its meticulous and exhaustive preparation for attacks makes al-Qaeda truly unique, clearly differentiating it from traditional terrorism. Al-Qaeda is not event-driven but campaign-driven—it does not believe in an immediate reaction to an attack carried out against it. Indeed, al-Qaeda doctrine stipulates that it should always wield the initiative and calmly decide when and where to attack. For example, after the United States fired seventy cruise missiles into Afghanistan following the East African embassy bombings in 1998, al-Qaeda decided to strike America's homeland using U.S. airplanes, an operation that would take three years to plan, prepare, and execute.[60]

Although al-Qaeda has appealed to Muslims across the world with its call that "it is the duty of every good Muslim to wage jihad," its primary tactical strength is an ability to meticulously study the gaps in security and patiently strike at targets that will have strategic implications. The challenge for intelligence services to prevent such attacks is extraordinary.

Sixth, parallel with building its conventional capabilities for "traditional"-style attacks, al-Qaeda has invested heavily in building a chemical, biological, radiological, and nuclear (CBRN) capability. A goal of mass destruction is a classic feature of the new terrorism, and al-Qaeda's structure includes a dedicated WMD Committee under its Military Committee. As far back as 1993, bin Laden asked his personal pilot, Essam al Ridi, to learn about crop dusting.[61] By the time the United States invaded Afghanistan in late 2001, al-Qaeda had established close links with Pakistani scientists, both nuclear weapons specialists and biochemists. The WMD Committee, led by Abdul Aziz al Masri, was dedicated to developing or acquiring a nuclear capability, but there were separate chemical and biological programs as well. Al-Qaeda planned to manufacture sarin at the Tanarak farm in Kabul, anthrax in Kandahar, and hydrogen cyanide in Darunta. The chemical program was led by an Egyptian and the biological program to manufacture anthrax by a Pakistani government scientist, and subsequently by a U.S.-trained Malaysian scientist/technician.[62] The overall supervisor of the biological program was Ayman al-Zawahiri.

The centralized al-Qaeda CNRB programs fell into disarray after the U.S. intervention in Afghanistan, but since the 1990s other like-minded groups have developed similar programs for the production of chemical and biological agents. They included clandestine programs in northern Iraq, in the Pankishi Valley in Georgia, and in the southern Philippines. In northern Iraq, Abu Musab al-Zarqawi, leader of the operation, used the Khurmal camp, a facility linked to Ansar al Islam,[63] to conduct research on toxins. Because al-Qaeda had invested significantly in training members of its associated groups in its camps in Afghanistan in the use of chemical and biological agents, both the jihadist intention and the capability to use unconventional agents have proliferated.

Al-Qaeda is an unpredictable adversary precisely because it draws from both the traditional and new forms of terrorism. An examination of its ideology and ideological evolution provides further insight into the group.

THE POLITICO-IDEOLOGICAL DIMENSION OF THE NEW TERRORISM

Most Western scholars, whether for or against the new terrorism argument, do not discuss the ideological dimension. Traditional terrorist groups used

violence as a means to a political end. Some scholars believe that the new terrorists aim at destruction as an end in itself. Although apocalyptic religious
groups such as Aum Shinrikyo belong in this category, most of the politico-
religious groups, including Islamist, are pragmatic. The politico-religious
ideology of al-Qaeda offers an insight into the thinking of Islamist groups.

In terrorism, the more strategic and long-term threat is the belief system. At
the heart of the sustained ideological campaign waged by al-Qaeda is the belief
that the United States, the West, and Israel are leading a global conspiracy
against Islam and Muslims. Al-Qaeda detests America's presence in the Arab
Peninsula, especially in Saudi Arabia; U.S. support for Israel and neglect of
the Palestinians; and U.S. assistance to pro-Western dictatorships around the
Middle East. Al-Qaeda holds the U.S. government, the American people, and
U.S. foreign policy responsible for bringing chaos to the Muslim world. The
only way the Muslim nation could live under the shade of Islam, al-Qaeda
ideologues argue, is to be united and work toward the establishment, by force
if necessary, of an Islamic caliphate. It is with this in mind that bin Laden
issued the 1998 fatwa. Since 9/11, the primary targets of the al-Qaeda movement have been U.S. allies—primarily Europe, Canada, and Australia—and
friends—primarily Muslim countries that support the West.

Although its long-term wish is to create a global Islamic caliphate, al-Qaeda's
immediate aim is to establish Islamic states wherever Muslims live. The methodology for achieving this goal is jihad.[64] Al-Qaeda's ideology is a composite of
writings and speeches of past and present ideologues. Muhammad bin Abdul
Wahhab, an eighteenth-century reformer, claimed that Islam became cor-
rupted a generation or so after the death of the prophet Muhammad. He
denounced any theology or customs developed after that as un-Islamic, and in
doing so tried to reform more than a thousand years of religious scholarship.
He and his supporters took over what is now Saudi Arabia, where Wahhabism
remains the dominant school of religious thought. Syed Qutb, the Egyptian
scholar, declared Western civilization an enemy of Islam and denounced leaders of Muslim nations for not following Islam closely enough. He preached that
jihad should be undertaken not just to defend Islam, but to purify Islam.

As an extension of these ideologies, the politically savvy al-Qaeda often
couches its grievances in "Third Worldist" terms familiar to any contemporary
antiglobalization activist and frames modern political concerns, including
social justice, within a divine and religious narrative. Jihad in the form of an
armed struggle in the name of God then becomes the means to attain freedom
and rid the *ummah* (community of Muslims) of injustice. The jihad they wage
is a "defensive jihad" in the face of perceived aggression by the enemies of
Islam. In this sense, the presence of U.S. and other non-Muslim troops in Saudi

Arabia after the 1991 Gulf War was a turning point in the life of bin Laden. He publicly criticized the Saudi royal family and alleged that their invitation of foreign troops to the Arab Peninsula constituted an affront to the sanctity of the birthplace of Islam and a betrayal of the global Islamic community.[65] After the Saudi government rendered him stateless, bin Laden advocated violence against it and the United States. Because it was difficult to strike inside Saudi Arabia, bin Laden increasingly focused his ire on the United States. After a period of exile in Sudan and Afghanistan, he sharpened his radical views. Jihad to al-Qaeda followers was deemed justifiable in order to defend the dignity and pride of the nation, a noble duty that had been neglected by Muslim leaders. Al-Qaeda's devotion to political ideology couched in religious terms is therefore not easily swayed by cheap promises and materialistic gains. So long as there is no sincere attempt to meet its demands, al-Qaeda will have sufficient support to continue the jihad.

Even though he did not possess Islamic religious credentials or authority, bin Laden issued the 1998 fatwa declaring jihad against the Jews and Crusaders. He claimed that the United States had made "a clear declaration of war on God, His messenger, and Muslims" through its policies in the Islamic world. This is another example of al-Qaeda's jihad ideology, which set the organization in motion.

With jihad comes the belief in martyrdom. Al-Qaeda operatives firmly believe that Allah guides and rewards those who sacrifice themselves for a noble cause. They are ever willing to sacrifice themselves without hesitation and often seek death as the best way to enter heaven.[66] When killed fighting for God, ideologues propagate that the "martyr" will enter paradise and receive an audience with God. In their ideological manuals, speeches, and one-on-one indoctrination, ideologues embellish the beauty of seventy-two virgins that would serve the "martyred Muslim hero" in paradise. As the "martyr" will be forgiven for his sins and vices, ideologues induce and exploit his fear of going to hell for wrongdoings on earth, compelling the gullible Muslim youth to kill and die. Furthermore, as the "martyr's" act will supposedly create the path for seventy relatives to enter paradise, some family members exposed to this ideology will clandestinely or openly support his mission to kill, maim, and injure.

The *baiah*, or pledge of allegiance, serves as an assurance that those affiliating themselves to the organization are committed to its ideology. By instituting it, the organization is freed from conceptual problems arising from differences in opinion. Through the *baiah* an acceptable level of uniformity is maintained which contributes to the organization's stability and ease of management and administration. *Baiah* unites all members to the notion that "true Islam or pure Islam" can only be established if the essence of Islamic society and its fundamentals are instituted. This requires the setting up of an Islamic state under *sharia,* or Islamic, law. Of course to achieve this end, the present Muslim society needs an Islamic movement which will provide leadership and the spiritual guidance.

Harnessing the forces of globalization, al-Qaeda has propagated the politico-ideological belief that Muslims worldwide belong to a one single global Muslim nation and has instilled the belief that whenever a group of Muslims suffer in any corner of the world, their brethren have a religious obligation to help. A convert to Islam, the American John Walker Lindh was motivated to travel to Afghanistan because as a "good Muslim" he felt a deep sense of obligation to help the "suffering Muslims to provide alms, train, and fight."[67] Despite international efforts to curb them, Muslim public sympathy, support, and participation in jihad are likely to continue and grow in coming years.

THE FUTURE OF AL-QAEDA

Today, al-Qaeda is in a period of consolidation. It has lost its territorial base—Afghanistan—but with the help of a new host, the Pakistani Taliban, al-Qaeda has reestablished itself. Together with some of its associated groups, al-Qaeda is operating from the Pakistani-Afghan border. On the Pakistani side, this region comprises the North-West Frontier Province (NWFP), the Federally Administered Tribal Areas (FATA), and Balochistan. FATA consists of seven agencies: Bajaur, Mohamed, Orakzai, Kurram, North and South Waziristan, and Khyber. Together with a dozen other groups, the core of al-Qaeda leadership has moved to the "ungoverned territories" of the NWFP and FATA-areas.

Al-Qaeda's global message increasingly appeals to a cross section of society—the old and young, men and women, the educated and the illiterate, the rich and the poor. Al-Qaeda maintains a high capacity to reach out, resonate, and radicalize segments of the Muslim masses. Graphic scenes of battles, spectacular and bloody bombings, periodic pronouncements, and striking messages, including explicit threats, are brought to life by al-Qaeda and its propagandists. Radicalization of the periphery of Muslim communities—territorial, migrant, and diaspora—will continue to result in some tacitly supporting violence and others directly participating in violence, fully believing that the pinnacle of Islam is martyrdom.

CONCLUSION: MORE CHANGE OR CONTINUITY?

Contemporary terrorist groups are in a phase of transition. Terrorism is constantly evolving. Is there more change than continuity? Considering the scale and frequency of attacks, the threat has increased. The earliest examples of attacks mounted by the new terrorists were the 1993 World Trade Center bombing in New York, the 1995 sarin gas attack in the Tokyo subway, the 1995 bombing of the federal building in Oklahoma, and the 1998 East Africa embassy bombings.[68] Ten years later, traditional terrorism still exists, and yet new terrorism is on the rise. Terrorist groups learn from one another; most are imitative, not innovative. Terrorism changes incrementally. There are neither typical traditional terrorist groups nor typical new terrorist groups. As such, the debate over the concepts of new and traditional terrorism will be ongoing.[69]

As described in this essay, al-Qaeda is certainly an illustration more of new terrorism than of old terrorism. But rather than label a terrorist group new or traditional, it is more useful to identify the characteristics that are new or traditional such as organizational structure, personnel, attitude toward violence, goals, and methods. As for al-Qaeda and its associated groups, research reveals that they are hybrids—picking among the most dangerous components of both old and new terrorism.

Moving forward, it is important to examine not only the Islamist strain of groups such as al-Qaeda or the Lebanese Hezbollah but the entire spectrum of threat groups. In addition to politico-religious groups such as Aum Shinrikyo, certain ethno-political and ideological groups have features of the new terrorism. For example, many ethno-nationalist groups such as the Tamil Tigers and Kurdistan Worker's Party have established state-of-the-art transnational networks. Wherever there are opportunities for harnessing the forces of globalization, terrorist groups will network with like-minded groups, cells, and individuals and create transnational networks.

At its core, the new terrorism is more resilient than traditional terrorism. Even if al-Qaeda the group is dismantled, al-Qaeda the movement is likely to survive as a network. Unless there is a concerted operational and ideological campaign at the global level, both al-Qaeda and its network cannot be dismantled. Although a network, unlike a hierarchy, cannot be destroyed by decapitation,[70] over time governments can develop a greater understanding of the operational environment and knowledge of such threat groups, thereby enabling their security and intelligence services and law enforcement agencies to fight the new terrorism. This battle will require a shift from cooperation to collaboration between national security and law enforcement agencies, joint training, joint operations, and the sharing of expertise, technology, and experience. Furthermore, it will require greater understanding of the adversary and the creation of platforms for both direct action and greater resource allocation for engagement.

Notes

1. These attributes form the bases of definitions of terrorism for both the United Nations Security Council (though, notably, not codified by the UN as a whole), as well as the U.S. government. See UN Security Council Resolution 1566 (S/RES/1566), 2004; and U.S. Department of State, *Country Reports on Terrorism 2008* (Washington, D.C.: Office of the Coordinator for Counterterrorism, U.S. Department of State, April 2009), chap. 7. For a detailed discussion of definitions of terrorism, see Bruce Hoffman, *Inside Terrorism,* rev. and exp. ed. (New York: Columbia University Press, 2006), 1–41.
2. Hoffman, *Inside Terrorism,* 3.
3. See, for example, Walter Laqueur, *The New Terrorism: Fanaticism and the Arms of Mass Destruction* (New York: Oxford University Press, 1999); and Steven Simon and Daniel Benjamin, "America and the New Terrorism," *Survival* 42 (Spring 2000): 59–75.
4. An extended version of this chapter will appear in Alexander Spencer, *The Tabloid Terrorist: The Predicative Construction of 'New Terrorism' in the Media* (Basingstoke, UK: Palgrave Macmillan, forthcoming).
5. Hoffman, *Inside Terrorism* (2006).
6. Walter Laqueur, *Terrorism* (London: Weidenfeld, 1977), 5.
7. Alex P. Schmid and Albert J. Jongman, *Political Terrorism: A New Guide to Actors, Authors, Concepts, Data Bases, Theories and Literature* (Amsterdam: North-Holland, 1988), 28.
8. Leonard Weinberg, Ami Pedahzur, and Sivan Hirsch-Hoefler, "The Challenges of Conceptualizing Terrorism," *Terrorism and Political Violence* 16, no. 4 (2004): 789.
9. Paul Wilkinson, "International Terrorism: New Risks to World Order," in *Dilemmas of World Politics,* ed. John Baylis and N. J. Rengger (Oxford: Clarendon Press, 1992), 230.
10. Kumar Ramakrishna and Andrew Tan, "The New Terrorism: Diagnosis and Prescriptions," in *The New Terrorism—Anatomy, Trends and Counter-Strategies,* ed. Kumar Ramakrishna and Andrew Tan (Singapore: Eastern Universities Press, 2002), 6.
11. Simon and Benjamin, "America and the New Terrorism," 65.
12. Ibid., 66.
13. Brian Jenkins, "International Terrorism: A New Mode of Conflict," in *International Terrorism: Fanaticism and the Arms of Mass Destruction,* ed. David Carlton and Carlo Schaerf (London: Croom Helm, 1975), 16.
14. Hans J. Horchem, "West Germany's Red Army Anarchists," in *The New Terrorism,* ed. William Gutteridge (London: Mansell Publishing, 1986), 199–217.
15. Described in Harry Henderson, *Global Terrorism—The Complete Reference Guide* (New York: Checkmark Books, 2001), 17.
16. Nadine Gurr and Benjamin Cole, *The New Face of Terrorism: Threats from Weapons of Mass Destruction,* (London: I. B. Tauris, 2000), 28–29.
17. Bruce Hoffman, "'Holy Terror': The Implications of Terrorism Motivated by a Religious Imperative," *Studies in Conflict and Terrorism* 18 (1995): 272.

18. Walter Laqueur, *The New Terrorism: Fanaticism and the Arms of Mass Destruction* (London: Oxford University Press, 1999), 81.
19. Matthew J. Morgan, "The Origin of the New Terrorism," *Parameters* 34, no. 1 (2004): 30–31.
20. Walter Enders and Todd Sandler, "Is Transnational Terrorism Becoming More Threatening? A Time-Series Investigation," *Journal of Conflict Resolution* 44, no. 3 (2000): 310.
21. Bruce Hoffman, *Inside Terrorism* (London: Indigo, 1998), 197.
22. David Tucker, "What's New about the New Terrorism and How Dangerous Is It?" *Terrorism and Political Violence* 15, no. 3 (2001).
23. Rohan Gunaratna, *Inside Al Qaeda: Global Network of Terror,* 3rd ed. (New York: Berkley Books, 2003).
24. Simon and Benjamin, "America and the New Terrorism," 70.
25. Other authors who support this line of argumentation include Thomas Copeland, "Is the New Terrorism Really New?" *Journal of Conflict Studies* 21 (Winter 2002/2003): 91–105; Tucker, "What's New about the New Terrorism," 1–14; and Isabelle Duyvesteyn, "How New Is the New Terrorism?" *Studies in Conflict and Terrorism* 27, no. 5 (2004): 439–454.
26. Hoffman, *Inside Terrorism* (1998), 87.
27. David C. Rapoport, "Fear and Trembling: Terrorism in Three Religious Traditions," *American Political Science Review* 78, no. 3 (1984): 659.
28. Audrey Kurth Cronin, "Behind the Curve: Globalization and International Terrorism," *International Security* 27 (Winter 2002/2003): 38.
29. Chris Quillen, "A Historical Analysis of Mass Casualty Bombers," *Studies in Conflict and Terrorism* 25, no. 5 (2002): 287.
30. Martin Miller, "The Intellectual Origin of Modern Terrorism in Europe," in *Terrorism in Context,* ed. Martha Crenshaw (University Park: Penn State University Press, 1995), 45.
31. William Powell, *The Anarchist Cookbook* (New York: Lyle Stuart, 1971).
32. Gavin Cameron, "Weapons of Mass Destruction Terrorism Research: Past and Future," in *Research on Terrorism-Trends, Achievement and Failures,* ed. Andrew Silke (London: Frank Cass, 2004), 81.
33. Laqueur, *The New Terrorism,* 72.
34. Robert Pape, "The Strategic Logic of Suicide Terrorism," *American Political Science Review* 97, no. 3 (2003): 343.
35. John Gearson, "The Nature of Modern Terrorism," in *Superterrorism—Policy Responses,* ed. Lawrence Freedman (Oxford: Blackwell Publishing, 2002), 14.
36. Rapoport, "Fear and Trembling."
37. Miller, "The Intellectual Origin of Modern Terrorism," 45.
38. Marie Breen Smyth, "A Critical Research Agenda for the Study of Political Terror," *European Political Science* 6 (2007): 260.
39. Ray Takeyh, "Islamism: R.I.P.," *National Interest* 63 (Spring 2001): 97–102.
40. Director of National Intelligence, "Letter from al-Zawahiri to al-Zarkawi," July 9, 2005, www.fas.org/irp/news/2005/10/dni101105.html .
41. Bruce Hoffman, "Change and Continuity in Terrorism," *Studies in Conflict and Terrorism* 24 (2001): 426.
42. Tucker, "What's New about the New Terrorism," 4.

43. Renate Mayntz, "Organizational Forms of Terrorism—Hierarchy, Network, or a Type sui generis?" MPIfG Discussion Paper 04/04, Max Planck Institute for the Study of Societies, Cologne, 2004, 11–12.

44. Richard Shultz and Andreas Vogt, "It's War! Fighting Post-11 September Global Terrorism Through a Doctrine of Preemption," *Terrorism and Political Violence* 15, no. 1 (2003): 10.

45. Craig Whitlock, "The New Al-Qaeda Central," *The Washington Post,* September 9, 2007.

46. Hoffman, *Inside Terrorism* (2006), 63. The advent of modern international terrorism dates to July 22, 1968, when the Popular Front for the Liberation of Palestine (PFLP) hijacked an Israeli El Al commercial flight en route from Rome to Tel Aviv.

47. In the 1990s, a few preeminent specialists brought the threat of a new terrorism to the attention of the world. They include Ian O. Lesser, Bruce Hoffman, John Arquilla, David Ronfeldt, Michele Zanini, and Brian Michael Jenkins, *Countering the New Terrorism* (Santa Monica, Calif.: RAND, 1999); Walter Laqueur, *New Terrorism*; and Steven Simon and Daniel Benjamin, "America and the New Terrorism," 59–75.

48. Stephane Leman-Langlois and Jean-Paul Brodeur, "Terrorism Old and New: Counter Terrorism in Canada," *Police Practice and Research* 6 (May 2005): 121–140.

49. Interview with Dennis Pluchinsky, Office of Intelligence and Threat Analysis, Bureau of Diplomatic Security, U.S. State Department, Washington, D.C., 2001.

50. Scholars and practitioners continue to debate the distinguishing features between new and traditional terrorism. For example, Russell Howard argues that the new terrorists are better trained, while David Tucker argues that they are amateurs. Russell D. Howard, "Understanding Al Qaeda's Application of the New Terrorism—The Key to Victory in the Current Campaign," in *Terrorism and Counterterrorism: Understanding the New Security Environment,* ed. Russell D. Howard and Reid L. Sawyer (Guilford, Conn.: McGraw-Hill/Dushkin, 2004), 75–76; Tucker, "What's New about the New Terrorism," 1.

51. Martha Crenshaw, "Old and New Terrorism: Lessons Learned" (paper presented at the Second IRRI Conference on International Terrorism, Jihadi Terrorism: Where Do We Stand? February 13, 2006).

52. Indeed, the first modern "religious" terrorist groups appeared in 1980, and, according to Bruce Hoffman, by 1992 eleven groups had strong religious affiliations, and by 1995 religious-based terrorist groups had grown to twenty-six out of fifty-six identifiable groups. Hoffman, *Inside Terrorism* (2006), 85–86.

53. "Al-Qaeda," *Jane's World Insurgency and Terrorism,* January 9, 2004, 1.

54. Gunaratna, *Inside Al Qaeda,* 2.

55. Ibid., 2–6.

56. The charter was published in April 1988 in *Al-Jihad,* the principal journal of the Arab mujahidin.

57. Azzam described his original concept as such: "Every principle needs a vanguard to carry it forward and, while focusing its way into society, puts up with heavy task and enormous sacrifices. There is no ideology, neither earthly nor heavenly, that does not require such a vanguard that gives everything it possesses in order to achieve victory for this ideology. It carries the flag all along the sheer, endless and

difficult path until it reaches its destination in the reality of life, since Allah has destined that it should make it and manifests itself. This vanguard constitutes Al-Qa'idah al-Sulbah for the expected society." See Abdullah Azzam, "Al-Qa'idah al-Sulbah," *Al-Jihad* 41 (April 1988): 46.

58. In addition to training its own group and support base, from 1989 to 2001 al-Qaeda trained more than 20,000 members in its camps in Afghanistan.

59. "Briefing on Operation Crevice," SO 13, New Scotland Yard, December 2004.

60. National Commission on Terrorist Attacks upon the United States, *The 9/11 Commission Report* (New York: Norton, 2004) provides information into the operation, including the different phases and timelines.

61. Interview with Essam al Ridi, Texas, December 2003.

62. While the United States believed that it had killed Abu Khebab al Masri, there are sufficient reasons to believe that he survived the attack. In December 2001, Rauf was arrested by Pakistan's Inter-Services Intelligence and Sufaat was arrested by the Malaysian Special Branch. The author interviewed members of ISI and MSB involved in their arrests and debriefings.

63. Ansar al Islam, a breakaway group of the Islamic Movement of Kurdistan, later evolved into Jayash Ansar al-Sunnah. Renamed Jamiaat Ansar al-Sunnah, it is one of the most active groups in Iraq.

64. Jihad has different meanings. For al-Qaeda and its followers, jihad means holy war.

65. Robert Fisk, "Interview with Saudi Dissident Bin Laden," *Independent* (London), July 10, 1996.

66. Rohan Gunaratna, "Unleashed: Wiser Not to Execute the Bali Bombers," *ABC News* (Australia), December, 17, 2007, www.abc.net.au/unleashed/stories/s2120383.htm.

67. Rohan Gunaratna, Debriefing of John Walker Lindh, Alexandria Prison, Alexandria, Va., 2002.

68. Simon and Benjamin, "America and the New Terrorism."

69. Duyvesteyn, "How New Is the New Terrorism?" 439–454.

70. Tucker, "What's New about the New Terrorism," 9.

2

does poverty serve as a root cause of terrorism?

NO: Poverty is a weak causal link
James A. Piazza, *University of North Carolina, Charlotte*

YES: Poverty is an important cause
Karin von Hippel, *Center for Strategic and International Studies*

The notion that poverty is a root cause of terrorist violence is widely asserted, particularly in the Western world. This assertion is not surprising considering how well it fits with basic liberal economic theory, which presupposes that individuals are motivated primarily by material well-being. Those who have opportunities to sustain and better themselves will likely accept the system in which they live and behave peacefully. By contrast, those confronting socioeconomic distress and deprivation are more likely to be drawn to radical and possibly violent movements, including terrorist movements.

This view has a long-standing pedigree. In 1994, for example, President Bill Clinton said that "the forces of terror and extremism . . . feed on disillusionment, on poverty, on despair." The way to end terrorism is, in his judgment, to "spread prosperity and security to all."[1]

After the attacks of September 11, 2001, the poverty-terrorism thesis was further bolstered. In December 2001, World Bank president James Wolfensohn remarked, "This war is viewed in terms of the face of bin Laden, the terrorism of al-Qaeda, the rubble of the World Trade Center and the Pentagon, but these are just symptoms. The disease is the discontent seething in Islam, and more generally, the world of the poor."[2] Secretary of State Colin Powell concurred, saying in 2002, "I fully believe that the root cause of terrorism does come from situations where there is poverty, where there is ignorance, where people see no hope in their lives."[3]

This thesis, however, has one glaring problem: it flies in the face of most evidence. Take the 9/11 hijackers. If one were to base an analysis solely on the biographies of those nineteen individuals, one would conclude that the root cause of terrorism is not poverty and despair, but privilege, education, and opportunity.[4] In fact, study after study, performed both before and after 9/11, confirms that most terrorists come from backgrounds more privileged than that of the average member of their national or regional population.[5] Furthermore, many of the poorest countries in the world experience no terrorism at all, while some of the wealthiest have been confronting terrorism for decades.

How can an assumption based on such deductive logic and enjoying such a renowned following be so wrong? The answer is that it may not be. Although both poverty and terrorism have been around for a long time, rigorous research into connections between the two is a relatively new phenomenon, and the jury is still out on definitive conclusions. Equally important, the criteria for judging the poverty-terrorism thesis may contain faulty assumptions—for example, perhaps poverty does not *directly* spawn terrorism, but rather provides an important *context* in which radicalism and other support structures of terrorism may benefit. Most terrorists may not come from poverty, but their radical movements—be they religious, ideological, territorial-separatist, and so forth—gain influence when the communities they purport to represent suffer under dire socioeconomic conditions.

In this chapter, James Piazza and Karin von Hippel agree that terrorism is a highly complex phenomenon and that uncovering silver bullet causal explanations is unlikely. They differ, however, on the relationship between poverty and terrorism. Piazza maintains that the critics of the poverty-terrorism thesis have it right. Using the most current data available, he shows there to be little (if any) connection between poverty and terrorism at the global, national, and individual levels. These findings will not bring comfort to policymakers who, he says, have treated the poverty-terrorism thesis as gospel. But it will allow for a more honest—and ultimately more fruitful—investigation into the real roots of terrorism.

Von Hippel agrees that there is a paucity of reliable data supporting the poverty-terrorism thesis. But this does not mean the evidence against it is any more reliable. In fact, she argues that most research to date has been too narrowly focused and does not include many relevant countries and regions, rendering current findings inconclusive. In addition, most analyses fail to account for the ways in which terrorist elites take advantage of impoverished communities in order to expand their support base. This, she says, illustrates the specific ways in which poverty may play an important role in increasing both radicalism and terrorism—both certainly vital public policy concerns.

Irrespective of its relationship with terrorism, addressing global poverty remains an important humanitarian goal. But in order to devise better strategies for reducing both poverty and terrorism, policymakers need to have clear, fact-based assessments on the relationship between the two. The authors of this chapter take crucial steps in that direction.

Poverty is a weak causal link
NO: James A. Piazza, *University of North Carolina, Charlotte*

Poverty and Terrorism: A Hypothesis in Search of Evidence

Poverty poses a serious threat to human life. It is responsible for an estimated one-third of all deaths each year worldwide. Roughly fifty thousand people die from poverty-related causes every day, and poverty has killed an estimated 270 million people since 1990, more than double the total casualties suffered by all sides during World Wars I and II.[6] Poverty also places a heavy toll on international security and political order. Poverty, unemployment, and income inequality have contributed to higher violent crime rates worldwide.[7] Unequal distribution of land and unequal access to material resources are key ingredients of civil wars, armed ethnic and sectarian conflicts, and riots.[8] Poverty and loss of livelihood help armed rebel movements and insurgencies with their recruitment efforts.[9] Economic distress as a result of poverty contributes to military coups, regime collapse, and the onset of nondemocratic rule.[10] Poverty also breeds social upheavals that produce refugees and illegal migrants, both of which have been linked to violence and armed conflict in the areas to which they migrate.[11]

But does poverty cause terrorism? In the wake of the September 11, 2001, terrorist attacks on the United States and subsequent attacks in Indonesia, Spain, Britain, Morocco, and Turkey, national politicians and United Nations officials were quick to identify poverty, global income inequality, unemployment, and low levels of education as key causes of terrorism. The reasoning behind their conclusion was straightforward: poor people who lack economic opportunities are resentful about their socioeconomic status and become alienated from mainstream society. This smoldering resentment is exacerbated by the large and growing gaps in living standards among rich and poor people, which result in intense feelings among the poor that they are being unfairly deprived of proper living standards and opportunities—a phenomenon that political scientist Ted Robert Gurr labeled "relative deprivation" and linked to increased likelihood of civil strife.[12] In this state of rage and hopelessness, the poor are more susceptible to the lures of political extremism.

Ordinary law-abiding citizens who are placed under economic distress or who are confronted with opulence while they struggle to make ends meet become primed to the anti–status quo message that is part and parcel of many terrorist group ideologies, and therefore they are more likely to sympathize with terrorists. This sympathy can even lead them to aid, shelter, and provide information to terrorists, to refuse to cooperate with government agents fighting terrorism, and to be more likely to join terrorist groups themselves.

Thus poverty and inequality are deemed the natural fertilizers for terrorism. It stands to reason that the appropriate response to the threat of terrorism, as argued by a surprisingly wide range of public officials, is to increase aid to impoverished countries to foster economic development and to bridge gaps in wealth. More aid would remedy what President Bill Clinton called the "dark side of globalization," the fact that nearly half of the world's population survives on roughly $2 a day, despite the remarkable economic growth worldwide over the last fifteen years. President George W. Bush outlined a new international security imperative affixed to the traditional moral imperative of foreign aid and poverty alleviation, famously stating before the 2002 Monterey Development Summit, "We fight poverty because hope is an answer to terror."

The alleviation of poverty *should* be a top priority for developed countries, and wealthy countries should increase their international development and aid budgets. Doing so will undoubtedly produce humanitarian benefits and will likely yield real security dividends. However, humanitarian and development aid is not likely to reduce the threat of terrorism. Despite the very well-intentioned statements of policymakers eager to address the root causes of terrorism in the modern world, there is an absence of hard evidence that poverty, socioeconomic inequality, or low levels of economic development cause terrorism or elicit public sympathy for terrorist movements. Indeed, the experts that study terrorism agree on very few root causes of terrorism, but they have begun to produce a consensus that terrorism is not the direct by-product of economic factors.[13] As social scientists gain access to more comprehensive and precise data on human living standards, or what is known among development economists as "human development indicators," as well as better statistics on terrorism and other types of political violence, the argument that poverty causes terrorism has begun to erode. Simply put, there is little empirical evidence to support the hypothesis that poverty, poor economic performance, or socioeconomic inequality are related to patterns of terrorism at any of the levels on which the causes of terrorism are traditionally investigated: the global level, the national level, and the individual level.

In this essay, I dissect and analyze the available empirical data to pinpoint vast evidentiary holes in the hypothesis that poverty causes terrorism. I do so from three perspectives: global, state, and individual. The essay concludes with a discussion of other possible root causes of terrorism that merit more attention.

TERRORISM AND GLOBAL POVERTY

The alleviation of global poverty has been a goal of the international community since the end of World War II. The urgent need to reduce poverty and to promote economic prosperity on the grounds that they both foment political extremism and increase the potential for violent conflict was a precept of the United Nations Charter drafted in San Francisco in 1945 and was a foundational concept upon which the U.S. Marshall Plan was built in 1947.

The threat of poverty to international order and the possibility that it could stoke terrorism was raised more recently in the negotiations that produced the 2000 United Nations Millennium Declaration. A by-product of this concern is a voluminous body of international statistics on poverty and on various types of political violence. Examination of these statistics reveals that global rates of terrorism, which increase and decrease in cyclical waves over time, are out of sync with changes in global poverty rates and measurements of global inequality, which do not show cyclical dynamics. As the percentage of the world's population living in poverty has steadily *declined* from about 66 percent in 1981 to about 47 percent in 2006,[14] the annual rate of transnational terrorist attacks has *fluctuated wildly*, exhibiting peaks of activity in the mid-1980s, around 1991, and between 2001 and 2005, and a steady decline in the mid- to late 1990s.[15] A similar pattern is found when one looks at casualties— persons injured or killed—in transnational terrorist attacks. By contrast, although global inequality, defined as differences in the gross domestic product (GDP) between the rich and poor countries of the world, has steadily increased since the 1970s,[16] the sharpest growth in the wealth gap, which occurred in the mid-1990s, was accompanied by the sharpest decrease in transnational terrorist attacks. It cannot be demonstrated that either economic good news—greater global prosperity—or economic bad news—a wide and growing gap in the global distribution of wealth—conforms to patterns of international terrorist activity.[17] This finding is a problem for the argument that poverty causes terrorism.

Another way to look at this argument is to examine the distribution of terrorism by regions of the world and by countries arranged by their level of economic development. Table 2-1 arranges terrorist activity by major world regions for the period 2000–2006. If economic privation were a cause of terrorism, it would be reasonable to expect that the poorer world regions would

Table 2-1

Regional Distribution of Terrorism, 2000–2006

	Sub-Saharan Africa	Middle East	East Asia and Pacific	Latin America	South Asia	Eastern Europe and CIS	Western Europe and North America
Total incidents of terrorism[a]	148	10,953	1,362	1,470	3,295	1,898	2,425
Total casualties due to terrorism[b]	1,806	59,180	6,355	3,758	17,586	4,714	6,787
"Source" incidents of terrorism[c]	258	328	171	128	56	370	283
Number of active groups[d]	79	320	92	133	143	75	380
2005 regional Human Development Index[e]	.493 (Low)	.699 (Medium)	.771 (Medium)	.803 (High)	.611 (Medium)	.808 (High)	.916 (High)
Number of countries	39	16	17	21	6	28	19

Source: United Nations Development Programme, *Human Development Report 2007/2008* (Washington, D.C.: UNDP, 2008); Rand-MIPT Terrorism Knowledge Base (www. tkb.org).

Note: CIS = Commonwealth of Independent States (former Soviet Union).

[a] Total terrorist attacks occurring within region.

[b] Total persons killed, injured, detained through a hijacking, or kidnapped through terrorist incidents within region.

[c] Total terrorist attacks launched against third countries, within or outside of the region, by locally based terrorist groups.

[d] Total groups listed by the U.S. Central Intelligence Agency (CIA) to have an active presence within countries in region.

[e] UNDP-reported 2005 Human Development Index measurement for region, accompanied by categorization of level of development: "High" (.968–.800), "Medium" (.798–.502), or "Low" (.499–.336).

experience the most terrorism and would produce or house a greater number of terrorists than wealthier regions. However, this is not the case. The poorest world region—determined by comparing regional United Nations Development Programme (UNDP) Human Development Index scores that incorporate GDP per capita with literacy and life expectancy rates[18]—is sub-Saharan Africa. This region also experienced the *fewest* number of terrorist attacks during the period, suffered the fewest number of casualties from terrorism, and, despite its poor level of economic development, can be said to be a relatively poor place for terrorist groups to operate. Compare Africa with the Middle East, a medium human development region home to several wealthy states that both sustains and produces the lion's share of contemporary terrorist activity in the world. It is also particularly striking that the wealthiest and most developed region, Western Europe and North America, countries in the Organisation for Economic Co-operation and Development (OECD), hosts the largest number of active terrorist groups, while sub-Saharan Africa hosts the second fewest. Again, the pattern expected by the popular wisdom—that poor regions are more likely to be afflicted with terrorism—is not evident.

Analogous results are produced when one sorts terrorism globally by rich, middle-income, and poor countries irrespective of region, as illustrated in Table 2-2. Nationals of *Low Human Development* countries, classified using the UNDP's Human Development Index, committed fewer transnational terrorist attacks than the global average, experienced fewer terrorist attacks than the global average, and saw their national territory used as a base of operations by fewer terrorist groups than the global average during the period 2000–2006. The *Medium Human Development* countries, not the poorest states, were the biggest contributors to transnational terrorism and the sites of the largest concentration of terrorist activity in terms of attacks.[19] By contrast, the wealthiest countries—that is, those classified by the UNDP as *High Human Development* countries—produced a higher average number of transnational attacks and sustained a higher average number of terrorist attacks than the *Low Human Development* countries. It is a particularly striking feature of Table 2-2 that the richest countries had the highest average number of active terrorist groups operating within national boundaries, while poor countries had the lowest.

TERRORISM AND POOR STATES

A closer look at individual states is revealing. Do the poorest and least-developed states produce and experience the highest levels of terrorism? Are socially stratified countries more likely to produce resentment that

Table 2-2

Distribution of Terrorism by Level of Human Development, 2000–2006

	Average transnational terrorist attacks produced by:	Average terrorist attacks occurring in:	Number of active terrorist groups operating out of:
High Human Development countries (n = 56)	4.8	108.3	10.3
Medium Human Development countries (n = 66)[a]	7.4	218.5	8.9
Low Human Development countries (n = 26)[b]	3.1	46.8	2.7
All countries (n = 146)	5.6	147.6	8.4

Source: United Nations Development Programme, *Human Development Report 2007/2008* (Washington, D.C.: UNDP, 2008); RAND-MIPT Terrorism Knowledge Base (www.tkb.org).

[a] Includes 1995 classification of North Korea, 1998 classification of Micronesia, and 1999 classification of Iraq.

[b] Includes 1993 classifications of Somalia and Afghanistan.

manifests itself in terrorist activity per the relative deprivation model? Do economically stagnant countries experience more terrorism, and can afflicted countries therefore *grow* their way out of terrorism through economic development?

In 2005 the ten poorest countries in the world, measured using the Human Development Index, were in order Sierra Leone (poorest), Burkina Faso, Guinea Bissau, Niger, Mali, Central African Republic, Mozambique, Chad, Ethiopia, and the Democratic Republic of Congo. Although many of these countries have indeed experienced civil war and serious political strife, terrorism has for the most part failed to appear in their lists of security challenges. Collectively, only 2 percent of all transnational terrorist attacks from 2000 to 2006 were committed by nationals of these least economically developed countries, and only one of them, Ethiopia, experienced significant terrorism within its borders (the perpetrators of most of these attacks were believed to be Muslim radicals of the al-Ittihad al-Islamiya movement based across the border in Somalia). Three of these countries—Guinea Bissau, Mozambique, and Central African Republic—experienced and produced no terrorism whatsoever during the period, while Sierra Leone, Burkina Faso, and Chad each saw only one transnational attack launched from their territory, all of which resulted in no casualties.

By contrast, the countries that face the most serious challenges from terrorism seem to have no coherent socioeconomic profile. Table 2-3 lists in rank order the ten most terrorism-afflicted countries from 2000 to 2006, along with some of their macroeconomic indicators. One of them, Afghanistan, is without a doubt acutely underdeveloped as a result of more than thirty years of severe political turmoil and internal armed conflict. Both Pakistan and Iraq also face significant economic challenges, though they are classified by the UNDP as *Medium Human Development* countries and are far wealthier than most sub-Saharan African countries. Indeed, Pakistan's economic growth rate consistently outstripped global averages from its independence in 1947 until the present day with a short pause in the 1990s. Iraq, prior to the imposition of UN sanctions in 1991, had an industrial, health, and educational infrastructure that was widely admired throughout the Arab world. The Russian Federation, India, Colombia, Thailand, and the Palestinian territories are also all middle-income countries characterized by pockets of significant poverty alongside industrial development, functioning educational systems, relatively high literacy rates, and, with the exception of Russia, rising rates of life expectancy. Two countries in Table 2-3, Spain and the United Kingdom, are OECD countries marked by the highest levels of economic development and relative affluence.

Table 2-3

Economic Development in the Most Terrorism-Challenged Countries, 2000–2006

	Number of transnational terrorist attacks produced	Number of terrorist attacks sustained	Number of active terrorist groups operating out of country	GDP per capita (2005 US$)	Gini coefficient	GDP growth, 1990–2005 (percent)
Iraq	140	7,327	77	$466	42.0[a]	n.a.
Palestinian territories	140	2,748	59	1,107	37.0[b]	−2.9
India	23	1,770	74	3,452	36.8	4.2
Colombia	39	1,212	15	2,682	58.6	0.6
Afghanistan	46	921	16	290	60.0[a]	n.a.
Pakistan	60	731	36	711	30.6	2.5
Spain	12	772	14	25,914	34.7	2.5
Thailand	16	826	15	2,750	42.0	2.7
United Kingdom	13	597	35	36,509	36.0	2.5
Russia	2	610	24	5,336	39.9	−.1
Group average	49.1	1,751.4	36.5	7,921	39.8	1.5
World average	5.6	147.6	8.4	9,221	40.8	1.7

Source: United Nations Development Programme, *Human Development Report 2007/2008* (New York: UNDP, 2008).; RAND-MIPT Terrorism Knowledge Base (www.tkb.org).

Note: n.a. = not available.

[a] Figure obtained from Global Peace Index, www.visionofhumanity.org/gpi/home.php.

[b] Figure obtained from Palestinian Central Bureau of Statistics, "Demographic and Socioeconomic Status of the Palestinian People," 2006.

The countries listed in Table 2-3 are not noticeably unequal societies, as indicated by the Gini coefficients—a measurement used by development economists to determine income inequality in countries; the coefficient ranges between 100, indicating pure inequality of distribution, and 0, indicating pure equality. The countries mirror closely the rates of inequality found in the rest of the world with two exceptions. Both Afghanistan and Colombia have extremely high Gini scores, placing them in the top ten most economically stratified societies in the world. However, it is necessary to recognize complexities regarding both of these countries that muddy a straightfoward relationship between inequality and terrorism. In the case of Afghanistan, it is difficult to determine whether economic inequality has been the source or the *product* of its acute security turmoil over the past several decades. The 1979 Soviet invasion prompted the emigration of six million Afghans, devastating the country's agricultural production, the mainstay of its employment and GDP, while exacerbating rural-urban gaps in development. Furthermore, Soviet counterinsurgency policy in the 1980s involved the destruction of irrigation infrastructure, roads, and communications in the rural areas of Afghanistan to weaken the armed resistance based there. This approach caused the standard of living to plummet in the hinterland relative to the cities, where the Soviet-backed Afghan regime was more firmly in control. The Soviet withdrawal in 1989 ushered in a decade-long civil war that chased away foreign aid and investment while giving rise to an opium industry that enriched local warlords. After removal of the Taliban regime by the United States and coalition forces in 2001, Afghanistan received a sizeable infusion of humanitarian and reconstruction aid from the international community. However, distribution of the aid monies remains uneven because of bureaucratic inefficiencies, corrupt Afghan politicians and officials, and the fact that security remains poor in the Taliban strongholds in the southern Pashtun regions bordering Pakistan.

As for Colombia, Latin American countries are traditionally characterized by high levels of socioeconomic inequality, and Colombia's Gini coefficient is close to the regional median of 53.7 and is indeed lower than that of Bolivia, Paraguay, and Brazil, three countries with insignificant levels of terrorism. Table 2-3, then, provides little indication that domestic inequality produces terrorism. This result is further validated by other evidence. On average, the twenty most unequal countries in the world actually produce fewer transnational attacks (3.1), sustain fewer terrorist attacks (72.8), and host fewer terrorist groups (5.3) than the world average.[20]

But what about growth? If a paucity of economic opportunities creates pools of disaffected and alienated people from which terrorists can garner support and recruit, then economic growth is surely a panacea for terrorism. Terrorism would then be a feature of countries with stagnating economies, whereas countries experiencing rapid economic growth would produce and sustain less terrorism. The countries listed in Table 2-3, as a whole, mirror worldwide GDP growth rates, though it is striking that many of them have experienced rapid GDP growth in the past decade and a half. One of them, India, a country with one of the most vibrant and rapidly growing economies in the world and with a burgeoning middle class, has endured some of the longest internal terrorism campaigns in the world, including a dramatic spike since the 1980s in Islamist-separatist terrorism related to the Kashmir crisis. Another, Thailand, has seen a resurgence since 2001 of intense separatist terrorism in its Muslim-majority Pattani region bordering Malaysia, even though it is one of the so-called East Asian Tigers—a group of Southeast Asian countries noted for their spectacular rates of economic growth and export-led rapid development in the 1980s and the 1990s. In the shorter term, Afghanistan grew by 12.4 percent in 2007 in the midst of an impressive spring offensive launched against Afghan government and North Atlantic Treaty Organization (NATO) troops by Taliban extremists.

Only the Palestinian territories conform with the stereotypical profile of a terrorism-plagued country. They have experienced negative economic growth, mostly attributable to the limitations imposed by the forty-year Israeli occupation, and are plagued by a notoriously corrupt domestic administration, the Palestinian Authority, and unemployment rates that reach 20 percent in Gaza. However, the Palestinian territories receive significant foreign assistance, benefit from preferential trade agreements from the European Union, and are marked by literacy rates higher than those found in other Arab countries. Thus the territories are solidly within the *Medium Human Development* cohort.

As was true for level of economic development, a broad survey of countries' economic growth rates also fails to reveal a pattern consistent with the argument that economic stagnation generates terrorism. Indeed, some of the data provide evidence to the contrary. Looking beyond the countries listed in Table 2-3, of the twenty-nine countries that experienced negative growth during the period 1990–2005, seventeen of them experienced no terrorism at all, while all but two—the Russian Federation and the Palestinian Occupied Territories— experienced significantly lower than average levels of terrorist activity. Yet the cohort of fastest-growing countries in 2007 includes a sampling of countries with significant terrorism challenges: Georgia, Jordan, Venezuela, Uzbekistan, the Philippines, and Sri Lanka. However, in general, countries that produced and experienced higher than average levels of terrorism from 2000 to 2006 are distributed across all levels of economic growth, from high growth (India and Algeria) to medium growth (Turkey and Thailand) to low growth (Nepal).

Finally, patterns of terrorist activity *within* states also fail to yield a discernible relationship between poor economic development and terrorism. The case of India is particularly useful here. At first glance, terrorist activity in India seems to vindicate the hypothesis that poverty and social class stratification incubate terrorist activity. Indeed, India has many poor people, and it has struggled for more than forty years against an internal Maoist terrorist insurgency—the Naxalites, recently renamed the People's War Group—that bases itself in impoverished rural communities and conducts terrorist attacks allegedly on behalf of peasants and low-caste Hindus exploited by rural landlords.[21] However, an examination of the distribution of terrorist incidents across the states of India demonstrates that contemporary (1998–2006) terrorism plagues *both* poor and wealthy areas and that the pattern of terrorist activity is inconsistent with regional economic development rates.

The lion's share of Indian terrorism, over 60 percent, occurs in the state of Jammu and Kashmir, a region whose status has been disputed by India and Pakistan since 1947. Today, Jammu and Kashmir is the seventh least economically developed state of India. However, before intensification of its separatist insurgency in 1989 it was a middle-income state with a thriving tourist industry. Terrorism in Jammu and Kashmir also has a transnational dimension that has little to do with the economic status of the residents of Jammu and Kashmir in that Kashmiri militants are alleged by Indian intelligence to be armed and trained by Pakistan (Pakistani officials counter that India is arming Baluchi separatists in Pakistan). Impoverished Indian states such as Assam and Chattisgahr share the dubious distinction of being high-terrorist activity states along with middle-income Andra Pradesh and wealthy Maharashtra and the Delhi municipality. The poorest Indian state, Madhya Pradesh, suffered *only one* terrorist attack between 1998 and 2006. The caste-based Naxalite terrorist movement accounts for most contemporary terrorist activity in the poor and middle-income states of Chattisgahr, Jharkhand, and Andra Pradesh. Terrorism in underdeveloped Assam is separatist-inspired and draws energy from ethnic conflict between the native Assamese population and recent immigrants from Bangladesh, whereas terrorism in rich Maharashtra and poor Uttar Pradesh is tied to religious-sectarian tensions between Hindus and Muslims in those states. This is all to say that empirical patterns of domestic terrorism in India mirror those found on the global level: poor places do not produce or experience more terrorism than rich places.

All of these outwardly contradictory empirical findings make sense once one considers the theoretical disadvantages poor societies foist upon terrorists as

opposed to the advantages that affluent societies offer terrorists. Like all organizations, terrorist groups need a stable, predictable environment in which to
operate. Political scientist Ken Menkaus provides important insight in explaining that severely underdeveloped states such as Somalia, one of the poorest
countries in the world, are actually suboptimal operational venues for terrorist
groups because these states offer poor infrastructure, a paucity of desirable
targets such as foreign firms or tourists, and expose terrorist cadres themselves
to harassment, extortion, or co-optation by corrupt authorities.[22] In theory,
more developed countries are more attractive to terrorist groups because these
countries have better transportation and communication infrastructures and
are more likely to be political democracies that afford their residents rights of
assembly and privacy and place constraints on police power. These features
facilitate the free movement of terrorists, terrorist recruitment, and organization and training activities, and they hamper police counterterrorism efforts.
More developed countries also contain an abundance of lucrative targets for
terrorist groups and are more likely to have free media that will cover terrorist
attacks when they occur, giving groups an outlet for their propaganda. In this
sense, it is not the poverty of underdeveloped countries that incubates terrorism but the opportunities afforded to terrorist entrepreneurs by wealthier
countries.

TERRORISM AND POOR PEOPLE

The release of the identities and biographies of the nineteen September 11
hijackers revealed a puzzling profile: all were well-educated young men with
middle- and upper-middle class family backgrounds who had traveled, some
extensively, in the West and had attended Western educational institutions. The
lead terrorist, Muhammad Atta, an Egyptian national who had lived for a time
in Hamburg, was a trained engineer. None of them seem to fit the profile of the
poorly educated, economically deprived, and socially marginal individual that
makes up the popular stereotype of a terrorist. The suspected perpetrators of
subsequent al-Qaeda attacks in Madrid, London, Casablanca, Istanbul, and
Bali also do not fit the popular profile. Notorious al-Qaeda leaders such as
Osama bin Laden, Ayman al-Zawahiri, 9/11 mastermind Khalid Sheikh
Muhammad, and the recently slain Abu Musab al-Zarqawi tend to be significantly better educated than their co-nationals—bin Laden holds a degree
in civil engineering, al-Zawahiri is a trained physician with surgery credentials, Khalid Sheikh Muhammad is a U.S.-educated mechanical engineer,
and al-Zarqawi for a time worked as a journalist—and to have been born to
economically comfortable families.

However, unlike tracking patterns of global, national, or subnational terrorist incidents, surveying socioeconomic profiles of individuals who join terrorist groups or participate in terrorist attacks is fraught with statistical difficulty. Because it is challenging for researchers to obtain a reliable and representative sample of individual terrorists, most surveys have been limited to specific groups or populations. Nevertheless, the existing studies of the socioeconomic backgrounds of terrorists and their supporters fail to provide evidence that poor people are more likely to become or to sympathize with terrorists. In fact, the opposite seems likelier. Statistical studies have shown that the individuals more likely to engage in terrorism are also more likely to come from materially better-off backgrounds, to have obtained higher levels of education, and to enjoy higher standards of living. And this finding seems to be consistent across groups, nationalities, and time periods.[23] The common experience for most terrorists has been recruitment while at university, rather than in the street, urban shanty, or poverty-stricken rural tract. The individuals who sympathize with terrorists—a critical population because many terrorist groups rely heavily on networks of noncombatant supporters who provide safe houses, material support, and information and who refuse to cooperate with police—are also not more likely to be poor, unemployed, or uneducated. Recent surveys of ordinary Palestinians and Lebanese Muslims show no correlation between income, employment status, and educational background and support for suicide bombings and the September 11 attacks.[24] As a consequence, constructing a discrete demographic profile that can be used to neutralize terrorism has been fruitless.

And, again, there are theoretical reasons that individuals with a higher socioeconomic status might be more likely to become terrorists than their downtrodden brethren. As counterintuitive as this observation may seem, terrorism expert Edgar O'Ballance explains that an effective terrorist operative must be able to carry out often complex logistical and technical tasks, must have sufficient intellectual sophistication to evade security personnel, must have the educational and social backgrounds—or have acquired the requisite social comfort—to appear inconspicuous when traveling abroad, and often must be able to communicate in one or more of the international business languages, particularly English.[25] In addition to being committed, terrorists need to be reliable, adaptable, and polished, not unlike an employee of a multinational business enterprise, in order to launch their attacks successfully. Officials of the Palestinian terrorist group Hamas admit that because they are presently inundated with volunteers for suicide missions, they have implemented tough selection criteria for prospective martyrs that include educational achievement, intellectual ability, and social and professional aptitude.

WHAT, THEN, CAUSES TERRORISM?

These assemblies of empirical information do not provide much comfort to those who wish to reduce terrorism by attacking poverty and remedying economic inequality. The idea that poverty and inequality promote terrorism is, in many ways, a very attractive one because it gives policymakers a cogent tool to use in the fight against terrorism—promotion of economic development—and it fortifies humanitarians' pleas for more attention to alleviating poverty. But there simply is no evidence of a direct relationship between poverty and terrorism.

So what does cause terrorism? A coherent answer to this question is obscured by the fact that terrorism is rare, erratic, and diverse in its manifestations. Terrorist group behavior, therefore, gives social scientists a small compendium of data points with which to work, and they are never sure it is a representative body of data. Terrorism is likely to be multicausal and is also likely to have multidirectional relationships with its causes. Is terrorism in a poverty-stricken area—for example, the underdeveloped northern region of Sri Lanka—prompted and sustained by the poor level of local economic development, or have thirty years of brutal attacks by Tamil separatists eroded local economic progress and increased poverty by scaring away investment? Terrorism scholars are only now starting to untangle these sorts of relationships.

I will, however, raise two potential precipitants of cross-national terrorist activity I uncovered in my own research that may have policy implications in the war on terrorism, and can at least partially explain the uneven success of America's counterterrorism efforts. First, there is some preliminary evidence that failed and failing states—states such as Afghanistan, Somalia, or Colombia that, because of severe political turmoil, are unable to govern or project power internally—are more likely to have their nationals join terrorist groups and commit attacks abroad and are more likely to suffer from high levels of domestic terrorist activity.[26] Of course, many failed and failing states, though not all, suffer from low levels of economic development and poor economic growth. But poverty and economic stagnation in these countries are more a consequence of the failure of state institutions and poor levels of internal security than the cause. The feature of failed and failing states that seems to correlate most strongly with terrorism is the presence of internally contested zones, more commonly referred to as stateless areas. These are swaths of territory in the hinterland of troubled states over which the central government has little or no control and in which nongovernmental actors such as rebels or terrorist movements operate with impunity. Some examples are the jungle provinces controlled by the Revolutionary Armed Forces of Colombia

(FARC),[27] the mountainous Federally Administered Tribal Areas (FATA) in northern Pakistan where Osama bin Laden is thought to be in hiding, and the remote northern border territory of Uganda out of which the violent Lord's Resistance Army terrorist movement operates. This situation suggests that bilateral or multilateral efforts to remedy state failures could meaningfully reduce terrorist activity.

Second, human rights abuses seem to exacerbate terrorism. In a cross-national empirical study, my colleague James Walsh and I found that countries with poor human rights records were significantly more likely to be victims of both transnational and domestic terrorist attacks.[28] Basic counterinsurgency theory helps to explain why this is the case. Governments that face security challenges posed by irregular armed groups, such as rebel movements and, we would add, terrorist organizations, can only effectively counter such groups by maintaining general public support for governmental efforts and by winning the hearts and minds of populations out of which militants operate. When governments resort to abuse, torture, arbitrary arrest and imprisonment, or extrajudicial killings in their campaigns against militants, they erode their own popular legitimacy. This erosion only weakens counterterrorist efforts by fueling domestic political opposition and alienating noncombatants who reside in the communities in which the terrorists are imbedded—that is, those who could otherwise provide critical intelligence and other assistance to security forces.

These two potential root causes of terrorism—state failure and human rights abuses—are supported by preliminary empirical evidence afforded by statistics on terrorist attacks worldwide. But, it is clear that scholars and others still have much to learn about patterns of terrorism, and they remain limited by the quality of their tools to examine those patterns.

Poverty is an important cause
YES: Karin von Hippel, *Center for Strategic and International Studies*

The Role of Poverty in Radicalization and Terrorism

Of all the debates on terrorism that have taken place in the eight-plus years since the attacks of September 11, 2001, the impact of poverty on terrorism has been the most emotional, the most anecdotal, and the least methodical. Several prominent economists and researchers have mined the data to demonstrate that—contrary to conventional wisdom—terrorists are not poor and uneducated. If anything, they tend to come from the ranks of the middle and upper classes—the "haves" rather than the "have-nots."[29] Alan Krueger concluded, "The bottom line . . . is that poor economic conditions do not seem to motivate people to participate in terrorist activities."[30]

Even when confronted by this research, world leaders tend to disregard it: they continue to blame poverty and its corollaries (alienation, humiliation, marginalization, and globalization) for "growing" terrorists, relying more on intuition rather than any rigorous research. At the March 2002 World Development Summit in Monterey, Mexico, leaders such as President George W. Bush and former UN secretary-general Kofi Annan declared that the fight against poverty was intrinsically linked to the fight against terrorism.[31] In his farewell address to the United Nations on September 23, 2008, President Bush remarked, "The extremists find their most fertile recruiting grounds in societies trapped in chaos and despair, places where people see no prospect of a better life. In the shadows of hopelessness, radicalism thrives. . . . Overcoming hopelessness requires addressing its causes: poverty, disease, and ignorance." These leaders' proclamations have, in turn, put enormous pressure on bilateral and multilateral development agencies to formulate policies and programs to counter radicalization, based on an insufficient empirical database.

Should we spend more time educating leaders and policymakers so that we can officially close the case on this debate and move on to the arguably more important, hard-edged counter-terrorist challenges, such as policing and intelligence sharing? Or is there a chance that the emotion-driven, data-poor poverty defenders may at least be partially correct, while the cold-hearted, data-rich number crunchers may be overlooking critical aspects in the debate?

This essay indeed posits that the focus of the research conducted thus far has been too narrow and not current enough to rule out poverty as a critical contributing factor in terrorism. In particular, such research has not taken into account the socioeconomic dynamics of the communities in which terrorists operate (their support base); it has not fully explored the drivers for the ordinary foot soldiers; nor has it taken into account recent manifestations of the terrorist threat. This is not to argue that poverty is *the* primary cause of terrorism, but rather that socioeconomic conditions are relevant to understanding the rise of radicalism and the development and support for terrorism in a growing number of situations. An improved understanding of the connections between economic vulnerability, on the one hand, and radicalism and terrorism, on the other, should help governments and multilateral agencies determine more appropriate and effective policies.

COMMUNITY DYNAMICS: THE ENABLING ENVIRONMENT

Today, it is well recognized that the more successful terrorist groups (and insurgents) thrive by building and expanding their constituencies. For the al-Qaeda network and movement, this "enabling environment"[32] includes potential sympathizers not only in the Arab and Muslim world, but also in Europe and North America. These adherents may not themselves use violence, but they either endorse the arguments and platforms of the terrorists or are intimidated into silence.

This wider community needs to be won over so that they *oppose* terrorism in their neighborhoods, cities, states, and critically, in the virtual world of the Internet, where many of the battles are taking place. Appealing to the enabling environment may be the only way in the long term to isolate terrorists and end terrorism. Severing the connection between terrorists and their constituents would allow the former to become much more vulnerable to informants and standard policing surveillance. Recent experiences in Northern Ireland, Greece, Yemen, and now even Iraq, demonstrate that this strategy can work, and that it can be internally or externally driven.

It is in the enabling environment that poverty is a factor. By providing the poor with social services, a number of nationally focused Islamist groups and political parties,[33] and the al-Qaeda movement more generally, have been able to significantly broaden their appeal. It is not yet clear whether this support has increased the numbers of people who have become fully radicalized, but evidence does exist that terrorist groups have expanded their influence in their constituencies because of the assistance.

The connection among religion, charity, and group solidarity is, of course, nothing new. In the late 1880s, the anticolonial Libyan insurgent hero and holy warrior Omar al-Mukhtar ("Lion of the Desert") belonged to a conservative Islamic order, influenced by the radical Wahhabi movement. He was able to gain converts through the provision of social services such as schools and wells. Likewise, Christian missionaries in Africa during the colonial period competed for souls by providing health care and education.

Charity has been central to the growth of the Muslim Brotherhood movement in Egypt and elsewhere in the Muslim world and of more nationally focused Islamist groups such as Hezbollah in Lebanon and Hamas in the Palestinian territories. Many Islamic charities and their affiliated parent organizations are perceived as not being corrupt, and these charities often are the first to arrive on the scene in a disaster or a war zone. For example, in the aftermath of the Pakistani earthquake, the charity group Jamaat ud-Dawa (JuD) was an early provider of relief.[34] JuD is accused of being affiliated with Lashkar-i-Taiba (LiT), a radical Islamist group fighting in Kashmir and an ally of al-Qaeda. LiT was blamed for several recent high-profile terrorist attacks, including the November 2008 attacks in Mumbai, India.

After the Israeli bombings in Lebanon in July and August 2006, the international press featured Hezbollah-sponsored charities bulldozing bombed-out areas and providing cash to families that had lost their homes, whereas international agencies and the Lebanese government were much slower off the mark. According to focus groups in Lebanon, Hezbollah's increasing popularity amongst the Shia population can be attributed to the view, as explained by one Shia resident, that "it is the only party that provides security and services while remaining transparent."[35]

The sentiments toward Hamas are similar. Haim Malka wrote: "The centrality of welfare to Hamas's broad social agenda of Islamizing society has been Hamas's most effective form of activism."[36] An International Crisis Group (ICG) report also concluded that "the leaders of the movement themselves ascribe a significant if not primary role to Islamic social welfare activism in explaining the growth and enduring popularity of the Islamist movement."[37] In the immediate aftermath of the intensive fighting between Israel and Hamas in Gaza that began in late December 2008 and lasted about three weeks, Hamas distributed compensation and reconstruction assistance.

In other parts of the world, the results are similar. Theodore Gerber and Sarah Mendelson conducted surveys in the North Caucasus region and concluded, "Whoever gets there first and delivers social goods—the Russian government, the West, or radical Islamists—will shape the political trajectory of this region."[38] In Somalia, again according to the ICG, the fundamentalist movements "owe their rapid growth since 1990 less to genuine popularity than access to substantial external funding."[39] Mark Bradbury added that "the success of [the radical Somali Islamist group] Al Ittihaad has, in part, been based on investing in a social and economic welfare program that the West will not fund."[40]

My interviews of Somalis and a review of the Somali press indicated that Somalis initially supported the radical Islamic Courts Union (ICU, which includes the former al-Ittihaad organization) when it took over much of southern Somalia in mid-2006, because the ICU established security for the first time since the state collapsed in 1991 and because of the social services provided by affiliated charities.[41] Public support for the ICU was also intended as a rebuke of many of the warlords, who were deeply unpopular, responsible for numerous human rights abuses and extortion, and perceived as uncaring about the suffering of ordinary Somalis.

Although some Islamic charities in Somalia—such as those managed by al-Islah—may not support extremist violence, other Somali Islamists, notably the Shabaab, a radical youth militia movement, do advocate more fundamental changes to Somali society and endorse violence as a strategy to achieve their goals.[42] Therefore, much like in other parts of the world, providing the poor with social services has helped to broaden the appeal of fundamentalist and violent interpretations of Islam inside Somalia.

Some observers have argued that extremist groups provide charitable services in order to expand their political power base. A variation on this argument posits that many of the more radical Islamic organizations purposely link assistance with politics because the two are an inextricable part of their overall worldview, identity, and purpose (help for the poor is indeed core to all religions). Whatever the motive, it is clear that affiliated charities fulfill critical state functions in places where the state does not. The result may be that they successfully realign community loyalty in the direction of radicalism.

When an extremist nongovernmental organization (NGO) is the only service provider in an area and a beneficiary refuses to wear a head scarf, for example, she may not get any service at all. Even if a recipient complies only temporarily to receive the aid, such pressures can transform societies over the long term.[43] Significantly, this aid monopoly often results in members of the public being reluctant to speak out against terrorist acts in their communities, or to help government authorities locate suspects.

Increased support for Somali, Algerian, or Pakistani terrorist groups does not necessarily imply that more Somalis, Algerians, or Pakistanis will themselves become terrorists. But if the goal is to isolate terrorists and reduce their appeal, then effective provision of basic social services would be one way to do this. At the most basic level, it is often simply the dearth of government-provided services or international donor support that makes some people and communities vulnerable and susceptible to extremist ideology.[44]

The sad fact is that the extremist charities in many fragile, weak, and even autocratic states receive very little competition from national capitals, Western donors, and multilateral agencies. The ideological viewpoint espoused by a radical group may not be the primary draw for many recipient families, but the lack of alternatives for schooling or health care fuels the growth of extremist movements. Because many developing states do not have the capacity to provide basic services for their inhabitants today and may not for the foreseeable future, Western assistance providers need to take a deeper look at their own approaches and funding mechanisms and elaborate more creative alternatives, especially when dealing with the "poor performers."

THE ORDINARY FOOT SOLDIER

In many instances, the provision of social services to the poor has shaped the environment in which terrorists operate. Here the linkages between poverty and terrorism are indirect, but compelling. More direct connections between the two can be found when examining the drivers for *some* volunteers and recruits: poor education and indigence have influenced decisions to volunteer (or be recruited or duped) for suicide bombing missions and also to enlist (or be conscripted) as a low-level operative. The changing nature of the terrorist threat has also shifted the issue of poverty into sharper focus.

Education and the Madrassa

A poor education (or no education) has been linked to terrorism, but it also has been determined not to be a crucial factor. According to some researchers, children who are educated in extremist madaris (plural for madrassa) are cannon fodder for terrorist organizations.[45] To the contrary, argue others, they do not have the requisite basic skills to carry out a terrorist attack.[46]

Either the data are not conclusive enough or both may be correct. The nineteen hijackers who committed the 9/11 atrocities and their spiritual father bin Laden were neither poor nor uneducated. Most members of the Muslim Brotherhood movement emerged from secular universities in Egypt. Palestinian and Lebanese members of Hamas and Hezbollah also tend to come from the ranks of the educated rather than the impoverished.

At the same time, some extremist madaris have provided recruits from the ranks of the impovershed for terrorist and militant organizations. Most madaris are heavily subsidized or free of charge. In addition to tuition, children also receive food, clothing, and books, at no cost to the family. Thus these schools are an attractive option for a poor family. In Pakistan alone, according to an International Crisis Group report, over one and a half million children attend madaris.[47]

Not all madaris have an extremist agenda; many also teach secular subjects and middle-class children. Yet the children who attend the more radical madaris are taught from an early age a violent worldview and to despise "corrupting western influences."[48] According to Ali Riaz, "Children are taught that Muslims all around the world . . . are under siege from sinister forces which they must fight to the death."[49] It is primarily in the Indian subcontinent (India, Pakistan, and Bangladesh) where these schools have been used to promote a political agenda—unlike in the Arab world where they do not play such a role.[50] Parts of Indonesia resemble the Indian subcontinent model rather than the Arab one, as do a growing number of regions in East and West Africa.

The Taliban leader Mullah Omar famously called on the Pakistani-based madaris to help with the fighting in Afghanistan during the Taliban takeover of the country in the late 1990s.[51] In response, in 1997 Maulana Samiul Haq shut down his famous Haqqania madrassa in the North-West Frontier Province of Pakistan and sent all 2,800 students to the frontline. The word *Talib* itself means religious student, and indeed an estimated one-third of the original Afghan Taliban were educated in Pakistan's madaris.

Some may argue that the madrassa students were not attacking the West during the fight against the Soviets nor during their national struggle against the Afghan warlords and other rebel leaders, and thus they are not relevant to a discussion of international terrorism. Since 9/11, however, these same madaris are sending students and graduates to kill NATO troops and civilians in Afghanistan. Some are also targeting Pakistani and expatriate civilians inside Pakistan. Christine Fair adds, "Pakistan's madaris in FATA—especially in North and South Waziristan—are deeply implicated in the recruitment of suicide attackers in both Afghanistan and Pakistan."[52] These madaris may also be providing short-term, "executive-level" education programs for European Muslims and other foreigners wishing to join the jihad (the July 2005 London bombers allegedly spent time in a Pakistani madrassa).

On a more general level, very few students from the world's madaris will become terrorists, even if there are some notable exceptions (such as in Afghanistan and Pakistan). And many of those who become terrorists will not be as skilled as their educated counterparts, accounting, perhaps, for some failed suicide bombing attempts. In many public schools in these same countries, students are also often offered a similarly violent worldview.

The madrassa has become the catchall for the debate on the root causes of terrorism, but as Fair and others point out, it is the quality of education—not whether it is religious or secular, public or private—that matters. As Fair explains, the available data suggest that in Pakistan's public schools, which educate 70 percent of Pakistan's children, "public school students have views only marginally more accommodating of domestic and external peace than those of madrassah counterparts. The same can be said of their teachers."[53] How many poorly educated public school students have joined terrorist groups is not known and should be an area of future inquiry.

Thus the data currently show that poverty and a lack of education can have a direct influence in some instances: some poor madrassa students do become terrorists. Poverty and lack of education also can play an indirect role:

the nonterrorist, impoverished student with a substandard education will gain few practical skills to prepare him or her for working in modern society.[54] These students and graduates will populate the enabling environment. Therefore, educational reform should become a top priority for counter-radicalization programs in the appropriate countries. The story is similarly nuanced for volunteers (or recruits) for suicide attacks.

Suicide Bombers

Because the families of "martyrs" are compensated by a number of charitable organizations (often very generously), it has been argued that the financial reward is an incentive for a poor family. Some families of suicide bombers are indeed elevated to a higher status in their communities, and receive financial help to start businesses or build new homes. Jessica Stern found from her interviews with those involved in the Kashmir dispute that "wealthy Pakistanis would rather donate their money than their sons to the cause, [and] families in poor, rural areas are likely to send their sons to 'jihad' under the belief that doing so is the only way to fulfill this spiritual duty."[55] Peter Bergen also reported on fees paid to families of suicide bombers who carried out attacks in Afghanistan, some earning $500, which Bergen described as "a good sum of money in a part of the world where many laborers only make a couple of dollars per day."[56]

A study of suicide attacks in Afghanistan from 2001 to 2007 conducted by the UN Assistance Mission in Afghanistan (UNAMA) found that children were recruited from both Afghanistan and Pakistan, and "these young children may be uneducated, ignorant, impressionable, brainwashed, and seeking money for their families."[57] Although suicide bombers may be motivated by a mix of greed, grievance, and ideology, they are largely drawn from the ranks of the poor. Whether they do it for money or belief is less relevant here than the fact that poverty led them into the hands of radicals in the first place. The UNAMA study concluded: "Poverty and lack of education figure in all but one [sic] the interviews of the confessed perpetrators."[58]

In Afghanistan and Pakistan, the connection appears to be direct. Evidence has also been found of indirect links. One study of the relationship among education, income, and support for suicide bombings in six Muslim countries (Indonesia, Jordan, Lebanon, Morocco, Pakistan, and Turkey) found that "increased education reduces the probability of support for suicide bombings . . . in the case of attacks on civilians, but not in the case of attacks on foreign forces and supporting civilians occupying Muslim lands."[59] Although this finding does not focus on the attackers themselves, it does fit into the enabling environment discussion and thus is also relevant. The researchers conclude that "educated Muslims identify and confront the moral dilemmas that come with the killing of civilians better than less educated ones. They are also more capable of dealing with the clear Islamic prohibition on suicide that some extremist Islamist ideologues have undermined by reinterpreting suicide as 'martyrdom.'"[60]

Another study carried out by researchers at the University of Jordan concurred with these results, though on a more general level. Polls carried out by the research team showed that the better educated were more likely to define Islamic Jihad, Hamas, al-Aqsa Martyrs Brigade, Hezbollah, al-Qaeda, and the Armed Islamic Group in Algeria as terrorist organizations. By contrast, the less educated were more likely to view these same organizations—notably al-Qaeda—as legitimate.[61]

On the other hand, some researchers have found conflicting results. Nasra Hassan discovered in her study of Palestinian suicide bombers that they were mostly educated, middle-class men.[62] Other studies seem to back her findings, though they tend to focus on longitudinal studies that stopped around 2001 or 2002 or only pertained to the Middle East.[63] Thus most of the research does not take into account the backgrounds of suicide bombers in Iraq since the U.S. invasion, the changing dynamics in Somalia, or the evolving situation in Pakistan and Afghanistan, where terrorists have attacked Western interests, soldiers, and citizens as well as local civilians. Motivation for these "new terrorists" will likely be a mix of factors, with poverty relevant in some instances and grievances or ideology in others.

The Peasants Revolt!

The research on the role of poverty is complex and demonstrates that there is no prototype terrorist. For example, at the leadership level most research has concluded that the bosses are typically educated and relatively affluent. Recent changes in the terrorist threat, however, indicate that there are more and more exceptions. Most of the leaders of the forty-plus militias in the loose network that comprises Pakistan's Taliban (Tehrek-e-Taliban), parts of which are now working with al-Qaeda, come from humble backgrounds. Baitullah Mehsud, the militia commander in South Waziristan and self-proclaimed head of the Pakistan Taliban, is himself from a poor peasant family, as is Manghal Bagh, the militia head in Khyber agency, who previously swept buses for a living.[64] Many other militant leaders in FATA, NWFP, and Balochistan also come from deprived backgrounds, as did Mullah Omar, the reclusive Afghan Taliban leader. Some would argue that warlords or militia heads should not be evaluated in the same way as terrorists, and yet today many of these leaders and groups have fused with al-Qaeda and are officially stamped with the terrorist label.

Although the leaders of terrorist organizations seem to come from both indigent and bourgeoisie backgrounds, that is not true of their humble servants. Strangely, most researchers recognize that poverty may be a factor among the lower ranks, but do not include the foot soldiers in their research or when aggregating data.

Returning to South Asia, the ordinary volunteer or recruit in Pakistan and Afghanistan has typically been poor. Daniel Markey explains, "In Pakistan, Taliban recruits are drawn from Afghan refugee camps and the network of extremist madrassas in the tribal areas. Taliban foot soldiers tend to be uneducated, poor Pashtuns with few other employment prospects."[65]

According to the UN study in Afghanistan, "Given the low development of FATA and paucity of employment opportunities, unemployed youth have joined these local militant groups as a way of both earning a livelihood and as a means of enhancing their social status."[66] Bergen learned that Taliban fighters were paid about $300 a month, "four times the wage of the average Afghan police officer."[67] Early indications are that at least one of the ten terrorists who committed the Mumbai attacks in November 2008 was motivated by poverty: the sole surviving gunman captured admitted that he joined LiT for the money.[68]

Deprivation seems to be a common factor among recruits elsewhere. The infamous impoverished town of Darnah in Libya sent a disproportionate number of young men to fight in Iraq, and an equally disproportionate number of them volunteered for suicide missions.[69] As Kevin Peraino explains, "There is no doubt that economic misery and its social consequences have scarred Darnah's young people."[70]

In Somalia—another country that has witnessed an unfortunate increase in al-Qaeda–inspired terrorism—poverty has convinced some young people to join the violent jihadist youth group Shabaab. Here the motivation for membership at the foot soldier level appears to be more about dollars than dogma. There are no reliable data to draw on in Somalia because of the eighteen years of state collapse, which also complicates efforts to disentangle the competing motivations for joining and leading such groups. The available data do indicate, however, that the lack of governance and inadequate economic opportunities have been persuasive at the lower ranks. Moreover, although the motivations at the leadership level may be a mix of ideology, opportunism, personal political ambition, greed, and grievance, the leaders have exploited the issue of poverty in Somalia as part of their public rhetoric and to attract more recruits to their movement.

CONCLUDING REMARKS

Returning to the question posed at the outset, it appears that the research on the relationship between poverty and terrorism is by no means conclusive and, if anything, reveals a mixed picture. Poverty plays a role in some instances and not in others. Certain terrorist movements have expanded their support base in the enabling environment by providing the poor with direct aid. Some volunteers for suicide missions and many ordinary foot soldiers come from impoverished backgrounds, and also attended the radical madaris. Thus poverty has played an indirect and direct role in the recruitment of terrorists in some critical cases.

Moreover, many of the more privileged terrorists use the plight of the poor as one justification for committing violence and for broadening their appeal. They claim to speak on behalf of the poor, just as other middle-class, well-educated ideologues have done in the past. This claim allows them to broaden their constituencies to include many marginalized communities throughout the world. Thus it is too early to shut the book on this debate, especially because poverty appears to be more relevant in today's hottest terrorist theaters, notably Afghanistan and Pakistan, which have become the main Taliban and al-Qaeda sanctuaries, breeding grounds, and training centers.

Indeed, over the past year in Pakistan militant activity and violence have spread throughout the poorest parts of the country, from South and North Waziristan into all seven agencies of the Federally Administered Tribal Areas, into settled parts of the North-West Frontier Province, and into Balochistan, where Afghan Taliban leaders regroup from fighting. The writ of the central government and traditional authority has steadily eroded in FATA, although proposals are on the table to integrate FATA into NWFP. This is not to say that the region is an "ungoverned territory" (an inappropriate term), but rather that this extremely impoverished and undergoverned region has been infiltrated by violent extremists over the years who have coerced, bribed, or killed local authorities when entrenching their authority.

Yet much like in Somalia, and because few Westerners and Pakistanis visit most of FATA, Pakistani and American analysts and officials have only a rudimentary understanding of the complicated alliances, dynamics, and threats posed by the numerous groups operating in these areas, especially the Pakistan Taliban, the Afghan Taliban, al-Qaeda, and other militant groups.[71] Nor does anyone seem to have a good grasp of who the "foreigners" are, and the alliances among and between Pakistanis, Afghans, Arabs, and Central Asians (for example, the Uzbeks, Chechens, Tajiks, Kazaks, and Uighirs). The lack of reliable data and information on this region (and other "ungoverned spaces") may account for why these areas have not been integrated into previous studies on the relationship between poverty and terrorism.

When examining the research on the role of poverty in terrorism, it is therefore important to consider the areas excluded from the analysis and what creative tools can be used to learn more about these no-go territories so that they can be included in ongoing research. If these areas were factored in, more researchers would find that poverty is indeed an important concern in some of today's most pressing terrorist hot spots.

Much of the previous research that supposedly debunked the poverty-terrorism thesis concentrated on international terrorism and terrorism that targeted the West, not on nationally focused insurgencies. Yet as most researchers know, the al-Qaeda movement and network are extremely fluid and rapidly mutating. Over the last few years, many of the national and international groups have fused. For example, today the Somali Shabaab, Afghan Taliban, Pakistan Taliban, and Algeria's Armed Islamic Group are very different creatures from their predecessors or earlier iterations. Such groups collaborate and learn from each other as well as from their counterparts in places such as Iraq, Chechnya, and even Colombia. Policymakers and researchers need to ensure that the debate and response are also fluid, flexible, and able to adapt in real time.

Notes

1. President Bill Clinton, remarks to the Jordanian Parliament, Amman, Jordan, October 26, 1994, www.presidency.ucsb.edu/ws/index.php?pid=49373.
2. Transcription of *La Stampa* interview with James D. Wolfensohn, World Bank, December 7, 2001.
3. Quoted in Claude Berrebi, "Evidence about the Link between Education, Poverty and Terrorism among Palestinians," *Peace Economics, Peace Science and Public Policy* 13, no. 1 (2007): 2.
4. For background on the 9/11 hijackers, see National Commission on Terrorist Attacks upon the United States, *The 9/11 Commission Report* (New York: Norton, 2004), esp. chap. 5; and Terry McDermott, *Perfect Soldiers* (New York: HarperCollins, 2005).
5. Daniel Pipes, "God and Mammon: Does Poverty Cause Militant Islam?" *National Interest* (Winter 2001/2002); Alan Kreuger and Jitka Maletkova, "Does Poverty Cause Terrorism?" *New Republic,* June 24, 2002.
6. World Health Organization, *World Health Statistics 2008* (Washington, D.C.: WHO, 2008).
7. Ching-Chi Hsieh and M. D. Pugh, "A Meta-Analysis of Recent Aggregate Data Studies," *Criminal Justice Review* 18, no. 2 (1993): 182–196.
8. James Fearon and David Laitin, "Ethnicity, Insurgency and Civil War," *American Political Science Review* 97 (2003): 75–90.

9. Leif Ohlsson, "Livelihood Conflicts: Linking Poverty and Environment as Causes of Conflict," Swedish International Development Cooperation Agency, 2000.

10. Adam Przeworski, Michael Alvarez, Jose Antonio Cheibub, and Fernando Limongi. *Democracy and Development: Political Institutions and Well-Being in the World 1950 to 1990* (New York: Cambridge University Press, 2000); J. B. Londregan and K. Poole, "Poverty, the Coup Trap and the Seizure of Executive Power," *World Politics* 42, no. 2 (1990): 151–183.

11. Aristide R. Zolberg and Peter M. Benda, *Global Migrants and Global Refugees* (New York: Berghahn Books, 2001).

12. Ted Robert Gurr, *Why Men Rebel* (Princeton, N.J.: Princeton University Press, 1971).

13. See, for example, James A. Piazza, "Rooted in Poverty? Terrorism, Poor Economic Development and Social Cleavages," *Terrorism and Political Violence* 18 (2006): 219–237; Alberto Abadie, "Poverty, Political Freedom and the Roots of Terrorism," *American Economic Review* 96, no. 2 (2006): 159–77; Claude Berrebi, "Evidence About the Link Between Education, Poverty and Terrorism Among Palestinians," *Peace Economics, Peace Science and Public Policy* 13, no. 1 (2007). Note, however, that Quan Li and Drew Schaub, in "Economic Globalization and Transnational Terrorism," *Journal of Conflict Resolution* 48, no. 2 (2004): 230–258, did find economically developed countries to be significantly less likely to experience terrorist attacks.

14. Figures derived from Shaohua Chen and Martin Ravallion, "How Have the World's Poorest Fared Since the Early 1980s?" *World Bank Research Observer* 19, no. 2 (2004): 141–169.

15. For an overview of these terrorist attacks, see the RAND-MIPT Terrorism Knowledge Base (www.tkb.org).

16. UNDP, *World Development Report* (various years).

17. The time-series line graphs for these data can be found in James A. Piazza, "Global Poverty, Inequality and Transnational Terrorism: A Research Note," *Perspectives on Terrorism* 1, no. 4 (2007).

18. Explanations for the Human Development Index and data tables are available at the United Nations Development Program's website, http://hdr.undp.org/en/reports/global/hdr2007-2008. The data used are from the UNDP's *Human Development Report 2007/2008: Fighting Climate Change: Human Solidarity in a Divided World*.

19. The results in Table 2-2 are made more dramatic by the inclusion of Iraq in the Medium Human Development category, a country that has seen a dramatic increase in domestic terrorism since the United States toppled the Saddam Hussein regime in 2003. The most recent Human Development Index score available for Iraq, 1999, places it firmly in the Middle category. Even if Iraq is excluded from the data in Table 2-2, the overall results are the same: Low Human Development countries still produce the least transnational terrorism, sustain the lowest level of terrorism, and host the fewest terrorist groups.

20. The twenty countries are, in order from the most unequal, Namibia, Lesotho, Sierra Leone, Central African Republic, Botswana, Bolivia, Afghanistan, Haiti, Colombia, Paraguay, South Africa, Brazil, Panama, Guatemala, Chile, Honduras, Ecuador, El Salvador, Peru, and the Dominican Republic.

21. For a full discussion of the Naxalites and their origins, see Dipak K. Gupta, "The Naxalites and Maoist Movement in India: Birth, Demise and Reincarnation," *Democracy and Security* 3, no. 2 (2007): 157–188.
22. Ken Menkhaus, "Quasi-States, Nation-Building and Terrorist Safe Havens," *Journal of Conflict Studies* 23, no. 2 (2003): 7–23.
23. Alan Krueger and Jitka Maleckova, "Education, Poverty and Terrorism: Is There a Causal Connection?" *Journal of Economic Perspectives* 17, no. 4 (2003): 119–144; Berrebi, "Evidence about the Link"; Charles A. Russell and Bowman H. Miller, "Profile of a Terrorist," *Studies in Conflict and Terrorism* 1, no. 1 (1977): 17–34.
24. Simon Haddad and Hilal Khashan, "Islam and Terrorism: Lebanese Muslim Views on September 11," *Journal of Conflict Resolution* 46 (2002): 812–828; Krueger and Maleckova, "Education, Poverty and Terrorism."
25. Edgar O'Ballance, *The Language of Violence: The Blood Politics of Terrorism* (San Rafael, Calif.: Presidio Press, 1979).
26. See James A. Piazza, "Incubators of Terror: Do Failed and Failing States Promote Transnational Terrorism?" *International Studies Quarterly* 52, no. 3 (2008): 469–488.
27. Though it should be noted that Bogota has made progress in increasing government control over rural regions in which the FARC operates since the inception of Plan Colombia, a U.S.-financed counterterrorism program that began in 1999.
28. James I. Walsh and James A. Piazza, "Why Respecting Physical Integrity Rights Reduces Terrorism," *Comparative Political Studies* (forthcoming 2010).
29. See Alan Kreuger, *What Makes a Terrorist* (Princeton, N.J.: Princeton University Press, 2007); Krueger and Maleckova, "Education, Poverty, Political Violence and Terrorism"; Piazza, "Rooted in Poverty?" 159–177; Tim Krieger and Daniel Meier-rieks, "What Causes Terrorism?" Working Papers Series No. 2008-05, Center for International Economics, Paderborn, Germany, June 2008.
30. Kreuger, *What Makes a Terrorist*, 12.
31. See "Poverty 'Fueling Terrorism,'" BBC News, March 22, 2002, http://news.bbc .co.uk/hi/english/world/newsid_1886000/1886617.stm.
32. Louise Richardson at Harvard University originally coined this term. Another useful term is *complicit society*.
33. Interestingly, some of the more successful Islamist political parties have a social service wing, whereas secular political parties do not.
34. John Lancaster and Kamran Khan, "Extremists Fill Aid Chasm after Quake: Group Banned in Pakistan Dispenses Relief," *Washington Post*, October 16, 2005.
35. National Democratic Institute, "Findings of Lebanon Focus Groups," NDI, Washington, D.C., 2007, 8.
36. Haim Malka, "Hamas: Resistance and Transformation of Palestinian Society," in *Understanding Islamic Charities*, ed. Jon Alterman and Karin von Hippel (Washington, D.C.: Center for Strategic and International Studies, 2007), 100.
37. "Islamic Social Welfare Activism in the Occupied Palestinian Territories: A Legitimate Target?" ICG Middle East Report No. 13, International Crisis Group, Brussels, April 2, 2003, 27.
38. Theodore P. Gerber and Sarah E. Mendelson, "Security through Sociology: The North Caucasus and the Global Counterinsurgency Paradigm," unpublished manuscript, November 2007.

39. International Crisis Group, "Somalia: Countering Terrorism in a Failed State," ICG Africa Report No. 45, Brussels, May 23, 2002, 13.

40. Mark Bradbury, "Somalia: The Aftermath of September 11th and the War on Terrorism," Oxfam Great Britain Report, February 2002, 25.

41. This point is difficult to demonstrate more conclusively because there are no reliable polling or survey data for Somalia. In general, since the state collapsed in 1991 statistics have been difficult to accrue because of the insecurities on the ground, because of the lack of regular and reliable data collection, and because up to half of the population is nomadic. Different organizations—both Somali and international—gather data in different ways, with no agreed methodology or reliable means of accumulating information over time.

42. See Andre LeSage, "Islamic Charities in Somalia," in Alterman and von Hippel, *Understanding Islamic Charities*.

43. See Shawn Teresa Flanigan, "Charity as Resistance: Connections between Charity, Contentious Politics, and Terror," *Studies in Conflict and Terrorism* 29 (2006): 641–655.

44. See Karin von Hippel, "Aid Effectiveness: Improving Relations with Islamic Charities" in Alterman and von Hippel, *Understanding Islamic Charities*.

45. See Jeffrey Goldberg, "Inside Jihad U.: The Education of a Holy Warrior," *New York Times Magazine*, June 25, 2000.

46. See, for example, Peter Bergen and Swati Pandey, "The Myth of the Madrassa," *International Herald Tribune*, June 15, 2005.

47. International Crisis Group, "Pakistan: Madrasas, Extremism and the Military," ICG Asia Report No. 36, Brussels, July 29, 2002, i.

48. See Craig Davis, "'A' is for Allah, 'J' is for Jihad," *World Policy Journal* (Spring 2002): 90.

49. Ali Riaz, "Global Jihad, Sectarianism and the Madrassahs in Pakistan," Working Paper 85, Institute of Defence and Strategic Studies, Singapore, August 2005, 20.

50. Uzma Anzar, "Islamic Education: A Brief History of Madrassas with Comments on Curricula and Current Pedagogical Practices," World Bank, Washington, D.C., March 2003, 17–18.

51. See Ahmed Rashid, *The Taliban: Islam, Oil and the New Great Game in Central Asia* (London: I. B. Taurus, 2002), 59, 72, 78.

52. C. Christine Fair, *The Madrassah Challenge: Militancy and Religious Education in Pakistan*, U.S. Institute of Peace, Washington, D.C., 2008, 7. See also United Nations Assistance Mission in Afghanistan, "Suicide Attacks in Afghanistan (2001–2007)," September 1, 2007, 6, 98.

53. See, for example, Fair, *Madrassah Challenge*, 97–98.

54. See Jessica Stern, "Meeting with the Muj," *Bulletin of the Atomic Scientists* 57 (January/February 2001): 42–51.

55. Jessica Stern, "Pakistan's Jihad Culture," *Foreign Affairs* 79 (November/December 2000): 122.

56. Peter Bergen, "Afghan Spring," *New Republic*, June 18, 2007.

57. United Nations Assistance Mission, "Suicide Attacks in Afghanistan (2001–2007)," 89.

58. Ibid., 79.

59. M. Najeeb Shafiq and Abdulkader H. Sinno, "Education, Income and Support for Suicide Bombings: Evidence from Six Muslim Countries," Indiana University Working Paper Series, July 2008, 1.

60. Ibid., 22.
61. Center for Strategic Studies, University of Jordan, "Revisiting the Arab Street Research from Within," Amman, February 2005, 75, 78–79.
62. Nasra Hassan, "An Arsenal of Believers," *New Yorker*, November 19, 2001, 36–41.
63. See, for example, Berrebi, "Evidence about the Link"; Krueger, *What Makes a Terrorist*; and Marc Sageman, *Understanding Terror Networks* (Philadelphia: University of Pennsylvania Press, 2004), 61–98.
64. Dexter Filkins, "Right at the Edge," *New York Times Magazine*, September 7, 2008.
65. Daniel Markey, "Securing Pakistan's Tribal Belt," CFR 36, Council on Foreign Relations, New York, July 2008, 11.
66. "Suicide Attacks in Afghanistan (2001–2007)," 84.
67. Bergen, "Afghan Spring," 2007.
68. Vikas Bajaj and Lydia Polgreen, "Suspect Stirs Mumbai Court by Confessing," *New York Times*, July 20, 2009.
69. Kevin Peraino, "Destination Martyrdom: What Drove So Many Libyans to Volunteer as Suicide Bombers for the War in Iraq? A Visit to Their Hometown—The Dead-end City of Darnah," *Newsweek International*, April 28, 2008.
70. Ibid.
71. As diplomat Richard Holbrooke remarked in congressional testimony on May 7, 2008, "I don't have a clue what's going on in the FATA. And if anyone ever comes before this Committee and says so, you'd better ask twice, because it is one of the most elusive areas in the world."

3

can terrorism ever be justified?

NO: Terrorist violence is never justified
Tamar Meisels, *Tel Aviv University*

YES: Terrorism is a just tool of the weak
Ted Honderich, *University College London*

There is a famous scene in Gillo Pontecorvo's 1966 film *The Battle of Algiers* in which the recently captured leader of Algeria's National Liberation Front (FLN), Larbi Ben M'Hidi, is brought before international journalists at a press conference. The year is 1957 and the FLN, a group committed to Algeria's full independence from French colonial rule, had recently launched a series of deadly bombings in civilian locations in the European quarter of Algiers.

French reporter: "Mr. Ben M'Hidi, isn't it a filthy thing to use women's baskets to carry explosives for killing people?"

Ben M'Hidi: "Doesn't it seem even filthier to drop napalm bombs on defenseless villages, wreaking even greater havoc? It would be better if we too had planes. Give me the bombers, and you can have the baskets."

This exchange, in a nutshell, brings to life two of the most contentious and politically charged issues surrounding terrorism: how and why groups choose—and justify—the killing of innocents as a means of achieving their goals and how is it determined who has the "legitimate" right to use violence in the first place.

Terrorism, by any definition, involves the use of violence in furtherance of a political cause.[1] But definitions are one thing, justifications quite another. In the subjective world of terrorism, when it comes to justifying killing, much depends on *who is doing the justifying*. The FLN and its supporters justified indiscriminant killing as a necessary means of achieving what they believed to be a legitimate political goal—ending French colonial rule. Opponents of the FLN and its tactics (though not necessarily its goals) argued the opposite: that such killing was "filthy" and illegitimate.

In accusing the French government of even more widespread killing of innocents, Ben M'Hidi raises a larger point: how can the French government claim legitimacy in its use of violence to maintain control of its colony, while those seeking independence are morally condemned for doing the same? In other words, how is it that states can use force in furtherance of their political goals—or, in the parlance of the military strategist Carl von Clausewitz, as "a continuation of politics by other means"—while aggrieved groups within those states cannot?[2]

Tamar Meisels and Ted Honderich delve bravely into these issues. Meisels argues that it is the calculated targeting of civilians that separates terrorism from other forms of substate violence (for example, guerrilla warfare) and eliminates the right of terrorists to claim moral justification for their actions. Yes, states sometimes kill civilians in the course of military operations, but they are rarely if ever the primary target; this is not the case with terrorists. Mesiels also takes issue with the presumption, offered by many defenders of terrorism, that aggrieved groups often have "no other option" than indiscriminate killing in order to achieve their goals. Nonviolence often pays far greater dividends, she argues.

Honderich, using the example of Palestinian terrorism as his primary resource, addresses these issues from a very different plane of logic. What, for example, is an "innocent civilian"—surely not those who support (and benefit from) an unjust occupation, whether or not they wear a military uniform? In addition, who determines whether and in what ways the use of violence may be "legitimate"? It cannot simply be the side that has the biggest guns. And if the term *terrorist* is to be used pejoratively, should states escape such description simply because they are, in fact, states?

The important issues raised in this chapter will not be resolved here. Perhaps they will never be. Terrorism, by its very nature, is a highly social phenomenon—passionate differences on the basic questions of definition, description, and justification will linger as long as terrorism itself remains on the world scene.

NO: Terrorist violence is never justified
Tamar Meisels, *Tel Aviv University*

Terrorism Can Never Be Justified

As terrorism penetrates liberal democracies, Western intellectuals, particularly left-leaning ones, seem increasingly confused, because traditional loyalties appear to pull in opposing directions. Liberals and leftists are accustomed to siding with the underdog and supporting the self-determination of peoples (most recently they are fervently committed to Palestinian independence). They customarily oppose violence and war and associate with peace movements. Most versions of modern liberalism include a complicated commitment to cultural pluralism and the toleration of cultures and societies, beliefs, and life choices, including those that appear dramatically alien to their own. Perhaps one man's terrorist is another's freedom fighter; one man's crime against humanity is another's resistance against oppression. Why, one might ask, are the desperate actions of militant groups dubbed illegitimate terrorism, while the military operations of established nation-states are considered legitimate warfare?

Such liberals often support a global application of equality standards, and they are therefore particularly sensitive to the plight of impoverished populations of developing nations. In the extreme, this sensitivity has led some to an overall antiglobalization stance or even to outright support of some forms of terrorism.

This essay looks at such questions of moral judgment, which have been thrust upon political philosophy by current events. Analyzing both the definition of terrorism and its possible justifications, the argument developed here calls for a unanimous liberal front against terrorism and its perpetrators.

IS TERRORISM EVER "RIGHT"?

There is a growing academic reluctance to define terrorism as a specific and fiendish deed. The considerable body of academic literature now available expresses sympathy, and at times outright justification, for Islamic (particularly Palestinian) terrorism. Among these apologetics of terrorism are well-known intellectual figures such as Noam Chomsky and the late French philosopher Jacques Derrida. One such leading scholar who offers a vigorous defense of modern-day terrorism is the philosopher Ted Honderich.

In his controversial book *After the Terror,* Honderich takes up the linguistic challenge of defining *terrorism,* alongside the moral issues that flow from it. Setting out with more basic terms such as *violence* in general, and *political violence* in particular, Honderich ultimately refrains from defining *terrorism* independently.[3] Choosing to make no distinction between various forms of political violence, Honderich speaks of either terrorism or political violence as "violence with a political and social intention, whether or not intended to put people in general in fear, and raising a question of its moral justification— either illegal violence within a society or smaller-scale violence than war between states or societies and not according to international law."[4]

In defense of this inclusive definition, Honderich argues that making people in general fearful is not a significantly distinctive factor between forms of violence. He believes that "the main thing is getting political and social change," and this goal characterizes all forms of political violence. The idea that certain forms of political violence are directed specifically at innocent people, and that this notion ought to be viewed as part of their particular condemnation as "terrorism," is also raised in passing and similarly dismissed out of hand. This common intuition that there is a particular wrong involved in the *intentional* killing of noncombatants, and that such attacks in particular ought to be singled out as "acts of terror," is no more than momentarily considered and subsequently denied in the name of consistency.[5] After all, Western states kill innocents, too, and do not condemn the death of some innocents as loudly as we denounce the death of other (our) innocents.

Honderich's self-professed excuse for not singling out and condemning the specific sort of violence usually called "terrorism" is that it is actually more like all other forms of political violence than it is distinct from them. Whatever their particular mode of operation, all terrorists aspire to bring about (or preserve) a social and political end by means of inflicting harmful force. In his view, then, there is nothing unique or particularly condemnable about any one specific type of political violence, aside from the prima facie assumption of possible wrongfulness, which applies to the infliction of all injury and harm.[6]

This perspective bears clear normative implications, because it "does not by itself morally condemn in a final way anything that falls under it. It leaves open the possibility that there was justification of, say, the particular terrorism that led to the existence of the state of Israel. So with the attempt on Hitler's life and attempts to kill Osama Bin Laden in the years before September 11."[7]

Because Honderich's view of "terrorism" makes no distinction between various forms of political violence, it justifies the subsequent comparison between these examples and the case that appears to form the foundation of Honderich's agenda: that Palestinian terror against Israeli civilians is in fact justified. As Honderich puts it: "I myself have no doubt, to take the outstanding case, that the Palestinians have exercised a moral right in their terrorism against the Israelis . . . and those who have killed themselves in the cause of their people have indeed sanctified themselves."[8]

As for the attacks of September 11, 2001, Honderich holds that "our definition of terrorism does not rule out the possibility that some terrorism could be justified as response to what others called structural violence." His overall political argument, developed throughout several publications, is that political violence, including terrorism, is justifiable in response to the wrongs done to individuals in the developing and Arab world—by the immoral omissions or direct commissions, particularly of the United States, associated with globalization, oil, and other capitalist interests and support of Israel.[9] For Honderich, "the conclusion is that there is no simple objection of a certain kind to terrorism against us, even the terrorism of September 11. We do not have a certain imagined moral high ground to stand on in condemning terrorism against us, in explaining our revulsion for the killers at the twin towers."[10]

Certainly, if terrorism is conceived so widely as to include all forms of political violence with no moral distinction between them, then that means "we are all terrorists," with the United States, Britain, and Israel leading a rotten bunch. Thus Noam Chomsky, who shares many of Honderich's assumptions, states clearly and repeatedly that the United States is a leading terrorist state.[11] Add to this the forms of "structural violence"—that is, America's alleged responsibility for the misfortunate lives in developing countries and among Arab populations—how then can one nonhypocritically oppose attacks against the United States by those harmed by its policies? On these question-begging assumptions, one cannot. Once terrorism is defined with a deliberate disregard for the element of fear—the literal terrorization of a civilian population— along with the element of targeting innocent noncombatants, the convenient outcome is inevitably going to be a striking formal similarity between killing soldiers, policemen, or officials, assassinating Adolf Hitler or targeting Osama bin Laden, and blowing up a café, a commuter bus, or a skyscraper. It would seem that, according to Honderich, these are "all in a good cause."

Nevertheless, Honderich regards the events of September 11, 2001, as wrong (as opposed to Palestinian terrorism aimed at Israelis), but only because they involved the use of violence *without any reasonable hope of achieving its justifiable goals,* understood as fighting off the effects of America's bad policies. Indeed, Honderich more than implies that if the attacks of 9/11 could reasonably have been conceived as an effective means of saving more misfortunate lives (say, in Africa) than taking the number of lives destroyed in New York, then such attacks would, in fact, have been justified. Furthermore, future attacks on American civilians that would explicitly have antiglobalization and ending U.S. exploitation as their goals, with reasonable hope of achieving this end, would be justified, perhaps even commanded by Honderich's "humanitarian" principles.

Honderich, of course, is not a lone voice. In an engaging dialogue with Giovanna Borradori, Jacques Derrida presents a somewhat more subtle, yet not dissimilar, evaluation of the events of September 11. He, too, discredits the commonly attempted distinctions between terrorism and other types of violence.[12] Aside from the terrorist excesses of states during wartime and otherwise, Derrida suggests that causing fear, anxiety, panic, and even outright terror among the citizens of a state, far from being unique to any specific type of political violence, actually characterizes the very authority of law and exercising of state sovereignty. Partly in view of "state terror," Derrida's comments imply that the civilian-military distinction between wartime killing and terrorism is misplaced, although, like Honderich, he pays this distinction little attention, remarking only in passing and in a somewhat offhand tone, that "the victims of terrorism are *assumed* to be civilians."[13] He also reminds readers of the undeniable fact that the predominant powers often use, and abuse, terminology and definitions opportunistically to suit their own partisan political advantage, and he attempts to move from this reminder to the disputable claim that terrorism therefore cannot be strictly defined. Derrida also reiterates the platitude "that terrorists might be praised as freedom fighters in one context . . . and denounced as terrorists in another," but without seriously scrutinizing this common aphorism.

In a similar vein as Honderich, Derrida then points out that both terrorists and states invoke self-defense as their excuse for exercising the type of violence that their adversaries regard as terrorism. And he alludes to the possibility that certain forms of Western-instigated "structural violence" associated with capitalism and globalization could in themselves be regarded by some observers as prior incidents of state terrorism. With this, Derrida joins Honderich in placing the distinctions between deliberate and unintentional actions as well as between acts and omissions in the philosophical wastepaper basket, alongside the earlier dismissal of the civilian-combatant distinction.[14] Thus he also questions whether terrorism need necessarily involve the deliberate act of killing, or whether the neglect of developing nations, for example, can in itself count as terrorism. As Derrida has said, "All situations of social or national structural oppression produce a terror."[15] Having "deconstructed" the notion of terrorism, Derrida's terminology is also deliberately inclusive, referring only to "violence" in a general fashion rather than to "war" or "terrorism." Ultimately, for these thinkers the normative evaluation of terrorism hinges on its prospects of success.

A DEADLY TRILOGY: GUERRILLA WARFARE, POLITICAL ASSASSINATION, AND TERRORISM

Furthering this discussion of general conceptions of terrorism, Michael Walzer's classic work *Just and Unjust Wars* offers a uniquely instructive (and contemporarily relevant) distinction between three categories of irregular warfare, each warranting a different moral attitude.[16] First, there are guerrillas, or partisans, who are undeniably irregular in that they do not wear uniforms or other revealing dress (such as identifying badges or caps)and conceal their weapons and militant identity, and so remain unprotected by international laws of war. They also endanger civilian populations in a variety of ways, such as by hiding among them. Guerrilla warfare, however, does not itself subvert the war convention by attacks on civilians. Indeed, guerrillas draw a fine line between military and civilian targets. For the most part, guerrillas uphold the distinction between combatants and civilians, primarily targeting combatants either by direct ambush or by means of espionage and sabotage. As a rule, Walzer tells us, guerrillas do not target innocent civilians.[17] This distinguishing feature of guerrilla warfare indicates, at least intuitively, that, though nonconventional, this kind of warfare warrants some legitimacy, even though it does not render its participants eligible for the protection of international conventions and the war rights of soldiers specified in them. Guerrillas make distinctions and although they do at times kill civilians (as do anti-guerrilla forces), civilians are not their primary targets. Guerrillas, then, may warrant moral respect, at least by those who identify with their cause. The French resistance to the German occupation in World War II is a classic case in point.

This vital distinction between modern terrorism and guerrilla warfare, along with its normative implications, was recently restated by Jurgan Habermas in slightly different terms. Habermas clearly distinguishes between "indiscriminant guerrilla warfare" and "paramilitary guerrilla warfare"—"the first is epitomized by Palestinian terrorism, in which murder is usually carried out by a suicide militant."[18] By contrast, only "the model of paramilitary guerrilla warfare is proper to the national liberation movements and is retrospectively legitimized by the formation of the state." Contra Derrida, then, indiscriminant guerrilla warfare cannot be retrospectively legitimized by political success. In Habermas's own words, "Palestinian terrorism . . . revolves around murder, around the indiscriminate annihilation of enemies, women and children—life against life. This is what distinguishes it from the terrorism that appears in the paramilitary form of guerrilla warfare."[19]

Next, political assassination, despite what Honderich would have people believe, is clearly distinguishable from terrorist strikes of the 9/11 type. When acting in the capacity of assassins, revolutionaries draw a moral distinction "between people who can and people who cannot be killed." Those who can be killed consist exclusively "of officials, the political agents of regimes, thought to be oppressive." Assassination, Walzer explains, necessarily involves "the drawing of a line that we will have little difficulty recognizing as the political parallel of the line that marks off combatants from non-combatants."[20] Crucially, assassins do not kill indiscriminately; ordinary private citizens remain immune from attack.[21] Although assassins cannot claim any of the soldiers' rights specified by international war conventions and treaties, they may gain some degree of respect simply because they do set limits to their actions. In his recent book *Terror and Liberalism*, Paul Berman makes a similar observation about the ethics of assassination. The "terrorists" of the past, such as the Russian anarchists who assassinated tzarist officials, took care to avoid incidental innocent casualties; they "were morally fastidious," even "delicate."[22]

Terrorism more strictly conceived, however, is distinct from both guerrilla warfare and assassinations. It allows for no fusion of terms or the kind of confusion of the various forms of political violence attempted by Honderich and Derrida. In sharp contrast with guerrillas who (as a rule) confront armies and assassins who target particular officials, modern terrorists uphold no distinctions. Terrorists do not kill civilians by accident, as an unfortunate consequence of their military activity. All armed forces admit and profusely regret (whether cynically or sincerely) the killing of (at times many) innocent civilians in the course of military strikes or operations. For terrorists, however, the killing of noncombatants is not a regrettable by-product or side effect; innocent victims are not an "occupational hazard." Instead, they are the be all and end all of this form of belligerency.

THE TROUBLE WITH TERROR

What, then, is so wrong about terrorism in particular? Terrorism, Walzer explains, "breaks across moral limits beyond which no further limitation seems possible, for within the category of civilian and citizen, there isn't any smaller group for which immunity might be claimed. . . . Terrorists anyway make no such claim; they kill anybody."[23] For Walzer, this is a crucial point about terrorism: it is not aimed at particular people.

Berman's evaluation of modern terrorism is similar. He marks an important transition within revolutionary movements in the twentieth century, which he eloquently describes as the point at which "the fastidious yielded to the not fastidious."[24] Berman describes the loss of what the Russian revolutionary

Boris Savinkov called a "terrorist conscience," which took care to aim at the victim. For modern-day terrorists, the murder is massive and anonymous, the nihilism unlimited, and the transgression total.

Crucially, terrorism is also a form of immoral free riding. All groups have at least some interest in upholding the distinction between civilian and military targets. It was precisely the growing realization of the dangers of war to civilian populations, probably more than any abstract moral principle, that pushed European statesmen in the nineteenth and twentieth centuries to negotiate and regulate the manners in which wars ought, and ought not, to be fought. As war became a more popular business, states were led, largely by the concern for the well-being of their own citizenry, to initiate international conventions and side with treaties that committed them to upholding distinctions between military and nonmilitary personnel, as well as between lawful and unlawful combatants, with the proviso that others do the same.

Such distinctions and codes of war, which are desirable for conventional armies and the states they represent, are in fact absolutely essential for terrorists and the success of their strategies. Terrorist tactics rely entirely on conventional armies maintaining these distinctions, while the terrorists themselves openly thwart them. Put differently, terrorism wholly depends on its opponents' upholding of a moral code that the terrorists themselves reject. Terrorists hitch a morally dubious free ride on their adversaries' moral code. If their adversaries were to match the terrorists' nihilism by denying the status of noncombatants and the distinction between belligerents and civilians, choosing to terrorize civilians with their superior force, they would once again have the upper hand, rendering the smaller-scale terrorism of the "underdog" totally ineffective.

In explaining why suicide terrorists almost exclusively target democracies, Robert Pape argues that "suicide terrorists . . . must also be confident that their opponent will be at least somewhat restrained. . . . [D]emocracies have generally been more restrained in their use of force against civilians, at least since World War II."[25] The Kurds, Pape points out, are a case in point:

> Although [pre-2003] Iraq has been far more brutal towards its Kurdish population than has Turkey, violent Kurdish groups have used suicide attacks exclusively against democratic Turkey and not against the authoritarian regime in Iraq. There are plenty of national groups living under authoritarian regimes with grievances that could possibly inspire suicide terrorism, but none have.[26]

To put all this more concretely, the instigators and perpetrators of 9/11 relied on the fact that the United States—for whatever its moral transgressions—

would not retaliate by, for example, using atomic weapons against civilian Arab populations in the Middle East. Palestinian terrorists rely on the fact that Israel, while at times killing civilians, is nevertheless bound in a web of international and internal pressures alongside moral restraints that prevent it from striking back at Palestinians with all its might with no regard for civilian life. Terrorists also rely on a set of civil liberties, which they often hold in contempt but which enable them to operate more freely than they could in the absence of such civil liberties. Terrorism's very livelihood depends on a reversal of the Kantian imperative to "act only on that maxim through which you can at the same time will that it should become a universal law."[27] Terrorists must will, and be assured of, the precise reverse. They rely wholeheartedly on their maxim not being universalized. Where terrorists are pursued in kind—that is, by a military force that shares their disregard for human rights and moral codes—they have no hope of success.

All this is less true of guerrillas and assassins, who need not be free riders. As noted earlier, guerrillas customarily take advantage of the local terrain, or civilian surroundings. Admittedly, they depend on their enemies to respect the lives of civilians and consequently to refrain from pursuit in civilian settings. However, at least for the most part, guerrillas themselves uphold the very same distinctions and standards they expect their enemies to maintain. Unlike terrorists, guerrillas draw the same fine line that their opponents do between combatants and civilians. Their strategic advantage derives from a difference in circumstances (such as familiarity with the local topography and enjoying the sympathies of the local population) and not from the evasion of any moral code.

As for assassins, the success of their operations does not, as with terrorism, depend on their opponents refraining from similar tactics—two can play at this game. To take a familiar case, Israel's policy of targeting wanted archterrorists does not invalidate the effectiveness of Palestinian attacks on Israeli officials, such as the 2001 assassination of Israeli minister Rechavaam Zeevi. When viewed from conflicting point of views, or from a neutral standpoint, the Palestinian gunman displayed the same moral code as the one upheld by Israel's assassination policy—kill an (allegedly) guilty oppressor while refraining (as much as possible) from harming the innocent. Israel's frequent reference to the assassination of Minister Zeevi as "terrorism" is an unfortunate example of inaccurate political speech (though the culpable organizations are legitimately dubbed "terrorists" by virtue of some of their other actions). A terrorist, as opposed to an assassin or guerrilla, is essentially a free rider on the moral codes and political liberties of others. They are, to say the least, free riders on the prohibitions to which civilized nations adhere.

LAST RESORT

One might respond to the preceding comments by observing that there are worse things in the world than free riding—oppression, persecution, occupation, and economic exploitation, to name just a few. Perhaps something further can be said along these lines in defense of terrorism, at least when it is employed in the pursuit of a "just cause." Honderich, who at least superficially renounces 9/11 (primarily for its predictable inefficiency), nevertheless defends "liberation-terrorism," understood as "terrorism to get freedom and power for a people when it is clear that nothing else will get it for them."[28]

This argument, whereby terrorism is justified as the only means of attaining particular political ends such as overthrowing repressive regimes, liberating oppressed peoples, and founding new nations, is not a new one. Terror apologists often point out that terrorism is a weapon of the weak. Terrorists are frequently portrayed by their sympathizers as the underdog, at times conjuring up images of the young biblical David. This comparative weakness, it is implied, can be overcome only through the use of unconventional tactics. Such arguments sometimes imply counterfactually that the only choice faced by disadvantaged groups engaged in conflict with a stronger power is between conventional warfare, at which they are inferior to their enemies, and terrorism. But, as just noted, this assertion is far from accurate. In *Just and Unjust Wars,* Walzer argues that the availability of alternative forms of irregular warfare—that is, guerrilla tactics and assassinations—attest to the falsity of this assertion.[29] Or, as Walzer put it more recently, following 9/11, "terrorism is a choice; it is a political strategy selected from among a range of options."[30]

Similarly, Habermas's distinction suggests that revolutionaries may resort to "paramilitary guerrilla warfare," which, unlike indiscriminant terrorism, is a proper course of action for a national liberation movement and is retrospectively legitimized with the formation of its state.[31] Paul Gilbert points out that, although "the militarily weaker side has little chance of obtaining victory by conventional military conflict, however justified its cause may be," still "there are several possible avenues open to it."[32] One such alternative is the use of guerrilla tactics, understood by Gilbert as well to be distinct from terrorism by virtue of its respect for the immunity of noncombatants. Freedom fighters have fastidious alternatives and are therefore unjustified in turning to terrorism under the pretenses of last-resort arguments.

Honderich's paradigmatic case, that of Palestinian terrorism against Israel, is particularly curious in this respect. Palestinians clearly have a variety of effective options. Aside from the occasional assassination, Palestinians regularly attack Israeli soldiers in operations that, despite Israeli rhetoric, are not, strictly speaking, terrorism, but rather guerrilla warfare to be judged on the merits of its political goals. There is no cause to believe that guerrilla tactics are less effective than terrorist strikes against civilians. In fact, guerrilla action bears the distinct advantage that it rarely warrants large-scale international condemnation, which often makes Palestinian terrorism appear counterproductive. In addition, quite apart from Walzer's, Gilbert's, and Habermas's alternative modes of nonconventional warfare, Palestinians also have the option of falling back on internationally supervised peaceful negotiations. Indeed, in the wake of the Camp David meetings that emerged from the 1993 Oslo peace process, in which a fully functioning Palestinian state was offered, to continue to construe Palestinian terrorism against Israel as "liberation-terrorism" is rather peculiar. Berman well makes this point when he questions the logic of Palestinians rejecting the Clinton plan in favor of suicide attacks:

> Clinton and Barak had already offered a Palestinian state. Perhaps the purpose of the suicide attacks was to widen the borders of the proposed new state—though, in that case, Arafat might have haggled at Camp David for an extra slice or two, and the question of slightly wider borders would at least have been broached. Or maybe the purpose was to widen the proposed new borders by more than a slice, to obtain a Palestinian state on a different scale altogether. But the whole point of negotiating during the eight years of Israeli-Palestinian talks, beginning at Oslo, was to work out a compromise. Or maybe the purpose of the attacks was, as Hamas and Islamic Jihad forthrightly proclaimed, to abolish Israel altogether and establish the reign of Shariah in every corner of the land. But this was not within the realm of reality. Actually, none of the imaginable purposes had any chance of being realized, and especially not after 9/11.... Suicide terror against the Israelis was bound to succeed in one realm only, and this was the realm of death. [33]

In contrast, Honderich's example is telling. The sheer absurdity of celebrating Palestinian terror in the post-Clinton era as "terrorism to get freedom and power for a people when it is clear that nothing else will get it for them"[34] casts a dark shadow on his very notion of "liberation-terrorism," which the Palestinian illustration is intended to personify. Even if there were such a thing as "liberation-terrorism," which (unlike 9/11) could be justified as the *only* available realistic means of achieving an essential noble end, Palestinian terrorism is clearly not a case in point. An additional oddity in attempting to justify Palestinian terrorism on the grounds that it rightfully aims to "liberate" Palestinians from Israeli domination is the fact that Arab terrorism against Jews in Palestine began in the 1920s and was notoriously supported by the Nazis in the 1930s, long before Jewish sovereignty was established over any of the land. The

Palestine Liberation Organization (PLO) and Fatah, dedicated to the "liberation of Palestine" by terrorist means, were established in 1964 and 1965, respectively, several years before Israel won the "occupied territories" from Jordan in 1967.

Anyone contemplating "liberation-terrorism" also might find it interesting to consider the paradigmatic case of desperate liberation movements—such as the internal struggle against Nazism—in which nothing resembling Palestinian terror tactics were ever employed. As Israeli prime minister Benjamin Netanyahu likes to point out, "It is instructive to note, for example, that the French Resistance during World War II did not resort to systematic killing of German women and children, although these were well within reach in occupied France."[35] Some years earlier he had noted: "No resistance movement in Nazi-occupied Europe conducted or condoned terrorist attacks against German civilians, attacking military and government targets instead."[36]

Finally, as for the concerns of Honderich, Chomsky, Derrida, and others about the plight of developing nations and their populations, however miserable their lives or the justness of their grievances, almost no terror is actually emanating from sub-Saharan Africa. The attempt to tie terrorism to globalization, U.S. exploitation, and so forth is similarly problematic. Of course, these critiques of Western policies were formulated long before 9/11 by scholars such as Honderich, as well as by Chomsky, who is notorious for his criticism of the United States and its actions. Although those views are certainly respectable, one must wonder, as Walzer said of terror apologists immediately after 9/11, whether these critics now do not simply "see a chance to use Islamic terrorism as a kind of 'enforcer' for their own political agenda. They attribute their agenda to the terrorists (what else could terrorists have in mind but what Western Leftists have always advocated?)."[37]

Can terrorism ever be justified as essential to liberation? It has sometimes been argued that the type of state terror bombing carried out by Allied forces during World War II on cities such as Dresden and Hamburg, and later the atomic attacks on Hiroshima and Nagasaki, were justifiable last-resort terrorism of the essential liberating type. Certainly, many of the bombings meet the strict definition of terrorism, and as such many liberals remain unconvinced that they can be altogether justified. It is possible that in some rare instances in which no other form of military strategy would have been effective, arguments of overriding necessity could conceivably be invoked in their defense. But clearly this was not usually the situation in World War II, and in most instances the resort to terrorism was based on calculations of utility or on indifference to civilian life on the enemy side. Possibly some of the Allied terror bombings, while unjustifiable, may be retrospectively excusable, considering the uniquely diabolical nature of the enemy on the European front. But such hindsight would still not amount to a justification of terrorism of any kind, and I doubt any useful analogies can be drawn from it.[38]

TERROR AND LIBERALISM

Finally, to restate the obvious, terrorism, by definition, attacks the defenseless, the prohibition of which is perhaps the most basic rule of just war theory. This violation is not merely conventional, nor is it based solely on the utilitarian consideration to narrow the overall scope of suffering in war. Terrorism, as discussed in the previous section, defies a most basic standard of liberal-humanistic morality (at least since Immanuel Kant and up to John Rawls), which fundamentally forbids the use of human beings as means only and commands their treatment as ends in themselves.[39] Certainly, this imperative would categorically prohibit the arbitrary use, and intentional killing, of innocents as mere means toward attaining practical ends. Perhaps this logic is not purely Western. Berman cites Sayyid Qutb's understanding of the concept of jihad as containing a similar ethical dimension:

> He [Qutb] quoted Mohammed's successor, Abu Bakr, the first Caliph, who told his army "Do not kill any women, children or elderly people." Qutb quoted the Koran, which says: "Fight for the cause of God those who fight against you, but do not commit aggression. God does not love aggressors." Qutb thought that ethical commandments were crucial to military victory. Writing about Muhammad and his companions, he said, "These principles had to be strictly observed, even with those enemies who had persecuted them." Jihad did have its rules. It was fastidious.[40]

Be that as it may, among liberals there can be little dispute about the moral status of terrorism and terrorists. It is precisely the unequivocal Kantian "thou shalt not" invoked earlier, prohibiting the arbitrary use of rational beings, that requires Honderich to take great pains toward obscuring the distinction between terrorism and other forms of political violence that do not fall so clearly under this liberal commandment. It is not an incidental feature of his argument that it involves discrediting many of the distinctions that are basic to liberal philosophies, particularly Kantian-based ones.[41] Aside from downplaying the conventional distinction between killing belligerents versus innocent noncombatants, Honderich's disregard for the distinction between civilian casualties incurred in war and terrorist victims entails obscuring the relationship between intentions and consequences and the difference between deliberate action and unintentional effects. The extent of blame he attributes to the citizens of prosperous nations for the misfortunate lives of inhabitants of the developing world (with the implication that they had 9/11 coming to them) is largely pitted against the traditional moral distinctions between acts and omissions and between perfect and imperfect duties.[42] Rawls's version of liberalism, at least as it appears in *A Theory of Justice,* is reduced by Honderich to no more than "a philosophical celebration of America."[43]

In the end, Honderich's views on terrorism and its causes require him to do away with liberalism, from Kant to Rawls, almost entirely. Quite a high price to pay, one might think, for the defense of suicide bombers. Nevertheless, in this one respect Honderich's intuitions are quite correct: in the end, it must be either terrorism *or* liberalism. Honderich makes his choice, and ultimately everyone else must make theirs.

Once again, terrorism, properly distinguished and defined, is the intentional random murder of defenseless noncombatants, with the intent of instilling fear of mortal danger within a civilian population as a strategy designed to advance political ends. This understanding cannot be "deconstructed," nor can it be inclusively obscured. Terrorism is a particularly objectionable form of free riding morally because it relies inherently on the moral restraints of others, and it is a paradigmatic instance of the ruthless use of individuals as a mere means toward ends that they cannot conceivably share. Regardless of its professed cause, terrorism is diametrically opposed to the requirements of liberal morality and can be defended only at the expense of relinquishing the most basic of liberal commitments.

YES: Terrorism is a just tool of the weak
Ted Honderich, *University College London*

Humanity, Terrorism in Palestine, Innocents

1. THE MORALITY OF HUMANITY

Plainly we are in our lives much concerned with right and wrong. The fact is not obscured by the extent to which our dim politicians and others talk a little vaguely and ambiguously of the *acceptable* and the *unacceptable,* and make use of other locutions. They proceed in this somewhat covert way, presumably, in order to try to conceal the uncertainty and vulnerability of judgments of right and wrong, theirs in particular, and to evade challenges to their judgments and themselves.[44]

In fact, to my mind, we are all yet more concerned with right and wrong than is shown by our overt and covert judgments. Right or wrong is not one option among several in thinking of what to do. Consider someone who gives as her reason for getting or keeping something that she is just "doing as everyone does," or that "everyone is selfish." Patently she is *justifying* her action, not opining about her society, not doing a little sociology or social psychology.

If we are to be confident about and persuasive in our judgments as to right and wrong, we need to be consistent and to show ourselves to be. In fact, to be inconsistent about something is to give and to have *no* reason for or against it. It is only by inconsistency that we actually fail to have reasons of right and wrong, but certainly we can do it. We do it a lot.

For consistency, we need a general principle of right and wrong. The principle, if it is to command respect and be useful, must be as literal, clear, specific and therefore as determinant as possible. Only then will it be resistant to self-interest and in particular to self-interest by way of self-deception.

One principle, the guiding principle of all or most of us in crucial circumstances where self-interest is not defeating our reason-giving natures, is the Principle of Humanity. Like *all* principles, despite an illusion to the contrary, it judges actions, policies, institutions, societies, and the like by the *consequences* of them. The principle is as follows:

> What is right is what, according to the best available information and judgment, is the rational means, which is to say the means that are effective and not self-defeating, to the end of getting and keeping people out of bad lives, with bad lives defined in terms of deprivation or frustration with respect to the great goods, the great desires of human nature—a decent length of conscious life, bodily or material well-being, freedom and power, respect and self-respect, the goods of relationship, and the goods of culture.[45]

It is, of course, a *maximizing* principle. It does not contemplate the monstrosity that there is nothing to choose between one and a thousand killings, torturings, or deaths by starvation or international sanctions because no individual suffers more than one of these. It is not the Principle of Utility or Greatest Happiness Principle, partly because it is particular and not abstract, partly because it prohibits exactly the victimization that the Principle of Utility sanctions.[46]

It is, of course, not the principle that the end justifies the means, if there is such a *principle*, since, as it states, the means must satisfy the requirement that what is done must not be likely to cause more distress than it prevents. Rather, it is a principle that the end *and* the means justify the means. It is a principle that does not make much difference between acts and omissions.[47] It is a principle that seeks to have the recommendation of decent philosophy, which is a concentration on ordinary logic.

It is clear and literal as against, say, Immanuel Kant's wholly uninstructive imperative that we are to treat each person never only as a means but also as an end. Can you treat someone in dire need as an end without giving them real help? Who knows? The Principle of Humanity, more than any other moral principle, has foundations in our human nature. It has what truth the attitudes that are our moral principles and moral judgments can have.[48]

The most difficult part of judging right and wrong in many circumstances is the making of necessary judgments as to facts. It is often more difficult to judge these factual propositions than it was to establish a general moral principle in the first place. These propositions include some about the bad or good lives of people now, these being owed in part to their recent histories. They also include propositions as to the probability of the consequences of things, say of terrorism, and comparisons of alternative possible consequences, say of terrorism as opposed to peaceful negotiation.

The subject of this essay is Palestinian terrorism, a judgment in support of it, and objections to that judgment having to do with the killing of innocents.

We can begin with a summary of the circumstances of the Palestinians and the Israelis now, partly in terms of their histories in living memory. The summary is not only factual. It also contains my judgments of right or wrong entailed by the Principle of Humanity with respect to the founding of Israel and Palestinian terrorism.

2. PALESTINE AND ISRAEL, A SUMMARY

Jews lived in the society of another people, the Germans, and through their enterprise and other strengths succeeded in it. They were at least resented. Use was made of this. Millions were horribly killed. Their having a place of their own in compensation was a kind of necessity placed on us all. It was not seen as a possibility that they could have such a refuge formed out of a part of Germany, which indubitably ought to have happened.

Having no state of their own, the Palestinians could be taken to be less than a people, and thus not open to a certain great injury. In 1948 a homeland for the Jews was taken from the Palestinians with the agreement of the victors in the war against the Germans. This was four-fifths of the historic homeland of the Palestinians, the indigenous people. They had had nothing to do with the Holocaust. They were driven from their homes and otherwise violated in terms of the great human goods.

The defense of the new Jewish homeland within roughly the 1948 borders, the project of *Zionism* in a clear sense of the word, subsequently acquired the further justification that the lives of the Jewish people had become deeply rooted in a land.

In 1967 there began the project of *neo-Zionism*. This was the terrorism that took from the Palestinians at least their freedom in the last one-fifth of their historic homeland. It was resisted by them. Their terrorism and self-defense, the intifadas, gave evidence that in fact they *had* been a people in 1948. This is a further part of the fact that they have suffered a kind of Holocaust at the hands of descendants of people who suffered the first one.

The Palestinians have continued to resist the terrorism of neo-Zionism by the only means that has a possibility of success, their terrorism. They have resisted the vileness that is the ongoing ethnic cleansing of neo-Zionism. Their struggle is as much to be reverenced as are the existence and life of Israel within its 1948 borders.

Against the Palestinians has been not only neo-Zionism in Palestine but the superpower and kept-ignorant population that is the United States. Against them, as well, has been the existence of Semitism, a prejudice in favor of Jews in all things, owed in part to the greater prejudice of anti-Semitism. Despite this, the Palestinians have the possibility of achieving some goal of their terrorism. Their killing is not pointless. With respect to their goals, it is worth remembering the Jews who fought hopelessly to the death in the Warsaw ghetto. They fought for those who came after them.

Given these various propositions, beginning with those on Germany, the Palestinians have had and now have a moral right to their terrorism against the ethnic cleansing of neo-Zionism in all of historic Palestine, including Israel.[49]

3. REMARKS ON RIGHT AND WRONG, LIBERALISM, FREE RIDERS, SUMMARY

There are four lines of thought and feeling in Tamar Meisels's essay about which I shall only make brief remarks.

One line, not developed, is indicated by the use of quotation marks around the word *right* in her subheading "Is Terrorism Ever 'Right'?" Are the scare quotes an indication of some known and indeed common attitude to the effect that the question of Palestine is one of self-interest that is universal, or of legality, or of *realpolitik*, or of *facts*, or whatever? Something other than right or wrong? I don't know. Any such assumption, while tempting for many Israelis and others, could only pretend that the question is other than it is. It would also stand in flat contradiction with what follows in her essay—overt and covert moral condemnation of what has been done and is being done by Palestinians. We do not escape the question of right and wrong.

A second line of thought and feeling in her essay, certainly a main implication of it, is to the effect that we need to judge right and wrong in Palestine on the basis of the ideology or morality of liberalism.

Liberalism, in my view, is a congeries of stuff. It is about selected individual rights, self-serving liberties or freedoms, the state and a limited role for it, democracy, maybe the mixed economy, maybe the market, and more. Authoritative summaries disagree. At best, liberalism is some decency, some feeling for good lives and bad lives, but a decency and feeling not carried into clarity and resolution.[50]

The liberalism of John Stuart Mill, perhaps its founder, or John Rawls for that matter, certainly has no overwhelming or even great recommendation by way of its connection with our merely hierarchic democracy.[51] Liberalism is forgetful about much—for example, the truth that its talk of individual rights, say to bequeath property, has the effect of concealing the fact that equal or general or social rights, the rights of all, say to medical treatment, are no less the rights of precisely individuals.

Why is a better principle not produced by Meisels in order to help us, say, to make a choice between innocents? There are innocents killed on both sides in Palestine, of course. If you say that a principle will not make such things simple, that is readily agreed. But do you propose not to have any general and determinant means of being consistent, of satisfying that first requirement of argument and humanity? Will you judge only by your loyalties? If so, surely you rule yourself out of serious discussion.

That liberalism is indeed a congeries of stuff, by the way, is indicated by what is close to the *raison d'être* of Meisels's essay. That is the proposition that liberals are now unsure whether it is their commitment to support the Palestinians, because of what has been and is being done to them, or instead to condemn them because of their violence. Liberalism is not made clearer by the essay's implied declaration in the end that basically it is against all terrorism, presumably including terrorism thought to be somehow "legitimated" by the eventual formation of a state.

A third line in the essay is that the Palestinians are guilty of "free riding" in attacking and killing innocent people. That is to say they are not paying their way by limiting themselves, as it is supposed others do, and in particular their opponents, to attacks on non-innocents. Evidently the argument depends on what can be said in defense of or explanation of killing innocents in particular and awful circumstances.

There is a gulf between the case of something like a fair society where (1) people in general pay their way in various senses while (2) some others don't—that subject of liberal rumination—and the case of a conflict where (1) a vicious ethnicism is killing, depriving, and degrading a people, almost all of them innocents, indubitably the indigenous people of a land, and (2) some of them engage in "free riding" by fighting back in the only way they can. Who can really say seriously that the two cases are usefully judged by saying that the latter people in their self-defense against destruction are *not paying their way?* Shall we also judge what the Germans did in the Holocaust by saying they were *not paying their way?*

A fourth line in the Meisels essay is about the history of Palestine, partly the proposition that the Palestinians have in fact had an alternative to their terrorism, that it has not been and is not their last resort. In so doing, she questions my above summary of the history of Palestine.

The factual propositions in the summary, to my mind, are in several senses a true account, one that is widely agreed, certainly agreed by the so honorable and courageous Israelis who stand out to their cost against neo-Zionism and Semitism. It is possible to have confidence in the factual propositions in the summary despite also believing what was said earlier, that factual premises for conclusions of right and wrong are more difficult to establish than a general premise of right and wrong. Truth exists. Truth does not always or even often have two sides to it. There are real rapes.

One last general thought pertaining to my summary of Palestine has to do with any conflict between the rich and the poor, also the powerful and the weak, and a history of no success in peaceful negotiations between them. The rich and powerful side had so much more to give up. They could easily have made concessions. If they did not give anything up, they showed themselves to be at least self-concerned in a way that demonstrates the necessity of recourse by the poor and weak to means other than negotiation.

4. DEFINITIONS OF TERRORISM

Here is a definition of *terrorism* in general, the definition used by me and others in connection with the varieties of terrorism in historic Palestine: "Terrorism is (i) violence, (ii) smaller in scale than war, (iii) social and political in aim, (iv) illegal, and (v) *prima facie* wrong since it is indeed killing, maiming and destruction."[52]

The definition does not define *terrorism* as violence against innocent persons or the like. Nor does it define it as pursuing its aim by way of fear or terror caused by the killing, maiming, and destruction.[53]

The definition does, of course, include *state terrorism,* on account of the illegality of it and its also satisfying the four other requirements. It therefore covers Israeli state terrorism. It is worth noting that the definition goes with another one, of *terrorist war.* That is different from terrorism only in being larger in scale. Neo-Zionism unquestionably is and has been all of terrorism, state terrorism and terrorist war, again in terms of satisfying the requirements. You can argue neo-Zionism is *more* against international law, incidentally, especially in the form of United Nations resolutions, than is Palestinian terrorism.

Here is the different definition of terrorism offered by Meisels:

> terrorism . . . is the intentional random murder of defenseless noncombatants, with the intent of instilling fear of mortal danger within a civilian population as a strategy designed to advance political ends.

5. OBJECTIONS TO THE FIRST DEFINITION

Passages in the Meisels essay convey strong expressions of a familiar sort of objection to the first definition and others like it. For example, she says:

> There is a growing academic reluctance to define terrorism as a specific and fiendish deed. The considerable body of academic literature now available expresses sympathy, and at times outright justification, for Islamic (particularly Palestinian) terrorism.

A distinction is reported by Meisels between kinds of what is called irregular warfare. There are campaigns by guerrillas, whose primary targets are military personnel and not civilians. There are the actions and campaigns of political assassins, whose targets are political officials. There are, thirdly, those irregular fighters—terrorists in her definition—who target civilians.

Meisels argues that since my definition of terrorism makes no distinction between various forms of political violence, it somehow justifies or seeks to justify my proposition that the Palestinians have had a moral right to their terrorism; terrorism that kills Israeli civilians.

She says that if terrorism, conceived so widely as to include all forms of political violence with no moral distinction between them, would essentially mean that "we are all terrorists."

Ultimately relying on the Kantian "Thou shalt not" prohibiting the arbitrary use of rational beings, she reiterates what she speaks of as the necessity of including the intentional random murder of defenseless noncombatants in any proper definition of terrorism.

6. WHO ARE THESE INNOCENTS?

Any rigorous analysis of the subject of Palestinian terrorism against innocents calls out for more attention than it can have here—and could have in the Meisels essay. Still, two subjects can perhaps be treated more explicitly and fully here. They are of particular relevance to the essence of her objections above. One subject has to do with innocents, as they are usually called, and the other subject has to do with what it is to do something intentionally, in particular kill someone intentionally.

Is the first subject really *innocents?* Or is it *civilians?* Or *innocent civilians,* or *noncombatants,* or *innocent noncombatants,* or *citizens,* or *private citizens?* All are mentioned and run together by Meisels. This is careless, or useful in argument, or both.

Innocents are persons not guilty of a crime or offence, not responsible for an event yet suffering it, free from moral wrong. We can suppose an innocent in the present context is in some sense all of the three things. So innocents here are such in virtue of not doing or not having done something or certain things. That is why they call for special attention, which they get in all decent moralities, most certainly including the morality of humanity.

The good records of innocents, present and past, obviously may be lacked by civilians, noncombatants, citizens, and private citizens. Members of all four of these categories, for a start, can instigate killings. The conclusion must be that an objection to terrorism must have to do with innocents rather than civilians, noncombatants, citizens, and private citizens.

We still have a question. Who are these innocents? *What is it that they do not do?* They cannot possibly be understood simply to be persons who do not commit crimes or offenses according to an existing legal system. Someone who hid a Jewish child from the Nazis, against the law, was certainly not guilty in the sense now relevant to us, but innocent and better than that. It cannot conceivably be Israel's positive law, the law of the land, or any other such law, that determines who are the innocents.

Nor are they to be understood as persons who do not kill or otherwise do violence to others. This understanding would for a start make all soldiers noninnocent, including Israeli soldiers.

Innocents, rather, are presumably persons who do not intentionally do other things, maybe kill under certain circumstances, or benefit from such killings. More generally, innocents do not act in or benefit from certain projects. What are the projects?

Needless to say, there is in the context of Palestine an answer that comes to many minds, and may be implied by Meisels herself, though she does not

offer an explicit answer herself. She may be taken to imply that the innocents are persons not actively engaged in the Palestinian-Israeli conflict,
more particularly Israelis not actively engaged in it. Innocents are people
not themselves killing or wounding Palestinians. It is indicative that in her
essay she regularly mentions noncombatants, and in fact it is noncombatants who are specified as the victims in her definition of terrorism quoted
earlier.

But it will not conceivably do to understand innocents as just noncombatants. As any tolerable morality or law asserts, those who instigate killers, pay
for them, defend them, profit from them, and so on are not innocents. I am not
innocent if I choose to benefit from killings of Palestinians in the neo-Zionist
cause. For a start, I thereby contribute to the probability or certainty of more
killings by the movement on which my benefits continue to depend. I can be
counted on not to condemn it.

The short answer in the present context to the question of who the innocents are, what it is that they do not do, must be along certain lines. The
innocents are those who do not intentionally somehow take forward the
project of neo-Zionism or choose to benefit from it when they could do
otherwise.

I readily allow that there is much more to be said of innocents generally and
of kinds of them.[54] Still, in sum, it is evident that there are greatly fewer such
innocents than is ordinarily supposed, and is supposed by Meisels. Some are
not very innocent.

It is my own present inclination, by the way, to take the innocents as not
including people who refrain from absolutely and explicitly condemning neo-
Zionism. Some of these speak of *understanding* neo-Zionism. Some take the
problem of Palestine to be complicated or the claims of both sides to be controversial. But what is right is simple—that Israel, without condition, qualifica-
tion, negotiation, delay, or any other such thing withdraws from and accords
to the Palestinians their freedom in the last one-fifth of their homeland and
otherwise recompenses them fully.[55]

7. INTENTIONAL ACTION

What is it intentionally to do something? The question arises not only in connection with our present discussion about innocents killed by terrorism, but
also in another connection of importance having to do with war and the like.

A man's wife leaves him. He goes to the apartment he knows she is in, with
glue for the door lock and gasoline. As he gets there, he sees someone else go
in, a cleaning woman. He sticks to his plan. The two women might have got out
of the burning apartment somehow, but they don't. In court he pleads guilty

to only one murder, on the ground that he did not intend to kill the cleaning woman. The judge disdains his argument and convicts him of two murders. The husband sends a note of condolence and excuse to the family of the cleaning woman. They loathe him for it.

Can he change the mind of an appeal court or change the feelings of the family by establishing that he did not intend the killing of the cleaning woman since in a sense he *wanted* only to kill his wife? No, he cannot.

Can he change the mind of the appeal court, more particularly, by establishing that *if* he had had the option of killing only his wife, maybe at that time, without killing anyone else, he *would* have taken that option? No, he cannot. He cannot begin to establish to the satisfaction of judges and family that he did not intentionally kill both women in the only relevant sense. It does not matter much that if he could have killed only his wife, he would have.

Can he change the minds of the judges and family by convincing them that when he poured in the gasoline and threw in the matches he was then *thinking* only of his wife, that he had only her on his mind and in his feelings? No, he cannot.

Can he do so by saying in some vague sense that he was *targeting* only his wife—maybe a sense related to the one in which it is said an American soldier firing a rocket has one person in the cross hairs of the telescopic aiming device and not the person he sees or knows to be a yard away who is also about to be killed? No, the husband cannot save himself this way, any more than the American soldier.

Can the husband change the mind of the appeal court by convincing the judges that he had natural justice or religion on his side with respect to his wife, that he was taken up with that *personal conviction?* No, he cannot.

Can he change their minds by producing a philosopher's analysis of what it is to intend something—say an analysis beginning from the proposition that an intention is a predictive belief about a future event based in a certain way on an instrumental or causal belief and a want?[56] No, he certainly cannot.

The example of the husband is as good as any other in reminding us that what it is to intentionally do something in the relevant sense is *to act with the foreknowledge or reasonable belief that a thing will be the probable or certain consequence of the action.* No other idea carries any significant weight with respect to intention in any decent court or in the human life that is codified by decent law.[57]

No other doctrine will begin to persuade the Israeli mother of a dead child that the Palestine suicide bomber who saw the child near the Israeli border guard did not intentionally bring about the death of the child.

The subject of the intentional killing of innocents is therefore the subject of actions known to carry at least the probability of deaths of innocents. It is not any other subject. Meisels offers no alternative. In my view she cannot.

8. OBJECTIONS HAVING TO DO WITH DEFINITIONS

Meisels objects, as noted earlier, that I and others take up a definition of terrorism that covers three kinds of irregular warfare, and that this has the effect of somehow excusing or reducing the culpability of one of them by associating it with the other two. That is, the objectionable general definition of terrorism covers guerrilla war, and political assassination, and intentionally killing the innocent. The third of these, intentionally killing the innocent, by inclusion in the single general subject matter, is in effect excused or made less culpable by the inclusion of the first and second. They are less condemnable—despite the fact that guerrillas and political assassins only *for the most part* do not kill or endanger innocents.

Is the gravamen of the objections by Meisels that a certain factual mistake was made by many of us, including the U.S. Army, in defining terrorism without specifying that it is intentional killing of the innocent? That is, is the gravamen of the objections that a definition is chosen that goes against the ordinary use of the term, whatever does or does not follow from that supposed mistake? That a definition is chosen that goes against dictionaries, whatever does or does not follow from that? Well, the best dictionary I know, *The New Oxford Dictionary of English*, defines *terrorism* as "the use of violence and intimidation in the pursuit of political ends."

Also, Meisels is not fully convincing in facing an embarrassment. In the course of her argument or implication that her definition is true to usage and dictionaries, she finds herself allowing that one author with whom she is in sympathy differs from another in that he uses the term *terrorism* to *include* political assassination, which purportedly does not much involve killing innocents. He is not alone. So too do her own countrymen and women include political assassination in terrorism. As she reports, if judgmentally:

> Israel's frequent reference to this assassination of Minister Zeevi as "terrorism" is an unfortunate example of inaccurate political speech.

There can be little doubt that contemporary English usage, whether or not it is inaccurate political speech, does not regard terrorism as necessarily consisting only in the killing or attacking of innocents.

But I leave this matter of usage, which is of much less importance than others. Survey dictionaries to get a better answer if you want. Hire a lexicographer.

The result, as I say, for reasons to be given in a moment in connection with any definition, will be unimportant.

Consider the fact of stipulation, that different definitions of terrorism, whatever their relation to usage, are to an extent stipulated or chosen. This is indeed the case with the two definitions we are contemplating, the first not mentioning the killing of innocents and the second doing so.

Meisels would agree, I am sure, that she does not intend something that is incredible in her objections about a definition. It is that those who use the first definition of terrorism take themselves thereby to be able to do something like *deduce* that some terrorism is justifiable. Or, maybe slightly less incredibly, they suppose their use of the first definition somehow *logically or conceptually* removes an objection to terrorism as they define it—the objection that it includes killing the innocent. It might be contemplated that they suppose this because they take a definition to specify *all* the properties of a thing, every last one.

This is easily dealt with. My definition of an automobile does not include every fact about one. More importantly, that my definition does not include the fact that it can used for murder does not remove part of my objection to murder by automobile. Nor, patently, does a definition of terrorism that leaves out the intentional killing of innocents remove anything at all of the objection to terrorism that it includes intentional killing of innocents.

I note that despite having taken up a definition of terrorism that does not mention killing the innocent, I have considered the objection that some terrorism is wrong, and more particularly that some Palestinian terrorism is wrong, because it is the killing of innocents.[58] The largest thing of immediate relevance to it, of course, is the circumstance that the killing of innocents seeks to change.

It may also be worth noting that there is no possibility whatever of Meisels getting straight from her definition of terrorism to the conclusion that terrorism is wrong. Let us assume that her including "intentional random murder" in her definition does not go so far as condemning all terrorism as wrong—say including the terrorism that was a part of the founding of the state of Israel in 1948. So there can be no logical step from the definition to any condemnation.

The general fact of this whole matter of definitions is that *any* definition of terrorism, at least any not useless and inane in argument, logically or conceptually allows for *any* judgment for or against what is singled out by the definition.

9. INQUIRY, PREJUDICE, ADVOCACY

Inquiry, that which is found in university lectures, good books and articles, and some exceptional journalism, directly relates to our discussion of definitions. Inquiry is not to be confused with *prejudiced contention* or just *prejudice.*[59]

With respect to inquiry, it is possible to believe, indeed to know, that definitions do not matter. So I believed in the past. They make no substantial difference, even no significant difference, with respect to the conclusions drawn. In particular, definitions do not matter in inquiry about terrorism, *thinking* about terrorism. Certainly definitions can be inconvenient or otherwise, get in the way of proceedings, give rise to confusion and so on, but, as you know, they do not determine outcomes.

Meisels's objections and also objections by Georg Meggle[60] have led me to a kind of change of mind. More particularly, their insistence on definitions that include killing of the innocent, however well supported their insistence, has led to this change of mind. It is also owed to my including Meisels, and certainly Meggle, in the class of inquirers.

The change of mind is not to the cynical proposition that there is no inquiry, that it does not exist, but to the proposition that there is a kind of inquiry that is not so pure as the rest of it. There is something other than *pure inquiry* in addition to prejudiced contention. It is what can be called *advocacy*.

It goes beyond reliance on logic as a means to factual truth and also the kind of truth or justification we can aspire to with respect to right and wrong. Advocacy aims to *influence*, notably by means of *persuasive definitions*.[61] Advocacy, which lies on a spectrum including pure inquiry, has the aim of getting a certain agreement of others with respect to right and wrong.

Evidently philosophers and others are sometimes engaged in advocacy. I have been engaged in it in the past, and am now. This essay is advocacy.

In this new realism, I am *more* content to persist in the definition of terrorism that does *not* include the killing of innocents. It would be contrary to my aim in my advocacy to do otherwise, an aim that has the distinction of having been made clear. To take up the definition that includes talk of innocents could have some effect in persuading you away from what I take to be an entailment of the Principle of Humanity having to do with justification of Palestinian terrorism. It could make you less ready to agree.

But since this is advocacy in which I am engaged, not prejudiced contention, I am also ready to give reasons in defense of my definition. As you may expect, and have heard already, they have to do with innocents and not-so-innocents, intentional killing, war, and also what is distinguished as guerrilla war and political assassination.

War intentionally kills innocents on an immeasurably greater scale than terrorism. In war, the deaths of innocents, often in very great numbers, are foreseeable probabilities. In our own lifetimes we needed only World War II as confirmation, but we have also had the American and British terrorist war on Iraq.

To come exactly to the point, the definition of terrorism in terms of killing innocents is motivated by and depends for its effect precisely on an explicit or inexplicit comparison with war and like things. The definition lives and breathes in that comparison. *It is a false comparison.* Terrorism is no worse than war in the given respect.

Given this consideration of war alone—forget about irregular warfare— there is full reason to persist in exactly the definition of terrorism that does not mention killing innocents. This is not the reason, of course, that this definition is at least as true to ordinary usage and dictionaries as the other one. It is that this definition serves the necessary and great purpose of advocacy of the morality of humanity.

You will recall that an additional item in the Meisels definition of terrorism was that it is what instills fear of mortal danger in a civilian population. I shall also persist in the definition not mentioning fear. The reason, you will know, is the same as with the killing of innocents. War does more to cause fear than terrorism ever did. The contrast is false, and against what it is right to do.

One final comment. If you were to persuade me to add the item about killing innocents to my definition, I would not add it alone. I would add other items. They would be as true to facts and would be no more questionable as items of advocacy or persuasion than mention of the killing of innocents.

One such addition, of course, would be to the effect that terrorism, in intentionally killing innocents, is not thereby different from war. A second addition would be that some terrorism, much of what the newspapers and politicians call terrorism, is a response to ethnic cleansing or another great violation of a people. A third addition would be that the terrorism that kills innocents and has the support of the Principle of Humanity is directed to the saving of other innocents as we ordinarily speak of them, more of them, and also innumerable other victims.[62]

OTHER INNOCENTS

Finally, let me bring together in a certain way the principal facts that must be the reality of any attempt to justify Palestinian terrorism.[63] They were touched on earlier, first in the summary of the circumstances of the Palestinians and the Israelis, then in connection with liberalism, and also a moment ago, but they can do with more explicit expression.

There is a necessary distinction to be made. It is between the innocents or innocent victims we have mainly had in mind so far and other innocent victims.

The innocent victims we have mainly had in mind are individuals killed or directly harmed by an explosion, shooting, or other piece of violence. More particularly, we have been thinking about Israelis killed or directly harmed by Palestinian terrorism, Israelis not themselves advancing or intentionally benefiting from neo-Zionism.

There is also the category of their counterparts among the Palestinians—the innocent Palestinians killed or directly harmed by Israeli terrorism, including state terrorism, and also Israeli terrorist war. They are innocent in the sense that they are not themselves somehow engaged in resistance to neo-Zionism and not gaining from this resistance. There are more of these Palestinian victims than Israeli victims, three or four times as many. This fact is important in several ways, but it is not the most important fact.

There is a category of innocents far larger than these two. It consists in Palestinian victims of neo-Zionism who have *not* been killed or been directly harmed by a piece of violence. They have not been shot by an Israeli soldier or settler. Rather, they have lost their lives or been indirectly harmed as a result of earlier events with general effects. They are victims of earlier neo-Zionist decisions to carry forward the ethnic cleansing of the last one-fifth of Palestine. They include victims whose lives have been degraded by the effective threat carried by earlier neo-Zionist killings and other actions. Some live in refugee camps. Some die for want of medical supplies stopped in neo-Zionist blockades.

These victims are exactly and absolutely as innocent as those we have had in mind up until this point. They are not engaged in resistance to neo-Zionism or gaining from this resistance. It is true that we do not immediately *call* them *innocent* victims. Maybe we do not *ordinarily* call them innocent victims. This is because of the absence of a particular piece of violence against an individual, or a few individuals, or because there is not a non-innocent victim on hand. This fact of language is nothing whatever to the point. They *are* innocent victims. A habit of the English language and maybe other languages does not even touch this fact.

The justification of Palestinian self-defense, their moral right to it, is most importantly this fact of these Palestinian innocent victims in their great numbers. The Palestinian people since 1967, to go back only that far, have been violated—they have been deprived by neo-Zionism of every great human good. All the Palestinians have been deprived of some or all of decent lengths of conscious life, bodily or material well-being, freedom and power, respect and self-respect, the goods of relationship, and the goods of culture. Means to these great goods have been transferred to Israelis since 1967.[64]

It is a recommendation of the Principle of Humanity that it is explicit in what is allowed by almost every human moral or political doctrine or project, certainly Zionism and neo-Zionism. That is that the killing of innocents can be forced upon us. The morality of humanity is more concerned with innocents, so named or not, than any of the large alternatives to it.[65]

Notes

1. For a detailed discussion of definitions of terrorism, see Bruce Hoffman, *Inside Terrorism*, rev. and exp. ed. (New York: Columbia University Press, 2006), 1–41.
2. For a discussion of states as terrorists, see, for example, Noam Chomsky, "International Terrorism: Image and Reality," in *Western State Terrorism*, ed. Alexander George (New York: Cambridge University Press, 1991), 12–38.
3. Ted Honderich, *After the Terror* (Edinburgh: Edinburgh University Press, 2002).
4. Ibid., 98–99.
5. Ibid., 103. Noam Chomsky repeatedly makes similar points concerning the inconsistent and self-serving use of the term *terrorism* on the part of the United States, which he regards as a terrorist state. See, for example, Noam Chomsky, *9–11* (New York: Seven Stories Press, 2001), esp., 23, 40–54, 57, 73–74, 90–91.
6. Honderich, *After the Terror*, 97–99. Note, in contrast, the overall thesis of Paul Berman, *Terror and Liberalism* (New York and London: Norton, 2003), which involves the suggestion that real world political or social change is not always the object of political violence.
7. Honderich, *After the Terror*, 99.
8. Ibid., 151.
9. In addition to *After the Terror*, also see Ted Honderich, *Terrorism for Humanity—Inquiries in Political Philosophy* (London and Sterling, Va.: Pluto Press, 1989, 2003).
10. Honderich, *After the Terror*, 115.
11. Noam Chomsky, *9–11*, 23, 40, 76, 84.
12. Jacques Derrida attempts to "deconstruct" the concept of terrorism in Giovanna Borradori, *Philosophy in a Time of Terror—Dialogues with Jurgan Habermas and Jacques Derrida* (Chicago and London: University of Chicago Press, 2003), 102–107, 152. Derrida died in 2004.
13. Ibid., 103 (emphasis added).
14. Honderich, *After the Terror*, 73–88, 97–99, 103.
15. Derrida in Borradori, *Philosophy in a Time of Terror*, 108.
16. Michael Walzer, *Just and Unjust Wars* (New York: Basic Books, 1977).
17. Ibid., 180. For a similar characterization of guerrilla warfare as opposed to terrorism, see Paul Gilbert, *New Terror, New Wars* (Edinburgh: Edinburgh University Press, 2003), 96–97.
18. Borradori, *Philosophy in a Time of Terror*, 56.
19. Habermas in Borradori, *Philosophy in a Time of Terror*, 33.
20. Walzer, *Just and Unjust Wars*, 198.
21. As Paul Gilbert puts it: "Assassination is, however, far from the worst offence against the prohibition on attacking civilians that we witness in new wars." Gilbert, *New Terror, New Wars*, 94.

22. Berman, *Terror and Liberalism*, 33–34.
23. Walzer, *Just and Unjust Wars*, 203.
24. Berman, *Terror and Liberalism*, 34.
25. Robert A. Pape, "The Strategic Logic of Suicide Terrorism," *American Political Science Review* 97 (August 2003): 350. See also 347–349.
26. Ibid., 350.
27. Immanuel Kant, *Groundwork of the Metaphysic of Morals*, trans. and analyzed by H. J. Paton (New York: Harper and Row, 1964), 88.
28. Honderich, *After the Terror*, 151.
29. Walzer, *Just and Unjust Wars*, 204.
30. Michael Walzer, "Five Questions about Terrorism," *Dissent* 49 (Winter 2002).
31. Habermas in Borradori, *Philosophy in a Time of Terror*, 56.
32. Gilbert, *New Terror, New Wars*, 97.
33. Berman, *Terror and Liberalism*, 132–133.
34. Honderich, *After the Terror*, 151.
35. Benjamin Netanyahu, *Fighting Terrorism* (New York: Farrar, Straus and Giroux, 2001), 9.
36. Benjamin Netanyahu, ed., *Terrorism—How the West Can Win* (New York: Farrar, Straus and Giroux, 1986), 204.
37. Walzer, "Five Questions about Terrorism."
38. For an illuminating discussion of the World War II terror bombings, see Walzer, *Just and Unjust Wars* 109–106, 255–268.
39. See Kant, *Groundwork of the Metaphysic of Morals*, 96; and John Rawls, *A Theory of Justice*, 9th ed. (London: Oxford University Press, 1989), chap 3, sec. 29, 179.
40. Berman, *Terror and Liberalism*, 98.
41. See, in particular, his section on liberalism in *After the Terror*, 46–50.
42. Honderich, *After the Terror*, esp. 73–88, 97–99, 103. Many of these classic distinctions are also called into question in connection with terrorism by Jacques Derrida in Borradori, *Philosophy in a Time of Terror;* see, for example, p. 108.
43. Honderich, *After the Terror*, 70.
44. I thank my wife, Ingrid Coggin Honderich, for her thoughtful and troubling objections to a draft of this essay. We remain in disagreement about the proposition that the Palestinians have a moral right to their terrorism.
45. Ted Honderich, *On Political Means and Social Ends* (Edinburgh: Edinburgh University Press, 2003), 103, 112–132; Ted Honderich, *Right and Wrong, and Palestine, 9/11, Iraq, 7/7* . . . (New York: Seven Stories Press, 2006), 61.
46. Ted Honderich, "The Principle of Humanity and the Principle of Utility," in *Consciousness, Reality and Value: Essays in Honour of T. L. S. Sprigge*, ed. Pierfransesco Basile and Leemon B. McHenry (Frankfurt: Ontos Verlag, 2007).
47. Ted Honderich, *After the Terror*, 2nd ed. (Edinburgh: Edinburgh University Press, 2003), 73–88.
48. Honderich, *On Political Means*, 1–57; Honderich, *Right and Wrong*, 58–83.
49. For some recent writings on these matters, related but not the same in inclination, see Noam Chomsky, *Fateful Triangle: The United States, Israel and the Palestinians* (London: Pluto Press, 1999); Noam Chomsky, "Simple Truths, Hard Problems: Some Thoughts on Terror, Justice and Self-Defence," *Philosophy* 80 (2005): 5–28; Ghada Karmi, *In Search of Fatima: A Palestinian Story* (London: Verso, 2002);

Karma Nabulsi, "Being Palestinian," www.ucl.ac.uk/~uctytho/Being_Palestinian. html; Ilan Pappe, *A History of Modern Palestine: One Land, Two Peoples* (Oxford, UK: Oxford University Press, 2004); Igor Primoratz, ed., *Terrorism: The Philosophical Issues* (Basingstoke, UK: Palgrave Macmillan, 2004); and essays by Noam Chomsky, Tomis Kapitan, G. A. Cohen, Ardon Lyon, William McBride, Tamar Meisels, Michael Neumann, and Timothy Shanahan in *Israel, Palestine and Terror,* ed. Stephen Law (London: Continuum, 2008). Many of the essays in this book comment on my opening essay, "Terrorisms in Palestine."

50. Honderich, *Right and Wrong,* 35–38.

51. Ibid., 38–58; Honderich, *After the Terror* (2003), 105–115; Honderich, *On Political Means,* 135–154.

52. Honderich, *After the Terror,* 97–100; Honderich, *Right and Wrong,* 86–92.

53. Compare the good consideration of definitions of terrorism in C. A. J. Coady, "Defining Terrorism," in Primoratz, *Terrorism.*

54. For a more detailed discussion, see Honderich, *After the Terror* (2003), esp. 158–162.

55. Michael Neumann, "Terror and Expected Collateral Damage: The Case for Moral Equivalence," in Law, *Israel, Palestine and Terror.* G. A. Cohen and I are not in full agreement about Palestine and Israel. I do not mean to conscript him to a cause, but do recommend his "Casting the First Stone: Who Can, and Who Can't?" in Law, *Israel, Palestine and Terror.*

56. Ted Honderich, *Mind and Brain* (Oxford: Oxford University Press, 1990), 216–231.

57. Honderich, *Right and Wrong,* 155–159.

58. Ibid., 111–115, 155–159; Honderich, *After the Terror* (2003), 158–162.

59. *Inquiry* is informed and restrained by ordinary logic, which consists in the large contribution toward truth that consists in clarity, consistency and validity, and completeness. The truth being served by this logic is not only factual truth but also whatever truth or justification we can aspire to with respect to right and wrong. In contrast, the aim of *prejudiced contention,* the sort of thing that happens in the politics of our democracies, in most of their media, in second-rate books and articles, on so much of the Internet, paradigmatically in what was to me the moral stupidity of Bush and Blair, and so on, is not truth but something else. Its relation to truth is at best the relation of *selling* to truth. Ted Honderich, *Conservatism: Burke, Nozick, Bush, Blair?* (London: Pluto Press, 2005).

60. Georg Meggle, "What Is Terrorism?" in *Terrorism: Moral, Legal, and Political Issues, Filozofski Godisnjak* 19 (2006) (edited by Jovan Babic): 11–24; Georg Meggle, "Terror and Counter-Terror: Initial Ethical Reflections," *Deutsche Zeitschrift fur Philosophie* 50 (2002): 149–162.

61. C. L. Stevenson, *Ethics and Language* (New Haven, Conn.: Yale University Press, 1944).

62. Honderich, *After the Terror* (2003), 1–29; Honderich, *Right and Wrong,* 94–105.

63. For greater discussions of the main parts of that advocacy, see Honderich, *After the Terror* (2003) (2003), 24–9, 155–186, 184; Honderich, *Right and Wrong,* 94–125; and Honderich, "Terrorisms in Palestine," in Law, *Israel, Palestine and Terror.*

64. For a view of the author on the recent Israeli military operations in Gaza, see www .counterpunch.org/honderich12312008.html.

65. Tamar Meisels is to be commended and has my admiration for not joining those who confuse or choose to confuse condemnation of neo-Zionism with anti-Semitism. She does not in this way give in to the prejudice of Semitism or too much defer to it. This just compliment to a philosopher is given more force by a comparison that perhaps understandably sticks in my mind in connection with my book she criticizes, *After the Terror*. When it was translated into German by the publisher Suhrkamp, having been recommended for translation by Jurgen Habermas, and known to have been recommended by him, he wrote a newspaper article on the charge of anti-Semitism against the book (www.ucl.ac.uk/~uctytho/ BrumlikHabermastrans.html). Habermas, to his credit, affirmed the book was not anti-Semitic. But he did so in such an apologetic style, and with such additions, as so to qualify his judgment and to be little defense of the book. Suhrkamp's decision the next day to "ban" the book as anti-Semitic was no surprise. The second German publisher of the book, Abraham Melzer, Jewish himself, was closer to truth and humanity.

does islam play a unique role in modern religious terrorism?

YES: Islam has a unique impact on modern terrorism
Andrew C. McCarthy, *National Review Institute*

NO: Islam itself is not the problem in the current wave of global terrorism
Fawaz A. Gerges, *London School of Economics*

Although terrorism in the name of religion has been around for millennia and has been growing as a phenomenon in recent years, on September 11, 2001, religious terrorism exploded onto the world scene.[1] Al-Qaeda, the group responsible for the 9/11 attacks, claimed to be acting on behalf of Islam, as guided by God. Shortly after the attacks, al-Qaeda leader Osama bin Laden said he had not expected the World Trade Center's twin towers to fully collapse, and credited God's will for the extra death and destruction.[2]

Despite the clear religious motives behind the attacks, President George W. Bush sought to quickly dispel any connections among the 9/11 terrorists, God, and the religion they claimed to represent. In an address before a joint session of Congress on September 20, 2001, he said, "[Islam's] teachings are good and peaceful, and those who commit evil in the name of Allah blaspheme the name of Allah. The terrorists are traitors to their own faith. . . . We are not deceived by their pretenses to piety."[3] Bush later remarked, "All Americans must recognize that the face of terror is not the true face of Islam. Islam is a faith that brings comfort to a billion people around the world. . . . It's a faith based upon love, not hate."[4]

Seeking to downplay the religious component of the 9/11 attacks and the role of Islam in the al-Qaeda movement was certainly understandable, and accurate. After all, the vast majority of Muslims in America and around the world were outraged by the attacks, and even more so by claims that they were committed on their behalf.

Yet understanding the central role of religion—particularly militant branches of Islam—for al-Qaeda, its affiliated organizations, and their millions of supporters and sympathizers around the world is vital in order to diagnose correctly the threat and fashion proper responses.[5] And it will help explain how and why religion has come to play such an important role in modern terrorism.

The fact is that thirty years ago there were virtually no identifiable terrorist organizations motivated primarily by religion. Today, however, most of the world's active terrorist groups are religion-based, the vast majority of which are Islamist.[6]

What accounts for the tremendous upsurge in religious, predominantly Islamic, terrorism in recent decades? Geostrategic contributors include the 1979 Islamic revolution in Iran, which showed the power of religion to achieve major political goals; the 1979 Soviet invasion of Afghanistan, which gave the impression of Islam under attack; decades of reckless and self-serving American and Western policies in the Middle East; and general social and economic malaise in Muslim countries.

But what about the role of Islam itself? Since 9/11, a passionate debate has raged over the nature and depth of spiritual support for al-Qaeda and other violent Islamic movements. Is the world in the midst of a modern-day global religious war, an existential battle between Muslim and Western belief systems? Or is Islamic terrorism merely an outgrowth of resentment felt across the Muslim world toward Western policies, corrupt governance, and economic backwardness, whereby addressing these grievances would quash whatever support exists for the small fraction of Muslims who engage in terrorist violence?

Andrew McCarthy says the answers lie within the religion of Islam. He argues that there are features unique to Islam that explain not just the current global outbreak of terrorism, but also its particularly vicious variety—filled with images of beheadings, suicide bombings, and mass-casualty attacks. The spiritual importance of violent jihad and martyrdom for tens of millions of adherents of militant Islam are not well understood by the West—or are conveniently papered over. This violent movement has been growing in strength for centuries; it is not simply an outgrowth of recent policies. The threat will cease only if the worldwide Muslim community redirects itself toward moderation and tolerance.

According to Fawaz Gerges, such moderation and tolerance already predominate in the Muslim worldview; most Muslims admire Western values and wish to coexist peacefully with the West. Muslims (religious or otherwise) do not detest Americans or Westerners for "who they are" but rather for "what they do"—their specific policies, which always seem to place their interests first and the interests of Muslims last. The world is not in the midst of an existential religious war: only a tiny minority of Muslims condone or engage in violence. If the West would endeavor to better understand the Muslim world and craft more thoughtful policies, support for militant movements would quickly dry up.

Islam is certainly not the only religion of late to witness heinous acts of violence committed on its behalf—the 1995 Oklahoma City bombing, for example, was perpetrated by individuals inspired by America's Christian militia movement. However, the ubiquity and tremendous global reach of militant Islamist movements have come to define the terrorism threat of the modern era, and such movements present the most daunting global challenge for the West since the Cold War. Grasping the specific roles played by Islamic radicalism, on the one hand, and other sociopolitical factors, on the other, can only help better inform the West's policy choices.

YES: Islam has a unique impact on modern terrorism
Andrew C. McCarthy, *National Review Institute*

Islam's Unique Impact on Modern Religious Terrorism

Wasn't the "jihad" he was clamoring for just a spiritual camouflage for *terrorism?*[7] Omar Abdel Rahman, more notoriously known as the "Blind Sheikh," the man who would inspire the 1981 murder of Egyptian president Anwar Sadat, the 1993 World Trade Center bombing, and the atrocities of September 11, 2001, did not mince words:

> What kind of name is this? Why are we afraid of it? Why do we fear the word *terrorist?* If the terrorist is the person who defends his right, so we are terrorists. And if the terrorist is the one who struggles for the sake of God, then we are terrorists. We . . . have been ordered with terrorism because we must prepare what power we can to terrorize the enemy of Allah and your enemy. The Qur'an [said] "to strike terror." Therefore, we don't fear to be described with "terrorism." . . . They may say, "He is a terrorist, he uses violence, he uses force." Let them say that. We are ordered to prepare whatever we can of power to terrorize the enemies of Islam.

Omar Abdel Rahman was indeed proud to be a terrorist. He was relentless in the cause of annealing his large international following to this purpose. It was a cause he traced to a centuries-old summons to revive the "true Islam" of its founders. It was also the cause of a lifetime, ever since he'd lost his sight to juvenile diabetes in 1942 at the age of four. Reared in the tiny Nile Delta town of al-Gamalia, the sickly boy memorized the Qur'an and became a stellar academic, earning renown as a scholar who had graduated from Cairo's venerable al-Azhar University, where he earned a doctorate, with distinction, in Qur'anic studies.

Now serving a sentence of life imprisonment after his conviction for sundry terrorism crimes, Abdel Rahman is old and infirm. Because of his various maladies, he has never been known to help build or plant a bomb, to hijack an airplane, or even to fire a gun. He is no grand military tactician or even capable of plotting out (as opposed to authorizing) the activities of an urban guerrilla cell. And yet he has been a colossus in the world of international terrorism for three decades—so much so that one attorney has been convicted for helping him continue to run his Egyptian jihadist organization, al-Gama'at al-Islamiyya, from his American jail cell, and Osama bin Laden has publicly credited him with having issued from that cell the fatwa (or religious edict) that authorized the 9/11 attacks. How can this be? It stems solely from his undeniable status as a globally recognized authority on Islamic jurisprudence.

In the modern world, the common denominator of the most savage terrorism is an amalgam of fundamentalist Islamic ideologies (cutting across the Sunni/Shiite divide) that is somewhat hopefully labeled "radical Islam," although, doctrinally and popularly, it is much less aberrational than the term *radical* suggests. And in that framework, the catalyzing power of doctrine is such that a man who would otherwise be of utterly no use to a terrorist organization is a driving force of global terrorism. Which is to say: after all that has occurred in the last thirty-plus years, to have to ask whether Islam has a unique impact on modern terrorism is something like asking whether the sky is really blue. The question can be answered, but its very asking highlights the extent to which self-delusion prevails in a world where the fear of giving offense has become direr than the fear of being rendered defenseless.

VANGUARD OF MODERN JIHAD

Trailing only Morocco's al-Karaouine among the world's oldest institutions of higher learning, al-Azhar University is the seat of the Sunni tradition vastly predominant among the world's 1.4 billion Muslims. In terms of influence, al-Azhar's grand imam is about as close a cognate as Islam has to the Roman Catholic papacy. The analogy, though, is far from perfect. Islam is bereft of a regimented clerical hierarchy, councils, or synods to provide standards of orthodoxy.[8] This omission, indeed, is the central challenge confronting Islamic moderates—that is, the hundreds of millions of Muslims who reject terrorism as barbaric and regard as libelous the perpetrators of terror who rely on Islam to justify themselves (holding in equally low esteem those who have the temerity to draw attention to that reliance). Muslim terrorists *do* rely on scripture and Muhammadan tradition—scripture and tradition that they do not need to twist or pervert in order to serve the purpose. For argument's sake, suppose the moderates are right: jihadists like the Blind Sheikh are betraying the core principles of the Muslim religion. Even if this is true, Islam gives the moderates no vehicle by which to say this with authority so that it will be accepted as such by Muslims and non-Muslims throughout the world. Islam provides no hierarchical structure for marginalizing terrorists as heretics—and, in view of the alarming number of influential Islamic scholars who actually contend that the terrorists are in the right, this challenge may be insuperable for the foreseeable future.

Instead of a hierarchy, Islam relies on a venerated consensus of its greatest *mujtahids*, the masters of its four established schools of thought. That consensus was set in stone even before al-Azhar's doors first opened in the middle of the tenth century. Although early Islam had enjoyed a tradition of *ijtihad*, free and independent inquiry into Islamic scripture by believers seeking to discern Allah's intended meaning, those authoritative schools determined by about 900 AD that all essential questions had been settled with finality. From then on, no one would be deemed qualified for independent reasoning. According to Joseph Schacht, "All future activity would have to be confined to the explanation, application, and, at the most, interpretation of the doctrine as it had been laid down once at for all."[9] The "gates of *ijtihad*" were closed.

It was to this task of interpretation that Abdel Rahman set himself. Never reaching the high station of grand imam, Abdel Rahman's accomplishments did include a prestigious stint as an al-Azhar lecturer, as well as the leadership of the vicious Egyptian terror organization al-Gama'at al-Islamiyya (Islamic Group), and great influence over the "Arab-Afghans," who joined the mujahidin resistance against the 1979 Soviet invasion of Afghanistan. As a result, he was dubbed the "pope of jihad" by some of the few Western investigators who followed such things in the early 1990s. Later it became clear, though, that "*emir* of jihad," employing the Arab term for "prince" or "commander," was the more apt and widely used honorific among the faithful.

The Blind Sheikh was undeniably a mufti, a specialist in Islamic law authorized to opine on points of doctrine and to issue fatwas.[10] His status as an emir, a position of high operational authority, did, however, evoke occasional dissent, including from a feisty young Ayman al-Zawahiri—his ally and sometime rival who would rise years later to become al-Qaeda's second-in-command—when the two, detained together in an Egyptian prison after the Sadat murder, squabbled over a Qur'anic verse that casts the sightless as unfit for command.[11] Such dissent, however, was rare and muted, owing to the awe Abdel Rahman's religious erudition inspired and the practical impossibility of cleaving the spiritual from the operational in radical ideology.

SPIRITUAL UNDERPINNINGS OF MODERN JIHAD

Perhaps the most profound influence on Abdel Rahman's scholarship, and thus the intellectual font of radical Islam's modern iteration, was the fourteenth-century Sunni docent Taqi al-Din Ahmad Ibn Taymiyyah. A controversial scholar in his time, Ibn Taymiyyah championed a literal interpretation of scripture and the concept that the original Islamic communities forged during the Prophet Muhammad's Medinan period were the ideal to which all humanity must aspire.[12]

Muslim reverence for the prophet is, of course, a given. The Qur'an endorses Muhammad as "an excellent model of conduct" (33:21), who exhibited an "exalted standard of character" (68:4). Obedience to him is repeatedly adjured—made, in fact, just as essential as obedience to Allah himself (4:80).[13] Ibn Taymiyyah's focus on the Medinan period, though, is of seismic significance. During this phase of Islamic development, Muslims were forced to flee from Mecca by powerful tribes, including the Prophet's native Quraysh, which refused to accept the new religion. This flight, the *Hijra,* is Islam's groundbreaking moment, the event by which time is marked.

In the preceding thirteen-year Meccan period, when Muhammad first endeavored to call converts to Islam, he had been highly solicitous of the existing tribes and their traditions. It should come as no surprise, then, that the more tolerant verses of the Qur'an can be traced to this early Meccan period, such as the injunction that there shall be "no compulsion in religion" (2:256)—the unparalleled favorite verse of moderates and Western elites bent on portraying Islam as "the religion of peace" regardless of the evidence to the contrary.

In Medina, things changed drastically. It was from there that Islam was principally spread not by intellectual persuasion but by the sword. The scriptures tending toward ecumenism and tolerance were superseded by divine commands that the Prophet "make war on the unbelievers and the hypocrites and deal rigorously with them. Hell shall be their home: an evil fate" (9:73). This command is not immediately apparent to the unschooled observer because the Qur'an is not arranged chronologically but according to the length of its *suras* (chapters). It is reflective, however, of the Islamic doctrine of abrogation (*naskh*), the concept that, as he sees fit, Allah refines or repeals his prior instructions.[14] Abrogation is essential to a proper understanding of the Medinan period and of the chasm between the Islam of Western fantasy and the one that actually exists.

The Muhammad of Medina—which is to say, the Muhammad of Ibn Taymiyyah—sought Islamic hegemony, not ecumenical coexistence. Enemy tribes that had tormented him were savaged, their leaders slain and decapitated, their pleas for mercy ignored.[15] Rejection of Islam was construed as an attack upon Islam to be met with brutal retribution, meted out more than once by the Prophet himself. For example, as jihad historian Andrew Bostom relates:

> According to Muhammad's sacralized biography by Ibn Ishaq, Muhammad himself sanctioned the massacre of the Qurayza, a vanquished Jewish tribe. He appointed an "arbiter" who soon rendered this concise verdict: the men were to be put to death, the women and children sold into slavery, the spoils to be divided among the Muslims. Muhammad ratified this

judgment stating that it was a decree of God pronounced from above the Seven Heavens. Thus some 600 to 900 men from the Qurayza were [led] on Muhammad's order to the Market of Medina. Trenches were dug and the men were beheaded, and their decapitated corpses buried in the trenches while Muhammad watched in attendance. Women and children were sold into slavery, a number of them being distributed as gifts among Muhammad's companions, and Muhammad chose one of the Qurayza women (Rayhana) for himself. The Qurayza's property and other possessions (including weapons) were also divided up as additional "booty" among the Muslims, to support further jihad campaigns.[16]

Jihad campaigns are, indeed, the phenomenon known today as Islamic radicalism. It being the preoccupation of many Muslim activists and Western intellectuals to deny the patent nexus between Islamic doctrine and terror, a controversy naturally has developed over the "true" meaning of jihad—a controversy that is itself ill-conceived because the salient question is not which construers of the term have the better of the argument, but whether there is enough persuasive force in the militant construction that, even if arguably wrong (and I do not think it is), it is sure to convince a meaningful number of Muslims.

Today's moderates and their intellectual allies grudgingly acknowledge that jihad is a tenet of Islam—although, they imply, not all that important a tenet because it is not one of the five "pillars" of the faith.[17] But while Muhammad himself made jihad—militaristic jihad—Islam's doctrinal *ne plus ultra,* declaring that no deed on earth could equal it in God's favor, today's solons are determined to portray jihadists as heretics who have perverted the "true" faith, relieving us of any need to concern ourselves over Islam, the 800-pound gorilla that is somehow always in the middle of the room when terror strikes.

Thus is a fable assiduously advanced, pitting the good (or "greater") jihad against the bad (or "lesser") jihad. This school of thought finds a fine exemplar in Marc Sageman, a forensic psychiatrist and former case officer of the U.S. Central Intelligence Agency (from the late 1980s when the agency was underwriting the Afghan mujahidin's jihad against the Soviets). A frequent adviser to federal and state agencies, Sageman writes:

> Like other great, long established religions, Islam is full of contentious issues, especially about some of its core concepts, such as *jihad,* which translates roughly as "striving" but denotes any form of activity, either personal or communal, undertaken by Muslims in attempting to follow the path of God. No single doctrine is universally accepted.
>
> In a world full of iniquities, the greater jihad is the individual nonviolent striving to live a good Muslim life, following God's will. It includes

adhering to the five pillars of Islam: profession of faith (*shahada*); praying regularly; fasting during Ramadan; being charitable; and performing the *hajj*, the pilgrimage to Mecca. It requires lifelong diligence and constant vigilance.[18]

How admirable, indeed. The "greater" jihad is the good jihad. That other jihad—he is too nuanced to suggest it is altogether bad—is the "lesser" jihad. Only this small subordinate species of the genus involves "the violent struggle for Islam." It is a vestige of an antiquated *Weltanschauung* that simplistically divided the world into "the land of Islam (*dar al-Islam*) and the land of conflict (*dar al-Harb*)," and saw jihad as the Muslim *ummah's* (Muslim community's) communal obligation "to expand dar al-Islam throughout the world so that all humankind could benefit from living within a just political social order."[19]

That old world, Sageman claims, is no more. The purportedly lesser jihad has been "diluted," he contends, by "one school of interpretation" which introduced the concept of a "land of treaty (*dar al-Suhl*)" in which jihad was forbidden in lands which had struck agreements with Muslims. Sageman conveniently glides by the rather obvious point that the existence of "one school of interpretation" implies that there are other schools following different interpretations—to say nothing of the facts that the Qur'an limits treaties to ten years' duration and that Muhammad reserved the right to break them whenever it was expedient to do so (since "war," as the Prophet observed, "is deceit"). Instead, Sageman plows ahead with the suggestion that this "lesser" jihad has been further marginalized by its division into "defensive" and "offensive" strivings. Individual Muslims are required to fight only in the former, which happens only if a Muslim land has been invaded and a competent authority has issued a fatwa declaring a "state of jihad."

MISREADING OFFENSE AND DEFENSE IN JIHAD

Self-defense, of course, is a natural human right and, by extension, a bedrock of international law. Who, then, could argue with "defensive" jihad, if that is all the "lesser" jihad is about? Well, even if one leaves aside the inconvenient empirical fact that what constitutes "defense," as opposed to pretext, is often in the eye of the beholder, the concept of "offensive" jihad remains. This, Sageman concedes, involves Muslims invading infidel lands to impose *sharia* and spread the faith. Shouldn't such a possibility raise concerns that many Muslims will feel validated in acting on what they rationally see as a divine injunction? Not according to Sageman. He rationalizes that "offensive" jihad is a *collective* obligation—that is, one in which only Islamic governments, not individual believers, will involve themselves. Thus scholars and others seem to think they can Jesuitically define out of existence the nexus between Islam and terror by asserting that "offensive" jihad cannot be performed by individuals, and therefore those individual terrorists must not be jihadists—QED, terrorism is un-Islamic.

Sageman is far from alone. In their invaluable account of al-Qaeda's rise, *The Age of Sacred Terror*, former Clinton administration National Security Council officials Daniel Benjamin and Steven Simon more accurately acknowledge that jihad grew up as "exclusively actual, physical warfare." They argue, however, that "the concept of jihad took on a new meaning" in the late eighteenth and early nineteenth centuries as Islam was beleaguered by the rise of imperial Western European powers and the decay of Ottoman Turkey. There was, they aver, a "domestication of jihad," rendering it "a struggle against evil impulses within the soul of a believer." The "greater jihad" became the internal struggle for personal betterment waged through "acts of charity, good works in society, and education." "Military jihad" fell in status. [20]

Benjamin and Simon forthrightly concede that this greater/lesser divide is a "modern-day distinction" that would have been unrecognizable to classical Muslim scholars such as Ibn Taymiyyah. Their argument is indistinguishable from that advanced by devotees of the "living Constitution," who contend, for example, that the Eighth Amendment's prohibition against "cruel and unusual punishments" operates to ban the death penalty notwithstanding several implicitly approving references to capital punishment elsewhere in the Constitution—that is, the Framers would not have understood themselves to be proscribing executions, but because we Americans (or at least some of us) have evolved, we should deem the Eighth Amendment to have evolved along with us. So too we should interpret jihad as reprogrammed to fit enlightened sensibilities, such that today's "real" jihads are noble efforts to rid societies of blights such as narcotics trafficking, hate speech, and intolerance.

Sadly, these new constructions are most persuasive to those desperate to be persuaded: Western intellectuals—many of whom look askance at religion and are insensitive to a believer's faith in what he takes to be transcendent, non-evolving values. In the ivory towers, the nexus between Islamic doctrine and modern terrorism can be whisked away by logic, enlightenment, and (mainly) the sheer desire that it disappear. Down here on planet Earth, though, the exercise is futile. The Muslim world is not populated by Western intellectuals hardwired to nuance white into black by legalistic arcana and historical massaging. In large swaths of the *ummah*, there is rampant illiteracy, education consists of a myopic focus on the Qur'an, and intolerance (especially anti-Semitism) is so rudimentary a part of everyday life that any jihad rooted in "good works in society" would not conceivably reflect what Western progressives mean by that well-intentioned term.

Progressive moderate Muslims would no doubt like the concept of jihad to vanish altogether. They are in a battle for authenticity with fundamentalists, and jihad would be far easier to omit than it is to explain away. Jihad, however, will not go away. There would be no Muslim world without it. When it comes to jihad, authenticity is simplicity, and, simply stated, jihad is and has always been about military conquest. As explicated by the West's preeminent scholar of Islam, Bernard Lewis:

> Conventionally translated "holy war" [jihad] has the literal meaning of striving, more specifically, in the Qur'anic phrase "striving in the path of God" (*fi sabil Allah*). Some Muslim theologians, particularly in more modern times, have interpreted the duty of "striving in the path of God" in a spiritual and moral sense. The overwhelming majority of early authorities, however, citing relevant passages in the Qur'an and in the tradition, discuss jihad in military terms.[21]

In fact, the erudite former Muslim with the nom de plume Ibn Warraq points out that even

> the celebrated *Dictionary of Islam* defines *jihad* as 'a religious war with those who are unbelievers in the mission of Muhammad. It is an incumbent religious duty, established in the Qur'an and in the Traditions as a divine institution, enjoined specially for the purpose of advancing Islam and of repelling evil from Muslims.'[22]

It is no wonder that this should be so. The Qur'an repeatedly enjoins Muslims to fight and slay non-Muslims. "O ye who believe," commands Sura 9:123, "Fight those of the disbelievers who are near you, and let them find harshness in you, and know that Allah is with those who keep their duty unto him." It is difficult to spin that as a call to spiritual self-improvement. Likewise, Sura 9:5 instructs: "But when the forbidden months are past, then fight and slay the pagans wherever ye find them. And seize them, beleaguer them, and lie in wait for them in every stratagem (of war)," relenting only if they have accepted Islam.[23] The *hadith*, lengthy volumes recording the words and traditions of the Prophet, are even more explicit, as in Muhammad's teaching that "a single endeavor (of fighting) in Allah's cause in the afternoon or in the forenoon is better than all the world and whatever is in it."[24]

This is the jihad of Islamic scripture. It is the jihad on which Ibn Taymiyyah insisted. The Caliphate's defeat and the suddenly dire straits of thirteenth-century believers stemmed from their deviation from the true Islam: the Islam of conquest, whose calling, whose *command*, was to bring about universal submission to Allah. For Ibn Taymiyyah, this divine mandate required both imposing the penalties of *sharia* (Islamic law) on Muslims who strayed and

> the punishment of recalcitrant groups, such as those that can only be brought under the sway of the Imam by a decisive fight. That then is the jihad against the unbelievers (*kuffar*), the enemies of God and his Messenger. For whoever has heard the summons of the Messenger of God, Peace be upon him, and has not responded to it, must be fought, "until there is no persecution and the religion is God's entirely."[25]

"Lawful warfare," Ibn Taymiyyah elaborated, "is essentially jihad." Because its purpose is to eradicate all obstacles to the obligatory spread of Islam (so that "the religion is God's entirely"), "those who stand in the way of this aim must be fought." Famously, Ibn Taymiyyah further inferred from this a duty to overthrow rulers who failed to govern in accordance with a fundamentalist construction of *sharia*—including rulers who were, at least nominally, Muslim.

Among the heirs of Ibn Taymiyya's thought—those who "swoon of death" while their enemies, as Osama bin Laden scoffs, cling desperately to life—was Muhammad bin Abdul Wahhab, the eighteenth-century fundamentalist. His atavistic Sunni Islam, known today as Wahhabism, became the Saudi royal family's creed—and, in the twentieth century, its second best-known export. But Ibn Taymiyya's influence was not confined to Sunnis. Iran's Grand Ayatollah Ali Khomeini, trailblazer of the most significant revolutionary movement in Shiite history, echoed Ibn Taymiyya in this blistering critique of those who would bowdlerize the true jihad:

> Islam makes it incumbent on all [able] adult males . . . to prepare themselves for the conquest of [other] countries so that the writ of Islam is obeyed in every country of the world. . . . [T]hose who study Islamic Holy War will understand why Islam wants to conquer the whole world. . . . Those who know nothing of Islam pretend that Islam counsels against war. [They] are witless. Islam says: Kill all the unbelievers just as they would kill you all! Does this mean the Muslims should sit back until they are devoured? Islam says: Kill them, put them to the sword and scatter [their armies]. . . . Islam says: Whatever good there is exists thanks to the sword and in the shadow of the sword. People cannot be made obedient except with the sword! The sword is the key to Paradise, which can be opened only for Holy Warriors! There are hundreds of [scriptures] urging Muslims to value war and to fight. Does all that mean Islam is a religion that prevents men from waging war? I spit upon those foolish souls who make such a claim.[26]

SAYYID QUTB AND GLOBAL RELIGIOUS WAR

From across the Arabian Peninsula and the Sunni/Shia divide, the Blind Sheikh admired the grand ayatollah and harbored dreams of an Egyptian replication of his Iranian coup d'état. Still, for Abdel Rahman, coming of age in a boiling cauldron of dissidence, the most striking of Ibn Taymiyya's legatees was Sayyid Qutb. The intellectual father of modern jihadism and an iconic figure in the formidable Muslim Brotherhood, Qutb was "martyred" by Gamal Abdel Nasser's Egypt in 1966, when Abdel Rahman was twenty-eight years old.

Qutb was an education scholar who studied from 1948 until 1950 in the United States, where he was repulsed by what he saw as America's racism, debauchery, and vulgar materialism. Presaging Khomeini, he rejected the revisionism that depicts jihad as a personal struggle, a purely "defensive" obligation, or an antiquated concept confined to the time and circumstances of the early Muslims. Islam, he explained, was not merely intended for Arabs, and, plainly, there would not be what today is known as the "Islamic world" (*dar al Islam*) unless Muslims had fought and conquered the preexisting regimes. "The religion," he wrote,

> is really a universal declaration of the freedom of man from servitude to other men and from servitude to his own desires, which is also a form of human servitude; it is a declaration that sovereignty belongs to God alone and that He is the Lord of all the worlds. It means a challenge to all kinds and forms of systems which are based on the concept of the sovereignty of man; in other words, where man has usurped the Divine attribute. . . . [Thus it] addresses itself to the whole of mankind, and its sphere of work is the whole earth.[27]

It is crucial to grasp this Islamic notion of *freedom,* for it is the obverse of the Western conception. Reckless indifference to this fact has led to such follies as the grand project to democratize the Islamic world. *Islam* means *submission* to God. *Freedom* in Islam must be understood in this context. It is not, as Westerners assume, free *choice;* it is the voluntary *surrendering of oneself* to Allah, unqualifiedly accepting the laws he has established—for, as Qutb instructed, "Legislation is a Divine attribute," so to concede it to other men is to "accept [them] as Divine," whether or not one actually considers them so, because the Qur'an equates obedience with worship. When Islam speaks of free will, as in Western intellectuals' much loved decree that there shall not be compulsion in religion, *this* is the sense of freedom it conveys. That freedom, Qutb taught, cannot be realized without establishment of the *sharia* system—the only system that removes all obstacles to the comprehension and, inexorably, the acceptance of the imperative to submit to Allah.

Qutb recognized that supplanting man's dominion with God's could never "be achieved only through preaching." Incumbent infidel regimes were plainly "not going to give up their power merely through preaching." Expelling them was the mission of jihad, highlighting its centrality as a core Islamic obligation, the *sine qua non* of, as Ibn Taymiyya put it, making the religion God's entirely—of cementing Islam as universally supreme. The purpose of jihad is "to wipe out tyranny and to introduce freedom to mankind." Whenever Islam is obstructed by "the political system of the state, the socio-economic system based on races and classes, and behind all these, the military power of the government," the religion, according to Qutb, "has no recourse but to remove them by force so that when [Islam] is addressed to peoples' hearts and minds they are free to accept or reject it with an open mind." All such impediments hindering human beings from achieving their highest calling are seen as persecution, implicating the Qur'anic injunction to "fight in the cause of Allah those who fight you . . . and slay them whenever you catch them, and turn them out from where they have turned you out, for persecution is worse than slaughter."[28]

The logic of Qutb's construction is patently circular, and frightening. *Sharia* is the precondition necessary to ensure perfect "freedom," but *sharia* cannot be established without the violent overthrow of regimes that refuse to adopt it voluntarily. And—again foreshadowing Khomeini—the "freedom" extended by Islam is not liberty of conscience, for the purportedly "complete freedom to accept or reject" the religion's tenets "does not mean [people] can make their desires their gods, or that they can choose to remain in the servitude of other human beings, making some men lords over others." No, the system in which this "choice" takes place must be based "on the authority of God, deriving its laws from him alone."

Thus the "free" decision to submit is made in an atmosphere of intimidation, where the Islamic battalions have supplanted their opposition and installed the *sharia* system. In this system, the choices of nonbelievers are to convert "voluntarily," or to remain infidels with the consciously humiliating status of *dhimmitude* (they were compelled to pay a tribute, the *jizya* tax, aimed primarily at constantly reminding *dhimmis* of their subjugation), or to die.

While obsessed with establishing *sharia* societies, Islam is never content with them. Islamic history is an inevitable progression. At times, Muslims refrained from jihad for tactical reasons (such as when Muhammad was first attracting converts in Mecca). At other times, Muslims employed jihad defensively because they actually were under armed attack. Nevertheless, none of that can obscure Islam's sacred quest for hegemony—to expand *dar al Islam,* the realm of the Muslims, throughout the world. For Qutb, history had reached this final phase of Islam's march, with war declared against all non-Muslims, in accordance with the command of Sura 9:29: "Fight those who do not believe in Allah nor the Last Day, nor hold that forbidden which hath been forbidden by Allah and His messenger, nor acknowledge the Religion of Truth from among the People of the Book, until they pay the *jizya* with willing submission, and feel themselves subdued."[29]

Echoing Ibn Taymiyyah, Qutb's jihad targeted not only declared nonbelievers but also those rulers who professed to be Muslim but did not adhere to the commands of the faith—the commands divinely required for the furtherance of "freedom." In many ways, such Muslims, particularly those in authority positions, were more responsible than declared infidels for the *ummah*'s descent into the dystopian condition of *jahiliyya*. This term, drawn from the Qur'an and Ibn Tamiyyah's theology, denoted the pre-Islamic phase of history, the dark pagan ignorance overcome by the incandescence of the Prophet's message. Qutb infused the concept with a connotation of oppressive, anti-Islamic corruption. The *jahiliyya* included all people, including Muslims, who failed to comport unflinchingly with *sharia*. There was but a single true Islam, which Allah had commanded his adherents to establish through jihad. Everyone and everything else was *jahiliyya*. By nature, they could not coexist with Islam. Therefore, in this the final phase of Islam's history there was a positive duty to eradicate them—not to wait for them to attack so that the jihad could be spun as "defensive," for their very existence was an affront to Allah.

CONCLUSION

Because discussions of the nexus between Islamic doctrine and modern terrorism are so infected with timidity, passion, and demagoguery, it bears emphasizing that there is no single Islam. There is a seemingly infinite variety of Islamic sects, to say nothing of the prevalent phenomenon— quite familiar to Westerners—of adherents who are at best culturally or nominally Muslim but care little about theology and its demands. That said, however, it is whistling past the graveyard to ignore or minimize the virulent strain of fundamentalist Islam that galvanizes jihadism. And it is positively fatuous to suggest that it stems from poverty, alienation, wounded pride, American policies, or whatever is the anything-but-Islam justification du jour. Take one recent example: the rioting jihadists in Indonesia who stoned and burned a mosque. Their anger was provoked by another sect of Muslims, the Ahmadi, who are deemed heretics because they do not accept Muhammad as the final prophet or jihad as a divine injunction.

It is simply not the case that a mere nineteen terrorists hijacked a peaceful religion, as President Bush hastened to assure Americans while smoke billowed from the Pentagon and lifeless bodies were pulled from the rubble of the twin towers of the World Trade Center. It is not the case, as the Clinton administration and its Justice Department were equally emphatic in mollifying the public when the World Trade Center was first bombed in 1993, that a rag-tag handful of miscreants had "perverted" the "true Islam." The species of Islam that has spurred these and other attacks has a long and distinguished pedigree. It is fourteen centuries old. It is rooted in the literal commands of the scriptures. It is a project that has engaged high intellects. And it is a belief system that continues to win the allegiance of the educated and illiterate, rich and poor, young and old, princes and peons. It is not the majority construction of the faith, but it is the creed of a sizable minority—and a dynamic one, underwritten by Saudi billions and catapulted by Khomeini's revolution. Even if it were representative of only 20 percent of the Muslim world (an estimate that probably sells it short), that would translate into over a quarter of a billion people.

We ignore this reality at our peril.

Islam itself is not the problem in the current
NO: wave of global terrorism
Fawaz A. Gerges, London School of Economics

What Osama bin Laden and George W. Bush Got Wrong about Muslims

After September 11, 2001, two questions dominated America's public debate: Why do Muslims hate Americans so much?[30] And where are the Muslim moderates? On the first question, commentators supplied easy, simplistic answers that appealed to the country's wounded egos and prejudices, not critical faculties and common sense. We Americans were told that "they" (Muslims in general, not just the tiny militant minority) hated our freedoms and way of life, and that they were jealous of our economic success, political influence, and international prestige. We had nothing to do with their twisted misperceptions of our country and foreign policy. In short, the root causes of anti-Americanism, asserted pundits, reveal more about the moral and political decay of Muslim societies than about American actions.

For many Americans, the answer to the second question was that there are not any moderates, that Osama bin Laden and the radicals were the exclusive representatives of Islam, and that the Muslim moderates were either a misnomer or a cowardly bunch who dared not challenge the bullies among them. Islam, it was believed, was a radical religion, with terrorist violence a natural outgrowth.

Political leaders and pundits reassured us that the United States neither played empire nor caused harm abroad; a beacon of light and catalyst for good, America was an innocent bystander in a cynical, jealous, and ungrateful world. We are hated because of who we are, not because of what we did—that was the received wisdom after September 11.[31]

But more than eight years later, embroiled in two wars in Muslim countries and deeply invested in political conflicts from Morocco to Indonesia, it is worth pausing to ask whether this received wisdom is entirely correct. Of course, the landscape has changed. Iraq, in particular, has become a new source of radicalization and a reason to hate American foreign policy. But the broader questions about what the world's one billion-plus Muslims think remain, and in many ways are even more pertinent today than ever before. After all, to understand Islam today, one must understand what Muslims actually think and how that compares with both what we believe and what al-Qaeda believes to be true. To those who assume that radical, violent interpretations of Islam inspire most Muslims, the answers will be most surprising.

MUSLIMS AND MODERATION

The very nature of the second question—where are the Muslim moderates?—is based on a fundamental misreading of Islam 101. Unlike, say, the Catholic Church, no organized, hierarchical clerical establishment exists in Islam. There is no intermediary—church or priest—between the believer and God. Religious scholars and leaders, then, derive their authority mainly by interpreting Islamic texts and jurisprudence. That authority is even contested with multiple interpretations and counterinterpretations. To be sure, Muslim puritans and radicals—and some of their Western counterparts—want those who study Islam to believe that it is a monolith, with a timeless essence. But it is a mistake to take their claims at face value, because the Muslim world is complex and fragmented, divided along ethnic, nationalist, and socioeconomic lines. The militant fringe claims as much legitimacy and authority in representing Islam and Muslims as do the political moderates, but scholars and others assume otherwise because they do not hear the latter as often, or as loudly.

Unfortunately, many U.S. commentators bought the rhetoric of bin Laden and his right-hand man, Ayman al-Zawahiri, who anointed themselves spokesmen for Islam and Muslims. Those commentators lost sight of the social and political turmoil shaking Muslim societies to their very foundation. Indeed, bin Laden represents not a new dominant Islam but a revolt inside it, directed as much against the clerical establishment as against the ruling elite. Bin Laden and Zawahiri aim to fill the vacuum of legitimate political authority in the Muslim world and challenge the unholy alliance between Muslim rulers and clerics. In other words, Muslims, not Americans, were intended to be the primary audience for the attacks of September 11.

The ensuing struggle was momentous—and completely ignored in the United States. Less than two weeks after September 11, I traveled to the Middle East and was pleasantly surprised by the almost universal rejection—from taxi drivers and bank tellers to fruit vendors and high school teachers—of al-Qaeda's terrorism. Everyone I met expressed genuine empathy with the American victims, even while highly critical of U.S. foreign policy.

The initial sympathetic Muslim response to September 11 received hardly any coverage in the U.S. media, which constantly replayed sensational images of a few Palestinian children and teens in refugee camps celebrating the fall of the twin towers.

If the "terrorism experts" had listened closely, they would have learned that, far from condoning the September 11 attacks, leading mainstream and, yes, radical clerics—such as Hassan al-Turabi, former head of the National Islamic Front and now with the People's Congress in Sudan (in the early 1990s he hosted bin Laden) and Sayyid Mohammed Hussein Fadlallah, the spiritual founding father of Lebanon's Hezbollah—had condemned the 9/11 attacks, recognizing that they were harmful to Islam and Muslims.[32]

Yusuf al-Qaradawi, an influential Egyptian-born conservative cleric now based in Qatar, even issued a fatwa denouncing al-Qaeda's "illegal jihad" and expressed sorrow and empathy with the American victims. "Our hearts bleed because of the attacks that have targeted the World Trade Center, as well as other institutions in the United States," he wrote on his Web site just after the September 11 attacks. Nothing could justify the attacks, he wrote, including "the American biased policy toward Israel on the military, political, and economic fronts." That may be cold comfort to the victims, but it was also a significant challenge to bin Laden.

To be fair, most political religious leaders did not criticize al-Qaeda's political ideology, only its terrorist methods. Bin Laden may occasionally revert to religious rhetoric, but it is his *political and ideological* rhetoric that truly resonates among Muslims of all persuasions and ranks who blame the United States for sustaining Israeli military occupation of Palestinian territories, as well as oppressive Arab autocrats. As countless polls show, and as I have found in my own research, the efficacy of al-Qaeda's anti-American (and anti-Western) message stems from politics and foreign policy, not culture and religion.

THE MYTH OF MONOLITHIC JIHAD

Equally important, September 11 opened up a wide cleavage between the local and global branches of the jihadist tribe. Contrary to the received wisdom, 9/11 did not turn out as bin Laden and al-Zawahiri had hoped. Far from reinvigorating and unifying jihadist ranks, taking on the United States widened the cleavages separating local jihadists from transnational jihadis, clear signs of the internal struggle that is now tearing the jihadist family apart. This war within has hardly been noticed, let alone critically examined, in the United States.

Instead of closing ranks against the "enemies of Islam," as bin Laden and al-Zawahiri had hoped, 9/11 put to rest any possibility of bridging the gulf between al-Qaeda's global jihadists and the army of deactivated local jihadists who far outnumber bin Laden's few thousand men. The bulk of local jihadists (numbering tens of thousands) refused to fight alongside al-Qaeda and condemned its reckless tactics. Neither the *ummah* (Muslim community worldwide) nor the army of decommissioned local jihadists was willing to join al-Qaeda's suicidal caravan, however much they empathize with its grievances against the international order and American foreign policy in particular.

Before the dust settled on the September 11 crime scene, cracks appeared within the jihadist front. Top jihadists opposed what bin Laden had done, some even within his own wing of the movement. One of the first, Abu al-Walid al-Masri, a senior member of the al-Qaeda *shura* (consultative) who had been a leading theoretician of the network and participated in its most significant decisions, saw the attacks of September 11 as a calamity. He was among the most senior of the Arab Afghans to break with bin Laden over September 11 and take his grievances public. He publicly lambasted bin Laden's "catastrophic leadership" and his underestimation of American willpower.

Based in Qandahar, Abu al-Walid had worked closely with both Taliban leader Mullah Omar and bin Laden, and he had supervised *The Islamic Principality*, a newsletter regarded as the mouthpiece of Mullah Omar. After the events of 9/11, he published a series of articles entitled *The Story of the Arab*

Afghans: From the Entry to Afghanistan to the Final Exodus with Taliban in Asharq al-Awsat, in which he paints a dark portrait of bin Laden as an autocrat, running al-Qaeda as he might a tribal fiefdom, and offers a stinging critique of bin Laden's vision of global jihad.

Abu al-Walid's withering criticism of bin Laden has been echoed by others, including Egypt's al-Jamaah al-Islamiyah organization. Whereas at the height of its strength in 2001, al-Qaeda's membership numbered about 4,000, al-Jamaah fielded almost 100,000 fighters in the 1990s.

Of all the Islamists, al-Jamaah's senior leaders (most of whom have been in prison in Egypt since the 1980s and 1990s and were recently released) presented the most comprehensive critique of al-Qaeda's strategy and methods. Since early 2002, they have released more than a dozen manuscripts in Arabic, two of which deal specifically with the September 11 attacks. The first, authored by Mohammed Essam Derbala and reviewed and approved by the entire leadership, is entitled "Al Qaeda Strategy: Mistakes and Dangers," and the other, authored by Nageh Abdullah Ibrahim, is entitled "Islam and the Challenges of the Twenty-First Century." Both were serialized in the Egyptian newspaper *Asharq Al-Awsat.* These vital historical documents shed light on the thinking of the biggest and most influential jihadist organization in the region. But neither of the manuscripts has been translated into English, and thus they have not received the attention they deserve.

At the time, Derbala, one of the leaders of al-Jamaah, was serving a life sentence in prison for his role in the 1981 assassination of Egyptian president Anwar Sadat. He drew on religious texts to show that al-Qaeda's attacks violated Islamic law, which "bans killing civilians" of any religion or nationality. Derbala and his associates denounced al-Qaeda for preaching that American and Muslim interests would never meet and that "the enmity is deeply embedded and the clash is inevitable." They cited several instances in the 1990s when the United States helped to resolve international conflicts, with results that benefited Muslims. For example, U.S. military and financial assistance in the Afghan war tipped the balance in favor of the mujahedin against the Russian occupiers; from 1990 to 1991 the United States helped Kuwait and Saudi Arabia expel Iraqi forces from Kuwait; in 1995 American military intervention put a stop to the persecution and massacre of Bosnian Muslims by Serbs; and in 1999 the United States led a North Atlantic Treaty Organization (NATO) military campaign to force Serbia to end ethnic cleansing in Kosovo.

All these examples showed clearly, al-Jamaah's senior leaders asserted, that American and Muslim interests can and do meet. History has proven that there is nothing inevitable about a clash of cultures between Islam and the West because Islam is a universal religion, fully integrated with other civilizations.

Derbala, Ibrahim, and their imprisoned colleagues condemned bin Laden and al-Zawahiri's religious justification for attacking the Americans, reminding them that Islam has always practiced—not just taught—peaceful coexistence as a permanent way of life. Religious coexistence is a strategic, not a tactical, goal in Islam, particularly when Muslims migrate to foreign lands and are welcomed by native inhabitants. What makes the crime of the September 11 suicide bombers uniquely un-Islamic, Ibrahim wrote, is that the U.S. government had admitted them as guests. This was a betrayal of the most fundamental spiritual obligation, the one practiced in shops, cafés, and homes throughout the Arab world. Had the bombers read the Sunnah (containing the deeds of the Prophet—the second source of Islam after the Qur'an), they would have respected peaceful coexistence.

Al-Jamaah's critique of the 9/11 attacks is all the more powerful because the credibility and legitimacy of its leaders cannot be questioned, even by al-Qaeda. Derbala, Ibrahim, Karem Zuhdi, Osama Hafez, Assem Abdel-Maged, and the rest who signed and blessed the two documents from which I have quoted extensively were the founding fathers of a major wing of the jihadist movement.

These leaders were not alone in their criticism. The majority of key Islamists and jihadists have now condemned al-Qaeda's internationalization of jihad and echoed al-Jamaah's view of September 11: that it was a catastrophic blunder.

The revolt against al-Qaeda's global jihad recently escalated into all-out civil war. Now heavyweights in the bin Laden group blame him directly for the turmoil engulfing the Muslim world. And in an open letter written in September 2007, one of his prominent Saudi mentors, the preacher and scholar Salman al-Oadah, publicly reproached bin Laden for causing widespread mayhem and killing.[33]

A few months later, in November 2007, al-Qaeda's former top ideologue and theorist, Sayyid Imam al-Sharif (known to those in the underground as Dr. Fadl, author of the dissenting manifesto *Rationalizing Jihad*), publicly criticized bin Laden and al-Zawahiri in another shattering blow to their authority. "Al Qaeda committed suicide on September 11," said Fadl.[34]

Unfortunately, the escalating war within jihadism has received hardly any coverage by the so-called terrorism experts, who still lump all Islamists together with bin Laden and his cohorts. Terrorism pundits look backward and pigeonhole Islamists and repentant local jihadists through the prism of al-Qaeda's global jihadists. Many U.S. terrorism experts invest little or no effort in analyzing the conceptual and operational differences and boundaries among mainstream (moderate) Islamists, local jihadis, and global jihadis such as al-Qaeda. Their stories blur the lines between Islamist, radical, militant, extremist, jihadi, and terrorist, and equate Islamists' offensive speech with jihadists' violent actions.

After September 11, terrorism pundits, eschewing scholarly analysis and balance, injected their commentaries with a heavy dose of ideology. They viewed themselves as foot soldiers in an existential struggle against terrorism and evil. In all fairness, an injured, angry America was not in the mood to examine nuances and differences within Islamism and jihadism, or to reflect on what went wrong with the country's foreign policy. Americans wanted bin Laden and his associates—those evildoers who visited horror and death on their shores—dead or alive.

Wittingly or not, after September 11 some observers and commentators endorsed the official agenda by portraying Islamism not just as jihadism, but as a mortal threat to the West, an aggressive and totalitarian ideology dedicated to random destruction and global subjugation. Others advocated an all-out war against all manifestations of Islamism or political Islam.

Ideological blinders clouded the vision of some terrorism experts and prejudiced their understanding of all things Islamic. Some of these experts fell prey to al-Qaeda's propaganda, while others let their ignorance of Middle Eastern languages and cultures distort their analysis. The result was half-baked truths deployed by the Bush administration to convince Americans of the urgency of expanding the war on terrorism worldwide.

Building on the consensus among independent observers and policy ideologues and ratcheting up the rhetoric, President George W. Bush grouped all mainstream (moderate) and militant Islamists together under the name "Islamo-fascists" and called on Americans to be prepared for a global war on terrorism, the "inescapable calling of our generation."

The global war on terrorism, Bush said, will eradicate the threat of Islamic radical terrorism (a loose and incoherent term) and target rogue states that sponsor terrorism or offer lodging to terrorists. Declaring an end to the post–World War II security system, Bush said that the United States will no longer observe international treaties and institutions that constrain its ability to wage a long struggle on its own terms. Set in sweeping ideological terms, Bush and Vice President Dick Cheney's global war on terrorism set the stage for the American-led invasion and occupation of Iraq, but it is doubtful whether the U.S. president and vice president could have sold their ambitious war to the public without the complicity of the foreign policy and security establishment.

WHAT REALLY MOTIVATES MUSLIMS

It does not help that Americans know very little about Islam and Muslims, and the little they do know is based more on stereotypes than on facts. For example,

44 percent of Americans say Muslims are too extreme in their religious beliefs. Less than half believe U.S. Muslims are loyal to the United States. Nearly one-quarter of Americans, 22 percent, say they would not want a Muslim as a neighbor. Thirty-two percent say they admire nothing about the Muslim world, and 25 percent admit they simply "don't know." Fifty-seven percent say they know either nothing or not much about the opinions and beliefs of Muslims.[35] Interestingly, the more Americans report knowing about Muslim societies, the more likely they are to hold positive views of those countries.

Fortunately, two evidence-based books, *Who Speaks for Islam? What a Billion Muslims Really Think* by John Esposito and Dalia Mogahed and *Al Qaeda in Its Own Words,* edited by Gilles Kepel and Jean-Pierre Milelli, shatter the conventional wisdom and set the record straight.[36]

Based on tens of thousands of hour-long, face-to-face interviews conducted by the Gallup Poll between 2001 and 2007 with residents of more than thirty-five predominantly Muslim nations, *Who Speaks for Islam?* lets the voices of a billion Muslims be heard. But it is more than a statistical research survey. Esposito—a leading scholar of Islam and the director of the Center for Muslim-Christian Understanding at Georgetown University—puts the data in context and makes sense of it. Few are as qualified as Esposito, who has written extensively on contemporary Islamic societies, to assess the findings and draw relevant public and foreign policy lessons.

Some of the findings will shock American readers. For example, according to the survey, only 7 percent of the respondents think the September 11 attacks were "completely" justified, and a majority of Muslims—including nine out of ten Muslims who are called "moderate"—condemned the killings on religious and humanitarian grounds. Forget what bin Laden and al-Zawahiri preach about jihad. For most Muslims, jihad—whether it means a struggle of the soul or the sword—must be a just and ethical struggle. It has only positive connotations, and does not sanction the killing of noncombatants.

Moreover, Esposito and Mogahed show clearly that many Western commentators assign too much weight to Islam and neglect the social and political factors that are the real drivers of both politically "moderate" and radicalized Muslims: to wit, according to the study, those 7 percent of respondents who condoned the attacks mentioned the West's politics, not its culture or its way of life, as justification. There was not a single mention of religion or culture, according to the data.

When asked what they admired most about the West, the politically radicalized and moderates alike most often mentioned three areas, all of which indicate admiration and respect for American values and way of life: (1) its achievements in technology; (2) its value system, including hard work, self-responsibility, rule of law, and cooperative ethic; and (3) its fair political system, democracy, respect of human rights, freedom of speech, and gender equality.[37]

The interviews put to rest the popular hypothesis that Muslims hate American freedom and success. Contrary to the conventional wisdom that extremists are antidemocratic, a significantly higher percentage of the politically radicalized (50 percent versus 35 percent of moderates) said "moving toward greater governmental democracy" will foster progress in the Arab/Muslim world. More surprisingly, the politically radicalized were as likely as moderates, if not more so, to express interest in improving relations between the world of Islam and the Christian West (58 percent versus 44 percent of moderates).[38]

Again, instead of religion or religious extremism, it comes down to foreign policy. Although the American way of life is prized by Muslims, American foreign policy is loathed. When Esposito and his colleagues asked respondents in ten predominantly Muslim countries how they viewed a number of countries, the attributes they most associated with U.S. foreign policy were ruthless (68 percent), scientifically and technologically advanced (68 percent), aggressive (66 percent), conceited (65 percent), and morally decadent (64 percent). When asked what about America they thought brought out these qualities, most respondents listed foreign policy such as the Palestinian-Israeli conflict and America's support for Muslim dictators. Much of these attitudes seem to have developed since September 11. Clearly, then, the war on terrorism has damaged American standing and reputation almost everywhere. In the poll, substantial majorities of Muslims believed that the United States was waging a "war against Islam" and that its goal is "to weaken and divide the Islamic world."[39] Majorities of moderate and radical Muslims alike viewed Western, particularly American, political, economic, military, and cultural hegemony as threats to Islamic identity and independence. Esposito is correct to conclude that the intensity and fear of radicalized Muslims predisposes them to have a more sympathetic ear for terrorists if their grievances are not addressed.

In my own interviews with politically radicalized activists over the years, many cited Western intervention as a primary driver of their decision to join extremist groups. They said they wanted the West to stop meddling in their countries' internal affairs and pay them respect. When asked by Gallup interviewers what they wanted from the West, a plurality of Muslims cited concrete changes in certain aspects of foreign policy and greater respect for Islam. Esposito groups Muslim grievances against the United States along three dimensions—perceptions of cultural disrespect and denigration of Islam, political domination, and the reality of acute conflicts—all of which he finds filtered through a focus on U.S. foreign policy. Regardless of whether respect can be granted as opposed to being earned, the important point is that Muslims do not demand that Westerners change who they are. As Esposito stresses, foreign policy grievances can be addressed if the United States and its Western allies possess the moral courage and proceed with caution, consistency, and respect.

THE MUSLIM WORLDVIEW

An important question remains: what sort of political worldview do Muslims hold? According to the Gallup survey, however diverse Muslim populations may be, large majorities (over 80 percent) of moderates and political radicals want *sharia* or Islamic law as a source of legislation in a democratic polity. Women are as likely as men to say that "religion is an important part of life" and that "attachment to spiritual and moral values is critical to their progress." Even in the "new" Iraq, 58 percent of Iraqi women opposed separation of religion from politics, and 81 percent said religious authorities should play a direct role in crafting family law.[40]

But it would be wrong to read too deeply into these findings. Such views are not a call for theocracy. Majorities of the politically radicalized and moderates said they did not want religious leaders to be directly in charge. Implementing *sharia,* according to many Muslims, would limit the power of rulers whom they regard as autocratic, "un-Islamic," and corrupt. And although many Western commentators and policymakers argue that *sharia* is antidemocratic, Muslims view it as a vehicle of liberation and counterweight against political authoritarianism at home and Western domination.

In short, the gaps between Western and Muslim worldviews are real, but they are bridgeable. Take the gulf between the perceptions of Westerners and Muslims of the status and plight of women in Muslim societies. Studies and surveys show that what Americans find most troubling about Islam is the "oppression of women" and that women readily accept second-class status. However, according to the Gallup survey, majorities of women in virtually every country surveyed say they deserve the same legal rights as men—to vote without influence from family members, to work at any job for which they are qualified, and to hold the highest executive position in government. In Saudi Arabia, one of the most religiously conservative Muslim countries, where women are not allowed to vote or drive, majorities of women say they should be able to drive a car by themselves (61 percent), vote without influence (69 percent), and choose the job for which they are qualified (76 percent).[41]

At the same time, although Muslim women challenge the entrenched patriarchal structure of their societies, the majority do not yearn to become like their Western counterparts. They favor gender parity, but they want it on their own terms and within their own cultural and religious contexts. They do not want to imitate the lifestyle of their Western feminist counterparts. They would like to have equality before the law but preserve their local traditions. Like their male counterparts, Muslim women say their most pressing priorities are economic development and political reforms, not gender issues. Moreover, the Gallup survey did not find that religiosity among Muslim men correlates with less egalitarian views toward women. In Lebanon, Morocco, and Iran, men who support women's rights tend to be more religious than those who do not support women's rights.[42] Plain old secular patriarchy, not Islamic principles—let alone Islamic extremism—accounts for the lagging status of women in much of the Muslim world.

As a result, for those seeking to understand women's issues within a Muslim context, what seems to be an intractable divide is, in fact, nothing of the kind. This holds true as well for similar gaps in understanding on issues such as religion, politics, and extremism.

Indeed, upon closer inspection such gaps are balanced by commonalities between the Muslim world and the West. A critical segment of both Americans and Muslims believe that religion is or ought to be a pillar of their society, informed and guided by the Bible or *sharia*. Both groups also emphasize the preservation of family values, are concerned about their economic futures, employment, and their abilities to support their families, and give high priority to human rights and broad-based political participation. Finally, both groups strongly support eradicating extremism and terrorism.[43]

UNDERSTANDING ISLAM

The possibility of better relations and mutual understanding is just that, a possibility, and one made less likely thanks to eight years of George W. Bush's global war on terrorism. The Bush ideologues, in their zeal to defeat the "enemy," alienated the very Muslim majorities that are American allies in the struggle against religious extremism and global terrorism. The war on terrorism has played into the hands of bin Laden and al-Zawahiri, who relentlessly portray themselves as the vanguard elite who speak for the *ummah* and defend it.

One would hope that the new U.S. presidential administration of Barack Obama would discard the terrorism prism and sweeping ideology through which its predecessor viewed America's relations with the world of Islam. The evidence so far has been most encouraging.[44]

In *Al Qaeda in Its Own Words,* Gilles Kepel—a renowned French scholar on contemporary Islam who has written extensively on Muslim militancy at the Institute for Political Studies (IPS) in Paris—has collected and annotated selected extracts by four radical leaders: bin Laden, al-Zawahiri, Abu Musab al-Zarqawi (the al-Qaeda chief in Iraq), and Abdullah Azzam, leader of the Afghan Arabs in the 1980s. Most of these documents are available in print or on the Web; the book's importance lies in the analytical essays written by Kepel's postgraduate colleagues on each of the four men.[45] The book is an excellent companion to Esposito and Mogahed's, because it illustrates and analyzes how our real enemy is manipulating the battlefield—that is, the Muslim public.

The insightful chapter in *Al Qaeda in Its Own Words* on bin Laden by the IPS researcher Omar Saghi argues convincingly that bin Laden has gained ground not by appealing to a monolithic form of dogmatism that should apply to all Muslims; to the contrary, he claims to tolerate multiple varieties of belief.[46] Rather, he justifies his claim to being the exclusive representative of the *ummah* by insisting that only a vanguard like al-Qaeda can carry out jihad on behalf of the *ummah* and take upon itself the duty of applying God's laws and preserving the Muslim community from sin. Bin Laden claims a much bigger tent than Western analysts give him credit for.

It is not as if his claim has gone unchallenged. A significant majority of Muslims—more than 90 percent, according to the Gallup interviews— condemn bin Laden's terrorism on religious grounds and thus reject his claim as a representative of Islam and Muslims. Moreover, on the run from U.S. forces for nearly a decade, bin Laden has been reduced to a static photo, a fading television image who fell victim to his own success.

As Saghi argues, al-Qaeda's large-scale, spectacular terrorism is a product of media consumption: "It is still a crime, but less and less effective as a political and military tool."[47] Meanwhile, increasingly bin Laden is being overshadowed by a galaxy of wannabes in Iraq, London, Spain, Lebanon, and Indonesia who call themselves al-Qaeda but have at best a tenuous connection to the group. Now, more and more Muslims view bin Laden's project through the monstrosity of killing of civilians around the world.

Al Qaeda in Its Own Words makes clear that the distinctions among the extremist groups typically lumped under the umbrella term *jihadists* are significant, and that understanding them is critical to assessing the relatively limited nature of the threat and constructing strategies to deploy the Muslim public in the struggle against extremists. For example, in his chapter on Azzam, Thomas Hegghammer, a Norwegian researcher who specializes in Muslim militancy, highlights the discontinuities between Azzam's radical ideas and those of bin Laden and al-Zawahiri.[48]

The conventional wisdom in the United States describes contemporary Salafi jihadism, or global Sunni jihad, as homogenous and historically continuous, beginning in Soviet-occupied Afghanistan and carried forth by Azzam's disciples bin Laden and al-Zawahiri after their mentor's 1989 assassination. In reality, the "global jihad movement" is a complex and fragmented political phenomenon that has witnessed radical ruptures and shocks since its inception. Although Azzam certainly influenced his two most famous acolytes, to equate his worldview with bin Laden and al-Zawahiri's total global war against "the alliance of Jews and crusaders," as many terrorism experts do, is to falsify history: Azzam opposed terrorism as a tool of war as well as aggression against noncombatants. His definition of *jihad* was the defense of Muslims under attack and occupation, not waging battle against Muslim rulers and the United States. In my interviews with Azzam's former lieutenants and confidantes, I was told that at the height of the Soviet occupation Azzam vetoed proposals by militants to attack Russian civilians, because it would tarnish the image of the mujahidin and jihad. Bin Laden and company, of course, have had no similar reservations.

BRIDGING THE DIVIDE

In the introduction to *Al Qaeda in Its Own Words,* Kepel describes a new "science of terrorism" that has emerged in the United States—a kind of cottage industry that props up wobbly theories while doing little to advance actual knowledge of the jihadist phenomena. But by focusing on radical Muslim terrorism, with all its fearful implications, analysts forestall inspection of the variety of distinctions and divisions that exist within Muslim society, and even among Muslim radicals.

Since September 11, 2001, the vast diversity of Islam and of mainstream moderate Muslims has been obscured by a murderous minority, particularly al-Qaeda and its prodigies, that claims it speaks for Islam and Muslims. Ironically, although the weight of evidence reveals that Muslims reject bin Laden's terrorist rhetoric and exclusive ownership of Islam, many in the West take bin Laden's claims for granted. The result is that the hyper and overmilitaristic American response to the events of September 11 alienated the moderate Muslim majority and reinforced a belief that the war against global terrorism is really a war against Islam.

Nevertheless, it is not too late to change tack and reach out to Muslim moderates. But doing so will require a more nuanced and subtle understanding of who they are and how they think. Policymakers interested in doing so should eschew ideology in favor of a more analytical and constructive approach, one that draws distinctions between the many faces of Islamism—a politico-religious ideology that accepts the rules of the political game—and jihadism—a tiny breakaway insurgent current that uses violence in the name of religion and seeks to seize power and Islamize society by autocratic fiat from the top down.

Notes

1. For overviews on the relationship between religion and terrorism, see David Rapoport, "Fear and Trembling in Three Religious Traditions," *American Political Science Review* 78 (September 1984): 658–677; and Jessica Stern, *Terror in the Name of God: Why Religious Militants Kill* (New York: HarperCollins, 2003).
2. "Pentagon Releases Bin Laden Videotape," National Public Radio, December 13, 2001, www.npr.org/news/specials/response/investigation/011213.binladen.tape.htm.
3. President George W. Bush, address to joint session of Congress, September 20, 2001, www.pbs.org/newshour/bb/military/terroristattack/bush_speech_9–20.html.
4. Remarks of President George W. Bush at a roundtable with Arab and Muslim American leaders, September 10, 2002, www.dhs.gov/xnews/speeches/speech_0026 .shtm.
5. For historical and contemporary background on militant Islamic movements, see John L. Esposito, *Unholy War: Terror in the Name of Islam* (New York: Oxford University Press, 2002).
6. Bruce Hoffman, *Inside Terrorism,* rev. and exp. ed. (New York: Columbia University Press, 2006), 85; U.S. Department of State, "Country Reports on Terrorism 2007," April 2008, chap. 6, "Terrorist Organizations," www.state.gov/s/ct/rls/ crt/2007/index.htm
7. This essay is adapted from Chapter 3, "We Are Terrorists," of my book, *Willful Blindness: A Memoir of the Jihad* (New York: Encounter Books, 2008), and from my essay "The Jihad in Plain Sight" (May 6, 2008), which was commissioned by the Hudson Institute on the occasion of the 2008 Bradley Symposium. The essay is available at www.hudson.org/index.cfm?fuseaction=publication_details&id=5567.
8. Bernard Lewis, *Islam and the West* (New York: Oxford University Press, 1993), 155; Ibn Warraq, *Why I Am Not a Muslim* (Amherst, N.Y.: Prometheus Books, 1995), republished in 2003.
9. Joseph Schacht, *An Introduction to Islamic Law* (New York: Oxford/Clarendon Press, 1982), 69–71; Robert Spencer, *The Politically Incorrect Guide to Islam (and the Crusades)* (Washington, D.C.: Regnery, 2006), 38.
10. Schacht, *Introduction to Islamic Law,* 73.
11. Lawrence Wright, *The Looming Tower* (New York: Knopf, 2006), 57, 138; see also Fawaz A. Gerges, *The Far Enemy—Why Jihad Went Global* (New York: Cambridge University Press, 2005), 100. As Wright recounts, Abdel Rahman is said to have tartly rebuked the younger al-Zawahiri, reminding him that the *sharia* also forbids a prisoner from being emir. Wright further describes how the rivalry between Abdel Rahman and al-Zawahiri, who ran competing (though at times cooperating) Egyptian terrorist organizations, became especially heated when they accused each other of treachery while jockeying for leadership positions in Afghanistan during the 1980s. After the Blind Sheikh's conviction and sentencing to life imprisonment, however, al-Zawahiri joined Osama bin Laden in vowing revenge if he died in American custody. See, for example, "Inside Al-Qaeda: A Window into the World of Militant Islam and the Afghani Alumni," *Jane's,* September 28, 2001, www.janes.com/security/international_security/news/misc/janes010928_ 1_n.shtml.

12. Ibn Taymiyyah is widely regarded as a theological eminence; see, for example, Schacht, *Introduction to Islamic Law,* 63, 72. For a decidedly contrary view, see Stephen Schwartz, *The Two Faces of Islam* (New York: Anchor Books, 2003), 60–62.

13. Robert Spencer, *The Truth about Muhammad—Founder of the World's Most Intolerant Religion* (Washington, D.C.: Regnery, 2006), 8.

14. Schacht, *Introduction to Islamic Law,* 115, 1n; Spencer, *Politically Incorrect Guide to Islam (and the Crusades),* 24.

15. Serge Trifkovic, *The Sword of the Prophet—Islam: History, Theology, Impact on the World* (Salisbury, Mass.: Regina Orthodox Press, 2002), 37–54; Spencer, *Truth about Muhammad,* 89–145.

16. Andrew Bostom, "The Sacred Muslim Practice of Beheading," *FrontPage Magazine,* May 13, 2004, www.frontpagemag.com/Articles/ReadArticle.asp?ID=13371.

17. Annemarie Schimmel, *Islam—An Introduction* (Albany: State University of New York Press, 1992), 35.

18. Marc Sageman, *Understanding Terror Networks* (Philadelphia: University of Pennsylvania Press, 2004), 1–2.

19. Ibid.

20. Daniel Benjamin and Steven Simon, *The Age of Sacred Terror—Radical Islam's War against America* (New York: Random House, 2003), 54–55.

21. Bernard Lewis, *The Middle East: A Brief History of the Last 2,000 Years* (New York: Simon and Shuster, 1996), 233.

22. Ibn Warraq, *Why I Am Not a Muslim,* 12.

23. See Andrew Bostom, ed., *The Legacy of Jihad—Islamic Holy War and the Fate of Non-Muslims* (Amherst, N.Y.: Prometheus Books, 2005), 125–126 (collected Qur'anic verses commanding warfare).

24. Ibid., 136–37, quoting the Sahih Bukhari Collection of Hadith, vol. 4, bk. 52, nos. 42 and 48.

25. Ibid. , 165, quoting Sura 2:193 and 8:39.

26. Amir Taheri, *Holy Terror* (Chevy Chase, Md.: Adler and Adler, 1987), 226–227; Ibn Warraq, *Why I Am Not a Muslim,* 12.

27. See Chapter 4, "Jihaad in the Cause of God," in Sayyid Qutb, *Milestones* (Cedar Rapids, Iowa: Mother Mosque Foundation, 1993), 57–58, 59–60. See also Bostom, *Legacy of Jihad,* 233, 235.

28. Qutb, *Milestones,* 58–59; see also Bostom, *Legacy of Jihad,* 234–237, and Benjamin and Simon, *Age of Sacred Terror,* 64–66. The passage, Sura 2:190–191, continues: "But fight them not at the Sacred Mosque, unless they first fight you there; but if they fight you, slay them. Such is the reward of those who reject faith."

29. Qutb, *Milestones,* 64; see also Bostom, *Legacy of Jihad,* 238.

30. A version of this essay appeared in *Democracy: A Journal of Ideas* 9 (Summer 2008).

31. At a joint session of Congress on September 20, 2001, President George W. Bush asked, "Why do they hate us? They hate what they see right here in this chamber—a democratically elected government. They hate us for our freedoms—our freedom of religion, our freedom of speech, our freedom to vote, and assemble, and disagree with each other."

32. For further elaboration on Muslim responses to 9/11, see the chapter "The Aftermath: The War Within," in Fawaz A. Gerges, *The Far Enemy: Why Jihad Went Global* (New York: Cambridge University Press, 2005).

33. Fawaz A. Gerges, "His Mentor Turns on bin Laden," *International Herald Tribune,* September 21, 2007.

34. I have examined in depth Oadah and Imam's critiques of al-Qaeda in the chapter "Beyond the Far Enemy," in Gerges, *Far Enemy.*

35. John L. Esposito and Dalia Mogahed, *Who Speaks for Islam? What a Billion Muslims Really Think* (Washington, D.C.: Gallup Press, 2008), 155.

36. Ibid.; Gilles Kepel and Jean-Pierre Milelli, eds., *Al Qaeda in Its Own Words* (Cambridge, Mass.: Harvard University Press, 2008).

37. Esposito and Mogahed, *Who Speaks for Islam?* 80–81.

38. Ibid., 81.

39. Ibid., 87.

40. Ibid., 101–102.

41. Ibid.

42. Ibid., 123.

43. Ibid., 154.

44. Notably, President Obama's first televised interview in the White House was with the al Arabiya news network based in Dubai. In that interview, Obama said he would be "very clear in distinguishing between organizations like Al Qaeda—that espouse violence, espouse terror and act on it—and people who may disagree with my administration and certain actions, or may have a particular viewpoint in terms of how their countries should develop. We can have legitimate disagreements but still be respectful." See www.alarabiya.net/articles/2009/01/27/65096.html.

45. Kepel and Milelli, *Al Qaeda in Its Own Words.*

46. Omar Saghi, in ibid..

47. Ibid., 39.

48. Thomas Hegghammer, in Kepel and Milelli, *Al Qaeda in Its Own Words.*

is suicide terrorism an effective tactic?

Suicide terrorism is a pragmatic choice
YES: Gordon H. McCormick and Lindsay Fritz,
Naval Postgraduate School

NO: Suicide terrorism rarely achieves its goals
Max Abrahms, *Stanford University*

From the attacks on the United States of September 11, 2001, through the 2002 Bali nightclub bombings, 2005 London transit bombings, 2008 Mumbai attacks, and scores of other recent terror incidents across the Middle East, South Asia, North Africa, and elsewhere, suicide attacks have come to symbolize the shockingly lethal terrorism of the modern age.

But has the ultimate sacrifice of hundreds of individual attackers and the deaths of thousands of innocent victims paid off in terms of suicide terror groups achieving, or moving closer to achieving, their stated goals?

This question goes to the heart of long-standing academic and policy debates over whether terrorism itself is an effective means of achieving political objectives.[1] Although this broader concern remains far from resolved, a specific focus on suicide terrorism is a constructive way to test the utility of terrorism itself. Because suicide attacks are far deadlier and more fear-inspiring than conventional attacks—compare the failed bombing of the World Trade Center in 1993 (six dead) with the successful suicide operation in September 2001 (nearly three thousand dead)—they are also presumably more politically effective than conventional attacks as well. Indeed, terrorist groups adopt suicide tactics for a simple reason: they believe they will work.[2]

Ever since a series of Hezbollah suicide bombings drove the United States and France out of Lebanon in the early 1980s, a mythology of success has surrounded suicide terrorism, leading dozens of different terror groups to since adopt the tactic. And although the use of suicide terrorism parallels the modern rise of religious, particularly Islamic, terrorism, many prominent non–religion-based groups have also ubiquitously employed the tactic—including the secular Palestinian Fatah organization, and the separatist Tamil Tigers in Sri Lanka, which committed more suicide attacks between the mid-1980s and 2001 than any other group in the world.

The authors of the first essay in this chapter, Gordon McCormick and Lindsay Fritz, agree with Max Abrahms, the author of the second essay, that suicide terrorism is a more lethal and fear-provoking form of terrorism than conventional terrorism. And they agree that groups employ suicide attacks for reasons beyond purely instrumental goal attainment—for example, powerful individual and group solidarity benefits are gained from having members willing to commit the ultimate act of sacrifice for the cause. Suicide tactics are, therefore, an understandably attractive option for terrorist organizations. The authors strongly disagree, however, on the question of whether suicide tactics are an effective means of achieving political ends.

McCormick and Fritz argue that terrorism is a tactic chosen by strategic actors who rationally calculate that it will maximize their chances of achieving objectives. Suicide attacks are employed for a similar reason: it is believed they offer a "higher return on investment" than conventional alternatives (the authors present eight factors that they say contribute to the greater utility of suicide terrorism). Terrorist groups do not always make perfect decisions (who does?), but, according to McCormick and Fritz, if one starts from the empirically grounded proposition that terrorists make rational (context-dependent) strategic choices—including the choice to employ suicide attacks—it is possible to efficiently isolate key variables and ultimately better understand the nature of terrorist decision making, including decisions that may appear to deviate from rationality.

By contrast, Abrahms believes that terrorism is a futile political strategy and that adding suicide attacks to the mix does nothing to alter its losing track record. Like McCormick and Fritz, he believes the choice of both terrorism and suicide tactics may be rational, but for reasons other than political goal attainment such as for ideological/organizational purposes. Indeed, Abrahms contends that suicide attacks against civilian populations tend to backfire, leaving groups further from their objectives rather than closer. As for the question of whether terrorists are strategically rational political maximizers, Abrahms says there is little evidence that terrorist groups carefully weigh their strategic options; they often reflexively shun nonviolent avenues with stronger track records of eliciting political change. He concludes that political scientists and policymakers need to reexamine assumptions that suicide terrorist groups behave as rational political actors.

The use of suicide as a tactic of war or terrorism is not new. For example, during World War II thousands of Japanese kamikaze pilots attacked American ships and military outposts across the Pacific. And in the nineteenth century, Russian anarchists often employed suicide tactics against the royal family and other government targets.[3] What is new is the widespread use of suicide attacks as a form of mass-casualty terrorism. A tremendous amount of death and destruction has been wrought by suicide terrorists over the last twenty-five years. Determining whether this carnage has paid political dividends for groups employing the tactic is not simply an academic exercise; it will inform policymakers' understanding of future terrorist strategies and help determine their strategies of response as well.

Suicide terrorism is a pragmatic choice
YES: Gordon H. McCormick and Lindsay Fritz,
Naval Postgraduate School

A Strategic Perspective on Suicide Attack

On a warm autumn morning in 2003, Hanadi Jaradat said goodbye to her parents in the West Bank city of Jenin. The twenty-nine-year-old apprentice lawyer had a reputation as an ambitious and independent young woman. She had grown up as the eldest daughter in a large family, studied law at Jareesh University in Jordan, and aspired to one day open her own law office. Hanadi was so driven to succeed, her mother later claimed, that she had turned down a succession of suitors to pursue her studies and career. Her parents therefore detected nothing out of the ordinary when she hurriedly bid farewell that morning, rushing off with a smile to close a real estate deal for her law office.

Six hours later, Hanadi quietly entered Maxim's, a restaurant in Haifa many miles from Jenin and on the other side of the security zone that separated Israel from the West Bank. Like her parents, the diners of the crowded seaside establishment did not perceive anything out of the ordinary. Hanadi had left her home in traditional dress, but she entered the restaurant in fashionable black jeans with her hair pulled back in a ponytail framing what witnesses said was a pretty "heart-shaped" face. She looked like any other casual lunchtime customer. Upon sitting down, Hanadi ordered a meal. After finishing her meal, she calmly got up and walked to the most crowded part of the restaurant. Situating herself between two families, she then detonated the 22 pounds of explosives laced with ball bearings that she had concealed under her clothing.[4]

In an instant, body parts of diners were strewn across the room. Hanadi's victims—twenty-one in total—included women and children, Jews and Arabs. Each of the two families that Hanadi had made sure was within the lethal blast radius of her explosives lost five members. All that remained to identify the young Palestinian woman was her head. Her attack proved to be one of the deadliest suicide attacks of the Second Palestinian Intifada.

It is reasonable to ask how a young woman of such great promise could take her own life. How could she do so, furthermore, for the express purpose of carrying out such a merciless and calculated attack? The portrait that first emerged of Hanadi Jaradat and the scene of devastation that she left in her wake—what Haifa's chief of police called "a vision of hell"—seemed incongruous. Once all the facts surrounding the incident were uncovered, however, it was clear that her actions, though dramatic, were in no way unique. Hanadi's attack was one of over two hundred suicide operations carried out in Israel during the Second Intifada (2000–2004) and one of at least a dozen such actions carried out by Palestinian women, including wives, mothers, and students. Since 1983, over 2,500 suicide attacks have been carried out worldwide.[5] The circumstances that surround these actions reveal a common underlying logic.

To uncover this logic, we must distinguish between the reasons why individuals are willing to die to kill others and the reasons why the groups that train, equip, and send them on their way choose to solicit or otherwise accept their sacrifice. At the level of the individual, the reasons for martyrdom vary widely. These reasons can be found in the realm of individual and social psychology and are beyond the scope of this essay. The task of this essay is to examine the *strategic* basis of suicide attacks. To do this, we will evaluate these operations at the level of the group.

We begin with the observation that terrorism is not a strategy per se, but a tactic that traditionally has been employed to support one of two alternative strategic programs: political coercion or political mobilization. We follow with a discussion of the specific nature and utility of suicide tactics. We conclude with a brief discussion of the meaning and limits of strategic behavior. Some of the confusion about the underlying strategic basis of terrorism begins with a prior misunderstanding of the nature of strategic action itself. A complete understanding of terrorist behavior requires a multilayered approach to terrorist decision making. The starting point for any such effort, however, must be the hypothesis that terrorist groups are rational agents that try to match means with ends to achieve their objectives.

TERRORISM, SIGNALING, AND STRATEGY

From a strategic perspective, terrorism can be thought of as a multistaged signaling game in which violent images are employed to communicate a group's ability and commitment to use violence in whatever form is necessary to achieve its goals.[6] The players in this game consist of a terrorist group and one or more target audiences. As in all signaling games, one or both sets of players act with incomplete information on the other. The terrorist group may or may not have a complete understanding of the relevant attributes of its target audiences, but its target audiences will always begin the game with an incomplete picture of the utility function, commitment, and capabilities of the group. It is this state of incomplete information that permits the group to manipulate external perceptions of its "type." The group can be seen as strong or weak. The targets of influence that the group wishes to impress evaluate its type based on what they see, which is what the group chooses to reveal through the "signals" it generates by its attacks. These attacks—as signals—are designed to shape audience perceptions of the payoff structure of the game in a way that advances the group's political agenda.[7]

Terrorism can be used to support two different strategic programs. The first is a strategy of political coercion or "dirty bargaining."[8] In such cases, terrorism is a means of gaining negotiating leverage over the state. The group begins by initiating attacks against high-value targets to establish that it is willing and able to continue its attacks into the foreseeable future. Having established its bona fides, the group then enters into (tacit or explicit) negotiations with the target government and offers to halt its campaign of violence in return for political concessions. Coercive campaigns are designed to convince the target regime that the costs of not complying with a group's wishes are greater than the costs of concession. Although the dynamics of dirty bargaining is a complicated subject in its own right, it is generally true that the degree of leverage a group will be able to exercise is directly related to the perceived level of damage it can threaten over time. This is a function, in turn, of the frequency, scale, and "media quality" of its attacks.

In the second strategic program, terrorism can play a significant role in supporting a strategy of political mobilization. Signaling attacks are designed to draw attention to the group's existence and purpose, sharpen popular views of the nature of the struggle, demonstrate the group's growing strength and the increasing weakness of the incumbent regime, and embolden people to begin to actively support the group's efforts to usher in a new political order. Such attacks are also regularly employed in the hope of provoking an extreme response. If successful, this strategy can have the effect of radicalizing and polarizing popular opinion, retroactively legitimating the group's use of violence, and making it easier for the group to mobilize popular support for its cause.[9] In contrast to a strategy of coercion, the ultimate objective of this program is not to gain a greater degree of leverage at the negotiating table, but to eventually displace the state altogether. To do so, a terrorist group must grow to the point that it can defeat the state on its own terms.

Each of these strategic programs is designed to shape the perceptions of a different primary audience. For a program of coercive bargaining to succeed, a terrorist group must establish itself as a plausible threat in the minds of state decision makers and their constituents, who must be made to believe that they will be subjected to an unacceptable level of continuing violence if a compromise settlement is not reached. In making this determination, state authorities will consider a number of factors that will bear on their decision, each of which is subject to manipulation. Is the group actually capable of carrying through on its threats? What would it cost the group to do so? Is it willing to incur these costs? Does it have the means to sustain a protracted campaign in the face of government countermeasures? What will these countermeasures cost? What costs will be incurred in defying the group's demands? What are the costs of compliance? The answers to these and related questions can be answered only after a group has begun to develop a track record for itself. Even at this point, the answers cannot be known with certainty. With this in mind, today's terrorists design their actions to magnify state perceptions of the threat it can expect to confront tomorrow.

The primary audience in a program of political mobilization is the group's own constituents. Violent opposition groups are generally composed of a hard-core minority and a much larger majority who are more or less committed to the cause. The much larger majority is made up of "conditional supporters"[10] whose willingness to back the opposition (and not the state) is based on their subjective estimates of the expected costs and benefits of their alternatives. These estimates, in turn, are based on their perceptions of the relative balance of power between the two players and their corresponding prospects. This process poses a mobilization challenge to violent opposition groups during the early days of their campaigns because of the state's obvious and overwhelming force advantage. Who would want to join such a high-risk enterprise? This challenge can be overcome through a program of symbolic violence designed to generate an exaggerated image of group strength and regime weakness. Terrorist actions, in this respect, are intended to create a self-fulfilling prophecy: if a group can convince enough people that it has the ability to effectively challenge the state, it can mobilize the support it needs to do so.[11]

Such efforts, as noted, are generally reinforced by a program of target provocation. High-profile attacks on the state and its constituents, in such cases, are carried out for the purpose of triggering indiscriminate counterattacks on a group's own political followers. The intention is to force the state into a Hobson's choice—either "retreat or unleash the struggle."[12] Regardless of what course of action it chooses, the state can be expected to improve the group's chances of expanding its base of support. In contrast to the demonstrative use of terrorism, which is designed to manipulate the *expectations* of the target audience, the provocative use of terrorism is designed to (indirectly) influence the *preferences* of that audience. As a practical matter, of course, many if not most terrorist actions serve both purposes at the same time. A series of terrorist attacks against high-value targets in the face of state efforts to keep such attacks from occurring will not only make the attacking group look strong and the government look weak, but also put increasing pressure on the state to use "every means at its disposal" to put an end to the violence. The provocative utility of such actions does not derive from their popularity among a group's constituency "but from the unpopularity of the ensuing repression."[13]

To accomplish these goals, terrorist groups must create a perceptual or subjective effect that is greater than the sum of the physical consequences of their attacks. This approach places a premium on conducting operations that are newsworthy enough to be picked up and transmitted to a larger audience by the mass media. The media, in this respect, play an essential intermediate role in amplifying the signal a group transmits every time it carries out an attack.[14] By analogy, this is the same role played by the amplifier in one's home sound system, television, or computer. The function of an amplifier is to take an initially weak audio signal and boost it to the point that it is strong enough to drive a speaker. The audience, then, is not listening to the sound of the initial signal, but that of an amplified signal strong enough to be heard. This is the function the media play in the aftermath of a terrorist attack. In the absence of a strong media boost, terrorist attacks have little or no effect beyond the immediate area of the event. With this boost, by contrast, they are international news. To paraphrase an old philosophical question: if a car bomb goes off in the forest and there is no one around to hear it, does it make any (political) noise? The answer, of course, is no. Terrorists, through their actions, either succeed in staying in the headlines or are out of the game.

As many observers have noted over the years, nothing is more likely to seize the headlines than a deliberately executed act of violence. Furthermore, the more graphic the violence is, the more prominently, broadly, and repeatedly it is likely to be reported.[15] To ensure the media boost they need to prevail, terrorist groups have a strong incentive to select targets and tactics that are as audacious as possible. Even violent acts of terrorism, however, can become routine. As they do so, their media value diminishes. To escape this trap, terrorist groups must continue to innovate and escalate to hold the attention of their target audiences over the course of their campaigns. As a practical matter, this tactic frequently results in greater levels of violence. Who is killed, how many are killed, the ways in which they are killed, and the frequency with which such killings take place—all influence the newsworthiness of a terrorist event. In an oft-quoted remark, terrorism expert Brian Jenkins claimed some years ago that "terrorists want a lot of people watching, not a lot of people dead."[16] The increasingly deadly nature of terrorism over the past decade, however, would appear to validate the counterclaim of McCormick's First Corollary to Jenkins's Rule: "If a lot of people are dead, a lot of *other* people are watching."

Regardless of the nature of its specific strategic program, every violent opposition group faces a similar challenge at the outset of its campaign: to "win," it must find a way to achieve an ambitious political agenda in the face of imposing resource constraints. This challenge is generally complicated by two competing requirements: the need to remain secure, on the one hand, and the need to continue to advertise itself, on the other.[17] In the first case, a group's small size makes it highly vulnerable to attack. Any significant breach in security can easily end the game before it starts. This factor places a premium on reducing a group's exposure to government counterattack by reducing its operating profile. However, this same constraint means that underground groups must make the most of the little they have. Should the group fail to maintain an effective presence before the state and in the minds of its constituents, it will not only result in a loss of influence, but also eventually destabilize the organization itself. The underground group, then, faces two ways to lose but only one way to win. To prevail, it must walk an often fine line between two competing types of operational errors.

Terrorist groups, in this respect, face a dual paradox. To carry out their strategic program, they must appear to be strong, but they must do so from a position of weakness. To create an appearance of strength, they must operate in a way that signals strength rather than weakness in the minds of those they wish to influence. This goal must be accomplished, however, in a manner that minimizes the risk that the state will exploit a group's weakness to eliminate it from the game. This paradox helps explain why violent opposition groups turn to terrorism in the first place. Terrorism, as high-profile symbolic violence, offers a way of balancing the competing requirements of influence and security in the face of constrained resources. It appears to offer a way of achieving a lot with a little at a relatively small price. From this perspective, of course, terrorism is not an expression of strength but a sign of weakness. To overcome this contradiction, terrorist groups must appear to be much stronger than they are using the same violent tactics that mark them as weak actors. Their objective strength in the long run will be directly proportional to the illusion of strength they are able to create for their target audiences along the way.

THE TACTICAL UTILITY OF SUICIDE ATTACKS

Suicide attacks, as noted earlier, can be evaluated at two different levels of analysis: the individual and the group. At the individual level, there is no consistent pattern. When the circumstances surrounding Hanadi Jaradat's attack came to light, for example, it was found that the young Palestinian woman was motivated by revenge. Four months before her attack, her brother and fiancé had been shot and killed by an Israeli assassination squad while drinking coffee on the family's front porch. Both men, it was alleged, had ties to Islamic Jihad.

The murder of her loved ones led her to offer herself to Islamic Jihad as a suicide bomber. Each case, however, is different. Although the desire for revenge is a common contributing factor in suicide attacks, it is by no means universal. Some individuals, it appears, are motivated by a sense of social and moral obligation, some make a deal with God, and still others are willing to trade their lives for a promise of financial support for their families. The reasons why people volunteer or allow themselves to be recruited for suicide attacks, in short, are as diverse, complex, and idiosyncratic as the individuals themselves.[18]

At the group level, which is what interests us here, the motivations underlying the use of suicide attacks are more consistent. The decision to employ suicide tactics at this level of analysis is a rational choice that can be evaluated through the same strategic lens that we have used to evaluate a group's decision to resort to terrorism in the first place. Both decisions are subject to a "logic of consequence," in which a group's strategic and tactical alternatives are evaluated in terms of their anticipated effects and potential utility.[19] Groups that employ suicide tactics under this logic do so because these attacks appear to offer a higher return on investment than their conventional alternative.

We have isolated eight key factors that explain the utility of suicide terrorism. First, suicide attacks are more lethal than their conventional counterparts. Conventional bombers depend on the unwitting cooperation of their targets to carry out their missions. The bomb itself is stationary. The target(s) of attack must come within the effective blast radius of the bomb before the explosion can have the intended effect. In the case of a timed detonation in particular, which constitutes the majority of bombings, the attacker has no control over who or how many are caught in the fragmentation pattern. The suicide attacker, by contrast, is a "smart bomb" with a "human guidance system."[20] He can vary the timing and vector of his attack to improve his chances of hitting his target and maximizing his intended effects. When Hanadi Jaradat got up from her table to move to a more crowded area of the restaurant, she did so to improve her chances of killing as many people as possible. This is not the exception but the norm in suicide operations. In one survey carried out several years ago, suicide attacks were estimated on average to be four times as deadly as conventional operations.[21]

Second, suicide operations have proven to be a highly effective way of gaining the spotlight, which is one of the reasons groups resort to terrorist tactics in the first place. The efficiency of suicide attacks stems not just from their greater average lethality, but also from the fact that the act itself is a newsworthy event in its own right. The self-destructiveness of these operations makes them attractive publicity stunts. At times, their inherent drama is further extended through a systematic follow-on program of symbolic exploitation.

Most groups such as Hamas, Islamic Jihad, and al-Qaeda that employ suicide operations as a standard tactic glorify and immortalize the attacker in videos, audiocassettes, posters, graffiti, and group Web sites. The Palestinian groups, in particular, regularly videotape the last will and testaments of their martyrs and distribute these tapes to local and international media. During the period of the Second Intifada, a number of these groups are reported to have even circulated calendars that featured a "martyr of the month." The heroism and self-sacrifice of the martyr are discussed in mosques and madrassas. The attacks are reenacted in playgrounds and on the streets.[22] A single suicide action, in this respect, can generate a significant level of second-order attention.

Third, in enabling social circumstances, suicide attacks can be a way of building solidarity with one's political base. The decision to use suicide terrorism does not occur *ex nihilo*, but in the context of a larger social and cultural environment that can either promote the use of suicide operations or restrict their use as a practical tactic. In the absence of facilitating social norms, suicide tactics would most likely be rejected by a group's own target audience. Indeed, the use of such tactics under these conditions is likely to do more harm than good, even assuming a group could find the recruits needed to carry out such attacks in the first place. In a facilitating environment, by contrast, a group finds not only ample recruits who are willing to die for the cause, but a ready audience for their sacrifice. A martyr's death, in this case, is a mutual loss for the group and the community that raised him. Honoring his memory requires honoring the cause and, by association, the group for which he sacrificed his life. This support, in turn, can be used as a means of building a stronger common bond between a terrorist group and its core supporters.

Fourth, and in a related vein, the use of suicide tactics can be a way of deflecting or reducing the possibility of backlash over civilian casualties. Terrorism by its nature is horrific—it is intended to be. Although suicide operations, as we have argued, can be useful, they also carry risks. One such risk is that it will be rejected by the very people it is supposed to impress. This risk can be acute in the case of deliberately chosen civilian targets. The fact that the goals of a group have widespread popular support does not mean that the methods it employs to achieve its goals will receive the same level of acceptance. Disputes over tactics can divide a group from its own self-defined constituency. Suicide operations, paradoxically, can prove to be a more acceptable alternative than conventional terrorist attacks—even when they prove to be more lethal. The reason for this, it is argued, is their built-in act of atonement.[23] The self-martyr only kills others at the cost of his own life. His willingness to do so justifies the event. In the right social setting, once again, this willingness can turn an act of murder into a necessary sacrifice. To the degree it does so, it can give a group the political space it needs to conduct its program without losing the support of its own followers.

Fifth, suicide attacks can be a useful instrument of "auto-propaganda,"[24] which, in turn, can help motivate and unify a group's internal membership. Extremist elements within violent opposition groups often reflect the underlying emotions of the group as a whole. Their actions, if properly calibrated, can tap into these emotions, give them definition, and, in doing so, contribute to forging a group's collective identity. They also personify the group's mission and its ideology in its purest form. Their example can be used to remind others of who they are, why they fight, and how they must fight to win. Martyrdom operations, and the cultivated ritual that almost universally surrounds these operations, serve this purpose admirably. Although those who are selected for suicide missions are typically marginal affiliates of their group in life, they are elevated into symbols of the group's purpose and motivation in death. Those who survive them are strengthened by their shared image and memories of their dead heroes and their mutual responsibility to live by the example of those who died for their convictions.

Sixth, suicide terrorism can be employed as an instrument of interorganizational competition, providing terrorist groups with a competitive advantage over their local rivals. Terrorists frequently compete for political market share. In such cases, suicide operations can be used as a means of signaling a group's relative attractiveness over groups that share the same or similar ideological goals but employ a more conventional tactical portfolio. This argument is supported by the work of Mia Bloom, who has shown that Palestinian suicide operations, and the events in their aftermath, have resulted in an increase in popular support for martyrdom attacks and a reduction in support for the Palestinian Authority.[25] Similar findings have been generated by Dipak Gupta and Kusum Mundra,[26] who have illustrated the way in which intra-Palestinian rivalries have influenced the timing of suicide operations, and Scott Atran, who has observed that although Hamas's suicide campaign during the Second Intifada actually prompted Israel to reoccupy the Palestinian territories, the organization's level of popular support increased substantially during the same time period, eventually eclipsing that of the Palestinian Liberation Organization (PLO). The September 11 attacks, Atran suggests, represent a similar case. Though it ultimately resulted in a significantly greater level of foreign intervention in the Muslim world, the 9/11 operation dramatically bolstered al-Qaeda's reputation as a global jihadist organization and significantly increased its leverage over rival jihadi groups.[27]

Seventh, suicide operations are cheap. As with any operation, suicide attacks require a preexisting infrastructure to select, prepare, and equip new recruits.

Once this is in place, however, the marginal cost of carrying out an attack is insignificant. The average improvised explosive device (IED) worn or carried by a suicide bomber, while increasingly sophisticated, probably still costs no more than $100 to $200 to produce.[28] Where explosives are plentiful, even vehicle-born IED attacks, which typically employ stolen vehicles, are a trivial expense. The bombers themselves are expendable assets. Often, as suggested earlier, they are not even members of the group, but individuals—like Hanadi Jaradat—who are recruited for the sole purpose of carrying out a single one-way mission. The costs of achieving the same effect with conventional means would often prove to be much higher. This was summarized nicely by a member of the Black Tigers, the suicide arm of the Liberation Tigers of Tamil Eelam (LTTE), who noted: "If we have a target and use conventional operations we normally lose 15 or 16 fighters. With self sacrifice we can achieve the same objective and only one dies."[29]

Finally, as economist Thomas Schelling observed years ago, it is sometimes rational to appear to be irrational. Many observers during the period in which suicide attacks first emerged as a terrorist tactic tended to classify them as irrational, or at least as nonrational acts. They were considered to be the actions of individuals who had lost the capacity to reason and were "crazy for the cause." Rational actors, as we have noted, weigh the consequences of their actions in relation to their goals and select the course of action that appears to offer the highest expected return. This gives them a measure of predictability. It also gives their opponents a way of influencing their behavior, at least in principle. One has only to identify and manipulate their incentive structure to get them to change their ways. Irrational actors, by contrast, are not motivated by incentives. They are guided by impulse and emotion and, as a consequence, often act in ways that undermine their own interests. They are not subject to manipulation in the same way that rational actors are. All things being equal, this frame of mind makes them more dangerous and more difficult to deter. The group that can gain a reputation for being "a little bit crazy" can enhance its leverage at the negotiating table and its reputation as an effective counterweight to the state.[30]

THE (IMPERFECT) STRATEGIC TERRORIST

The strategic perspective on terrorist decision making in general, and the use of suicide tactics in particular, is not without its challengers. Terrorists, we are told, always lose, and a strategic actor would never adopt a course of action with a losing track record. The critics, therefore, conclude that terrorists are not strategic agents.[31] This argument has a number of shortcomings. The first is empirical. Terrorists, in fact, sometimes win. Three examples include the Irgun Zvai Leumi in Israel, the Ethniki Organosis Kyprion (EOKA) in Cyprus, and the National Liberation Front (FLN) in Algeria. Each of these groups played a pivotal role in displacing a colonial occupier and establishing an independent political order. Terrorism was an important tool in each organization's larger strategic program. This conclusion is echoed by Robert Pape, who lists a series of successful or partially successful terrorist campaigns over the last twenty-five years that specifically employed suicide tactics. His examples include Hezbollah's campaign to force the United States and France out of Lebanon (1983), Hezbollah's efforts to force Israel's withdrawal from Lebanon (1983–1985), and Hamas versus Israel (1994–1995).[32] A recent RAND study focusing on how terrorist campaigns end found that roughly 10 percent of the 268 terrorist groups that have come and gone since 1968 disbanded after achieving all or some of their political objectives. A much larger percentage ended after being incorporated into the mainstream political process which, for some of these groups, represented a partial victory in its own right.[33] In evaluating such cases we must recognize that the operative goals of terrorist groups are frequently more complex, differentiated, and nuanced than their public agendas might otherwise suggest.[34]

Some of the cases just cited, one might argue, are actually examples of guerrilla or insurgent organizations rather than terrorist groups, and therefore somehow do not count.[35] For the purposes of this discussion, this is a distinction without a difference. As suggested earlier, one of the principal ways violent opposition groups use terrorism is to jump-start the mobilization process by attempting to polarize society and reshaping popular images of the relative power and prospects of the opposition and the state. Most "insurgent" organizations, in this respect, initiate their campaigns with the liberal use of high-profile violence, much of it directed against nonmilitary and, often, explicitly civilian targets. Examples include such groups as the Viet Cong, Shining Path, Tupac Amaru Revolutionary Movement (MRTA), Farabundo Martí National Liberation Front (FMLN), the Tamil Tigers, and the contemporary Taliban, to name just a few. Many so-called terrorist groups, by the same token, remain hopeful of transforming their campaigns into a full-fledged insurgency. Terrorism, in such cases, is a means of "bootstrapping" themselves into a position of eventual strength by expanding their popular bases.[36] Most insurgent organizations, in short, begin their operational life as "terrorists," and many terrorist groups think of themselves as future "insurgents."

Strategic actors, furthermore, do not only pursue long-range goals, they have short-range goals as well. These short-range, or proximate, objectives are intermediate goals that must be achieved to implement their larger strategic program. In the case of terrorist groups, such objectives include advertising a group's presence and political agenda; raising popular consciousness about the terms of the struggle; discrediting the target regime; revealing the "inner contradictions" of the state; creating fissures and confusion within the governing bodies of the state and between the government and its internal and external political constituencies; finding outside allies to support the inside struggle; and polarizing popular political attitudes and creating the conditions needed to mobilize popular support. As the record of the past fifty years has demonstrated, terrorism—including suicide terrorism—is a well-established means of achieving such goals. Even when a group ultimately fails, it frequently succeeds in achieving many of its intermediate objectives along the way. As with conventional strategic actors, these tactical achievements can give the illusion of strategic progress and motivate a group to continue the struggle long after the possibility of a final victory has faded.

A recent and dramatic example of such a situation is offered by al-Qaeda in Iraq (AQI), a group that has relied heavily on suicide attacks. Before his death, Abu Musab al-Zarqawi stated that one of his objectives was to incite widespread internecine violence between the Shiite and Sunni communities in Iraq as a means of expanding his own base of support within the Sunni population. "If we succeed in dragging the [the Shia] into a sectarian war," he declared, it "will awaken the sleepy Sunnis who are fearful of destruction and death at the hands of the Shi'ia."[37] One of the single most provocative attacks he carried out to support this objective was the February 2006 bombing of the al-Askari mosque in Samarra.[38] Few targets could have been as well chosen to catalyze the polarization process that al-Zarqawi believed would enable him to grow his base. Within a week of the attack, hundreds of Sunni and Shia had been killed in spontaneous and orchestrated outbreaks of sectarian violence, and some two hundred Sunni mosques were reported to have been damaged or destroyed.[39] The incident marked the beginning of a brutal and highly destabilizing cycle of violence, fed by the continuing AQI conventional and unconventional attacks against Shia population targets, which had the intended effect of further dividing Iraqi society and pushing the country to the brink of civil war.

The next six months leading up to al-Zarqawi's death in June was probably the high-water mark of AQI's strength. Growing Sunni fears about the consequences of a Shiite-dominated Iraq, due in part to the Shiite backlash catalyzed by al-Zarqawi's operations, resulted in an upsurge in Sunni-initiated violence throughout the country. The fact that, in the end, AQI did not succeed in carrying out its larger game plan is not evidence of a lack of strategic focus under al-Zarqawi's leadership. In fact, much of the support AQI was able to gather within the Sunni community was attributable to the very reason he foresaw. After his death, to be sure, AQI effectively lost its way as a unified organization, fragmenting into a series of poorly coordinated and locally motivated factions under second-tier commanders. This fragmentation, coupled with a series of bad tactical decisions (and corresponding good decisions by U.S. forces), led AQI into the situation in which it finds itself today: standing on the wrong side of many of its former allies.[40] Although AQI, in the end, made some poor choices that ultimately alienated many of its previous supporters within the Sunni community, it was the calculated use of violence that allowed it to achieve its position of influence in the first place.

AQI's rapid decline in the years after al-Zarqawi's death illustrates the essential role that strong central leadership plays in keeping a group on course. Terrorist groups, like every other organization, are made up of individuals and cliques with a wide range of interests, motives, and worldviews. Many if not most of these factors are likely to be in sync with, complementary to, or at least not incompatible with a group's objectives and planning assumptions. Others, however, will certainly contradict them. The presence of such internal contradictions represent a continual (if often hidden) challenge to a terrorist group's strategic program, as it does for all strategic actors. One of the roles of group leadership, in this respect, is to ensure that the diverse motives of a group's members are harnessed to its mission rather than allow its mission to be effectively defined by the individual motives of its members. As a rule, few strategic actors ever completely live up to this ideal. Equally few, however, end up at the other end of the spectrum and lose any semblance of strategic direction. Those groups that begin to drift in this direction, as AQI did in the wake of al-Zarqawi's death, tend to either disintegrate internally because of their own centrifugal forces or are otherwise eliminated from the game before they arrive.

This bounded view of terrorist rationality does not invalidate the argument that terrorism can be viewed as a strategic, or more specifically an instrumentally tactical, activity. A strategic choice is one that selects the best means of achieving specified ends. The strategic nature of the choice does not depend on the nature of these ends, whether the individual making the decision fully and accurately understands his environment, whether he appreciates what his alternatives are, or whether he understands what the consequences of his alternative courses of action might be in relation to his goals. It depends only on whether he selects the best course of action based on his beliefs. Beliefs, of course, are perceptually grounded and subject to error. To the degree that the assumptions underlying one's decisions are in error, any instrumental choices that follow from these assumptions are likely to be suboptimal. This situation does not make these choices any less strategic or rational. The strategic view of terrorist decision making, in this sense, does not address the outcome or consequences of group decisions, but the nature of the decision process itself.

Terrorist groups are imperfect strategic agents, just like everyone else. A complete understanding of why terrorists do what they do, at the level of the group and certainly at the individual level, must account for organizational and psychological factors that are deliberately excluded by the strategic frame. The strategic model, in this sense, is not an inaccurate depiction of terrorist decision making; it is incomplete. It is one of a number of competing models that can be usefully employed to evaluate terrorist events. All have their strengths and weakness, based on what they include and what they exclude. In different situations, at different times, and in relation to different cases, one approach is likely to provide greater insights into the decision processes of a group than others. In most cases, however, each has something to contribute. As long as the nonstrategic factors that influence terrorist choices follow a discernible pattern, they can be identified, weighted, and factored into a hybrid of terrorist behavior. Even in this case, however, the strategic approach to terrorist decision making, including the tactical decision to employ suicide attacks, must serve as the baseline frame of reference to identify and evaluate any apparent deviations from rationality.

NO: Suicide terrorism rarely achieves its goals
Max Abrahms, *Stanford University*

Dying for Nothing? The Political Ineffectiveness of Suicide Terrorism

Why do groups turn to suicide terrorism? Two competing explanations have shaped the debate. Steeped in the rationalist tradition of microeconomics, political scientists generally assume that terrorist groups employ a particular violent tactic for a purpose—to advance their stated political goals.[41] Palestinian Islamic Jihad is thus said to practice suicide terrorism to attain a Palestinian state, and the Kurdistan Workers' Party (PKK) supposedly does it for a Kurdish national homeland. The general public, by contrast, typically views suicide terrorism not as an aggressive form of politically motivated violence, but as deadly madness. According to this viewpoint, pervasive in the media, suicide terrorist groups do not aim to accomplish anything at all. In the parlance of political science, their attacks are noninstrumental; suicide terrorism is simply an expression of craziness or fanaticism. Neither school of thought has much empirical support. The evidence suggests that suicide terrorism is an ineffective tactic for achieving political objectives. However, although this tactic does not induce political concessions, members of suicide terrorist groups benefit from their actions in a variety of other ways. In short, suicide terrorism is politically useless, but quite useful for obtaining a range of nonpolitical ends.

This essay makes four main points in support of my argument. First, I show that suicide terrorist groups that target civilians systematically fail to achieve their policy demands. Despite its added lethality, suicide terrorism is no more effective than conventional terrorism in forcing target countries to make political concessions. In fact, suicide terrorism tends to be politically counter-productive. Second, I explain why no suicide terrorist group has ever accomplished its political platform by attacking civilians. Third, I demonstrate that even though suicide terrorism is a losing tactic politically, groups that use it do not consistently seize alternative nonviolent opportunities for political change. Fourth, I show how all members of suicide terrorist organizations—from leaders to foot soldiers—can benefit from their politically pointless violence in other important ways. I conclude by briefly exploring the policy implications of fighting a highly lethal terrorist enemy that is rational, albeit oftentimes surprisingly apolitical.

THE POLITICAL INEFFECTIVENESS OF SUICIDE TERRORISM

Political scientists generally assume that groups adopt terrorism for its effectiveness in coercing political concessions. This assumption is especially common for suicide terrorist groups. By deploying individuals who are indifferent to their personal fates, suicide terrorist groups tend to be extralethal and difficult to defend against. Compare the two attacks on the World Trade Center: the 2001 suicide attack was a far greater operational success than the 1993 conventional attack, largely because of the willingness of the perpetrators to martyr themselves. But destructiveness is one thing; political gain quite another. How successful are terrorist groups in achieving their policy demands? And does the use of suicide terrorism increase the likelihood of government compliance? The answer to both questions appears to be no.

Terrorism does not pay politically, say authorities on political violence. In the 1980s, Martha Crenshaw asserted that terrorist groups do not obtain "the long-term ideological objectives they claim to seek, and therefore one must conclude that terrorism is objectively a failure."[42] The RAND Corporation also remarked at the time that "terrorists have been unable to translate the consequences of terrorism into concrete political gains. . . . [I]n that sense terrorism has failed. It is a fundamental failure."[43] Thomas Schelling made a similar observation in the 1990s, noting that acts of terrorism "surely attract attention and publicize grievances," but "never appear to accomplish anything politically significant."[44]

In 2006 I conducted the first study to analyze a large number of terrorist groups in terms of their political accomplishments. I found that none of the twenty-eight most important terrorist groups according to the State Department have accomplished their political platforms by targeting civilians. This lack of political success is particularly telling for two reasons. First, the groups had been practicing terrorism on average for twenty-eight years; the majority of them had engaged in terrorism since the 1960s, and only four of them were established after 1990.[45] Second, the groups that I analyzed—the so-called foreign terrorist organizations—tend to be endowed with far greater capabilities than other groups that use terrorism.[46] This is the main reason that the U.S. government singles out these groups with this special designation in the first place. In 2008 RAND examined the universe of terrorist groups since the advent of international terrorism in 1968. Using a similar methodology, RAND found that of the 648 groups to ever use terrorism, only 4 percent achieved their policy demands. "Perhaps more importantly," the authors emphasize, "terrorism had little or nothing to do with the [favorable] outcome." Just because a terrorist group achieved its political goals does not mean that the terrorism helped to achieve them; for example, numerous groups happened to achieve their platforms only by dint of the Soviet Union unraveling.[47]

Suicide terrorist attacks are roughly ten times more lethal than conventional terrorist attacks,[48] but even with that extra punch, groups that deploy suicide attackers fare no better politically. In my study, suicide terrorist groups had a political success rate of 0 percent. And in the RAND study, none of the groups that happened to achieve their given political demands dispatched a single suicide terrorist. Robert Pape contends that suicide terrorist campaigns are a chillingly effective way to compel political concessions, but his confirming examples are actually guerrilla campaigns.[49] By definition, terrorist campaigns are directed mainly against the target country's civilians, whereas guerrilla campaigns are directed mainly against its military. As Jeff Goodwin points out, "It is a mistake, therefore, to refer to these [guerrilla] campaigns as 'terrorist' in nature, as Pape does."[50] In the accompanying essay, McCormick and Fritz make the same mistake, citing the anticolonial campaigns by the Irgun in Israel, the

EOKA in Cyprus, and the FLN in Algeria as evidence of terrorist campaigns that successfully coerced government concessions. Yet those campaigns also exacted concessions from the target countries by attacking their militaries, not their civilian populations. As Walter Laqueur explains, the anticolonial campaigns used "little or no terrorism" against the occupiers, though "a great deal of guerrilla warfare, which is something quite different."[51] Page Fortna recently found that guerrilla campaigns are significantly less likely to be politically successful when they also use some terrorism by attacking civilians.[52]

Not only do terrorist groups fail to advance their political platforms by targeting civilians, but governments tend to do the political *opposite* of whatever the terrorists demand. The political impact of terrorism, then, is generally negative regardless of whether the perpetrators die in their violent acts. Polls show, for example, that after the Irish Republican Army attacked British civilians in conventional bombings, the British people became significantly less likely to favor withdrawing from Northern Ireland. Similar trends in public opinion have been registered after suicide attacks in Egypt, Indonesia, Israel, Jordan, the Philippines, and Russia. For the terrorists and their communities, the adverse political consequences are often long-term. During the al-Aqsa Intifada, for example, Israel erected a security wall on the West Bank to prevent suicide bombers from sneaking into the country. If a Palestinian state is established, this wall will limit its size.

Al-Qaeda neatly illustrates the political perils of using suicide terrorism. Its leaders have come to favor "the method of martyrdom operation" because it "is the most successful way of inflicting damage against the opponent."[53] But what is the political return? According to Osama bin Laden, the political purpose of the attacks of September 11, 2001, was fourfold: (1) to force the United States to withdraw its troops from the Persian Gulf; (2) to deter the United States from supporting military interventions that kill Muslims; (3) to sever U.S. relations with pro-Western Muslim rulers; and (4) to destroy U.S.-Israeli relations. From a political perspective, the 9/11 suicide attack was an unmitigated political disaster.[54]

Instead of forcing a U.S. retreat from the Gulf, the events of 9/11 provided the strategic rationale for Operation Iraqi Freedom and was the critical enabler for securing the support of the American public. The main selling point for regime change in Baghdad was not that Iraq would itself attack the United States or its allies, but that, using Iraqi weapons of mass destruction, "the terrorists" could one day launch a mega-attack on the U.S. homeland. Even before September 11, 2001, President George W. Bush and top-level officials had considered removing Iraqi dictator Saddam Hussein from power. The American public, however, did not support the invasion until August 2002, when the administration began ratcheting up its rhetoric linking Saddam to terrorism. From this point until the invasion in March 2003, two-thirds of the American public supported Bush's Iraq policy in the context of the wider war on terrorism. In the absence of the attacks of 9/11, it is impossible to imagine that the United States would have increased its troop presence in the Gulf by a factor of fifteen. Although the number of coalition forces has recently been reduced, they would not have deployed there in the first place without the suicide terrorist attacks on the American homeland.

Rather than protecting the global Muslim population (or *ummah*), the 9/11 attacks brought on the proverbial war on terrorism, which has killed countless innocent Muslims around the world. About four thousand Afghan civilians were killed in the course of Operation Enduring Freedom. In Iraq, the number of Muslim deaths has been orders of magnitude greater. Washington responded to the 9/11 attacks not only with an aggressive counterterrorism campaign that has inadvertently killed tens of thousands of Muslim civilians; the Bush administration also broadened its definition of the terrorism threat. The catch-all slogans of the "global war on terror" and "global struggle against violent extremism" did not distinguish between terrorist enemies of the United States and asymmetric conflicts around the world of limited strategic importance to either the United States or al-Qaeda. With this expansive definition, the Bush administration turned a blind eye toward foreign governments engaged in localized crackdowns against their Muslim civilians, such as in Russia and India. Specifically, the Bush administration dropped its demand for Moscow to reach a peaceful settlement with Chechnya, and it refrained from criticizing President Vladimir Putin when Russian forces flattened Grozny, the rebel stronghold. In the wake of 9/11, the Bush administration was likewise mum on the massacre of two thousand Muslims in Gujarat by Hindu rioters. As part of its global campaign on terrorism, the United States also directly assisted numerous Muslim countries in capturing and killing al-Qaeda affiliated operatives, with untold civilian losses.

Quite the opposite of severing U.S. relations with pro-Western Muslim rulers, the Bush administration used the events of 9/11 to bolster them. Almost overnight, the governments of Algeria, Egypt, Jordan, Pakistan, and Saudi Arabia became critical allies in the war on terrorism, sharing real-time intelligence on the movements of al-Qaeda and its affiliates. Because of this unprecedented strategic convergence, Washington increased both its dependence and influence on these governments; in short, U.S. ties with al-Qaeda's so-called near enemy deepened. After the September 11 attacks, the Bush administration publicly attributed terrorism to autocratic regimes. Yet notwithstanding its newfound commitment to democracy promotion, the Bush administration only selectively pressured Muslim governments to reform. As realists would predict, leaders who supported the war on terrorism were exempt from making reforms that might threaten their survival. In fact, if anything, the events of 9/11 provided a disincentive for removing pro-American Muslim rulers. For the Bush administration, the fear of Taliban-like regimes assuming power across the globe was evidently more threatening than inflaming the Muslim street.

Finally, instead of breaking U.S.-Israeli relations, the 9/11 attacks strengthened the "special relationship." Bush suddenly granted the government of Ariel Sharon unprecedented leeway to reoccupy the West Bank, detain Yasser Arafat in his Ramallah compound, authorize targeted assassinations, and construct the security wall on the West Bank. The American public shared Bush's pro-Israel reaction. Before September 11, 2001, 41 percent of Americans expressed support for Israel and 13 percent for Palestinians. After the attack, 55 percent backed Israel, while support for Palestinians dropped by almost half, to 7 percent. Such high approval levels for Israel had not been seen since 1991, when Saddam Hussein had launched dozens of Scud missiles at the Jewish state. Predictably, the American public also became less supportive of Washington engaging in the peace process. In other words, not only did 9/11 fail to end al-Qaeda's stated political grievances, but the suicide attacks actually exacerbated them.

In summary, the evidence strongly suggests that terrorist groups do not achieve their political platforms by attacking civilians. Terrorism is not simply politically unprofitable; target countries typically respond to terrorists by rendering more urgent their official political grievances—even when the perpetrators sacrifice themselves in the course of their attacks.

WHAT MAKES SUICIDE TERRORISM SO POLITICALLY INEFFECTIVE?

Like conventional terrorism, the more lethal suicide variety empowers hard-liners who are ideologically opposed to accommodating the terrorists. In 1993 Christopher Hewitt noted that "the public favors hard-line policies against terrorism. Conservative parties are more likely to advocate hard-line policies. Therefore, the public will view conservative parties as the best on law and order."[55] For this reason, RAND observed in 2009 that "terrorism fatalities, with few exceptions, increase support for the bloc of parties associated with a more-intransigent position toward terrorism and territorial concessions."[56] This trend has been carefully documented within Israel, such as in 2001 when a series of suicide bombings helped to elect hard-liner Ariel Sharon to the post of prime minister.[57] This trend is also apparent within the United States. The mere release of a bin Laden videotape the weekend before the 2004 presidential election boosted George W. Bush's electoral lead by two percentage points over his comparatively dovish opponent, Sen. John Kerry. Similarly, in the run-up to the 2008 presidential election, staffers for the Republican nominee, Sen. John McCain, acknowledged that another 9/11-type attack on the homeland would benefit their candidate, not the more gun-shy Democratic alternative, Sen. Barack Obama. That electorates tend to shift to the right in the face of terrorism goes a long way toward explaining why it does not work politically.

Even more than conventional terrorist groups, suicide terrorist groups are notoriously poor at conveying their presumed policy preferences. In theory, spectacular terrorist acts highlight the group's policy demands so that the target country can then comply. Yet most terrorist attacks—particularly suicide attacks—are anonymous. Since 1968, 64 percent of worldwide terrorist attacks have been carried out by unknown perpetrators. Anonymous attacks have been rising in tandem with suicide terrorism, as three out of four terrorist incidents have gone unclaimed since September 11, 2001. Clearly, target governments are constrained from making concessions without knowing which group committed the attack. Furthermore, specific policy demands are rarely forthcoming even when the terrorist group divulges its identity to the target country. Writing in 1991, Schelling captured this point: "Usually there is nothing to negotiate. A soldier is killed in a disco in Germany. A bomb explodes in front of an Israeli consulate. Japanese Black Septembrists unpack automatic weapons in the Lod airport and start shooting. The perpetrators don't ask anything, demand anything."[58] This tendency for terrorist groups to refrain from issuing policy demands increased in the late 1990s with the ascendance of suicide terrorism, leading Bruce Hoffman to conclude that its political logic is "seriously flawed."[59] It is still unclear, for example, what political aspirations the suicide terrorists could have hoped to achieve by blowing up the three hotels in Amman, Jordan, in November 2005. In fact, it is not even known which government the violence was supposedly intended to pressure. People say the attacks were aimed perhaps at the Hashemite monarchy or the United States or Israel or the broader international community.

Not only is terrorism counterproductive for winning concessions, but even the weakest terrorist groups have the preposterous habit of issuing wildly unrealistic demands. The Japanese Red Army, for example, had about six hard-core members in the 1970s, but that did not stop it from demanding that the Japanese government adopt Marxism. Compared with conventional terrorist groups, suicide terrorist groups tend to have even more ambitious, and thus unrealistic, demands.[60] The bulk of al-Qaeda's criticisms have focused on a handful of unpopular U.S. policies in the Muslim world. But bin Laden and his lieutenants have also suggested at times that the endgame is to resurrect the caliphate—a single global state under *sharia* rule. Such maximalist pronouncements only dissuade countries from even considering making concessions. Paul Wilkinson has found that in deciding whether to negotiate with terrorists, the target government first assesses whether the terrorists' demands are "corrigible" or "incorrigible." When terrorists are deemed corrigible, the government is inclined to engage in a roots debate—an assessment of the pros and cons of negotiation. But when terrorists are found to be incorrigible, concessions are rejected outright because the demands are seen as so extreme that they fall outside of the realm of consideration. In Wilkinson's terminology, incorrigible terrorists are not categorically implacable, but placating them would exact a prohibitive cost.[61] With their occasional loose talk of resurrecting the caliphate, al-Qaeda and its affiliates are generally viewed as incorrigible.

This perception that terrorist groups are politically incorrigible is fueled by their tendency to abruptly shift their political rationales. This tendency applies to conventional terrorist groups such as France's Action Directe, which from 1979 to 1986 altered its political rationale from opposing Israel to nuclear energy to the Catholic Church. Similarly, the Basque Fatherland and Liberty (ETA) claimed it was fighting to overturn Spain's dictatorship, but with its passing, proceeded to target the emergent democratic government—a progression similar to that followed by the Shining Path, Peru's most notorious terrorist organization.[62] Such political capriciousness is perhaps even more common in suicide terrorist groups. In her article "The Protean Enemy," Jessica Stern charts al-Qaeda's transitory political platform as the movement morphed rapidly and unpredictably from waging defensive jihad against the Soviets in Afghanistan to fighting local struggles in Bosnia, the Philippines, Russia, Spain, and Muslim countries to eventually targeting the American "far enemy" in the late 1990s.[63] Al-Qaeda members have frequently noted the inconsistency of their own organization's jihadi message. Al-Qaeda's military strategist Abu'l-Walid observed that with its "hasty changing of strategic targets," his organization was engaged in "random chaos."[64] Other al-Qaeda members have acknowledged that their organization espouses political objectives that seemingly "shift with the wind."[65] Audrey Kurth Cronin sensibly notes, "It is hard to conceive of al-Qaeda fully achieving its aims, in part because those aims have evolved over time."[66] Naturally, the "opportunistic" nature of al-Qaeda's political platform has led scholars to question the movement's dedication to achieving it. Al-Qaeda is hardly the only suicide terrorist group to rapidly overhaul its political rationale. The Kurdistan Workers' Party—Turkey's most dangerous contemporary suicide terrorist group—has vacillated between advocating jihad, a Marxist revolution, and a Kurdish homeland governed without Islamist or Marxist principles.[67] Similarly, Hezbollah remains a potent suicide terrorist group, despite the fact that its guerrilla attacks on the Israel Defense Forces succeeded in liberating southern Lebanon in May 2000, which was its stated goal for nearly twenty years. Today, Hezbollah's official goal is not to merely defend Lebanon, but also to destroy the "Zionist Entity" within Israel's own borders.

Finally, often the target selection of terrorist groups makes no sense for exacting the relevant political concessions. In the early years of the Algerian War, the National Algerian Movement and the National Liberation Front mainly attacked each other, not their French occupiers. Terrorist groups likewise undermined their political platforms by targeting each other more than their mutually declared enemies in the violent clashes in Aden between the Liberation of Occupied South Yemen and the National Liberation Front in 1967; in Argentina between Marxist terrorist organizations in the late 1970s; and in the Gaza Strip between Palestinian groups fighting for a common cause during the first intifada.

Suicide terrorist groups follow the same politically irrational pattern. The Tamil Tigers, for example, did not target the Sinhalese government in the mid-1980s. Instead, it engaged in a "systematic annihilation" of other Tamil organizations "espousing the same cause" of national liberation.[68] Pape concedes that the "apparent implication" of the Tigers' target selection is that the violence had "little to do with the political grievances of Tamil society or the relationship between the Tamils and their Sinhalese opponents."[69] Ami Pedahzur agrees: "In contrast to what might be expected from a guerrilla or a terrorist organization whose [expressed] goals were national liberation, the first violent actions initiated by the Tigers were not aimed at any army forces or Sinhalese politicians. . . . [T]he Tigers systematically liquidated leaders and sometimes activists of other [Tamil] organizations."[70] Similarly, in Iraq, the Mecca of suicide terrorism from 2003 to 2008, one would have expected the attacks to be directed against the occupying U.S. troops. In reality, though, the most lethal suicide attacks targeted Shias, Kurds, and Sufis, ultimately uniting them against the terrorists. One of the biggest suicide attacks did not even take place within the country, but when Iraqi terrorists crossed into Jordan to bomb its civilians, again drying up local support for the terrorists. Indeed, in recent years suicide attacks have rocked Bangladesh, Indonesia, Morocco, Saudi Arabia, Turkey, and Uzbekistan, even though these countries are not occupied.[71] Together, these politically irrational tendencies help to explain why conventional and suicide terrorist groups alike have such a poor record of advancing their political demands.

SUICIDE TERRORISTS AS POLITICAL MINIMIZERS?

Political scientists like to say that terrorist groups are political maximizers—that is, they adopt terrorism because the political gains are superior to those of alternative forms of protest. In truth, not only is terrorism a manifestly ineffective political instrument, but the groups that use it rarely seize promising alternatives for inducing political change. Like conventional terrorist groups, the suicide variety does not even consistently survey its political options.

Terrorist groups never lack political alternatives.[72] Studies show that only the most oppressive totalitarian states have been immune from terrorism. The number of terrorist groups operating in a country is actually positively associated with its freedom of expression, assembly, and association—conditions conducive to effecting peaceful political change. Yet suicide terrorist groups seldom go out of the terrorism business by embracing national elections. Instead, they generally toil alongside peaceful parties, refuse to lay down their arms after participating in elections, or sabotage open elections that would have yielded political gains, such as the Sunni suicide squads in postwar Iraq. In dismissing voting as apostasy, al-Qaeda leaders instruct their followers to abstain from a mechanism of altering the political status quo with a far better track record than that of terrorism. Furthermore, in electing to use suicide terrorism, these groups regularly choose to abstain from nonviolent strategies such as symbolic protests, labor strikes, and economic boycotts that also have proven to be superior to terrorism at inducing government concessions. Unlike terrorism, nonviolent strategies do not tend to rouse target countries into going ballistic on the aggrieved group and digging in their political heels.[73]

As a rule, suicide terrorist groups also do not compromise with the target country. On the contrary, they typically derail negotiations by ramping up their attacks. This aversion to compromise is again not politically rational. In many cases, these terrorist groups could have achieved their political platforms by entering into talks. The al-Aqsa Martyrs' Brigades, for example, claims to be motivated to establish a Palestinian state on the West Bank and Gaza Strip. Yet the group responded with an unprecedented wave of suicide terror to Israel's January 2001 offer of the Gaza Strip and nearly all of the West Bank. Because of this decision, the Martyrs ended up with no Palestine at all. Suicide terrorist groups with more openly extreme policy demands fail to accomplish even part of them because of this refusal to compromise. Hamas, for example, may oppose surrendering claims to all of historic Palestine. But the terrorist group still claims to value the West Bank and Gaza Strip. If acting to optimize its political platform, Hamas would therefore be expected to accept the Palestinian territories in exchange for peace. Hamas, however, acts as a spoiler, depriving its members of policy goals that the group purports to support. In summary, if suicide terrorist groups actually behaved as political maximizers then they would compromise—even if that means securing only partial concessions over continued deadlock—but they rarely do.

Why do terrorist groups reject these political opportunities? This behavior is puzzling in light of terrorism's political inefficacy. The answer of terrorism specialists is that these groups seem partial to violence—that is, they possess "an innate compulsion" to engage in terrorism and an "unswerving belief" in its desirability over nonviolence.[74] This observation certainly applies to al-Qaeda and its affiliates. After the Soviets withdrew from Afghanistan in the late 1980s, jihadist leaders began exporting suicide terrorism around the globe without even considering nonviolent tactics.[75] As Peter Bergen concluded from his interviews with the al-Qaeda leader, "Bin Laden acts on impulse . . .paying little attention to the potential [political] consequences of his actions."[76]

SUICIDE TERRORISTS AS IRRATIONAL ACTORS?

It would be easy to conclude that suicide terrorists and their leaders are irrational. Suicide terrorism is politically unprofitable behavior. When their civilians are attacked or even threatened with terrorist violence, governments do not ameliorate the terrorist groups' professed political grievances. On the contrary, governments tend to do the opposite by rendering them more urgent as their electorates shift to the right. In many cases, the target government does not even know the putative political purpose of the attack. When the government does know what is demanded of it, the demands are generally wildly unrealistic, such as to transform a liberal democratic country into a tyrannical Islamist regime. The perception that suicide terrorist groups are implacable is fueled by their tendencies to abruptly change the nature of their demands and to prey on countries that have nothing to do with their given political problems. To be sure, suicide terrorism is a superb way to blow things up. But there is precious little empirical evidence that groups turn to suicide terrorism to maximize the political return. These groups are notorious for reflexively eschewing elections, compromise proposals, and other nonviolent avenues with a much stronger record than terrorism of eliciting political change. Clearly, political scientists need to reexamine their reflexive assumption that suicide terrorist groups behave as rational political actors.

These observations do not imply that members of suicide terrorist organizations are irrational. Interviews with prospective suicide bombers and biographical information on operationally successful bombers indicate that they did not have higher rates of psychopathology than the general population. The leadership actually vets out unstable suicide terrorists for reasons of organizational security.[77] So how can suicide terrorists and their leaders be rational, and yet consistently partake in politically inefficacious behavior at such seemingly high costs to themselves?

Suicide terrorism does not work politically, but that does not mean it accomplishes nothing at all. It is effective and thus rational for achieving many nonpolitical ends. Ironically, suicide terrorism can help to preserve the organization. Suicide terrorist attacks are relatively cheap, requiring fewer personnel and resources because of the enhanced precision. Equally important, the suicide terrorist cannot be captured and then coerced into revealing organization threatening secrets. Suicide terrorism's greater visibility also helps to "outbid" rival organizations and thereby win over new members.[78] Perpetuating the organization directly benefits the leadership by maintaining its prestige, legitimacy, and identity.

Even the suicide attackers themselves can benefit from their actions by

- Enjoying the camaraderie and social solidarity of participating in a tight-knit group, even if temporarily
- Paying tribute to ideologies that are consistent with their worldviews, even if these will never be realized
- Avenging the mistreatment of kin, friends, or strangers with whom they empathize
- Relishing the violation of societal norms
- Receiving financial compensation, at least for their families
- Assuming positions of responsibility
- Gaining respect within their communities, which often appreciate their personal sacrifice
- Delighting in the attention that their violence will invariably attract, even if no longer around to witness the fallout
- Feeling closer to their god
- Ending their personal state of despair.

CONCLUSION

Determining what makes terrorists tick is not an academic exercise; scholars cannot expect to cure a malady until they understand its underlying causes. If people participate in suicide terrorist groups for the social solidarity, then governments should promote nonviolent social outlets, such as moderate places of worship. If people participate for vengeance, then governments should think twice before authorizing counterterrorism measures that are liable to harm the local population. If people participate for empowerment then the media should resist elevating them with generous post-attack coverage. If people participate to honor an idealized ideology, then the international community should discredit it by highlighting its pernicious real-world consequences. If people participate for the financial compensation to their family, then governments are presumably able to buy some of them off. If people participate to find their god, then moderate religious authorities need to underscore the relevant religious passages that condemn the taking of life, including their own. And if people participate to alleviate their depression, then the international community should invest in identifying and treating at-risk populations, particularly in cultures that value martyrdom. Clearly, continued research on the motives of suicide terrorist members is vital to formulating effective counterterrorism strategies. In all likelihood, terrorism is an equifinal phenomenon in that people gravitate to it for diverse reasons.[79] Terrorist foot soldiers and their leaders surely derive different payoffs from suicide terrorism, but its political return is not one of them.

For that reason, the most common counterterrorism strategies have not worked on any systematic basis: within the policy community it is assumed that suicide terrorists are mainly committed to achieving political concessions. The three most prevalent counterterrorism strategies therefore try to reduce terrorism by divesting it of its political utility. The predominant counterterrorism strategy is to deter terrorism by adopting a strict no-concessions policy. Like most heads of state, President George W. Bush believed that terrorism will end when its practitioners realize that "these crimes only hurt their [political] cause."[80] Although target governments rarely appease terrorists, the second most common strategy is to defuse them through political accommodation. Proponents of this strategy urge rekindling stalled peace processes, for example, to deny prospective political benefits from using terrorism. The third most common strategy is promoting democracy, which is designed to decrease terrorism's value by empowering citizens to peacefully address their country's political problems.

And yet all three counterterrorism strategies have poor track records. Suicide terrorist groups generally resist disbanding in the face of consistent political failure, when presented with promising alternatives for political gain, and even after their original political rationale has became moot because of factors unrelated to terrorism. Political solutions are not a panacea for suicide terrorism, because it is manifestly not intended to achieve concrete political aims. If this were the point of participating in suicide terrorist groups, then their members would be profoundly irrational, especially those who traded their lives and ruined dreams for nothing.

Notes

1. See, for example, Alan M. Dershowitz, *Why Terrorism Works: Understanding the Threat, Responding to the Challenge* (New Haven, Conn.: Yale University Press, 2002); and Seth G. Jones and Martin C. Libicki, *How Terrorist Groups End: Lessons for Countering al Qa'ida* (Santa Monica, Calif.: RAND, 2008).
2. Ehud Sprinzak, "Rational Fanatics," *Foreign Policy* (September/October 2000): 66–73.
3. Indeed, Tsar Alexander II was assassinated in 1881 by a suicide bomber dispatched by the group People's Will.
4. For details on Hanadi Jaradat's attack, see John F. Burns, "The Mideast Turmoil: The Attacker; Bomber Left Her Family with a Smile and a Lie," *New York Times,* October 7, 2003; John Ward Anderson and Molly Moore, "For 2 Families in Haifa, 3 Generations of Victims," *Washington Post,* October 6, 2003; and Robert Baer's documentary *The Cult of the Suicide Bomber 2,* Many Rivers Films, 2008.
5. Suicide Attack Database: 1983–Present, Department of Defense Analysis, Naval Postgraduate School, Monterey, Calif.
6. Earlier versions of some of the arguments presented in this chapter can be found in Gordon H. McCormick, "Signaling and the Logic of Suicide Terrorism," Occasional Paper, Department of Defense Analysis, Naval Postgraduate School, Monterey, Calif., May 2003; and Bruce Hoffman and Gordon H. McCormick, "Terrorism, Signaling, and Suicide Attack," *Studies in Conflict and Terrorism* 27 (2004): 243–381.
7. For a general discussion, see Jeffrey S. Banks, *Signaling Games in Political Science* (New York: Harwood Academic Publishers, 1991). For an application to terrorism, see Harvey E. Lapan and Todd Sandler, "Terrorism and Signaling," *European Journal of Political Economy* 9 (August 1993): 383–397.
8. Hoffman and McCormick, "Terrorism, Signaling, and Suicide Attack," 245–246.
9. Gordon H. McCormick and Frank Giordano, "Things Come Together: Symbolic Violence and Guerrilla Mobilisation," *Third World Quarterly* 28, no. 2 (2007): 295–320.
10. Ibid., 306.
11. For further discussion, see Gordon H. McCormick and Guillermo Owen, "Revolutionary Origins and Conditional Mobilization," *European Journal of Political Economy* 12 (1996): 377–402.
12. Ernesto Guevara, *Guerrilla Warfare* (Lincoln: University of Nebraska Press, 1985), 189.
13. Quoted in Nathan Leites, "Understanding the Next Act," *Terrorism* 3 (1979): 1–46.
14. The relationship between terrorists and the media is, in this respect, a symbiotic one. Terrorist groups need someone to tell their story; the media, for their part, need a story to tell.
15. See, for example, the discussion in Brigitte Nacos, *Terrorism and the Media* (New York: Columbia University Press, 1996).
16. Brian Michael Jenkins, "International Terrorism: A New Mode of Conflict," in *International Terrorism and World Security*, ed. David Carlton and Carlo Schaerf (London: Croom Helm, 1975), 15.

17. This trade-off is examined in detail in Gordon H. McCormick and Guillermo Owen, "Security and Coordination in a Clandestine Organization," *Mathematical and Computer Modeling* 31 (2000): 175–192; and J. Bowyer Bell, "Revolutionary Dynamics: The Inherent Inefficiency of the Underground," *Terrorism and Political Violence* 2 (Summer 1990): 193–211.

18. For a good discussion of some of the individual motives that underlie suicide attacks, see Mohammed M. Hafez, *Manufacturing Human Bombs: The Making of Palestinian Suicide Bombers* (Washington, D.C.: United States Institute of Peace Press, 2006), 33–52.

19. For a general discussion of this logic, see James March, *A Primer on Decision Making* (New York: Free Press, 1994), 2–3. This logic is applied to the problem of terrorism in Gordon H. McCormick, "Terrorist Decision Making," *Annual Review of Political Science* 6 (June 2003): 481–486.

20. Suzanne Goldenberg, "The Men behind the Suicide Bombers," *Guardian*, June 12, 2002.

21. Bruce Hoffman, "The Logic of Suicide Terrorism," *Atlantic Monthly*, June 2003. According to Robert A. Pape, suicide attacks accounted for 3 percent of terrorist incidents from 1980 to 2003, but 48 percent of all fatalities, making an average suicide attack twelve times deadlier than other forms of terrorism. See Pape, *Dying to Win* (New York: Random House, 2005), 6.

22. Nasra Hassan, "Letter from Gaza: An Arsenal of Believers," *New Yorker*, November 19, 2001, 39.

23. Speaking of the People's Will, for example, Camus noted that "for them, as for all rebels before them, murder is identified with suicide. A life is paid for another life, and from these two sacrifices springs the promise of a value." Albert Camus, *The Rebel: An Essay on Man in Revolt* (New York: Vintage Books, 1956), 169.

24. Bonnie Cordes, "When Terrorists Do the Talking: Reflections on Terrorist Literature," *Journal of Strategic Studies* 10 (December 1987): 164.

25. Mia Bloom, *Dying to Kill: The Allure of Suicide Terror* (New York: Columbia University Press, 2005). For anecdotal evidence of Palestinian groups, see Barbara Victor, *Army of Roses* (New York: Rodale Books, 2003).

26. Dipak K. Gupta and Kusum Mundra, "Suicide Bombing as a Strategic Weapon: An Empirical Investigation of Hamas and Islamic Jihad," *Terrorism and Political Violence* 17 (Winter 2005): 573–598.

27. Scott Atran, "The Moral Logic and Growth of Suicide Terrorism," *Washington Quarterly* 29 (Spring 2006): 132.

28. See Christoph Reuter, *My Life Is a Weapon* (Princeton, N.J.: Princeton University Press, 2004), 87; and Hoffman, "Logic of Suicide Terrorism."

29. Quoted in Rosemarie Skaine, *Female Suicide Bombers* (London: McFarland, 2006), 85.

30. This statement is, of course, ironic. The implication is that the less open to incentive-based manipulation a terrorist group appears to be (that is, the "crazier" it seems), the more dangerous it will appear and the stronger the state's incentive will be to come to terms with it. Thus the less open a group is to a negotiated compromise, the more likely it is to be offered a compromise and the more attractive that compromise is likely to be.

31. In the companion piece to this essay, for example, Max Abrahms states that in 2006 he "conducted the first study to analyze a large number of terrorist groups in terms of their political accomplishments." The groups he examined were the twenty-eight organizations that were listed by the State Department as *active* terrorist groups in 2001. In 2006 these groups were still active. Based on the assumption that these groups had already had "ample time" to achieve their goals, he concludes that they must not be strategic actors. There must be something else that is motivating them. This argument is problematic. First, circumstances rather than outside observers, determine how much time is necessary to achieve one's objectives, whatever these might be. It took the Chinese Communist Party (CCP) twenty-eight years to assume power in China in 1949. We would have been in error if we had stated in 1939 that Mao and the CCP were not strategic actors because they had already had eighteen years to achieve their goals and had not yet done so. Second, should we be surprised that terrorist groups that have not yet achieved their objectives are still in the fight? This is what you would expect from strategic actors who still believed that the game was worth the candle. If the author wishes to test his claim that those actors who use terrorism never achieve their goals, he needs to examine the list of groups that are *no longer active* to determine whether or not any have been successful, not look at the list of groups that have not yet been successful and are therefore still active. For the original discussion, see Max Abrahms, "Why Terrorism Does Not Work," *International Security* 31 (Fall 2006): 42–78.

32. Pape, *Dying to Win*, 64–65.

33. Jones and Libicki, *How Terrorist Groups End* (2008). This percentage, quite appropriately, is based on the outcome of terrorist campaigns that have "ended"; it does not consider ongoing campaigns—that is, those that have not yet ended. A recent study of how political insurgencies end has found that the success rate for insurgent campaigns, most of which employed various forms of terrorism, is slightly higher over a longer time frame. Just over 14 percent (n = 34) of the insurgent conflicts that came and went between 1945 and 2007 ended with either an outright insurgent victory or a nominal negotiated settlement with the incumbent government that codified its de facto defeat. See Gordon H. McCormick, Steven B. Horton, and Lauren A. Harrison, "Things Fall Apart: The Endgame Dynamics of Internal Wars," *Third World Quarterly* 28 (March 2007): 321–367.

34. In the end, of course, the success rate of groups that employ terrorism is ultimately irrelevant to the discussion of whether terrorism is strategically motivated. What is important is whether a group chooses to use terrorist tactics based on the belief that terrorism is a means to its ends and that the net expected benefits of pursuing such a course of action exceed those of its alternatives.

35. See, for example, the accompanying essay by Abrahms. How one labels a group—"terrorist" or "guerrilla"—of course, is again irrelevant to the point of this discussion, which focuses on the utility of terrorist tactics in the eyes of the organizations that employ these tactics, regardless of what one chooses to call these groups after the fact.

36. If terrorist groups grow in strength in relation to the state, their tactical options will increase accordingly. The mix of tactics they employ under these circumstances will become more diversified. Terrorists and insurgents, in this respect, do not generally

employ different tactics; they tend to employ a different mix of tactics. As a historical matter, over the last fifty years few insurgent organizations have not employed terrorist tactics at some point in their life cycles, and few abandon such tactics completely as they grow.

37. Quoted in Mary Anne Weaver, "Inventing Al-Zarqawi," *Atlantic Monthly,* July/August 2006, 98.

38. The al-Askari mosque was ultimately attacked twice by AQI. The first attack, in February 2006, destroyed its golden dome and severely damaged its main structure. A second attack in June 2007 destroyed its two minarets.

39. See, for example, Patrick Cockburn, "Ten Imams Murdered in Iraq as Sectarian Killings Intensity," *Independent*, February 24, 2006.

40. AQI's fall from grace, so to speak, began when it tried to impose a social fundamentalism in its zones of control and challenge the traditional authority of Sunni tribal leaders, many of whom had been among al-Zarqawi's strongest early allies. These errors were then compounded by the organization's efforts to enforce its dicta at the point of a gun. AQI's anti-Shiite attacks are not considered to be a reason for its decline in Sunni support. To the contrary, AQI was originally considered to be an important shield against Shiite domination because of its revealed willingness and ability to protect Sunnis against a Shiite majority. Al-Zarqawi successfully cultivated these fears and used them to expand AQI's influence.

41. I have labeled this school of thought the Strategic Model. For a more extensive description and critique of this model, see Max Abrahms, "What Terrorists Really Want: Terrorist Motives and Counterterrorism Strategy," *International Security* 32 (Spring 2008): 78–105.

42. Martha Crenshaw, "Theories of Terrorism: Instrumental and Organizational Approaches," in *Inside Terrorist Organizations,* ed. David Rapoport (New York: Columbia University Press, 1988), 15.

43. Bonnie Cordes, Bruce Hoffman, Brian M. Jenkins, Konrad Kellen, Sue Moran, and William Sater, *Trends in International Terrorism, 1982 and 1983* (Santa Monica, Calif.: RAND, 1984), 49.

44. Thomas C. Schelling, "What Purposes Can 'International Terrorism' Serve?" in *Violence, Terrorism, and Justice*, ed. R. G. Frey and Christopher W. Morris (New York: Cambridge University Press, 1991), 20.

45. Max Abrahms, "Why Terrorism Does Not Work," *International Security* 31(Fall 2006): 42–78.

46. Greg Bankoff, "Regions of Risk: Western Discourses on Terrorism and the Significance of Islam," *Studies in Conflict and Terrorism* 26 (Fall 2003): 423-424; and Paul F. Deisler, "A Perspective: Risk Analysis as a Tool for Reducing the Risks of Terrorism," *Risk Analysis* 22 (Spring 2002): 406.

47. To be clear, the study found that since 1968 10 percent of terrorist groups that have ended achieved their political platforms. This is not the same as saying that terrorism had a 10 percent success rate. Most terrorist groups in the sample have remained active despite failing to make any political progress, and in the coercion literature the persistent absence of political progress is considered evidence of campaign failure. Furthermore, the study stresses that the small minority of terrorist groups that achieved their platforms did not do so as a result of terrorism. Jones, Libicki, *How Terrorist Groups End* (RAND), 15, 33.

48. Author's conversation with Nicholas Ayers, U.S. Military Academy at West Point, February 11, 2009.

49. Robert A. Pape, *Dying to Win: The Strategic Logic of Suicide Terrorism* (New York: Random House, 2005), 40–41. For a discussion of his methodology and the wider literature on terrorism's political efficacy, see Abrahms, "Why Terrorism Does Not Work," 44–46.

50. Jeff Goodwin, "A Theory of Categorical Terrorism," *Social Forces* 84 (June 2006): 317.

51. Walter Laqueur, "Left, Right, and Beyond: The Changing Face of Terror," in *Understanding the War on Terror*, ed. James F. Hoge Jr. and Gideon Rose (New York: Norton, 2005), 154.

52. Page Fortna, "Terrorism, Civil War Outcomes, and Post-War Stability" (paper presented at the annual meeting of the American Political Science Association, Boston, August 28, 2008).

53. Quoted in Abdel Bari Atwan, *The Secret History of Al Qaeda* (Los Angeles: University of California Press, 2006), 99.

54. For a lengthier analysis of how 9/11 backfired politically, see Max Abrahms, "Al Qaeda's Scorecard: A Progress Report on Al Qaeda's Objectives," *Studies in Conflict and Terrorism* 29 (June 2006): 509–529. Al-Qaeda's supporters agree that 9/11 was politically counterproductive. See Fawaz A. Gerges, *The Far Enemy: Why Jihad Went Global* (New York: Cambridge University Press, 2005), 228.

55. Christopher Hewitt, *Consequences of Political Violence* (Sudbury, Mass.: Dartmouth, 2003), 98.

56. Claude Berrebi, "The Economics of Terrorism and Counterterrorism: What Matters and Is Rational-Choice Theory Helpful?" in *Social Science for Counterterrorism: Putting the Pieces Together*, ed. P. K. Davis and K. Cragin (Santa Monica, Calif.: RAND, 2009), 189–190.

57. Claude Berrebi and Esteban F. Klor, "Are Voters Sensitive to Terrorism? Direct Evidence from the Israeli Electorate," *American Political Science Review* 102 (August 2008): 279–301.

58. Schelling, "What Purposes Can 'International Terrorism' Serve?" 24.

59. Bruce Hoffman, "Why Terrorists Don't Claim Credit," *Terrorism and Political Violence* 9 (Spring 1997): 1.

60. James A. Piazza, "A Supply-Side View of Suicide Terrorism: A Cross-National Study," *Journal of Politics* 70 (January 2008): 28–39.

61. Paul Wilkinson, "Security Challenges in the New Reality," lecture, Tufts University, Medford, Mass., October 16, 2002.

62. See Martha Crenshaw, "An Organizational Approach to the Analysis of Political Terrorism," *Orbis* 29 (Fall 1985): 71.

63. Jessica Stern, "The Protean Enemy," *Foreign Affairs* 82 (July/August 2003).

64. Quoted in Vahid Brown, "Cracks in the Foundation: Leadership Schisms in al-Qaeda from 1989–2006," Combating Terrorism Center Report, West Point, N.Y. September 2007, 10.

65. Omar Nasiri, *Inside the Jihad: My Life with Al Qaeda, A Spy's Story* (New York: Basic Books, 2006), 295.

66. Audrey Kurth Cronin, "How al-Qaeda Ends: The Decline and Demise of Terrorist Groups," *International Security* 31 (Summer 2006): 41–42.

67. See Ami Pedahzur, *Suicide Terrorism* (Cambridge, UK: Polity Press, 2005), 87, 89. See also Bloom, *Dying to Kill*, 112.

68. Shri D. R. Kaarthikeyan, "Root Causes of Terrorism? A Case Study of the Tamil Insurgency and the LTTE," in *Root Causes of Terrorism: Myths, Reality, and Ways Forward*, ed. Tore Bjorgo (New York: Routledge, 2006), 134.

69. Pape, *Dying to Win*, 139–140.

70. Pedahzur, *Suicide Terrorism*, 81–82.

71. Assaf Moghadam, "Suicide Terrorism, Occupation, and the Globalization of Martyrdom: A Critique of Dying to Win," *Studies in Conflict and Terrorism* 29 (2006): 719.

72. Martha Crenshaw, "How Terrorists Think: What Psychology Can Contribute to Understanding Terrorism," in *Terrorism: Roots, Impact, Responses*, ed. Lawrence Howard (New York: Praeger, 1992), 71.

73. Maria J. Stephan and Erica Chenoweth, "Why Civil Resistance Works: The Strategic Logic of Nonviolent Conflict," *International Security* 33 (Summer 2008): 7–44.

74. Bruce Hoffman, *Inside Terrorism*, rev. and exp. ed. (New York: Columbia University Press, 2006), 245; Cronin, "How al-Qaeda Ends," 11.

75. Jason Burke, *Al-Qaeda: The True Story of Radical Islam* (New York: I. B. Tauris, 2004), 290.

76. Quoted in Khalil Hasan, "Postcard USA: Osama bin Laden Unveiled," *Daily Times*, February 26, 2006.

77. Robert J. Brym and Bader Araj, "Suicide Bombing as Strategy and Interaction: The Case of the Second Intifada," *Social Forces* 84 (June 2006): 1970–1971.

78. Bloom, *Dying to Kill.*

79. Karen Rasler, "Review Symposium: Understanding Suicide Terror," *Perspectives on Politics* 5 (February 2007): 118.

80. Quoted in "Pledge to 'Liquidate' Pearl Killers," BBC.com, February 22, 2002.

is nuclear terrorism a real threat?

YES: The threat is very real
Matthew Bunn, *Harvard University*

NO: The threat is overblown
Susan B. Martin, *King's College London*

Prior to the attacks of September 11, 2001, the possibility of terrorists utilizing weapons of mass destruction, particularly the most potentially devastating weapon, a nuclear device, received a good deal of attention.[1] The conventional wisdom at the time, even among those who were warning of the growing danger, was that the possibility of a nuclear terrorist attack was a "low probability, high consequence" threat.[2] Nuclear terrorism was generally considered a low-probability threat because of issues related to supply, demand, and technical feasibility. It would be extremely difficult for a terrorist group to obtain materials for a tactical nuclear device. Successfully carrying out an attack meant leaping over another set of technical and logistical hurdles. And wouldn't a terrorist group create a counterproductive backlash against itself (and its cause) if it callously massacred hundreds of thousands of people?

After the events of 9/11, these purported constraints were urgently rethought. For one thing, the brazen and catastrophic nature of the 9/11 attacks (and many since) gave new credence to the idea that al-Qaeda and similarly inspired religious and millennial groups actively seek maximum casualties. In addition, with the growing global proliferation of nuclear materials and know-how, obstacles to filling in the supply and technical side of the equation have been greatly reduced. In 2005 Sen. Richard Lugar, chairman of the Senate Foreign Relations Committee, issued a report that estimated the likelihood of a nuclear terrorist attack somewhere in the world in the next ten years to be as high as 29 percent.[3] A 2008 presidential commission on the subject concluded that "it is more likely than not" that a biological or nuclear weapon of mass destruction will be used in a terrorist attack in the next five years.[4]

There is, however, another side to the story. Each year that passes without a nuclear terrorist attack breathes life into arguments that frightening predictions may be used simply as predictions to frighten.[5] The possibility of nuclear terrorism must, of course, be acknowledged, and efforts must be made to prevent it. But overstating and oversimplifying the threat may only make matters worse by, for example, increasing the incentives for terrorists to try to accomplish this bold act and by diverting valuable resources from other areas of diplomacy and counterterrorism.

Matthew Bunn and Susan Martin each bring their own unique professional insights (and predictions) into the debate over nuclear terrorism. Although careful not to overstate the threat, Bunn lays out in detail why he believes nuclear terrorism to be a real risk, based on technical plausibility and the mass-casualty motivations of some terrorist groups. Martin views issues of capabilities and motives through a different lens, arguing that the hurdles for a terrorist group to detonate a nuclear device remain prohibitively high in terms of both technical and political considerations. Although they may disagree on many core issues, there is one thing on which all can agree: that this debate will stay firmly in the realm of the hypothetical.

YES: The threat is very real
Matthew Bunn, *Harvard University*

The Real Risk of Nuclear Terrorism

On the night of November 8, 2007, two teams of armed men attacked the Pelindaba nuclear facility in South Africa, where hundreds of kilograms of weapons-grade highly enriched uranium (HEU) are stored. One of the teams was reportedly chased off by site security forces, but the other team of four armed men disabled the detection systems at the site perimeter, got through the 10,000-volt security fence without setting off any alarm, and went to the emergency control center and shot a worker there in the chest. The injured worker then raised the alarm for the first time. This team spent forty-five minutes inside the secured perimeter without ever being engaged by site security forces, and then disappeared through the same hole they had cut in the fence. No one on either team was shot or captured. South African officials later arrested three individuals, but soon released them without charge.[6] The South African government, which has not released important details of its investigation of the attack, had earlier refused U.S. offers to remove the HEU at Pelindaba or to help improve security at the facility, and has continued to do so since.

Although it is not known whether the attackers were after the HEU, this incident is nevertheless a potent reminder that inadequately secured nuclear material is a global problem, not one limited to the former Soviet Union, which typically gets most of the attention in the discussion of "loose nukes." It is also a reminder that the world is still a long way from overcoming the obstacles to sensitive nuclear security cooperation.

Perhaps most important, Pelindaba illustrates just how vulnerable the world remains to the threat that terrorists intent on committing acts of mass destruction may acquire the means to do so.

INTRODUCTION: THE THREAT OF NUCLEAR TERRORISM

Nuclear terrorism poses a very real and urgent threat to U.S. and world security.[7] Mother Nature has been both kind and cruel in setting the laws of physics that frame the nuclear predicament the world faces. She has been kind in that the essential ingredients of nuclear weapons, highly enriched uranium and plutonium, do not occur in significant quantities in nature and are quite difficult to produce. Making them is well beyond the plausible capabilities of terrorist groups. Thus if all of the existing stockpiles could be effectively guarded, nuclear weapons terrorism could be reliably prevented: no material, no bomb. (Because of this factor, nuclear weapons are quite different from chemical and biological weapons, whose essential ingredients can be found in nature.) Mother Nature has been cruel in that, although it is not easy to make a nuclear bomb, it is not as difficult as many believe once the needed materials are in hand. Most states, and even some particularly well-organized terrorist groups, could do it. Mother Nature has also been cruel in that HEU and plutonium, though radioactive, are not radioactive enough to make them difficult to steal and carry away, or to make them easy to detect when being smuggled across borders. Therefore, the best defense is keeping these items from being stolen in the first place.

Getting and using a nuclear bomb would be the most technically challenging operation any terrorist group has ever carried out. The *probability* of nuclear terrorism is surely far lower than the probability of many other types of terrorist attack. But the *risk* posed by nuclear terrorism—the probability multiplied by the immense consequences of such an attack—is unacceptably high. Fortunately, practical and affordable actions can be taken to drastically reduce the risk—beginning with a fast-paced global campaign to ensure that nuclear stockpiles everywhere are protected effectively from both insider and outsider attempts to steal them. Implementation of many of the needed measures is already under way.

Unfortunately, that progress is being slowed by widespread complacency about the threat. Many key policymakers and nuclear managers around the world simply do not believe that nuclear theft and nuclear terrorism are real dangers. Until they are convinced that nuclear theft and terrorism are real threats to *their* countries' security, worthy of a major investment of their attention and resources, they are highly unlikely to take the actions needed to prevent nuclear terrorism. Some academics have contributed to this complacency—and thereby have increased the difficulty of reducing the risk—by making unfounded arguments that the threat of nuclear terrorism is vanishingly small.[8]

The answers to the following series of "frequently asked questions" will help to clarify the risk of nuclear terrorism. After exploring those questions, and their implications for the overall risk of nuclear terrorism, this essay concludes with a few thoughts on where to go from here.

NUCLEAR TERRORISM Q&A

1. Do terrorists want nuclear weapons?

For a small set of terrorists, the answer is clearly "Yes." By word and deed, al-Qaeda and the global movement it has spawned have made it clear they want nuclear weapons. Osama bin Laden has called the acquisition of nuclear weapons a "religious duty,"[9] and al-Qaeda operatives have made repeated attempts to buy the nuclear material for a nuclear bomb and to recruit nuclear expertise. These attempts include the well-known case in which two extremist Pakistani nuclear weapons scientists met with bin Laden and his deputy Ayman al-Zawahiri in the summer of 2001 to discuss nuclear weapons, which reportedly included handing over a sketch of a nuclear bomb design and discussing other Pakistani scientists who might be recruited for the effort.[10]

In his memoir, George Tenet, a former director of the Central Intelligence Agency (CIA), argues that long after the removal of al-Qaeda's Afghanistan sanctuary, bin Laden and the rest of al-Qaeda's top leadership remained "singularly focused" on obtaining nuclear, chemical, or biological weapons, and that they "desperately want" a nuclear bomb in particular.[11] He tells of a case in 2003 in which the CIA received a "stream of reliable reporting" that al-Qaeda was negotiating to purchase three Russian nuclear weapons—reports that were sufficiently alarming that Tenet was directed to call personally Russian defense minister Sergei Ivanov and to dispatch the CIA's top expert on al-Qaeda's nuclear, chemical, and biological efforts to Moscow to seek cooperation from Russia's intelligence services.[12]

Rolf Mowatt-Larsen, head of intelligence for the U.S. Department of Energy (DOE), testified to the U.S. Senate in the spring of 2008 that "al-Qaida's nuclear intent remains clear," citing, among other things, bin Laden's successful effort in 2003 to get a radical Saudi cleric to issue a religious ruling, or fatwa, authorizing the use of nuclear weapons on U.S. civilians.[13] Mowatt-Larsen warned that the world's efforts to prevent terrorists from gaining the ability "to develop and detonate a nuclear weapon" are likely to be "tested" in "the early years of the 21st century."[14] Before al-Qaeda, the Japanese terrorism cult Aum Shinrikyo had also tried to obtain nuclear weapons, which, like al-Qaeda's efforts, included attempts to buy stolen nuclear warheads or nuclear material from the former Soviet Union.[15] With at least two groups actively going down the nuclear path in the last fifteen years, others are also likely do so in the future.

Should terrorists succeed in getting a nuclear bomb, there would be a terrible danger that they would use it, incinerating the heart of a major city. Indeed, an al-Qaeda spokesman has argued explicitly that al-Qaeda has the "right" to kill four million Americans in response to what the group sees as U.S. aggressions against the Islamic world.[16]

2. Could a terrorist group plausibly get the materials needed for a nuclear bomb?

The answer here is also "Yes." Nuclear weapons or their essential ingredients can be found in hundreds of buildings in dozens of countries, protected by security measures that range from excellent to appalling—in some cases, no more than a night watchman and a chain-link fence. No specific and binding global standards for how these stockpiles should be secured exist.

Remarkably, another thing that does not exist is a comprehensive, prioritized list of which nuclear stockpiles around the world pose the highest risk of nuclear theft—though the U.S. government is now preparing such a list under the Nuclear Materials Information Program (NMIP).[17] Based on the information available in the public domain, I believe the highest risks of nuclear theft today are in the former Soviet Union, in Pakistan, and at HEU-fueled research reactors around the world.

Nuclear security in Russia and the rest of the former Soviet Union has improved dramatically in the last fifteen years; at many sites, the difference between the security in place today and the security in place in 1994 is like night and day. But Russia has the world's largest stockpiles of nuclear weapons and materials, scattered in the world's largest number of buildings and bunkers, and some serious security weaknesses remain, ranging from poorly trained, sometimes suicidal guards to gross underfunding of nuclear security. The upgraded security systems must handle huge threats, from insider theft conspiracies, which are cropping up everywhere in Russia, to large-scale outsider attacks. Within Russia, terrorist surveillance teams have carried out reconnaissance at secret nuclear weapon storage sites; a Russian businessman has offered $750,000 for stolen weapons-grade plutonium; and the Beslan school massacre reconfirms terrorists' ability to strike in force, without warning or mercy.[18] As just one indicator of the insider threat, in 2006 Russian president Vladimir Putin fired Maj. Gen. Sergey Shlyapuzhnikov, deputy chairman of the section of the Ministry of Internal Affairs (MVD) responsible for guarding the closed nuclear cities and other secured locales, because, according to the Russian state newspaper, he was helping to organize smuggling in and out of these closed areas—in particular, giving out passes that allowed people to go in and out without being checked.[19]

In contrast to those in Russia and the rest of the former Soviet Union, Pakistan's nuclear stockpile is small, stored at a limited number of sites, and is thought to be heavily guarded, with substantial security upgrades in recent years, in part with U.S. help. The unrest in Pakistan since 2007 does not appear to have substantially increased the risks of theft, because it apparently has not undermined the cohesion of the military and the security services. But if violent Islamic extremists continue to improve their abilities to strike in force, and to do so not just in the tribal areas but elsewhere in the country, and if sympathies for them within the Pakistani military and nuclear establishments increase, the danger of nuclear theft will surely rise. Already, Pakistani security systems face immense threats, from nuclear insiders with a demonstrated willingness to sell practically anything to practically anybody (including some with demonstrated sympathies for radical Islam) to armed attack potentially by scores or hundreds of jihadists. In at least two cases, serving Pakistani military personnel working with al-Qaeda came within a hair's breadth of assassinating former Pakistani president Pervez Musharraf. If the people guarding the president cannot be trusted, how much confidence can one have in the people guarding the nuclear weapons?[20]

HEU-fueled research reactors typically have comparatively modest stockpiles of material, but they also have some of the world's weakest security measures for those stocks. Roughly 130 research reactors in more than thirty countries around the world still use HEU as their fuel. Most of this HEU is in forms that would require chemical processing to recover the uranium for use in a bomb, but the processing needed is straightforward—probably simpler than the steps required to make pure heroin from opium poppies. Moreover, the processing steps have been widely published. Even irradiated research reactor fuel poses a threat: most of this material is still HEU, it is in small, easily carried fuel assemblies, and it is not radioactive enough to pose any significant deterrent to theft by suicidal terrorists.[21] And yet remarkably, years after the 9/11 attacks, with overwhelming evidence that terrorists are seeking stolen nuclear weapons material, security for these and other stockpiles of fissile material remains left almost entirely to the discretion of the country in which the materials are located.

Although stocks in Russia, in Pakistan, and at HEU-fueled research reactors are the three highest risk categories, virtually every country in possession of nuclear materials—including the United States—has more to do to ensure that these stocks are effectively protected against the kinds of threats that terrorists and criminals have shown they can pose. The recent incidents in which nuclear weapons were improperly handled by members of the U.S. Air Force—which led to the firing of both the air force secretary and the air force chief of staff—are only the most recent reminder that effective nuclear security requires eternal vigilance.[22]

Theft of HEU and plutonium is not a hypothetical worry; it is an ongoing reality. As a recent example, in February 2006 Russian citizen Oleg Khinsagov was arrested in Georgia (along with three Georgian accomplices) with some 79.5 grams of 89 percent enriched HEU. He claimed he had several more kilograms available for sale.[23] The International Atomic Energy Agency (IAEA) has confirmed eighteen incidents of the theft or loss of HEU or separated plutonium.[24] Other incidents are known to have occurred—the thieves were captured, tried, and convicted—but they have nevertheless not been confirmed by the states concerned.[25] What is not known, of course, is how many thefts may have occurred that were never detected; it is a sobering fact that nearly all of the stolen HEU and plutonium seized over the years was not missed before it was seized.[26] In 2005 former CIA director Porter Goss testified to Congress that, in view of the amount of material that could not be accounted for, he could provide no assurances that enough material for a bomb had not been stolen.[27]

Another unsettling factor is that the amounts of fissile material required for a bomb are small. The Nagasaki bomb contained some 6 kilograms of plutonium, which would fit easily in a soda can. A similar HEU bomb would require only about three times as much. For a simpler but somewhat less-efficient design, roughly 50 kilograms of HEU would be needed—about the size of a six-pack of beer.[28] In either case, the material for a nuclear bomb could easily be transported across borders in already manufactured parts that would be small and easy to hide, but which could be assembled in a matter of hours at the target. Even a fully assembled bomb of the crude type terrorists might make could fit in a truck, a fishing boat, a small plane, or the hold of a yacht.

3. Could a sophisticated terrorist group make a crude nuclear bomb if it was able to steal or buy HEU or separated plutonium?

Unfortunately, the answer here is also "Yes." Those who discount the threat of nuclear terrorism often fail to grasp a crucial fact: the most difficult part of making a nuclear bomb is acquiring the nuclear material. As one leading critic has argued, "Actually building [a crude nuclear weapon] is extremely difficult. A number of countries with vast resources and expertise, such as Iraq, have struggled unsuccessfully to produce one. It is difficult to imagine that a small terrorist group would find bomb-building any easier."[29] Similarly, the security chief of Russia's Federal Agency for Atomic Energy has publicly stated that "even having any nuclear material does not mean that an explosive device can be made [by terrorists]. This is absolutely impossible."[30]

These arguments are simply incorrect. They conflate the difficulty of producing the nuclear material—the key step on which Iraq spent billions of dollars—with the difficulty of making a bomb once the material is in hand. These critiques also fail to make the crucial distinction between the technical and scientific challenge of building safe, reliable, and efficient nuclear weapons suitable for delivery by a missile or a fighter aircraft and the far simpler task of making a single crude, unsafe, and unreliable terrorist nuclear explosive that might be delivered by truck or boat.

If a sophisticated terrorist group obtained HEU or plutonium, making at least a crude nuclear bomb might well be within its capabilities. According to one study by the (now-defunct) congressional Office of Technology Assessment, "A small group of people, none of whom have ever had access to the classified literature, could possibly design and build a crude nuclear explosive device. . . . Only modest machine-shop facilities that could be contracted for without arousing suspicion would be required."[31] Indeed, even before the revelations from seized al-Qaeda documents after the fall of the Taliban in Afghanistan, U.S. intelligence concluded that "fabrication of at least a 'crude' nuclear device was within al-Qa'ida's capabilities, if it could obtain fissile material."[32] Mowatt-Larsen told Congress that an al-Qaeda nuclear bomb effort "probably would not require the involvement of more than the number of operatives who carried out 9/11" and would be "just as compartmented," making it extraordinarily difficult for the intelligence community to detect and stop.[33]

The simplest type of nuclear bomb that terrorists could build is the gun-type bomb, which involves little more than slamming two pieces of HEU together at high speed. The bomb that incinerated the Japanese city of Hiroshima, for example, was a cannon that fired a shell of HEU into rings of HEU.[34] Building such a bomb usually requires some ability to cast and machine uranium, a reasonable knowledge of the nuclear physics involved, and a good understanding of cannons and ballistics. An ability to undertake some chemical processing may also be needed (for example, to dissolve research reactor fuel containing HEU in acid, separate the HEU, and reduce the HEU to metal), but the chemical processing required is no more sophisticated than some of the processing criminals routinely undertake in the illegal drug industry.

It is impossible, however, to achieve a substantial nuclear yield with a gun-type bomb made from plutonium, because the neutrons emitted from plutonium will set off the nuclear chain reaction prematurely, causing the bomb to blow itself apart. Thus, if terrorists only had plutonium available, they would have to attempt the more challenging task of designing and building an implosion-type device, such as that used at Nagasaki in which explosives arranged around nuclear material compress it to a much higher density, setting off the nuclear chain reaction. Although terrorists' likelihood of success in making such a bomb would be lower than for a gun-type bomb, the danger certainly cannot be ruled out.

If the terrorists working to make a nuclear bomb were able to get help from someone with direct experience in matters such as machining uranium metal weapons components, their chances of succeeding would be higher. But repeated U.S. government studies have concluded that terrorists might well be able to make a crude bomb without such knowledgeable help. To slam two pieces of HEU together, unwritten "tacit knowledge" is not likely to be crucial, in contrast to more complex endeavors such as getting the many finicky pieces of a uranium enrichment centrifuge to work properly. In any case, al-Qaeda has been working to recruit such knowledgeable help, and, if it succeeds, the world may never know until it is too late.

Al-Qaeda's ability to plan and carry out large, complex operations has undoubtedly been disrupted by the fall of the Taliban and the death or capture of many senior al-Qaeda leaders, including in July 2008 Abu Khabbab, who had headed al-Qaeda's chemical and biological weapons efforts.[35] But al-Qaeda has been reconstituting its ability to plan and direct large, complex operations from the tribal areas of Pakistan. As Director of National Intelligence (DNI) Michael McConnell told the Senate in February 2008:

> Al-Qa'ida's top leaders Usama Bin Ladin and Ayman al-Zawahiri continue to be able to maintain al-Qa'ida's unity and its focus on their strategic vision of confronting our allies and us with mass casualty attacks around the globe. . . .
>
> [A]l-Qa'ida and other terrorist groups are attempting to acquire chemical, biological, radiological, and nuclear weapons and materials (CBRN). We assess al-Qa'ida will continue to try to acquire and employ these weapons and materials. [36]

No one knows for sure what the current status of al-Qaeda's nuclear effort is—or how much the group may have learned from past failures that may increase its chance of future success.[37] But if it could acquire the needed HEU or plutonium, there is no basis for confidence that it could not put together and deliver a crude but devastating nuclear bomb.

4. Could a terrorist group likely deliver a bomb to Washington, New York, or other major cities around the world?

Here, too, unfortunately, the answer is "Yes." If stolen or built abroad, a nuclear bomb might be delivered to the United States, intact or in ready-to-assemble pieces, by boat or aircraft or truck. The length of the U.S. border, the diversity of means of transport, the vast scale of legitimate traffic across national borders, and the ease of shielding the radiation from plutonium or especially from HEU all operate in favor of the terrorists. Building the overall system of legal infrastructure, intelligence, law enforcement, border and customs forces, and radiation detectors needed to find and recover stolen nuclear weapons or materials, or to interdict these as they cross national borders, is an extraordinarily difficult challenge. In particular, the radiation detectors being put in place today at ports and border crossings worldwide simply cannot detect HEU metal even modestly shielded, and, in any case, it seems very likely that al-Qaeda operatives, known for carefully collecting intelligence on adversary defenses and means to overcome them, would choose one of the myriad possible routes for moving their nuclear material that did not pass through a monitored border crossing equipped with large, readily observable radiation detectors.

5. What would happen if terrorists set off a nuclear bomb in a U.S. city?

Here, the answers are nothing short of terrifying. A bomb with the explosive power of 10,000 tons of TNT—that is, 10 kilotons, which is somewhat smaller than the bomb that obliterated Hiroshima—could easily be delivered in an ordinary truck. If set off in midtown Manhattan on a typical workday, such a bomb could kill half a million people and cause $1 trillion in direct economic damage.[38] Neither the United States nor any other country is remotely prepared to cope with the aftermath of such an attack—caring for tens of thousands of burned, wounded, and irradiated victims, evacuating hundreds of thousands of people in the path of the fallout, restoring essential services to a partly burned and irradiated city, and much more.[39]

Terrorists—either those who committed the attack or others—would certainly claim they had more bombs already hidden in U.S. cities (whether they did or not), and the fear that this might be true could lead to panicked evacuations of major U.S. cities, creating widespread havoc and economic disruption. If the bomb went off in Washington, D.C., large fractions of the federal government would be destroyed, and effective governance of the country would be very much in doubt.

Devastating economic aftershocks would reverberate throughout the country and the world—global effects that in 2005 UN Secretary-General Kofi Annan warned would push "tens of millions of people into dire poverty," creating "a second death toll throughout the developing world."[40]

Politically, confidence in the U.S. government would be profoundly, perhaps irrevocably, shaken, because no one could be certain that the government that had failed to protect its citizens from such a devastating attack would succeed in protecting them from another. Far more than after 9/11, U.S. policies on eavesdropping, handling of terrorist suspects, and the legitimacy of attacking foreign countries to prevent possible future attacks would change dramatically. America and the world would be transformed forever—and not for the better.[41]

NUCLEAR TERRORISM: THE RISKS

To understand the risks of nuclear terrorism, it is important to put these aspects of the real danger in a broader context, balancing both the bad news and the good news—and there is good news in this story as well.

The Good News

First, there is no convincing evidence that any terrorist group has yet acquired a nuclear weapon or the materials needed to make one, or that al-Qaeda has succeeded in pulling together the expertise needed to make a bomb. Indeed, to the contrary, there is some evidence of confusion and lack of nuclear knowledge by some senior al-Qaeda operatives.[42]

Second, as already noted, making and delivering even a crude nuclear bomb would be the most technically challenging and complex operation any terrorist group has ever carried out. The effort could fail at any one of many different points, and the obstacles may seem daunting even to determined terrorists, convincing them to focus more of their efforts on conventional (if nevertheless creative) tools of terror—as al-Qaeda appears to have done.[43] Both al-Qaeda and Aum Shinrikyo appear to have encountered a variety of difficulties in trying to fulfill their nuclear ambitions, demonstrating that building or acquiring a nuclear bomb is a difficult challenge, even for large and well-financed terrorist groups with ample technical resources.

Third, as described earlier, the overthrow of the Taliban and the disruption of al-Qaeda's old central command structure in Afghanistan certainly reduced its chances of pulling off such a complex operation—though that capability may be growing again as al-Qaeda reconstitutes in the mountains of the Afghanistan-Pakistan border.

Fourth, there is now a very real debate, even within the community of violent Islamic extremists, over the moral legitimacy of the mass slaughter of innocents. One of the founders of al-Qaeda, who wrote two of the books on which the organization has long relied for its ideological justification for violent jihad, has written a new book that argues that most forms of terrorism—and particularly the indiscriminate killing of bystanders—are forbidden by Islamic law, and that violent jihad is permissible only under very rare circumstances. "There is nothing that invokes the anger of God and His wrath like the unwarranted spilling of blood and wrecking of property," this key al-Qaeda ideologist argues.[44] Al-Qaeda was sufficiently concerned about this frontal assault by one of its founders that Ayman al-Zawahiri rushed out a 188-page response only two months after the book was released. Moreover, when al-Qaeda organized an electronic question-and-answer session with al-Zawahiri, many of the questions al-Zawahiri chose to answer focused on bitter criticisms of al-Qaeda's killing of innocent people. He was at pains to argue that al-Qaeda fighters would kill innocents only when doing so was unavoidable, quoting bin Laden as instructing fighters to "make sure that their operations targeting the enemies are regulated by the regulations of the Shari'ah and as far as possible from Muslims."[45] A nuclear bomb, of course, is the apotheosis of indiscriminate mass slaughter, making no distinction between the innocent and the guilty, between Muslims and non-Muslims. These debates are not likely to convince bin Laden and al-Zawahiri, but the more the broader community of extreme Islamists views the nuclear level of mass slaughter as a moral crime, the more difficult it is likely to be for al-Qaeda to recruit experts and raise money to help it build a nuclear bomb.

Fifth, nuclear security is improving. Although a great deal has yet to be done, at scores of sites in Russia, the rest of the former Soviet Union, and elsewhere security is dramatically better than it was fifteen years ago. Security upgrades were completed for most Russian nuclear warhead and nuclear material sites by the end of 2008. HEU is being removed from sites all around the world, permanently eliminating the risk of nuclear theft at those sites. An alphabet soup of programs and initiatives—the Cooperative Threat Reduction (CTR) effort, the Materials Protection, Control, and Accounting (MPC&A) program, the Global Threat Reduction Initiative (GTRI), the Global Initiative to Combat Nuclear Terrorism (GI), the IAEA's Office of Nuclear Security, the Domestic Nuclear Detection Office (DNDO), and many more—are each making real contributions.[46] There can be no doubt that America and the world face a far lower risk of nuclear terrorism today than they would have had these efforts never begun.

Sixth, it is highly unlikely that hostile states would consciously choose to provide terrorist groups with nuclear weapons or the materials needed to make them. Such a decision would mean transferring the most awesome military power the state had ever acquired to a group over which it had little control—a particularly unlikely step for dictators or oligarchs obsessed with controlling their states and maintaining power. If the terrorists actually used the transferred capability against the United States or one of its allies, the source of the weapon or material would most likely be traced back to the state that provided it, and the resulting retaliation would probably be overwhelming, almost certainly obliterating the government that decided on such a transfer.

All of this good news comes with a crucial caveat: "as far as we know." The gaps in knowledge remain wide. Some intelligence analysts argue that the lack of hard evidence of an extensive current al-Qaeda nuclear effort simply reflects the group's success in compartmentalizing the work and keeping it secret. It is sobering to remember that Aum Shinrikyo was simply not on the radar of any of the world's intelligence agencies until *after* it perpetrated its nerve gas attack in the Tokyo subways.

Probabilities

So, taking the good news with the bad, what are the chances of a terrorist nuclear attack? The short answer is that nobody knows. Former secretary of defense William Perry and former assistant secretary of defense Graham

Allison are among those who have estimated the chance at more than 50 percent over the next ten years.[47] In 2006 I published a mathematical model that provided a structured, step-by-step way of thinking through the problem. A set of plausible illustrative values for the input parameters resulted in a 29 percent ten-year probability estimate—by coincidence, the same as the median estimate of the ten-year probability of a nuclear attack on the United States in a survey of national security experts by Sen. Richard Lugar's office a few years ago.[48] Because there are large uncertainties in each of those inputs, however, the real probability could well be either higher or lower. But if these estimates are even within a factor of three to five of being correct, and if, as I believe, there is a large chance that such an attack would be directed at Manhattan or Washington, D.C., then the danger of nuclear terrorism is high enough to have a significant effect on the life expectancy of everyone who lives and works in downtown Washington or midtown Manhattan.

The fact is that estimates and models of fundamentally unknown probabilities only go so far. Even a 1 percent chance of nuclear terrorism over the next ten years would be enough to justify substantial action to reduce the risk, given the unimaginable scale of the consequences. No one in his right mind would operate a nuclear power plant upwind of a major city that had a 1 percent chance over ten years of blowing sky-high—the risk would be understood by all to be too great. But that, in effect, is what countries are doing—or worse—by managing the world's nuclear stockpiles as they do today, and by not doing nearly as much as they should to address the multifaceted threat of nuclear terrorism.

CONCLUSION

To motivate and guide the actions needed to prevent nuclear terrorism, policy-makers and nuclear managers around the world must understand the scope and urgency of the threat. Complacency is the enemy of effective response.

The critical first step in an effective response is clear: do everything possible to ensure that *all* caches of nuclear weapons and the materials needed to make them, wherever they may be, are secured and accounted for to standards sufficient to ensure that they are defended, in ways that will work and will last, against the threats that terrorists and thieves have demonstrated they can pose. Improving nuclear security is the one step that will most reduce the overall risk of nuclear terrorism, because once a nuclear weapon or nuclear material has left the facility where it is supposed to be, it could be anywhere, and all the subsequent layers of defense are variations on looking for needles in haystacks.

Although securing nuclear weapons and materials at their source is the most effective way in which to reduce the risk, it will not be perfect. Most of the past successes in seizing stolen nuclear material have arisen from conspirators informing on each other and from good police and intelligence work, not from radiation detectors. The United States and other concerned countries should undertake a substantially stepped-up effort to build police and intelligence cooperation. This effort should concentrate on stopping nuclear smuggling around the world, including additional sting operations and well-publicized incentives for informers to report on such plots in order to make it even more difficult for potential nuclear thieves and those who would like to buy stolen material to connect. The United States should also work with key nations to ensure that they put in place laws that make any participation in nuclear terrorism or in real or attempted theft or smuggling of nuclear weapons or weapons-usable materials crimes with penalties comparable to those for murder or treason.

Internationally, countries should focus on stopping the other elements of a nuclear plot—the recruiting, fund raising, equipment purchases, and other activities that inevitably would be required. Because of the complexity of a nuclear effort, it would offer a bigger and more detectable profile than many other terrorist conspiracies. The best chances to stop such a plot lie not in exotic new detection technologies but in a broad approach to counterterrorism—targeting and disrupting those groups with the skills and ambitions to attempt nuclear terrorism, while also addressing the roots of anti-American hatred that make recruiting and fund raising easier and make it more difficult for governments to cooperate with the United States.[49]

President Barack Obama has an historic opportunity: a chance to reduce the risk of nuclear terrorism to a small fraction of what it is today. Accomplishing that objective will require sustained, high-level leadership, focused every day on nuclear terrorism as what it is—a real, urgent, but preventable danger.

NO: The threat is overblown
Susan B. Martin, *King's College London*

The Threat of Nuclear Terrorism Is Overblown

The possibility of nuclear terrorism is real, but a terrorist attack using nuclear weapons is not inevitable and is in fact unlikely.[50] In this essay, I will explain how I arrive at this assessment of the probability of nuclear terrorism, and then address what the consequences of this are for policymaking in general on this issue.

The current debate on the risks of nuclear terrorism is heated, and the stakes are high. An underestimation of the risk can lead to inadequate polices that, in turn, may raise the risk of such an attack. But an overestimation of the risks can also be dangerous, and these dangers are too often ignored. An overestimation can lead to inappropriate and costly policies that can decrease instead of increase security, such as the 2003 war against Iraq. It can lead as well to an unfounded and harmful sense of fear and vulnerability. And it is also possible that the hyperbole surrounding nuclear terrorism make it more likely through both demand and supply effects. The insistence that nuclear terrorism is only a matter of time suggests that there is a demand for fissile material, and this postulated demand might then create supply, encouraging those who are desperate or mercenary enough to try and steal it. In addition, the portrayal of nuclear terrorism both as inevitable and as the thing that frightens people most encourages terrorists to think that such an attack is both possible (I can imagine them thinking, "If someone can do it, why not us?" or "If someone is going to do it, it should be us") and necessary to have a major impact ("If this is what they are most afraid of, this is what we have to do").[51]

Participants in the current debate generally agree on the appropriate starting point for the discussion.[52] The risk of a nuclear terrorist attack is defined as a product of the probability of such an attack times the consequences of such an attack. All agree that the consequences of a nuclear attack would be horrific. Estimates of the immediate fatalities from a 10-kiloton, Hiroshima-sized bomb range from thousands to hundreds of thousands, with the precise effects dependent on the size of the explosion and other characteristics of the attack, including the population density of the target area. Even here, though, hyperbole poses a danger. For example, some have warned that a terrorist nuclear attack, in addition to causing death and destruction, would "end American civil liberties."[53] But other experts have testified to Congress that a nuclear attack would affect only part of a major city, and it is clear that other sorts of effects, including on civil liberties, would depend not on the terrorists but on Americans themselves.[54]

The other component of risk, probability, is a function of motives and capabilities. The difficulty is that the probability of a nuclear terrorist attack is essentially unknowable. The possibilities and uncertainties seem endless. There are many levels of capability and many different paths to acquiring those capabilities. There are hundreds of different terrorist groups, and although only one or two may be discussed as likely candidates for a nuclear capability today, an estimation of probability unbounded by time has to include groups that might emerge or change in the future. Even if analysts tried to limit probability to the possibility of a nuclear attack by al-Qaeda in the next ten years, the unknowables are still immense. For example, estimates of the size and capability of al-Qaeda vary enormously today, and open source information is not even clear about whether Osama bin Laden is still alive. Despite these difficulties, estimates of the probability of a terrorist nuclear attack can be and are made. But it is important to keep in mind the degree of fundamental uncertainty in these estimates.

In assessing the risk of a terrorist nuclear attack, I proceed by analyzing the probability of such an attack, looking first at capabilities and then at motives. I then conclude with a discussion of the policy dilemma posed by the uncertain threat of nuclear terrorism.

PROBABILITY OF A TERRORIST ATTACK WITH NUCLEAR WEAPONS

No one with knowledge of the subject argues that a terrorist attack with nuclear weapons is impossible, and few are willing to say that a terrorist attack with nuclear weapons will never happen.[55] Most analysts hedge a bit, with the doubters arguing that such an attack is unlikely.[56] Others, including Graham Allison and Matthew Bunn, argue that the consequences of such an attack would be so horrendous that the probability does not really matter.[57] And still others argue that such an attack is nearly inevitable.[58] I find the argument that such an attack is unlikely the most persuasive for reasons centered on both motives and capability. And I argue that this low probability does matter, and it should be taken into account when making policy decisions about how to respond to the threat.

The first task is to specify what is meant by a terrorist nuclear attack. The possibilities include food or water contaminated with nuclear material; a conventional bomb that disperses radioactive material, otherwise known as a radiological or dirty bomb; an attack on a nuclear power plant; an attack with a stolen nuclear weapon; or an attack with an improvised nuclear device (IND), a crude nuclear bomb that terrorists construct themselves.

Analysts generally, although not universally, agree that governments are deterred from giving a nuclear weapon to a terrorist group both by the fear that the weapon could be turned against the government or its interests and by the retaliation that would follow if the terrorist group used the weapon and its source was identified.[59] Analysts also acknowledge that a terrorist group would find it very difficult to steal or buy a nuclear weapon, and that, even if it managed to do so, the group would have to overcome additional difficult hurdles before it could use a purloined bomb.[60]

Other scenarios are more possible but also less alarming. There seem to be no large hurdles to terrorist acquisition of radioactive material that could be used to contaminate food or water or that could be used in a dirty bomb. But no open source examples of these sorts of attacks are available, suggesting that terrorists lack the motives to carry them out. A handful of non-nuclear attacks on food have taken place in the past, but they were not very effective, and contaminating food or water with radioactive materials would not cause mass casualties or create spectacular media images. A radiological dirty bomb would inflict a heavy economic toll and could cause great disruption, but the death toll would be small. Similarly, an attack on a nuclear power plant is likely to be within the capability of at least some terrorist groups, and such an attack is frightening in its environmental, economic, and long-term health costs. But the number of direct deaths caused by such an attack would be low, and the motive for such attacks appears to be small.[61]

This leaves the possibility of a terrorist attack with an IND. How does one estimate the probability of such an attack? Probability is a function of capability and motives, so the following sections will look at each of these in turn.

Capability

The two main categories of nuclear devices, gun-type and implosion-type, largely use two kinds of nuclear material, highly enriched uranium, or HEU, and plutonium. The simplest device is the gun-type, which requires HEU. An implosion device is more challenging technically, and it can use either HEU or plutonium. Most analyses focus on a gun-type device using HEU as the simplest, and therefore most likely, path to a terrorist nuclear bomb, and because of space considerations I will do the same.[62]

There are two chief hurdles to the construction of any nuclear device: acquisition of the necessary fissile material and the specialized knowledge and expertise required to construct a bomb using that material. For a gun-type device, a terrorist group would have to obtain about 50 kilograms (110 pounds) of HEU, although the amount needed varies with "the level of enrichment of the uranium used in the weapon, the explosive yield desired, and the technical sophistication of the bomb design."[63]

Acquiring the fissile material. No one expects a terrorist group to attempt to produce this material on its own; to construct a bomb a group would have to either steal the material or purchase it on the black market.[64]

The factors that suggest that such a theft or purchase is possible include the enormous amount of fissile material produced since 1945 and the lack of an accurate inventory or record of this material;[65] the lack of adequate security arrangements for much of the fissile material known to exist, which creates an opportunity for theft as well as the possibility that such theft will go undetected, at least for a time;[66] economic and political instabilities in countries, which can create both incentives (disaffection, economic hardship) and opportunity (corruption, criminal gangs) for theft; and the record of trafficking incidents since 1993.[67]

However, there are serious obstacles to the acquisition through theft or purchase of the fissile material necessary for an IND. The record of trafficking incidents is at least somewhat comforting on this score. None of the known incidents has come close to the quantity necessary for a gun-type device. The largest reported incident is a failed attempt to steal 18.5 kilograms of HEU from Russia in December 1998; this amount is less than half of what would be necessary for a gun-type device.[68] In an incident reported in 2007, 79.5 grams of uranium enriched to 89 percent were seized in Georgia.[69] Although the enrichment level of this material is alarming, and although the smuggler allegedly claimed to have 2–3 kilograms of this material, this amount is still far short of what would be required for a gun-type device. In addition, policies have been and are being enacted to make the trafficking of nuclear materials more difficult now than it was in the past.[70]

Another obstacle to the theft of fissile material is the complicated nature of the task.[71] Theft of fissile material requires identifying a vulnerable source of HEU, stealing that material from what is likely to be at least a somewhat guarded site, and then transporting the material, most likely across international borders, to the location where the bomb will be constructed. As John Mueller has pointed out, this scenario will surely include some people who are not committed to the terrorists' cause (facility insiders or smugglers motivated only by money), and so the conspirators must maintain their silence, even in the face of the rewards offered for information on the theft of such materials or planned terrorist acts.[72] They also must avoid arousing the suspicions of others in the vicinity. To the extent that a series of such thefts are needed to accumulate the required amount of material, the same gauntlet of obstacles must be run each time. Mixing and matching different sources of uranium would also increase the technical challenge of constructing a bomb, because sophisticated analysis would be needed to identify the isotopes in each batch of uranium, and additional processing of the fissile material might be required.[73] Attempting to steal the required amount in one go also would be difficult, however, because such an amount is less likely to go unnoticed and may give facilitators (such as facility insiders) pause.

All this applies if the terrorists themselves steal the material. Purchasing material requires that someone else undertakes all the steps just described; that the seller and the buyer are able to find each other, avoiding any sting operations; that they are able to negotiate a deal for the purchase; that the material for sale is actually fissile material and not fake goods; and that the deal is not discovered or reported for the reward money.

Clearly, acquiring sufficient fissile material is a complicated, risky (and expensive) undertaking. Even though I do not think I can say with certainty that a terrorist group would *never* be able to achieve all of this, I do know that the acquisition of the required amount of fissile material by a terrorist group would be a very complicated undertaking, requiring careful planning and research, good management, and a lot of luck. And even if a terrorist group does succeed in acquiring the necessary material, it will find itself only partway toward achieving a usable nuclear device.

Building the bomb. How likely is it that, having acquired the requisite amount of nuclear material, a terrorist group would be able to construct a nuclear device? In looking at this question, it is important to remember that I am not examining the ability of a terrorist group to acquire a sophisticated nuclear arsenal but whether it could build one nuclear bomb.

Analysts generally agree that it is within the realm of possibility that a subnational group could build a gun-type device, especially if the group is not concerned with the efficiency and reliability of the weapon.[74] In 1977 the U.S. Office of Technology Assessment (OTA) estimated that an improvised nuclear device could be built by a minimum of two people, and Anna Pluta and Peter Zimmerman agree that this is plausible, as long as the uranium is enriched to at least 50 percent.[75] When constructing a scenario of how a terrorist group would build a nuclear bomb, Peter Zimmerman and Jeffrey Lewis assume it would take nineteen people and argue that it would take them up to a year.[76]

But just because it is feasible that terrorists could construct a nuclear device does not mean that any particular group would be successful, or that the construction of a device by some group in the future is inevitable. Substantial hurdles are involved. Even while arguing forcefully that a terrorist group could build a nuclear bomb, Matthew Bunn cautions that "making and delivering even a crude nuclear bomb would be the most technically challenging and complex operation any terrorist organization has ever carried out."[77] And the OTA also cautions against oversimplifying the construction of a gun-type device, arguing that

> although the gun assembly may be conceptually simpler [than an implosion device], the difficulty of actually constructing a nuclear explosive is roughly equivalent whether a gun or implosion assembly is used. The difficulties of the gun assembly are often not appreciated: a large mass of high density must be accelerated to a high speed in a short distance, putting quite unusual requirements on the gun design.[78]

This means that not just anyone can build a nuclear bomb. Furthermore, one cannot learn how to do so by reading a book. Tacit knowledge or learning by doing is important. No matter what blueprints have been obtained and what publications have been read, adjustments must be made when designing and building a bomb, which requires an ability to carry out experiments and to use the information gained from these experiments. But will terrorists be able to do this? And even if they can, there will be little room for learning by doing because both time and the necessary materials will be scarce.

The difficulty in assessing the likelihood of a terrorist nuclear attack is that one can spin scenario after scenario. Yes, it is possible that a terrorist group can figure out a way to acquire the necessary nuclear material. Yes, it is possible that a terrorist group can manage to recruit the people with the requisite knowledge and skills. Yes, it is possible to imagine that this group will be able to work together well, and that it will overcome the technical challenges, making all the necessary precise measurements and identifying any errors so that they can be corrected.

But how likely is it that all of this will happen at the right time without any discovery? How likely is it that the fissile material is acquired at the same time the group of experts is recruited? If there is a time lag, the risk of things going wrong increases—for example, the stolen material may be discovered (or may be stolen by someone else); one of the experts may have a change of heart or become unable to participate; someone from outside may discover or stumble upon the plot.

The bottom line is that, although it is certainly possible that a terrorist group could build a nuclear bomb, the chances of its doing so successfully are small. But even extremely difficult tasks can be accomplished if one is motivated enough, and so motives are the subject of the next section.

Motives

As noted earlier, analysts such as Graham Allison and Matthew Bunn argue that the consequences of a terrorist nuclear attack would be so horrendous that even an extremely low probability of such an attack does not decrease the risks. If one follows this logic, then the motives of a group to carry out such an attack become irrelevant. All that matters is that such an attack is possible, because the very possibility, given the consequences, is all that is required to justify action to prevent it. But I do not think motives can be dismissed so easily. After all, a strongly motivated group will be more likely to overcome the hurdles involved in building a bomb than a weakly motivated group, which may give it a try, but turn back at the first failure or obstacle.

It is clear that some terrorist groups have an interest in nuclear weapons. The Japanese group Aum Shinrikyo first tried to buy a nuclear weapon, and then, when that attempt failed, recruited scientists and engineers to help in its pursuit of nuclear as well as chemical and biological weapons.[79] What is most significant about the Aum example, however, is not that the group tried to get nuclear weapons but that it failed. Due in part to the technological challenges—and despite the enormous financial and scientific resources available to this group, which dwarf those available to other known groups except perhaps al-Qaeda—its efforts to acquire nuclear weapons were unsuccessful. In addition to illustrating the difficulty of acquiring nuclear weapons, the Aum example is also suggestive because of the light it sheds on motives for use. When the group decided to launch a chemical weapons attack on the Tokyo subway, using the sarin nerve gas that it was able to make, it did so in the pursuit of tactical aims and not to maximize destruction.[80]

There is also evidence that al-Qaeda has at least some interest in nuclear materials.[81] This evidence includes reported attempts by al-Qaeda operatives to purchase fissile material as well as statements by Osama bin Laden. Perhaps the statement most cited is bin Laden's assertion that it is a "religious duty" for Muslims to acquire nuclear weapons. But note that in this statement bin Laden focuses on acquisition, not use, as the duty for Muslims and suggests that nuclear weapons could be used for the prevention of harm (perhaps deterrence):

> Acquiring weapons for the defense of Muslims is a religious duty. If I have indeed acquired these weapons, then I thank God for enabling me to do so. And if I seek to acquire these weapons, I am carrying out a duty. It would be a sin for Muslims not to try to possess the weapons that would prevent the infidels from inflicting harm on Muslims.[82]

Other statements, however, can be read as suggesting that al-Qaeda might try to justify the use of nuclear weapons on the United States by reference to Hiroshima and Nagasaki.[83] And indeed, from al-Qaeda's perspective, a nuclear attack could conceivably be "just," part of a defensive jihad against the West or a "preventive" attack, intended to prevent future attacks on Muslims.[84]

But it is difficult to use statements such as these from Osama bin Laden to gauge al-Qaeda's motives and intentions. These sorts of public statements can serve different functions and be intended for different audiences. They may be intended to recruit Muslims to bin Laden's cause. They also may be intended to terrorize the West as part of al-Qaeda's strategy to generate fear. Thus they are not necessarily an accurate statement of al-Qaeda's aims and strategies.

The issue of strategy raises the question of whether a nuclear attack would be a rational choice for a terrorist group—that is, could such an attack serve its aims and objectives? This question assumes that terrorist groups are rational in the sense that they choose their means with an eye to their ends. And, indeed, this seems to be a reasonable assumption, because groups that fail to meet this limited definition of rationality would have a hard time organizing, managing, and completing a project to acquire nuclear weapons.

In addressing the question of rational choice, I will focus on al-Qaeda as the most prominent terrorist group alleged to be pursuing nuclear weapons today. The general argument, however, would apply to other groups as well.

Al-Qaeda wants to punish the United States and to compel it to change its policies in the Middle East—to end its support of Israel and "corrupt" Arab governments, to withdraw its troops from the region, and to allow the establishment of *sharia* in Muslim lands. But it is unlikely that an al-Qaeda nuclear attack on the United States, which would be limited to one or two nuclear weapons, would accomplish these objectives. The Middle East and the oil it contains are a vital national security interest of the United States. A nuclear attack on the United States and the economic damage it would inflict would probably make it even more important that the United States not suffer another economic blow from a disruption to its oil supply. As a consequence, a terrorist nuclear attack is unlikely to compel the United States to withdraw from involvement in the Middle East. And even if a nuclear attack on the American homeland somehow led to the establishment of a regime and territory controlled by al-Qaeda, it would simply provide a target for retaliation by the United States.

There is no reason to think that after a nuclear attack the United States would be unwilling or unable to retaliate. Contrary to what bin Laden has implied, America would not be in the situation of Japan in August 1945.[85] The nuclear attack in 1945 came after Japan had fought a long war and its military was close to defeat. By contrast, a terrorist nuclear attack would have no ability to destroy the military capabilities of the United States. In the aftermath of such an attack, the U.S. military, supported by the American people, would be determined to retaliate and to bring the perpetrators to justice.

Nor is there any reason to conclude that a nuclear attack would succeed in undermining liberal democracy in the United States, which is often stated as one of al-Qaeda's primary aims. How the United States responds and how that response affects the health of democracy are in the hands of American policymakers and the American people. Even if the first impulse is to sacrifice civil liberties in the name of security, the response to the events of 9/11 is beginning to demonstrate that such excesses can be challenged and overturned.[86]

In addition, any terrorist group that launched a nuclear attack would likely be the subject of the most intensive international effort to find and punish those responsible the world has ever seen. Nuclear weapons have not been used since 1945, and any group or state that breaks this tradition of nonuse would be shunned and outcast not just by the victim of the attack but also by people and states around the world. The tradition of nonuse is generally held to be in the interest of all; no one wants nuclear weapons to become a "normal" weapon of war. In addition, no state can afford to be seen harboring a terrorist group that launched a nuclear attack for fear that it would be held responsible. Again, unlike Japan in 1945, the United States and other states opposed to the use of nuclear weapons would be in a position to retaliate. Al-Qaeda has to ask itself if unleashing such a response is really in its interest.

To the extent that a group like al-Qaeda is interested in fueling divisions between Muslims and the West, the use of a nuclear weapon seems risky. If, as just argued, the nonuse of nuclear weapons is a common interest, not just in the West but around the world, then the use of nuclear weapons would unite most if not all the world into a coalition against the group. Al-Qaeda might hope that the response provoked by its nuclear attack would weaken or shatter this coalition. Although this is possible, the nuclear character of the attack makes it unlikely. In addition, the 9/11 attacks demonstrate that there are less drastic and easier means of creating divisions between Muslims and the West.

It is also possible to question whether a nuclear attack would serve other goals of terrorist groups, including recruitment and increased support from passive sympathizers. Although the use of a nuclear weapon may make the group seem powerful and attract some additional recruits, I believe the use of such a weapon would also make passive sympathizers and perhaps even potential recruits question the wisdom of supporting al-Qaeda.[87]

In a world of more than two nuclear powers, no state has been able to devise a strategy for the first use of nuclear weapons that serves its interests. It may be possible that some terrorist group will succeed where states have failed, but luckily I think this prospect is unlikely. Nuclear weapons are useful for deterrence, and perhaps when possessed but not used for "getting a seat at the table." But it is not clear how the first use of nuclear weapons can advance any substantive goals.

If terrorists are interested in inflicting pure destruction, they may be better off sticking with what they know. The empirical record thus far suggests that attacks with "weapons of mass destruction" have done less damage than more conventional attacks.[88] A successful terrorist nuclear attack is clearly the most destructive attack imaginable. But a failed nuclear attack, where much time, effort, and money are devoted to a failed effort to acquire or build a nuclear bomb, would be much less effective than that same amount of effort put into attacks using more accessible means.

This observation suggests that the motives for a terrorist nuclear attack are not nearly as strong as those in the West are often led to believe. Ironically, the strongest motivation for such an attack is probably the attention that the possibility of a terrorist nuclear attack receives in the West. To the extent that the West continues to portray the terrorist nuclear threat as the thing it fears most—to the extent that the West continues to portray it as inevitable and as only a matter of time—it nurtures the idea that a nuclear attack is what terrorists must do if they want to be taken seriously.

This is not to say that if the world ignores the possibility of nuclear terrorism it will go away—the possibility exists and needs to be addressed. But I do think that analysts and policymakers need to lower their rhetoric and approach the problem carefully so that they do not inspire the very attacks they are trying to prevent.

CONCLUSION

In view of the difficulties involved in terrorists' acquisition of a nuclear weapon, the paucity of motives for a nuclear attack, and the reasons why such an attack would not be in the interests of a terrorist group, I judge the probability of such an attack to be low.

But even if a terrorist attack with nuclear weapons is unlikely, the possibility cannot be ignored for two reasons. First, the consequences of such an attack would be catastrophic, so that some effort to prevent it is justified. Second, many of the hurdles that terrorists face today in carrying out a nuclear attack flow from the various policies governments around the world have put in place to prevent nuclear terrorism.

The most important policies are those aimed at preventing the theft of fissile material and tracing and recovering that material if prevention fails. In addition to securing sources of fissile material, reducing the potential sources of such material is also important.[89] The costs of carrying out these policies are both financial and political. The financial costs are obvious. The political costs arise when cooperation from other countries is needed to implement these policies, as this may require compromise on other issues. Policies that are "international" rather than "American" or "Western" may help to lower these political costs, and the establishment of global standards for the security of stockpiles of fissile material, as suggested by Matthew Bunn, could be very helpful in this regard.

However, tensions between policies that address the terrorist nuclear threat and other policies will still exist, which is where the policy dilemma arises. How does one determine the best policy to counter such an uncertain threat? And how does one weigh the possible benefits of a policy to decrease the likelihood of a terrorist nuclear attack against the benefits of policies to counter other more likely threats? After all, states do not possess unlimited resources, and therefore they must trade off one policy against others.

Analysts such as Matthew Bunn and Graham Allison emphasize the possibility of a nuclear attack in order to overcome what they see as the complacency of governments. There are sensible, effective policies that should be enacted to increase the difficulty of a terrorist nuclear attack, but these policies require government activity and financing and may be neglected if the possibility of a terrorist nuclear attack is not emphasized.

Other analysts such as John Mueller and William Arkin emphasize the low probability of an attack in an effort to counter what they see as an overreaction to the threat. In the extreme, this overreaction can contribute to events such as the 2003 war against Iraq, which I and others believe has increased and not decreased the terrorist threat. An overreaction can also contribute to a lack of preparedness to meet other threats, whether natural disasters such as Hurricane Katrina or, more likely, other military threats.[90]

Caught on the horns of the policy dilemma are the policymakers who are responsible for making the decisions and who have to act even in the face of the uncertainties. They are also the ones who will be held to account if a terrorist nuclear attack does occur, and this political reality is a contributing factor to overreaction.

In all likelihood, nations will continue to be both over- and underprepared for a terrorist nuclear attack. Overreaction may occur if the threat is overhyped or if it is manipulated in order to serve other interests. Underreaction may occur if sensible but relatively nonexciting policies such as increasing the security of fissile material are underfunded. A way must be sought between these two dangers, which requires continued scholarly analysis and debate as well as informed discussion among both policymakers and the general public. The possibility of a terrorist nuclear attack is real, but the likelihood of such an attack and the efficacy and costs of proposed policies to counter that threat demand careful analysis and thorough discussion.

Notes

1. See, for example, Richard Falkenrath, Robert Newman, and Bradley Thayer, *America's Achilles' Heel: Nuclear, Biological, and Chemical Terrorism and Covert Attack* (Cambridge, Mass.: MIT Press, 1998).
2. Ibid., 2. Also see Ashton Carter, John Deutch, and Philip Zelikow, "Catastrophic Terrorism: Tackling the New Dangers," *Foreign Affairs* 77 (November/December 1998): 80–94.

3. Sen. Richard Lugar, "The Lugar Survey on Proliferation Threats and Responses," Office of U.S. Senator Richard Lugar, Washington, D.C., June 2005, http://lugar .senate.gov/reports/NPSurvey.pdf.

4. Commission on the Prevention of WMD Proliferation and Terrorism, *World at Risk: The Report of the Commission on the Prevention of WMD Proliferation and Terrorism* (Washington, D.C.: Commission on the Prevention of WMD Proliferation and Terrorism, December 2008), www.preventwmd.gov/report.

5. See, for example, John Mueller, "Radioactive Hype," *National Interest* (September/ October 2007): 59–65.

6. Micah Zenko, "A Nuclear Site Is Breached: South African Attack Should Sound Alarms," *Washington Post*, December 20, 2007. See also Rob Adam, "Media Briefing: Security Breach at Necsa on 08 November 2007," Nuclear Energy Corporation of South Africa, November 13, 2007.

7. This essay focuses on terrorist use of an actual nuclear explosive—either detonating a nuclear weapon from a state stockpile or making a crude bomb from weapons-usable nuclear materials. It does not address, for example, sabotage of major nuclear facilities intended to disperse large quantities of radioactive material, or dispersal of radioactive material in a so-called dirty bomb. For a discussion of other nuclear-related types of terrorism, such as sabotage of major nuclear facilities, and of dispersal of radioactive material in a dirty bomb, see, for example, Charles D. Ferguson and William C. Potter, with Amy Sands, Leonard S. Spector, and Fred L. Wehling, *The Four Faces of Nuclear Terrorism* (Monterey, Calif.: Center for Nonproliferation Studies, Monterey Institute of International Studies, 2004). Nor does this essay address other terrorist options for causing catastrophic harm, many of which would be less challenging for terrorists than a nuclear attack. But the massive, assured, instantaneous, and comprehensive destruction of life and property that would result may make nuclear weapons a priority for terrorists despite the difficulties. A substantial literature on the danger of nuclear terrorism is now available. For one comprehensive (and alarming) look, see Graham T. Allison, *Nuclear Terrorism: The Ultimate Preventable Catastrophe* (New York: Times Books/Henry Holt, 2004). For a less alarming examination, see Michael Levi, *On Nuclear Terrorism* (Cambridge, Mass.: Harvard University Press, 2007).

8. See, for example, John Mueller, "Radioactive Hype," 59–65; and Robin M. Frost, "Nuclear Terrorism after 9/11," *Adelphi Papers*, no. 378 (2005). For replies to some of the myths of the nuclear terrorism skeptics, see Matthew Bunn and Anthony Wier, "Debunking Seven Myths of Nuclear Terrorism and Nuclear Theft," in *Securing the Bomb: An Agenda for Action* (Cambridge, Mass., and Washington, D.C.: Project on Managing the Atom, Harvard University, and Nuclear Threat Initiative, 2004); and Anna M. Pluta and Peter D. Zimmerman, "Nuclear Terrorism: A Disheartening Dissent," *Survival* 48 (Summer 2006).

9. Rahimullah Yusufzai, "Interview with Bin Laden: World's Most Wanted Terrorist," *ABC News*, 1999.

10. Kamran Khan and Molly Moore, "2 Nuclear Experts Briefed Bin Laden, Pakistanis Say," *Washington Post*, December 12, 2001; Peter Baker, "Pakistani Scientist Who Met Bin Laden Failed Polygraphs, Renewing Suspicion," *Washington Post*, March 3, 2002.

11. George Tenet, *At the Center of the Storm: My Years at the CIA* (New York: Harper Collins, 2007), 279.
12. Ibid., 264–268.
13. For an English translation of this fatwa, see Nasir Bin Hamd al-Fahd, "A Treatise on the Legal Status of Using Weapons of Mass Destruction against Infidels," May 2003, www.carnegieendowment.org/static/npp/fatwa.pdf. Al-Fahd, who has since been arrested, has publicly renounced some of his previous rulings, including this one.
14. Rolf Mowatt-Larssen, testimony to the Senate Committee on Homeland Security and Governmental Affairs, 110th Cong., 2nd sess., April 2, 2008. Before taking over as head of DOE intelligence, Mowatt-Larssen led the CIA's efforts to track al-Qaeda's weapons of mass destruction programs. Mowatt-Larssen now chairs an intelligence community-wide working group on nuclear terrorism.
15. For a summary of the al-Qaeda and Aum Shinrikyo efforts, see Matthew Bunn and Anthony Wier, with Joshua Friedman, "The Demand for Black Market Fissile Material," in *Nuclear Threat Initiative Research Library: Securing the Bomb* (Cambridge, Mass., and Washington, D.C.: Project on Managing the Atom, Harvard University, and Nuclear Threat Initiative, 2005). See also Sara Daly, John Parachini, and William Rosenau, *Aum Shinrikyo, Al Qaeda, and the Kinshasa Reactor: Implications of Three Case Studies for Combating Nuclear Terrorism* (Santa Monica, Calif.: RAND, 2005).
16. Suleiman Abu Gheith, quoted in "'Why We Fight America': Al-Qa'ida Spokesman Explains September 11 and Declares Intentions to Kill 4 Million Americans with Weapons of Mass Destruction," MEMRI Special Dispatch Series 388, Middle East Media Research Institute, Washington, D.C., June 12, 2002.
17. For a discussion of NMIP, see Mowatt-Larssen, testimony to the Senate Committee on Homeland Security and Governmental Affairs.
18. See Matthew Bunn, *Securing the Bomb 2008* (Cambridge, Mass., and Washington, D.C.: Project on Managing the Atom, Harvard University, and Nuclear Threat Initiative, 2008), 7–8 and 23–32. www.nti.org/securingthebomb.
19. "The President Issued a Decree to Dismiss Deputy Chairman of the MVD Department in Charge of Law and Order in Closed Territories and Sensitive Sites, Major General Sergey Shlyapuzhnikov," *Rossiyskaya Gazeta,* June 2, 2006 (translated by Anatoly Dianov).
20. See Bunn, *Securing the Bomb 2008,* 7, 26–32.
21. Ibid., 8–9, 40–44.
22. Thom Shanker, "2 Top Leaders of Air Force Pushed Out after Inquiry," *New York Times,* June 6, 2008.
23. For an especially useful account of this case, see Michael Bronner, "100 Grams (and Counting): Notes from the Nuclear Underworld," Project on Managing the Atom, Harvard University, Cambridge, Mass., June 2008. (The material was roughly 100 grams of HEU oxide, containing 79.5 grams of actual uranium.) See also Laurence Scott Sheets, "A Smuggler's Story," *Atlantic Monthly,* April 2008; and Elena Sokova, William C. Potter, and Cristina Chuen, "Recent Weapons Grade Uranium Smuggling Case: Nuclear Materials Are Still on the Loose," Center for Nonproliferation Studies, Monterey Institute of International Studies, Monterey, Calif., January 26, 2007.
24. For the International Atomic Energy Agency's most recent list of incidents confirmed by the states concerned, see *Incidents Involving HEU and Pu Confirmed to*

the ITDB, 1993–2006 (Vienna: IAEA, 2007). Eighteen incidents are on this list, but three of them appear to involve inadvertent losses rather than thefts. Some incidents that were on the list have been removed: one plutonium incident involved such a small amount of material that it was reclassified as a radioactive source incident, and one incident previously tracked as an HEU case was confirmed to be a low-enriched uranium (LEU). Richard Hoskins, IAEA Office of Nuclear Security, personal communication, October 2006.

25. Perhaps the best summary of the available data on nuclear and radiological smuggling is "Illicit Trafficking in Radioactive Materials," in *Nuclear Black Markets: Pakistan, A. Q. Khan, and the Rise of Proliferation Networks: A Net Assessment* (London: International Institute for Strategic Studies, 2007), 119–138. (Lyudmila Zaitseva was the principal author.)

26. The U.S. National Intelligence Council continues to assess that "it is likely that undetected smuggling has occurred, and we are concerned about the total amount of material that could have been diverted over the last 15 years." U.S. National Intelligence Council, *Annual Report to Congress on the Safety and Security of Russian Nuclear Facilities and Military Forces* (Washington, D.C.: Central Intelligence Agency, 2006).

27. See his testimony in Senate Select Committee on Intelligence, "Current and Projected National Security Threats to the United States," 109th Cong., 1st sess., February 16, 2005. Goss was not saying that the CIA had definite information that enough material for a bomb was missing, only that the accounting uncertainties are large enough that he could not confirm that was not the case. The same is true in the United States; some two tons of U.S. plutonium, for example, enough for hundreds of nuclear bombs, is officially considered "material unaccounted for." See U.S. Department of Energy, *Plutonium: The First 50 Years: United States Plutonium Production, Acquisition, and Utilization from 1944 through 1994* (Washington, D.C.: DOE, 1996).

28. This is especially disconcerting when considering that world stockpiles of separated plutonium and HEU exceed 500 metric tons and 2,000 metric tons, respectively— enough to make about 200,000 nuclear weapons. See International Panel on Fissile Materials, *Global Fissile Material Report 2007* (Princeton, N.J.: IPFM, 2007).

29. Karl-Heinz Kamp, "Nuclear Terrorism Is Not the Core Problem," *Survival* 40, no. 4 (1998): 168.

30. Aleksandr Khinshteyn, "Secret Materials," Russian Center TV, November 29, 2002.

31. U.S. Congress, Office of Technology Assessment, *Nuclear Proliferation and Safeguards* (Washington, D.C.: OTA, 1977), 140.

32. Commission on the Intelligence Capabilities of the United States Regarding Weapons of Mass Destruction, *Report to the President* (Washington, D.C.: WMD Commission, 2005), 276. For discussions of official assessments of the complexity of the operation and the number of people required, see Matthew Bunn and Anthony Wier, "Terrorist Nuclear Weapons Construction: How Difficult?" *Annals of the American Academy of Political and Social Science* 607 (September 2006). For a particular scenario involving a cell of nineteen people working for roughly a year (probably more than is actually required for some types of crude bomb), see Peter D. Zimmerman and Jeffrey G. Lewis, "The Bomb in the Backyard," *Foreign Policy* 157 (November/December 2006): 32–39.

33. Mowatt-Larssen, testimony to the Senate Committee on Homeland Security and Governmental Affairs.

34. For a more detailed discussion of the difficulty of making a crude nuclear bomb, see Bunn and Weir, "Terrorist Nuclear Weapons Construction." Scientists working on the Manhattan Project were so certain of success using this mechanism that they did not bother to test it before its use over Japan.

35. See, for example, Steven Graham, "Pakistan Investigates Reports Senior Al-Qaeda Figure Killed by Missile Strike on Afghan Border," Associated Press, July 25, 2008. Al-Qaeda–linked Web sites later confirmed Abu Khabbab's death.

36. DNI Michael McConnell, "Annual Threat Assessment of the Intelligence Community," testimony to the Senate Committee on Armed Services, 110th Cong., 2nd sess., February 27, 2008.

37. For a discussion of both the possibility that multiple terrorist failures may contribute to eventual success and the difficulty that insular terrorist groups have in changing their approaches (and replacing ineffective experts), see Richard Danzig, "Limitations of Terrorists . . . and Ourselves" (paper presented to "Pivot Point: New Directions for American Security," Center for a New American Security, Washington, D.C., June 11, 2008).

38. See Matthew Bunn, Anthony Wier, and John Holdren, *Controlling Nuclear Warheads and Materials: A Report Card and Action Plan* (Cambridge, Mass., and Washington, D.C.: Project on Managing the Atom, Harvard University, and Nuclear Threat Initiative, 2003), 15–19.

39. Ashton B. Carter, Michael M. May, and William J. Perry, *The Day After: Action in the 24 Hours Following a Nuclear Blast in an American City,* report based on a workshop hosted by the Preventive Defense Project, Harvard and Stanford Universities, Cambridge, Mass., and Palo Alto, Calif., May 2007).

40. Kofi Annan, "A Global Strategy for Fighting Terrorism: Keynote Address to the Closing Plenary," in *The International Summit on Democracy, Terrorism and Security* (Madrid: Club de Madrid, 2005).

41. For a meditation arguing that such an attack would leave the very notion of the sovereignty of nation-states in tatters, see Stephen D. Krasner, "The Day After," *Foreign Policy* 146 (January/February 2005): 68–70.

42. For example, both Khalid Sheikh Muhammed and Abu Zubaydah reportedly believed that uranium, which is only weakly radioactive, would be a good material for a dirty bomb. Bunn and Wier, "Demand for Black Market Fissile Material."

43. For the most comprehensive available account of this argument, see Levi, *On Nuclear Terrorism.*

44. The new book is from Sayyid Imam al-Sharif, sometimes known as "Dr. Fadl," an original member of the al-Qaeda ruling council. See Lawrence Wright, "The Rebellion Within," *New Yorker,* June 2, 2008, 37–53.

45. "The Open Meeting with Shaykh Ayman al-Zawahiri," As-Sahab Media, 1429–2008. As-Sahab is al-Qaeda's media arm.

46. For a detailed discussion of these programs, see Bunn, *Securing the Bomb 2008.*

47. Allison, *Nuclear Terrorism.*

48. Lugar, "Lugar Survey on Proliferation Threats and Responses."

49. For a detailed agenda to prevent nuclear terrorism, see Bunn, *Securing the Bomb 2007,* 97–141.

50. I wish to thank James Acton, Wyn Bowen, Chris Hobbs, and Stuart Gottlieb for their valuable comments and suggestions.

51. That discussions in the West can have such effects is suggested by a memo on an al-Qaeda computer found in Afghanistan. The memo states that al-Qaeda "only became aware of [chemical and biological weapons] when the enemy drew our attention to them by repeatedly expressing concern that they can be produced simply." See Alan Cullison et al., "A Computer in Kabul Yields a Chilling Array of al-Qaeda Memos," *Wall Street Journal* December 31, 2001.

52. Key works in this debate include Levi, *On Nuclear Terrorism;* Robin Frost, *Nuclear Terrorism after 9/11* (London: Routledge/International Institute for Strategic Studies, 2006); Allison, *Nuclear Terrorism;* Bunn and Wier, "Seven Myths of Nuclear Terrorism"; Bunn and Weir, "Terrorist Nuclear Weapon Construction"; Christoph Wirz and Emmanuel Egger, "Use of Nuclear and Radiological Weapons by Terrorists?" *International Review of the Red Cross* 87 (September 2005); William Langewiesche, *The Atomic Bazaar: The Rise of the Nuclear Poor* (New York: Farrar, Straus and Giroux, 2007); and John Mueller, "The Atomic Terrorist: Assessing the Likelihood" (paper prepared for presentation at the Program on International Security Policy, University of Chicago, January 15, 2008), http://polisci.osu.edu/faculty/jmueller/ APSACHGO.PDF. See also Brian Michael Jenkins, *Will Terrorists Go Nuclear?* (New York: Prometheus Books, 2008), a new and important contribution to the debate by one of the first analysts to look at the possibility of nuclear terrorism.

53. Lee H. Hamilton, director of the Woodrow Wilson International Center for Scholars in Washington, D.C., is one person who has warned that a nuclear terrorist attack could end civil liberties. See "There's No End to the Threat from Terrorist Weapons," *Indianapolis Star,* January 31, 2005. For other examples of hyperbole about the effects of a terrorist nuclear attack, see Mueller, "Atomic Terrorist."

54. On the physical effects of a nuclear attack, see "Lieberman, Collins Survey Consequences of Terrorist Nuclear Attack," press release, Office of Senator Joseph Lieberman, April 15, 2008, http://lieberman.senate.gov/newsroom/release.cfm?id=296161. See also "Nuclear Attack on D.C. a Hypothetical Disaster," *Washington Times,* April 16, 2008; and Nuclear Threat Initiative, "Securing the Bomb: Blocking the Terrorist Pathway to the Bomb; Nuclear-Weapons Effect," www.nti.org/e_research/cnwm/ overview/technica13.asp.

55. William Arkin is one exception, arguing that after the events of September 11, 2001, terrorists will not be able to acquire the materials necessary to build a nuclear weapon. See William M. Arkin, "The Continuing Misuses of Fear," *Bulletin of Atomic Scientists* (September/October 2006): 43.

56. Examples here include Karl-Heinz Kamp, "Nuclear Terrorism: Hysterical Concern or Real Risk?" Aussenpolitik: German Foreign Affairs Review 46, no. 3 (1995): 211–219; Frost, *Nuclear Terrorism after 9/11;* Gavin Cameron, "Nuclear Terrorism Reconsidered," *Current History* 99 (April 2000): 154–157; Langewiesche, *Atomic Bazaar;* and Mueller, "Atomic Terrorist."

57. Graham Allison, "The Failure of Imagination," *Bulletin of Atomic Scientists* (September/October 2006): 36; Matthew Bunn's essay in this chapter.

58. See Graham Allison, "Nuclear Attack a Worst-Case Reality?" *Washington Times,* April 23, 2008; Rob Edwards, "Top Police Officer Warns that Nuclear Attack Is Inevitable," *Sunday Herald* (Scotland), November 25, 2007.

59. Although it is not universally agreed that states will not pass nuclear weapons to terrorists—the George W. Bush administration was a notable exception—even those such as Matthew Bunn who worry about terrorists' use of nuclear weapons argue that states are unlikely to supply them. See his accompanying essay in this chapter.

60. On the hurdles in using a stolen weapon, see Mueller, "Atomic Terrorist"; Wirz and Egger, "Use of Nuclear and Radiological Weapons by Terrorists?" 502; Robin Frost, "Nuclear Terrorism Post 9/11: Assessing the Risks," October 2003, www.cda-cdai .ca/symposia/2003/frost.htm.

61. This does not mean that there has been no interest in these sorts of attacks. For example, the *Washington Post* reported that in 2003 Canada arrested nineteen people who allegedly planned to destroy a nuclear power plant. Cited in Charles D. Ferguson and William C. Potter, *The Four Faces of Nuclear Terrorism* (New York: Routledge, 2005), 2.

62. For background on nuclear weapons and materials, see the overview provided by the International Panel on Fissile Materials and Nuclear Weapons, www.fissilema terials.org/ipfm/pages_us_en/fissile/fissile/fissile.php; Gary T. Gardner, *Nuclear Nonproliferation: A Primer* (Boulder, Colo.: Lynne Rienner, 1994); U.S. Congress, Office of Technology Assessment, *Technologies Underlying Weapons of Mass Destruction,* OTA-ISC-559 1993 (Washington, D.C.: Government Printing Office, December 1993), www.wws.princeton.edu/~ota/ns20/pubs_f.html; Peter D. Zimmerman "Technical Barriers to Nuclear Proliferation," *Security Studies* 2 (Spring/ Summer 1993): 345–355; and Randall Forsberg et al., *Nonproliferation Primer* (Cambridge, Mass.: MIT Press, 1996).

63. The quote is from the Nuclear Threat Initiative, "Chapter 2: Two Types of Fission Nuclear Weapons Designs," Nuclear Terrorism Tutorial, www.nti.org/h_learnmore/ nuctutorial/chapter02_05.html. As a point of comparison, Little Man, the gun-type device dropped on Hiroshima, used 60 kilograms of HEU enriched to 80 percent. The Union of Concerned Scientists estimates that 40–50 kilograms of HEU enriched to 90 percent would be required to build a bomb. See the Union of Concerned Scientists, "Weapons Material Basics," www.ucsusa.org/nuclear_weapons_ and_global_security/nuclear_terrorism/technical_issues/fissile-materials-basics. html. See also Owen R. Cote Jr., "Appendix B: A Primer on Fissile Material and Nuclear Weapon Design," in *Avoiding Nuclear Anarchy: Containing the Threat of Loose Russian Nuclear Weapons and Fissile Material,* ed. Graham T. Allison, Owen Cote Jr., Richard A. Falkenrath, and Steven E. Miller (Cambridge, Mass.: MIT Press, 1996), 203–228.

64. A state would have as little reason to supply a terrorist group with fissile material as it would to supply it with a nuclear weapon.

65. See Siegfried S. Hecker, "Toward a Comprehensive Safeguards System: Keeping Fissile Materials Out of Terrorists' Hands," *Annals of the American Academy* 607 (September 2006): 121–132; and David Albright and Mark Gorwicz, "Tracking Civil Plutonium Inventories: End of 1999," *ISIS Plutonium Watch* (October 2000).

66. The attack on Pelindaba, described by Matthew Bunn in this chapter, is a vivid example of vulnerable security arrangements. See also the National Intelligence Council's "Annual Report to Congress on the Safety and Security of Russian Nuclear Facilities and Military Forces," December 2004, www.dni.gov/nic/special_ russiannuke04.html.

67. See William C. Potter and Elena Sokova, "Illicit Nuclear Trafficking in the NIS: What's New? What's True?" *Nonproliferation Review* (Summer 2002): 112–120. See also the Web site of the IAEA Illicit Trafficking Database, www-ns.iaea.org/security/itdb.htm, and of the Nuclear Threat Initiative's Newly Independent States (NIS) Nuclear Trafficking Abstracts Database, www.nti.org/db/nistraff/index.html.

68. Reported in Pluta and Zimmerman, "Nuclear Terrorism," 58. They describe this amount as "nearly enough for a nuclear bomb," but that is true only if the bomb in question is a far more complex implosion device.

69. See Elena Sokova, William C. Potter, and Cristina Chuen, "Recent Weapons Grade Uranium Smuggling Case: Nuclear Materials Are Still on the Loose," CNS Research Story, January 26, 2007, http://cns.miis.edu/pubs/week/070126.htm; and IAEA Staff Report, "Georgian Authorities Report Seized Illicit Nuclear Material," www.iaea.org/NewsCenter/News/2007/georgia_material.html.

70. Examples here include Cooperative Threat Reduction and various other international programs. For an overview by the IAEA, see *Combating Illicit Trafficking in Nuclear and Other Radioactive Material*, IAEA Nuclear Security Series No. 6. (Vienna: IAEA, 2007), www-pub.iaea.org/MTCD/publications/PDF/pub1309_web.pdf. For information on Cooperative Threat Reduction, see the Defense Threat Reduction Agency's Web site, www.dtra.mil/oe/ctr/index.cfm. See also Gloria Duffy, "Cooperative Threat Reduction in Perspective," in *Dismantling the Cold War: US and NIS Perspectives on the Nunn-Lugar Cooperative Threat Reduction Program*, ed. John M. Shields and William Potter (Cambridge, Mass.: MIT Press, 1997), 23–29; and Rose E. Gottemoeller, "Cooperative Threat Reduction beyond Russia," *Washington Quarterly* 28 (Spring 2005): 145–158.

71. This section draws on John Mueller's "The Atomic Terrorist," which provides a very useful breakdown of all the obstacles that would have to be overcome for a terrorist group to build a nuclear weapon.

72. The U.S. "Rewards for Justice Program" is one example of the rewards offered for information on terrorist activities. See www.rewardsforjustice.net for further information on this program.

73. The point is not that this sort of processing is necessarily beyond the capabilities of a terrorist group, but that the need for this additional step requires additional skills and knowledge and so is just one more hurdle for the group to overcome.

74. *Efficiency* refers to the efficiency with which a bomb uses the fissile material in the resulting explosion; *reliability* refers to whether the bomb would produce the expected force when exploded.

75. See U.S. Congress, Office of Technology Assessment, *Nuclear Proliferation and Safeguards*, 17, 140–141; Pluta and Zimmerman, "Nuclear Terrorism."

76. Zimmerman and Lewis, "Bomb in the Backyard." Note that Pluta and Zimmerman estimate that a terrorist group could build a gun-type IND in as little as sixty days. Pluta and Zimmerman, "Nuclear Terrorism," 64.

77. See Matthew Bunn, "The Risk of Nuclear Terrorism—and Next Steps to Reduce the Danger," testimony to the Senate Committee on Homeland Security and Governmental Affairs, 110th Cong., 2nd sess., April 2, 2008.

78. Office of Technology Assessment, *Nuclear Proliferation and Safeguards*, 142. See also Mueller's discussion in "The Atomic Terrorist," where he quotes Steven M.

Younger on the difficulty of designing and constructing a nuclear device. Younger is former head of the Defense Threat Reduction Agency and former senior fellow at Los Alamos National Laboratory, where he was in charge of nuclear weapons research and development. Younger's arguments can also be found in his book *Endangered Species: How We Can Avoid Mass Destruction and Build a Lasting Peace* (New York: Ecco, 2007).

79. On Aum Shinrikyo's attempt to obtain nuclear weapons, see Sara Daly, John Parachini, and William Rosenau, *Combating Nuclear Terrorism: Lessons from Aum Shinrikyo, Al Qaeda and the Kinshasa Reactor* (Santa Monica, Calif.: RAND, 2005). For a more general discussion of Aum, see David E. Kaplan, "Aum Shinrikyo (1995)," in *Toxic Terror: Assessing Terrorist Use of Chemical and Biological Weapons*, ed. Jonathan B. Tucker (Cambridge, Mass.: MIT Press, 2001), 207–226.

80. On the tactical nature of Aum's attack, see Jonathan B. Tucker, "Chemical and Biological Terrorism: How Real a Threat?" *Current History* 99 (April 2000): 150.

81. For an overview of al-Qaeda's nuclear attempts, see Jack Boureston, "Assessing Al Qaeda's WMD Capabilities," *Strategic Insight* (Center for Contemporary Conflict), September 2, 2002; and Daly et al., *Combating Nuclear Terrorism*.

82. "Interview with *Time Magazine*, December 23, 1998: 'Wrath of God: Osama bin Laden Lashes Out against the West.'" *Time Magazine*, January 11, 1999, www.time .com/time/asia/asia/magazine/1999/990111/osama1.html. See also Hamid Mir, "Osama Claims He Has Nukes: If US Uses N-arms It Will Get Same Response," *Dawn Internet Edition* (Karachi, Pakistan), November 10, 2001. In this interview, bin Laden states explicitly that al-Qaeda has chemical and nuclear weapons "as a deterrent."

83. For example, see the quote from bin Laden that appeared in the October–November 1996 issue of *Nida'ul Islam* magazine, as reported in "Calls to Action," *Washington Post*, August 23, 1998. See also the transcript of a May 1998 bin Laden interview with John Miller, www.pbs.org/wgbh/pages/frontline/shows/binladen/who/interview.html.

84. Osama bin Laden has been careful to portray al-Qaeda's attacks as a response to previous attacks by the West on Muslims—as part of a defensive jihad. See John Stone, "Al-Qaeda, Deterrence and Weapons of Mass Destruction," *Studies in Conflict and Terrorism*, 32 (September 2009): 1–13, for a discussion of bin Laden's attempt to justify his actions to the global Muslim community and the way in which the need to justify his actions may limit the types of attacks that al-Qaeda undertakes.

85. See Steve Coll, "What Bin Laden Sees in Hiroshima," *Washington Post*, February 6, 2005.

86. Examples include the international and domestic pressure to close the detention center at Guantanamo Bay, as well as various court challenges to Bush administration policies, including the U.S. Supreme Court's ruling that acknowledges the right of detainees at Guantanamo to habeas corpus hearings. See Sue Pleming, "U.S. Ponders Guantanamo Closure as Bush Term Ends," *International Herald Tribune*, May 2, 2008; and Robert Barnes, "Justices Say Detainees Can Seek Release," *Washington Post*, June 13, 2008.

87. Even al-Qaeda's current conventional violent tactics have been the subject of debate and condemnation. See, for example, Rich Gardella, "Insurgent Groups Condemn

al-Qaeda Tactics," *NBC Nightly News*, October 16, 2007, www.msnbc.msn.com/id/21267335.

88. John V. Parachini, "Comparing Motives and Outcomes of Mass Casualty Terrorism Involving Conventional and Unconventional Weapons," *Studies in Conflict and Terrorism* 24 (2001): 389–406.

89. One important example here is the ongoing effort to replace research reactors that use HEU with research reactors that use less dangerous fissile material. See Nuclear Threat Initiative, "Past and Current Efforts to Reduce Civilian HEU Use," www.nti.org/db/heu/pastpresent.html.

90. See Arkin, "Continuing Misuses of Fear," for a discussion of these and other dangers of an overzealous focus on the terrorist nuclear threat.

counterterrorism strategies: do we need bombs over bridges?

NO: There is a need to focus more on building bridges
Brigitte L. Nacos, *Columbia University*

YES: More creative military strategies are needed
Michael Rubin, *American Enterprise Institute*

Since taking office, President Barack Obama has engaged in an unprecedented campaign of outreach to Muslims around the world. In January, Obama chose the Arabic satellite television station al-Arabiya for his first formal televised interview as president, where he called for a "new partnership" between America and the Muslim world "based on mutual respect and mutual interest." This interview was followed by speeches in Turkey and Egypt, where he quoted verses from the Qur'an and promised Muslims worldwide that the United States would "listen carefully, bridge misunderstanding, and seek common ground."

President Obama also has authorized dozens of targeted executions of suspected Islamic terrorists in Afghanistan, Pakistan, and elsewhere. The strikes, usually by unmanned drone aircraft using guided missiles, have killed scores of terrorist leaders and lower-level operatives. The diplomatic price, however, has been tremendous: wives, children, and hundreds of innocent bystanders have also been killed or maimed in the strikes, provoking mass outrage and protests across Pakistan and other Muslim countries.[1]

Though these two examples might appear to be contradictory, what they in fact show is that counterterrorism is rarely an either/or proposition. Effectively confronting a robust terrorist movement requires the deployment of a whole range of options and initiatives, some of which may seem in direct opposition.[2]

At its core, the goal of counterterrorism is to weaken the strike capacity of terrorist organizations and to undercut their base of support. Although both hard power (such as military force) and soft power (such as diplomatic endeavors) will play a role in any comprehensive counterterrorism strategy,[3] choices of emphasis will inevitably be made: Is the threat best handled in a more warlike fashion, where the elimination of terrorist leadership, destruction of physical bases of operation, and direct confrontation with state sponsors form the basis of the approach? Or should emphasis be placed on more diplomatic efforts, such as global law enforcement cooperation, aid and outreach to affected communities, and direct negotiations with state sponsors and possibly terrorist organizations themselves?

Both approaches have their benefits, and potential pitfalls. Hard-line tactics can put terrorist leaders on the run and weaken their organizations, but if relied upon too heavily such tactics can inflame and alienate local populations, possibly laying the foundation for another round of fighting. Softer approaches can win legitimacy and the moral upper hand, but savvy terrorist groups will spin such efforts as signs of weakness, creating a potential boon for terrorist recruiters.

And both approaches have their passionate supporters among counterterrorism experts and professionals, each armed with facts and evidence to show that their preferred strategies are more likely to lead to the reduction or elimination of the terrorist threat.

Brigitte Nacos and Michael Rubin recognize the need for balance in counterterrorism policy—effectively confronting modern terrorism will require both an ability to build bridges as well as the wherewithal to occasionally blow some up. They strongly disagree, however, on the strengths and weaknesses of hard power versus soft power in counterterrorism, and especially on which approach should guide the effort.

Nacos believes that the use of hard power—for example, missile strikes against terrorist camps or commando raids to free hostages—tends to accomplish only limited objectives; hard power tactics are unlikely to destroy a terrorist organization or dry up its support. She argues that such tactics should be a rarely used adjunct to a broader strategy based on "traditional diplomatic mechanisms and soft power approaches." Specifically, she supports the use of multilateral economic and political sanctions against state sponsors of terrorism and cooperative policing against terrorist groups as the most effective means of destroying those groups and networks. In addition, she promotes aggressive public diplomacy and generous foreign aid as the most promising tools to steal hearts and minds away from terrorist groups.

Rubin does not disagree that hearts and minds can be won through direct political, economic, and humanitarian assistance. But he argues that such efforts are doomed to fail or to backfire unless besieged communities feel secure from terrorist violence—security that can come only from the defeat of the terrorist groups in their midst. Rubin says that reliance on soft power strategies aimed at state sponsors and terrorist groups will only perpetuate terrorist movements. Indeed, it will bring back the 1990s mindset in which prosecution and punishment after attacks were the main objective of counterterrorism policy. In this age of catastrophic terrorism, preventing attacks—not responding after the fact—must be the primary goal, and this can be accomplished only when aggressive military and intelligence efforts are leading the way.

The rise of modern mass-casualty terrorism has placed a tremendous existential premium on crafting effective counterterrorism strategies. Although there is no such thing as perfect security against terrorism, reducing the scale and scope of attacks and weakening or eliminating groups require skillful and thoughtful policymaking. Success will depend on a mixture of both hard and soft strategies—strong enough to disrupt and deter terrorist groups and their sponsors and temperate enough to secure global allies and win hearts and minds. As the essays in this chapter make clear, finding the right balance is one of the most critical—and challenging—aspects of any counterterrorism initiative.

There is a need to focus more on
NO: building bridges
Brigitte L. Nacos, *Columbia University*

Soft Power Trumps Hard Power in Counterterrorism

July 28, 2008

A missile strike against an al-Qaeda compound in Pakistan's South Waziristan region kills Abu Khabab al-Masri, a top commander of the terrorist organization. Three other members of al-Qaeda Central die along with al-Masri, the mastermind of the terrorist attack on the USS *Cole* eight years earlier. Because similar U.S. attacks are periodically launched on terrorist targets in the tribal border region near the Afghan border, it is most likely that the U.S. military is responsible for this particular strike, which "neutralizes" a terrorist with a $5 million bounty on his head from the United States.

March 1, 2008

A predawn air strike by the Colombian military against a jungle camp of the Revolutionary Armed Forces of Colombia (FARC) just inside neighboring Ecuador kills Paul Reyes, one of the most influential leaders and the most prominent spokesperson of FARC. Sixteen other members, among them Reyes's female partner, are also killed in the air raids. The well-planned and well-executed military move strikes the core of one of the most durable and most dangerous terrorist organizations.

October 7, 2001

Less than a month after the September 2001 terrorist attacks on the United States, American and British forces launch military operations against targets in Afghanistan. The declared goal of the invasion is the removal of the Taliban regime that allowed Osama bin Laden and his organization to establish headquarters and training camps inside Afghanistan and, of course, the destruction of al-Qaeda. The initial military operations end the Taliban's rule, tear down al-Qaeda's camps in Afghanistan, and force al-Qaeda to flee into Pakistan. But the Taliban as well as al-Qaeda's central organization regroup in Pakistan's tribal region along the Afghan border.[4]

Whether responding to domestic and transnational terrorism carried out by nonstate actors or dealing with states that sponsor terrorists, governments should not exclude military options altogether. Just as military force and the mere threat of force are factors in international politics, hard power has a place in counterterrorism.[5] The opening summaries of actions against FARC and al-Qaeda operatives and the Taliban regime are cases in point. And yet successful attacks against terrorist camps, missiles fired from unmanned drones, commando raids to free hostages, and even invasions tend to meet only limited objectives (the destruction of training camps, the decimation or displacement of a group's or regime's leadership, the freeing of hostages). They are far less likely to destroy terrorist organizations or dry up state support for terrorism.

The distinct differences between terrorist organizations and state sponsors of terrorism require different counterterrorism approaches. In this essay, I will therefore discuss first counterterrorism options vis-à-vis state supporters of terrorist violence and thereafter responses to the terrorist groups themselves. It is my argument that both are more effectively dealt with using the traditional diplomatic mechanisms and "soft power" approaches rather than the more aggressive, military-dominant measures.

DEALING WITH STATE SPONSORS OF TERRORISM

As one would expect in view of the wars in Afghanistan and Iraq, the Pentagon's 2008 *National Defense Strategy* left no doubt that, as a last resort, the U.S. military must be prepared to use force against state sponsors of terrorism and rogue states.[6] To be sure, retaliatory or preventive military actions with and without formal declarations of war are options in the most serious of conflicts between two or more states. When it comes to state sponsors of terrorism, the problem is that neither all-out war nor limited attacks guarantee a reduction in terrorist activities; indeed, they can have the opposite effects. The Iraq War, sold by the Bush administration as a preemptive move against a state sponsor of terrorism that was accused of being in bed with al-Qaeda, is an instructive case. No doubt, Saddam Hussein and his government supported terrorists and their violence. For many years, the Baghdad regime provided safe harbor for Abu Abbas, Abu Nidal, and other leaders of secular Palestinian terrorist groups; it also promised and paid out substantial sums of money to the families of Palestinians that committed deadly suicide attacks against Israelis. Furthermore, Iraq hosted and supported the Mujahadeen-e-Khalq, a large group that opposed the Islamic Republic of Iran and carried out terrorist attacks on Iranian targets.

However, even though it was supporting anti-Israeli and anti-Iranian terrorism and harboring some prominent Palestinian terrorists, Iraq was not a breeding ground of terrorists and did not allow foreign extremists from all over the Arab world to enter the country and unleash lethal violence against civilians. In stark contrast, during the years after Iraq's defeat Iraqi and foreign militants carried out waves of terrorist attacks—not only against members of the occupation forces but most of all against the civilian population in many parts of the country. If Iraq was indeed the most important front in the so-called global war on terrorism, as the Bush administration claimed, it stemmed directly from the resentment and anger in the Arab and Muslim world triggered and nourished by the military invasion and occupation of Iraq. In 2007, for example, more than 6,000 (43 percent) of the more than 14,000 terrorist incidents worldwide occurred in Iraq, and more than 13,000 (60 percent) of the more than 22,000 persons killed by terrorists around the globe died in terrorist attacks in that country.[7]

The dramatic decline in terrorist attacks in 2008 and 2009—more than 90 percent below 2006 and 2007 levels—can be attributed to the U.S. troop surge in the summer of 2007, the so-called Anbar Awakening, in which large numbers of Sunnis turned against foreign extremists of al-Qaeda in Iraq, choosing instead to cooperate with the U.S. military, as well as Shia cleric Moqtada al-Sadr's decision to rein in his Mahdi Army and focus on gaining power in the political process.[8]

As mentioned earlier, the Bush administration justified the U.S. invasion of Iraq in 2003 as a preemptive counterterrorist measure. Prior to the Iraq War, U.S. military actions against nation-states were typically immediate responses to specific terrorist incidents. For example, the interception of an Egyptian plane by U.S. Air Force jets in 1985 was an immediate reaction to intelligence that Egypt intended to use the plane to fly to safety the Palestinian terrorists who had hijacked the cruise ship *Achille Lauro* and killed an American passenger. Instead, the plane was forced to land in Italy. And, as described in the next section, Washington has utilized both hard and soft power against Libya, with the latter more effective than the former.

Disengaging and Reengaging State Sponsors of Terrorism: The Case of Libya

In the summer of 2008, twenty-eight years after the United States and Libya broke off diplomatic relations and five years after some diplomatic ties were reestablished, the two countries were ready to restore full diplomatic relations. Actually, Libya was removed from the U.S. State Department's list of state sponsors of terrorism in 2003, when its leader, Muammar al-Qadhafi, agreed to give up his weapons of mass destruction (WMDs) program and any involvement in international terrorism and promised to compensate the families of victims who perished in Libya-sponsored terrorist incidents. By settling outstanding lawsuits on behalf of American families against the Libyan government and by

Libyan civilians killed during U.S. air raids on Tripoli and Benghazi in 1986, the U.S. and Libyan governments removed the final obstacle on the way to full diplomatic relations.

During the 1980s and beyond, the U.S. government considered Libya one of the most flagrant sponsors of international terrorism. After intercepted phone calls implicated Libyan agents in the 1986 bombing of the La Belle Disco in Berlin, a favorite of American GIs stationed in the then-divided city, President Ronald Reagan ordered the retaliatory bombing of two Libyan cities. Forty-one Libyans, including Qadhafi's adopted daughter, were killed, but the attacks did not persuade Qadhafi to end Libya's involvement in terrorism. Instead, Libya continued to support terrorists and was behind one of the most lethal acts of terrorism in history: the downing of Pan Am Flight 103 over Lockerbie, Scotland, just days before Christmas 1988. All 259 persons on board and 11 more on the ground died.

What eventually convinced Qadhafi to abandon his support for terrorism and his ambition to develop weapons of mass destruction were not actual and threatened military measures but concerted American, European, and United Nations sanctions that isolated Libya economically and politically. In one expert's judgment, "Libya represents probably the best case of sanctions helping to shape a state sponsor's behavior on terrorism-related matters."[9]

The families of the Pan Am 103 victims also played an important role in Libya's metamorphosis from a sponsor of terrorism to a state willing to shed its pariah status. By relentlessly lobbying the U.S. government and the United Nations to pressure Qadhafi into admitting his government's role in the Pan Am 103 bombing by handing over two incriminated Libyan agents to the Scottish High Court, they kept the limelight on Qadhafi's misdeeds and reinforced the rationale for tough sanctions against Libya.

Disengaging a state sponsor of terrorism from important players in the political and economic community of nations and reengaging the state's leadership in direct diplomacy worked in the case of Libya.

Enticing Other State Sponsors

Joint diplomatic efforts, not military might, brought North Korea, another longtime member of the State Department's list of terrorism sponsors, to the negotiating table as well during the Clinton and George W. Bush administrations. As a result of the "six-party talks" by the United States, China, Japan, Russia, and South Korea, Pyongyang took its first small steps toward dismantling its Yongbyon nuclear reactor and promised a long-delayed declaration of its nuclear program and acceptance of a verification regime. In turn, the United States pledged to lift economic sanctions, remove North Korea from its list of terrorist sponsors, and open the door for international aid once the verifiable denuclearization process was in place. In October 2008, after North Korea was indeed scratched from the State Department's terror list, Helene Cooper of the *New York Times* wrote:

> The decision to remove North Korea from the terror list was a dramatic moment for President Bush, who had called the country part of an "axis of evil" and had only reluctantly ordered administration officials to engage in negotiations, saying that the United States had made deals with the nation's leaders before without winning enough concessions. That calculus changed in 2006, when North Korea exploded a nuclear device.[10]

Although it was far from clear whether North Korea would ever agree to give international inspectors full access to its nuclear facilities and eventually abandon its nuclear weapons, a difficult and protracted negotiation process had brought about some positive result. As Secretary of State Condoleezza Rice put it, "The North Koreans took 30 years to get a nuclear weapons program, I think it might take more than a couple to unravel it."[11]

Indeed, in April 2009, less than three months into the Obama presidency, North Korea expelled the inspectors of the International Atomic Energy Agency and announced that it was reactivating all of its nuclear facilities. This step came in reaction to the U.N. Security Council's criticism of North Korea's several missile launches and the adoption of a tougher sanction regime against Pyongyang. That same month, North Korea arrested two American journalists, Laura Ling and Euna Lee, for allegedly entering its territory across its border with China. But after trying and sentencing the women to twelve years of hard labor, North Korea signaled in August 2009 once again a desire for diplomacy by freeing the two Americans during former president Bill Clinton's visit in Pyongyang where he met with Kim Jong Il and his top nuclear negotiator, Kim Kye-gwan.[12]

But traditional diplomacy is not the whole story in the changing relationship between Washington and Pyongyang. Just as "ping-pong diplomacy" in the early 1970s opened the door for President Richard Nixon's China visit in 1973 and the eventual normalization of diplomatic relations between the two countries, cultural diplomacy in the form of the New York Philharmonic's concert in Pyongyang in early 2008 was a prelude to North Korea's subsequent reengagement in six-party talks.

The stick-and-carrot tactic of traditional diplomacy does not guarantee immediate wholesale behavioral changes on the part of state sponsors of terrorism, but it does offer the best possibility of small victories one at a time.

For example, in 1994, under pressure from U.S. and UN sanctions, the Sudanese government allowed French agents to fly Illich Ramirez Sanchez, better known as Carlos the Jackal, from his hideaway in Khartoum to Paris, hoping that the United States would reward this cooperative act by removing Sudan from its list of terrorism sponsors. Instead, Washington continued to pressure the Sudanese government to deny safe havens to terrorists, among them Osama bin Laden.[13]

At the request of the Sudanese government, bin Laden and his closest aides left Khartoum in 1996 and relocated in Afghanistan. Unlike in the case of Carlos the Jackal, when French agents were invited to take custody of one of the most notorious terrorists of the 1970s and 1980s, Khartoum did not arrange for U.S. agents to arrest bin Laden. Nevertheless, in the following years the Sudanese government was less hospitable to terrorists and actually signaled its willingness to counter transnational terrorism.

In 2001 the UN Security Council lifted terrorism-related sanctions against Sudan. Washington, too, recognized a sea change in Sudan's policies with the exception of the government's continued support for the Palestinian Hamas organization. At the time, Khartoum's friendly ties to Hamas kept Sudan on the list of state sponsors of terrorism. According to the State Department's "Country Reports on Terrorism" for 2007:

> With the exception of HAMAS, the Sudanese government does not appear to openly support the presence of terrorist groups in Sudan. The Sudanese government has taken steps to limit the activities of these organizations. As an example, Sudanese officials have welcomed HAMAS members as representatives of the Palestinian Authority (PA), but have limited their activities to fundraising. The Sudanese government has also worked hard to disrupt foreign fighters from using Sudan as a logistics base and transit point for extremists going to Iraq.[14]

And what about the Islamic Republic of Iran? Since the Islamic revolution in 1979, the Iranian government has been the most flagrant sponsor of terrorism in the region. The Tehran government was instrumental in the establishment of the Lebanese Hezbollah and has supported the organization ever since. Hamas has been another beneficiary of Iran's support for terrorists, as have groups in Africa and elsewhere. At a time when several terrorist organizations are trying hard to get their hands on weapons of mass destruction, the Iranian government's nuclear program has raised alarms in Washington, Jerusalem, and the capitals of several Arab countries. The question was and remains how to discourage the mullahs in Iran from developing nuclear weapons and how to dissuade their support for regional and global terrorist groups.

Since the Nixon presidency, American administrations have insisted that they will not negotiate and not make deals with terrorists and state sponsors of terrorism like Iran. But in reality, they have conducted negotiations and struck deals with state sponsors even during ongoing terrorist incidents, typically through third parties. One of the most obvious examples was the deal by the U.S. and Iranian governments—negotiated by Algerian diplomats—to end the Iranian hostage crisis. It secured the release of fifty-two Americans in January 1981 after 444 days of captivity in the U.S. embassy in Tehran.

The George W. Bush administration sent contradictory signals on Iran. In a May 2008 speech to the Israeli Knesset, immediately after mentioning Iranian president Mahmoud Ahmadinejad President Bush said:

> Some seem to believe that we should negotiate with the terrorists and radicals, as if some ingenious argument will persuade them they have been wrong all along. We have heard this foolish delusion before. As Nazi tanks crossed into Poland in 1939, an American senator declared: "Lord, if I could only have talked to Hitler, all this might have been avoided." We have an obligation to call this what it is—the false comfort of appeasement, which has been repeatedly discredited by history.[15]

Yet two months after the president categorically nixed suggestions to open a dialogue with Iranian leaders and attacked those who recommended direct talks, the U.S. State Department's third-ranking official, William J. Burns, traveled to Geneva to participate, along with representatives of the European Union, in talks with Iran's nuclear negotiator, Saeed Jalili. Although the Geneva meeting ended without any tangible results, there were reports that the Bush administration and the Iranian government were considering opening interest sections in each other's capitals. Comments in Washington and Tehran on the possibility of informal diplomatic representations were in substance and tone a marked respite from President Ahmadinejad's and President Bush's usually combative rhetoric and Vice President Dick Cheney's long practice of saber rattling.

In fact, before Secretary of State Condoleezza Rice met with Libya's Qadhafi in early September 2008 to discuss common interests, State Department officials had expressed the hope that Iran and North Korea would take note of the changed U.S.-Libyan relationship. According to one of her deputies, Rice was eager to demonstrate "that even sworn enemies who have inflicted pain on Americans can reap dividends by conclusively changing their ways."[16]

For decades, Iran was a model of the limits of economic and political sanctions against state sponsors of terrorism. Indeed, as sanctions against Iran demonstrated, unless there is broad international support for tough sanction regimes, authoritarian rulers in particular can simply ignore even the harmful effects of measures meant to inflict pain and change behavior. Like Iraq under Saddam Hussein, Iran under the mullahs has not changed its support for terrorists because of sanctions. Thus, short of military conflict that could destabilize the whole region, the advantages of negotiations in such cases are twofold: first, there is always a chance that common ground can be found—not in one single meeting but during ongoing exchanges; second, if talks ultimately fail in spite of serious efforts by the party seeking to engage a state sponsor of terrorism, the failure may well work in favor of the rejected side. As one expert in favor of negotiations with Iran suggested, "If Tehran rebuffs an opportunity to have meaningful talks with Washington, it will increase its own isolation and put itself under greater international pressure, while the United States will improve its own standing."[17]

Traditional Diplomacy and Media Diplomacy

An important diplomatic pathway to influencing rogue states and state sponsors of terrorism is the media. Simply by reporting what high officials in various countries are saying about each other's positions, the news media enable actors around the world to communicate effectively with each other. During the Iran hostage crisis, for example, President Jimmy Carter and the Ayatollah Khomeini, the U.S. administration and the Iranian government, and U.S. officials in Washington and the hostage holders in Tehran communicated frequently via the news media.

Throughout the buildup to the first Persian Gulf War in 1990–1991 and during the short hostilities, President George H. W. Bush and Saddam Hussein exchanged mass-mediated messages. Before the Iraq invasion of 2003, President George W. Bush and other U.S. officials communicated with Saddam Hussein and other Iraqi officials in the same manner.

But media diplomacy is not a substitute for old-fashioned diplomacy, which requires personal contacts. The mass media highlight negative, not positive, news and prefer sound bites of division, conflict, threat, anger, and nightmare scenarios.

Nothing constructive was achieved by mass-mediated exchanges between Washington and Pyongyang during the first years of George W. Bush's presidency, which focused on the most extreme outbursts of both sides. However, when the two sides agreed to direct diplomatic contacts, some progress was made on the issue of North Korea's nuclear program. Although it will never be known, would traditional diplomacy have convinced North Korea not to develop nuclear weapons in the first place?

In short, even though today's global media and communication networks are ideal vehicles for media diplomacy, traditional government-to-government diplomacy has its advantages—even when engaging state sponsors of terrorism.

DEALING WITH TERRORIST GROUPS

Dealing with nonstate terrorist entities is far more difficult than responding to state sponsors both for hard and soft power. Unlike states that sponsor or harbor terrorists, terrorist organizations are difficult targets for military action—especially if they are small or geographically dispersed. Even if a sizable guerrilla or terrorist organization controls a chunk of real estate, these fighters are not easily defeated by traditional military force as the examples of the FARC in Colombia and the Tamil Tigers in Sri Lanka attest.

In one military expert's view, "most of the tools and expertise developed for fighting military organizations will have limited utility in fighting al-Qaeda and similar groups, until and unless they are fixed in place geographically."[18] If there is reliable intelligence on training camps, hideouts, or other locations frequented by terrorists, surgical air strikes or commando operations can be successful. One proponent of what he calls "offensive action and offensive military capabilities" argues that "even unsuccessful offensive actions, which force terrorist units or terrorist cells to stay perpetually on the move to avoid destruction, will help reduce their capability," and that the "threat of offensive action is critical to exhausting the terrorists, whether they are with units in the field in Afghanistan or hiding out in cities and empty quarters across the world."[19]

But targeting terrorists who fight within larger military units—not exactly typical for terrorist organizations—is very different from using offensive military force against terrorists or insurgents who hide among civilians in cities, towns, or villages. One of many tragic examples of high-risk offensive actions against terrorists or insurgents during the war on terrorism was an August 2008 ground operation by U.S. Special Operation Forces backed by air strikes in the Afghan village of Azizabad. When the dust settled, more than ninety civilians—most of them women and children—were dead along with three dozen or so insurgents.[20] The damage to America's reputation in the Afghan village, in all of Afghanistan, and in the international community was once again far greater than the benefit of eliminating a few terrorists or insurgents. Military actions, especially when they involve the death of innocent bystanders, tend to rally supporters and recruit new ones. Thus the surgical strike against the leading al-Qaeda operative al-Masri and his companions in Pakistan was followed by a surge in violence in Afghanistan and Pakistan by the Taliban and other al-Qaeda allies.

Recognizing the inherent negative utility of this "shoot first" approach, one leading counterterrorism expert promotes a softer terrorism-as-crime understanding rather than the aggressive terrorism-as-war paradigm:

> Terrorism is a phenomenon that is global in its range, constant in its presence, and inevitably involves the commission of crime. Any national or international mechanism to counter it must be predicated on that understanding. Liberal democracies have well-developed legislation, systems, and structures to deal with crime; consequently, the criminal justice system should be at the heart of their counterterrorism efforts.[21]

Over time, conventional criminal justice work or policing has been far more successful in weakening and destroying terrorist groups than offensive military actions. Italy's Red Brigade, Germany's Red Army Faction, the United States' Weather Underground, and similar groups in the West ended because their leaders and many rank-and-file members were arrested, tried, and imprisoned.

A recent study of all terrorist groups active worldwide from 1968 through 2006 found that 7 percent ceased to exist because of military force, 40 percent because of policing, and 10 percent because they realized their typically very limited objectives. According to the same research, 43 percent of these organizations terminated their violence because of political solutions or settlements.[22] In other words, traditional criminal justice approaches and efforts to bring terrorist groups into the political process were far more successful in ending terrorism than military actions.

Engaging Group Leaders in Negotiations

In the past, negotiations with terrorist groups were most likely during hostage situations, when governments were under pressure to free their citizens and save their lives. Most governments, however, are reluctant to admit they ever negotiate with terrorists. In the negotiated release of the Iranian hostages, for example, both the Carter administration and the Iranian authorities pretended that an autonomous group of students took over the U.S. embassy in Tehran and held Americans captive rather than a group with direct links to the new radical regime in power. Later, the arms-for-hostages deal pursued by the Reagan White House was justified as a transaction with Iranian officials who had contacts and influence with but not control over the Hezbollah hostage-holders in Lebanon. Many governments and many corporations have struck deals with terrorists to free hostages without admitting such bargains. The practice continues to this day.

I am not in favor of negotiating with terrorists who hold hostages and offering them something tangible in return for the release of their captives: history has shown that such bargains encourage further hostage taking by the same groups or by other organizations. But negotiating the abandonment of terrorism and bringing groups into the domestic or international political process are another story. Northern Ireland is an excellent example. After decades of bloody violence and a long, protracted peace process, Northern Ireland finally turned the corner in early 2007 when Sinn Fein, the political wing of the Irish Republican Army (IRA), and the Democratic Union Party, representing the Protestant majority, formed a government in which Ian Paisley, the longtime Protestant opponent of any meaningful political role for the Catholic minority, became the first minister and Martin McGuinness, a former IRA commander, the deputy first minister.

As Northern Ireland demonstrates, negotiated peace agreements rarely hold after the first try; instead, it is far more likely that the road to peace is paved with broken accords and renewed outbreaks of violence. Cease-fire agreements between the Sri Lankan government and the Tamil Tigers, between Spain's government and the Basque Fatherland and Liberty (ETA), and between the Israeli government and Hamas have been repeatedly negotiated and broken. Yet in view of the poor track record of military actions in ending terrorism, the criminal justice approach and the negotiation route are the most promising options.

However, the goals and the ideologies of terrorist organizations determine whether there are opportunities for common ground and compromises. Separatist groups may be inclined to settle for a significant degree of political, economic, and social autonomy short of full independence if only because such a compromise satisfies their supporters. By contrast, organizations with uncompromising objectives will not compromise on their ultimate goals. Although it was possible in the 1970s and 1980s to negotiate with Marxist militants such as the Baader-Meinhof terrorists in Germany about the release of their hostages in return for freeing some of their imprisoned comrades, it would have made little sense to talk about the group's final solution: the destruction of capitalism and democracy in Germany and elsewhere in the West.

Religious terrorists, too, tend to have absolute demands and goals that defy compromise—they also have far greater longevity than nonreligious groups. Thus, although 62 percent of all terrorist organizations ended between 1968 and 2006, only 32 percent of religious groups ceased to exist and not one of them realized its objectives.[23] A comparison between Yasser Arafat's secular Palestinian al-Fatah, a terrorist organization before—at least officially—abandoning terrorism, and the religious Palestinian Hamas is instructive. Even though al-Fatah has been open to a compromise two-state solution with Israel, Hamas has stuck to its ultimate objective—the violent removal of Israel from the map of the Middle East.

What, then, are the prospects for persuading groups such as al-Qaeda to forsake terrorism through negotiations? On this issue, I side with those who reject talks with Osama bin Laden or his lieutenants because of the organization's non-negotiable goals. As one observer wrote:

> There is no sign that al Qaeda has changed its thinking on the utility of violence. And it is hard to conceive of a viable process of primary negotiations in which al Qaeda could be included. Al Qaeda has global aspirations and no firm territorial base, and there is no clearly defined territory in which its aims could be satisfied through constitutional means. Under these conditions, opening negotiations would be a counterproductive move: it would provide al Qaeda with political legitimacy. [24]

But opposing viewpoints deserve consideration as well. Noting that her take on this is unpopular, Louise Richardson favors negotiations with al-Qaeda for the following reasons:

> By overcoming our reluctance to talk, we could discover a great deal about our adversaries, the importance they assign to particular goals, about how they make decisions, and about their assessment of their own position. Such talks do not have to be public, nor do they have to be direct. They could be conducted through intermediaries, but it is very difficult to know your enemies if you don't try to engage them.[25]

A more promising course of action, one that Richardson recommends as well, would concentrate on weakening support and sympathies among those Arabs and Muslims in whose name al-Qaeda, its affiliates, and like-minded groups claim to act. Terrorists need community support to sustain their activities. When that support fades, terrorists' support lines and recruitment reservoirs dry up. The most effective way to engage in this endeavor would be to focus attention and resources on effective public diplomacy.

PUBLIC DIPLOMACY AND COUNTERTERRORISM

Even though the Bush administration used military force in its war on terrorism, the Pentagon's 2008 *National Defense Strategy* recognizes the limits of hard power in response to terrorism carried out by nonstate actors:

> The use of military force plays a role, yet military efforts to capture or kill terrorists are likely to be subordinate to measures to promote local participation in government and economic programs to spur development, as well as efforts to understand and address grievances that often lie at the heart of insurgencies.[26]

Although it is far from clear that democratic participation and economic development prevent or decrease terrorism, public diplomacy may well be the best hope to diminish terrorists' natural reservoirs of recruits, supporters, and sympathizers. The three pillars of American public diplomacy during the Cold War era—the spread of information via foreign language broadcasts into the communist world, cultural exchanges, and educational exchanges—should be adapted to the global realities of the twenty-first century.[27] In the age of information, when a multitude of global television and radio networks and the Internet provide instant news, information, and communication, the successful broadcast strategies of the past will no longer work. There are more vehicles for and opportunities to reach and engage larger audiences overseas than ever before—but only by means of innovated programs conceived, produced, and presented by professionals who speak the languages and know the cultures of the target audiences and, of course, the public relations goals of the United States.

So far, American public diplomacy efforts via television, radio, and Internet have not been success stories. For example, although well financed, the U.S. government's Arab-language television network, al-Hurra, and radio station, al-Sawa, have neither displayed the excellence of their Cold War predecessors, such as Voice of America or Radio Free Europe, nor found promising new approaches for a completely different media and communication environment. Established by the George W. Bush administration to cultivate a positive image of the United States in the Arab world, al-Hurra and al-Sawa were overseen by bosses who either did not speak Arabic or had no experience in broadcasting. As a result, they made incredible blunders, such as airing "anti-American and anti-Israeli viewpoints" and showcasing pro-Iranian policies and giving "air time to a militant who called for the death of American soldiers in Iraq."[28]

An investigation by the media watchdog *ProPublica* and CBS News's *60 Minutes* found that the two outlets had "an untrained, largely foreign staff with little knowledge of the country whose values and policies they were hired to promote. There appeared to be little oversight of the daily operations."[29] Certainly not a recipe for effective public diplomacy.

As for the Internet, U.S. Secretary of Defense Robert Gates was right on target when he said:

> Public relations was invented in the United States, yet we are miserable at communicating to the rest of the world what we are about as a society and a culture, about freedom and democracy, about our policies and our goals. It is just plain embarrassing that al-Qaeda is better at communicating its message on the internet than America. As one foreign diplomat asked a couple of years ago, "How has one man in a cave managed to

out-communicate the world's greatest communication society?" Speed, agility, and cultural relevance are not terms that come readily to mind when discussing U.S. strategic communications.[30]

A modernized public diplomacy model must focus on the Internet's ample opportunities for virtual cultural and educational exchanges, but it should never do so at the expense of direct physical, cultural, and educational exchanges. Most important, the United States has a big opportunity to influence the attitudes of foreign publics if Washington decision makers, not just in the Department of State, are committed to developing new approaches to public diplomacy and making them part of their policy deliberations.

When it comes to the Arab and Muslim world, public opinion polls in Pakistan, Saudi Arabia, Indonesia, and several other countries reveal that the strong support for Osama bin Laden and his causes has a soft underbelly and could be softened more so with the right public diplomacy approaches. Kenneth Ballen, president of the organization Terror Free Tomorrow, which has conducted extensive surveys in Muslim countries, found significant resentment toward the United States and yet the potential for a dramatic turnaround in favor of America without drastic policy adjustments.[31]

Take the example of Pakistan, where 80 percent of respondents in a June 2008 survey said that al-Qaeda's top goal was "standing up to America," and 57 percent agreed with that objective. The same survey revealed that only one-third of Pakistanis had a favorable opinion of bin Laden and al-Qaeda. When asked what would improve their opinion of the United States, the vast majority pointed to educational scholarships and visas to the United States, free trade between the two countries, and American disaster relief, medical aid, and resources to build schools and train teachers. The most surprising result was that a larger percentage of bin Laden supporters than of nonsupporters reacted positively to U.S. measures deemed likely to improve Pakistanis' attitudes toward America and Americans.

Or take Indonesia, where public opinion became much more favorable toward the United States and much less positive toward bin Laden after the American-led relief efforts in the wake of the deadly tsunami of 2005. With these and similar results in other Muslim countries in mind, Ballen wrote:

> What our surveys uncovered is that the U.S. would witness dramatic improvements in the view of the United States among the overwhelming majority of Muslims, including those who express support for al Qaeda and Bin Laden, if we demonstrate respect and caring for people in their daily lives through practical, relatively achievable steps such as increasing direct humanitarian assistance (medical, education, food), visas and better trade terms.[32]

CONCLUSION

Although military actions against state sponsors and terrorist groups are appropriate in certain circumstances, they tend to be stop-gap measures. As the Iraq War has demonstrated, massive military force can result in a recruiting bonanza for terrorists. And as ground and air operations against al-Qaeda and Taliban figures in Pakistan's tribal region showed, such strikes can trigger further waves of terrorist attacks.

In the long run, widely supported economic and political sanctions against state sponsors and policing against terrorist groups are the most hopeful approaches to ending state sponsorship of terrorism and destroying terrorist groups and networks. In addition, soft power in the form of new mass-mediated and personal public diplomacy as well as generous disaster relief and targeted foreign aid are the most promising tools for depriving terrorists of their lifeblood: the popular support and breeding grounds among those in whose interest they claim to act.

YES: More creative military strategies are needed
Michael Rubin, *American Enterprise Institute*

Military Tactics Are Essential for Fighting Terrorism

Anti-Americanism peaked under President George W. Bush because the international community disapproved of his war on terrorism. Yet while promising a new beginning, Bush's successor in office, Barack Obama, acknowledges that "we are indeed at war with al Qaeda and its affiliates." He nevertheless suggests that cooperative diplomacy toward state sponsors and criminal prosecutions of terrorists is the best way in which to counter terrorism, the predominant view before September 11, 2001.[33]

Soft power and police investigations are not effective counterterrorism strategies absent intelligence and military force. Obama believes that "our courts and juries . . . are tough enough to convict terrorists." But these convictions require evidence available only after the attack; they are meaningless to prevention, the essence of effective counterterrorism. Diplomats and academics embrace both multilateralism and soft power and shun unilateralism and military force, but in the wake of the destruction of the World Trade Center, many U.S. policymakers concluded they should eschew theory and recognize the reality: military tactics are the best means to counter terrorist threats.

THE NATURE OF TERRORISM CUES STRATEGIES FOR RESPONSE

Terrorism is a tactic. It is not simply an asymmetric strategy or an approach used by the weak against the strong. This is particularly true for terrorist groups under the tutelage of state sponsors. Stephen Sloan, a terrorism expert at the University of Oklahoma, has noted that although terrorism traditionally seeks to resist state oppression from within, state sponsors of terrorism use the tactic to amplify force.[34] For example, during the Cold War the Soviet Union sponsored the Baader-Meinhof Gang in West Germany and the National Liberation Army of Bolivia. Algerian support enabled the Polisario Front to challenge the Moroccan army from 1976 until the late 1980s. Only when observers remove these groups from the context of their sponsors can they be considered weak. The Kurdistan Workers' Party (PKK) is only David to Turkey's Goliath if the supply and support of Greece, Syria, and Iran are ignored. Without the support of Venezuela, it is doubtful that the Revolutionary Armed Forces of Colombia, or FARC, would continue its insurgency.

Political movements employ terrorism to achieve aims. They engage in terrorism because it is a tactic that can maximize gain with relatively little cost. Even minor military deployments by states are expensive. Each M1 Abrams battle tank carries a replacement cost of $4.1 million, and each UH-60L Black Hawk helicopter costs $5.9 million. By contrast, Matthew Levitt, a former terrorism finance analyst at the U.S. Treasury Department, estimated that the November 27, 2001, shooting attack on the Afula central bus station in northern Israel cost the terrorist group executing the attack $31,000, and the July 31, 2002, bombing of a Hebrew University cafeteria that killed seven, including five Americans, cost $50,000. Andrew Garfield, an influence operations specialist with experience in both Iraq and Afghanistan, estimated that the production of terrorists' martyrdom videos cost only $2,000.[35]

The modern media amplify the effectiveness of terror, especially when the target is a democracy. The proliferation of satellite television networks across the globe wins terrorists a global audience for every hijacking, car bomb, or kidnapping, which undercuts a target's will to fight. In the 1990s, Chechen units operated in cells of five: four to carry weapons and fight and one whose only responsibility was to film a unit's exploits to amplify perception of effectiveness. Terrorist violence in Iraq—especially videos depicting the murders of kidnapped foreigners—undercut public support for Operation Iraqi Freedom, enabling analogies to Vietnam and leading to increasingly high-profile calls for unilateral withdrawal. In Chechnya, Iraq, and, more recently, Afghanistan, terrorists employ the media to undercut the morale of the population of the country deploying armed forces. Thus not only is terrorism cheap, but, by enabling its sponsors plausible deniability, it also allows sponsors to avoid costly accountability and to reap the benefits of diplomatic legitimacy that soft power too often bestows.

A fuller understanding of the nature of terrorism, its cost-effectiveness, and its support structures lead to one conclusion: reliance on soft power strategies will only perpetuate terrorist movements. This is true of the actions aimed at sponsors of terrorism and at terrorist groups themselves.

THE SOFT POWER FALLACY

Proponents of soft power argue that military force alone cannot effectively counter terrorism. Joseph S. Nye Jr., a Harvard political scientist who coined the phrase in 1990, later revisited the topic in the context of the war on terrorism. "The United States cannot confront the new threat of terrorism without the cooperation of other countries," he wrote. "Of course, other governments will often cooperate out of self-interest. But the extent of their cooperation often depends on the attractiveness of the United States."[36] As for Islamic terrorism, Nye adopted the metric articulated by Secretary of Defense Donald Rumsfeld in February 2003: "Are we capturing, killing or deterring and dissuading more terrorists every day than the madrassas and the radical clerics are recruiting, training and deploying against us?" The key to success, Nye argued, is to appeal more to moderate Muslims so that they gain the upper hand against extremists.

Nye's approach is naïve. Countering terrorism is not a popularity contest. As the 2006 "Quadrennial Defense Review" stated, "This is both a battle of arms and a battle of ideas," not one or the other.[37] As I wandered through the Taliban's Afghanistan in March 2000, ordinary Afghans told me they chafed under Taliban rule. However, because the Taliban had monopolized force, they could do little. Iraqis living under Muqtada al-Sadr's grip in Najaf likewise had little ability to express their views freely as long as his Mahdi militia retained its local dominance. Only after the U.S. and Iraqi armies routed Sadr's militia in November 2004 did moderate Iraqis emerge from hiding. Hezbollah in Lebanon and Hamas in Gaza pursue similar reigns of terror.

Soft Approaches to the Root Causes of Terrorism

Too often, Western officials seek to address terrorism by speculating about root causes. Misidentifying these, however, undercuts any soft power antidote. For example, as Taliban fighters advanced on Buner, just sixty miles from the Pakistani capital, on April 22, 2009, Secretary of State Hillary Clinton declared, "The government of Pakistan must begin to deliver government services, otherwise they are going to lose out to those who show up and claim that they can solve people's problems."[38] This statement indicates that the secretary had misread the Islamist threat. Should Pakistan embark on land reform, the Taliban would simply switch to a new talking point to distract local attention while they pursue centuries-old ideological aims with force of arms.

As discussed in detail in an earlier chapter of this volume, the notion that poverty breeds terrorism lacks evidence. Indeed, sub-Saharan countries are among the poorest on earth, but they do not produce the terrorists; rather, Saudi Arabia, Pakistan, and Libya do. Poverty exists in these countries as well, but the well-educated and middle class are more likely than the poor to pursue terrorism. The 9/11 hijackers, for example, had university educations and lived comfortable lives. Elite Palestinian institutions such as the Islamic University of Gaza and Bir Zeit University in the West Bank serve as breeding grounds. British security services reports suggest that in the United Kingdom, universities (and not soup kitchens) are incubators of extremism.

Basing counterterrorism on economic development and poverty eradication, as was done to some extent in Sri Lanka, is counterproductive, even though development assistance is the chief weapon in the soft power arsenal. Not only is foreign aid ineffective in battling terrorism, it also often exacerbates the problem. In 2000 the Palestinian Authority launched its second intifada, a decision that led to a 40 percent drop in government revenue. Rather than hold the Palestinian leadership accountable for its decision to pursue its aims through terrorism rather than diplomacy, the international community doubled direct financial assistance. As Palestinian Authority chairman Yasir Arafat began to realize that the international community would not allow his constituents to suffer as a result of his decisions, the violence increased. Between 1999 and 2006, international assistance to the Palestinian Authority and incidences of terrorism are directly proportional.[39] In May 2009, the U.S. Government Accountability Office reported that it was unable to certify that U.S. taxpayer dollars did not subsidize Palestinian terrorists or underwrite their propaganda.[40]

Even if foreign aid does not pad terrorists' coffers, prioritization of development over security wastes funds. In numerous reports between 2004 and 2009, the special inspector general for Iraq reconstruction detailed how security concerns constrained the multibillion dollar reconstruction effort. When terrorists undermine stability, development aid is at best ineffective and at worst encourages corruption.

"Understanding" Terrorists' Grievances

If targeting economic development does little to reduce (and in fact it may exacerbate) terrorism, what about addressing directly the demands and grievances that terrorists say underpin their actions? The fact is that soft power strategies to address demands and grievances are counterproductive for two reasons. First, responding to terrorism with diplomatic outreach or responding to demands incentivizes terror. The core of the Iran-contra affair, for example, was the Reagan administration's attempt to trade arms for American hostages held by Iranian proxies in Lebanon. At first, it seemed to work: between June 9, 1985, and September 9, 1986, these militias kidnapped no Americans. But no sooner did the Reagan administration deliver the last shipment of spare parts, then kidnappers seized three more Americans.[41] William Quandt, a Middle East aide in the Nixon and Carter administrations, acknowledged as much: "This provides a perverse incentive to Iran to keep some hostages."[42]

The second reason gearing counterterrorism strategy to grievance removal is ineffective is that declared complaints do not always correlate with goals. The PKK used the cause of realizing Kurdish cultural rights and an independent state as justification for its bloody struggle in Turkey. However, throughout the entire conflict the PKK staged more attacks on fellow Kurds than on Turkish soldiers. The goal of its leader, Abdullah Öcalan, was power, not Kurdish freedom. In March 1987, for example, Öcalan ordered some Kurdish villages in Turkey to be burned in order to subjugate the region to his authority. No amount of "outreach" or "understanding" of the PKK's purported grievances and goals had a positive effect on reducing PKK terrorism.

Terrorists' objectives expand as they achieve aims; they do not discard effective tools. As Turkey liberalized its Kurdish policy during the 1989–1993 presidency of Turgut Özal, and again during the premiership of Recep Tayyip Erdo an (2002–present), the PKK accelerated its attacks, at least until Ankara responded with cross-border military strikes on safe havens. Hezbollah also demonstrates the tendency of terrorists to manufacture grievance once they fulfill initial goals. On May 24, 2000, Israel pulled its forces out of southern Lebanon, a withdrawal that the UN secretary-general subsequently certified complete. Israel's occupation of southern Lebanon was the reason for Hezbollah's birth in 1982, and yet rather than disband, Hezbollah asserted new claims to the Shebaa Farms and seven villages in Galilee in order to justify its continued existence.

The primary problem with soft solutions is that the ideologies that spark terrorism—whether Hezbollah's or al-Qaeda's Islamism or the Shining Path's Maoism—are so extreme that they allow no solution other than surrender or victory. Sometimes, there are simply no alternatives to military solutions. A

Vietnamese invasion, not a donors' conference, ended Pol Pot's reign of terror in Cambodia; a Tutsi invasion, not the United Nations, ended the Rwandan genocide. Terrorist groups often operate in such a world of extremes. In an October 22, 2002, speech at Haret Hreik, Hezbollah's secretary-general, Hassan Nasrallah, declared, "If they [Jews] all gather in Israel, it will save us the trouble of going after them worldwide."[43] When the solution to grievance is genocide, compromise is untenable. Bush recognized this after the September 11, 2001, attack on New York and Washington. Addressing a joint session of Congress on September 20, he declared, "The terrorists practice a fringe form of Islamic extremism. . . . The terrorists' directive commands them to kill Christians and Jews, to kill all Americans and make no distinctions among military and civilians, including women and children."[44]

Many scholars resist the idea that ideology or religion actually motivates terrorism. Robert Pape, a University of Chicago political scientist, challenged the idea in his 2005 book *Dying to Win: The Strategic Logic of Suicide Terrorism*, which asserts that pragmatic grievance—specifically resistance to occupation—motivates suicide bombers.[45] His assumption that all terrorism shares common core motivations is problematic. Indeed, his theory does not conform to radical Muslims' own statements of motivation voiced in martyrdom videos and last wills.[46]

Terrorist "successes"—the multinational peacekeepers' withdrawal from Beirut in 1983 after a series of devastating bomb attacks; the U.S. withdrawal from Somalia after the "Black Hawk down" incidents in 1993; Israel's withdrawal from Lebanon in 2000; and Israel's unilateral disengagement from Gaza in 2005—have only emboldened terrorist groups. A willingness to turn the other cheek and not respond militarily to terrorism does little to break cycles of violence. The U.S. refusal to respond militarily to an al-Qaeda attack on the USS *Cole* in 2000 did not prevent the group from striking again on 9/11. Only when countries show greater commitment to denying and defeating the terrorists can counterterrorism strategies succeed.

HARD POWER: RAISING THE COST

The key to an effective counterterrorism strategy is to raise the price of engaging in terrorism so that the costs to terrorists and their sponsors outweigh the benefits. Even if material resources are unlimited, conducting terrorist attacks is never a cost-free, risk-free process. Any terrorist attack—whether a rocket strike, improvised explosive device, or suicide bombing—leaves forensic evidence. Rocket trajectories can be calculated, electrical components tracked, and contacts of suicide bombers identified. By striking at terrorists and their sponsors militarily, states amplify the cost to any group or government seeking to achieve its aims through terrorism.

The experience of Israel offers an instructive case. Rather than accept Israel's independence, her neighbors pursued a policy of attrition and harassment, providing safe-haven to terrorists who would strike across the border. In the 1950s, Israeli prime minister David Ben-Gurion and chief of staff Moshe Dayan embraced a disproportionate military response to induce Israel's neighbors to restrain Palestinian terrorists in their territories. For example, an October 14, 1953, Israeli raid on the West Bank town of Qibiyah quieted the Jordanian front until March 1956. And although the Egyptian-controlled Gaza Strip was a hotbed of *fidayin* activity through the early 1950s, Israel's participation in the 1956 Sinai campaign stopped all terrorist attacks launched from Egypt and the Gaza Strip until 1967. Retaliation did not end terrorism, but it did raise the cost of sponsorship.

More recently, Israel's targeted strikes against Palestinian terrorists and the U.S. drone missile attacks on insurgents in Iraq, Taliban targets in Afghanistan and Pakistan, and al-Qaeda leaders in Yemen and East Africa offer a template for effective hard power counterterrorism strategies aimed at weakening terrorist organizations and denying them bases of operation from which to strike.

Targeted Killings

In the early 1970s, the Israeli military began to assassinate terrorists such as those who attacked Israel's Olympic team at Munich in 1972. Future prime minister Ehud Barak gained fame when, dressed as a woman, he led a hit squad to assassinate Arafat's deputy in the heart of Beirut. The April 1988 raid on Tunis that killed Khalil al-Wazir (Abu Jihad), the Palestine Liberation Organization's second-in-command, convinced Arafat that distance did not bring security. Diplomats might have wrung their hands over cycles of violence, but it was Israel's ability to make Palestinian leaders face a high personal cost for their decision to engage in terrorism that opened a window for diplomacy. Had the Israeli military not crushed the first intifada (1987–1993), it is doubtful that Arafat would have acceded to the Oslo peace process. The Palestinian leadership chose diplomacy only after the costs of terrorism became too great to bear.

With the peace process deadlocked, in September 2000 the Palestinian Authority launched the second intifada, seeking to gain through force what it could not gain at the negotiating table. In the months that followed, Palestinian terrorists launched hundreds of attacks on the Israeli public. The Israeli government responded by using helicopter gunships or even fighter bombers to assassinate terrorist leaders. The international community condemned the practice, but Jerusalem's policy was effective: terrorist attacks inside Israel declined by over 90 percent.

It is a fallacy that terrorist recruitment from an antagonized population negates the benefit of killing terrorist leaders. Striking at terrorist leaders undercuts a group's effectiveness. Because most terrorist groups organize in cells, killing organizers can disrupt both hierarchical and lateral communications. Repeated assassinations—often executed only after receiving information from informants—also spread paranoia among terrorist leaders, hampering their effectiveness. Time spent on their own security (for example, seeking the next safe house) is energy diverted from operations.[47]

As much as targeted assassinations erode terrorist capabilities, they also enhance counterterrorism in two ways: first, elimination of recruiters and trainers degrades effectiveness and, second, in their desire for revenge terrorists accelerate the dispatch of bombers. The result is easier detection. For example, after Israel commenced targeted assassinations, Israeli bus drivers and guards encountered terrorists who, lacking complete psychological preparation, exposed themselves by sweating profusely or fumbling with wiring, enabling denial of access to the target or their disarming.

Denial of Safe Havens

Although the debate over counterterrorism strategies can strike partisan rancor, there is a bipartisan consensus that denial of safe haven is central to effective counterterrorism. As the 9/11 Commission concluded, "Terrorists should no longer find safe-haven where their organizations can grow and flourish."[48] The question then becomes how best to deny safe haven, especially in failed states. In theory, diplomacy-centric foreign assistance and aid organizations can prevent states from descending into failure, but, in reality, the track record of foreign ministries and nongovernmental organizations is poor. Few have any strategy other than to cocoon themselves when confronting lawlessness. In 1994, as violence increased in Rwanda and genocide loomed, Kofi Annan, then head of UN peacekeeping, ordered his forces to stand down. Occupation is one solution, but military deployments, whether to Haiti or Somalia or East Timor, are expensive and cannot be undertaken without governments' willingness to sanction kinetic strategies to maintain force protection. For example, although the United Nations condemned the al-Qaeda–affiliated Islamic Courts Union attacks on the recognized government in Somalia, it was only the willingness of Ethiopia to deploy troops that forced the extremists to scatter. Targeted military strikes, however, enable states to deny safe haven to terrorists without costly deployments. Taliban officials in Pakistan acknowledged in 2009 that the only counterterrorism strategy they feared was drone attacks, because they negated the safe haven they enjoyed.[49]

Preventing the Proliferation and Use of WMDs by Terrorists

Al-Qaeda and other apocalyptic terrorist organizations have a clear desire and willingness to kill on a massive scale. On May 25, 2008, for example, Islamic extremists uploaded a video entitled "Nuclear Jihad: The Ultimate Terror" onto the al-Ekhlaas jihadist forum. The video declared, "Terror in their [Western] countries must involve human losses and these human losses must be with WMD's."

The 9/11 attacks convinced national security experts that they could no longer assume that terrorists' lack of advanced delivery systems offered protection from weapons of mass destruction (WMDs). If terrorist groups could use airplanes as missiles, then they could just as easily use hijacked container ships or airplanes as delivery systems for WMDs. A jihadist on the Ekhlaas video explained, "It's not that you put [some explosives] in the metro and kill a woman who is walking her dog at the end of the night, and say we killed two people. . . . You can, in any European village, make up a gas canister, and go and put it in a bomb or parachute or fire truck, and you go and blow it in a stadium that has 120,000 spectators, and get 70,000 dead. This is called terrorism."[50]

Proponents of soft power solutions argue that the fight against terrorism is more appropriately left to the police, but there is a huge difference between threats to kill two people and threats to wipe out tens of thousands. Chemical, biological, and nuclear weapons are military threats, not criminal justice concerns. Indeed, the Clinton administration underscored this conclusion when, on August 20, 1998, a U.S. cruise missile strike destroyed the Shifa factory in Khartoum, Sudan. Debate continues about whether the factory produced chemical weapons or pharmaceutical products. By ordering the strike, however, Clinton showed that the deciding factor should be military suspicion rather than criminal proof. Regardless of whether U.S. intelligence was accurate, the Sudanese government understood that there would be costs for even the appearance of involvement with terrorism and unconventional weapon development.

The recognition that the confluence of terrorism and technology had created a new paradigm infused the 2002 U.S. "National Security Strategy." "The gravest danger our Nation faces lies at the crossroad of radicalism and technology," President Bush wrote in his introduction to the document, explaining, "As a matter of common sense and self-defense, America will act against such emerging before they are fully formed."[51] It was this broader concept of preemption—not simply allegations of Iraqi ties to al-Qaeda—that motivated the White House to topple the Iraqi government when it would not cooperate with international inspections of its decades-old WMD programs.

Some critics fear that whatever the risks of WMDs falling into the wrong hands, accepting preemption undercuts international law and justifies interventions like the 2003 U.S.-led invasion of Iraq. This view is overly simplistic. UN Secretary General Ban Ki-moon, speaking to students at the 2009 commencement of the Johns Hopkins University School of Advanced International Studies, emphasized the importance of timing: "If we can intercede early to prevent conflict, we save lives and forestall the need for a vastly more expensive peacekeeping mission down the road," he explained, while also asserting the simultaneous need for diplomacy.[52] Waiting until threats develop magnifies the costs of intervention. It is best to intervene early against WMD threats, as Israel did against Iraq in 1981 and against Syria in 2007, than to wait for threats to grow.

ONLY HARD POWER CAN LAY THE FOUNDATION FOR EFFECTIVE SOFT POWER

Soft power strategies have utility, but they are ineffective absent hard power. Here, the case of Iraq is instructive. On January 11, 2007, President Bush announced that the United States would deploy additional military forces to Iraq. The "surge" occurred at the same time as the engagement with and empowerment of Sunni Arabs in al-Anbar, Iraq's insurgency-ridden western province. The subsequent decline in violence surpassed expectations. Because of the strategy's success, critics of the Bush administration argued that its earlier refusal to diplomatically engage Baathists and insurgents exacerbated violence. "If the compromises accepted later by the Bush administration had been accepted when a rapprochement was first broached by the Sunnis, in 2004, some 2,000 Americans and thousands more Iraqis might not have died," wrote David Rose, a British journalist.[53]

The problem with such a conclusion, however, is that it employs anachronism. Sunni attitudes did not remain constant over time. Rose ignores earlier engagement initiatives that undercut his thesis. After Sunni fighters ambushed four American contractors and mutilated their bodies on March 31, 2004, in Fallujah, a hotbed of insurgency, U.S. forces surrounded the city. Rather than seize the city and risk collateral damage, U.S. Marine general James Conway crafted a deal to lift the siege of Fallujah and empower the Fallujah Brigade, a unit of former Baathists and insurgents, to restore order. It backfired. Islamists interpreted the deal as a victory over the United States. Minaret-mounted loudspeakers lauded "victory over the Americans." The cost to innocent Iraqis of the outreach was devastating. Between April 6 and April 30, 2004, the period of siege, there were five bombings in Fallujah. In the twenty-four days after the creation of the Fallujah Brigade, there were more than thirty bombings, killing and wounding hundreds.

Gen. David Petraeus also preached reconciliation throughout his tenure in Iraq, during which he served as the commanding general of the multinational force. Eventually, he was successful, but not on his first tries. "The coalition must reconcile with a number of the thousands of former Ba'ath officials . . . giving them a direct stake in the success of the new Iraq," he declared on April 7, 2004.[54] While commanding the 101st Airborne in Mosul, Petraeus appointed senior Baathists to high positions in defiance of both the Iraqi government and the Coalition Provisional Authority. For example, he assigned Gen. Mahmud Muhammad al-Maris to lead Border Police units guarding the Syrian border, and he appointed another Baathist general, Muhammad Khairi Barhawi, as chief of police. Both used their positions to undermine security. Maris facilitated terrorist infiltration from Syria into Iraq, and only after Mosul erupted in insurgency in November 2004 did Petraeus learn that Barhawi had organized insurgent cells in the city. So why did the Sunnis accept reconciliation in 2007? Becoming the prime target of U.S. military force convinced them that the costs of armed struggle were too great to bear. Only after Iraqi Sunni leaders concluded that they would gain little through bombs and boycotts did they agree to participate in Iraq's political reconstruction. The willingness by the White House to deploy additional troops to Iraq despite significant opposition inside the United States convinced many holdouts that they simply could not outlast U.S. willpower.

Across the globe, from Peru to Sri Lanka, military force has succeeded where soft power has failed. Through the 1980s, the Shining Path, a Maoist group, waged a bloody campaign against the Peruvian government, killing between thirty and seventy thousand people. By 1991 the Shining Path controlled much of the countryside in central and southern Peru, and had begun to strike in the heart of Lima. Peru was on the brink. The tide turned only when President Alberto Fujimori launched a military response. On September 12, 1992, Peruvian police captured the Shining Path's leaders. Within weeks, the group collapsed.

In Colombia, too, military force succeeded where diplomacy could not. For forty-five years, Colombia has battled a FARC insurgency. Using both Mexican and Venezuelan intermediaries, the Colombian government sought negotiation, but to no avail. On November 7, 1998, President Andrés Pastrana granted FARC a 16,200-square-mile safe haven—an area larger than Switzerland—as a confidence-building measure. But instead of reducing the violence, the compromise encouraged FARC to ramp up pressure. It was only when President Álvaro Uribe abandoned diplomacy and resorted to military measures that Colombia not only contained the terrorist threat, but also created a cascade of momentum that unraveled decades of FARC gains. A March 1, 2008, raid into Ecuador killed a senior FARC commander and led to the capture of three laptops containing valuable intelligence that enabled further targeted operations. On July 2, 2008, Colombian soldiers raided a FARC camp, freeing fifteen hostages, including a former Colombian presidential candidate and three American contractors, some of whom had been held for six years. Simply put, military force succeeded where diplomacy and soft power failed.

Turkey is another example. The PKK insurgency cost thirty thousand deaths. Many European officials leaned on Turkey to improve human rights, implement reforms, and even tolerate the group's political proxies. No amount of reform, however, appeased the PKK, largely because it remained sheltered from the consequence of its actions by the safe haven provided by Syria. After Damascus ignored Ankara's diplomatic entreaties for two years, the Turkish military mobilized along the Syrian border in September 1998. Recognizing that the cost of continuing to provide safe haven to a terrorist leader would be greater than the geopolitical gain, the Syrian government expelled Öcalan.[55] He fled to Europe and then, with Greek government facilitation, to Kenya. His saga ended on February 15, 1999, when a crack Turkish unit seized him in Nairobi. Just as the Shining Path crumpled after the capture of its leadership, so too did the PKK insurgency collapse. Underscoring this point, the PKK staged a brief resurgence beginning in 2003, when the Kurdistan Regional Government in Iraq extended the PKK safe-haven as a diplomatic chit to play against Turkey. Over the next four years, Turkey unsuccessfully sought diplomatic remedy. Finally, after a series of attacks in the fall of 2007, the Turkish army crossed into northern Iraq. For Masud Barzani, president of Iraqi Kurdistan, the cost of terrorism sponsorship grew too high; he abandoned the PKK and the movement fizzled. Again, military action accomplished what diplomacy could not.

Sri Lanka underlines this conclusion. From 1976 to 2009, the Liberation Tigers of Tamil Eelam (LTTE), or Tamil Tigers, waged a bloody insurgency and terrorist campaign marked by suicide attacks, rape, impressments, bombings of buses and trains, and ethnic cleansing, altogether killing more than seventy thousand people. Throughout this period, the international community sought to mediate. Norwegian mediation failed after the LTTE broke its 2001 ceasefire to launch an offensive. The same pattern was repeated in 2005 and 2006. What diplomats hailed as chances for peace, the Tamil Tigers saw as tactical pauses to regroup and resupply. In 2008 the Sri Lankan government ordered its military to advance. Amid hand-wringing and condemnation by both UN agencies and the U.S. government, the Sri Lankan army pushed its offensive forward, routing the LTTE and eliminating its leadership. In May 2009, brute military force ended a thirty-three-year civil war. Had the Sri Lankan government listened to UN officials, European diplomats, or the White House, thousands more civilians might have perished as the LTTE pursued its terrorist campaign. President Obama even sought to withhold $1.9 billion in International Monetary Fund assistance unless the Sri Lankan government accepted a cease-fire that would have only allowed the Tamil Tigers to live to fight another day. Ironically, Joseph Nye had cited Sri Lanka as a test case for soft power.[56] Reconstruction and reconciliation are important, but they do not ameliorate conflict; they are effective only after its conclusion.

Military strategies need not be violent. The value of military force is that its demonstration—and the adversary's belief that the threat is credible—is often enough to coerce a change of behavior. Many proponents of diplomacy like to cite Libyan leader Qadhafi's decision to abandon terrorism and his weapons of mass destruction program as an example of soft power's efficacy. Efforts to coerce Libya spanned several U.S. administrations. On December 20, 2003, the *Washington Post* ran the headline "Two Decades of Sanctions, Isolation Wore Down Gaddafi." To credit diplomacy for Tripoli's agreement, however, is a stretch. As columnist Charles Krauthammer observed,

> Yeah, sure. After 18 years of American sanctions, Gaddafi randomly picks Dec. 19, 2003, as the day for his surrender. By amazing coincidence, Gaddafi's first message to Britain—principal U.S. war ally and conduit to White House war councils—occurs just days before the invasion of Iraq. And his final capitulation to U.S.-British terms occurs just five days after Saddam is fished out of a rat hole.[57]

CONCLUSION

Despite the high-minded rhetoric of the United Nations and other international bodies, coercion—the threat of force and, if necessary, its use—remain a critical element of counterterrorism. It may be comforting to believe that diplomacy with state sponsors of terrorism and with terrorist groups themselves can alone alter their behavior, but such wishful thinking is dangerous. The United States has learned this lesson. In 1997 the Clinton administration engaged the Taliban. The militant group "indicated a willingness to negotiate with the opposition and agreed on the need for a broad-based government. . . . They repeated their pledge to prevent terrorists from using Afghanistan to launch attacks on others."[58] Even though hindsight is 20/20, the Taliban's insincerity was always clear. Had the Clinton administration preempted the terrorist threat rather than pursued charade engagement, perhaps al-Qaeda would not have enjoyed a safe haven to plot its attacks. Symbolism—onetime missile strikes against empty camps in the wake of the East Africa embassy bombings—is not enough to defeat terrorists or ensure security.

So how then should counterterrorism strategies be crafted? U.S. military academies teach the DIME paradigm: every strategy should have diplomatic, informational, military, and economic components. Recognizing the necessity to confront terrorists with military force does not mean dispensing with diplomacy. Diplomacy is important because transnational terrorists respect no boundaries. It is always preferable to win the other country's cooperation through diplomacy, thereby minimizing cost. But as Colombia learned about Ecuador, Turkey about Syria, and the United States about al-Qaeda, diplomacy itself should not be an excuse to inaction. And as the Libya example shows, sometimes it is the willingness to use military force rather than simply engage that enables diplomacy to succeed.

A military-based strategy also does not mean eschewing aid and development. Both the 2002 "National Security Strategy" and the 2003 and 2006 "National Strategy for Combating Terrorism" recognized the importance of combining force with development. It was in this context, for example, that Bush formulated the Millennium Challenge Account. But even though aid and development have a role, absent security they are counterproductive. As the United Nations discovered in Somalia, dispatching aid to insecure zones bolsters warlordism, not rule of law. It is all well and good that the German army builds schools in Afghanistan. But that it flees when fired upon helps no one.

Police investigate crimes; militaries preempt and neutralize threats. As technology advances and access to it increases, terrorism becomes a more deadly phenomenon. Police pursuit might have contained the Weather Underground, the Baader-Meinhof Gang, or Red Army Faction, but transitional terrorists enjoying safe haven and sophisticated military munitions pose a far deadlier threat, one that only a robust strategy centered on military force can counter.

Notes

1. David Kilcullen and Andrew McDonald Exum, "Death from Above, Outrage Down Below," *New York Times,* May 17, 2009.
2. For an excellent overview of the basic instruments of counterterrorism policy—diplomacy, criminal justice, military force, intelligence, and financial controls—see Paul R. Pillar, *Terrorism and U.S. Foreign Policy* (Washington, D.C.: Brookings, 2003), chap. 4.

3. See, for example, White House, "National Strategy for Combating Terrorism," September 2006, http://georgewbush-whitehouse.archives.gov/nsc/nsct/2006.

4. For years the Afghanistan war was widely hailed as a success story in the fight against terrorism, even though neither the Taliban nor al-Qaeda was mortally wounded. As the United States shifted its interest and military assets from Afghanistan to Iraq, Taliban and al-Qaeda forces were able to regroup in their hiding places across the border with Pakistan and to mastermind violent attacks in Afghanistan and elsewhere.

5. For excellent overviews and examples of "hard" and "soft" counterterrorism strategies, see Pillar, *Terrorism and U.S. Foreign Policy*; and Audrey Kurth Cronin and James M. Ludes, eds., *Attacking Terrorism* (Washington, D.C.: Georgetown University Press, 2004). For a classic discussion of "soft power" in international relations, see Joseph S. Nye Jr., *Soft Power: The Means to Success in World Politics* (New York: Public Affairs, 1994).

6. U.S. Department of Defense, *National Defense Strategy* (Washington, D.C.: DOD, June 2008).

7. According to the *2007 Report on Terrorism* (Washington, D.C.: National Counterterrorism Center, June 2008).

8. As the *Washington Post* reported before the release of Bob Woodward's most recent book, *The War Within: A Secret White House History, 2006–2008*, the surge "was not the primary factor behind the steep drop in violence" in Iraq. Woodward mentions intelligence and military officials' "new covert techniques" that helped to locate and target leading terrorists and insurgents, besides the "Anbar Awakening" and the restraint of the Mahdi Army. See Steve Luxenberg, "U.S. Spied on Iraqi Leaders, Book Says," *Washington Post*, September 5, 2008. In his response, National Security Adviser Stephen Hadley insisted that the troop surge of 2007 was the decisive factor that made the other improvements possible. For the Hadley statement, see http://georgewbush-whitehouse.archives.gov/.

9. Pillar, *Terrorism and U.S. Foreign Policy*, 167. For an in-depth account of the role of diplomacy versus force in America's relations with Libya over twenty-five years, see Bruce Jentleson and Christopher Whytock, "Who 'Won' Libya? The Force-Diplomacy Debate and Its Implications for Theory and Policy," *International Security* 30 (Winter 2005/2006): 47–86.

10. Helene Cooper, "U.S. Declares North Korea Off Terror List," *New York Times*, October 23, 2008.

11. Roger Runningen and Mark Drajem, "Talks on North Korea's Nuclear Program to Be Held," Bloomberg, November 23, 2008, www.bloomberg.com/apps/news?pid=20601089&sid=aAu80wL_lvCw.

12. I was among those who did not applaud Bill Clinton's humanitarian mission to Pyongyang because the former president's visit offered North Korea's leadership the opportunity for a major propaganda coup. It had rejected a less prominent special envoy's visit and insisted on the former president to meet with Kim and others. For more on this, see my post at www.reflectivepundit.com/reflectivepundit/2009/08/bill-clinton-and-the-freed.

13. Saudi Arabia, too, pressured Sudan's government to stop supporting bin Laden. For more on this, see Simon Reeve, *The New Jackals* (Boston: Northeastern University Press, 1999), chap. 9.

14. The U.S. Department of State's "Country Reports on Terrorism" for 2007 is available at www.state.gov/s/ct/rls/crt/2007/index.htm.
15. The transcript of President George W. Bush's speech on 15 May 15, 2008, is available at http://georgewbush-whitehouse.archives.gov.
16. Howard LaFranchi, "Rice's Visit to a Changed Libya," *Christian Science Monitor*, September 4, 2008.
17. Richard Holbrooke, "The Next President: Mastering a Daunting Agenda," *Foreign Affairs* 87 (September/October 2008): 18.
18. Timothy Hoyt, "Military Force," in Cronin and Ludes, *Attacking Terrorism*, 173.
19. Barry R. Posen, "The Struggle against Terrorism: Grand Strategy, Strategy, and Tactics," *International Security* 26 (Winter 2001/2002): 47.
20. Carlotta Gall, "Evidence Points to Civilian Toll in Afghan Raid," *New York Times*, September 9, 2008.
21. Lindsay Clutterbuck, "Law Enforcement," in Cronin and Ludes, *Attacking Terrorism*, 141.
22. Seth Jones and Martin Libicki, *How Terrorist Groups End: Lessons for Countering al Qa'ida* (Santa Monica, Calif.: RAND, 2008), chap. 2.
23. Ibid., 36.
24. Peter Neumann, "Negotiating with Terrorists," *Foreign Affairs* 86 (January/February 2007): 136.
25. Louise Richardson, *What Terrorists Want* (New York: Random House, 2006), 214.
26. U.S. Department of Defense, *National Defense Strategy*, 8.
27. For public diplomacy in the information age, see Geoffrey Cohen and Amelia Arsenault, "Moving from Monologue to Dialogue to Collaboration: The Three Layers of Public Diplomacy," in "Public Diplomacy in a Changing World," ed. Geoffrey Cohen and Nicholas J. Cull, *The Annals* 616 (March 2008): 46–52.
28. Dafna Linzer, "Lost in Translation: Alhurra—America's Troubled Effort to Win Middle East Hearts and Minds," *ProPublica*, June 22, 2008.
29. Ibid.
30. The remarks were made during the Landon Lecture at Kansas State University, November 26, 2007, www.defenselink.mil/speeches/speech.aspx?speechid=1199.
31. For survey summaries and news accounts about them, see Terror Free Tomorrow's Web site, www.terrorfreetomorrow.org.
32. Kenneth Ballen, "Even al Qaeda Supporters Can Be Won Over," *Los Angeles Times*, June 14, 2008.
33. Barack Obama, "Remarks by the President on National Security," delivered at the National Archives, Washington, D.C., May 21, 2009.
34. Stephen Sloan, "Terrorism and Asymmetry," in *Challenging the United States Symmetrically and Asymmetrically*, ed. Col. Lloyd Matthews (Carlisle Barracks, Pa.: U.S. Army War College, Strategic Studies Institute, 1998), 176.
35. Matthew Levitt. *Hamas: Politics, Charity, and Terrorism in the Service of Jihad.* (New Haven, Conn.: Yale University Press, 2006), 55; Andrew Garfield, "Winning the War of Ideas: Cultural Understanding, and Influence Operations," Lecture at I Corps headquarters, Ft. Lewis, Wash., April 29, 2008.
36. Joseph S. Nye Jr. "The Decline of America's Soft Power," *Foreign Affairs* 83 (May/June 2004): 16–20.
37. U.S. Department of Defense, "Quadrennial Defense Review," February 3, 2006, 22.

38. "Pakistan Giving Up to Militants: Hillary," *Dawn.com* (Karachi), April 23, 2009.

39. Steven Stotsky, "Does Foreign Aid Fuel Palestinian Violence?" *Middle East Quarterly* 15 (Summer 2008): 23–30.

40. U.S. Government Accountability Office, "Foreign Assistance: Measures to Prevent Inadvertent Payments to Terrorists under Palestinian Aid Programs Have Been Strengthened, but Some Weaknesses Remain," GAO-09-622, May 2009, 15–19.

41. *The Tower Commission Report* (New York: Bantam, 1987), 47–48.

42. Quoted in Bernard Gwertzman, "Why President Ended Silence on Iran Policy," *New York Times*, November 14, 1986.

43. *Daily Star* (Beirut), October 23, 2002.

44. White House, "President George W. Bush's Address to a Joint Session of Congress Concerning the Sept. 11, 2001 Terrorist Attacks on America," September 20, 2001.

45. Robert Pape, *Dying to Win: The Strategic Logic of Suicide Terrorism* (New York: Random House, 2006.)

46. Jonathan Fine, "Contrasting Secular and Religious Terrorism," *Middle East Quarterly* 15 (Winter 2008): 59–69.

47. Gal Luft, "The Logic of Israel's Targeted Killing," *Middle East Quarterly* 10 (Winter 2003).

48. National Commission on Terrorist Attacks Upon the United States, *The 9/11 Commission Report*, July 22, 2004, 364, www.gpoaccess.gov/911/Index.html.

49. Jane Perlez and Pir Zubair Shah, "Porous Pakistani Border Could Hinder U.S.," *New York Times*, May 4, 2009.

50. Transcript provided by SITE Intelligence Group, no. 2008052701, May 27, 2008.

51. George W. Bush, Introductory Letter, in White House, "The National Security Strategy of the United States of America," September 2002, http://georgewbush-whitehouse.archives.gov/nsc.

52. Ban Ki-Moon, "Global Leadership in a Time of Crisis," Commencement Address at the Paul H. Nitze School of Advanced International Studies, Washington, D.C., May 21, 2009.

53. David Rose, "Heads in the Sand," *Vanity Fair*, May 12, 2009.

54. Gen. David Petraeus, "Lessons of the Iraq War and Its Aftermath," Washington Institute for Near East Policy, April 9, 2004.

55. Ely Karmon, "A Solution to Syrian Terrorism," *Middle East Quarterly* 6 (June 1999).

56. "Joseph Nye on Smart Power," John F. Kennedy School of Government, Web site interview, July 3, 2008.

57. Charles Krauthammer. "Aftershocks of War," *Washington Post*, December 26, 2003.

58. "Afghanistan: Meeting with the Taliban," State Department cable no. 231842, December 8, 1997. Republished in the National Security Archives Web site, www.gwu.edu/~nsarchiv/NSAEBB/NSSAEBB97/index.htm#doc24.

8

can spreading democracy help defeat terrorism?

NO: Democracy promotion is problematic as a counterterrorism priority
F. Gregory Gause III, *University of Vermont*

YES: Promoting democracy can combat terrorism
Jennifer L. Windsor, *Freedom House*

In the early morning of January 26, 2006, Secretary of State Condoleezza Rice was enjoying her regular workout on an elliptical trainer while watching the morning news on television. Suddenly, the news crawl at the bottom of the screen reported something that caused her to halt her workout: "In wake of Hamas victory, Palestinian cabinet resigns." As the *New York Times* reported on the episode:

> "I thought, 'Well, that's not right,'" Ms. Rice recalled. When the crawl continued, she got off the elliptical trainer and called the State Department.
> "I said, 'What happened in the Palestinian elections?'" Ms. Rice recalled. "And they said, 'Oh, Hamas won.' And I thought, 'Oh my goodness, Hamas won?'"[1]

The 2006 Palestinian elections had been heralded by the Bush administration as a symbol of the stirrings of democracy in the Middle East, and as a way to counteract extremist groups like Hamas that engage in terrorism. Instead, the Hamas landslide victory over Mahmoud Abbas's moderate Fatah party became an important illustration of the frustrating complexity encountered in trying to combat extremism and terrorism through the spread of democracy.

Indeed, the promotion of democracy as a means of addressing the important root causes of terrorism in the Arab and Muslim world—corrupt autocratic regimes and disenfranchised, disaffected populations that fuel the popularity of radical religious groups—was a vital part of the Bush administration's post-9/11 national security and counterterrorism strategies. The 2002 and 2006 versions of the "National Security Strategy" and 2006 "National Strategy for Combating Terrorism" each promoted the spread of freedom and democracy as a "long-term antidote to the ideology of terrorism."[2]

Yet as the wars in Afghanistan and Iraq have shown, fashioning democracies through direct military intervention and occupation is rife with cost and controversy, leaving the final outcomes, at best, uncertain (although, in fairness, the primary justification for these wars was not the creation of democracy).

And as revealed by the 2006 Palestinian election, and other recent elections in Lebanon, Saudi Arabia, Egypt, Yemen, and elsewhere, Islamist parties— some with ties to active terrorist groups—often fare very well. Should Egypt or Saudi Arabia permit truly free and fair elections, the results would likely be Islamist, and extremely anti-American, governments.

So, although the idea of transforming countries that breed terrorism into democracies may be attractive in theory, in practice it remains a very uncertain long-term proposition.

But perhaps that is the point. Perhaps it is the very *process* of opening up political systems in the Arab and Muslim world—with all of the uncertainty this often entails—that will eventually lay a path for stable, legitimate political structures that can marginalize radical groups. There are certainly examples of former terrorist organizations becoming moderated by inclusion in open political processes—including the Irish Republican Army in Northern Ireland and the African National Congress in South Africa. And there are examples of radical Islamist parties faring very poorly in elections in Muslim countries, including Jordan and Indonesia.

As the Obama administration rethinks America's policy toward the Middle East, a debate has reemerged over the utility of democracy promotion as a tool of counterterrorism. How much of the Bush administration's "freedom agenda" should be scrapped, and how much, if any, should be saved? Should other democracy promotion initiatives toward the Middle East be developed?

Gregory Gause argues that promoting democracy in the Arab world is counterproductive, and that such efforts should be dropped. He claims that democratic governments have not been shown to reduce or eliminate terrorism. Moreover, groups such as al-Qaeda have declared democracy promotion a new tool of Western imperialism, and they use such outside meddling to draft new recruits. Gause contends that even if free elections were permitted across the Arab world, the types of governments they would produce would likely be more anti-American than they are now. If the United States cannot cease all pro-democracy efforts, then at a minimum, he suggests, it should shift its emphasis away from elections that will simply bring Islamists to power and toward encouraging the development of secular political organizations.

Jennifer Windsor agrees that democracy is not a panacea for social unrest and possible terrorist activities. But, she argues, democratic governments are far more responsive to their citizens and far more capable of ameliorating conditions that breed violence than autocracies. In the Arab and Muslim world, she believes democratization can address conditions that facilitate radical Islamist movements: governments that support human rights and the rule of law, and encourage political participation, will drain the recruitment pool for groups like al-Qaeda. Although Americans may not celebrate the outcome of every election, Windsor says holding regular, lawful elections offers a slow but sure way to ease the development of moderate political and social institutions. She concludes that supporting elections, along with encouraging progress in government accountability and respect for individual rights, are initiatives the United States should maintain and bolster in its policies toward the Middle East.

Debates over the relationship between democracy and global peace and security have been around since at least the days of Immanuel Kant. The role of democracy in addressing terrorism is a much more recent policy paradigm. As the authors of the essays in this chapter make clear, the stakes in this ongoing debate are high—not only for U.S. counterterrorism policy, but also for citizens of the Arab and Muslim world.

NO: Democracy promotion is problematic as a counterterrorism priority
F. Gregory Gause III, *University of Vermont*

Democracy, Terrorism, and American Policy in the Arab World

Much has changed since the heady days of 2003 and 2004, after the fall of Saddam Hussein's regime and of the notion that the United States could remake the Middle East.[3] The Bush administration's and its supporters' initial enthusiasm for democratic change in the region as a central element of "draining the swamp" that produced the terrorism of September 11, 2001, has been tempered by the realities of Islamist victories at Arab polls. Still, the American debate about the Middle East remains characterized by the belief that democratic reform will ameliorate the root causes of terrorism. Because it was not just President George W. Bush who held these ideas, it is useful to consider both the theoretical argument about the relationship between democracy and terrorism more generally and the effects of real democratic reform in the Arab world for American interests there.

Two questions present themselves in this context. First, is there a relationship between terrorism and democracy such that the more democratic a country becomes, the less likely it is to produce terrorists and terrorist groups? In other words, is the security rationale for democracy promotion in the Arab world based on a sound premise? Second, what kind of governments would likely be generated by democratic elections in Arab countries? Would they be willing to cooperate with the United States on important policy objectives in the Middle East, not only in curbing terrorism but also on Arab-Israeli, Gulf security, and oil issues?

Unfortunately, the answer to the first of these questions appears to be "No." Although the state of scholars' knowledge about terrorism is admittedly incomplete, and thus subject to revision as more research is done, the data available now do not show a strong relationship in general between democracy and an absence of or reduction in terrorism. It seems that terrorism stems from much more specific political and social factors than from regime type. When it comes to the current opponents of the United States in the global struggle against terrorism, it is even clearer that democratization would not end their campaign against the United States. Al-Qaeda and like-minded groups are, of course, not fighting for democracy in the Muslim world; in fact, they have declared the promotion of democracy a new tool of Western imperialism. Instead, they are fighting to impose their notions of an Islamic state. They oppose democracy on both doctrinal and practical grounds. Democratic change in Arab countries will not change their course. Whether such change would reduce the number of potential recruits to al-Qaeda and similar organizations is a matter of speculation. But, if the Arab democracies that the United States wants to encourage pursue foreign policies amenable to Washington—if they cooperate with American military operations, host American military forces, make peace with Israel, and generally follow the American foreign policy line—then there would be ample incentives for anti-American terrorist organizations to continue to be able to recruit followers in Arab societies.

On the second question, scholars have a good idea of what kinds of governments would be produced in the first elections in real Arab democracies. Based on Arab public opinion surveys and recent elections in the Arab world, democratic elections are likely to produce Islamist governments that would be much less likely to cooperate with the United States than their authoritarian predecessors on a whole range of issues, including the global struggle against terrorism.

The answers to these two questions should lead to a rethinking of the American strategy of promoting democracy in the Arab world. My preference would be to drop these efforts altogether, both on the principled grounds that the United States should not be interfering in the domestic affairs of other countries and out of the prudential concern that U.S. meddling in the domestic affairs of others usually turns out very differently than intended. Washington cannot micromanage political change in countries that it only imperfectly understands. If the United States must promote democracy in the Middle East, it should shift its emphasis away from elections and toward encouraging the development of secular, nationalist, and liberal political organizations that can compete on an equal footing with Islamist parties.

TERRORISM AND DEMOCRACY

President Bush was absolutely clear about why the promotion of democracy in the Muslim world generally and the Arab world more specifically is not only consistent with American values, but also central to American interests. He laid out that logic in an address in March 2005 at the National Defense University:

> Our strategy to keep the peace in the longer term is to help change the conditions that give rise to extremism and terror, especially in the broader

Middle East. Parts of that region have been caught for generations in the cycle of tyranny and despair and radicalism. When a dictatorship controls the political life of a country, responsible opposition cannot develop and dissent is driven underground and toward the extreme. And to draw attention away from their social and economic failures, dictators place blame on other countries and other races and stir the hatred that leads to violence. This status quo of despotism and anger cannot be ignored or appeased, kept in a box or bought off.[4]

President Bush's analysis of the link between the lack of democracy in the Arab world and terrorism is shared across the political spectrum in the United States. In 2004 the Democratic presidential candidate, John Kerry, also highlighted the need for greater political reform in the Middle East as an integral part of the war on terrorism.[5] *New York Times* columnist Thomas Friedman, one of America's leading commentators on foreign affairs, has done more to propound this logic to the attentive American public than anyone else.[6] In a prominent mea culpa published in 2002, Martin Indyk, a senior Middle East policymaker in the Clinton administration, said that the strategy President Bill Clinton pursued of focusing on Arab-Israeli peace while downplaying democracy in the region was a mistake and urged a new American policy focused on political reform. Morton Halperin, the director of policy planning in the Clinton State Department, was the lead author of a 2004 book that argued that the roots of al-Qaeda are in the poverty and educational deficiencies of Saudi Arabia, Egypt, and Pakistan. These deficiencies arose from the authoritarian nature of those states and can be overcome only by their democratization.[7] The argument underlying the Bush administration's emphasis on political reform in the Middle East as a necessary part of the struggle against terrorism is widely accepted in Washington, and it has not disappeared since Bush and the neoconservatives left office.

Terrorism and Democracy: The Empirical Evidence

The academic literature on the relationship between terrorism and other sociopolitical indicators such as democracy is surprisingly scant. Very good case studies of terrorists and terrorist organizations and overall surveys of the phenomenon are available, but little that tries to answer the question posed earlier: does democracy lead to less terrorism? Analysts are hamstrung, in particular, by the quality of the data available. There is a bias in the data toward international terrorist incidents—attacks that have a cross-border element and tend to be reported more completely in the Western press—and away from home-grown terrorist attacks in developing countries that might not make it into the *New York Times*. The most widely used datasets tend to identify the location of a terrorist incident, but they are not as reliable or complete in identifying the perpetrator. If an attack occurs in a democracy but is perpetrated by people from a nondemocratic country or countries, as were the 9/11 attacks, analysts would want to know more about the countries of origin of the attackers than about the target country to test whether nondemocratic political systems are more likely to produce terrorists than democratic political systems.

Because of these data constraints, only preliminary conclusions from the academic literature are possible. However, those conclusions call into question the close link between terrorism and lack of democracy that underpinned the Bush administration's justification of the democracy initiative in the Arab world. In their widely cited study of terrorist events in the 1980s, William Eubank and Leonard Weinberg found that during that period the most common type of terrorist incident was one that occurred in a democracy, and both the victims and perpetrators were citizens of democracies.[8] In a more recent look at the same dataset for the period 1975 and 1997, Quan Li found that although higher levels of democratic political participation correlate negatively with terrorist attacks, the kind of restraints on executive power associated with liberal democracy seem to encourage terrorist actions.[9] In *Dying to Win: The Strategic Logic of Suicide Terrorism*, Robert Pape finds that democracies are almost always the targets of suicide bombers, but that the motivations of the groups behind those bombings is to fight against military occupation and for self-determination. It is not the lack of democracy that drives suicide terrorism, but opposition to what is seen as foreign domination.[10]

A quick look at the numbers published by the American government also does not appear to bear out a close link between terrorism and the lack of democracy. Between 2000 and 2003, based on the State Department's annual *Patterns of Global Terrorism*, 269 major international terrorist incidents occurred in countries classified as "Free" in Freedom House's *Freedom in the World* annual report; 119 occurred in countries classified as "Partly Free;" and 138 occurred in countries classified as "Not Free."[11] This is not to argue that free countries are more likely to produce terrorists than other countries. Rather, it seems that terrorist incidents are distributed somewhat proportionately according to the number of people governed by countries in the three categories, or perhaps even randomly, indicating no necessary relationship between terrorism and the degree of freedom enjoyed by citizens. These numbers certainly do not indicate that democracies are substantially less susceptible to terrorism than other forms of government.

But, of course, terrorism is not distributed randomly. Only a few countries account for the vast majority of terrorist incidents, according to the official U.S. government data. Terrorist incidents in India account for fully 75 percent of all terrorist incidents in free countries (as defined by Freedom House) in the four years surveyed. It is fair to assume that some of those terrorist incidents, particularly in Kashmir, are perpetrated by groups based in Pakistan, though clearly not all of the terrorist attacks in India are foreign in origin. A significant number of the terrorist incidents in the country are far from Kashmir, reflecting other local grievances against the central government. A vibrant democracy with the full range of political rights available to its citizens, India has rightly been held up as an example of the possibility of democracy outside the context of wealthy Western countries. And yet as strong as Indian democracy is, one Indian prime minister was assassinated (Indira Gandhi, by a Sikh extremist) and a former prime minister campaigning to regain the office was assassinated (her son, Rajiv Gandhi, by Tamil extremists). If democracy reduces the prospects for terrorism, India's numbers should not be so high. It is also interesting to note that in 2003 two countries classified as "Not Free" by Freedom House accounted for 50 percent of the international terrorist incidents reported in *Patterns of Global Terrorism* in "Not Free" countries—Iraq and Afghanistan. At least for that year, movement toward democracy did not lessen the incentives for terrorists to operate in those countries; indeed, Iraq witnessed a tremendous spike in terrorist incidents over the next four years even as real democratization accelerated.

The comparison between India, the world's most populous democracy, and China, the world's most populous authoritarian state, highlights the difficulty in assuming that democracy can solve the terrorism problem. The *Patterns of Global Terrorism* data for 2000–2003 report 203 international terrorist incidents in India and none in China. A more comprehensive list of terrorist incidents between 1976 and 2004 compiled by National Memorial Institute for the Prevention of Terrorism in its Terrorism Knowledge Base contains over four hundred incidents in India and only eighteen in China.[12] If the relationship between authoritarianism and terrorism were as strong as the Bush administration implied, the discrepancy in terrorist incidents between China and India would run the other way.

More anecdotal evidence also calls into question a necessary relationship between regime type, particularly democracy, and terrorism. In the 1970s and 1980s, democratic countries generated some brutal terrorist organizations: the Red Brigades in Italy, the Provisional Irish Republic Army in Ireland and the United Kingdom, the Japanese Red Army, and the Red Army Faction (Baader-Meinhof Group) in West Germany. The transition to democracy in Spain did not eliminate the terrorism perpetrated by the Basque Fatherland and Liberty (ETA). Turkish democracy suffered through a decade of mounting political violence from the late 1960s through the late 1970s. The strong and admirable democratic system in Israel has been the subject of terrorist assault, but it also has produced its own terrorists, including the assassin of Prime Minister Yitzhak Rabin. And then there is the memorial in Oklahoma City testifying to the fact that U.S. democracy has not been free of domestic terrorism.

All in all, there is no solid empirical evidence of a strong link between democracy, or any other regime type, and terrorism, in either a positive or a negative direction. In the first edition of Bruce Hoffman's widely quoted survey of the phenomenon, *Inside Terrorism*, published in 1998, the word *democracy* does not even appear in the index.[13] Jessica Stern, in her highly praised post-9/11 study of religious militants, *Terror in the Name of God,* argues that "democratization is not necessarily the best way to fight Islamic extremism," because that transition to democracy "has been found to be an especially vulnerable period for states across the board."[14] Terrorism springs from sources other than form of government. There is, therefore, no reason, based on this evidence, to believe that a more democratic Arab world will, simply by virtue of being more democratic, generate fewer terrorists.

Terrorism and Democracy: Logic, Theory, and al-Qaeda

Logical and theoretical problems, as well as these empirical problems, surround the argument bolstering the American push for democracy as part of the struggle against terrorism. The logic underlying the assertion that democracy will reduce terrorism is the belief that, if able to participate openly in competitive politics and have their voices heard in the public square, potential terrorists and terrorist sympathizers will not feel the need to resort to violence to achieve their goals. Even if they lose in one round, the confidence that they will be able to win in the future will inhibit the temptation to use extrademocratic means. To put it another way, the habits of democracy will ameliorate extremism.

Well, maybe. But it is just as logical to assume that terrorists, who rarely represent political agendas that could mobilize electoral majorities, would reject the very principles of majority rule and minority rights on which liberal democracy is based. If they cannot achieve their goals through democratic politics, why should it be assumed that they will privilege the democratic process over those goals? It seems more likely that, having been mobilized into politics by a burning desire to achieve a goal, a desire so strong that they are willing to take up arms and kill and maim defenseless civilians, terrorists and potential terrorists will attack democracy and its processes if those processes do not produce the desired result. Respect for American democracy did not stop southern slaveholders and their supporters from taking up arms in 1861. Respect for the nascent Iraqi democracy, despite very successful elections in January and December 2005, has not stopped Iraqi and foreign terrorists from their campaign against the new political order in that country. If the goal is important enough, it will trump democracy for some militants, who, in turn, might become terrorists.

Another factor is that the primary terrorist organizations that threaten the United States are not mass-based; they are small and secretive. And they are not organized or based on democratic principles; they revolve around strong leaders and a cluster of committed followers, willing to take actions from which the vast majority of people, even people who might support their political agendas, would rightly shrink. It seems unlikely that simply being outvoted would deflect them from their path.

America's major foe in the struggle against terrorism, al-Qaeda, certainly would not close up shop if every Muslim country in the world were to become a democracy. Osama bin Laden has been very clear about democracy—he does not like it. His political model is not democratic; it is the early years of the Muslim Caliphate. The Taliban regime in Afghanistan was the closest in modern times to that model in bin Laden's view. In an October 2003 "message to Iraqis," bin Laden castigated those in the Arab world who are "calling for a peaceful democratic solution in dealing with apostate governments or with Jewish and crusader invaders instead of fighting in the name of God." He referred to democracy as "this deviant and misleading practice," and "the faith of the ignorant."[15] His view of American democracy is equally negative: "The majority of you [Americans] are vulgar and without sound ethics or good manners. You elect the evil from among you, the greatest liars and the least decent."[16] Bin Laden's ally in Iraq, Abu Musab al-Zarqawi, was even more direct in his reaction to the Iraqi election of January 2005: "The legislator who must be obeyed in a democracy is man, and not God. . . . That is the very essence of heresy and polytheism and error, as it contradicts the bases of the faith and monotheism, and because it makes the weak, ignorant man God's partner in His most central divine prerogative—namely, ruling and legislating."[17]

Al-Qaeda is not fighting for democracy. Its leaders profoundly distrust democracy, and not just on ideological grounds. There is absolutely no reason to believe that a move toward more democratic Arab states would deflect them from their course. There is also no reason to believe that they would not be able to recruit followers in more democratic Arab states, as long as those more democratic Arab states continued to have good relations with the United States, made peace with Israel, and generally behaved in ways that Washington hopes that they will. It is the American agenda in the Middle East, as much if not more than democracy itself, to which al-Qaeda objects. Even though Washington hopes that a democratic Middle East will be a Middle East that continues to accept a major American role and cooperates with American goals, it is simply foolish to think that democracy will dry up support for al-Qaeda, as will be demonstrated in the next section.

When it works, liberal democracy is the best form of government. It affirms the dignity of each person in the right to vote. It provides the check of popular elections on those in power, along with other constitutional and legal barriers to the abuse of power. It provides for an independent judiciary to guarantee those rights and curb the abuses that inevitably come with great power. There is much to recommend it. But there is no evidence that it reduces terrorism or prevents terrorism. Regrettably, it seems that regime type has no relationship to the development or prevalence of terrorism. There is strong evidence that the current opponents in the struggle against terrorism will not be placated by democracy in their home countries. Thus a fundamental assumption of the push for democracy in the Arab world as part of this struggle is seriously flawed.

ARAB DEMOCRACY: WHAT TO EXPECT

Would democratically elected Arab governments be as cooperative with the United States as the current authoritarian incumbents? That is highly unlikely. To the extent that public opinion can be measured in these countries, the polls reveal that Arabs are very supportive of democracy. When they have a chance to vote in real elections, they generally turn out in percentages far greater than Americans. However, today the United States remains distinctly unpopular in the Arab world. If Arab governments were to reflect more accurately their public opinion, they would be more anti-American. Moreover, in recent free elections in the Arab world the Islamists have done very well. Moves toward Arab democracy will, at least for the foreseeable future, most likely generate Islamist governments that will be less likely to cooperate with the United States on important American policy goals, including American basing rights in the region, peace with Israel, and the campaign against terrorism.

Arab Public Opinion: Yes to Democracy, No to the United States

Arabs in general do not have any problem with democracy, though some Islamist ideologues do. The Pew Global Attitudes Project conducted public opinion surveys in several Arab countries in 2003, asking whether "democracy is a Western way of doing things that would not work here" or whether "democracy would work" in that country. In Kuwait, 83 percent said democracy would work there, and only 16 percent thought it would not. In Jordan, 68 percent said democracy would work there; 25 percent disagreed. In the Palestinian Authority, 53 percent thought democracy would work there, but 38 percent disagreed.[18] In a 2002 poll by Zogby International, majorities of those polled in five Arab states—Egypt, Kuwait, Lebanon, Saudi Arabia, and the United Arab Emirates (UAE)—had a favorable attitude toward American freedom and democracy, even while holding very unfavorable attitudes toward U.S. policy in the Arab world.[19] In that same Zogby International poll, in seven Arab countries "civil/ personal rights" ranked as the most important political issue among those polled, exceeding health care, the Palestinian issue, and economic questions.[20]

These positive views toward democracy are borne out on the ground. Turnout in Arab states for real elections is regularly very high. Despite the boycott by most Sunni Arabs (roughly 20 percent of the population) and threats of violence, Iraqi turnout for the January 2005 parliamentary elections was 53 percent of registered voters. Turnout in the December 2005 Iraqi elections, with the Sunni boycott lifted, was much higher—nearly 80 percent of registered voters. Algerians turned out at a rate of 58 percent for their April 2004 presidential election. Official figures put Palestinian turnout for the January 2005 presidential election at 73 percent, despite Hamas's refusal to participate. Again, with Hamas participating in the Palestinian parliamentary elections of 2006, turnout was a bit higher, 78 percent of registered voters. In 2003, 76 percent of eligible Yemeni voters cast their ballots in the legislative elections; 59 percent of Jordanian voters did the same in their 2003 parliamentary elections.[21] Turnout in the Kuwaiti parliamentary elections is regularly over 70 percent. Although anti-democratic forces are certainly at work in the Arab world, and some Arab elections are characterized by low turnout or low voter registration rates,[22] in general Arabs are enthusiastic about voting and elections.

The problem for the United States in promoting democracy in the Arab world is not that Arabs do not like democracy, it is that Washington will probably not like the governments that Arab democracy would produce. If it is assumed that more democratic Arab governments will be more affected by public opinion than the incumbent Arab regimes, Arab democracy should produce more anti-American foreign policies. In a February–March 2003 poll conducted in six Arab countries by Zogby International and the Anwar Sadat Chair for Peace and Development at the University of Maryland, overwhelming majorities held either a very or somewhat unfavorable attitude toward the United States. Lebanon had the highest percentage—32 percent—of those polled who viewed the United States in either a very or somewhat favorable light. The overall favorable rating of the United States in Egypt was 13 percent, in the United Arab Emirates 10 percent, in Morocco and Jordan 6 percent, and in Saudi Arabia 4 percent.[23]

These numbers most certainly were affected by the Iraq War, which was either under way or about to begin as the poll was conducted. However, these numbers are not that much different from those found in less comprehensive polls conducted before and after the Iraq War. In a Gallup poll conducted in early 2002 in several Muslim countries, strong majorities in Jordan (62 percent) and Saudi Arabia (64 percent) gave the United States an unfavorable rating. Only in Lebanon did favorable views of the United States roughly balance unfavorable views.[24] In a Zogby International poll conducted in seven Arab countries at about the same time, unfavorable ratings of the United States ranged from a low of 48 percent in Kuwait (a plurality of those polled) to highs of 87 percent in Saudi Arabia and the UAE, with unfavorable ratings in Egypt of 76 percent and Jordan of 61 percent.[25] In a Pew Global Attitudes poll conducted in March 2004, one year after the Iraq War began, 93 percent of Jordanians had either a somewhat unfavorable or a very unfavorable attitude toward the United States; 68 percent of Moroccans had similar views.[26] Even the recent stability in Iraq has not improved America's numbers. A March 2008 poll by Zogby International found America's unfavorability to be over 80 percent in Egypt, Saudi Arabia, and Jordan, and over 70 percent in Lebanon, Morocco, and the UAE.[27]

Although the available poll data do not allow analysts to pinpoint the precise sources of anti-American feeling in the Arab world, there are indications that it is American policy in the region, not rejection of American ideals, that drives Arab anti-Americanism. In the February–March 2003 poll by the Sadat Chair at the University of Maryland and Zogby International, those polled in every Arab country except the UAE said that their attitudes toward the United States are based more on American policy than on Americans' values. In Egypt, 46 percent identified American policy as the source of their feelings; 43 percent identified Americans' values. In the other countries polled—Saudi Arabia, Morocco, Lebanon, and Jordan—no fewer than 58 percent said their views on America were based on American policy.[28] Arab publics are particularly cynical about the American policy of promoting democracy in their region. In the May 2004 poll conducted by the Sadat Chair and Zogby International, only in Lebanon did a substantial percentage of those polled (44 percent) believe that the promotion of democracy was an important motive in the American war against Iraq. Twenty-five percent of Jordanians polled saw democracy as an important motive for the war. In the other four countries polled—Morocco, Saudi Arabia, Egypt, and the UAE—fewer than 10 percent saw democracy as one of America's motives for the war. For majorities in most of the countries, the war was motivated by an American desire to control oil, weaken the Muslim world, and protect Israel.[29] In the less extensive Pew Global Attitudes Survey of 2004, only 17 percent of Moroccans and 11 percent of Jordanians polled thought that the American war on terrorism was a sincere effort, not a cover for other goals.[30] No poll is needed to know that American policy on Arab-Israeli questions is very unpopular in the Arab world.

Public opinion is a fickle thing. Anti-American feelings in the Arab world could change markedly with events; these numbers are not written in stone. It is possible (though there are few data to test the assertion) that Arab anti-Americanism would decline if Washington no longer supported authoritarian Arab governments. It certainly seems, from anecdotal evidence, that in non-Arab Iran the public has a more favorable impression of the United States than does the anti-American government. That more pro-American public opinion did not, however, translate into votes in the June 2005 presidential election for the candidate who favored rapprochement with the United States. There is also little to indicate that Syria's public, whose government is even more authoritarian than Iran's and equally out of favor with Washington, is pro-American. It is hard, then, to escape the conclusion that the United States is very unpopular in the Arab world because of all of its policies there, and not simply because of its strong relations with unpopular governments. Thus Arab governments more in tune with their public opinion, as democratic governments must be, will feel enormous pressure to distance themselves from the United States. And from all available evidence, there has been little, if any, Obama effect in the domestic politics of Middle East states.

Arab Elections: The Recent Record

It is very likely, based on past performance, that real democratic elections in Arab states will redound to the benefit of Islamist candidates, groups, and parties. In many recent Arab elections, the Islamists did very well, either winning elections outright or emerging as the leading political force in opposition to the government. This very brief survey of relatively free Arab elections is also an overview of how Islamist parties have performed:

• In the January 2006 Palestinian parliamentary elections, Hamas—the political wing of the Palestinian Muslim Brotherhood—won a stunning victory against the long-dominant Fatah, the Palestinian nationalist movement founded by Yasir Arafat. Hamas carried 56 percent of the seats against Fatah's 34 percent and 7 percent for liberal, leftist, and other nationalist parties.[31]

• Nearly two-thirds of candidates elected to the Iraqi parliament in December 2005 won on platforms that called explicitly for a greater role for Islam in politics. Among the 215 Arab parliamentarians elected (the others were Kurds and smaller minority group representatives), 81 percent campaigned on lists that were sectarian and Islamist; only 9 percent came from former interim prime minister Iyad Allawi's explicitly secular, nonsectarian, and multiethnic Iraqi National List.[32] In the January 2005 Iraqi parliamentary elections, the list put together by Ayatollah Ali al-Sistani, a Shiite, won 51 percent of the vote and

140 of the 275 seats. The two more overtly secular Arab lists, headed up by Prime Minister Iyad Allawi and President Ghazi al-Yawir, gained a total of 16.3 percent of the vote and forty-five seats. The unified Kurdish list, not particularly Islamist, won 27 percent and seventy-five seats. Sunni Arabs largely boycotted this round of the voting.[33]

• In Egypt's parliamentary elections in November and December 2005, the Egyptian Muslim Brotherhood won eighty-eight seats, or 20 percent of the 444 elected seats, despite progressively greater government interference over the three rounds of balloting. That figure understates the significance of the Brotherhood's showing. The group had fielded only about 150 candidates as part of a tacit agreement with the government that allowed Brotherhood candidates to campaign openly, and so it won almost 60 percent of the seats it contested. Liberal, leftist, and nationalist opposition parties won a paltry eleven seats, less than 3 percent of the total.[34]

• In the Kuwaiti parliamentary election of 2008, Sunni (Muslim Brotherhood and Salafi-Wahhabi) and Shia Islamists combined to win twenty-one of the fifty seats, with twelve more independent candidates closely identified with the various Islamist groups also winning seats. Liberal candidates won only four seats.[35]

• In the Jordanian parliamentary election of 2007, pro-government independents swept 104 of the 110 seats. The major Islamist group, the Islamic Action Front (the political arm of the Jordanian Muslim Brotherhood), won only six seats amid charges of fraud.[36]

• In the Yemeni parliamentary election of 2003, the party of President Ali Abdallah Salih, the General People's Congress, won 238 of the 301 seats. The Yemeni Reform Group (al-Islah), a combination of Islamist and tribal elements, won forty-six seats and forms the opposition.[37]

• In the Moroccan parliamentary election of 2007, the Islamist Justice and Development Party won 46 of the 325 seats, making it the second largest party in the parliament. This was a disappointing result, because earlier public opinion polls had indicated that it could become Morocco's dominant political party. Very low turnout, below 40 percent, apparently hurt the party's fortunes.[38]

• In the Bahraini parliamentary election of 2006, in two rounds of voting Islamist candidates (Sunni and Shiite) took thirty-eight of the forty seats. Some of these, mostly among the Sunnis, campaigned as government allies; some Sunni and all the Shiite Islamists campaigned as opposition to the government. But whether pro-government or in opposition, successful candidates identified themselves to the voters as Islamists.[39]

- In the 2005 Saudi municipal elections, informal Islamist tickets won six of the seven seats in Riyadh and swept the elections in Jeddah and Mecca. Candidates backed by Sunni Islamists also won control of the municipal councils in a number of mixed Sunni-Shia towns in the Eastern Province. Tribal and clan ties seemed to be the most important element in municipal elections outside the major cities.[40]

The trend in Arab elections is absolutely clear. In the free elections in Palestine, Iraq, Kuwait, Bahrain, and Saudi Arabia, Islamists of various hues win. In elections in which there is a governing party or a royal preference—Egypt, Jordan, and Yemen—Islamists run second and form the opposition. Only in Morocco, where more secular-left parties have a long history and organizational presence was there an organized non-Islamist political bloc, independent of the government, that could compete with Islamist forces. And even there, in the 2007 election most observers detected a palace tilt against the Islamists.

CONCLUSION

It is hard to avoid the conclusion that an American push for democracy in the Arab world is unlikely to have much effect on its anti-American terrorism, but such a push could help bring to power governments that will be much less cooperative with the United States on a whole range of issues—including cooperation in the struggle against terrorism, the Arab-Israeli peace process, and military-strategic issues—than the current Arab regimes. An American democracy initiative can be defended as an effort to spread American democratic values, whatever the cost, or as a long-term gamble that the realities of governance will either moderate Islamists or lead to public disaffection from them once they are in power, which may be happening in Iran. However, the emphasis on electoral democracy cannot be said to serve immediate American interests either in the campaign against terrorism or in other important policy areas in the region. Unfortunately, right now, the United States has no reasonable alternative to working with the authoritarian Arab governments who are willing to work with it.

If Washington continues down the road of promoting democracy in the Arab world, at least it can take a lesson from the variety of electoral experiences briefly reviewed here. Where there are strongly rooted non-Islamist parties, such as in Morocco, Islamists have a harder time dominating the field. This is also true in non-Arab Turkey, where the Islamist political party has moderated its message over time to contend with the power of the secular army and with the well-established, more secular Turkish parties. Likewise, the confessional mix in Lebanon will prevent Hezbollah and other Islamists from dominating elections there. Conversely, where non-Islamist political forces have been suppressed, such as in Saudi Arabia and Bahrain, Islamist parties and candidates can dominate the field. Washington should take no comfort from the success of ruling parties in Yemen, Algeria, and Egypt against Islamist challengers. Once stripped of their patronage and security control levers, ruling parties do not do very well in democratic transitional elections.

It was not only the focus on elections that was troubling in the Bush administration's democracy initiative in the Arab world. Equally troubling was the unjustified confidence that Washington could predict, and even direct, the course of domestic politics in other countries. No one in the administration would sign on, at least in public, to the naïve view that Arab democracy would produce governments that would always cooperate with the United States. But there was precious little appreciation for the likelihood that democratic Arab governments would actively oppose American policy on important issues, including the Arab-Israeli conflict and the campaign against terrorism. That is why the Hamas victory in the 2006 Palestinian elections shocked Washington. Those who advocate democracy seem to assume that the transitions like those in Eastern Europe, Latin America, and East Asia produce pro-American governments. However, in those areas the major ideological challenge to liberal democracy and market capitalism—Soviet-style communism—was thoroughly discredited. In the Arab world, there is a real ideological competitor to liberal politics: the movement that claims as its motto "Islam is the solution." The hubris that says America can direct the domestic politics of foreign countries should have been exploded in Iraq, where even the presence of 140,000 U.S. troops could not guarantee that politics would go the way the policymakers back home wanted. The lack of humility in the Bush administration's approach to the democracy initiative bespoke a lack of reality about the extent to which the United States can control the political future of societies about which it knows very little. And it will hopefully serve as a fruitful lesson for President Obama as he fashions a new American approach to the Arab and Muslim world.

YES: Promoting democracy can combat terrorism
Jennifer L. Windsor, *Freedom House*

U.S. Support for Democratization in the Middle East: Revisiting the Democracy and Terrorism Debate

Soon after entering office, President Barack Obama broke dramatically from several of his predecessor's most frequently criticized policies. He ordered a ban on dubious detention and interrogation techniques, publicly announced plans to close the Guantanamo detention center, set a date to withdraw most combat troops from Iraq, launched high-profile diplomatic efforts, and engaged actively with multilateral institutions. However, the future of the Bush administration's "freedom agenda" is still uncertain. The Obama administration continues to grapple with the question of what changes need to be made in U.S. support for democratization and human rights around the world.

There are distinct strands of discourse in the discussions about what the new policy should be. In one strand, the democracy promotion community writ large has urged a "decontamination," which would involve dropping the most problematic aspects of the Bush administration's freedom agenda, along with some of its counterterrorism policies.[41] However, the community does not support a reduction in U.S. backing for democratization and human rights.[42] Another strand tends to settle on quite a different policy prescription: the Obama administration should clearly distance itself from the Bush program, even if it means de-emphasizing the promotion of human rights and democracy in U.S. foreign policy. Some have even exhumed the mantra of political nonintervention that was popular some three decades ago.[43] Calls for a "development first" approach also seem to be back in vogue. According to this approach, democracy should happen only *after* a state has alleviated poverty, eliminated corruption, enhanced its rule of law, and seen a tolerant political culture emerge.[44] But perhaps most worrying is the argument that the United States should refocus on its "core" national security interests in its relations with other states, unencumbered by concerns of repression or abuses committed by those governments against their own people.[45]

The human rights and democracy promotion communities were enormously uncomfortable with the Bush administration's public linkage of the freedom agenda and the war on terrorism on several levels.[46] First, the decision by Bush's speechwriters to portray U.S. efforts in Iraq and the fight against insurgents there as the cornerstone of the freedom agenda was devastating for American groups that had been working for decades to support democratization around the world.[47] Second, the inconsistent implementation of the freedom agenda, in which some allies in the war on terrorism were subject to criticism while others were apparently exempt, led to understandable charges of hypocrisy by advocates for strong U.S. human rights policies. Finally, the administration's failure to uphold international human rights commitments in its own conduct of the war on terror, and turning a blind eye to the proliferation of laws and practices—undertaken by countries including China, Russia, Ethiopia, Egypt, and Jordan, aimed at restricting freedom of expression and association in the name of combating terrorism—undermined decades of work by U.S. human rights and democracy advocates.

In a parallel strand of discourse, those in the realist camp argued that the freedom agenda was disrupting U.S. relations with important allies including Saudi Arabia and Egypt, whose cooperation was vital to implementing an international strategy to combat terrorism, as well as to advancing other foreign policy objectives. (Such arguments echo the long-standing claims of those and other authoritarian regimes in the Middle East, which have warned that the alternatives to their continued rule are much worse.)

Realist critics (and others) questioned the underlying assumption that there was a positive relationship between more freedom or democracy and less terrorism.[48] Scholarly analyses—based on multiple regression models and involving a wide range of datasets and definitions of the variables—proliferated, each coming up with different conclusions.[49] After the electoral gains by Hamas in Palestine, Hezbollah in Lebanon, and other Islamist movements in Egypt, Iraq, and the Gulf, realists from both parties ratcheted up their rhetoric on the dangers of supporting democratization in the Middle East.[50] Although President Bush's personal embrace of freedom continued, and the 2006 "National Security Strategy" was as strong and nuanced a statement of U.S. goals in promoting freedom as any democracy advocate could wish for, there was a notable decline in enthusiasm within the State Department for vigorously implementing the freedom agenda.[51] One could see the change of heart particularly in the shifts in U.S. policy toward Egypt (Pakistan, of course, was never subject to any significant pressure from the Bush administration to return to a democratic path).[52]

With a new administration reviewing policies across the board, there is an opportunity to step back and assess American strategies to promote democratization and combat terrorism. It is also an opportunity to reexamine the relationship between those two goals. It is well past time to examine underlying assumptions, review former practices and results, and make the appropriate adjustments.

In doing so, it is important to be fair. The Bush administration made multiple serious mistakes, but the totality of what it advocated for and did under the broad rubric of the freedom agenda should not simply be discarded for the sake of change. The Obama administration clearly needs to distance itself from certain aspects of that agenda, and would receive strong backing from the human rights and democracy communities for doing so. But the last administration's decision to incorporate democracy and governance indicators into the allocation of U.S. foreign assistance, and its long-delayed inclusion of the Middle East in U.S. efforts to strengthen democracy and human rights, were noteworthy advances that should be built upon rather than abandoned. In fact, few within the democracy promotion and human rights communities believe that terminating official American support for political freedom is necessary to extricate the "freedom agenda" from its disrepute. Instead, the new leadership should find a way to drop the "agenda" but retain the goal of advancing freedom as a U.S. policy goal.

Certainly, any further sweeping public pronouncements that U.S. support for democracy is linked to its counterterrorism strategies is not advised. But the administration and the policy community should acknowledge that democratization, properly defined and supported, can help to address some of the conditions that have led to the rise of radical and sometimes violent elements within the Middle Eastern and other Muslim majority communities and societies. Transnational terrorist movements like al-Qaeda have been able to tap into such extremism to promote their own causes, especially by winning recruits, encouraging the continued use of violence, and generating broader sympathy for their own ambitions and worldview.[53]

Before an elaboration of the rationale behind this argument, it is important to go back to basics and define the key terms. Surprisingly, it still seems necessary to reiterate what democratization is and to clarify what U.S. support for democracy abroad entails. Similar if not greater confusion arises when one attempts to link democracy with counterterrorism strategies. It is hard to make coherent policy choices and measure trade-offs without clarifying the two main variables—democracy and terrorism.

DEFINING DEMOCRATIZATION AND ITS PROMOTION

The process of democratization is aimed at increasing a government's accountability to the governed. Therefore, it is about regular elections and all that is necessary for an electoral process to be fair and meaningful, including but not limited to freedom of association, freedom of speech, genuine political choices for the people, and access to independent news media. Beginning with the 1948 Universal Declaration of Human Rights and reinforced by subsequent regional and global covenants and agreements, the international community has largely accepted that progress on all of these fronts must be part of becoming a democratic and rights-abiding society. The process of democratization also involves a broader range of vital institutions that hold governments accountable after elections: an independent judiciary, a viable parliament, security forces that defer to the authority of elected civilian leaders, and protections against the diversion of public resources for private gain. In addition to these processes and institutions, democratization requires the majority of citizens to accept the overall rules of the "political game" and to embrace fundamental democratic principles such as the preservation of minority rights in the face of majority rule, tolerance of diversity (ethnic, religious, linguistic, political), and fair application of the law to all members of society.[54]

No country ever becomes perfectly democratic, but there has been substantial progress in the world over the last quarter-century. Governments have become more transparent, more accountable, more representative, and more respectful of individual freedoms and the rule of law. This tremendous growth in freedom has proven that no culture or society is impervious to citizens' yearnings for justice and the ability to exercise fundamental freedoms of expression, association, and belief. Over the years, almost every region in the world—including Asia, Africa, Latin America, and the Middle East, which is home to societies shaped by religious traditions including Catholicism, Confucianism, and Islam—has been considered inhospitable to democratic progress. Yet in each of these regions notable advances have been made.[55]

The U.S. and other governments typically use a variety of tools to encourage more respect for human rights and to support those who are committed to establishing or strengthening a democratic system, whether from inside or outside the existing power structure. Diplomatic pressure can be exerted through multilateral institutions, such as the United Nations, the Organization for Security and Cooperation in Europe, and the Organization of American States. This pressure can include strengthening the international recognition of democracy as a universal right and urging dictators to respect free and fair elections. Bilateral contacts can be used to advocate the adoption of laws and behavioral changes that result in greater respect for human rights and a more open political space. Incentives can come in the form of sticks (targeted sanctions against leaders, bans on military training or equipment) or carrots (the valuable linkage of U.S. foreign assistance to democratic performance through the Millennium Challenge Account).

Democratization can also be supported indirectly, and in this sense the democracy promotion toolbox is quite deep. The U.S. government, private foundations, and other donors have funded programs that involve the provision of training, citizen and academic exchanges, facilitation of the flow of information and expertise between democracy activists within and between societies, on-site advice and encouragement, visible demonstrations of solidarity, and emergency humanitarian and legal assistance for local activists and human rights defenders who face repression by their governments.[56] The underlying premise of such assistance is that even though democracy can ultimately be brought about and maintained only by a country's own citizens, external support that is properly designed and applied can make a difference.[57]

In a welcome departure from past U.S. practices in the Middle East, the Bush administration placed greater democratization and freedom alongside other U.S. objectives, mainly by utilizing bilateral diplomatic dialogues and increasing funding for political reform in the region. However, as many critics have correctly noted, this policy was not applied consistently. Tunisia and Algeria were never taken to task, despite ongoing human rights abuses; Saudi Arabia was largely given a free pass after its flawed local elections; and U.S. pressure on Egypt greatly decreased beginning in 2006.[58] Unfortunately, the positive steps that were taken to open up political space and encourage respect for human rights in other countries (including Morocco, Jordan, Kuwait, and Bahrain) were drowned out by the storm of criticism surrounding the war in Iraq. Indeed, the decision by the Bush administration to identify Iraq as the centerpiece of its freedom agenda was a terrible mistake, because its missteps in Iraq overshadowed the more positive steps it took to advance and defend freedom in other parts of the world. Finally, the Abu Ghraib scandal solidified in many people's minds the idea that the Bush administration was willing to abuse the very rights and values it espoused in the name of fighting terrorism.

DEFINING THE THREAT AND CLARIFYING THE CURRENT U.S. COUNTERTERRORISM STRATEGY

There may be even greater confusion when it comes to defining and conceptualizing the terrorist threat the United States faces today. Definitional debates within the United Nations and other bodies as to what constitutes terrorism have gone on for decades, and varying definitions appear in articles and policy analyses.[59] But at its core terrorism is a method by which nonstate actors use acts or threats of violence to advance political, religious, or ideological goals. Such methods can be—and have been—utilized by individuals and groups against civilians within their own societies as well as against the civilian populations of other countries. The 2002 U.S. "National Security Strategy" defines terrorism as "premeditated, politically motivated violence perpetrated against innocents."[60] The British government's latest counterterrorism strategy notes that

> the current international terrorist threat is quite different from the terror- ist threats we faced in the past. Contemporary terrorist groups claim a religious justification for their actions and have a wide-ranging religious and political agenda; they are no longer concerned with a single issue. Many seek mass civilian casualties and are prepared to use unconven- tional techniques (including chemical or radiological weapons); they conduct attacks without warning; they actively seek to recruit new mem- bers in the UK and elsewhere around the world.[61]

Especially for those outside of the immediate counterterrorist community, the recommended goal and approach of U.S. counterterrorism efforts vary widely. Some argue for a narrow definition—that is, the prevention of a recur- rence of attacks, either within the United States or against other democracies. Others focus on a reduction in all transnational terrorist attacks, although some worry that including lingering regional conflicts in the mix is mixing apples and oranges. Still others would further broaden the strategy to include a reduction in violent extremism within countries. And finally, some have sought to expand the U.S. strategy to include countering the rise of radical Islamist movements in the Middle East and elsewhere. The difficulty of distin- guishing between these objectives has led to commentators talking past one another and to many inaccurate perceptions—inside and outside of the United States—of the particular approaches and goals of U.S. counterterrorist strategy under the prior administration.

In examining the linkage between democratization and terrorism and how the concepts have been connected in practice in U.S. policy, it is useful to sepa- rate transnational terrorism from violent extremism and radical Islamism within societies. These are distinct issues that overlap only at the margins. Regional conflicts are a murkier area, because they involve "conveyor-belt groups" that feed into the larger international terrorist networks.[62]

In countering the current threat of transnational terrorism (including attacks against the United States)—which seemed to be the main focus of the Bush administration—the U.S. government primarily taps its military and intelligence capabilities to identify and eradicate terrorist enclaves, employing surveillance and law enforcement mechanisms to identify and detain suspected collaborators and choking off the flow of funding to terrorist groups by moni- toring and restructuring the international financial system.[63] Established democracies in Europe and elsewhere have been the country's natural and most reliable partners in this effort, and at times they have faced more of a threat than the United States.

Rhetorically, the "war on terrorism" and the "freedom agenda" were linked by President Bush himself in multiple sets of remarks delivered from 2001 to 2005. But by the time the 2006 "National Security Strategy" was released, the goals of promoting freedom and combating terrorism were being portrayed as distinct endeavors. Promoting freedom was the first U.S. foreign policy priority—a historically unprecedented elevation of that goal. The second priority was to make the United States safer by combating the international terrorist threat. The strategy did note that the two goals were mutually reinforcing.[64] Democracies make better partners in countering international terrorism, which, in turn, makes democracies more secure from violence. And in the long term, the strategy argued, democratization could help by addressing some of the underlying conditions and arguments used by al-Qaeda and others to win recruits and popular support.

In practice, even in the early part of the administration U.S. government officials who were tasked with supporting democratization in the Middle East were not part of the core interagency group that focused on counterterrorism, and there were few areas of overlap between the two policies. In the Middle East Partnership Initiative (MEPI), a new assistance program for the Middle East established under the Bush administration, one would be hard-pressed to find any program that explicitly integrated terrorism and democracy objectives. Within the U.S. Agency for International Development (USAID), some officials tried to connect their conflict mitigation and democracy programs (especially in the Horn of Africa and in Pakistan) with U.S. counterterrorism goals, but to the great discomfort of democracy experts within USAID and outside who argued that connecting the two was inappropriate and dangerous. Perhaps most seriously damaging for the success of U.S. democratization strategies, USAID sought to institute a noxious and overly intrusive system to "vet" partners, including their board members, to ensure that they were not in any way connected to terrorism, violent extremism, or radical Islamism.

Public diplomacy was the U.S. foreign policy vehicle that commingled the two goals the most. Various speeches by President Bush portrayed the September 11, 2001, attacks as an assault on "freedom." Successive public diplomacy strategies sought to produce new messages that promoted democracy as a political system, touted America's track record in incorporating Muslim immigrants, and presented all U.S. foreign policy efforts as the products of sincere and benevolent intentions. Needless to say, these initiatives were widely seen as amateurish and unsuccessful. At the end of the administration, U.S. public diplomacy correctly refocused on efforts to undercut the popularity of the use of violence and terrorism within Muslim majority communities and countries.[65]

WHAT DEMOCRACY CAN AND CANNOT DO IN PREVENTING TERRORISM

Now it is time, having defined basic terms, to revisit the question of what plausible linkages exist between democracy and terrorism—and the more pertinent issue of whether democratization in the broader Middle East can contribute to the goal of preventing al-Qaeda–style terrorism and the more diverse forms of violent extremism.

Democracy is not a vaccine against terrorism. Democracy in India prevented neither the recent attacks in Mumbai nor the ongoing violence in Kashmir. Violent extremists have also emerged within democracies, including those in alienated Muslim communities in Western Europe. Many individuals involved in transnational terrorist networks grew up or were even born in democracies (although one could plausibly assert that they felt excluded from the power structures of their societies). Of course, no matter what protections for human rights or mechanisms for political input are in place in democracies, there will always be men and women who are consumed with hatred and committed to killing innocents to prove a point. And yet, even though Timothy McVeigh, the perpetrator of the 1995 Oklahoma City bombing, and violent groups such as the Irish Republican Army and Basque Fatherland and Liberty (ETA) do emerge from or persist in democratic systems, their appearance is relatively rare because of the availability of numerous alternatives and often more successful means for addressing grievances and achieving political aims.

Established democracies provide an outlet for participating, channeling dissent, debating policies, and seeking peaceful resolution of grievances. They offer mechanisms for the regular exercise of citizen choice and changes of government. Within repressive systems, individuals have no clear and effective recourse for their frustrations. Such governments cut off legitimate and peaceful forms of political dissent, with no allowance for public debate. The primary goal of an undemocratic regime is to maintain its monopoly on power at all costs. Civil society and peaceful political opposition are typically weakened by severe legal restrictions and coercive methods. Politics is driven underground. Although it is arguably effective in the short term, the use of brutal repression can also help to further radicalize individuals, swell the ranks of extremists, and marginalize or destroy the moderate elements within society.

Thus repressive, unaccountable, and unresponsive systems create an enabling environment for violent extremism.[66] And the Middle East today remains the most repressive region in the world, despite incremental gains over the last several years in some countries. No Arab country in the Middle East demonstrates enough respect for political rights and civil liberties to be considered "Free" in the classification system of Freedom House's annual survey of political rights and civil liberties around the world.[67]

Because of the repression, often extremely brutal, that has prevailed in the Middle East, it is no surprise that effective organized democratic forces have yet to emerge, especially in the political arena. Parties have had little political space in which to operate and few opportunities to hone their skills or to translate their largely intellectual platforms into popular political messages. Islamist movements, however, have been able to continue to function even under repressive conditions, and they have done a better job of shepherding their message and organizations, frequently without the complications and compromises that come with full participation in the political process or government.

Meanwhile, transnational terrorist networks can and do profit from the combustible mix of lack of socioeconomic opportunities, political stagnation, and repression that characterize many societies in the region. Recruiters for extremist groups have been able to play effectively on the sense of humiliation, injustice, and powerlessness felt by those—especially the younger generation—who lack a voice and perceive that they have no ability to make their own future.[68]

That sense of frustration is amplified and aggravated by the wider exposure to outside information and the increased presence of foreign cultural and commercial products. Regimes have used their remaining control over information flows to try to divert their populations' attention away from domestic failings and toward the evils outside their borders. The closed nature of political systems and media environments in the Middle East have allowed these leaders to disseminate inaccurate, polemical versions of the news that are manipulated to serve narrow political interests. The introduction of Arab satellite stations has eroded government information monopolies in these countries, although the programming on many of the networks remains sensationalist and reinforces al-Qaeda's arguments that the West is trying to humiliate or subjugate Islam.

As emphasized in both American and British counterterrorism strategies, in their most recent spate of transnational terrorist attacks organizations have utilized an extreme, distorted version of Islam in their self-presentation and efforts to gain popular support. When the expression of even peaceful dissent entails extreme risks to life and limb, religious motivations, however poorly grounded, are often essential in organizing violence against the state.[69]

In the face of this volatile and worrying mixture of religious extremism and repression, the process of democratization in the Middle East is not without risks. In any society, changes in the prevailing power structure are by definition destabilizing in the short term. Established elites realize that their political (and sometimes economic) status will be lost, and they take action to protect their positions. Opposition movements are often peopled not only by those seeking a more democratic political system, but also by those who have thoroughly undemocratic leanings. Despite using the language of democracy, Islamist opposition movements have certainly not yet demonstrated that they would be willing to accept and play by the rules of a democratic system. As evidenced by other parts of the world, especially during an electoral process, both government and opposition often appeal to religious, regional, or ethnic differences to mobilize support for their parties or, in some cases, to create a climate of disorder and violence that discourages any further attempts at change.[70]

ARE "EARLY" ELECTIONS TO BLAME FOR RISING EXTREMISM IN THE MIDDLE EAST?

So is it time to give up on elections in the Middle East? It is a truism to state that genuinely free and fair elections in many societies in the world may produce leaders who prove problematic. In the worst case, leaders use democratic elections to gain power and then systematically attempt to dismantle the institutions that facilitated their ascent. Echoing Fareed Zakaria's admonitions about "illiberal democracies," Gause and others argue that early elections in the Middle East are responsible for political gains by Islamist extremists. Elections, they argue, should be delayed until the rule of law and a liberal democratic culture are established and an organized, viable secular democratic alternative emerges in the region.[71]

In fact, Islamist political gains were not caused by elections that were held "too early." Elections are the occasion to measure, not the cause of, the popularity of political groups within a society. The 2006 Palestinian elections were not "early"—in fact they were five years late—and they are not to blame for the ascension of Hamas. The blame lies squarely on Fatah and the Palestinian Authority, which was widely seen as corrupt, unresponsive, and ineffective in addressing the real needs of the population. The United States turned a blind eye for years to the corruption and unaccountable governance of President Yasir Arafat and his colleagues. Moreover, the driving force for the holding of elections in Iraq was not the U.S. government, but Grand Ayatollah Ali al-Sistani.[72]

Whether it wants to do so or not, the United States cannot stop elections in the Middle East, or anywhere else for that matter. Virtually every country in the world, with a few exceptions among the Arab Gulf states, have and are going to have national elections on a recurring basis for their own reasons and in their own time. The only question is whether the elections will be more or less genuine reflections of voters' preferences.

The reasons for the gains and the fairness of the electoral systems are quite varied,[73] and there are critical differences between the groups themselves. Hamas and Hezbollah clearly represent serious threats to U.S. interests in the region, and they can feed recruits into transnational terrorist networks. But other Islamist movements within the region are distributed across a wider political spectrum; they are not internally monolithic. Analysts have documented splits within these groups and struggles between extremist and moderate elements.[74] That does not mean that their political effectiveness is not problematic for the future of democratization in the region—the platforms of even the mildest Islamist groups are troubling in terms of respect for women's rights, freedom of expression, religious freedom, and equality before the law.

However, the answer to the Islamist dilemma is exactly the opposite of the suggestions offered by Gause and others—not fewer but *better* elections are needed.[75] Although the recent balloting in some Middle Eastern countries featured improvements in the electoral environment or ended long stretches without any elections at all, it would be an overstatement at best to declare that the voting was "free and fair."[76] The current situation will not be remedied by a moratorium on elections. Ordinary political parties will not get stronger if they have no opportunity to run for office regularly. Only through such trials can they strengthen their message, outreach, and appeal to populace. The political implications of electoral system design cannot always be identified in advance (although the ability of legislators to predict the political impact of gerrymandering and redistricting within the United States seems to be well honed).

Meanwhile, elections alone, as has been repeatedly affirmed, do not constitute democratization. Democratization requires strengthening the institutions—legislatures and independent judicial systems—that counter excessive executive powers. And it requires more freedom of expression and association—that is, a freer environment in which a society can generate alternatives to oppressive governments and aspiring authoritarians. And civil society must be strengthened; the members of that society play a key role in civic education, raising awareness of human rights and helping to cultivate more tolerant political attitudes.

For the United States, the promotion of democracy has never been about elections alone, but it should always include elections. U.S. policymakers have yet to find a better mechanism for citizens to choose their governments and hold them accountable. Free elections are an exercise in self-determination, and democratization can encourage the emergence of new executive and legislative leaders who are less pliable and more complex in dealings with the

United States and other democratic states than a single autocrat who can approve a U.S. military base with the stroke of a pen. But elected leaders benefit from the support of the citizenry and a degree of inherent legitimacy, which makes them stronger allies in the long run. Elections also greatly improve long-term stability, because course corrections and political successions are managed peacefully and at a measured pace, without resort to civil conflicts and military coups.

What really is the alternative? The maintenance of the status quo in the Middle East is not necessarily beneficial to U.S. national interests. The past is replete with examples of governments in the Middle East, including those of Iran, Syria, and Saudi Arabia, that have actively backed violent transnational movements to advance their own domestic interests and foreign policy goals in the region.[77] Moreover, most of the regimes in the region lack the popular legitimacy or the political will to address the underlying conditions that spawn violent extremism within their societies, including allowing genuine mechanisms of political accountability. And as a recent RAND report persuasively argues, the partial political liberalization that has occurred in the Middle East poses even more dangers if it is stymied or reversed. Violent extremism may in fact increase in that scenario, as the relative moderates within Islamist movements are edged out by radicals who argue that they have no real shot at influencing the political system by peaceful means.[78]

A WAY FORWARD

So what is the way forward? For the foreseeable future, American counterterrorism strategy will continue to rely primarily on military, intelligence, and financing approaches to disrupt and weaken al-Qaeda and other terrorist groups. Clearly, the Obama administration should avoid rhetorically linking the goals of supporting democratization and U.S. counterterrorism strategy. In the ideal world, U.S. policy to strengthen respect for human rights, the advance of freedom, and more democratization should be an end in itself, not a mere instrument for achieving American national interests. But given the realities in Washington, it is likely that future national security and government strategies will need to spell out how support for democracy contributes to U.S. security and prosperity and how democratization can reinforce the nation's efforts in diplomacy, defense, and development. So it is appropriate for the next U.S. national security strategy to include a discussion of how advancing political as well as economic and social reform abroad—including the Middle East—can contribute to reducing the virulent extremism that fuels the recruitment efforts of al-Qaeda and its ilk.

There is obviously a need to recalibrate U.S. policies and approaches toward democratization in the Middle East. That said, it is a very difficult time to assess the future of political reform in the region. Time will tell whether the changes in some countries in the region are simply further examples of the political manipulations that authoritarian governments like that in Egypt have used for decades to "blow off steam" while mitigating any fundamental alteration of the power structure. And although some progress has been made in Iraq, Morocco, Kuwait, and elsewhere, there is still a long row to hoe before any of those countries could be considered a robust democracy.

It is also hard to predict whether the current popularity of some Islamist groups will continue in the future. But certainly the Obama administration can improve upon the strategy embraced by its predecessors by adopting a more nuanced approach toward the range of Islamist groups that have emerged in the region.[79] An all-out embrace of Islamists is obviously inappropriate, but the United States should incorporate in its planning a more in-depth knowledge of these groups and their memberships and appeals. Broader U.S. engagement with the groups that are not violent should be considered, so long as it does not send a signal to the non-Islamist opposition and civic groups that they are being undercut in any way.

The U.S. government does not have to do everything itself. To reduce risks, it should allow nongovernmental organizations and other groups that are well versed in this business to operate with more autonomy and to explore relationships with new interlocutors. In the past, as the promotion of democracy became more of a priority, the U.S. government sought to be publicly affiliated with every initiative, requested more detailed work plans, and attempted to choose or vet participants in every seminar and study mission. The zeal within some parts of the U.S. government to exert excessive control over the nongovernmental work that they fund has backfired in the region and made the situation more—not less—politically volatile.

As for elections, the United States certainly cannot stop them in the Middle East region. The citizens of every country have the right to elect whom they want to represent them. But the U.S. government is not obliged to embrace all of the leaders produced by those contests—nor to agree to the policies that those leaders then adopt. The United States retains the right, indeed the obligation, to choose its allies and identify its adversaries according to its own national interests. The corrective power of regular democratic elections simply makes it more likely that practical and effective international partners will emerge in the future and more likely that forces of radicalism and terror will lose the primary foundations of their support structures—corrupt, unaccountable, illegitimate, repressive governance.

At this critical juncture, the new administration has a unique opportunity to rebrand freedom and democracy and the U.S. government's role in supporting its advance in the world. President Obama's historic election has allowed the world to see the transformative power of the ballot box and citizen participation, and his government can add substance to these positive impressions by not only promising but also delivering robust support for democratic activists and by reiterating the right of all individuals to be free, no matter where they live.

Notes

1. Elisabeth Bumiller, "Behind Rice's Shift on Leading Mideast Peace Efforts," *New York Times,* November 26, 2007.
2. White House, "National Strategy for Combating Terrorism," September 2006, 1, http://georgewbush-whitehouse.archives.gov/nsc/nsct/2006/. Also see the 2002 and 2006 versions of the "National Security Strategy of the United States of America" at http://georgewbush-whitehouse.archives.gov/nsc/nss/2002/index.html and http://georgewbush-whitehouse.archives.gov/nsc/nss/2006.
3. This essay is a revised and updated version of F. Gregory Gause III, "Can Democracy Stop Terrorism?" *Foreign Affairs* Vol. 84, No. 5 (Sept./Oct. 2005): 62–76.
4. President George W. Bush, remarks at National Defense University, March 8, 2005, http://georgewbush-whitehouse.archives.gov.
5. Candidate Kerry said, "We must support the development of free and democratic societies in the Arab and Muslim worlds to win the war of ideas. . . . In a Kerry Administration, America will be clear with repressive governments in the region that we expect to see them change, not just for our sake but for their own survival," www.johnkerry.com/issues/national security/terrorism.html.
6. For example: "Because if it is impossible for the peoples of even one Arab state to voluntarily organize themselves around a social contract for democratic life, then we are looking at dictators and kings ruling this region as far as the eye can see. And that will guarantee that this region will be a cauldron of oil-financed pathologies and terrorism for the rest of our lives." Thomas Friedman, "The Country We've Got," *New York Times,* January 6, 2005.
7. Martin Indyk, "Back to the Bazaar," *Foreign Affairs* 81 (January/February 2002): 75–88. Morton H. Halperin, Joseph T. Siegle, and Michael M. Weinstein, *The Democracy Advantage: How Democracies Promote Prosperity and Peace* (New York: Routledge for the Council on Foreign Relations, 2004), chap. 5. Halperin said, "In short, even as new security threats emerge in the twenty-first century, one thing remains constant: authoritarian governments are at the source" (121).
8. William Eubank and Leonard Weinberg, "Terrorism and Democracy: Perpetrators and Victims," *Terrorism and Political Violence* 131 (Spring 2001).
9. Quan Li, "Does Democracy Promote or Reduce Transnational Terrorist Incidents?" *Journal of Conflict Resolution* 49 (April 2005).
10. Robert Pape, *Dying to Win* (New York: Random House, 2005). Pape's findings are summarized in Robert Pape, "Blowing Up an Assumption," *New York Times,* May 18, 2005.

11. Calculations from U.S. Department of State, *Patterns of Global Terrorism,* 2000–2003, www.state.gov/s/ct/rls/pgtrpt; and Freedom House, *Freedom in the World* (Washington, D.C.: Freedom House, 1999–2000, 2000–2001, 2001–2002, 2003), www.freedomhouse.org. I excluded from this count terrorist incidents that occurred in Israel, because they were overwhelmingly perpetrated by Palestinians, not Israelis (or Israeli Arabs), and would have skewed the count of incidents in democratic countries. I also excluded the September 11, 2001, attacks on the United States from the count, because they were not perpetrated by Americans.

12. On India, see www.tkb.org/Category.jsp?catID=8494; on China, see www.tkb.org/Category.jsp?catID=8352. The National Memorial Institute for the Prevention of Terrorism was established by Congress after the Oklahoma City bombing of 1995.

13. Bruce Hoffman, *Inside Terrorism* (New York: Columbia University Press, 1998).

14. Jessica Stern, *Terror in the Name of God: Why Religious Militants Kill* (New York: Harper Collins, 2003), 287–288.

15. Message broadcast on al Jazeera television, October 19, 2003, http://english.aljazeera.net/NR/exeres/ACB47241-D25F-46CB-B673-56FAB1C2837F.htm.

16. From a message broadcast on al Jazeera television on October 18, 2003, http://english.aljazeera.net/NR/exeres/8E8EA580-943C-4FBF-9ABD-21B47627FECD.htm.

17. Middle East Media and Research Institute, Special Dispatch Series, No. 856, February 1, 2005.

18. Pew Global Attitudes Project, "Iraq Vote Mirrors Desire for Democracy in Muslim World," February 3, 2005, http://people-press.org/commentary/pdf/107.pdf.

19. James J. Zogby, "What Arabs Think: Values, Beliefs and Concerns," Zogby International and the Arab Thought Forum, September 2002, 63–64.

20. Ibid., 33–34.

21. International Foundation for Electoral Systems (IFES), "Election Guide" Web site, various country pages, www.electionguide.org.

22. In the Riyadh area, only about 30 percent of eligible voters registered to cast their ballots in the February 2005 municipal elections. Neil MacFarquhar, "Asterisk Aside, First National Vote for Saudis," *New York Times,* February 10, 2005.

23. "Arab Public Opinion Survey" public opinion poll conducted by Shibley Telhami, Anwar Sadat Chair for Peace and Development, University of Maryland, in cooperation with Zogby International, February 19–March 11, 2003, www.bsos.umd.edu/sadat/pub/survey2003.htm.

24. Heather Munson, "Poll of Islamic World: Favorability toward U.S., Britain," Gallup Organization, February 26, 2002, www.gallup.com/poll/content/?ci=5722.

25. Zogby, "What Arabs Think," 61.

26. Pew Research Center for the People and the Press, "Chapter 7: Global Opinion: The Spread of Anti-Americanism," *Trends 2005,* http://people-press.org/commentary/pdf/104.pdf.

27. See James Zogby, "Arab Opinion of the U.S. Declined in 2008," March 2008, www.arabamericannews.com/news/index.php?mod=article&cat=Opinions&article=1048.

28. "Arab Public Opinion Survey."

29. "Arab Attitudes Towards Political and Social Issues, Foreign Policy and the Media," public opinion poll conducted by Shibley Telhami, Anwar Sadat Chair for Peace

and Development, University of Maryland, in cooperation with Zogby International, May 2004, www.bsos.umd.edu/SADAT/pub.

30. Pew Research Center, "Chapter 7."

31. Official results from Palestinian Central Elections Commission, www.elections.ps/pdf/Final_Result_distribution_of_PLC_seats-EN.pdf.

32. Ellen Knickmeyer, "Iraq Election Results Show Sunni Gains," *Washington Post,* January 21, 2006.

33. *Al-Hayat,* March 17, 2005, 5.

34. Hani Shukrallah, "Egypt: Stormy Elections Close a Turbulent Year," *Arab Reform Bulletin* (December 2005).

35. *Al-Hayat,* May 19, 2008.

36. Ellen Knickmeyer, "Jordan Vote Reflects Islamic Parties' Slide," *Washington Post,* November 27, 2007.

37. Daniel Brumberg, "Liberalization versus Democracy: Understanding Arab Political Reform," Middle East Series-Working Paper 37, Democracy and Rule of Law Project, Carnegie Endowment for International Peace, Washington, D.C., May 2003, www.ceip.org/files/pdf/wp37.pdf.

38. Ellen Knickmeyer, "In Morocco, a Hush at the Polls," *Washington Post,* September 12, 2007.

39. F. Gregory Gause III, "As You Chart It—Bahrain Parliamentary Election Results," *International Journal of Middle East Studies* 39 (May 2007).

40. Nasser al-Salti and Raid Qusti, "Riyadh Election Winners Named," *Arab News,* February 12, 2005; *al-Hayat,* February 12, 2005, 1, 6; Ali Khalil, "Sectarian Lists Circulate for Second Round of Saudi Polls," *Daily Star* (Beirut), March 3, 2005; Joe Avacena, "Dammam, Qatif Voters Pick Businessmen," *Saudi Gazette,* March 6, 2005; Steven Coll, "Islamic Activists Sweep Saudi Council Elections," *Washington Post,* April 24, 2005.

41. For the first use of the term *decontamination,* see Thomas Carothers, *U.S. Democracy Promotion during and after Bush* (Washington, D.C.: Carnegie Endowment for International Peace, 2007).

42. See Arch Puddington, "Freedom in the World 2009: Setbacks and Resilience, Selected Data from Freedom House's Annual Survey of Political Rights and Civil Liberties," 11, www.freedomhouse.org. Also see Richard Gephardt and Vin Weber, "Democracy Promotion in Obama's Reign," *Politico,* March 29, 2009; Thomas Carothers, "Democracy Promotion under Obama: Finding a Way Forward," Policy Brief No. 77, Carnegie Endowment for International Peace, Washington, D.C., 2009; and Larry Diamond, "Supporting Democracy: Refashioning U.S. Global Strategy," in *Democracy in U.S. Security Strategy: From Promotion to Support,* ed. Alexander Lennon (Washington, D.C.: Center for Strategic and International Studies, 2009), 24.

43. See F. Gregory Gause III, "Can Democracy Stop Terrorism," *Foreign Affairs* 84 (September/October 2005): 62–76; Gause, "Beware of What You Wish For," *foreignaffairs.com,* February 8, 2006. For a somewhat different spin on noninterventionism, see Charles Kupchan and Adam Mount, "The Autonomy Rule," *Democracy: A Journal of Ideas* (Spring 2009).

44. Ronald Inglehart and Christian Welzel, "How Development Leads to Democracy: What We Know about Modernization," *Foreign Affairs* 88 (March/April 2009):

33–48. Past arguments about the primacy of alleviating poverty and securing weak states were addressed in Jennifer Windsor, "Breaking the Poverty-Insecurity Nexus: Is Democracy the Answer?" in *Too Poor for Peace: Global Poverty, Conflict and Security in the 21st Century*, ed. Lael Brainard, and Derek Chollet (Washington, D.C.: Brookings, 2007); and at the August 2006 Aspen Institute conference on "The Tangled Web: The Poverty-Insecurity Nexus."

45. See Joshua Muravchik and Stephen M. Walt, "The Neocons vs. the Realists," *National Interest*, September 3, 2008. In "Democracy Promotion under Obama," Carothers urged that there was no need for a realistic "correction" in U.S. democracy promotion.

46. The democracy promotion and human rights organizations operate in separate realms. The democracy promotion group—which emerged after the mid-1980s when the Reagan administration began providing assistance for democracy— designs and carries out programs to build the capacity of local actors to advance reform, often with U.S. government funds. The human rights community has largely eschewed any U.S. government assistance, which began a decade earlier. It analyzes the deficiencies between government practice and international legal standards within societies, as well as advocates more respect for fundamental human rights in U.S. foreign policy and that of other countries. Freedom House, founded in 1941, bridges both communities and predates the emergence of either group.

47. Independent democracy promotion groups (even those funded by private individuals such as George Soros) have routinely been accused of being pawns of the Central Intelligence Agency (CIA) or instruments of American imperialism. In recent years, new accusations arose about such groups working toward "regime change" to advance U.S. interests. In some countries in the Middle East, U.S. support for democracy (including women's rights) was seen as part of a broader scheme by a U.S. government bent on attacking, subjugating, or diminishing the Muslim faith. See Carothers, "U.S. Democracy Promotion"; and Francis Fukuyama and Adam Garfinkle, "A Better Idea: Promote Democracy and Prevent Terrorism— But Don't Conflate the Two," *Wall Street Journal*, March 27, 2006.

48. See Gregory Gause's essay in this chapter. This notion is also endorsed by Thomas Carothers in "U.S. Democracy Promotion during and after Bush."

49. Gause relies heavily on Quan Li, "Does Democracy Promote or Reduce Transnational Terrorist Incidents," *Journal of Conflict Resolution* 49 (April 2005): 1–20. Although carefully researched and argued, Li's dataset in terms of terrorism measures is dated, and he shows limited knowledge of Freedom House's methodology. Alan Kruger makes a more compelling argument in *What Makes a Terrorist: Economics and the Roots of Terrorism* (Princeton, N.J.: Princeton University Press, 2006).

50. See Jennifer Windsor, "Advancing the Freedom Agenda: Time for a Recalibration?" *Washington Quarterly* 29 (Summer 2006): 21–34; and Thomas Carothers, "The Backlash against Democracy Promotion," *Foreign Affairs* 85 (March/April 2006): 55–68.

51. White House, "National Security Strategy of the United States of America."

52. See the work of Tamara Wittes, including *Freedom's Unsteady March: America's Role in Building Arab Democracy* (Washington, D.C.: Brookings, 2008.) The Carnegie Endowment Democracy and Rule of Law Project has an extensive series that explores both U.S. policy and events in the region.

53. I first made this argument in Jennifer Windsor, "Promoting Democratization Can Combat Terrorism," *Washington Quarterly* 26 (Summer 2003): 43–58. This essay draws heavily from that piece, while updating it to include more recent events and discussion. Also see Dalia Dassa Kaye, Frederic Wehrey, Audra K. Grant, and Dale Stahl, "More Freedom, Less Terror? Liberalization and Political Violence in the Arab World," RAND Corporation, Santa Monica, Calif., 2008, www.rand.org/pubs/monographs/MG772.

54. Freedom House has a long-standing, well-established methodology for measuring freedom that includes a broad array of measures of political rights and civil liberties. A country cannot make it into the Free category only by holding elections that are considered free and fair. It must also meet clear standards related to accountable governance and respect for fundamental rights, including freedoms of expression, association, and religious belief, and show a commitment to the rule of law. See the methodology at www.freedomhouse.org.

55. See the historical tables in Freedom House, *Freedom in the World 2009*.

56. Thomas O. Melia "The Democracy Bureaucracy: The Infrastructure of American Democracy Promotion," Princeton Project on National Security, September 2005, www.princeton.edu/~ppns/papers/democracy_bureaucracy.pdf.

57. The U.S. Agency for International Development recently spent millions of dollars trying to prove that U.S. aid has an impact on democratization; see www.usaid.gov/our_work/democracy_and_governance/publications/pdfs/impact_of_democracy_assistance.pdf.

58. See Jennifer Windsor, "Advancing the Freedom Agenda: Time for a Recalibration," and Michelle Dunne, "Democracy Promotion: Three Fallacies," at http://blogs.law.harvard.edu/mesh/2008/10/democracy_promotion_three_fallacies.

59. In my 2003 article "Promoting Democratization Can Combat Terrorism," I did not adequately clarify the nature of the terrorist threat by blending both transnational attacks against the United States and violent extremism more generally.

60. White House, "National Security Strategy of the United States of America."

61. Government of Britain, "The United Kingdom's Strategy for Countering International Terrorism," March 2009, 34, www.security.homeoffice.gov.uk/news-publications/publication-search/general/HO_Contest_strategy.pdf?view=Binary.

62. This broader approach is taken by the Task Force on Confronting the Ideology of Radical Extremism in "Rewriting the Narrative: An Integrated Strategy for Counterradicalization" (Washington, D.C.: Washington Institute for Near East Studies, 2009).

63. See the 2006 versions of the "National Security Strategy," and the "National Strategy for Combating Terrorism."

64. The 2006 "National Security Strategy" sets out two distinct goals—promoting freedom and defeating global terrorism. The connection between the two is set out in the second section, where lack of accountability of the state to the people is seen as one of four contributing factors to the current terrorist threat. The reference to the role of democracy is that it can help in the long run to counter all four factors.

65. See Task Force on Confronting the Ideology of Radical Extremism, "Rewriting the Narrative," 11.

66. For more in-depth treatment of this point, see Karin von Hippel's essay in Chapter 2 of this volume.

67. Of the eighteen countries in the Middle East and North Africa, Freedom House rates eleven as "Not Free," which means they have severely limited rights and political persecution. Saudi Arabia, Libya, and Syria are among the sixteen countries considered to be the most repressive in the world. See "Worst of the Worst" at www.freedomhouse.org. Note that Israel's actions in the Palestinian territories are scored separately. They receive next to the lowest possible scores and are rated Not Free.

68. Jessica Stern, *Terror in the Name of God* (New York: Harper Collins, 2003).

69. As Ethan Bueno de Mesquite notes, all religious extremists (not just Muslims) are likely to succeed in creating violent factions because their organizational structure is well suited to solving the fundamental problems that terrorists face—the need to mobilize support and to weed out those with uncertain commitment. See Ethan Bueno de Mesquita, "The Political Economy of Terrorism: A Selective Overview of Recent Work," *Political Economist* 10 (Winter 2008): 1–11.

70. See, for example, Jack Snyder, *From Voting to Violence: Democratization and Nationalist Conflict* (New York: Norton, 2000).

71. See Fareed Zakaria, *The Future of Freedom: Illiberal Democracy at Home and Abroad* (New York: Norton, 2004); and Nathan Sharansky, "The Price of Ignoring Palestinian Needs," *International Herald Tribune,* February 1, 2006. For an incisive critique of the "sequencing" argument and a defense of the reasonable amount of funding that the U.S. government has actually put toward elections, see Thomas Carothers, "The Sequencing Fallacy," *Journal of Democracy* 19 (January 2007): 12–27.

72. See Diamond, "What Went Wrong in Iraq."

73. Marina Ottaway and Amr Hamzawy, "Islamists in Politics: The Dynamics of Participation" (Washington, D.C.: Carnegie Endowment for International Peace, 2008).

74. See Mona Yacoubian, "Engaging Islamists and Promoting Democracy," U.S. Institute for Peace, Special Report 190, August 2007, for an examination of the evolution of the Islamist movement in Morocco, Jordan, and Yemen; and Mona Makram–Ebeid, in *Countering Islamists at the Ballot Box: Alternative Strategies,* Policy Focus No. 61, ed. David Schenker (Washington, D.C.: Washington Institute for Near East Studies, November 2006).

75. Turkey offers an apt example. For many years, successive American administrations were reluctant to hold Turkey to account for its poor human rights record and the denial of basic ethnic minority rights. Still, the United States did insist that Turkey's armed forces return political power to civilians after military coups and did support Turkey's regular process of elections. These elections led to frequent changes in government, which, along with the institution building required by Turkey's European Union bid, have helped to develop and deepen Turkish democracy.

76. None of the countries even qualifies as electoral democracies according to Freedom House. See page 3, "Setbacks and Resilience, Selected Data from Freedom House's Annual Survey of Political Rights and Civil Liberties," in Freedom House, *Freedom in the World 2009,* for a definition of what constitutes an electoral democracy.

77. For example, long before the 9/11 attacks and the rise of al-Qaeda, the Egyptian and Saudi regimes regularly highlighted their opposition to Islamist extremism in order to maintain American support while clearly coddling Islamist groups. Also, a treasure trove of documents captured in Iraq after 2003 illustrates the great extent

to which Saddam Hussein went in examining whether enhanced relations with extremist groups could serve Iraqi interests.

78. Kaye et al., "More Freedom, Less Terror?"

79. Under the Bush administration, the U.S. government forbade U.S. groups to come into contact with any individual or group that might be connected to Islamist groups, even nonviolent organizations. The exception was Iraq, as Brian Katulis notes in his excellent overview of U.S. democracy policy toward the Middle East, which provides a number of new approaches that the Obama administration should consider adopting. See Brian Katulis, *Democracy Promotion in the Middle East and the Obama Administration*, (New York: The Century Foundation, 2009), www.americanprogress.org/issues/2009/02/tcf_report.html.

9

can the united nations make a difference in fighting terrorism?

NO: The UN is limited in its ability to play a role
Zachary C. Shirkey, *St. John Fisher College*

YES: The UN has vital roles to play in countering terrorism
Eric Rosand, *Center on Global Counterterrorism Cooperation*

On December 15, 1999, the United Nations Security Council adopted a unanimous resolution demanding that Afghanistan's Taliban government close all terrorist training camps, stop providing sanctuary for international terrorists, and arrest and extradite Osama bin Laden and other indicted al-Qaeda members to countries where they could be brought to justice.[1] This resolution was followed on December 19, 2000, by an even more strongly worded condemnation and threats of new international sanctions against the Afghan government for noncompliance with the first resolution.[2]

Less than nine months later, on September 11, 2001, Afghanistan served as the springboard for the most destructive terrorist attack in history.

As this example illustrates, the United Nations' ability to directly combat terrorism has its shortcomings. If the UN could not act effectively against a known international terrorist group that for years was openly plotting and planning from within a member state, could it ever do so?

This assessment, however, may not be entirely fair. After all, the UN was created in 1946 not to replace states as the primary actors in world politics, but rather to help facilitate interstate cooperation and compliance with international obligations. So shortcomings in the UN's ability to directly address global security threats such as terrorism are built into the system.

Acknowledging structural limitations in the UN's ability to lead counterterrorism efforts should certainly temper expectations about UN-based solutions. But it is also true that the organization has often undermined its own ability to play a credible role. For example, despite decades of trying, the UN has yet to agree on a common definition of *terrorism*. States can, then, pick and choose which terrorist groups or state sponsors they will act against and which they will not. And the UN's track record of objectivity in dealing with terrorism is spotty at best: in 1974 the UN granted the Palestinian Liberation Organization "observer status" in the General Assembly, despite the assertions by Israel and other member states that the group was a terrorist organization.

After the 9/11 attacks, the UN found itself in a novel position in relation to terrorism. The advent of globalized mass-casualty terrorism in the form of al-Qaeda—a group with footholds in dozens of countries and that targets dozens more—called out for action by the world's leading political and security organization.

Indeed, since the events of 9/11 the UN has strived to become a more effective player in combating terrorism. For example, Security Council Resolution 1373 (September 28, 2001) requires member states to adopt strict regulations against terrorism and enhance their own counterterrorism readiness. The organization also has created new bodies, such as the Counter-Terrorism Committee, to monitor and assist counterterrorism efforts by member states. And in 2006 the General Assembly adopted its first Global Counter-Terrorism Strategy, which pulls together all preexisting UN counterterrorism resolutions and treaties into one approved framework.

So does this mean the UN has become a key player in the global fight against terrorism?

Not according to Zachary Shirkey, who argues that, despite laudable efforts, the UN remains hamstrung by its inherent shortcomings: failure to coordinate a common acceptance of what constitutes terrorism (and who is a terrorist), failure to punish noncompliance with UN mandates, and failure to create effective legal frameworks that states will take seriously. Shirkey recognizes that terrorism can be countered successfully only through coordinated global action. And he believes that the UN plays an important role in international politics. But he says that when it comes to terrorism—an acute security challenge often involving parochial passions—states will inevitably need to take the lead. Indeed, should the UN overreach on this issue, it may well hinder rather than help effective global counterterrorism efforts.

Eric Rosand does not disagree that states will take the lead in counterterrorism. But he differs with Shirkey over the degree to which the UN can assist in these efforts. Rosand argues that the UN has a comparative advantage in many important global counterterrorism functions, such as creating universal lists of terrorist groups and individuals against whom sanctions might be targeted. And the UN is in a unique position to serve as a global "norm-setter" for counterterrorism programs and initiatives and to assist states in building up their counterterrorism capacities (not every state has the counterterrorism resources of the United States or Britain, for example). Although the UN may never replace states in combating terrorism, the organization can and will continue to assist in the fight. And with further reforms and more funding, the UN is poised to assist even more.

The United Nations serves as a valuable organization to help deal with a plethora of global challenges in the twenty-first century. If it is to play an effective role in combating terrorism, its members need to both balance their expectations and boost the areas in which it can best contribute. The authors in this chapter offer a road map in this direction.

NO: The UN is limited in its ability to play a role
Zachary C. Shirkey, *St. John Fisher College*

Why the UN Is Ill-Suited to Help Defeat Terrorism

Terrorism, especially global terrorist movements like al-Qaeda, can be successfully confronted only through international cooperation. States must work together on collecting intelligence, capturing and extraditing terrorists, tracking and stanching the flow of terrorist funding, and even military actions designed to curb terrorism. Without such cooperation, counterterrorism efforts will be much more difficult, take longer to work, and be far less effective. For example, without cooperation states may fail to learn of impending attacks as terrorists plot against them from foreign lands, or they may watch as terrorist suspects remain free because of lack of extradition agreements or sharing of evidence. And without cooperation, terrorist financial networks would remain fluid and robust as groups simply play off different states with varying and uncoordinated degrees of financial oversight and enforcement.

Because sustained bilateral and multilateral cooperation is needed to avoid such undesirable scenarios, it seems logical that states would turn to international organizations to overcome the free riding and coordination problems inherent in such multilateral efforts.[3] Although claims about the benefits of institutions are not unchallenged,[4] institutions such as the World Bank, International Monetary Fund (IMF), World Health Organization, and European Union have been used widely in attempts to overcome the problems that generally bedevil international cooperation. It follows, then, that states also should turn to the United Nations to help coordinate counterterrorism efforts and that the UN may well be essential to winning the war on terrorism.

Surprisingly, such a conclusion is wrong. The reason, in part, is that broad-based cooperation in security matters is difficult to achieve. Narrower security cooperation through alliances such as the North Atlantic Treaty Organization (NATO) is common, but broad-based cooperation is much rarer. This is not to say that organizations that seek broad-based cooperation, such as the UN, are failed or useless. Yes, the UN has its share of flaws and would benefit from reform, but it has helped the international community cope with security issues as diverse as interstate and civil wars, refugee flows, and human rights violations. It would be difficult to argue that greater cooperation or better results would have been achieved had the UN left these problems to be tackled by others. Why then is the UN poorly equipped to bring about cooperation for the specific purpose of combating terrorism?

To answer this question, it is necessary to think about what the UN could conceivably do to fight terrorism. First, it could provide a common legal framework and enhance law enforcement capabilities for apprehending and prosecuting terrorists worldwide. Second, it could mediate and verify agreements struck with terrorist groups. Third, it could overcome free riding by coordinating interstate cooperation in intelligence gathering and synthesis and by synchronizing states' individual tactical responses to terrorism. In practice though, each of these three approaches has serious flaws. First, the legal approach is problematic because the UN's structure is not geared toward dealing with nonstate actors such as al-Qaeda and because of the UN's inability to even define terrorism. Second, mediation and verification mean little in a world in which states are wary of negotiating with terrorists. Third, the UN would likely be incapable of facilitating counterterrorism cooperation because, despite the widely shared interest in fighting the phenomenon of terrorism, states often do not share an interest in fighting specific terrorist groups. This essay will delve into these three areas of possible UN efforts in fighting terrorism and discuss in detail each of their shortcomings.

WHY THE UN CANNOT PROVIDE A LEGAL FRAMEWORK

Couldn't the UN help by coordinating the international legal efforts against terrorism? After all, the UN is capable of creating binding international law and its court, the International Court of Justice (ICJ), is the most prestigious body in the realm of international jurisprudence. And yet despite these apparent advantages, the UN is ill-suited to aid the legal battle against terrorism because successful legal action requires at least three things: reasonably clear definitions of what is legal and what is not; a means of apprehending suspected perpetrators; and a body to adjudicate competing claims and convict the guilty. The UN lacks all three.

First, the UN has yet to even define terrorism.[5] The failure to take this necessary first step arises because every state naturally wants UN policy to first benefit its interests rather than any common good. Thus states that back groups whose actions could potentially be labeled as terrorist would want to define terrorism in order to exclude those groups. This is the old saw "one man's terrorist is another man's freedom fighter" in action. For example, Hugo Chavez of Venezuela has consistently rejected the notion that the Revolutionary Armed Forces of Colombia (FARC) is a terrorist organization or that its actions are in any way illegitimate.[6] Similarly, Iran certainly would resist any attempt to have its protégé Hezbollah labeled as a terrorist group. States that face guerrilla insurgencies would want such movements classified as terroristic, whereas many Arab states would want to include actions by states and not just groups in order to label Israel as engaging in terrorism. All that said, whether states truly believe their own claims about who is or is not a terrorist, or simply make them out of self-interest, is irrelevant. Because of their reluctance to have groups they support labeled as terrorists, and thus violators of international law, it is extremely difficult, if not impossible, to achieve a broad-based international consensus on how terrorism should be defined.

As far back as the failed effort of the League of Nations in 1937, such conflicting interests have paralyzed repeated efforts to define *terrorism*.[7] Since 1997, the UN General Assembly has failed repeatedly to pass resolutions that would define terrorism, such as Resolution 51/210 in 1999.[8] Debates in the General Assembly on a definition in the immediate post-9/11 period also went nowhere, so discouraging Secretary-General Kofi Annan that he urged the Assembly to give up the search for legal precision.[9] Again in 2005, even after the shocking attack by a Chechen group on a school in Beslan, Russia, the Assembly made no headway in its attempt to define terrorism, largely because of opposition from states in the Organization of the Islamic Conference.[10] Nor is it defined in the UN's Global Counter-Terrorism Strategy (2006).[11] Even narrow UN bodies focused specifically on global security have failed. Most notably, Security Council Resolution 1373 (2003), which created the UN's main counterterrorism committee, does not define terrorism.[12]

Worse than the definitional impasse is the fact that many UN members have been willing to tolerate terrorist groups, provided their goals are seen as admirable. Perhaps the most striking example of this was the success of the Palestine Liberation Organization (PLO) in obtaining observer status at the UN beginning in the early 1970s, at a time it was clearly viewed by many as a terrorist organization. Thus even if the UN were to agree on a definition, many UN members would probably decline to denounce terrorism itself as always being illegitimate. If universal condemnation cannot be achieved, it will be impossible to target terrorism generally, and the notion of equality before the law will be undermined. It is not at all clear how the UN can impose legal constraints on terrorist activity if it cannot even agree on what it is trying to make illegal or that all terrorist activity is inherently wrong.

Second, the UN currently has no body to act as a law enforcement agency or police force, and it is unlikely to create such a body. The UN could call on member states to provide such forces on an ad hoc basis, but it is not clear how such an arrangement would be more effective than states simply acting without UN involvement. In fact, to the extent that UN involvement would add another layer of bureaucracy to the process, it might slow and reduce the effectiveness—secrecy is often required—of such actions. Thus even if the UN could pass effective laws, enforcement would, by necessity, be left to member states. This would not be an improvement over the status quo.

Finally, the UN lacks a body to rule on terrorism cases. The ICJ accepts only *states* (not institutions, businesses, individuals, or terrorist groups) as parties to a case. Raising the profile of terrorist groups to the level of a state so that the ICJ could address them would be counterproductive, because it would give groups the attention, prestige, and legitimacy they desperately seek. Thus the ICJ cannot actually deal with terrorism, except in the case of a suspected state sponsor. Even then, the ICJ lacks the means to enforce its decisions. Although the ICJ charter says that the opinions of the ICJ are "final and without appeal," it is completely silent on how compliance is to be brought about. In practice, compliance occurs when states wish to be seen as playing by the rules. But because state sponsors of terrorism are already often operating outside of the normative and often legal rules of the international system, such considerations are unlikely to compel them to comply. In any event, under the UN Charter the ICJ cannot directly impose sanctions. In cases in which states fail to voluntarily comply with a ruling, the aggrieved party can ask the Security Council to enforce the decision under Article 94(2) of the UN Charter, but the Security Council is not required to take such action. As described later in this essay, the Security Council's track record in dealing with state sponsors of terrorism is spotty at best. Worse, many states refuse to accept the ICJ's jurisdiction in any matter involving national security: the United States and France, for example, have refused to comply with ICJ rulings affecting national security based on other states' refusal to admit jurisdiction over such matters.[13]

Not surprisingly, the UN has made little headway in its attempts to combat terrorism by imposing binding mandates on members. The UN's main effort has centered on creating two permanent committees within the Security Council: the 1267 Committee and the Counter-Terrorism Committee (CTC), created, respectively, by Resolutions 1267 (October 15, 1999) and 1373 (September 28, 2001). The UN's more recent effort, its Global Counter-Terrorism Strategy (2006), essentially enjoins member states to comply with previous UN statues on terrorism and pledge to try to create more effective measures in the future.[14] Thus it effectively adds nothing new to the UN's counterterrorism toolkit. The 1267 Committee specifically targets individual members of al-Qaeda and the Taliban and forbids states from providing funding, safe haven, or weapons to any of some five hundred members whose names appear on the proscribed list. Although this interdiction may sound impressive, al-Qaeda alone has over four thousand known members, and no other terrorist groups are targeted by the committee.[15] Thus most terrorists escape UN sanctions. Furthermore, new names can be added only with the unanimous consent of the Security Council, a condition that has rarely been met except in the immediate aftermath of the 9/11 attacks, as illustrated by the fact that nearly half of the names on the list were added in September 2001.[16]

Even as it pertains to the listed members, the effectiveness of the 1267 Committee is unclear. Although terrorist groups' finances may have been interrupted to some degree, there is little evidence that the safe haven travel ban has been enforced, suggesting that rules passed by the 1267 Committee have little, if any, bite. The 1267 Committee's own monitoring group observed that "there have been no reports yet from any State that a designated individual has sought entry into or has been stopped from entering or transiting their country."[17] Worse, the committee has no mandate to bring any of these listed members to justice, and fully one-third of UN members have not even bothered to report whether they are in compliance with the committee's requirements.[18]

The CTC's efforts have not been much more successful. It is charged with confronting terrorism in general and has issued binding rules for UN members to follow when dealing with terrorist groups. However, because no UN body has created a global list of terrorist groups, member states retain great latitude in which groups they consider to be terrorists.[19] It is not clear, then, what sort of requirements CTC mandates actually place on UN member states. Like the 1267 Committee, the CTC has no actual enforcement powers, though at least it has moved most of the work on terrorism from the General Assembly to the Security Council. Beyond providing expert legal advice on tightening national antiterrorism laws, the CTC has no authority to punish state sponsors, identify terrorist groups, or prosecute actual terrorists.[20] The CTC's data gathering, though useful, in part duplicates work already being done by the United Nations Office on Drugs and Crime (UNODC).[21]

Even to the extent that international institutions in general can play a role in constructing legal or procedural tools for combating terrorism, the UN is often not the most appropriate institution. Better institutional options exist for arresting, prosecuting, and cutting off the finances of individual terrorists and terrorist groups. For example, in the area of terrorist financing—an area of emphasis of both the 1267 Committee and CTC—an institution such as the IMF may well be better suited to the task. The IMF routinely deals with financial transactions and has created programs such as the Financial Action Task Force on Money Laundering to fight terrorism-related financial activities.[22] The IMF, which deals directly with banks and governmental financial organs on a daily basis, has built a vast reservoir of contacts, expertise, and leverage. It would be easier to enhance such programs rather than create new ones out of whole cloth.

Likewise, in the legal battle against terrorism it would be far better to let organizations such as the International Criminal Court (ICC) and Interpol take the lead. Unlike the ICJ, the ICC is designed to deal with individuals who break international law and has the authority—though not necessarily the capacity—to indict, apprehend, convict, and punish individual terrorists. Similarly, Interpol has the capacity and experience to coordinate law enforcement operations across many countries and actually capture suspected terrorists.[23]

This is not to say, however, that these other international organizations are a panacea to terrorism. They also must overcome many of the same challenges as the UN. The ICC, for example, faces a host of difficulties. Most notably, the United States is not, nor soon likely to be, a member. This absence reduces the organization's capabilities and legitimacy. In addition, the ICC and the various ad hoc human rights and war crimes tribunals that preceded it have often moved at a snail's pace—if at all. The slow pace may be acceptable in some issue areas, but terrorism is not one of them, because inaction or slow action may cost many lives, even if terrorists are ultimately brought to justice. Finally, although the ICC can put terrorists on trial and convict them, like the UN it lacks an ability to apprehend terrorists. Two well-known examples of indicted war criminals able to avoid trial before the ICC and its predecessors are former Bosnian Serb military leader Ratko Mladić and Sudanese president Omar al-Bashir. Thus, although other international organizations are better suited than the UN to engage in counterterrorism efforts, they, too, have significant limitations.

WHY THE UN CANNOT MEDIATE AND VERIFY AGREEMENTS WITH TERRORISTS

Rarely do states reach accommodation with terrorist groups. Indeed, they tend to be reluctant to even recognize terrorist groups out of fear of giving them legitimacy. For example, the United States and Israel have refused to treat Hamas as the *de jure* government of the Palestinian Authority despite Hamas's clear electoral triumph in 2006. Of course, the same can be said of guerrilla groups, and UN-led mediation with such groups has sometimes proved profitable.[24] The fundamental problem in mediation with terrorists is that many groups have unlimited, and arguably unattainable, aims. Such groups cannot be accommodated and will simply use any concessions offered as leverage to try and extract even more. For example, al-Qaeda quickly pivoted to other, more expansive goals after its initial demand that the United States withdraw its troops from Saudi Arabia was met. Similarly, Hezbollah has only grown in ambition since achieving its primary goal of pushing Israel out of southern Lebanon.

Unfortunately, groups with the most significant global reach—that is, the ones most likely to bring about widespread coordination among states in a body such as the UN—are the very groups that tend to have these maximalist, nonnegotiable demands.[25] No amount of skillful mediation or inventive verification can make accommodation with such groups possible. This problem is not limited to negotiating with Islamic groups. Perhaps the best example of the dangers of signing agreements with terrorists is when, from 1998 to 2002, Colombia granted a safe zone to FARC so that peace talks could begin. Not only did the talks ultimately fail, but FARC exploited the safe zone to greatly increase its strength. Although there is no reason to think all negotiations would be equally disastrous, the risk is real.

This is not to say, of course, that mediation between states and terrorist groups with limited demands is never possible. Such negotiations have occurred and have been profitable. Britain's cease-fire with the Irish Republican Army (IRA) illustrated that successful compromises can be struck with some terrorist organizations. However, such opportunities will be rare, and even when they do emerge the UN may not be the organization preferred for mediation. Because UN involvement generally raises the profile of an issue and governments and possibly the terrorists themselves will likely want to keep negotiations quiet—at least in the early stages—UN involvement could be detrimental. The Oslo negotiations between Israel and the PLO, for example, began with secret meetings in Madrid and not through high-profile talks. Even in the latter stages of mediation or in the monitoring phase, it may not be clear that the UN would be the preferred organization. For example, when the IRA and British government reached a settlement in the Good Friday Accords in 1998 the two sides chose to set up a new body, the Independent Monitoring Commission, to verify the agreement rather than invite the UN to do the job. To the extent that local capacity exists for verification or that the involvement of a great many outside powers is undesirable, UN involvement may well be unattractive.

WHY THE UN CANNOT COORDINATE STATE RESPONSES TO TERRORISM

As noted earlier, international organizations like the UN are thought to be able to help states coordinate their responses to shared problems. Such organizations can help build state capacity, overcome free-rider problems, and assist states in aligning policies for maximum effectiveness. But the UN's structure, its past performance in dealing with state sponsors, and the nature of the terrorist challenge all cast significant doubt on the UN's ability to perform such functions in the realm of counterterrorism. Specifically, the UN has little capacity to lend to states, and the nonstate nature of terrorist groups will foil UN attempts to coordinate counterterrorism efforts. Beyond this, the main obstacle to successful cooperation in counterterrorism efforts remains not free riding, but a lack of shared state interests.

Inability to Assist Capacity Building and Coordination

Even if states wanted to comply with UN counterterrorism mandates or confront terrorism on their own, many lack the capacity to do so. It has been suggested that the UN could provide expertise and capacity-building tools to countries that are willing but unable to fight terrorism—and that such efforts would be more politically palatable coming from the UN rather than, say, the United States.[26] To the extent that the UN has tried to build counterterrorism capacity, it has been the work of the CTC, whose efforts have met with little success. The reason, in part, is that it is not clear in what sort of capacity building the CTC could engage. As mentioned earlier, the UN lacks its own policing or enforcement mechanisms. Therefore, it cannot lend that capacity to states. In addition, the CTC is not authorized to provide direct financial assistance to states; it can only put states in contact with donors and other providers of assistance.[27] Thus even if the CTC's funding situation improved, it would not be able to provide direct financial aid to states.

One area in which the CTC could engage in state capacity building might be intelligence. Many states lack sufficient, actionable counterterrorism intelligence. Perhaps this deficit could be overcome if the UN acted as a clearinghouse for intelligence gathered by its member states, which could be done without having to create new UN intelligence assets. However, it is unlikely that the CTC or any other organ of the UN would be able to share intelligence with states to help them fight terrorism because most actionable counterterrorism intelligence is closely guarded by the states that gather it (they want to protect their sources and their ongoing counterterrorism operations).

Proponents of an intelligence clearinghouse might argue that the International Atomic Energy Agency (IAEA), a UN-affiliated body, has been able to collect a good deal of information on the nuclear programs of states and thus a similar agency could be created to deal with terrorism. Unfortunately, the tasks faced by the IAEA and any counterterrorism intelligence organization are quite different. The IAEA relies heavily on voluntary information and voluntary compliance, elements not common to counterterrorism intelligence gathering. Thus intelligence does not seem to be an area in which the UN can have much success at building state counterterrorism capacity.

Even simply trying to coordinate states' responses rather than building their capacity is problematic because of the public nature of UN action. Many states may wish to keep their cooperation with other countries against certain terrorists groups from becoming public. For example, governments of states in which terrorists maintain some popular support may well refuse to cooperate unless their actions remain secret or at least receive minimal publicity. And the reactions of EU member states in June 2006 to the revelation of their roles in a secret U.S.-led terrorist financing tracking program suggest that policies even suspected of violating privacy or civil liberties may not survive public disclosure, at least in Western democracies.[28] Joint UN actions are, almost by definition, highly visible. To the extent that this visibility would reduce governments' willingness to collaborate against terrorist groups, the UN's involvement would, if anything, be counterproductive.

States versus Nonstate Actors

A major challenge the UN faces in attempting to combat terrorism is that it is structured to deal with states rather than nonstate actors. The UN has had its greatest successes in confronting states that have run afoul of the will of the international community and in mediating between member states—though, of course, the UN has also had its share of failures in these areas.[29] Dealing successfully with nonstate actors, such as terrorist groups, would require a realignment of UN thinking and probably significant institutional changes as well. Such changes are notoriously hard to undertake. For example, the UN still has a permanent committee to deal with Trust Territories (a leftover from the League of Nations), even though the committee has not met since 1994 when the last territory became independent. It has simply been easier to let the committee continue to exist on paper than to attempt to alter the UN's structure. Similarly, the UN Charter still refers to Japan as a "former enemy."[30] If such a commonsense realignment that does not harm the interest of any member is too difficult to undertake, a more controversial significant realignment seems very unlikely.

The UN has tried to deal with nonstate actors using its current structure. The best examples have been peacekeeping missions, such as in Cambodia and Bosnia, where the UN has dealt with guerrilla and rebel groups with mixed success. However, groups such as the Khmer Rouge and the Bosnian Serb nationalist movement served as de facto governments for large swaths of territory, making them significantly different from transnational terrorist groups, such as al-Qaeda, or groups that have no governmental aspirations, such as the Earth Liberation Front. True, some terrorist groups, such as Hezbollah and Hamas, have governed territory much like guerrillas, but that is the exception rather than the rule. Even in such select cases, problems remain, because when the UN has dealt with nonstate actors it has mainly been helpful in aiding mediation and enforcing cease-fires, which, as noted earlier, is unlikely to be a popular or helpful avenue for dealing with terrorist groups.[31] Thus even when the UN occasionally gets around the difficulties posed by the nonstate nature of terrorist groups, the discussion must return again to the obstacles to effective UN counterterrorism efforts.

Targeting State Sponsors of Terrorism

Combating state sponsors of terrorism is the area in which the UN should be best equipped to help. Unfortunately, the UN's track record in dealing with such states leaves much to be desired. To the extent that sponsors such as Syria, Libya, Iran, and Sudan have been punished for backing terrorist groups, it has mostly occurred outside the purview of the UN system, such as the U.S. strikes on Libya in 1986 and Sudan in 1998. This situation is not surprising because the terrorism these states sponsor generally affects only a few states. For example, although Lebanon, Israel, and the United States may be especially concerned about Iran's support for Hezbollah, how many other states are truly affected? The ability to link Iran's support for Hezbollah to nuclear proliferation may bring some additional states along, but it will not likely be enough to move the Security Council or General Assembly into taking truly meaningful actions. Simply proceeding on the Iranian nuclear proliferation issue alone has proven exceedingly difficult for the UN.[32]

Meanwhile, as Venezuela's and Ecuador's growing support for FARC in Colombia reveals, the international community's past responses to state sponsors have not been sufficient to deter new states from becoming sponsors. Indeed, during the March 2008 dispute over Colombia's raids on FARC bases in Ecuador, most members of the Organization of American States—to say nothing of the UN—were more favorably disposed toward Ecuador and Venezuela than Colombia.[33] Despite the repugnant nature of terrorism, states will react to it and its sponsorship based on their own national interests. Because one terrorist group rarely threatens a large number of states, forming the kind of broad-based coalitions necessary to bring about meaningful UN sanctions or UN military actions under either Chapters 6 or 7 of the UN Charter will be extremely difficult, if possible at all.

Al-Qaeda is unusual in that it does actually threaten a great many states, including all five permanent members of the Security Council, each of whom confronts varying degrees of Islamic extremism. Thus the international response to al-Qaeda's former state sponsor, Taliban-controlled Afghanistan, was swift and decisive—at least initially. Yet even in this case, although the UN endorsed the post-9/11 Afghan war by means of Resolutions 1368 and 1373, it was NATO rather than the UN that coordinated the invasion and occupation, and even NATO's mission has had serious coordination problems. For example, many NATO members outside of the United States have placed major restrictions on their troops' participation.[34] And even though the contributions of NATO members increased as the situation in Afghanistan worsened, the mission has not succeeded in stabilizing Afghanistan or eliminating al-Qaeda's Taliban ally. The war in Afghanistan has been one of the most robust post-9/11 counterterrorism actions, and NATO is arguably the world's most unified, coordinated, and powerful security organization. How then can there be much optimism for the average UN action against recognized state sponsors that will likely be bedeviled by greater conflicts of interest, lack of proper planning, and lack of deployable assets?

Combating Terrorist Groups as Opposed to Combating Terrorism

Perhaps the biggest problem for the UN lies in the assumption that all states share an equal interest in combating terrorism. The UN does not require unanimity to act, but it does require a broad consensus to be effective. Even leaving aside the serious problem of state sponsors, it is extremely difficult to form broad coalitions to fight terrorism because states are not threatened by terrorism in general, but rather by specific terrorist groups. There is no all-encompassing "war on terrorism." Rather, many counterterrorism battles are being waged against specific terrorist groups. For example, Colombia certainly would be interested in measures that would help combat FARC, but it probably would have little interest in using its limited resources to combat groups such as al-Qaeda, which do not currently target the Colombian government. Thus UN efforts would be limited to studies and attempts at capacity building rather than targeting actual terrorists, because these kinds of actions would be the only ones that coincide with widely shared interests. Not surprisingly, these are exactly the kinds of limited measures in which the UN has been engaging.[35]

The lack of shared interests is apparent in past and ongoing UN attempts to address other security issues, such as Iran's current nuclear program or Iraq's violation of UN resolutions in the decade following the Persian Gulf War. The split over how to confront Iraq prior to 2003 is now infamous on both sides of the Atlantic.[36] And despite widespread and long-standing concerns about Iran's nuclear program—concerns that have been confirmed by the IAEA[37]—little in the way of meaningful action has taken place. Although neither issue was directly tied to terrorism, it is not at all clear why concerns about terrorism would bring about more unity of action in the UN than these other security issues. For example, some of the leading states have continued to pursue their own interests and have often failed to agree on the severity of the Iranian threat.[38] It is clear, then, that terrorism will always be only one of the many issues that states face, and it often will not be the most important.

CONCLUSION

The UN has and will continue to have great difficulty in aiding counterterror-ism efforts. The interests of member states differ in their relations with terror-ist groups, and the UN's institutional structures are not well suited for dealing with nonstate actors. These two factors undermine the UN's efforts to create a global legal framework for coping with terrorism and to help build states' counterterrorism capacities. These problems do not affect the UN's ability to engage in mediation, but negotiating with terrorists is not the norm. Further-more, because of the high levels of attention UN involvement brings to an issue—as well as the legitimacy UN involvement may give to the terrorist groups involved—the UN is often an unattractive mediator even when nego-tiations with terrorist groups may otherwise prove profitable. Thus UN coun-terterrorism efforts face severe limitations.

These limitations do not stem primarily from funding issues. Funding is certainly inadequate, but the CTC, 1267 Committee, and other UN organs are limited by their mandates in what they can do. Increasing funding will not eliminate these restrictions. Indeed, the deep divisions among member states about which terrorists groups to target, as illustrated by the debates on defining terrorism, almost certainly ensure that these restrictions are not likely to be removed. They exist because a sufficiently broad consensus on fighting terror-ism does not exist within the UN—states focus on specific groups rather than on the phenomenon as a whole.

This argument is not one against the UN or international organizations in general. International organizations, and the UN in particular, can help solve many problems. Similarly, it is not an argument against cooperative efforts in counterterrorism. Quite the contrary, whenever possible states should and must form coalitions dedicated to combating specific terrorist groups, includ-ing coalitions that take advantage of existing, more narrowly focused organiza-tions and alliances.

Rather, it is an argument against putting too much hope into combating ter-rorism through the UN. UN efforts may produce some results, but the resources employed to get those results may well go further if used in the more traditional state-centered ways. Certainly, if the UN could produce a fairly comprehensive list of terrorists and their groups or contribute to building state capacity, it would be helpful. Unfortunately, past UN efforts in these areas are not encouraging. Whatever efforts are taken at the UN, it should first ensure that those efforts are not duplicating work being done by other organizations, such as the IMF, or other parts of the UN, such as the UN Office on Drugs and Crime. Narrow UN efforts with limited expectations will likely have the best return on states' investments. Whatever tasks the UN undertakes they should be adjuncts to, rather than central planks in, global counterterrorism strategies.

YES: The UN has vital roles to play in countering terrorism
Eric Rosand, *Center on Global Counterterrorism Cooperation*

The UN Is Poised to Assist against Global Terrorism

Eight years after the September 11, 2001, attacks, transnational and home-grown Islamist terrorist networks continue to pose serious challenges to international peace and security.[39] Attacks and thwarted attacks in Algeria, Germany, Indonesia, Pakistan, India, Indonesia, Mauritania, Morocco, the Philippines, Turkey, the United Kingdom, and elsewhere, often planned by individuals with ties to multiple regions, underscore the reality of a complex global phenomenon that requires a comprehensive, coordinated global response. With the upsurge in terrorist violence, even the most economically and militarily powerful of countries now recognize that no single state or coalition of states can effectively fight this threat alone.

Although the primary response to international terrorism has come from national governments, which carry the principal responsibility for protecting their citizens, multilateral bodies at the international and regional levels can, if properly structured, mandated, and resourced, make an important contribution as well. In fact, successes in the global campaign against terrorism frequently have been the result of the cooperation and mutual support shown by governments, often facilitated by and through engagement in multilateral settings.[40]

Traditionally, nationalist or separatist groups that resort to terrorist violence—for example, the Kurdistan Workers' Party (PKK) in Turkey, the Tamil Tigers in Sri Lanka, or the Revolutionary Armed Forces of Colombia (FARC)—have generated limited responses at the multilateral levels. Only with the emergence of al-Qaeda, with its global reach and ability to operate across national boundaries—and more precisely the September 2001 attacks on the United States—did counterterrorism rise to the top of the agenda in multilateral institutions, mostly as a result of U.S. pressure. This was particularly so in the UN Security Council, which through the extraordinary powers granted to it under the UN Charter to impose binding obligations on all UN member states and its relatively streamlined decision-making processes, offered the United States the quickest route for globalizing the fight against terrorism. Ever since both the Security Council and General Assembly condemned the attacks on the United States, with the smoke from the ruins of the World Trade Center visible from the windows of the United Nations, a standard talking point for leaders of countries big and small, from North and South, has been to place the UN at the center of global efforts to counter terrorism.[41] This message was echoed on behalf of all fifteen members of the Security Council in its president's statement after the November 2008 attacks in Mumbai, India.[42]

Despite rhetorical support from the highest levels, many U.S. policymakers and counterterrorism experts remain skeptical of what the United Nations can actually contribute in concrete terms to combating terrorism because it does "not have any of the personnel needed to gather intelligence on activities and movements of suspected terrorists, nor to patrol border crossings or arrest alleged perpetrators—all of which [are] functions that governments should perform."[43] In addition, the UN is deemed unable to serve as a mechanism for intelligence sharing among governments. Skeptics also point to the fact that although UN member states have joined together to condemn terrorism in general, many continue to differentiate between terrorists and "freedom fighters," thereby blocking universal agreement on a definition of terrorism.

Even though all of this is true, it has not prevented the UN system, which includes its principal organs such as the Security Council, General Assembly, and Secretariat, as well as its programs and specialized agencies, from working to reinforce national and regional counterterrorism efforts.[44]

Although there will always be a great deal of multilateral cooperative counterterrorism activity at the global, regional, and subregional levels that does not (and should not) involve the UN, that does not take away from what the UN and only the UN, because of its global membership and legitimacy, can provide.

However, any serious discussion of the UN's comparative advantages in this area must keep in mind the human and financial resources devoted to an issue that many member states do not view as a top priority. After briefly addressing this issue, this essay will identify some of the ways in which the UN system can make, and in many cases has made, concrete contributions to reinforcing national and regional efforts to respond to the terrorist threat. These contributions consist of short-term law enforcement and other security-related preventative measures and longer-term efforts to address the conditions conducive to the spread of terrorism or what is often labeled terrorism's root causes.

Much of the security-related preventive work has been carried out by the "traditional" UN counterterrorism actors—the Security Council's counterterrorism-related bodies and groups of experts and the UN Office on Drugs and Crime's Terrorism Prevention Branch (TPB) based in Vienna. The essay will also refer to some of the contributions that the UN's nontraditional counterterrorism actors, such as the United Nations Development Programme (UNDP) and the United Nations Educational, Scientific, and Cultural Organization (UNESCO), have made to longer-term efforts that seek to address conditions conducive to the spread of terrorism such as lack of development, poverty, social and economic marginalization, unresolved conflicts, and human rights abuses. Although generally not labeled or identified as "counterterrorism" work, many of the activities of these parts of the UN system, which often have robust field presences, nevertheless contribute to the longer-term efforts to address the threat.

Finally, this essay will show that although the UN is contributing in many ways to the global efforts to combat terrorism, its impact is being impeded by a few structural flaws. These include the lack of a broad-based forum to give a wide range of countries a sense of ownership over the UN's counterterrorism program and the continuing lack of coordination among the many bodies or offices scattered around the globe and operating under distinct and often overlapping mandates. The essay will conclude by suggesting manageable reforms that would allow the UN to develop broader, and yet more streamlined, credible and effective counterterrorism initiatives.

BACKGROUND: BUDGET AND STAFF

Many UN member states have been victimized by terrorism, and nearly all seem to recognize the global dimension of today's threat. However, despite the fact that a majority of the victims are from Muslim-majority nations, most states tend to view Islamist terrorism as primarily a Western problem, seeing it as less salient to their own concerns than, for example, poverty, lack of development, HIV/AIDS, and ordinary crime. Only some $15 million from the $2 billion UN regular budget is allocated to the traditional UN counterterrorism efforts. Most of this goes to support the three Security Council counterterrorism-related bodies, each composed of Council member states and their respective group of experts.

The Counter-Terrorism Committee and its Executive Directorate (CTED), which has about twenty-five counterterrorism experts, are responsible for monitoring national efforts to implement Security Council Resolution 1373, adopted shortly after September 11, 2001, which requires all states to adopt a series of measures to enhance their counterterrorism readiness, and Security Council Resolution 1624, adopted after the London attacks in July 2005, which addresses the problem of incitement of terrorist acts. The Council's Al-Qaida/Taliban Sanctions Committee and its Analytical Support and Sanctions Monitoring Team supervise the implementation of financial, travel, and arms sanctions the Council has imposed against al-Qaeda, the Taliban, and related groups and individuals. And the Council's Non-Proliferation Committee and its group of eight experts monitor national efforts to implement Resolution 1540, which mandates states to take a series of steps to prevent weapons of mass destruction (WMDs) and their means of delivery from getting into the hands of terrorists.

In addition to these Council bodies, the UN's Terrorism Prevention Branch in Vienna receives some $1 million from the UN's regular budget, and an additional $9 million in "voluntary" contributions from largely Western donors to support the work of its forty experts and consultants. They provide countries with the technical assistance they need to join and implement the UN counterterrorism instruments, which are discussed in more detail shortly. Apart from a few human rights and counterterrorism officers in the UN Office of the High Commissioner on Human Rights and three or four people assigned to work on counterterrorism issues within the UN Secretariat, this is largely the extent of the resources within the United Nations that have been earmarked for counterterrorism (or counterterrorism-related) activity, nearly all of which goes to staff salaries and travel.

Thus, when determining the appropriate role for the United Nations in global counterterrorism efforts and assessing its performance to date, one needs to be mindful of the limited resources it has at its disposal to carry out the "counterterrorism" programs under its global remit, particularly when compared with certain bilateral actions. For example, among bilateral donors active in Southeast Asia, Japan's budget for Grant Aid for Cooperation on Counter-Terrorism and Security Enforcement was some $66 million for the 2007 fiscal year; it is largely distributed to individual countries in Southeast Asia. Australia's counterterrorism assistance budget is estimated to be around $68 million per year, with most of it targeted to Southeast Asia. And the United States allocated some $150 million in 2007 for the Department of

State's Anti-Terrorism Assistance program, which is only a small slice of U.S. counterterrorism assistance activity.[45]

In addition to the significant resource discrepancy between the United Nations and bilateral donors in counterterrorism programs, differences exist in the types of activities these resources are used to fund. The United Nations focuses more on assessing needs, providing assistance with the drafting of counterterrorism legislation, and training judges and prosecutors on how to implement the legislation. The bilateral donors tend to concentrate on strengthening operational capabilities at the national level. For example, in Indonesia, Australia has helped to train the Indonesian police in intelligence analysis and surveillance techniques and assisted in the establishment of the Indonesian police's Transnational Crime Centre in Jakarta and Indonesia's Financial Intelligence Unit.[46] In the Philippines, the United States has provided funding to the newly formed Attorney General's Task Force on Terrorism and Transnational Crime, which has taken a leading role in the prosecution of terrorists in that country. U.S. prosecutors and FBI agents also provided training to thirty-four representatives of the Philippine Anti-Terrorism Council aimed at assisting the Philippines in implementing the 2007 Human Security Act. And the United States helped the Philippines establish interagency intelligence fusion centers to support maritime interdictions against transnational criminal/terrorist organizations and a "Coast Watch" system in Mindinao.[47]

WHERE DOES THE UN'S COMPARATIVE ADVANTAGE LIE IN THE FIGHT AGAINST TERRORISM?

The UN offers a number of comparative advantages in the effort to combat and prevent terrorism. These advantages include its ability to (1) serve as a global norm-setter and assistance provider, (2) convene experts from around the world, (3) address conditions conducive to the spread of terrorism, (4) serve as a "legitimizer" and interlocutor, (5) act as an assessor of national counterterrorism efforts around the globe, and 6) develop a counterextremist narrative.

The United Nations as a Global Norm-setter and Assistance Provider

The UN system has contributed to the development of a global legal and technical framework that is directly related to efforts to combat terrorism, and it has provided countries with the technical assistance they need to implement the framework.

In addition to the Security Council resolutions adopted after the events of 9/11 that imposed a range of counterterrorism-related obligations on all states,[48] the United Nations and its specialized agencies have helped develop a global counterterrorism legal framework consisting of sixteen international treaties that criminalize nearly every imaginable terrorist offense and facilitate international legal cooperation in this area. Negotiations on the comprehensive convention against international terrorism remain deadlocked over differences surrounding the definition of terrorism. However, the existing instruments have laid important normative foundations in a number of counterterrorism-related fields through which the UN system has created a broad framework of international criminal law. The instruments provide essential tools for extradition and mutual legal assistance (MLA) that national authorities can use in assisting the state parties that ask for help. The national authorities can conduct investigations on their behalf and pass the information, evidence, and possibly even the accused over to that country and help ensure that there are no safe havens from prosecution and extradition.

In the absence of an extradition or MLA treaty for criminal matters at the global level, the international conventions and protocols are the only instruments providing a universal legal basis for cooperation on terrorism matters, which highlights the importance of working toward universal participation. Although certain regions such as Africa, the Caribbean, and the Middle East continue to lag behind other regions, since the attacks of 9/11 there has been a dramatic increase in the number of countries joining and implementing these instruments. For example, the number of countries that have ratified the twelve instruments in force prior to 9/11 has risen from two (Botswana and the United Kingdom) to ninety-eight as of December 2007. This increase is attributable to a various factors, but perhaps, most important, to the technical assistance that the UN's Terrorism Prevention Branch has provided on how to join and implement the global counterterrorism legal framework embodied in these instruments.[49] Partly as a result of this training, twenty-one countries have adopted new or amended existing counterterrorism laws, including Afghanistan, Argentina, Burundi, Colombia, Niger, and Tunisia.[50]

In addition to this legal framework, UN specialized agencies such as the International Civil Aviation Organization (ICAO), the International Maritime Organization (IMO), and the World Customs Organization (WCO) have developed new security standards and programs, many of which deal specifically with security in the context of the terrorist threat, often at the urging and with the assistance of the United States and its G8 partners. For example, global standards and best practices have been adopted in areas such as travel documents issuance and security and aviation and airport facilities security (ICAO),[51] international supply chain security (WCO),[52] and maritime and port facilities security (IMO).[53]

The IMO's International Ship and Port Facility Security Code, adopted after 9/11, has "been implemented by 158 Member States, representing 99 per cent of the world's merchant fleet (around 40,000 ships) engaged in international voyages. Close to 10,000 port facilities have their security plans developed and approved."[54]

Implementing the technical framework set forth by UN bodies often requires human expertise and significant financial resources to purchase and operate high-cost, technologically advanced security equipment, the cost of which developing countries either cannot afford or find disproportionate to the equipment's value. As a result, many of these bodies have developed capacity-building programs, including region-specific ones. ICAO, for example, conducts training and provides other technical assistance through its regional offices in Bangkok, Cairo, Dakar, Lima, Mexico City, Nairobi, and Paris. The technical training carried out by ICAO and other UN technical bodies is often carried out by or in close cooperation with national technical experts from partner countries such as Canada, the United States, and the United Kingdom.

The capstone of the UN normative counterterrorism effort was the September 2006 adoption by the General Assembly of the first-ever *global* counterterrorism strategy. The UN Global Counter-Terrorism Strategy pulls together all UN counterterrorism resolutions and treaties into a single, coherent, and universally adopted framework supported by the entire UN membership.[55] The strategy also incorporates long-term efforts to address conditions conducive to the spread of terrorism, thereby moving beyond the Council's emphasis on law enforcement and other security measures, and it underscores the need for all states to respect human rights and promote the rule of law while fighting terrorism. Finally, the strategy acknowledges the wide range of stakeholders beyond states, such as regional bodies and the private sector, that have a role to play in its implementation and is the first UN document on counterterrorism to include a role for civil society.

Although like other resolutions adopted by the General Assembly the strategy is not a legally binding document, it is already being used by countries such as Bangladesh, Indonesia, and South Africa and by the UN itself as a vehicle to stimulate national efforts both to develop counterterrorism strategies that include a wide range of government departments and agencies and to deepen interagency cooperation and coordination at the national level.

The United Nations as Convener

The United Nations has a convening power that is often underestimated. It can bring together national experts from within a particular region or from different regions to allow them to share information and experiences on a range of thematic issues related to addressing today's terrorist threat. This function is particularly important in regions where there is no effective regional organization or mechanism or where the lack of a common percep-tion of the threat has otherwise limited interstate cooperation.

The UN system's potential in this area, however, has not been fully realized, largely because of the lack of a broad-based and effective counterterrorism body within the United Nations for discussing the wide range of issues included in the UN's Global Counter-Terrorism Strategy. For example, the UN has never brought together national counterterrorism experts from around the world to share experiences and lessons learned in trying to understand and counter the growing violent radicalization and extremism that helps fuels Isla-mist terrorism. This issue is further addressed in the conclusion to this essay.

The UN's Role in Addressing Conditions Conducive to the Spread of Terrorism

Different parts of the UN system, whether in areas such as development, human rights, or education, can contribute to addressing some of the under-lying conditions that may help facilitate the rise of terrorism, whether it be poverty, underdevelopment, lack of rule of law, human rights abuses, or political, social, and economic marginalization.

A number of different parts of the UN system, though they are not coun-terterrorism actors as such, are nevertheless helping states address these conditions. One example is UNDP and its initiatives to combat corruption, strengthen civil society, promote local development, train the media, and build the capacities of administrative and parliamentary bodies. Although all impor-tant in their own right, many of these programs have counterterrorism benefits as well.

Unfortunately, UNDP has generally been reluctant to involve itself or associ-ate its activities with combating terrorism for fear that a counterterrorism label might unduly politicize its work on the ground. A significant exception is a Danish-funded UNDP project in Kenya, which UNDP is currently carrying out in cooperation with the United Nations Office on Drugs and Crime (UNODC) and the Kenyan National Counter-Terrorism Centre (NCTC) under the Office of the President. The project was designed to help promote the adoption and effective implementation of national counterterrorism legislation that safe-guards human rights and to raise awareness among the general public of the reasons why such a law is needed.[56] Although UNDP has conducted public awareness-raising workshops in different parts of Kenya, much of the work has yet to take place because many of the project's activities were contingent upon the passage of the counterterrorism bill, which remains stalled in parliament because of objections that the draft targets Muslims and expands the powers of a police force already accused of abusing its current powers.

UNDP is the best-represented UN agency on the ground. Its resident representatives often serve as the UN resident coordinators responsible for promoting coherence among the different parts of the UN system operating in a particular country. UNDP may be the UN entity best placed to coordinate in-country technical assistance programs and serve as a focal point for a range of in-country UN counterterrorism-related activities. Finding ways to convince UNDP to be less reflexively anti-counterterrorism is thus critical to getting the UN to become more active at the country level in this field.

Like UNDP, UNESCO is also reluctant to give its programs a counterterrorism label, but it is nevertheless contributing to efforts to address some of the conditions conducive to the rise and spread of terrorism. Through its capacity-building center in Africa and training institutes and centers around the world, UNESCO is working with countries to update and revise education and cultural policies and facilitate teacher training and the revision of textbooks and curricula to help ensure they are not being used to fuel radicalization.[57] In June 2008, UNESCO and the Kingdom of Bahrain co-organized a conference, "Youth@the Crossroads: A Future without Violent Radicalization," that brought together more than a hundred representatives of community-based and national programs from all regions of the world. Participants shared experiences and analysis of some fifty best-practice examples of different approaches to countering the violent radicalization of youth.[58]

The United Nations as a "Legitimizer" and Interlocutor

Soon after the 9/11 attacks, UN Secretary-General Kofi Annan reminded the Security Council that one of the prerequisites to getting countries to take action to combat terrorism is that the "global struggle against terrorism [be] seen as necessary and legitimate by their peoples—and that such universal legitimacy is something the United Nations can do much to confer."[59] As evidenced by its rush to the United Nations in the immediate aftermath of the attacks, the United States saw the value and the need to have the UN's backing of its response to the attacks. In most parts of the world, it is easier to convince a country to take action if one can point to a UN resolution or treaty calling for such action rather than relying exclusively on bilateral or informal group pressure.

Particularly now that the broad-based UN Counter-Terrorism Strategy is in place, the UN's seal of approval can offer legitimacy to a wide range of counterterrorism programs and initiatives, thereby reinforcing the bilateral efforts of the United States and other countries outside of the United Nations. Working through UN agencies and programs can offer major counterterrorism actors and donor states the necessary platform for building coalitions and help to overcome the stigma attached to bilateral relations between certain states and the growing skepticism and distrust among many Muslim nations and communities. Such an approach may be not only more cost-effective because existing expertise and programs can be leveraged, but also more politically acceptable in the recipient country and thus more likely to be implemented. The reason is that for many countries in the developing world the United Nations is generally seen as an objective and politically neutral player not associated with the global war on terrorism.

The United Nations as Global Assessor

The United Nations, with its global membership and its adoption in 2006 of a global counterterrorism strategy, is uniquely placed to provide a universal assessment of how all countries are doing in their efforts to combat terrorism. This information can benefit all governments. The United States and other donor countries often have a particular security interest that leads them to focus on assessing the terrorist threat and counterterrorism capacities in particular countries or regions—for example, Australia, Japan, and New Zealand focus much of their counterterrorism attention on Southeast Asia. However, dozens of other countries and some regions, including much of sub-Saharan Africa, would end up falling through the cracks were it not for the United Nations.

Although currently no single UN entity is undertaking national assessments covering the breadth of issues now included in the UN Global Counter-Terrorism Strategy, some are making contributions to this effort within their limited mandates. Most significantly, since it was established in October 2001, the Security Council's CTC, with the help of its thirty-five-member Executive Directorate, has analyzed more than eight hundred country reports detailing efforts to implement the range of counterterrorism requirements the Council imposed via Resolution 1373 on all countries after the events of 9/11, and it maintains a database that contains more than 300,000 documents related to national and regional efforts to implement the resolution and related analyses of capacity gaps. The CTC has also prepared Preliminary Implementation Assessments (PIAs) of all 192 UN members. The PIAs provide a comprehensive overview of national efforts to implement Resolution 1373. Finally, in June 2007 the CTC produced the first ever global survey of the implementation of Resolution 1373. It looks at how countries in all regions and subregions are proceeding in their counterterrorism efforts generally, where they are encountering difficulties, and what gaps and vulnerabilities have yet to be addressed in particular regions.[60]

In addition to the CTC, the Council's Non-Proliferation Committee and its group of experts have produced matrices for some 150 states that identify the different steps the states have taken to implement Resolution 1540 (it imposes obligations on all countries to prevent terrorists from getting their hands on WMDs) and the additional steps that need to be taken. Like the CTC's PIAs, these documents are being used as the basis for an ongoing dialogue with states and potential assistance providers to help ensure the identified capacity gaps are filled.

The Council's monitoring team has produced high-quality reports that offer assessments of global efforts to implement the financial, travel, and arms sanctions the Council has imposed on al-Qaeda, the Taliban, and related individuals and entities. These targeted sanctions are among the UN's most effective counterterrorism tools and have been used successfully to globalize the fight against al-Qaeda, the Taliban, and associated groups. After the November 2008 Mumbai attacks, for example, the Security Council placed these sanctions on four members of the Pakistani militant group Lashkar-e-Taiba as well as on the charitable organization Jamaat-ud-Dawa, which, according to Indian and U.S. officials, serves as Lashkar's financial front.[61]

The eight-member monitoring team has provided rigorous analyses of the terrorist threat and numerous recommendations on how existing measures could be refined and what new measures should be adopted. Although since 2004 it has presented more than two hundred recommendations to its parent committee, the Al-Qaeda/Taliban Sanctions Committee, few of those recommendations have been adopted because the fifteen members of the committee have had difficulty reaching the required consensus to adopt them. Nevertheless, the committee has endorsed some significant ones such as the monitoring team's call for the Security Council to address the growing problem of criminal misuse of the Internet to provide support for terrorism.

The monitoring team's reports are the only place in which serious analysis is undertaken by the United Nations or any multilateral body on the evolving nature of the threat posed by al-Qaeda and the Taliban. And they raise interesting points that should be discussed by the wider UN membership rather than limited to the fifteen members of the Al-Qaeda/Taliban Sanctions Committee as it currently stands. For example, the most recent report addresses issues such as the use by non-Muslim commentators and politicians of religious terms when describing al-Qaeda, the role of the media in disseminating al-Qaeda propaganda, and the porous borders, absence of any formal financial system, and limits to government authority in Afghanistan that make it particularly difficult for the government to implement the sanctions measures within its territory.[62]

As a result of their global mandates, these Council mechanisms are well placed to identify common shortcomings and challenges in different parts of the world and identify ways of addressing them, drawing on best practices and experiences from different regions such as Southeast Asia, South Asia, North Africa, and Europe. However, these mechanisms continue to suffer from a lack of legitimacy among the wider membership, a lack of transparency that makes it difficult for non-Council members and technical assistance providers to access their analytical work, and overpoliticization that stems from being within the Security Council. The expert groups have a large body of analysis and a wealth of expertise to offer UN member states. The challenges are how to make better use of these resources and how to offer states a unified UN Global Counter-Terrorism Strategy implementation assessment.

The current fragmented institutional arrangements within the UN make achieving progress on the latter challenge exceedingly difficult. The current internal coordinating mechanism, the UN Counter-Terrorism Implementation Task Force, which brings together twenty-three entities in the UN system—plus Interpol—with some involvement in countering terrorism (either directly or indirectly), lacks the resources and expertise in its small secretariat, and the needed mandate, to be able to undertake a unified assessment, let alone compile the ones being prepared by its constituent members. The creation of a single UN counterterrorism office or department that would include the resources and expertise currently being allocated to the three Security Council counter-terrorism expert groups would partially address this shortcoming, because the new entity could provide effective support to the implementation task force.

The UN's Role in Developing and Promoting a Counterextremist Narrative

Perhaps the most significant long-lasting contribution the United Nations could make to global counterterrorism efforts, and the area in which it may have so far contributed the least, is in the development and promotion of a narrative to counter the one of hate and violence being espoused by extremists. The UN could do so by promoting peace, tolerance, dialogue among cultures and religion, and through far-reaching efforts to address some of the social, political, and economic marginalization that, in part, motivate young people to turn to violence. In fact, much of the work of the UN system is directly devoted to these issues, whether it be UNDP, UNESCO, the Office of the High Commissioner for Human Rights (OHCHR), the World Bank, the UN Children's Fund, the UN Population Fund, the UN Development Fund for Women, the World Food Programme, the World Health Organization, or the work of the Department of Political Affairs in preventing conflict and the Department of Peacekeeping in helping to pick up the pieces in postconflict situations.

However, these UN bodies or offices are scattered around the globe, operating under distinct mandates, and no single senior UN official is responsible for fashioning a coherent counterextremist narrative. Furthermore, partly because the Security Council has dominated the UN's counterterrorism agenda for much of the post-9/11 period, there is a lingering perception that the Council's agenda is largely dictated by the United States. Rather than offering a coherent alternative to the narrative being put forward by al-Qaeda and other violent extremists or an alternative to the former Bush administration's war on terrorism, the UN effort has often been viewed as reinforcing this unpopular U.S. strategy.

Nevertheless, the adoption of the UN Global Counter-Terrorism Strategy, with its holistic, human rights-based approach, offers a unique opportunity for the United Nations to develop a more coherent counterterrorism narrative and one that reflects the range of tools in its extensive tool kit. For this to happen, however, the turf wars and dysfunctionality that characterize the current UN approach needs to end.

CONCLUSION

As this essay has detailed, the United Nations has comparative advantages that have allowed it to make important contributions to the global campaign against terrorism. It has been a global norm-setter, capacity builder, assessor, "legitimizer," and contributor to addressing the conditions conducive to the spread of terrorism.

However, certain aspects of the UN effort are limiting its overall impact on counterterrorism. For example, there is a lack of effective coordination and collaboration among the relevant UN system actors, both at UN headquarters and in the field and an absence of leadership from within the United Nations on this issue. In addition, a more representative intergovernmental mechanism is needed within the United Nations that would allow counterterrorism policymakers and practitioners from countries in the global North and South to engage, build trust, and share information and expertise. The current approach, in which much of the day-to-day counterterrorism work is being carried out by the Security Council's various counterterrorism-related bodies and expert groups, impedes the UN's ability to confer the universal legitimacy that is perhaps its single greatest comparative advantage in this field. In the end, however, despite these flaws, the question is not whether the United Nations can contri-bute—as it can and does—but rather how it can do so more effectively than it has done since 9/11 to ensure that its rhetoric is matched with effective action.

With a broad-based consensus framework finally in place, the UN counterterrorism architecture needs to be streamlined and reformed to create an appropriately designed intergovernmental body. That body should be supported by a properly resourced counterterrorism department in the UN Secretariat, headed by an official at the under-secretary-general level who is dedicated to supporting implementation of the UN Global Counter-Terrorism Strategy. The new body should be designed to have a technical focus and allow for the regionally balanced participation of some forty to fifty countries.[63] The new senior UN counterterrorism official—perhaps called a UN high commissioner for counterterrorism or a special representative of the secretary-general on counterterrorism—would spearhead the UN system's largely incoherent counterterrorism program. The UN has high commissioners or special representatives of the secretary-general in more than a dozen thematic areas, many of which were created to improve both the coordination within the UN of a number of relevant programs and the coherence of the message the United Nations is projecting to the world as it works in the particular field. And yet on an issue as important as terrorism that is at the top of the world body's agenda and that requires a whole system response at the national, regional, and global levels, the United Nations is faceless.

Notes

1. See UN Security Council Resolution 1267. S/RES/1267, 1999.
2. See UN Security Council Resolution 1333. S/RES/1333, 2000.
3. For a sampling of the vast literature on how institutions can help foster cooperation, see Kenneth A. Oye, ed., *Cooperation under Anarchy* (Princeton, N.J.: Princeton University Press, 1986); Elinor Ostrom, *Governing the Commons* (Cambridge, UK: Cambridge University Press, 1990); and Robert O. Keohane and Lisa M. Martin, "The Promise of Institutional Theory," *International Security* 20 (Summer 1995): 39–51.
4. See, for example, Joseph M. Grieco, "Anarchy and Limits of Cooperation: A Realist Critique of the Newest Liberal Institutionalism," in *Neorealism and Neoliberalism: The Contemporary Debate*, ed. David A. Baldwin (New York: Columbia University Press, 1993); and John J. Mearsheimer, "The False Promise of International Institutions," *International Security* 19 (Winter 1994/1995): 5–49.
5. Kennedy Graham, "The Security Council and Counterterrorism: Global and Regional Approaches to an Elusive Public Good," *Terrorism and Political Violence* 17 (2005): 37–65. Graham highlights many of the issues that have bedeviled the UN's attempts to create an overarching definition of terrorism that can serve as the basis for UN actions.
6. Jenny Carolina González and Simon Romero, "Marches Show Disgust with a Colombian Rebel Group," *New York Times*, February 4, 2008.
7. United Nations Office on Drugs and Crime, "Definitions of Terrorism," http://web.archive.org/web/20070129121539 and www.unodc.org/unodc/terrorism_definitions.html.
8. Ibid.
9. Jayantha Dhanapala, "The United Nations' Response to 9/11," *Terrorism and Political Violence* 17, no. 1 (2005): 17–23.

10. Joshua Muravchik, "The U.N.'s Terrorism Gap," *Los Angeles Times*, September 18, 2005.

11. United Nations, "UN Action to Counter Terrorism," www.un.org/terrorism/strategy-counter-terrorism.shtml.

12. Eric Rosand, "Security Council Resolution 1373, the Counter-Terrorism Committee, and the Fight against Terrorism," *American Journal of International Law* 97, no. 2 (2003): 733–741.

13. For example, see *U.S. Statement of January, 1985*, 24 I.L.M. 246 (1985), related to its dispute with Nicaragua, or the French position in the *Nuclear Test Cases* (Austl. v. Fr.; N.Z. v. Fr.), 1973 I.C.J 99, 135 (June 22); 1974 I.C.J. 253, 257 (December 20).

14. United Nations, "UN Action to Counter Terrorism."

15. Eric Rosand, "The Security Council's Efforts to Monitor the Implementation of Al Qaeda/Taliban Sanctions," *American Journal of International Law* 98, no. 4 (2004): 745–763.

16. Ibid.

17. Security Council Resolution 1455, Second Report, *Supra* note 3, at 5.

18. Rosand, "Security Council's Efforts."

19. Graham, "Security Council and Counterterrorism."

20. Rosand, "Security Council Resolution 1373."

21. Dhanapala, "United Nations' Response to 9/11."

22. International Monetary Fund, "The IMF and the Fight against Money Laundering and the Financing of Terrorism," IMF Factsheet, April 2008, www.imf.org/external/np/exr/facts/aml.htm.

23. For a general background on Interpol, see Malcolm Anderson, *Policing the World: Interpol and the Politics of International Police Co-operation* (Oxford, UK: Clarendon Press, 1989).

24. Virginia Page Fortna, "Does Peacekeeping Keep Peace? International Intervention and the Duration of Peace after Civil War," *International Studies Quarterly* 48, no. 2 (2004): 269–292.

25. Justine Rosenthal, "Jigsaw Jihadism," *National Interest* 87 (2007): 61–66.

26. See, for example, Shashi Tharoor, "Why America Still Needs the United Nations," *Foreign Affairs* 82 no. 5 (2003): 67–80.

27. Dhanapala, "United Nations' Response to 9/11."

28. Eric Lichtblau and James Risen, "Bank Data Is Sifted by US in Secret to Block Terror," *New York Times*, June 23, 2006.

29. For a discussion of UN successes and failures, see Joshua Muravchik, *The Future of the United Nations: Understanding the Past to Chart a Way Forward* (Washington, D.C.: AEI Press, 2005); and David Cortrigh and George A. Lopez, *The Sanctions Decade: Assessing UN Strategies in the 1990s* (Boulder, Colo.: Lynne Reiner, 2000).

30. James Brooke, "Japan to Cut Contribution to the Budget of the UN," *New York Times*, January 22, 2003.

31. Fortna, "Does Peacekeeping Keep Peace?"

32. "Iran Unmoved on Nuclear Stance in Face of Sanctions," *Washington Post*, August 10, 2008.

33. Juan Forero, "Latin American Crisis Resolved; Colombia Apologizes at Region Summit," *Washington Post*, March 8, 2008.

34. Helene Cooper, "NATO Allies Wary of Sending More Troops to Afghanistan," *New York Times*, January 27, 2007.

35. Rosand, "Security Council Resolution 1373"; Rosand, "Security Council's Efforts."

36. Rick Fawn and Raymond A. Hinnebusch, eds., *The Iraq War: Causes and Consequences* (Boulder, Colo.: Lynne Reiner, 2006).

37. Karen DeYoung, "Iranian Defiance of U.N. Detailed; Nuclear Enrichment Continues, Report Says," *Washington Post*, May 24, 2007.

38. Elaine Sciolino, "Russia and West Split on Iran Nuclear Issue," *New York Times*, March 8, 2006.

39. The author would like to thank Alistair Millar and Jason Ipe of the Center on Global Counterterrorism Cooperation for their helpful comments on previous versions of this essay. All errors or omissions are the author's.

40. William P. Pope, "European Cooperation with the United States in the Global War on Terrorism," remarks to the House International Relations Committee, Subcommittee on Europe and International Terrorism, Nonproliferation and Human Rights, Washington, D.C., September 14, 2004.

41. For example, the Group of Eight industrialized nations have "recognized the central role of the United Nations in the fight against terrorism," noting that "the UN is the sole organization with the stature and reach to achieve universal agreement on the condemnation of terrorism and to effectively address key aspects of the terrorist threat in a comprehensive manner." "G8 Justice and Home Affairs Ministerial Declaration on Capacity Building Assistance," G8 Justice and Home Affairs Ministerial Meeting, Hokaido Toyako, Japan, June 11–13, 2008; "G8 Summit Statement on Counter Terrorism—Security in the Era of Globalization," Heiligendamm, Germany, June 8, 2007.

42. The Security Council president stated that "the Security Council emphasizes the central role of the United Nations in the global struggle against terrorism," "Statement by the President of the Security Council," UN Doc. S/PRST/2008/45, December 9, 2008.

43. Jeffrey Laurenti, "The United Nations and Terrorism," in *Democratic Responses to Terrorism,* ed. Leonard Weinberg (New York: Routledge, 2008), 76.

44. Examples of the programs and agencies are the UN Development Programme (UNDP), UN Educational, Science and Cultural Organization (UNESCO), UN Office of the High Commissioner for Human Rights (OHCHR), International Maritime Organization (IMO), and International Civil Aviation Organization (ICAO).

45. For U.S. figures, see U.S. Government Accountability Office, "Combating Terrorism: State Department's Antiterrorism Program Needs Improved Guidance and More Systematic Assessments of Outcomes," U.S. GAO Report, February 2008, 8.

46. AusAID in Indonesia, "Counter-terrorism Capacity Building Initiative," May 22, 2007, www.indo.ausaid.gov.au/projects/counterterrorism.html.

47. Office of the Coordinator for Counterterrorism, U.S. Department of State, "Country Reports on Terrorism," April 30, 2008, chap.2, "East Asia and Pacific Overview."

48. These include Resolution 1373 (2001), Resolution 1390 (2002), Resolution 1456 (2003), Resolution 1535 (2004), Resolution 1540 (2004), Resolution 1617 (2005), and Resolution 1624 (2005).

49. "Report of the Secretary-General: United Nations Global Counter-Terrorism Strategy: Activities of the United Nations System in Implementing the Strategy," UN Doc. A/62/998, July 7, 2008, para. 51.

50. The UN's Terrorism Prevention Branch has trained over 6,700 criminal justice officials in over one hundred countries. "Note on Programme Implementation:

Delivering Technical Assistance for Strengthening the Legal Regime against Terrorism, January 2003–December 2008," UN Office of Drugs and Crime, Terrorism Prevention Branch, Vienna, December 8, 2008, 19 [copy on file with author].

51. ICAO standards and programs on travel documents and aviation security facilitation are available at www.icao.int/atb/sfbranch/index.asp.

52. The WCO Framework of Standards to Secure and Facilitate Global Trade, when implemented, should "contribute positively to economic and social development, act as deterrent to international terrorism, secure revenue collections and promote trade facilitation world-wide." Further details are available at www.wcoomd.org.

53. A list of the IMO conventions on safety and security are available at www.imo.org/ Conventions.

54. "Report of the Secretary-General: United Nations Global Counter-Terrorism Strategy: Activities of the United Nations system in Implementing the Strategy," UN Doc. A/62/998, July 7, 2008, para. 31.

55. UN General Assembly Resolution 60/288, 2006.

56. The project has worked since 2006 to assist with the finalization of Kenya's antiterrorism bill, which has still not been passed by parliament, and an anti-money laundering bill; convene sensitization and awareness-raising workshops; organize training workshops for officers from the judiciary and the security sectors; assist in the establishment of a Financial Investigation Unit; and produce and disseminate informational materials. UNDP e-mail communication with author, December 7, 2007.

57. For information on UNESCO's Institutes and Centers for Education, see http:// portal.unesco.org/education.

58. "Youth@the Crossroads: A Future without Violent Radicalization: The Manama Findings," http://portal.unesco.org/en/ev.php-URL_ID=42682&URL_DO=DO_TOPIC&URL_SECTION=201.html. UNESCO also has facilitated the establishment of the Greater Horn Horizon Forum, an independent research forum coordinated in close collaboration with the Intergovernmental Author on Development (IGAD) and the Djiboutian government. The forum is designed to foster dialogue on the future of the Horn of Africa in order to facilitate the formulation and implementation of policies conducive to mutual understanding, regional integration, and peace in the region. See www.greater-horn-horizon.org.

59. "Secretary-General, Addressing Council Meeting on Counter-Terrorism, Says United Nations 'Stands Four-Square' Against Scourge," UN press release, January 18, 2002.

60. United Nations Security Council, Survey of the Implementation of Resolution 1373 (2001): Report of the Counter-Terrorism Committee," UN Doc. S/2008/379, June 10, 2008.

61. "UN: Pakistani Charity Was Terrorist Front: Security Council Imposes Sanctions on Group Linked to Mumbai Attacks," CBS News, December 11, 2008.

62. United Nations Security Council, Report of the Analytical Support and Sanctions Monitoring Team Pursuant to Resolution 1735 (2006) Concerning Al-Qaida and the Taliban and Associated Individuals and Entities," UN Doc. S/2008/324, May 14, 2008.

63. Designers of these forums can draw on different models, including the UN Development Programme's Governing Board, the Peacebuilding Commission, the UN Office of the High Commissioner's Executive Committee, and the Human Rights Council.

is an outright ban the best way to eliminate or constrain torture?

YES: Torture violates U.S. and international law and should never be allowed
Michael H. Posner, *U.S. Department of State*

NO: There is a need to bring an unfortunate practice within the bounds of law
Alan M. Dershowitz, *Harvard Law School*

In April 2009, President Barack Obama sparked an impassioned national debate on torture when he released four previously top secret memos drafted by Bush administration lawyers that offered guidelines for "enhanced interrogations" by the U.S. Central Intelligence Agency (CIA) of al-Qaeda operatives in the wake of the attacks on the United States on September 11, 2001.[1] The release of the memos followed Obama's earlier executive order banning harsh interrogation practices and requiring all U.S. personnel, including CIA agents, to abide by the *Army Field Manual*'s noncoercive guidelines.

The Obama administration's reason for releasing the memos and its justification for banning coercive interrogations centered on three points. First, torture violates American law and values. Second, it hurts America's image abroad. And, third, such practices are unnecessary because, according to Obama, "we can effectively obtain the intelligence we need" without resorting to torture.

However, soon after the release of the Bush memos, a controversy erupted when a private internal memo written by Obama's director of national intelligence, Dennis Blair, was leaked to the press. The memo stated: "High value information came from interrogations in which those [coercive] methods were used and provided a deeper understanding of the al Qa'ida organization that was attacking this country."[2]

Blair quickly issued a public statement to clarify his words: "The bottom line is these techniques have hurt our image around the world, the damage they have done to our interests far outweighed whatever benefit they gave us and they are not essential to our national security."

Therein lies the policy dilemma over the use of torture. On the one hand, many if not most national security professionals recognize that harsh interrogations can glean actionable intelligence and will likely be used in extreme cases. Indeed, President Obama himself has ordered a secret task force to determine whether the CIA may require "additional or different guidance" on interrogations in the event of special circumstances.[3] On the other hand, it is equally clear that the use of torture incurs tremendous strategic costs in terms of a nation's reputation.

The classic case of the 1957 Battle of Algiers bears this out. Relying on brutal interrogation tactics, the French army was able to destroy the hardened National Liberation Front (FLN) in Algiers in a matter of months. Yet at the same time, the legitimacy of France to maintain its Algerian colony was left in tatters, contributing to France's loss of Algeria just a few years later.

The bottom-line question is this: if President Obama (or any future president) should find himself in the position of facing an imminent terrorist attack and having suspects with possible knowledge of the plot in custody, should he—indeed, *would* he—refrain from ordering coercive efforts to extract information? Put differently, would knowledge of the long-term strategic costs of engaging in a nefarious practice that violates America's laws and values outweigh the tactical imperative to do everything possible to prevent a potentially catastrophic attack?

Michael Posner offers a morally and legally consistent answer to this question. He argues that under no circumstances should the use of torture or cruel, inhuman, or degrading treatment in interrogations be accepted as a matter of policy, law, or practice. His "zero-tolerance" approach applies equally to "ticking bomb" scenarios—which he says are "rare or almost nonexistent"—through stressful battlefield conditions where there may be a strong temptation to use rough tactics to glean quick operational intelligence. According to Posner, any use of torture under any circumstances will ultimately undermine America's security. Not only does torture often evoke false or misleading information, but its use makes Americans less safe by emboldening their enemies and alienating their allies. Thus an outright ban is required not simply on grounds of law and morals, but also on grounds of security.

Alan Dershowitz approaches the question from a more policy-centered perspective. He agrees with Posner that torture should be illegal and never be used by a democracy committed to the rule of law. But he also argues that it is unrealistic to expect a president to refrain from utilizing some form of torture if he believes it might prevent an imminent mass-casualty attack. Dershowitz believes that the standard approach by democracies—declare torture illegal, but, in the words of torture opponent Sen. John McCain, "do what you have to do" in extreme cases—actually weakens the rule of law and makes the use of torture more likely. He proposes ending this dangerous "off-the-books" approach by enacting a "torture warrant statute," authorized by Congress and sanctified by the courts, that would permit the president to temporarily suspend the prohibition against torture in extreme cases. This way, he says, an age-old tension between fundamental values and necessities of security can be resolved within a rule of law framework.

Both authors of this chapter have identical goals in mind: upholding the rule of law and keeping the country safe. The fact that they view torture so differently is indicative of the legal and moral complexities of this important issue. Yet the real debate over the use of torture will not take place in the pages of a book during a time of relative calm. Should the United States enter another period like that surrounding 9/11, urgent decisions on the treatment of terror suspects will be required, and the thoughtful arguments of these authors will be front and center.

Torture violates U.S. and international law
YES: and should never be allowed
Michael H. Posner, *U.S. Department of State*

The Case for an Outright Ban on Torture

More than eight years after the attacks of September 11, 2001, the United States continues to debate a wide range of national security policies.[4] Perhaps no issue has stirred greater debate and controversy than the adoption of policies authorizing the use of torture and other coercive interrogation techniques to gather intelligence. And no other aspect of the Bush administration's counterterrorism policies was more damaging to America's internal commitment to uphold the rule of law and to its reputation and standing in the world. As the Obama administration and Congress grapple with these issues, they must recognize that enforcing the ban on torture and cruel treatment is the only effective way to end these abuses. President Barack Obama strongly signaled his intent to follow this approach during his first week in office when he signed an executive order that bans all forms of torture and cruel treatment.[5]

The debate on this issue is set in a broader context, one in which the government has employed security measures to prevent or greatly reduce the risks of future attacks. Preventive measures are essential. The U.S. government has the right, indeed the duty, to protect its people. Since the attacks on 9/11, the government, mindful of this obligation, has devoted significant resources and attention to enhancing airport security and increasing financial and other support for America's front line defenders—police, firefighters, and emergency medical providers. It has taken a series of measures to step up inspections of shipping containers coming into this country. The government also has adopted additional means of protecting other aspects critical to the national infrastructure, such as nuclear power facilities, electrical grids, the water supply, and America's food production and distribution system.

On a parallel track, officials have made efforts to improve and better coordinate intelligence gathering by federal and state governmental entities, having realized that better intelligence can prevent attacks and save lives. The federal government aided this effort by creating a new post, the director of national intelligence. These measures and more were examined by the 9/11 Commission, an independent, bipartisan group established by the president and Congress. The commission made a series of useful recommendations for enhancing the safety of Americans that were prudent, thoughtful, practical, and wise. Everything recommended was rights-neutral and clearly within the bounds of the law.[6]

But the focus of this essay is on another, much more troubling component of this broader context: the government's reliance on and attempt to justify coercive means, torture, or other forms of cruel, inhuman, or degrading treatment as an appropriate way to extract information from suspected members of al-Qaeda and other terrorist groups. Since 2002, reliance on such coercive interrogations by the CIA and other agencies has harmed America's reputation in the world. Rather than enhancing intelligence gathering, it has undermined these efforts. Rather than increasing the nation's security, this reliance has emboldened America's enemies, strained relations with its closest allies, and put its troops around the world at greater risk. The relaxation of rules on interrogations has undermined discipline within the military. As a consequence, the introduction of official cruelty as government policy has made the United States weaker and more vulnerable to attack.

To restore America's reputation and image, to support its troops, and to reaffirm relations with its allies, the U.S. government must, as President Barack Obama has directed, stop all forms of torture and cruelty, adopting a zero-tolerance approach. The use of torture or cruel, inhuman, or degrading treatment in interrogations should never be tolerated, regulated, or justified as a matter of official policy, law, or practice.

THE PRECEDENT FOR TREATING PRISONERS HUMANELY

The United States has a proud history of requiring the humane treatment of all enemy prisoners, a tradition dating back to Gen. George Washington. In January 1777, Washington ordered his troops to treat captured British soldiers "with humanity," writing, "Let them have no reason to complain of our copying the brutal example of the British army."[7]

Washington's admonition to his troops reflected a broader commitment by the Founders to set a high ethical standard and to adhere to the rule of law. As Thomas Jefferson later wrote to James Madison, "It has great effect on the opinion of our people and the world to have moral right on our side."[8]

This commitment has been reinforced at key junctures in U.S. history. In the Civil War, Lincoln appointed Columbia law professor Francis Lieber, under sponsorship of the army's general-in-chief, Henry Halleck, to develop a set of minimum standards for the military that forbade suffering, disgrace, cruel imprisonment, want of food, mutilation, death, or other barbarity. The Lieber Code, as it came to be known, required Union forces to treat prisoners of war "with humanity" and to "be strictly guided by the principles of justice, honor, and humanity—virtues adorning a soldier even more than other men, for the very reason that he possesses the power of his arms against the unarmed."[9]

The Lieber Code served as a basis for the development of the law of armed conflict, which the U.S. military has taken a leading role in developing and promoting on the international stage. Influenced by the Lieber Code, Theodore Roosevelt urged at the time of the Philippine-American War that "determined and unswerving effort must be made to find out every instance of barbarity on the part of our troops, to punish those guilty of it, and . . . to prevent the occurrence of all such acts in the future."[10]

The Lieber Code also guided those U.S. officials who, after World War II, took a lead in the international negotiations that led to the promulgation of the Geneva Conventions of 1949. Each of the four Geneva Conventions contains an identical provision, Common Article 3, which specifically prohibits "violence to life and person, in particular murder of all kinds, mutilation, cruel treatment and torture" and "outrages upon personal dignity, in particular humiliating and degrading treatment."[11]

In 1950 Secretary of Defense George Marshall spelled out the application of the humane treatment standard to U.S. officials in a book entitled *The Armed Forces Officer*. In it, he lists twenty-nine propositions that govern American conduct at war, explaining that

> the United States abides by the laws of war. Its Armed Forces, in their dealings with all other peoples, are expected to comply with the laws of war, in the spirit and to the letter. In waging war, we do not terrorize helpless non-combatants, if it is within our power to avoid doing so. Wanton killing, torture, cruelty or the working of unusual hardship on enemy prisoners or populations is not justified under any circumstances. Likewise respect for the reign of law, as that term is understood in the United States, is expected to follow the flag wherever it goes.[12]

Consistent with General Marshall's words, the U.S. military applied the humane treatment standard of the Geneva Conventions to all prisoners in its custody, even those like the Viet Cong who neither recognized nor abided by the Geneva Conventions and did not qualify as prisoners of war under the Geneva Conventions.

Members of the military still hold to these precedents. Over the last five years, some retired senior U.S. military leaders and Defense Department officials have become increasingly outspoken critics of U.S. interrogation practices. In September 2006, about fifty members of this group wrote a letter to the Senate Armed Services Committee in favor of strict adherence to Common Article 3 in the interrogation of al-Qaeda prisoners:

The framers of the Geneva Conventions, including the American representatives in particular, wanted to ensure that Common Article 3 would apply in situations where a state party to the treaty, like the United States, fights an adversary that is not a party, including irregular forces like al Qaeda. The United States military has abided by the basic requirements of Common Article 3—even to enemies that systematically violated the Geneva Conventions themselves.[13]

THE CASE AGAINST TORTURE AND COERCIVE TACTICS: WHY AN ABSOLUTE BAN IS ESSENTIAL

The case against torture and official cruelty is clear. For starters, these techniques are an ineffective and even counterproductive way to gather intelligence. As experienced interrogators from the military and intelligence agencies have said repeatedly, these techniques are not the best way to obtain actionable intelligence. Joe Navarro, a twenty-year veteran of the Federal Bureau of Investigation (FBI) with wide experience in counterterrorism investigations, said, "The only thing torture guarantees is pain. It never guarantees the truth. It's a technique that we in the FBI have never used, we don't need, . . . [M]ost of the military interviewers that I've worked with don't subscribe to it."[14]

Navarro teaches interrogators at the CIA and FBI that torture results in fear, contempt, and resistance. Although prisoners may occasionally volunteer useful information when tortured, they will not cooperate in the long run, and far more vital information will then be lost. Instead, an interrogator should "convince an informant to release information, not threaten" and remember "that acts of kindness help to build informants' confidence in the interrogator."[15]

As images and stories of torture and mistreatment by U.S. officials have spread and gained currency since the events of 9/11, potential sources of intelligence and even America's close allies in the world have turned and refused to cooperate with its intelligence-gathering efforts, making America less safe. Reacting to the U.S. government's recent reliance on harsh interrogations, fifteen senior interrogators, interviewers, and intelligence officials in the U.S. military, FBI, and CIA issued a public statement on this matter in June 2008. They concluded that

> the use of torture and other inhumane and abusive treatment results in false and misleading information, loss of critical intelligence, and has caused serious damage to the reputation and standing of the United States. The use of such techniques also facilitates enemy recruitment, misdirects or wastes scarce resources, and deprives the United States of the standing to demand humane treatment of captured Americans.[16]

Torture and coercive interrogation practices also run counter to the fundamental principles upon which the United States was founded and betray its citizens' religious and ethical ideals as a people. Those who have experienced torture at the hands of their enemies are often the most passionate advocates on this point. For example, Sen. John McCain, who was imprisoned and tortured by the North Vietnamese during the Vietnam War for almost six years, led the fight in Congress in 2005 against the Bush administration's coercive interrogation policy.[17]

As mentioned earlier, torture and cruel treatment also violate U.S. national and international law obligations. The Geneva Conventions are complemented by a set of human rights standards, including a provision in the International Covenant on Civil and Political Rights that bars all forms of torture and cruel, inhuman, and degrading treatment.[18] The Convention Against Torture and Other Cruel, Inhuman or Degrading Treatment or Punishment, which entered into force in 1987 and was ratified by the United States in 1994, elaborated on this standard.[19] All of these international standards serve as a minimum baseline, a floor beneath which the U.S. government cannot sink, and conform with and reinforce U.S. law.

Torture and mistreatment carried out by U.S. soldiers or intelligence agents also invite retaliatory treatment when U.S. citizens are detained abroad. The U.S. military has been a staunch advocate of the Geneva Conventions because these standards protect American soldiers in the field. If the U.S. government adopts policies that sanction "enhanced interrogation techniques," how can the United States object when similar policies are applied to its own citizens?[20]

Reliance on cruelty also engenders a broader climate of lawlessness and ill discipline by those who engage in such practices. An effective military relies on discipline and adherence to the rules. When commanders begin to relax these rules, especially on something as basic as the treatment of prisoners, soldiers will inevitably take it upon themselves to stretch the meaning of other rules as well. This is a prescription for a breakdown of discipline and control.

The resort to torture also has profound international implications. Because the United States is such a powerful country and has long presented itself to the world as a leader on human rights, a U.S. retreat from those standards has a devastating effect on others—a ripple effect that in recent years has provided a convenient excuse for dictatorial regimes around the world to follow suit. To cite just two examples:

• Former president of Georgia Eduard Shevardnadze stated in October 2002, after being criticized for colluding with Russia in violating the human rights of Chechens, that "international human rights commitments might become pale in comparison with the importance of the anti-terrorist campaign."[21]

• In September 2003, Malaysia's justice minister, Rais Yatim, defended detaining more than one hundred alleged terrorists without trial by citing the U.S. government's detention of individuals at Guantanamo Bay.[22]

In a similar vein, opportunistic governments expressed support for the fight against terrorism after the 9/11 attacks, while presenting their own domestic insurgencies as conflicts perpetrated by terrorist groups analogous to al-Qaeda. For example, Syria and Egypt, both notorious for their human rights abuses, encouraged the United States to emulate their "successful" strategies for fighting terrorism. Syria's minister of information, Adnan Omran, declared that Syria was "ahead [of the United States] in fighting terrorism," and Syrian president Bashar al-Assad invited the United States to "take advantage of Syria's successful experiences."[23] Similarly, Egypt's prime minister, Atef Abeid, responded to criticism of his country's use of torture by rejecting criticism of Egypt's rights record and linking Egypt's challenges to those of the United States:

> The U.S. and U.K., including human rights groups, have, in the past, been calling on us to give these terrorists their "human rights." You can give them all the human rights they deserve until they kill you. After these horrible crimes committed in New York and Virginia, maybe Western countries should begin to think of Egypt's own fight against terror as their new model.[24]

Today, America's longtime pursuit of human rights around the world has been tarnished by prisoner abuses, particularly the use of coercive interrogations, in the years since 9/11. Intangible but vitally important assets—such as U.S. standing in the world, its soft power, and its moral authority to lead— have been severely damaged. This was put most eloquently by Sen. John McCain:

> We are Americans. We hold ourselves to humane standards of treatment no matter how terribly evil or awful they [enemy combatants] may be. To do otherwise undermines our security, and it also undermines our greatness as a nation. We are not simply any other country. We stand for a lot more than that in the world: a moral mission, one of freedom and democracy and human rights at home and abroad. . . . The enemy we fight has no respect for human life or human rights. They don't deserve our sympathy. But this is not about who they are. . . . It is about who we are. These are values that distinguish us from our enemies.[25]

JUSTIFICATION FOR TORTURE AND COERCIVE INTERROGATIONS: THE BUSH ADMINISTRATION'S GLOBAL WAR ON TERRORISM

James Madison once wrote, "War is in fact the true nurse of executive aggrandizement."[26] His admonition was borne out by the Bush administration's assertions that in a new "global war on terror," war trumps law, and laws become a luxury, not a necessity, binding on the executive.

In the aftermath of the 9/11 attacks, the Bush administration departed from U.S. tradition and instituted draconian policies that allowed for and even encouraged official cruelty, including torture. This shift was part of what Vice President Dick Cheney called the "new normalcy," a concept he believed reflected an "understanding of the world as it is."[27] In an interview five days after the 9/11 attacks, the vice president asserted that to obtain information about al-Qaeda and to prevent future attacks, the U.S. government would

> have to work, though, sort of the dark side, if you will. We've got to spend time in the shadows of the intelligence world. A lot of what needs to be done here will have to be done quietly, without any discussion. . . . [I]t's going to be vital for us to use any means at our disposal, basically, to achieve our objective.[28]

By using this framework and asserting that it was fighting a new kind of enemy, the administration was claiming that existing laws were impediments to fighting this new war. The thrust of the government's approach to the public was essentially this: "Trust us—we will do what is necessary to keep you safe."

In 2002 White House Counsel Alberto Gonzales provided a legal underpinning to the administration's approach to interrogations. He instructed the Office of Legal Counsel in the Justice Department (DOJ) to provide a legal definition of torture in order to give legal cover to interrogators from the CIA and other agencies who were fearful that their reliance on "enhanced interrogation techniques" could lead to future criminal prosecutions. In August 2002, the DOJ presented its memo, authored by Jay S. Bybee. It concluded that to constitute torture, an act "must inflict pain that is difficult to endure . . . equivalent in intensity to the pain accompanying serious physical injury, such as organ failure, impairment of bodily function or even death."[29]

Four months later, Secretary of Defense Donald Rumsfeld took his cue from the Bybee memo. Frustrated by the military's failure to obtain good intelligence from detainees at Guantanamo,[30] Rumsfeld authorized a series of harsh techniques, including the use of dogs, to intimidate detainees and to get better information. In the spring of 2003, he authorized twenty-four new interrogation methods for prisoners at Guantanamo, part of the administration's gloves-off approach to interrogations.[31] Rumsfeld subsequently authorized the extension of these harsh, often illegal techniques for use in the interrogation of prisoners in Afghanistan and Iraq.

On a parallel track, the CIA developed what President Bush called "an alternative set of procedures," which were intended to give the CIA greater latitude in questioning high-value detainees in its custody.[32] These "enhanced interrogation techniques," more aggressive and often more abusive, were carried out in secret detention facilities under the CIA's control and reportedly included painful stress positions, temperature manipulation, forced nudity, sexual humiliation, sleep deprivation, physical abuse, and, in some cases, a form of simulated drowning known as waterboarding.

The combination of illegal interrogation rules and secret detentions led to serious abuses. These abuses became front-page headlines in the spring of 2004 when the news media released photographs showing the abuse and humiliation of prisoners at Abu Ghraib prison in Baghdad.[33] But these photos only revealed a small slice of the problem. A 2006 study conducted by Human Rights First revealed that more than one hundred prisoners have died in U.S. custody in Iraq, Afghanistan, and other places. The Pentagon has classified thirty-four of those one hundred cases as criminal homicides. Of those thirty-four, none occurred at Guantanamo and only one at Abu Ghraib prison. Human Rights First also documented that eleven of the one hundred cases were prisoners who literally were tortured to death.[34]

Both Congress and the Supreme Court attempted to check the Bush administration, but they met intense resistance. In 2005 Congress overwhelmingly passed the Detainee Treatment Act with a provision that explicitly prohibits any cruel, inhuman, or degrading treatment of detainees in U.S. custody.[35] Although the president signed the bill into law, he included a signing statement that stripped it of its essential meaning, asserting that there would be compliance with the law so long as it did not compromise national security.[36]

In June 2006, the Supreme Court entered the debate, ruling in *Hamdan v. Rumsfeld* that all detainees in U.S. custody are entitled to humane treatment, as defined by Common Article 3 of the Geneva Conventions.[37] The administration, however, rejected the court's ruling by proposing the Military Commissions Act (MCA) in September 2006. Though ostensibly aimed at bringing the procedures of Guantanamo's military commissions into conformity with the *Hamdan v. Rumsfeld* (2006) decision, the MCA included a provision that exempted the CIA, granting it latitude to continue using "enhanced interrogation techniques." At a press conference announcing this new initiative, President Bush made the case for circumventing the court's decision, claiming that he was simply proposing "that there be clarity in the law so that our professionals will have no doubt that that which they are doing is legal . . . [and so that] our professionals [cannot] be held to account based upon court decisions in other countries."[38]

Although there was pushback from Congress, which principally came from Republican senators John Warner, John McCain, and Lindsey Graham, all former military servicemen, Congress ultimately passed the MCA, adding a requirement for the president to issue an executive order spelling out how the CIA would comply with Common Article 3.[39] Again, the administration ignored the clear intent of the congressional directive and sought to avoid any restraints on the CIA. The executive order, issued by the president in July 2007, prohibits torture and asserts that the CIA program "fully complies" with Common Article 3, but significantly limits the circumstances in which acts of abuse are strictly prohibited and only prohibits other forms of cruel, inhuman, or degrading conduct if the purpose of such abuses is to humiliate or degrade.[40] Commenting on this provision, Gen. P. X. Kelley, retired U.S. Marine Corps commandant, and Prof. Robert Turner wrote, "The president has given the CIA carte blanche to engage in 'willful and outrageous acts of personal abuse.'"[41]

Responding to the executive order, Congress passed in 2007 a provision as part of the Intelligence Authorization Act for Fiscal Year 2008 that would have required the CIA to follow the army standard. Although the provision passed both chambers of Congress, yet again the administration recoiled, and the president vetoed the bill in March 2008.[42] President Obama explicitly revoked this executive order on January 22, 2009.[43]

In December 2008, a month before Obama took office, the Senate Armed Services Committee released a report placing responsibility for abuses committed in Guantanamo, Abu Ghraib, and other detention centers squarely on the shoulders of top Bush administration officials, including Secretary Rumsfeld. Issued jointly by Senators Carl Levin and John McCain, the report states:

> Secretary of Defense Donald Rumsfeld's December 2, 2002 authorization of aggressive interrogation techniques and subsequent interrogation policies and plans approved by senior military and civilian officials conveyed the message that physical pressures and degradation were appropriate treatment for detainees in U.S. military custody. What followed was an erosion in standards dictating that detainees be treated humanely.[44]

TICKING BOMBS AND RED HERRINGS: WHY TORTURE IS NEVER LEGITIMATE

Despite the sound advice of many senior military officers and national security experts and practitioners, some policymakers, academics, and others continue to make the case for some form of officially sanctioned torture or abuse.[45] One such proponent is Prof. Alan Dershowitz. In a series of articles and books in recent years, he has argued that because coercive questioning will inevitably occur in the new national security environment, it should be regulated through the use of torture warrants.[46] Professor Dershowitz believes that torture warrants would not only limit torture but also ensure openness and accountability because oversight and monitoring would be built into the system.[47] His argument for these warrants is based on the notion that in a war against terrorists, it is no longer sufficient for the United States to be on the defensive. Thus he argues, as he did in a March 2003 interview, that the U.S. government needs to have at its disposal a series of aggressive measures, including coercive interrogation techniques, to prevent terrorist acts:

> We should never under any circumstances allow low-level people to administer torture. If torture is going to be administered as a last resort in the ticking-bomb case, to save enormous numbers of lives, it ought to be done openly, with accountability, with approval by the president of the United States or by a Supreme Court justice.[48]

Professor Dershowitz frequently cites this ticking bomb hypothetical to make his point. In such cases, he argues, a torture warrant would actually be a form of protection because it

> puts a heavy burden on the government to demonstrate by factual evidence the necessity to administer this horrible, horrible technique of torture. I would talk about nonlethal torture, say, a sterilized needle underneath the nail, which would violate the Geneva Accords, but you know, countries all over the world violate the Geneva Accords . . . secretly and hypothetically. . . . If we ever came close to doing it, and we don't know whether this is such a case, I think we would want to do it with accountability and openly and not adopt the way of the hypocrite.[49]

The logic behind the use of torture warrants as a protective measure is flawed. Coercive interrogations tarnish the legal right to a presumption of innocence. With a presumption of guilt instead of innocence comes poor treatment and conditions, and the burden of proof is shifted to the detainee. In these situations, the detainee has the burden of providing information to his interrogators in order to stop the maltreatment. Torture warrants also promote and sustain an environment of hysteria and fear and open the door to more abuse, not less.

Professor Dershowitz has also theorized, "We won't know if he is a ticking-bomb terrorist unless he provides us information, and he's not likely to provide information unless we use certain extreme measures."[50] Although this may be an interesting law school exercise, national security experts warn against using this scenario as a basis for making official policy.

They make two points. First, the ticking bomb scenario in this country is rare or almost nonexistent. As such, it is not a sound basis for making law or policy. As Stephen Holmes, a professor at New York University School of Law, writes:

> Although neither realistic nor representative, the hypothetical [ticking bomb] is nevertheless revealing. For one thing, the idea that authorities might get a dangerous terrorist into their custody, after he has planned an attack but before he has executed it, is a utopian fantasy. The elusiveness of these criminal conspirators is intensely frustrating and naturally gives rise, among counter-terrorism officials, to daydreams of superman-style rescues. To set policies on the basis of such far-fetched scenarios would be folly.[51]

However, viewed from the battlefield, stressful situations akin to the ticking bomb seem to occur every hour of every day. As retired major general Paul Eaton testified before Congress:

> The argument, the "ticking time bomb," Jack Bauer, the program "24 Hours" gets a lot of press for his solutions to the threats of our Nation. Recently, his performance under the pressure of the ticking time bomb scenario was favorably received by many people, with criminal behavior excused for the greater good. . . . [S]quad leaders in Iraq are faced with a ticking time bomb scenario every day. The question is: Do we want our soldiers and Marines to play Jack Bauer?[52]

These stresses of combat, however, rarely if ever lead to situations in which a single interrogation leads to the discovery and dismantling of a ticking time bomb, though movies and television shows like 24 would have us believe otherwise. In Jack Bauer's world on 24, he and other interrogators often are presented with a detainee or suspect, and the evidence makes it seem as if he has time-sensitive information. That is the world of entertainment; in the real world, the choices are never so clear or simple.

Thus, according to two retired U.S. marine generals, Charles Krulak and Joseph Hoar, it is important for hard and fast rules to be established for interrogations and the battlefield so that interrogators and military personnel know how to react and what they can and cannot do. In 2007 General Krulak, former commandant of the U.S. Marines, and General Hoar, former commander in chief of the U.S. Central Command, wrote: "Complex situational ethics cannot be applied during the stress of combat. The rules must be firm and absolute; if torture is broached as a possibility, it will become a reality."[53]

Along these same lines, in September 2006 forty-eight retired generals, admirals, and other senior military leaders wrote a public letter to members of the Senate Armed Services Committee warning that "a flexible, sliding scale that might allow certain coercive interrogation techniques under some circumstances, while forbidding them under other others . . . will only create further confusion."[54] If torture is sanctioned, allowed, or even winked at by a high-ranking official, including the president or a Supreme Court justice, there will be a trickle-down effect with disastrous results—one need only look at Abu Ghraib and its aftermath to see how information and practices can flow down the chain of command, become distorted, and then lead to undesirable, unforeseen results.[55]

Finally, military experts and other national security professionals reject the misguided notion that because other countries or violent extremist groups rely on torture, the United States can too. As Rear Admiral John Hutson, a former judge advocate general of the U.S. Navy, testified to Congress in 2005:

> We must not be deterred just because our enemy in a war on terror doesn't comply with the [Geneva] Conventions. Our unilateral compliance will aid in the peace process. Moreover, it should have been understood that violations of the Conventions, or ignoring them, doesn't help bring an end to the war. To the contrary, as we have seen, this only adds ferocity to the fighting and lengthens the war by hardening the resolve of the enemy. Our flagrant disregard for the Conventions only serves as a recruiting poster for this enemy and for our enemies for generations to come.[56]

The experiences of other democratic societies such as Israel and Britain support Admiral Hutson's warning. In 1987 the Landau Commission examined interrogation methods of General Security Services (GSS), a department of the Israeli government that investigates individuals suspected of committing crimes against the security of the country. The commission found that interrogation methods used against those suspected of "hostile terrorist activity" would be allowed so long as the methods were not lied about. Specifically, the commission wrote:

> The means of pressure should principally take the form of non-violent psychological pressure through a vigorous and extensive interrogation, with the use of stratagems, including acts of deception. However, when these do not attain their purpose, the exertion of a moderate measure of physical pressure cannot be avoided.[57]

A study conducted by B'Tselem, a human rights group based in Jerusalem, found that the GSS interrogated 1,000–1,500 Palestinians a year and that 85 percent of those, about 850, were tortured.[58] Such figures and hundreds of petitions to the Supreme Court by detained Palestinians who complained of physical force and psychological pressure led to a change in policy. In September 1999, twelve years after the Landau Commission was appointed, the Israeli Supreme Court banned the use of torture and cruel treatment during interrogations.[59] In its order, Prime Minister Ehud Barak wrote on behalf of the Court, "Indeed, violence directed at a suspect's body or spirit does not constitute a reasonable investigation practice."[60]

Similarly, there has been a shift in thinking in the United Kingdom where, during the height of the troubles in Northern Ireland, coercive interrogation methods were used against suspected members of the Irish Republican Army and others. In recent years, UK officials have relied on noncoercive methods, a shift in policy that has served Britain well. According to Louise Richardson of the University of St. Andrews, who has studied British interrogation practices in-depth, the United States has much to learn about interrogation: "The U.S. is repeating the same mistakes that other democracies [like Britain] have made. They overreact initially by relying on force and over time learn that force is not the most productive response."[61]

PREVENTING THE SLIPPERY SLOPE: RECOMMENDATIONS FOR THE OBAMA ADMINISTRATION

In the long run, the struggle against al-Qaeda or other terrorist groups will not be won by resorting to torture and abuse. To the contrary, such methods make Americans less safe and are likely to actually prolong the struggle. As Generals Krulak and Hoar wrote:

> This war will be won or lost not on the battlefield but in the minds of potential supporters who have not yet thrown in their lot with the enemy. If we forfeit our values by signaling that they are negotiable in situations of grave or imminent danger, we drive those undecideds into the arms of the enemy.[62]

In its first days in office, the Obama administration took bold and decisive steps to begin restoring America's reputation. The series of executive orders issued by the administration embraced strong, effective counterterrorism policies, which include the establishment of a single interrogation standard based on humane treatment and the closure of secret prisons, policies that are consistent with the nation's core civil liberties precepts.

As the Obama administration acts to implement these directives and formulates future policy in this important area, its actions will be guided in part by the findings of the Special Interagency Task Force on Interrogations and

Transfer Policies. Chaired by the attorney general, the task force will make recommendations to the administration on whether the interrogation practices and techniques outlined in the *Army Field Manual* provide "appropriate means of acquiring the intelligence necessary to protect the nation." If not, the task force is charged with recommending additional or different guidance for other departments or agencies.

President Obama's task force should follow his lead and make recommendations consistent with his commitment to uphold America's legal and ethical values. As President Obama stated in his remarks at the National Archives Museum in May 2009, we Americans "cannot keep this country safe unless we enlist the power of our most fundamental values."[63] To help the president take full advantage of what he described as "our best national security asset," the task force should urge a permanent ban on torture and all forms of cruel treatment by all U.S. agencies.

The president and Congress also should work together to find the appropriate way to review all U.S. government interrogation policies and practices since 9/11. One option proposed by Sen. Patrick Leahy and others would be to establish a commission based on the 9/11 Commission to review the past as a basis for making recommendations on how to avoid future abuses. As Senator Leahy has stated, "We need to be able to read the page before we turn the page."[64]

These steps will serve to enhance national security and to ensure the protection of basic civil liberties. In so doing, they will go a long way toward restoring America's moral standing in the world.

NO: There is a need to bring an unfortunate practice within the bounds of law
Alan M. Dershowitz, *Harvard Law School*

Why an Absolutist Approach toward Torture Is Bad for Democracy

In this essay, I will first identify the points of agreement and disagreement between the absolutist approach represented by Michael Posner to reducing or eliminating torture and my own quite different approach. I will then describe and defend the idea of requiring torture warrants, and explain why the enactment of a torture warrant statute will minimize instances of torture and strengthen America's democratic values.

POINTS OF AGREEMENT

There are many areas of agreement between the most vocal advocates of an absolute ban on torture and myself. We agree that torture is bad and should not be used by democracies committed to the rule of law. We agree that under current law—both domestic and international—all forms of torture are prohibited under all circumstances. We agree that torture should be defined broadly to include waterboarding (a form of simulated drowning) and other physical measures that induce pain, cause injury, or risk death. We agree that it is important not to legitimate any form of torture. We agree that all nations should take whatever steps are necessary to eliminate or reduce torture. We agree that it would be a much better world if torture were no longer practiced or even considered as an option by civilized nations or individuals.

I am sure we also agree that torture is currently practiced by many, if not most, countries in the world, including many American allies such as Egypt, Jordan, the Philippines, and Pakistan. It is also practiced by the Palestinian Authority, Hamas, Iran, and other rogue nations and groups. I doubt we would disagree that torture has been employed by the United States not only during the Bush administration but also during the Vietnam War, the Korean War, the Second World War, the First World War, and probably during other periods in U.S. history. I think we would also agree that if there ever were a situation perceived by the administration to be a real ticking bomb case involving a captured terrorist who had information that could prevent a mass-casualty attack, some form of torture would *in fact* be used if it was thought likely to save numerous lives, regardless of the law.

Nor would torture be resorted to in the ticking bomb situation only by Republican, conservative, or "bad" presidents. Consider what former president Bill Clinton said when asked by National Public Radio, as someone "who's been there," whether the president needs "the option of authorizing torture in an extreme case":

> Look, if the president needed an option, there's all sorts of things they can do. Let's take the best case, OK. You picked up someone you know is the No. 2 aide to Osama bin Laden. And you know they have an operation planned for the United States or some European capital in the next . . . three days. And you know this guy knows it. Right, that's the clearest example. And you think you can only get it out of this guy by shooting him full of some drugs or waterboarding him or otherwise working him

over. If they really believed that that scenario is likely to occur, let them come forward with an alternate proposal.

We have a system of laws here where nobody should be above the law, and you don't need blanket advance approval for blanket torture. They can draw a statute much more narrowly, which would permit the president to make a finding in a case like I just outlined, and then that finding could be submitted even if after the fact to the Foreign Intelligence Surveillance Court.[65]

Clinton was then asked whether he was saying there "would be more responsibility afterward for what was done." He replied: "Yeah, well, the president could take personal responsibility for it. But you do it on a case-by-case basis, and there'd be some review of it." Clinton quickly added that he did not know whether the ticking bomb scenario "is likely or not," but he did know that "we have erred in who was a real suspect or not."

In the interview, Clinton summarized his views in the following terms:

If they really believe the time comes when the only way they can get a reliable piece of information is to beat it out of someone or put a drug in their body to talk it out of [him], then they can present it to the Foreign Intelligence Court, or some other court, just under the same circumstances we do with wiretaps. Post facto. . . .

But I think if you go around passing laws that legitimize a violation of the Geneva Convention and institutionalize what happened at Abu Ghraib or Guantanamo, we're gonna be in real trouble.

I have little doubt—as a matter of *fact,* not *law* or *morality*—that presidents would condone some forms of torture if they truly believed it was the only option available to prevent an act of mass-casualty terrorism. Nor do I have much doubt that intelligence operatives on the ground would resort to torture under such circumstances. No law or proclamation would change this cruel reality.

Some people have argued that the entire debate about torture is foolish and unnecessary because torture never works, because it always produces false and useless information from suspects who will say anything to stop the pain.

It is in my view dishonest, though politically correct, to claim, as an empirical matter, that torture *never* works—that it *never* produces reliable and useful real time information that could save lives. It can certainly be argued, though subject to empirical testing, that torture *rarely* works, that it *generally* produces false information, that there are *better* ways to secure such information, or that *on balance* any good it accomplishes is more than offset by the evil it produces. All of these are reasonable, and perhaps even true, statements.

But it defies history, science, common sense, logic, and what is known about human behavior to deny that under *some* circumstances *some* people will produce *some* useful and truthful information that could in fact save lives. Indeed, in numerous instances torture has produced truthful information.[66] It is not a question of seeking to use the fruits of torture to convict someone of a crime based on his own confession. Nor is it a question of merely verbal pronouncements of a person under torture. It is a question of the torturer who insists that his victim take him to where the bomb is hidden or take some other action that is self-proving. Too many brave men and women—in the French Resistance and other such organizations—disclosed the location of friends, loved ones, and even relatives under torture to doubt its effectiveness under some circumstances.

I do not believe that there is much room for disagreement with any of the above. Although Michael Posner argues in this chapter that "torture and coercive interrogation tactics are ineffective and even a counterproductive way to gather intelligence,"[67] he does not deny that it could, in some instances, produce truthful and self-proving information that could prevent a mass-casualty terrorist attack. The important point, however, is not whether Mr. Posner or I believe this, but whether the person who must make the decision to authorize or employ torture—the president or an intelligence official on the ground— might believe or be persuaded that in a given case torture is the best—or least worst—option available.

POINTS OF DEPARTURE

The major point of disagreement between my approach and the approach represented by Mr. Posner is about means, not ends. We both want to prevent any recurrence of what happened at Abu Ghraib. We both want to put an end to what happened under the Bush administration: publicly proclaiming that torture would never be used, while quietly encouraging "whatever it takes" to get intelligence information deemed necessary to prevent another act of mass-casualty terrorism. We both want to see torture ended, or—at the very least— reduced as much as humanly possible.

Mr. Posner believes that the best way to accomplish these admirable goals is by a blanket, unqualified, absolute prohibition on all torture, "adopting a zero-tolerance approach." More specifically, he insists that "the use of torture or cruel, inhuman, or degrading treatment in interrogations should never be tolerated, regulated, or justified as a matter of official policy, law, or practice."

I would agree—if I believed that this approach would work. But that is precisely the approach the United States has used for more than a century, and it has failed miserably. The twentieth century was the century in which the laws of virtually every nation and international body followed the Posner approach. And yet the twentieth century can fairly be characterized as the "Torture Century" in which torture was used extensively throughout the world, not only by evil nations such as Hitler's Germany, Hirohito's Japan, Stalin's Soviet Union, Mao's China, Castro's Cuba, and Pol Pot's Cambodia, but also by Britain, France, the United States, Israel, and other democracies.

Mr. Posner cites George Washington, Thomas Jefferson, James Madison, Abraham Lincoln, Franklin Roosevelt, George Marshall, and others in support of the myth that throughout American history the U.S. military has refrained from abusing prisoners of war. Although it is true that Americans have talked the talk of refraining from employing torture, the reality is that the U.S. military has tortured captured enemy soldiers to obtain real-time intelligence in every war it has fought. During the Vietnam and Korean Wars, torture was routine and pervasive, and these wars were fought after the enactment of the Geneva Conventions outlawing all forms of torture under all circumstances.

Saying they are against all forms of torture under all circumstances—even when it is believed that torture may be the only way to save thousands of innocent lives—makes Americans feel good. Announcing such a policy may make them look good. But the reality is that all democracies will close their eyes to torture in some extreme circumstances. In my view, that is an unacceptable option for a democracy. If torture is ever to be used—and it will be—it must be authorized as an explicit exception to the general law and with democratic accountability.

The strongest argument against my preference for candor and accountability is the claim that it is better for torture—or any other evil practice deemed necessary during emergencies—to be left to the low-visibility discretion of low-level functionaries than to be legitimated by high-level, accountable decision makers. Judge Richard Posner makes this argument:

> Dershowitz believes that the occasions for the use of torture should be regularized—by requiring a judicial warrant for the needle treatment, for example. But he overlooks an argument for leaving such things to executive discretion. If rules are promulgated permitting torture in defined circumstances, some officials are bound to want to explore the outer bounds of the rules. Having been regularized, the practice will become regular. Better to leave in place the formal and customary prohibitions, but with the understanding that they will not be enforced in extreme circumstances.[68]

The classic formulation of this argument was offered by Supreme Court justice Robert Jackson in his dissenting opinion in one of the Japanese detention camp cases stemming from World War II:

Much is said of the danger to liberty from the Army program for deporting and detaining these citizens of Japanese extraction. But a judicial construction of the due process clause that will sustain this order is a far subtler blow to liberty than the promulgation of the order itself. A military order, however unconstitutional, is not apt to last longer than the military emergency. Even during that period a succeeding commander may revoke it all. But once a judicial opinion rationalizes such an order to show that it conforms to the Constitution, or rather rationalizes the Constitution to show that the Constitution sanctions such an order, the Court for all time has validated the principle of racial discrimination in criminal procedure and of transplanting American citizens. The principle then lies about like a loaded weapon ready for the hand of any authority that can bring forward a plausible claim of an urgent need. Every repetition imbeds that principle more deeply in our law and thinking and expands it to new purposes. All who observe the work of courts are familiar with what Judge Cardozo described as "the tendency of a principle to expand itself to the limit of its logic." A military commander may overstep the bounds of constitutionality, and it is an incident. But if we review and approve, that passing incident becomes the doctrine of the Constitution. There it has a generative power of its own, and all that it creates will be in its own image.[69]

Experience has not necessarily proved that Justice Jackson's fear or Judge Posner's prediction to be well founded. The very fact that the Supreme Court expressly validated the Japanese detentions contributed to its condemnation by the verdict of history. Today, the Supreme Court's decision in *Korematsu* stands alongside decisions such as *Dred Scott, Plessy v. Ferguson,* and *Buck v. Bell* in the high court's Hall of Infamy. Though never formally overruled, and even occasionally cited, *Korematsu* serves as a negative precedent—a mistaken ruling not ever to be repeated in future cases. Yet had the Supreme Court merely allowed the executive decision to stand without judicial review, a far more dangerous precedent might have been established: that executive decisions during times of emergency will escape review by the Supreme Court. That far broader and more dangerous precedent would then lie about "like a loaded weapon" ready to be used by a dictator without fear of judicial review. That comes close to what happened during the Ronald Reagan, George H. W. Bush, and George W. Bush administrations. Those administrations denied they were acting unlawfully, while aggressively resisting any judicial review of their actions.

TORTURE WARRANTS AS THE BEST MEANS OF MINIMIZING TORTURE

My own belief is that a warrant requirement, if properly enforced, would probably reduce the frequency, severity, and duration of torture. I cannot see how it could possibly increase it, since a warrant requirement simply imposes an additional level of prior review. Two examples demonstrate why I think there would be less torture with a warrant requirement than without one. Recall the case of the alleged national security wiretap being placed on the phones of Martin Luther King Jr. by the Kennedy administration in the early 1960s. This was in the days when the attorney general could authorize a national security wiretap without a warrant. Today, no judge would issue a warrant in a case as flimsy as that one. When al-Qaeda suspect Zacarias Moussaoui was detained a month before the 9/11 attacks after trying to learn how to fly an airplane without wanting to know much about landing it, the government did not even seek a national security wiretap because its lawyers believed that a judge would not have granted one. If Moussaoui's computer could have been searched without a warrant, it almost certainly would have been.

It should be recalled that in the context of searches the Framers of the Fourth Amendment to the U.S. Constitution opted for a judicial check on the discretion of the police by requiring a search warrant in most cases. In *Johnson v. United States* (1948), the Supreme Court explained the reason for the warrant requirement as follows: "The informed and deliberate determinations of magistrates . . . are to be preferred over the hurried actions of officers." Justice Robert Jackson, who delivered the opinion of the Court, then elaborated:

> The point of the Fourth Amendment, which often is not grasped by zealous officers, is not that it denies law enforcement the support of the usual inferences, which reasonable men draw from evidence. Its protection consists in requiring that those inferences be drawn by a neutral and detached magistrate instead of being judged by the officer engaged in the often-competitive enterprise of ferreting out crime. Any assumption that evidence sufficient to support a magistrate's disinterested determination to issue a search warrant will justify the officers in making a search without a warrant would reduce the Amendment to nullify and leave the peoples' homes secure only in the discretion of police officers.[70]

Although torture is very different from a search, the policies underlying the warrant requirement are relevant to whether there is likely to be more torture or less if the decision were left entirely to field officers, or if a judicial officer had to approve a request for a torture warrant.

The major downside of any warrant procedure would be its legitimization of a horrible practice. But in my view it is better to legitimate and control a *specific* practice that will in fact occur than to legitimate a *general* practice of tolerating extralegal actions so long as they operate under the table of scrutiny and beneath the radar screen of accountability. Judge Posner's "pragmatic" approach would be an invitation to widespread (and officially—if surreptitiously—approved) lawlessness in "extreme circumstances." Moreover, the very concept of "extreme circumstances" is subjective and infinitely expandable. Jordan, which denies that it ever uses torture, has, in fact, tortured the innocent relatives of suspected terrorists. And when U.S. agents captured 9/11 mastermind Khalid Sheikh Muhammad, they reportedly also took into custody his two elementary school-age children—and let him know that they had them.

There is a difference in principle, as Jeremy Bentham noted more than two hundred years ago, between torturing the guilty to save the lives of the innocent and torturing innocent people. A system that requires an articulated justification for the use of nonlethal torture and approval by a judge is more likely to honor that principle—and other important ones—than a system that relegates these decisions to low-visibility law enforcement agents whose only job is to protect the public from terrorism.

Strengthening Democratic Principles

Several important values are pitted against each other in this conflict over the role of torture in national security and counterterrorism policy. The first is the safety and security of a nation's citizens. Under the ticking bomb scenario, this value may argue for the use of torture if that were the only way to prevent the ticking bomb from exploding and killing large numbers of civilians. The second value is the preservation of civil liberties and human rights. This value requires that Americans not accept torture as a legitimate part of their legal system.

In my debates with two prominent civil libertarians—Floyd Abrams and Harvey Silverglate—both acknowledged that they would want nonlethal torture to be used if it could prevent thousands of deaths, but they did not want torture to be officially recognized by the U.S. legal system. As Floyd Abrams put it: "In a democracy sometimes it is necessary to do things off the books and below the radar screen."

The former presidential candidate Alan Keyes has taken the position that although torture might be *necessary* in a given situation, it could never be *right*. He suggested that a president *should* authorize the torturing of a ticking bomb terrorist, but that this act should not be legitimated by the courts or incorporated into the legal system. He argued that wrongful and indeed unlawful acts might sometimes be necessary to preserve the nation, but that no aura of legitimacy should be placed on these actions by judicial imprimatur. Prof. Jean Elshtain makes a similar point. Although she strongly favors the use of nonlethal torture in certain extreme cases, she does not want "a law to cover such cases." Indeed, she characterizes my proposal for a torture warrant as "a stunningly bad idea." She prefers instead to have each individual "grapple with a terrible moral dilemma" rather than have any open debate and then codify its results.[71]

This understandable approach is in conflict with the third important value: open accountability and visibility in a democracy. Off-the-book actions "below the radar screen" are antithetical to the theory and practice of democracy. Citizens cannot approve or disapprove of government actions of which they are unaware. Indeed, the lesson of history teaches that off-the-book actions can produce terrible consequences. President Richard Nixon's creation of a group of "plumbers" led to the Watergate affair, and President Reagan's authorization of an off-the-books foreign policy in Central America led to the Iran-contra scandal. And these are only the ones everyone knows about!

Perhaps the most extreme example of this hypocritical approach to torture comes—not surprisingly—from the French experience in Algeria. The French army used torture extensively in seeking to prevent terrorism during France's brutal war between 1955 and 1957. An officer who supervised this torture, Gen. Paul Aussaresses, wrote an account of what he had done and seen, including the torture of dozens of Algerians. "The best way to make a terrorist talk when he refused to say what he knew was to torture him," Aussaresses boasted.[72] Although the book was published decades after the war was over, the general was prosecuted—but not for what he had *done* to the Algerians. Instead, he was prosecuted for *revealing* what he had done and seeking to justify it.

In a democracy governed by the rule of law, its citizens should never want their soldiers or president to take any action that they deem wrong or illegal. A good test of whether an action should or should not be done is whether those undertaking the action are prepared to have it disclosed—perhaps not immediately, but certainly after some time has passed. No legal system operating under the rule of law should ever tolerate an off-the-books approach to necessity. Even the defense of necessity must be justified lawfully. The road to tyranny has always been paved with claims of necessity made by those responsible for the security of a nation. The U.S. system of checks and balances requires that all presidential actions, like all legislative or military actions, be consistent with governing laws. If it is necessary to torture in the ticking bomb case, then the governing laws must accommodate this practice. If Americans refuse to change their laws to accommodate any particular action, then their government should not take that action. Requiring that a controversial, even immoral, action be made openly and with accountability is one way of minimizing resort to unjustifiable means.

Carefully Choosing Security

Only in a democracy committed to civil liberties would a triangular conflict of this kind exist. Totalitarian and authoritarian regimes experience no such conflict, because they subscribe to neither the civil libertarian nor the democratic values that come in conflict with the value of security. The hard question is: which value is to be preferred when a clash occurs? One or more of these values must inevitably be compromised in making the tragic choice presented by the ticking bomb case. If the United States does not torture, it compromises the security and safety of its citizens. If the country tolerates torture, but keeps the decisions to torture off the books and below the radar screen, it compromises principles of democratic accountability. If it creates a legal structure for limiting and controlling torture, it compromises its principled opposition to torture in all circumstances and creates a potentially dangerous and expandable situation.

In 1678 the French writer François de La Rochefoucauld said that "hypocrisy is the homage that vice renders to virtue." In this case, there are two vices: terrorism and torture. There are also two virtues: civil liberties and democratic accountability. Most civil libertarians I know prefer hypocrisy, precisely because it appears to avoid the conflict between security and civil liberties. But by choosing the way of the hypocrite these civil libertarians compromise the value of democratic accountability. Such is the nature of tragic choices in a complex world. As Bentham put it more than two centuries ago: "Government throughout is but a choice of evils." In a democracy, such choices must be made, whenever possible, with openness and democratic accountability, and subject to the rule of law.

Consider another terrible choice of evils that could easily have been presented on September 11, 2001, and may well be presented in the future: a hijacked passenger jet is on a collision course with a densely occupied office building, and the only way to prevent the destruction of the building and the killing of its occupants is to shoot down the jet, thereby killing its innocent passengers. This choice now seems easy because the passengers are certain to die anyway and their somewhat earlier deaths will save numerous lives. The passenger jet must be shot down. But what if it were only *probable*, not certain, that the jet would crash into the building? Say, for example, cell phone transmissions indicate that the passengers are struggling to regain control of the hijacked jet, but it is unlikely they will succeed in time. Or say there is no communication with the jet and all that is known is that it is off course and heading toward Washington, D.C., or some other densely populated area. Under these more questionable circumstances, the question becomes *who* should make this life and death choice between evils—a decision that may turn out tragically wrong?

No reasonable person would allocate this decision to a fighter jet pilot who happened to be in the area or to a local airbase commander—unless, of course, there was no time for the matter to be passed up the chain of command to the secretary of defense or the president. A decision of this kind should be made at the highest level possible, with visibility and accountability.

Why is this not also true of the decision to torture a ticking bomb terrorist? Why should that choice of evils be relegated to a local policeman, FBI agent, or CIA operative rather than to a judge, the attorney general, or the president?

It may be better to have each individual "grapple with a terrible moral dilemma" in a philosophy class. In a democracy, such grappling must occur in the open and be made by those accountable to the demos, not to the professorate.

Basically, four options are available to a democracy faced with what its leaders honestly believe is a ticking bomb situation that can be prevented only by torture. The first is to bravely do "the right thing": do not torture and accept responsibility for not having prevented the possibly preventable murders of thousands of innocent civilians. I might wish it were otherwise, but I am certain, as a matter of fact, that no democratic leader would knowingly accept that option.

The second option is to lie and claim that torture *never* works, that is why it was not tried, and that is why the president is not responsible for not having prevented the murder of thousands of civilians. No president would do that because the public would not believe him—and for good reason. They would insist that it should have been tried.

The third option has been called "the way of the hypocrite." The president would not "authorize" torture, but neither would he prevent its use. He would give himself—or his staff would give him—"plausible deniability." He would stick his head in the proverbial sand and engage in "willful ignorance." This is the option most presidents probably would prefer, because they can have their cake and eat it too. But in a democracy, such evasion of accountability in choosing among evil decisions raises profoundly disturbing questions.

The fourth option is for the president to declare that the nation is in a situation of dire necessity requiring temporary suspension of the absolute prohibition against torture. Such a declaration would have to be authorized by Congress (just like suspension of the writ of habeas corpus). It would have to be based on preexisting law and justified by evidence. Criteria would have to be spelled out in advance by Congress and then found to exist by a justice of the Supreme Court. All three branches of government would have to agree. All three branches would have to dirty their hands by participating in this terrible choice of evils. But that is how democracy requires those who live under it to confront and choose between or among horrible evils.

Notes

1. These memos are available at www.aclu.org/safefree/general/olc_memos.html.
2. Peter Baker, "Banned Techniques Yielded 'High Value Information,' Memo Says," *New York Times,* April 22, 2009.
3. "Close the Torture Loophole," *Los Angeles Times,* April 18, 2009.
4. The author wishes to thank Emily Stanfield for her extensive research assistance. He also wishes to thank Devon Chaffee, Sharon Kelly, Elisa Massimino, and Gabor Rona for their helpful suggestions. Views expressed are those of the author and do not necessarily represent official views of the U.S. Department of State.
5. President Obama signed three executive orders on January 22, 2009, that put a halt to the CIA's "enhanced" interrogation program, ended secret detentions, guaranteed Red Cross access to prisoners, imposed a one-year deadline for closing the detention facilities at Guantanamo Bay, Cuba, and set a single U.S. standard for all prisoners in U.S. custody—a standard that is contained in the *Army Field Manual on Human Intelligence Collector Operations.* The executive order on lawful interrogations makes clear that every person in U.S. custody must be treated humanely and not subjected to torture or any other forms of cruel, humiliating, or degrading treatment. See White House, "Executive Orders to Date," January 23, 2009, http:/// www.whitehouse.gov/executive-orders-to-date.
6. National Commission on Terrorist Attacks upon the United States, *The 9/11 Commission Report: Final Report* (Washington, D.C.: Government Printing Office, 2004).
7. David Hackett Fischer, *Washington's Crossing* (New York: Oxford University Press, 2006), 379.
8. Jefferson to James Madison, Monticello, April 19, 1809, in *The Works of Thomas Jefferson, Federal Edition,* Vol. 11, ed. Paul Leicester Ford (New York: G. P. Putnam's Sons, 1905), 107.
9. Frances Lieber, *Instructions for the Government of Armies of the United States in the Field* (Washington, D.C.: Government Printing Office, 1898), sec. 111, art. 76, and sec. 1, art. 4. These instructions were promulgated by Abraham Lincoln as General Orders No. 100, April 24, 1863. See Dietrich Schindler and Jiří Toman, eds., *The Laws of Armed Conflicts* (Boston: Martinus Nihjoff, 1988), 3–23.
10. President Theodore Roosevelt, speaking on May 30, 1902, to veterans at Arlington National Cemetery. See Joseph Bucklin Bishop, *Theodore Roosevelt and His Time Shown in His Own Letters* (New York: Charles Scribner's Sons, 1920), 192.
11. "Geneva Convention Relative to the Treatment of Prisoners of War," United Nations, Geneva, 1949.
12. U.S. Office of Information for the Armed Forces, U.S. Department of Defense, *The Armed Forces Officer* (Washington, D.C.: Armed Forces Information Service, 1975), 191.
13. Gen. John Shalikashvili et al., letter to Sen. John Warner and Sen. Carl Levin, September 12, 2006, www.humanrightsfirst.info/pdf/06913-etn-military-let-ca3.pdf.
14. "'Hardball with Chris Matthews' for November 22," msnbc.msn.com, November 23, 2005, www.msnbc.msn.com/id/10175425.
15. "Treating Terrorists with Respect," Talkradionews.com, June 2008, http://talkradio news.com/2008/06/treating-terrorists-with-respect.

16. Human Rights First, "Top Interrogators Declare Torture Ineffective in Intelligence Gathering," June 24, 2008, http:///www.humanrightsfirst.org/media/etn/2008/alert/313/index.htm.

17. In November 2005, Senator McCain wrote, "Our enemies didn't adhere to the Geneva Convention. Many of my comrades were subjected to very cruel, very inhumane and degrading treatment, a few of them even unto death. But every one of us . . . knew and took great strength from the belief that we were different from our enemies, that we were better than them, that we, if the roles were reversed, would not disgrace ourselves by committing or countenancing such mistreatment of them." See John McCain, "Torture's Terrible Toll," *Newsweek*, November 21, 2005.

18. "International Covenant on Civil and Political Rights," United Nations, New York, 1966, part 3, art. 7,

19. American Civil Liberties Union, "FAQ—The Convention Against Torture," April 27, 2006, www.aclu.org/safefree/torture/25353res20060427.html.

20. In a letter to members of the Senate Armed Services Committee in September 2006, a group of retired military leaders wrote: "If degradation, humiliation, physical and mental brutalization of prisoners is decriminalized or considered permissible [by the United States] under a restrictive interpretation of Common Article 3, we will forfeit all credible objections should such barbaric practices be inflicted upon American prisoners." See Shalikashvili et al., letter to Sen. John Warner and Sen. Carl Levin.

21. Naomi Klein, "Bush's War Goes Global," *Globe and Mail* (Toronto), August 27, 2003.

22. Human Rights First, "Defending Security: The Right to Defend Rights in an Age of Terrorism" (preliminary draft), Human Rights First, New York, 2004, 8, www.humanrightsfirst.org/us_law/PDF/behind-the-wire-033005.pdf.

23. Human Rights First, *A Year of Loss: Reexamining Civil Liberties since September 11* (New York: Human Rights First, 2002), 42.

24. Ibid., 43. Egyptian president Hosni Mubarak claimed in 2001 that U.S. policies implemented after September 11 "prove that we were right from the beginning in using all means" to combat terrorism.

25. National Defense Authorization Act for Fiscal Year 2006, H.R. 1815, 109th Cong., 1st sess., Congressional Record 102 (July 25, 2005): S 8792.

26. Alexander Hamilton and James Madison, "Helvidius Number IV," in *The Pacificus-Helvidius Debates of 1793–1794: Toward the Completion of the American Founding*, ed. Morton J. Frisch (Indianapolis, Ind.: Liberty Fund, 2007).

27. White House, "Vice President Cheney Delivers Remarks to the Republican Governors Association," October 25, 2001, http://georgewbush-whitehouse.archives.gov.

28. White House, "The Vice President Appears on Meet the Press with Tim Russert," September 16, 2001, http://georgewbush-whitehouse.archives.gov..

29. Jay S. Bybee, memorandum to Albert R. Gonzales, counsel to the president, August 1, 2002. http://f11.findlaw.com/news.findlaw.com/hdocs/docs/doj/bybee80102mem.pdf.

30. Commenting on the insulation of these practices from court review, a member of the "working group" assembled by the vice president and his attorney David Addington during the aftermath of September 11 called Guantanamo "the legal equivalent of outer space"—a "lawless" universe. See Michael Isikoff and Stuart Taylor Jr., "The Gitmo Fallout," *Newsweek*, July 17, 2006.

31. Donald Rumsfeld, memorandum to the commander, U.S. Southern Command, April 16, 2003, www.gwu.edu/~nsarchiv/NSAEBB/NSAEBB127/03.04.16.pdf.

32. White House, "President Discusses Creation of Military Commissions to Try Suspected Terrorists," September 6, 2006. http://georgewbush-whitehouse.archives.gov.

33. "Abu Ghraib," Times Topics, *New York Times,* http://topics.nytimes.com/top/news/international/countriesandterritories/iraq/abu_ghraib/index.html.

34. Human Rights First, *Command's Responsibility: Detainee Deaths in U.S. Custody in Iraq and Afghanistan* (New York: Human Rights First, 2006), 1.

35. Eric Schmitt, "House Backs McCain on Detainees, Defying Bush," *New York Times,* December 15, 2005.

36. The signing statement stated specifically: "The executive branch shall construe these sections in a manner consistent with the constitutional authority of the President." See White House, "President's Statement on Signing of H.R. 2863, the 'Department of Defense, Emergency Supplemental Appropriations to Address Hurricanes in the Gulf of Mexico, and Pandemic Influenza Act, 2006,'" http://georgewbush-whitehouse.archives.gov.

37. Linda Greenhouse, "Justices, 5–3, Broadly Reject Bush Plan to Try Detainees," *New York Times,* June 30, 2006.

38. White House, "Press Conference of the President," September 15, 2006, http://georgewbush-whitehouse.archives.gov.

39. *Military Commissions Act of 2006,* Public Law 109-366, 109th Cong., 2nd sess. (October 17, 2006), 2632, 2637.

40. The language of the executive order specifically reads: "willful and outrageous acts of personal abuse done for the purpose of humiliating or degrading the individual in a manner so serious that any reasonable person, considering the circumstances, would deem the acts to be beyond the bounds of human decency, such as sexual or sexually indecent acts undertaken for the purpose of humiliation, forcing the individual to perform sexual acts or to pose sexually, threatening the individual with sexual mutilation, or using the individual as a human shield; or acts intended to denigrate the religion, religious practices, or religious objects of the individual." See White House, "Executive Order: Interpretation of the Geneva Conventions Common Article 3 as Applied to a Program of Detention and Interrogation Operated by the Central Intelligence Agency," July 20, 2007, http://georgewbush-whitehouse.archives.gov.

41. P. X. Kelley and Robert F. Turner, "War Crimes and the White House: The Dishonor in a Tortured New 'Interpretation' of the Geneva Conventions," *Washington Post,* July 26, 2007.

42. In a statement to the U.S. House of Representatives, the president wrote, "I am returning herewith without my approval . . . the 'Intelligence Authorization Act for Fiscal Year 2008.' The bill would impede the United States Government's efforts to protect American people effectively from terrorist attacks and other threats because it imposes several unnecessary and unacceptable burdens on our Intelligence Community." He went on to write: "Section 327 of the bill would harm our national security by requiring any element of the Intelligence Community to use only the interrogation methods authorized in the Army Field Manual on Interrogations. It is vitally important that the Central Intelligence Agency (CIA) be allowed to

maintain a separate and classified interrogation program. . . . [M]y concern is the need to maintain a separate CIA program that will shield from disclosure to al Qaeda and other terrorists the interrogation techniques they may face upon capture." See www.fas.org/irp/congress/2008_cr/veto.html.

43. For the full text of President Obama's executive order revoking the Bush order, see www.whitehouse.gov/the_press_office/EnsuringLawfulInterrogations.

44. "Senate Armed Forces Committee Inquiry into the Treatment of Detainees in U.S. Custody," December 11, 2008, http://levin.senate.gov/newsroom/supporting/2008/Detainees.121108.pdf. The report pointedly rejects the administration's notion that using these coercive interrogation techniques keeps the country and its troops safe.

45. For a defense of the Bush administration's post-9/11 interrogation policy, see George Tenet, *At the Center of the Storm* (New York: HarperCollins, 2007).

46. Alan Dershowitz, "Want to Torture? Get a Warrant," January 22, 2002, www.alandershowitz.com/publications/docs/torturewarrants2.html.

47. Ibid.

48. "Dershowitz: Torture Could Be Justified," CNN.com, March 3, 2003, www.cnn.com/2003/LAW/03/03/cnna.Dershowitz.

49. Ibid.

50. Ibid.

51. Stephen Holmes, "Is Defiance of Law a Proof of Success? Magical Thinking in the War on Terror," in *The Torture Debate in America*, ed. Karen J. Greenberg (New York: Cambridge University Press, 2006), 127–128.

52. Senate Committee on Foreign Relations, "Extraordinary Rendition, Extraterritorial Detention and Treatment of Detainees: Restoring Our Moral Credibility and Strengthening Our Diplomatic Standing," hearing, 110th Cong., 1st sess., www.fas.org/irp/congress/2007_hr/rendition2.pdf.

53. Charles C. Krulak and Joseph P. Hoar, "It's Our Cage, Too; Torture Betrays Us and Breeds New Enemies," *Washington Post*, May 17, 2007.

54. Shalikashvili et al., letter to Sen. John Warner and Sen. Carl Levin.

55. Alberto Mora, former general counsel to the U.S. Navy from 2001 to 2005 and a principled dissenting voice on these issues, stated in an interview with *Vanity Fair* magazine, "I will also tell you that there are general-rank officers who've had senior responsibility within the Joint Staff or counterterrorism operations who believe that the number-one and number-two leading causes of U.S. combat deaths in Iraq have been, number one, Abu Ghraib, number two, Guantanamo, because of the effectiveness of these symbols in helping recruit jihadists into the field and combat against American soldiers." See Cullen Murphy and Todd S. Purdum, "Farewell to All That: An Oral History of the Bush White House," *Vanity Fair*, February 2009.

56. "Testimony of John D. Hutson before the United States Senate Committee on the Judiciary Concerning the Nomination of Alberto Gonzales for Confirmation as Attorney General of the United States," January 6, 2005, http://judiciary.senate.gov/hearings/testimony.cfm?id=1345&wit_id=3937.

57. "Background on the High Court of Justice's decision," www.btselem.org/english/Torture/Background.asp.

58. Ibid.

59. "Israel Supreme Court Bans Interrogation Abuse of Palestinians," CNN.com, September 6, 1999, www.cnn.com/WORLD/meast/9909/06/israel.torture/.

60. A. Barak, "Text of Israeli Supreme Court Decision on GSS Practices," Totse .com, September 6, 1999, www.totse.com/en/politics/foreign_military_intelligence_ agencies/ua92170.html.

61. Quoted in Josh Meyer, "CIA Should Tape More, Experts Say," *Los Angeles Times,* December 23, 2007.

62. Krulak and Hoar, "It's Our Cage, Too."

63. Remarks of President Barack Obama, National Archives Museum, Washington D.C., May 21, 2009, www.whitehouse.gov/the_press_office/Remarks-by-the-President-On-National-Security-5-21-09.

64. Sen. Patrick Leahy, "Take Action: Support a Truth and Reconciliation Commission," Office of Sen. Patrick Leahy, Truth Commission petition, http://ga3.0rg/campaign/ btcpetition?qp_source=btc_dk.

65. National Public Radio, *Morning Edition,* September 21, 2006.

66. For several such examples, see Alan Dershowitz, *Why Terrorism Works* (New Haven, Conn.: Yale University Press, 2002), chap. 4.

67. Posner cites Joe Navarro, a twenty-year FBI veteran, for the proposition that on balance torture is far less useful than other tactics. He also quotes a statement by fifteen senior interrogaters that torture "results in false and misleading information" and "loss of critical information."

68. Richard Posner, "The Best Offense," *New Republic,* September 2, 2002.

69. *Korematsu v. United States,* 323 U.S. 214 (1944), http://www.law.cornell.edu/supct/ html/historics/USSC_CR_0323_0214_ZD2.html.

70. *Johnson v. United States,* 333 U.S. 10 (1948), http://supreme.justia.com/us/333/10/ case.html.

71. Sanford Levinson, ed., *Torture: A Collection* (New York: Oxford University Press, 2004), 84.

72. Paul Aussaresses, *Battle of the Casbah: Terrorism and Counter-terrorism in Algeria, 1955–1957,* trans. Robert L. Miller (New York: Enigma, 2002).

counterterrorism and the constitution: does providing security require a trade-off with civil liberties?

YES: The United States needs to reasonably limit civil liberties and bolster executive powers
John Yoo, *University of California at Berkeley School of Law*

NO: Respecting civil liberties and preventing executive overreach are critical to preserving America's security and its ideals
David Cole, *Georgetown University Law Center*

In 1864 Abraham Lincoln was unexpectedly reelected president of the United States amidst the savagery of the Civil War. Though best known for freeing the slaves and saving the Union, during the war Lincoln came under fire for his aggressive use of presidential powers, including suspending habeas corpus in defiance of the Supreme Court, ordering the incarceration of thousands of citizens without charges, and blockading southern ports without congressional authorization.

Aware of the contradictions inherent in his actions to both preserve and when necessary limit liberty, he sought in his 1864 election victory speech to offer an explanation. He opened by saying, "It has long been a grave question whether any government, not too strong for the liberties of its people, can be strong enough to maintain its own existence, in great emergencies."

Eight years after the attacks of September 11, 2001, one of the most important public policy questions of the day parallels the one that confronted Americans during the time of Lincoln: what is the proper balance between safety and civil liberties in times of national threat? Indeed, it is a question that spans the life of the republic itself. In 1775 Ben Franklin framed one answer, saying, "Those who would give up essential liberty to purchase a little temporary safety, deserve neither liberty nor safety." Nearly two hundred years later, Supreme Court justice Robert Jackson framed a very different answer when he warned the Supreme Court that unless it tempered its notion of absolute rights with "a little practical wisdom," it risked converting the Constitution "into a suicide pact."

In fact, the tendency in U.S. history has been for wartime presidents to do what Lincoln did—assume vast executive powers that often run roughshod over civil liberties and test the very bounds of the Constitution. Witness President Woodrow Wilson's signing of the Espionage and Sedition Acts and the subsequent mass arrests during and after World War I. And then there is President Franklin Roosevelt's internment of tens of thousands of U.S. citizens of Japanese descent during World War II and his blatant violations of America's Neutrality Acts leading up to the war.

What differentiates past conflicts from the current threat of terrorism, however, is that the earlier ones were of limited duration—extraordinary executive powers quickly receded after the wars. Modern terrorism has created a potentially open-ended challenge to American democracy, threatening the delicate balance of power between branches of government and between government and citizen. Supreme Court justice Sandra Day O'Connor, though generally supportive of robust presidential wartime powers, noted the perilous circumstances: "Have we ever had a situation like this, where presumably this status, warlike status, could last 25 years? 50 years? Whatever it is?"[1] She called for clear safeguards to prevent executive overreach in the fight against terrorism.[2]

Justice O'Connor's warning of the inherent danger to individual rights in the age of terrorism—that the government in general, and the executive branch in particular, might use the threat to justify continued expansion of its powers at the expense of civil liberties—was certainly apt. But there is an equally acute second danger: that after years without another domestic attack, pressure will mount to return to some variation of pre-9/11 policies that were highly deferential toward civil liberties, but proved insufficient against an enemy like al-Qaeda.[3]

John Yoo and David Cole both recognize the enormous stakes in this debate. And, as in the previous debate over torture, both have the safety and security of the nation foremost in mind. Yet they agree on little else.

Yoo says that because the United States is at war with al-Qaeda, the president is constitutionally obligated to protect the nation using all necessary tools. And unlike previous wars on traditional battlefields, this conflict has a significant domestic dimension, with covert cells seeking to infiltrate the country to kill on a mass scale. This means, Yoo argues, that aggressively gathering and acting on intelligence is a critical priority—an executive branch function that, in wartime, will inevitably butt up against individual rights. Yes, civil liberties must be protected, but Yoo says that compared with prior national emergencies, the post-9/11 policies were measured and tempered. And though Congress should be consulted, the executive must maintain its flexibility to act swiftly and decisively in order to prevent another attack, the aftermath of which would certainly be evermore devastating for civil liberties.

Cole rejects outright this "preventive paradigm" developed under George W. Bush, which he says offers a lesson in "how not to fight terrorism." By employing aggressive anticipatory actions—seizing private records under the USA PATRIOT Act (Uniting and Strengthening America by Providing Appropriate Tools Required to Intercept and Obstruct Terrorism), wiretapping Americans without a warrant, engaging in preemptive war—the administration turned the law's traditional approach to state coercion (responding after specific wrongdoing has occurred) on its head. Worse, it substantially compromised U.S. security. Shirking the rule of law led to vast discrimination against Muslims, CIA "black sites," torture, Abu Ghraib, and the Iraq War, thereby creating a loss of legitimacy that made allies less cooperative and has spawned new enemies and inspired those already against Americans to adopt more radical tactics. Cole outlines ways to aggressively fight terrorism and abide by the rule of law at the same time, which, he argues, is the only way to ensure long-term success.

The 9/11 attacks revealed to one and all that a crafty enemy could orchestrate heinous acts of violence using the architecture of America's openness—liberal visitor and immigration laws, unfettered freedom of communication, unrestricted domestic travel, and open financial networks. In the wake of 9/11, it was inevitable that some individual and collective freedoms would be tempered and that some warfare measures would be adopted, a practical reality recognized by President Obama.[4] Finding the delicate balance of which Lincoln spoke—a government not too strong for the liberties of the people, but strong enough to safeguard the nation—will be the great test of the current president and presidents to come.

The United States needs to reasonably limit
YES: civil liberties and bolster executive powers
John Yoo, *University of California at Berkeley School of Law*

Executive Power, Civil Liberties, and Security: Constitutional Trade-offs in Fighting Global Terrorism

After the September 11, 2001, terrorist attacks, the United States went to war against the al-Qaeda terrorist organization. On that day in September, al-Qaeda operatives hijacked four commercial airliners and used them as guided missiles against the World Trade Center towers in New York City and the Pentagon in the nation's capital. Resisting passengers brought down a fourth plane that appeared to have been headed toward either the Capitol or the White House. The attacks sent about three thousand people to their death, disrupted air traffic and communications within the United States, and drained the economy of billions of dollars in losses. Both the president, in his military order of November 13, 2001, and Congress, in its September 18, 2001, authorization to use military force, agreed that these attacks marked the beginning of an armed conflict between the United States and the al-Qaeda terrorist network. Indeed, al-Qaeda's attack amounted to a classic decapitation strike designed to eliminate the political, military, and financial leadership of the country.

The unconventional nature of the war, and of the enemy, has called upon the U.S. government to undertake a full spectrum of domestic and international responses.[5] An important dimension of the conflict has been the war abroad in which U.S. armed forces and U.S. intelligence agencies have played an offensive role aimed at destroying the terrorist network. In October 2001, the United States launched a military campaign in Afghanistan that within a few short weeks rooted al-Qaeda from its bases and removed from power the Taliban militia that had harbored it.[6] Today, military operations continue in Afghanistan because Taliban resistance has intensified. There, as well as in Pakistan and Yemen, U.S. intelligence agencies and military forces are using unmanned aerial vehicles to launch pinpoint missile strikes on terrorist leaders and assets. In fact, the United States is conducting operations against al-Qaeda terrorists not only in Afghanistan, Pakistan, and Yemen, but also in the Philippines and other parts of Africa. Meanwhile, the U.S. military has detained hundreds of al-Qaeda and Taliban fighters at the U.S. naval base at Guantanamo Bay, Cuba, and has sought to prosecute some for war crimes using special military commissions rather than civilian courts. It also has subjected a few high-level al-Qaeda leaders to coercive interrogation procedures that critics charge violate a federal statute criminalizing torture.

Unlike previous conflicts, the war against al-Qaeda has a significant domestic dimension. In previous modern American conflicts, hostilities were limited to a foreign battlefield, and the United States home front remained safe behind the distances of two oceans. In this conflict, the strict division between the front and home has blurred. Al-Qaeda has not only taken to the battlefield against the United States in somewhat conventional warfare, but also sought to infiltrate covert cells of operatives into the United States to carry out surprise attacks on civilians. Al-Qaeda operatives launched the initial salvo against the United States from within the United States, and it shows no inclination to lessen its efforts to pull off another attack within the United States on the scale of September 11. The Justice Department has discovered al-Qaeda cells in cities such as Buffalo, New York, and Portland, Oregon; detained a resident alien who had intended to destroy the Brooklyn Bridge; intercepted at least one American citizen in Chicago who had planned to explode a radiological dispersal device, known as a "dirty bomb," in a major American city; and in September 2009 uncovered an al-Qaeda cell in New York with apparent plans to detonate bombs on the New York City transit system. After the attacks of September 11, the federal government investigated and detained hundreds of illegal aliens within the United States with possible links to the terrorists. Many were deported.

Perhaps the most controversial aspect of the Bush administration's domestic efforts to combat terrorism was in the area of intelligence gathering. Congress enacted legislation, the USA Patriot Act, to enhance the powers of the Federal Bureau of Investigation (FBI) and the intelligence community to collect and share intelligence on international terrorists within the United States. Most of these statutory changes modified and improved the Foreign Intelligence Surveillance Act (FISA) of 1978, which requires the FBI to seek a warrant from a special federal court when it wishes to intercept the electronic communications of a target inside the United States suspected of links to terrorist groups. In 2002 Congress created a new Department of Homeland Security to consolidate twenty-two separate domestic agencies with responsibilities for domestic security. After these legislative changes, the president issued an executive order directing the National Security Agency (NSA) to engage in an expanded surveillance effort, without going through the FISA warrant process, to intercept suspected terrorist communications entering the United States from abroad.

Critics have challenged the policy merits and the legality of almost all of these decisions. Their basic claim attacks the president's authority to carry out these policies either on his own authority acting alone, or when inconsistent with congressional statutes. They argue that Congress must authorize the president's actions in wartime, the president cannot act inconsistently with statutes or treaties or international law, and post-9/11 counterterrorism policy has violated basic individual rights and civil liberties. The NSA surveillance program is usually identified as the clearest example, because the government's intelligence gathering clearly did not comply with FISA's requirement for a judicial warrant when conducting electronic surveillance within the United States or on U.S. persons. In this essay, I will explain that these critics have it wrong. Instead of an imperial presidency, the executive branch has acted within its constitutional authorities—indeed, it has fulfilled the purpose of its original design by taking action to protect the citizens and territory of the United States from attack. Furthermore, instead of acting in violation of basic rights and liberties, the administration's exercise of executive power in the wake of 9/11 was measured and tempered—especially when compared with the actions of presidents during prior periods of national emergency.

FOUNDATIONS OF EXECUTIVE AUTHORITY

As commander in chief, the president has the constitutional power and the responsibility to wage war in response to a direct attack upon the United States. During World War II, the Supreme Court recognized that once war has begun, the president's authority as commander in chief and chief executive gives him access to the tools he needs to effectively wage war. The president has the power "to direct the performance of those functions which may constitutionally be performed by the military arm of the nation in time of war" and to issue military commands using the powers to conduct war "to repel and defeat the enemy."[7] In the wake of the September 11 attacks, even Congress agreed by enacting a law that declared "the President has authority under the Constitution to take action to deter and prevent acts of international terrorism against the United States."[8] This statement recognizes the president's authority to use force, and any powers necessary and proper to that end, to respond to al-Qaeda.

The shift of power to the executive branch in wartime is not just an inference from the constitutional text and structure, but a lesson of history. In the Civil War, for example, President Lincoln raised an army, withdrew money from the Treasury, and launched a blockade on his own authority in response to the Confederate attack on Fort Sumter—moves that Congress and the Supreme Court later approved.[9] Presidents of both political parties have waged war numerous times, in places ranging from Korea to Kosovo, on their own constitutional authority to protect the national security of the United States without congressional authorization. Past wartime presidents have also exercised tremendous unilateral powers within the borders of the country, including the suspension of habeas corpus, creation of military tribunals, and broad spying on private communications.

Even legal scholars who argue against this historical practice concede that once the United States has been attacked, the president can respond with force on his own.[10] The ability to direct military operations, detain the enemy, and collect intelligence is intrinsic to the use of military force. It is inconceivable that the Constitution would vest in the president the power of commander in chief and chief executive, give him the sole responsibility to protect the nation from attack, but then disable him by preventing him from using the means most effective to defeat the enemy. The Framers understood the Constitution to grant the government every ability to meet a foreign danger. James Madison wrote in *Federalist* No. 41 that "security against foreign danger is one of the primitive objects of civil society." Therefore, the "powers requisite for attaining it must be effectually confided to the federal councils."[11] As the Supreme Court declared after World War II, "This grant of war power includes all that is necessary and proper for carrying these powers into execution."[12]

During the writing of the Constitution, some Framers believed that the president needed to manage intelligence because only he could keep secrets. Several Supreme Court cases have recognized that the president's role as the sole organ of the nation in its foreign relations and as commander in chief must include the power to collect intelligence.[13] These authorities agree that intelligence rests with the president because the office's structure allows it to act with unity, secrecy, and speed.

Take the issue of surveillance. Presidents have ordered electronic surveillance without any judicial or congressional participation. More than a year before the Pearl Harbor attacks, but with war clearly looming with the Axis powers, President Franklin Roosevelt authorized the FBI to intercept any communications, whether wholly inside the country or international, of persons "suspected of subversive activities against the Government of the United States, including suspected spies."[14] FDR was concerned that "fifth columns"—those people believed to be loyalists who clandestinely undermine the nation—could wreak havoc on the war effort. "It is too late to do anything about it after sabotage, assassinations and 'fifth column' activities are completed," FDR wrote in his order.[15] FDR ordered the surveillance even though a Supreme Court decision and a federal statute at the time prohibited electronic surveillance without a warrant.[16] FDR continued to authorize the interception of electronic communications even after Congress rejected proposals for wiretapping for national security reasons.[17]

Until FISA, presidents continued to monitor on their own authority the communications of national security threats, even in peacetime.[18] If presidents in time of peace could order surveillance of spies and terrorists, as President Roosevelt did in 1940, or as presidents from Truman through Carter did during the Cold War, then executive authority is all the more certain now, after the events of September 11. This is a view that Justice Departments have not just held under President Bush; the Clinton Justice Department held a similar view of the executive branch's authority to conduct surveillance outside the FISA framework.[19] And in his confirmation hearing before the Senate Judiciary Committee, President Obama's attorney general, Eric Holder, agreed that the president's constitutional authority to engage in intelligence surveillance may not be subject to limitation by statute, including FISA.[20]

Courts have never opposed a president's authority to engage in warrantless electronic surveillance to protect national security. When the Supreme Court first considered this question in 1972, it held that the Fourth Amendment required a judicial warrant if a president wanted to conduct surveillance of a purely domestic group, but it refused to address surveillance of foreign threats to national security.[21] In the years since, every federal appeals court to address the question, including the FISA Appeals Court, has "held that the President did have inherent authority to conduct warrantless searches to obtain foreign intelligence information."[22] The FISA Appeals Court did not even feel it was worth much discussion. It took the president's power to do so "for granted" and observed that "FISA could not encroach on the President's constitutional power."[23]

In 1980 in *United States v. Truong Dinh Hung,* the Fourth Circuit observed that "the needs of the Executive are so compelling in the area of foreign intelligence, unlike the area of domestic security, that a uniform warrant requirement would, following *Keith,* 'unduly frustrate,' the President in carrying out his foreign affairs responsibilities."[24] The Fourth Circuit held that the government is relieved of the warrant requirement when the surveillance involves both a foreign power and a foreign intelligence motive. First, warrants are not required when the object of the search or surveillance is a foreign power, its agents, or its collaborators, because such cases are "most likely to call into play difficult and subtle judgments about foreign and military affairs." Second, "when the surveillance is conducted 'primarily' for foreign intelligence reasons" warrants are unnecessary for two reasons: first, "once surveillance becomes primarily a criminal investigation, the courts are entirely competent to make the usual probable cause determination," and, second, "individual privacy interests come to the fore and government foreign policy concerns recede when the government is primarily attempting to form the basis for a criminal prosecution."[25] Several other circuits have employed a similar logic, and no other federal appeals courts have taken a different view.[26] The factors favoring warrantless searches for national security reasons are compelling under the current circumstances created by the war on terrorism. After the attacks on September 11, 2001, the government's interest in conducting searches related to fighting terrorism were perhaps of the highest order—the need to defend the nation from direct attack. As the Supreme Court pointed out in 1981, "It is 'obvious and unarguable' that no governmental interest is more compelling than the security of the Nation."[27]

It is true that the NSA program might be unusual in its reliance on the president's power alone. But, in fact, for the most important issue of going to war the Bush administration went to Congress for approval of the use of force in Afghanistan and Iraq. For some other counterterrorism initiatives, the president could plausibly rely on Congress's support in the September 18, 2001, Authorization for Use of Military Force (AUMF). It is sweeping; it has no limitation on time or place; it authorizes the president to pursue al-Qaeda and those connected to the 9/11 attacks. Its passage was proof that the president and Congress fully agreed that military action would be appropriate. Congress's support for the president cannot just be limited to the right to literally use force, but to all the necessary subcomponents that permit effective military action. Congress's approval of the killing and capture of al-Qaeda must obviously include the tools to locate them in the first place and to detain them after they are captured.

Critics have argued that post-9/11 detention and surveillance measures are illegal violations of individual rights because the AUMF did not explicitly mention detentions, wiretapping, or surveillance. Even though the AUMF does not mention detentions, the Supreme Court later upheld the holding of enemy combatants in the war on terrorism as authorized by Congress, in spite of a law on the books known as the Anti-Detention Act.[28] Critics essentially argue that Congress must enact a grocery list of specific powers, and that, otherwise, the president cannot fight a war. For example, FISA prohibits electronic surveillance within the United States without congressional permission. However, in the AUMF Congress authorized the president "to use all necessary and appropriate force" against those "he determines" were involved with the 9/11 attacks, or those who aid, support, or harbor those involved in order to "prevent any future acts of international terrorism against the United States." The power to use force impliedly *includes* lesser powers such as surveillance and detention to find the targets and avert future attacks. As the critics see it, Congress authorized the president to pull the trigger, but also ordered him to wear a blindfold.

Congress cannot legislate in anticipation of every circumstance that may arise in the future. That is one of the reasons, along with the executive branch's advantages in expertise and structural organization, why Congress delegates authority. Those who consider themselves legal progressives generally support the administrative state and vigorously defend broad grants of authority from Congress to the agencies of the executive branch. Agencies such as the Federal Communications Commission or the Environmental Protection Agency exercise powers over broad sectors of the economy under the incredibly vague and broad congressional mandate that they regulate in the "public interest." These agencies make decisions with enormous effects, such as which parts of the radio spectrum to sell or how much pollution to allow into the air, all with little explicit guidance or thought from Congress.

Yet when Congress delegates broad authority to the president to defend the nation from attack, critics demand that Congress list everything. Although the threats to individual liberty may be greater otherwise, those threats must be balanced against the potentially tragic cost of insufficiently safeguarding the homeland. It makes little sense to place Congress under a heavier burden to describe every conceivable future contingency that might arise when the country is fighting a war, perhaps the most unpredictable and certainly most dangerous of human endeavors. Rather, Americans would expect and want Congress to delegate power to that branch, the executive, that is best able to act with speed to threats to national security. War is too difficult to plan for with fixed, antecedent legislative rules, and war also is better run by the executive, which is structurally designed to take quick, decisive action. If the AUMF authorized the president to detain and kill the enemy, the ability to aggressively search for the enemy is probably included.

EXECUTIVE INITIATIVE IN TIMES OF WAR AND NATIONAL EMERGENCY

Even accepting, for the moment, the claim that executive policies in the war on terrorism are in conflict with the wishes of Congress and civil libertarians, this acceptance does not make the former illegal, and it does not mean there is a practical alternative to decisive executive action. Everyone would prefer that the president and Congress agree on war policy; it was one of the reasons the Bush administration sought the AUMF in the first place. The nation will wage war more effectively if the executive and legislature share a unified purpose.

But conflict between the branches of government is commonplace. The president and Congress have pursued conflicting war policies in many wars. Congress passed the Neutrality Acts of 1935, 1937, and 1939 before World War

II in a largely futile effort to restrain FDR from assisting the Allies. Vietnam, Nicaragua, and Kosovo are just the most recent examples of wars in which Congress tried to frustrate or micromanage executive war policy.[29]

The Constitution not only anticipated this struggle—it was written to ensure it. The Framers did not give the president or the Congress complete control over war, foreign policy, and national security, but instead designed each branch differently and gave them different powers that could be used to cooperate or fight. The president is the commander in chief and chief executive, while Congress has the power over funding, legislation, the creation and discipline of the military, and the power to "declare war." The power over national security is dramatically unlike other government powers, such as passing a statute, appointing a judge, or making a treaty, for which the Constitution sets out a precise, step-by-step process for the roles of the different branches of government.

Critics of executive wartime policy appeal to the Constitution as it works in peacetime when Congress authorizes a policy and the president carries it out. They imagine that the Constitution requires the president to check back with Congress on every strategy and tactic in the war on terrorism to, among other things, ensure that basic rights and liberties are protected. The NSA program, Guantanamo Bay, the use of force, and detention policies are illegal, they say, because President Bush neglected to get yet another law approving them. It is true that Congress offers more transparency and perhaps greater accountability to the public. But it should also be clear that, over time, the presidency has gained the leading role in war and national security because of its superior ability to take the initiative in response to emergencies. Indeed, the Framers designed the executive branch precisely so that its powers could grow to protect the country in times of crisis from external threat.

The Framers well understood that war's unpredictability makes unique demands for decisive and often secret action. They rejected extreme republicanism, which concentrated power in the legislature, and created an executive with its own independent powers to manage foreign affairs and address war and emergencies. The power to protect the nation, Alexander Hamilton wrote in *Federalist* No. 23, "ought to exist without limitation," because "it is impossible to foresee or define the extent and variety of national exigencies, or the correspondent extent & variety of the means which may be necessary to satisfy them."[30] It would be foolhardy to limit the constitutional power to protect the nation from foreign threats. "The circumstances that endanger the safety of nations are infinite; and for this reason no constitutional shackles can wisely be imposed on the power to which the care of it is committed."

The Framers located the responsibility to respond to emergency and war in the presidency because of its functional advantages. In *The Federalist*

Papers, Hamilton observed that "decision, activity, secrecy, and dispatch will generally characterise the proceedings of one man, in a much more eminent degree, than the proceedings of any greater number." He went on to say: "Energy in the executive is essential to the protection of the community against foreign attacks."[31] Wartime, that most unpredictable and dangerous of human endeavors, therefore ought to be managed by the president. "Of all the cares or concerns of government, the direction of war most peculiarly demands those qualities which distinguish the exercise of power by a single hand."[32]

If ever there were an emergency that Congress could not prepare for, it was the war brought upon the United States on September 11, 2001. FISA, for example, was a law written with Soviet spies working out of their embassy in Washington, D.C., in mind. The Geneva Conventions of 1949 were adopted when there were two types of conflicts—international wars between nation-states and civil wars. No one in 1949 or 1978 anticipated war with an international terrorist organization wielding the destructive power of a nation. The presidency was the institution of government best able to respond quickly to the 9/11 attacks and to take measures to defeat al-Qaeda's further efforts. Although the certainty and openness of a congressional act would certainly be desirable, the success of counterterrorism policies depend on secrecy and agility, two characteristics that Congress as an institution lacks.

But, critics respond, Congress foresaw that war might increase the demands for domestic wiretapping or military commissions or detentions and interrogation, and still did not authorize (or even prohibited) the president from taking those measures. Why should not Congress's view here, as in any other domestic question, particularly those of such basic sensitivity, prevail?

It is simply not the case that the president must carry out every law enacted by Congress. The Constitution is the supreme law of the land, and neither an act of Congress nor an act of the president can supersede it. If Congress passes an unconstitutional act, such as a law ordering the imprisonment of those who criticize the government, the president must give force to the higher law, that of the Constitution. Thomas Jefferson did just that regarding the Alien and Sedition Acts that were passed in 1798 during an undeclared naval war with France. He took the position that he, "believing the law to be unconstitutional, was bound to remit the execution of it, because that power has been confided to him by the constitution."[33] That does not mean that the president "is above the law"; it only means that the Constitution is above the Congress and the president. FISA might be unconstitutional if it were read to forbid the president from gathering information necessary to prevent attacks on the United States in wartime.

If the critics are right and presidents are duty bound to obey any and all acts of Congress, Congress could have ordered FDR not to attempt an amphibious landing in France in World War II, Truman to attack China during the Korean War, or JFK to invade Cuba in 1962. But presidents such as Jefferson, Jackson, Lincoln, and FDR believed they had the right to take action, within their own constitutional authorities, to follow their interpretation of the Constitution rather than the views of Congress or the Supreme Court, especially in their role as commander in chief.

Although Congress has the sole power to declare war, neither presidents nor Congresses have acted under the belief that a declaration of war must come before military hostilities abroad. And both the president and Congress generally agree that the legislature should not interfere in the executive branch's strategic and tactical decisions. Congress attempted to prevent presidents from using force abroad in the Nixon-era War Powers Resolution by prohibiting the insertion of troops into hostile environments abroad for more than sixty days without legislative approval. But the resolution has been a dead letter. Presidents and Congresses alike have since realized that the War Powers Resolution made little practical sense, and instead represented congressional overreaching into presidential expertise and constitutional authority in foreign affairs.

Presidential leadership has always included control over the goals and means of military campaigns. As the Supreme Court has observed, the president has the authority to "employ the armed forces in the manner he may deem most effectual to harass and conquer and subdue the enemy."[34] President Lincoln did not seek a law from Congress on whether to defend Washington, D.C.; President Roosevelt did not ask Congress whether he should make the war in Europe a priority over the war in the Pacific; President Truman did not seek legislative permission to drop nuclear bombs on Japan. The same applies to the application of presidential authority at home—from ordering conscription to directing private industries to support the war effort. Obviously, presidents should not ignore congressional leaders—a wise president will consult with them at the right time—but the Constitution does not force the president to get a letter from Congress every time he makes an important decision about wartime strategy or tactics, at home or abroad.

Nor is Congress powerless. It has ample powers to block wartime initiatives. It has total control over funding and the size and equipment of the military. If it disagrees with wartime strategy, it can cut off funds, reduce the size of military units, or refuse to provide supplies. War would be impossible without Congress's cooperation or at least acquiescence. This is even more so in the age of modern warfare, whose demands require constant congressional budgetary support.

Critics claim that Congress ought to have the upper hand in war to prevent military adventurism, to check war fever, to guarantee political consensus, and to safeguard values and rights. This sounds plausible, but it neglects the benefits of executive action during time of foreign threat, and it downplays Congress's faults, such as delay, inflexibility, and lack of secrecy. World War II clearly demonstrated that presidential initiative has been critical to the protection of American national security. When Europe plunged into war, Congress enacted a series of Neutrality Acts designed to keep the United States out of the conflict. In 1940 and 1941, FDR recognized that America's security would be threatened by German control of Europe, and he and his advisers gradually attempted to bring the United States to the assistance of Britain and the Soviet Union.[35] FDR stretched his authority to cooperate closely with Britain in protecting convoys in the North Atlantic and providing the British with fifty "obsolete" destroyers, among other things. Administration pressure on Japan to withdraw from China helped to trigger the war in the Pacific, without which America's entry into World War II might have been delayed by at least another year, if not longer.[36] With what they now know, most Americans would agree that earlier U.S. entry into World War II would have been much to the benefit of the United States and to the world.

Critics also ignore how poor Congress's independent judgment can be on national security matters. Congress led the country into two "bad" wars, the 1798 quasi-war with France and the War of 1812. And Congress does not always bring consensus. The Vietnam War, one of the wars initially supported by Congress, did not meet with a consensus over the long term, but instead provoked some of the most divisive politics in American history. It is also difficult to claim that the congressional authorizations to use force in Iraq, either in 1991 or 2002, reflected a deep consensus over the merits of the wars there. Indeed, the 1991 authorization barely survived the Senate, and the 2002 authorization received significant negative votes and became a deeply divisive issue in national politics.

Legislative deliberation can breed consensus in the best of cases, but it also can stand in the way of speed and decisiveness. Terrorist attacks are more difficult to detect and prevent than those posed by conventional armed forces and nations, and weapons of mass destruction (WMDs) allow them to inflict devastation that once only could have been achievable by a nation-state.[37] To defend itself from this threat, the United States will have to use force earlier and more often than at the time when nations generated the primary threats. To forestall a WMD attack or to take advantage of a window of opportunity to strike at a terrorist cell, the president needs the flexibility to act quickly. By acting earlier, perhaps before WMD components have been fully assembled or before an al-Qaeda operative has left for the United States, the executive branch might also be able to engage in a more limited, more precisely targeted use of force.

Critics of counterterrorism policy want to overturn American historical practice in favor of a new and untested theory about the wartime powers of the president and Congress. For too long, the U.S. system delayed aggressive measures to preempt terrorist attacks.[38] But seeking to give Congress the dominant hand in setting wartime policy would render the country's tactics against al-Qaeda less, rather than more, effective. It would slow down decisions, make sensitive policies and intelligence public, and encourage risk aversion rather than risk taking. It ignores the reality of the al-Qaeda challenge to require the president to first seek congressional permission every time he wants to make an important policy change.

Claims that terrorism policies amount to presidential violation of the Constitution appeal to an entirely different concern, not one about law but about politics. Those critics worry that if the president is waging a war and the war has slipped into the United States itself, terrorism policies will centralize too much power in the presidency over domestic affairs. The response to 9/11, however, does not signal that Americans live under a dictator, or that the separation of powers has failed, the exaggerated claims of civil libertarians notwithstanding.

Instead, the other branches of government have powerful and important tools to limit the president should his efforts to defeat terrorism slip into domestic oppression. Congress has total control over funding and significant powers of oversight. It could do away with the NSA or the Central Intelligence Agency (CIA) as a whole; it could close any detention facility. Congress need not engage in anything as drastic as doing away with the NSA, of course. It could easily eliminate surveillance, detention, and interrogation programs themselves—on which congressional leaders of both parties were secretly briefed no fewer than thirty times in the months and years after 9/11—simply by cutting off funding. It could also link approval of administration policies in related areas to agreement on changes to terrorism policies. Congress could refuse to confirm cabinet members, subcabinet members, or military intelligence officers unless its wishes prevail. It could hold extensive hearings that bring to light perceived abuses, backed up by the power of subpoena, and require officials to appear and be held to account. So far, Congress has not taken any of these steps, and in fact passed up an obvious chance when it confirmed Gen. Michael Hayden to head the CIA in 2006. Congressional silence should not be mistaken for opposition to the president's terrorism policies.[39]

Courts can exercise their own check on presidential power, although it is one that is not as comprehensive as Congress's. Any effort to prosecute an al-Qaeda member or a terrorism suspect within the United States will require the cooperation of the federal courts. If federal judges believe that terrorism policies are unconstitutional, they can grant a writ of habeas corpus to any detainee not properly held as an enemy combatant. In fact, the Supreme Court has taken steps to expand the habeas corpus jurisdiction of the courts over the detainees held at Guantanamo Bay, and demanded that Congress explicitly authorize military commissions (which it swiftly did).[40] Although they have not yet ordered the release of any detainees, and have been overruled by Congress twice, the courts retain limited measures to frustrate counterterrorism policies. Even in areas such as the NSA surveillance program or military commissions, the courts can maintain a check by refusing to admit any evidence gathered in violation of the Fourth Amendment and to order the release of any detainees convicted by military courts that have used unconstitutional procedures.

THE SYSTEM WORKS

The claims of an unchecked imperial presidency have been vastly overblown. Throughout American history, times of crisis have called forth broad uses of presidential power, episodes invariably accompanied by loud protests that the president arrogated the powers of a king. Yet history portrays such moments as times of challenge and presidential greatness. In the darkest depths of the Civil War, Abraham Lincoln invoked his powers as commander in chief to issue the Emancipation Proclamation and free the slaves of the Confederacy, acting wholly without the approval of Congress and in the face of contrary statutes. Yet Lincoln also took extraordinary measures to raise and fund an army without congressional appropriations, used military force against the seceding states, suspended habeas corpus, and instituted military trials for civilians suspected of working with the Confederacy. He was dogged throughout his presidency by harsh criticism that he was seeking "absolute power" with acts "subversive of liberty and law, and quite as certainly tending to the establishment of despotism."[41] Civil liberties did suffer, and perhaps he went too far at times, but Lincoln led the Union through the terrible crisis of secession, slavery, and Civil War.

The same is true for Franklin Roosevelt, whose creative use of executive power is credited with pulling the nation out of the Great Depression and putting it on the path to victory in World War II. Yet FDR also tested the very bounds of presidential authority, as with his secret executive order directing the internment of tens of thousands of American citizens of Japanese descent.

Exercises of presidential power can go badly wrong, of course. Richard Nixon is the most salient example of presidential authority used for ill, having ordered the covert surveillance of political opponents, the infiltration of anti-war groups, and the harassment of critics—all on grounds of national security that were strained at best and at worst criminally deceitful. He used executive privilege to conceal information from criminal investigators in the Watergate scandal, fired special Justice Department prosecutors, and ultimately resigned before his almost certain impeachment by the House of Representatives. After he left office, Nixon defended his actions in a television interview with David Frost saying, in a damning overgeneralization, "When the president does it, that means that it is not illegal."[42] Nixon, Lyndon Johnson, and John Kennedy came to symbolize an "imperial presidency" grown out of control during the 1960s and 1970s, to the point that it seemed to fundamentally threaten American liberty.

Post-Watergate efforts to restrict the executive branch have not made the American president less central to the political universe. This is particularly true in the realm of national security: the threats of the modern age—most notably the threat of catastrophic terrorism—require tremendous executive flexibility and decisive executive action. To those who argue that this is an unacceptable trade-off—that the robust exercise of executive power in times of war comes at too great an expense to fundamental rights and values—I would ask them to consider the potentially tremendous costs of restricting such action.

I would also remind them that the broad exercise of presidential power is not unique to the twentieth or twenty-first centuries, but represents the growth over two centuries of the constitutional powers of the office. It started with the Framers' efforts to avoid executives who might slip into monarchy or dictatorship. By the time of the Constitution's ratification, however, the Framers' views had evolved in favor of an independent, forceful president. The Framers devoted much of their attention to listing the powers of Congress, whereas they deliberately paint the president's powers in broad strokes. The nation's greatest presidents, from George Washington on, have filled in these sketchy outlines in the ways in which they have met national challenges, both foreign and domestic. Presidential power has grown as the nation's power has grown, both in constitutional law and in prestige and substantive power. It is that power that has allowed presidents to respond forcefully to challenges like the 9/11 attacks, and will allow future presidents, if they so wish, to rapidly change course as well.

NO:
Respecting civil liberties and preventing executive overreach are critical to preserving America's security and its ideals
David Cole, *Georgetown University Law Center*

Securing Liberty in the Face of Terrorism

> In order to fight and to defeat terrorism, the Department of Justice has added a new paradigm to that of prosecution—
> a paradigm of prevention.
>
> —U.S. Attorney General John Ashcroft, speech to
> the Council on Foreign Relations, February 10, 2003

As President Barack Obama took office in January 2009, he rejected "as false the choice between our safety and our ideals," and proclaimed that he would not sacrifice U.S. ideals "for expedience's sake."[43] That message was understood as marking a sharp departure from his predecessor's approach to the "war on terrorism" in which some of the nation's—and indeed the world's—most cherished ideals were abandoned in the name of security. The Bush administration authorized waterboarding and other forms of torture to interrogate suspects; "disappeared" others for years at a time into secret CIA prisons, known as "black sites," where they were held incommunicado and brutally abused; claimed the power to hold anyone labeled an "enemy combatant" indefinitely without abiding by the most basic protections guaranteed by the laws of war, including a fair hearing and humane treatment; asserted the right to violate in secret federal criminal statutes outlawing torture and warrantless wiretapping of Americans; and "rendered" suspects to countries with long records of torture to be interrogated with even more extreme tactics than our own agents were authorized to employ. All of this was done in the name of the "war on terror," which President Bush defined as a war against all terrorist organizations of potentially global reach.

On his second day in office, President Obama began to make good on his promise, issuing executive orders that halted the CIA's use of cruel, inhuman, and degrading interrogation tactics; closed the CIA's secret prisons; and ordered the closure of the military detention center at the Guantanamo Bay naval base. Shortly thereafter, former vice president Dick Cheney warned that

Guantanamo was "necessary" and that Obama's new measures might put the country at high risk of future terrorist attacks.[44]

Cheney's criticism reflected the central premise of the Bush administration's approach to fighting terrorism: that harsh preventive measures are both warranted and necessary to keep the United States secure. The Bush administration pursued what Attorney General John Ashcroft dubbed a "paradigm of prevention." The now-familiar argument is that when one faces an enemy like al-Qaeda, the nation is justified in employing highly coercive and intrusive measures—warrantless wiretapping, detention, coercive interrogation, even war itself—preemptively, not based on hard evidence of past or current wrongdoing, but on the basis of predictions about future threats. All of these measures were said to be warranted by the need to prevent a future terrorist attack—as was the Iraq War, launched on claims that Saddam Hussein had weapons of mass destruction and might deliver them to terrorists who might use them against the United States at some unspecified point in the future.

The preventive approach, at least as applied by the Bush administration, entailed widespread sacrifices in prior commitments to U.S. ideals. Ideals such as due process and the right not to be subjected to inhumane treatment, the government's defenders argued, were not absolutes, and at the end of the day the nation's survival required a recalibration of the balance between its ideals and its security. As federal judge and conservative law scholar Richard Posner reminded Americans in a book defending this approach, the Constitution is "not a suicide pact."[45]

The challenge for the Obama administration—and for liberal democracies generally—is how best to counter terrorist threats without unduly compromising the ideals that form the foundation of the rule of law. A review of the Bush administration's "preventive paradigm" provides an important object lesson in how not to fight terrorism. Abandoning the nation's ideals is not only normatively flawed but also undermines its security in the long run. Whatever else the Bush administration accomplished, it surely demonstrated that claims that respecting basic liberties necessarily undermines the nation's security are grossly reductive. In fact, hewing to basic rights may increase the nation's security in the long run.

THE PREVENTIVE PARADIGM AND RULE OF LAW VALUES

In isolation, neither the goal of preventing future attacks nor the tactic of using coercive measures is particularly novel or troubling. All law enforcement, after all, seeks to prevent crime, and coercion is a necessary element of state power. The force of law depends in part on the threat that violations will trigger a coercive response such as arrest, prosecution, and punishment. But the rule of law generally requires that the state restrict its use of such measures to situations in which it has established through fair processes that a specific wrong has been committed. The Bush administration's "preventive paradigm," by contrast, employed anticipatory state violence—that is, preventive measures were undertaken before any wrongdoing had actually occurred and often without good evidence for believing that any wrongdoing would in fact occur. That approach not only placed tremendous stress on the ideals that the nation and the world associate with the rule of law, but also compromised the nation's security.

The preventive rationale made thinkable tactics that have long been unthinkable in the United States. No one defends coercive interrogation, disappearances, and renditions as permissible forms of investigation or punishment for past crimes; rather, they are invariably defended with some version of the familiar "ticking bomb" hypothetical, in which extreme measures such as torture are said to be warranted to defuse a bomb and thereby save thousands of lives. What would be unacceptable as punishment suddenly becomes acceptable, at least to some, when information is urgently needed to forestall some future hypothetical catastrophe.

The Bush administration even invoked the preventive paradigm to alter the grounds for starting a war. Established international law permits individual nations to go to war only in self-defense, meaning in response to an armed attack or an imminent armed attack. In its 2002 "National Security Strategy," the Bush administration pronounced this standard too constraining in an era of suicide terrorists and weapons of mass destruction, and maintained that the country is justified in going to war even when it has not been attacked and faces no threat of imminent attack.[46] An "emerging" threat is enough, the document insists. The administration relied on this theory to justify the attack on Iraq in 2003, at a time when Iraq had neither attacked the United States nor posed any threat of imminent attack.

This strategy of employing force anticipatorily, either at home or abroad, before there is evidence of wrongdoing and before wrongdoing occurs, turns the law's traditional approach to state coercion on its head. With narrow exceptions, the rule of law generally reserves invasions of privacy, detention, punishment, and use of military force for those who have been shown—on the basis of sound evidence and fair procedures—to have committed some wrongful act in the past. The police can invade privacy by tapping phones or searching homes, but only when there is probable cause to believe that a crime has been committed and that the search is likely to uncover evidence of the crime. Arrest, too, requires probable cause of crime. People can be preventively detained pending trial, but only when there is both probable cause of past wrongdoing and concrete evidence that they pose a danger to the community or are likely to abscond if left at large. Individuals can be punished only upon proof of guilt beyond a reasonable doubt. And nations may use military force unilaterally only in response to an objectively verifiable attack or threat of imminent attack. Meanwhile, the rule of law absolutely prohibits other forms of state coercion—such as disappearances and torture—even when it can be shown without a doubt that an individual has broken the law.[47]

The preventive paradigm rejects these constraints on coercive state intervention into people's lives. In the USA Patriot Act, the Bush administration obtained expanded powers to demand private records on suspects without showing a judge that there was probable cause to suspect the individual of criminal activity. It authorized a sweeping warrantless wiretapping program, run by the National Security Agency, that gathered up international phone calls between American citizens living in the United States and other persons thought to be living abroad—again without establishing probable cause or seeking judicial approval.

The preventive paradigm requires so many compromises in fundamental principles of legality that it renders the rule of law virtually unrecognizable. The rule of law, after all, is designed to subject state power to careful checks, to scrupulously enforce the line between guilt and innocence, and to hold government officials accountable to clear rules. These ideals mix uneasily with the strategies of the preventive paradigm, which generally demand sweeping executive discretion, eschew questions of guilt or innocence (because no wrong has yet occurred), and substitute secrecy and speculation for accountability and verifiable fact. Where the rule of law insists on objective evidence of wrongdoing, the preventive paradigm relies on predictions about future behavior. Such predictions generally cannot be proved true or false; frequently rest on questionable assumptions, stereotypes, and preconceptions; and are especially vulnerable to pretextual manipulation. In times of crisis, moreover, the increased fear of a false negative—allowing a real terrorist to go free— becomes so great that high rates of false positives—detaining or punishing innocents or attacking countries that do not intend to attack us—are deemed increasingly acceptable.

Where the rule of law demands fair and open procedures, the preventive paradigm employs truncated processes that are often conducted in secret, denying suspects a meaningful opportunity to respond to the charges against them. The need for preemptive action is said to justify the secrecy and the shortcuts, whatever the cost to targeted individuals. Where the rule of law demands that people be held accountable only for their own actions, not for their ethnic identity or religious or political views, the preventive paradigm paints in broad brushstrokes, frequently employing guilt by association and ethnic profiling to target suspected future wrongdoers. And where the rule of law absolutely prohibits torture and disappearances, the preventive paradigm maintains that these measures should be viewed as lesser evils to defuse the proverbial ticking bomb. In short, the preventive paradigm treats the rule of law's most fundamental commitments as luxuries that the nation cannot afford in the face of a catastrophic threat.

The impetus toward prevention is understandable. All other things being equal, preventing a terrorist act is preferable to responding after the fact—all the more so when the threats include weapons of mass destruction and adversaries are difficult to detect, are willing to kill themselves, and seemingly are unconstrained by any considerations of law, morality, or human dignity. There is nothing wrong with prevention itself as a motive or a strategy; think, for example, of preventive medicine. And plenty of preventive counterterrorism initiatives do conform to the rule of law such as more protective measures at borders and around vulnerable targets, institutional reforms designed to encourage better analysis of data and information sharing among the many government agencies responsible for the country's safety, prosecutions for conspiracies to engage in terrorist acts, and even military force and military detention when employed in self-defense. The real problems arise when the state seeks to inflict highly coercive measures—depriving individuals of their life, liberty, or property or going to war—on the basis of speculation about the future, without adhering to the processes long seen as critical to regulating and legitimating such force.

THE FAILURE OF THE PREVENTIVE PARADIGM

Abandoning the rule of law is not just wrong as a matter of principle. It is wrongheaded as a practical matter of security. The Bush administration's turn to preventive coercion appears to have made the United States more vulnerable to attack, not more secure. Even if one were to accept as a moral or ethical matter the "ends justify the means" rationales advanced for the preventive paradigm, the paradigm fails its own test: there is little or no evidence that the Bush administration's coercive preemptive measures made the United States safer, and there is substantial evidence that they exacerbated the dangers the nation faced.

Consider the most costly example of the administration's preventive paradigm: the war in Iraq. Precisely because the preventive doctrine turns on speculation about nonimminent events, it permitted an administration—

which for its own reasons had persistently sought to topple Saddam Hussein—to turn its focus from al-Qaeda, the organization that actually attacked the United States, to Iraq, a nation that did not. The Iraq War has, by virtually all accounts, made the United States, the Iraqi people, many U.S. allies, and for that matter much of the world, more vulnerable to terrorists. By targeting Iraq, the Bush administration not only siphoned off massive resources and expertise from the struggle against al-Qaeda, but also played into al-Qaeda's hands by reinforcing its anti-American propaganda and by creating a golden opportunity to inspire, recruit, and train terrorists to attack U.S. and allied targets. In February 2005, CIA director Porter Goss told Congress that "Islamic extremists are exploiting the Iraqi conflict to recruit new anti-U.S. jihadists."[48]

Although Iraq had nothing to do with the so-called war on terrorism before the United States attacked it, the invasion and continued U.S. presence there turned Iraq into the world's premier training ground for terrorists. As Goss admitted, "Those who survive will leave Iraq experienced and focused on acts of urban terrorism. They represent a potential pool of contacts to build transnational terrorist cells, groups, and networks."[49] For years, the insurgents in Iraq repeatedly attacked the U.S. and Iraqi military and police forces. These attacks were often videotaped and disseminated worldwide via the Internet to inspire those in the widely dispersed diaspora who might take the initiative to commit their own atrocities—as the world witnessed in the Madrid bombing in 2004 and the London bombing in 2005. In terms of direct costs, as of February 2009 over four thousand Americans and nearly 100,000 Iraqi civilians had been killed in Iraq since the war began.[50] Though the level of insurgent violence in Iraq has fallen over the last two years, virtually everyone agrees that the war made the United States less safe.

What is less widely recognized is that the preventive paradigm in other aspects of the war on terrorism has been no more effective. According to U.S. figures, terrorist attacks worldwide increased by 300 percent between 2003 and 2004.[51] In 2005 alone, there were 360 suicide bombings, resulting in three thousand deaths, compared with 472 such attacks spread over the five preceding years.[52] And since then, total terrorist attacks worldwide have risen from 11,156 in 2005 to roughly 14,500 in 2006 and in 2007, and deaths as a result of terrorism rose from 14,616 in 2005 to 20,872 in 2006 and 22,685 in 2007.[53] These figures hardly constitute progress in the global war on terrorism.

Still, Bush administration supporters frequently note that, other than the anthrax mailings in 2001, there was not another terrorist attack in the United States during the more than six years it served after 9/11. The real question, though, is whether the administration's coercive preventive measures can be credited for that fact. After all, eight years passed between the first and second attacks on the World Trade Center. Stationing U.S. troops in Baghdad where they could be blown up by suicide bombers may have *diverted* terrorist attacks, but their presence could hardly be said to have *prevented* terrorism. In fact, there is little reason to believe that the preventive paradigm worked. Take Guantanamo, once said to house the "worst of the worst." A 2006 study of the Defense Department's own findings on the detainees held at Guantanamo revealed that only 8 percent of the detainees held at that time were even *alleged* to be fighters for al-Qaeda or the Taliban, and fewer than half of the detainees were alleged to have engaged in any hostile act against the United States.[54]

As for terrorist cells at home, the FBI admitted in February 2005 that it had yet to identify a single al-Qaeda sleeper cell in the entire United States, and it has not publicly identified any since then.[55] The Justice Department under President Bush claimed to have charged more than four hundred persons in "terror-related" cases, but its own inspector general criticized these figures as inflated and inaccurate. The vast majority of the cases involved no charges of terrorism whatsoever—only minor nonviolent offenses such as immigration fraud, credit card fraud, or lying to an FBI agent.[56] Many of the administration's most highly touted "terrorism" cases disintegrated under close scrutiny, most notably those against Capt. James Yee, a Muslim chaplain at Guantanamo initially accused of being a spy; Sami Al-Arian, a computer science professor acquitted on charges of conspiracy to kill Americans; Sami al-Hussayen, a Saudi student acquitted on charges of aiding terrorists by posting links on a Web site; and Yaser Hamdi and José Padilla, the two U.S. citizens held for years as enemy combatants, but released from military custody when the government faced the prospect of losing in court.[57]

In preventive paradigm immigration initiatives, the Bush administration called in 82,000 foreign nationals to be fingerprinted, photographed, and registered, simply because they came from predominantly Arab or Muslim countries. It sought out another eight thousand young men from the same countries for FBI interviews, and placed more than five thousand foreign nationals in preventive detention in just the first two years after 9/11. And yet today *not one of these individuals stands convicted of a terrorist crime.* The government's record, in what is surely the biggest campaign of ethnic profiling since the Japanese internment of World War II, is 0 for 95,000.[58]

One might object that this is the wrong way to measure success. If the Bush administration's measures succeeded in preventing terrorism, there would not be terrorist convictions because the terrorism itself will never occur. It is possible that some of these preventive paradigm measures deterred would-be terrorists from attacking the country, or perhaps helped to foil terrorist plots before they could come to fruition. But if real plots had been foiled and real terrorists identified, one would expect to see at a minimum criminal convictions for conspiracy or attempt to engage in terrorism. Thus, when FBI agents successfully foiled a plot by Sheikh Omar Abdel Rahman (popularly known as the "Blind Sheikh") and others to bomb bridges and tunnels around Manhattan in the 1990s, it convicted the plotters and sent them to prison for life.[59]

President Bush boasted that his administration foiled many terrorist plots after 9/11, but identified remarkably few terrorists brought to justice for these purported plots. The administration's claims of success were often questioned by people with inside knowledge. In October 2005, for example, President Bush claimed that the United States and its allies had foiled ten terrorist plots.[60] Later, however, the *Washington Post, Los Angeles Times,* and *USA Today* each reported that intelligence experts seriously questioned President Bush's claims.[61]

One of the most frequently heard criticisms of the FBI in the wake of 9/11 was that it was too "backward-looking," overly concerned with amassing evidence in order to try alleged criminals for past crimes and not sufficiently intelligence-focused, or "forward-looking." But this criticism ignores the fact that traditional measures of law enforcement investigation are often forward-looking and backward-looking at the same time, and that traditional tools are perfectly capable of disrupting plots and bringing would-be bombers to justice before bombs go off. It is traditional law enforcement methodology, for example, to conduct surveillance on a group of suspected criminals for an extended period of time before arresting them in order to assess the scope of the threat the individuals pose, to identify others who may pose even greater threats, and to develop sufficient evidence so that once individuals are apprehended they can be successfully prosecuted and incapacitated. It was just such traditional police work, for example, that enabled British authorities in the summer of 2006 to avert an alleged plot to explode numerous aircraft traveling from Britain to the United States and bring the asserted perpetrators to trial, three of whom were convicted and sentenced to 30 years to life in prison in September 2009.

Wars against countries that do not pose a threat and broad-brush measures that sweep up thousands of people who have nothing to do with terrorism consume scarce financial and human resources. Just as the U.S. military would have been put to better use had it concentrated on al-Qaeda in Afghanistan and the border regions of Pakistan, the law enforcement agents and resources used to track down 95,000 Arabs and Muslims in the United States, none of whom were terrorists, would have been more effectively deployed had they targeted those for whom there was some reason to believe actually posed a threat— beyond their mere ethnicity or religion. Registering 82,000 people whose only connection to terrorism is that they are Arab and Muslim immigrants is a colossal waste of resources. So, too, apparently, was the National Security

Agency's warrantless wiretapping program, which, according to frustrated FBI agents, generated thousands of leads that were virtually all "dead ends or have led to innocent Americans."[62]

Because the Bush administration was so focused on swaggeringly aggressive and coercive forms of prevention, it devoted insufficient resources and attention to less glamorous but more effective preventive initiatives. It spent more in a day in Iraq than it did annually on some of the most important defensive initiatives here in the United States.[63] In December 2005, the bipartisan 9-11 Commission gave the Bush administration failing or near-failing grades on many of the most basic homeland security measures, including assessing critical infrastructure vulnerabilities, securing weapons of mass destruction, screening airline passengers and cargo, sharing information between law enforcement and intelligence agencies, ensuring that emergency first-responders have adequate communications, and supporting secular education in Muslim countries.[64] These measures were plainly not the Bush administration's priority.

COLLATERAL CONSEQUENCES

The preventive paradigm also had other collateral consequences. When the government chose to "disappear" al-Qaeda suspects into secret prisons and to use waterboarding to compel them to talk, it is certainly conceivable that it might have obtained useful intelligence, although one can never actually know whether the same information might have been obtained through lawful means. But one can know with certainty that such tactics foreclosed any real possibility of bringing the suspects to justice for their alleged crimes, because evidence obtained in a "black site" would taint any attempt to prosecute. The Bush administration was repeatedly stymied in its attempts to obtain convictions for war crimes against Guantanamo detainees. The head of military prosecutions at Guantanamo specifically ordered a high-profile prosecution dismissed because she concluded that the defendant, Mohammed Al-Qahtani, suspected of being the "twentieth hijacker" on 9/11 had been tortured by military interrogators acting under Defense Secretary Donald Rumsfeld's orders. There is debate about whether torture ever results in reliable intelligence—but there can be no debate that it radically curtails the government's ability to bring a terrorist to justice.

The goal of protecting innocent civilians from terrorist violence is indisputably legitimate. When laudable goals are pursued through dubious means, however, the legitimacy of the entire enterprise is compromised. That loss of legitimacy makes potential allies less eager to work with the United States, creates new enemies, and inspires those already arrayed against America to adopt more radical tactics. Assuming that the principal terrorist threat at this juncture comes from a violence-prone fundamentalist strain of Islam and that the "enemies" in this struggle are largely composed of Arab and Muslim men, it is all the more critical that the United States develop close positive ties with Arab and Muslim communities here and abroad. We Americans need their eyes and ears if we are going to find the small number of persons actually planning to use violence against us. And we need their support if we are to succeed in isolating al-Qaeda from the wider circle of potential supporters. When we impose on these communities measures that we would not tolerate for ourselves, measures that fail to treat them with the respect and dignity owed all human beings, we sow distrust and enmity that impede the communication and cooperation we need and simultaneously fuel the anti-Americanism that we cannot afford.

Nothing could more perfectly meet the recruitment needs of al-Qaeda and its supporters than the abuse U.S. forces meted out to prisoners at Abu Ghraib prison, the legal black hole that is Guantanamo, the policy of rendering foreign nationals to third countries for torture, the practice of "disappearing" suspects into a network of secret CIA detention centers, or the war in Iraq. Defense Secretary Rumsfeld identified the critical question in an October 2003 internal Pentagon memo: "Are we capturing, killing or deterring and dissuading more terrorists every day than the madrassas and the radical clerics are recruiting, training and deploying against us?"[65] Although there is no certain metric for answering Rumsfeld's question, there can be little doubt that the preventive tactics adopted by the Bush administration were a boon to terrorist recruitment throughout the world.

One telling sign of the damage to America's image was that after the report of CIA black sites surfaced in November 2005, Russia, among several other countries, promptly issued a press release claiming that it had nothing to do with the sites.[66] When Russia feels the need to distance itself from the United States out of concern that its human rights image might be tarnished by association, we Americans know we have fallen far. The fact that European nations may have housed some of the black sites and cooperated in renditions has caused a firestorm of controversy in that region and will undoubtedly complicate future cooperation. Italy and Germany, for example, have indicted CIA agents for their part in the kidnapping and rendition of their residents.[67] And Spain's national security court has opened a formal criminal investigation of Bush administration attorney John Yoo, former White House counsel and attorney general Alberto Gonzales, former counsel to the vice president David Addington, and the former general counsel to the Department of Defense for their part in authorizing torture of a Spanish citizen at Guantanamo.[68]

In short, under the Bush administration's preventive paradigm the United States went from being the object of the world's sympathy immediately after the events of 9/11 to being the country most likely to be hated the world over. The Bush administration squandered all the support Americans had in the wake of the attacks and its tactics caused anti-Americanism to climb to all-time highs. In some countries, Osama bin Laden had a higher approval rating than the United States.[69] Once widely admired for its record of safeguarding civil liberties and human rights, the United States under President Bush became the object of sweeping condemnations by the United Nations Human Rights Committee, international nongovernmental organizations, and judges and political leaders across the globe. These developments are linked; much of the anti-Americanism was tied to the perception that the United States pursued its war on terrorism in an arrogant, unilateral fashion, defying the very values that the nation had long championed.

PREVENTION WITHIN THE RULE OF LAW

Because the rule of law is a central element of popular conceptions of justice, those who adhere to it are likely to gain legitimacy and support in the all-important struggle for hearts and minds. But that is not how the Bush administration saw it. In March 2005, the Pentagon warned in its *National Defense Strategy* that "our strength as a nation state will continue to be challenged by those who employ a strategy of the weak using international fora, judicial processes, and terrorism."[70] The proposition that judicial processes and international accountability—the very essence of the rule of law—were to be dismissed as a strategy of the weak, aligned with terrorism itself, makes clear that the Bush administration viewed the rule of law as an obstacle, not an asset, in its effort to protect citizens from the threat of terrorist attack. Such an attitude can only breed still more anti-Americanism, and still more terrorists willing to sacrifice their lives in striking a blow against the United States.

If the Obama administration is to turn this tide, it must recognize that the long-term security of the United States does not require illegal spying on Americans; locking up thousands of "suspected terrorists" who turn out to have no connection to terrorism; forcing suspects to bark like dogs, urinate and defecate on themselves, and endure sexual humiliation; attacking countries that have not threatened to attack America; or claiming that the president as commander in chief can ignore congressional and constitutional restrictions on his authority.[71] Security rests not on exceptionalism and double standards but on a renewed commitment to fairness, justice, and the rule of law. A nation abiding by the rule of law has many options available for preventing terrorism.

But it will succeed only if it sees the rule of law values as an asset in that campaign, not an obstacle. Aharon Barak, president of Israel's Supreme Court, said it best in a case forbidding the use of "moderate physical pressure" in interrogating Palestinian terror suspects:

> A democracy must sometimes fight terror with one hand tied behind its back. Even so, a democracy has the upper hand. The rule of law and the liberty of an individual constitute important components in its understanding of security. At the end of the day, they strengthen its spirit and this strength allows it to overcome its difficulties.[72]

The preventive paradigm, by jettisoning fundamental commitments to the rule of law, compromised the nation's spirit, strengthened its enemies, and left the United States simultaneously less free and less safe. If the Obama administration is ready to learn from prior mistakes, there is a way forward—through, rather than in spite of, a recommitment to the rule of law.

Notes

1. Oral arguments of Sandra Day O'Connor in *Hamdi v. Rumsfeld* (542 U.S. 507), April 28, 2004.
2. See Justice O'Connor's controlling opinion in *Hamdi v. Rumsfeld*, June 28, 2004.
3. National Commission on Terrorist Attacks on the United States, *The 9/11 Commission Report* (New York: Norton, 2004), chap. 3
4. Charlie Savage, "To Critics, New Policy on Terror Looks Old," *New York Times,* July 2, 2009.
5. This essay originally appeared as chapter 5 of John Yoo, *War By Other Means* (New York: Grove Atlantic, 2006). All rights reserved c/o Writers Representatives LLC, New York, NY.
6. For a broader treatment of the issues raised by the war on terrorism, see John Yoo, *War by Other Means* (New York: Atlantic Monthly Press, 2006). For an earlier discussion of the legal issues surrounding the Afghanistan war, see Robert J. Delahunty and John Yoo, "The President's Constitutional Authority to Conduct Military Operations against Terrorist Organizations and the Nations that Harbor or Support Them," *Harvard Journal of Law and Public Policy* 25 (2002): 487.
7. *Ex Parte Quirin*, 317 U.S. 1, 28 (1942).
8. Authorization for Use of Military Force, Public Law 107-40 (September 18, 2001).
9. *Prize Cases*, 67 U.S. 635, 670 (1863).
10. See, for example, Louis Fisher, *Presidential War Power* (Lawrence: University of Kansas Press, 1995), 11; and Michael J. Glennon, *Constitutional Diplomacy* (Princeton, N.J.: Princeton University Press), 17. But also see John Yoo, *The Powers of War and Peace: The Constitution and Foreign Affairs after 9/11* (Chicago: University of Chicago Press, 2005), 143–160.

11. Alexander Hamilton, James Madison, and John Jay, *The Federalist Papers*, intro. Clinton Rossiter (New York: New American Library, 1961).
12. *Johnson v. Eisentrager*, 339 U.S. 763, 788 (1950).
13. See, for example, *United States v. Curtiss-Wright Export Corp.*, 299 U.S. 304 (1936); and *Chicago & S. Air Lines v. Waterman S.S. Corp.*, 333 U.S. 103, 111 (1948). In a post–Civil War case, recently reaffirmed, the Court ruled that President Lincoln had the constitutional authority to engage in espionage. The president "was undoubtedly authorized during the war, as commander-in-chief . . . to employ secret agents to enter the rebel lines and obtain information respecting the strength, resources, and movements of the enemy." *Totten v. United States*, 92 U.S. 105, 106 (1876). On *Totten's* continuing vitality, see *Tenet v. Doe*, 544 U.S. 1, 8–11 (2005).
14. Franklin D. Roosevelt, President, Confidential Memorandum for the Attorney General, May 21, 1940, reprinted in Appendix A, *United States v. United States District Court*, 444 F.2d 651, 669–670 (6th Cir. 1971).
15. Id.
16. See *Nardone v. United States*, 302 U.S. 379 (1937), interpreting Section 605 of the Federal Communications Act of 1934 to prohibit interception of telephone calls.
17. See Robert H. Jackson, *That Man: An Insider's Portrait of Franklin D. Roosevelt* (New York: Oxford University Press, 2003), 68–69.
18. Foreign Intelligence Surveillance Act of 1978: Hearings on H.R. 5764, H.R. 9745, H.R. 7308, and H.R. 5632 Before the Subcommittee on Legislation of the House Commitee on Intelligence, 95th Cong., 2nd sess., 15, 1978 (statement of Attorney General Griffin Bell).
19. Most notably, Clinton deputy attorney general Jamie Gorelick testified before Congress that the Justice Department could carry out physical searches for foreign intelligence purposes even though FISA at the time did not provide for them. Amending the Foreign Intelligence Surveillance Act: Hearings Before the House Permanent Select Comm. on Intelligence, 103rd Cong., 2nd sess., 61, 1994. Clinton's Office of Legal Counsel issued a legal opinion that the president could order the sharing between the Justice Department and intelligence agencies of electronic surveillance gathered through criminal wiretaps, even though this sharing was prohibited by statute. Sharing Title III Electronic Surveillance Material with the Intelligence Community, OLC Preliminary Print, 2000 WL 33716983, October 17, 2000.
20. See Executive Nomination of Eric Holder, Hearing Before the Senate Judiciary Committee, January 15, 2009. In an exchange, Republican senator Orrin Hatch of Utah asked Holder if he believed "that the President has . . . inherent authority under Article II of the Constitution to engage in warrantless foreign intelligence surveillance, or, in your opinion, does FISA trump Article II?" Holder replied, "Well, the President obviously has powers under the Constitution that cannot be infringed by the legislative branch."
21. *United States v. United States District Court* ("Keith"), 407 U.S. 297 (1972).
22. *In re Sealed Case*, 310 F.3d 717, 742 (For. Intel. Surv. Ct. Rev. 2002) (footnote omitted).
23. Id.
24. 629 F.2d 908, 913 (4th Cir. 1980).
25. Id. at 915.
26. See also *United States v. Brown*, 484 F.2d 418 (5th Cir. 1973), cert. denied, 415 U.S. 960 (1974); *United States v. Buck*, 548 F.2d 871 (9th Cir.), cert. denied, 434 U.S. 890

(1977); *United States v. Clay*, 430 F.2d 165 (5th Cir. 1970), rev'd on other grounds, 403 U.S. 698 (1971).

27. *Haig v. Agee*, 453 U.S. 280, 307 (1981).

28. *Hamdi v. Rumsfeld*, 542 U.S. 507, 518 (2004) (plurality opinion). Although a plurality opinion, five justices agreed on this point because Justice Clarence Thomas, in dissent, also concluded that the president had the constitutional authority to detain enemy combatants and that Congress had authorized this. Id. at 587. The Anti-Detention Act was passed in response to the detention of Japanese Americans in World War II and prohibits the detention of U.S. citizens without authorization by Congress. The Supreme Court has thus acknowledged that the AUMF suffices for this authorization.

29. See, generally, John Yoo, "Kosovo, War Powers, and the Multilateral Future," *University of Pennsylvania Law Review* 148 (2000): 1673.

30. Hamilton, *Federalist* No. 23, 147.

31. Hamilton, *Federalist* No. 70, 471.

32. Hamilton, *Federalist* No. 74, 500. James Iredell (later an associate justice of the Supreme Court) argued in the North Carolina ratifying convention that "from the nature of the thing, the command of armies ought to be delegated to one person only. The secrecy, despatch, and decision, which are necessary in military operations, can only be expected from one person." "Debate in the North Carolina Ratifying Convention," in *The Debates in the Several State Conventions on the Adoption of the Federal Constitution*, Vol. 4, 2nd ed., ed. Jonathan Elliot (Manchester, N.H.: Ayer Company Publishers, 1987 [1888]), 107. See also Joseph Story, *Commentaries on the Constitution of the United States* (Buffalo, N.Y.: William S. Hein, 1994 [1833]), 341, arguing that in military matters, "unity of plan, promptitude, activity, and decision, are indispensable to success; and these can scarcely exist, except when a single magistrate is entrusted exclusively with the power."

33. Letter from Thomas Jefferson, President, to Mrs. John Adams (September 11, 1804), in *The Writings of Thomas Jefferson*, Vol. 8, ed. Paul L. Ford (New York: Putnam's Sons, 1892–1899), 310–311. President Andrew Jackson expressed the same view in 1832, vetoing a bill that he regarded as unconstitutional even though the Supreme Court had upheld it as constitutional. "It is as much the duty of the house of representatives, of the senate, and of the president to decide upon the constitutionality of any bill or resolution, just as with the Supreme Court when the law arises in a case before them," he wrote. Andrew Jackson, Veto Message (July 10, 1832), in *A Compilation of the Messages and Papers of the Presidents, 1789–1897*, Vol. 2, ed. James D. Richardson (Washington, D.C.: Government Printing Office,1896–1899), 582. Abraham Lincoln, in the aftermath of the case of the slave Dred Scott, famously announced in his first inaugural that henceforth he would not follow the rule that a slave would not be free once in northern territory, though he chose to obey the Supreme Court's order in the *Dred Scott* case itself. See First Inaugural Address of Abraham Lincoln (March 4, 1861), in *Abraham Lincoln, Speeches and Writings, 1859–1865*, ed. Don E. Fehrenbacher (New York: Literary Classics, 1989), 221.

34. *Fleming v. Page*, 50 U.S. (9 How.) 603, 615 (1850).

35. For a standard historical source on the period. see Robert Dallek, *Franklin D. Roosevelt and American Foreign Policy, 1932–1945* (New York: Oxford University

Press, 1979). See also Robert Divine, *Roosevelt and World War II* (Baltimore: Johns Hopkins University Press, 1969); Gaddis Smith, *American Diplomacy during the Second World War* (New York: Wiley, 1965); Frederick W. Marks III, *Wind over Sand: The Diplomacy of Franklin Roosevelt* (Athens: University of Georgia Press, 1988); and Warren F. Kimball, *The Juggler: Franklin Roosevelt as Wartime Statesman* (Princeton, N.J.: Princeton University Press, 1991).

36. Marc Trachtenberg, "The Bush Strategy in Historical Perspective," in *Nuclear Transformation: The New U.S. Nuclear Doctrine*, ed. James Wirtz and Jeffrey Larson (New York: Palgrave Macmillan, 2005).

37. National Commission on Terrorist Attacks on the United States, *9/11 Commission Report*, 361–362.

38. Ibid., 399–419.

39. "Congress cannot anticipate and legislate with regard to every possible action the President may find it necessary to take or every possible situation in which he might act," the Supreme Court has said. "Such failure of Congress . . . does not, 'especially . . . in the areas of foreign policy and national security,' imply 'congressional disapproval' of action taken by the Executive." *Dames & Moore v. Regan*, 453 U.S. 654, 678 (1981) (quoting *Haig v. Agee*, 453 U.S., 280, 291 [1981]).

40. See, for example, *Rasul v. Bush,* 542 U.S. 466 (2004); *Hamdan v. Rumsfeld*, 548 U.S. 557 (2006); *Boumediene v. Bush*, 128 S. Ct. 2229 (2008).

41. See "To Erastus Corning and Others, June 12, 1863," in *The Collected Works of Abraham Lincoln*, Vol. 6, ed. Roy P. Basler (New Brunswick, N.J.: Rutgers University Press, 1953), 261

42. Transcript of the third Nixon-Frost interview, *New York Times*, May 20, 1977.

43. Much of this essay is adapted from David Cole and Jules Lobel, *Less Safe, Less Free: Why America Is Losing the War on Terrorism* (New York: New Press, 2007). The arguments made herein are elaborated and supported with greater detail in that book.

44. John Harris, Mike Allen, and Jim Vandehei, "Cheney Warns of New Attacks," Politico.com, February 4, 2009, www.politico.com/news/stories/0209/18390.html.

45. Richard Posner, *Not a Suicide Pact: The Constitution in a Time of National Emergency* (New York: Oxford University Press, 2006).

46. White House, "National Security Strategy of the United States of America," September 17, 2002, http://georgewbush-whitehouse.archives.gov/nsc/nss/2002.

47. The Convention Against Torture and Other Forms of Cruel, Inhuman and Degrading Treatment or Punishment prohibits torture under all circumstances and provides that "no exceptional circumstances whatsoever" can justify it. The prohibition on disappearances has been recognized as having the status of jus cogens, similar to torture, and similarly permitting no exceptions. See *Forti v. Suarez-Mason*, 694 F. Supp. 707 (N.D. Cal. 1988).

48. Senate Select Committee on Intelligence, Hearing on Current and Projected National Security Threats to the United States, 109th Cong., 1st sess., February 16, 2005.

49. Ibid.

50. "Iraq War Casualties," *Washington Post*, February 21, 2009.

51. Susan B. Glasser, "Global Terrorism Statistics Debated," *Washington Post*, May 1, 2005.

52. David Sands, "Suicide Bombing Popular Terrorist Tactic," *Washington Times*, May 8, 2006.
53. U.S. Department of State, "Country Reports on Terrorism 2007," April 30, 2008, www.state.gov/s/ct/rls/crt/2007/index.htm.
54. Mark Denbeaux and Joshua Denbeaux, "Report on Guantánamo Detainees: A Profile of 517 Detainees through Analysis of Department of Defense Data," Seton Hall Public Law Research Paper No. 46, February 2006, http://law.shu.edu/news/guantanamo_report_final_2_08_06.pdf; Corine Hegland, "Who Is at Guantánamo Bay?" *National Journal*, February 3, 2006.
55. "Secret FBI Report Questions Al-Qaeda Capabilities," ABC News, March 9, 2005, http://abcnews.go.com/WNT/Investigation/story?id=566425&page=1.
56. Dan Eggen and Julie Tate, "U.S. Campaign Produces Few Convictions on Terrorist Charges," *Washington Post*, June 12, 2005.
57. In 2004 the Justice Department released Hamdi to Saudi Arabia on the face-saving but unenforceable promise that he surrender his U.S. citizenship and stay in Saudi Arabia, where he also held citizenship. In January 2008, after a civilian criminal trial, Padilla was sentenced to seventeen years in prison for conspiracy and material support of terrorism overseas. Padilla was never tried for his alleged role in any plot to engage in terrorism in the United States.
58. See David Cole, *Enemy Aliens: Double Standards and Constitutional Freedoms in the War on Terrorism*, 2nd ed. (New York: New Press, 2004), xx–xxiii, 25.
59. *United States v. Rahman*, 189 F.3d 88 (2nd Cir. 1999).
60. See Peter Baker and Susan Glasser, "Bush Says 10 Plots by Al-Qaeda Were Foiled," *Washington Post*, October 7, 2005; "Mueller: More than 100 Terror Attacks Foiled Worldwide," CNN.com, March 4, 2003, www.cnn.com/2003/ALLPOLITICS/03/04/terror.war.congress/; U.S. Department of Justice, "Waging the War on Terror," www.lifeandliberty.gov/subs/a_terr.htm.
61. Josh Meyer and Warren Vieth, "Scope of Plots Bush Says Were Foiled Is Questioned," *Los Angeles Times*, October 8, 2005; Sara Kehaulani Goo, "List of Foiled Plots Puzzling to Some," *Washington Post*, October 23, 2005; John Diamond and Toni Locy, "White House List of Disrupted Terror Plots Questioned," *USA Today*, October 26, 2005.
62. Lowell Bergman, Eric Lichtblau, Scott Shane, and Don Van Natta Jr., "Spy Agency Data after September 11 Led F.B.I. to Dead Ends," *New York Times*, January 17, 2006.
63. Matt Brzezinski, "Red Alert," *Mother Jones*, September–October 2004, www.motherjones.com/news/feature/2004/09/08_400.html.
64. 9/11 Public Discourse Project, www.9-11pdp.org.
65. Memorandum from Donald Rumsfeld to Dick Myers et al., "Re: Global War on Terrorism," October 16, 2003, www.globalsecurity.org/military/library/policy/dod/rumsfeld-d20031016sdmemo.htm.
66. Dana Priest and Josh White, "Policies on Terrorism Suspects Come Under Fire," *Washington Post*, November 3, 2005.
67. Tracy Wilkinson, "Italy Issues Arrest Warrants for 3 CIA Officers in 'Rendition' Case," *Los Angeles Times*, July 6, 2006; Mark Landler, "German Court Confronts U.S. on Abduction," *New York Times*, February 1, 2007.
68. Scott Horton, "Bush Torture Lawyers Targeted in Criminal Probe," *Harper's Magazine Online*, March 28, 2009, www.harpers.org/archive/2009/03/hbc-90004640.

69. See Thomas Powers, "Bringing 'Em On," *New York Times,* December 25, 2005 (reports a 65 percent approval rate for Osama bin Laden in Pakistan); and Pew Research Center for the People and the Press, "A Year after Iraq War: Mistrust of America in Europe Ever Higher, Muslim Anger Persists," March 16, 2004 (reports that only 21 percent of Pakistanis had a favorable opinion of the United States), http://people-press.org/reports/pdf/206.pdf.

70. U.S. Department of Defense, *National Defense Strategy* (Washington, D.C.: DOD, March 2005), www.globalsecurity.org/military/library/policy/dod/nds-usa_mar2005_ib.htm.

71. In this chapter, John Yoo defends an expansive view of presidential power during wartime. While a lawyer in the Office of Legal Counsel after 9/11,Yoo wrote numerous memos asserting similarly expansive theories. Those memos have been widely repudiated, including by subsequent heads of the Office of Legal Counsel under President Bush. See Jack Goldsmith, *The Terror Presidency: Law and Judgment Inside the Bush Administration* (New York: Norton, 2007), which describes Yoo's August 1, 2002, memo on the CIA's use of coercive interrogation tactics as "wildly broader than was necessary," "tendentious [in] tone," and lacking "care and sobriety." Also see U.S. Dept of Justice, Office of Legal Counsel, Memorandum "Re: Status of Certain OLC Opinions Issued in the Aftermath of the Terrorist Attacks of September 11, 2001," www.usdoj.gov/opa/documents/memostatusolcopinions01152009 .pdf, in which OLC head Stephen Bradbury notes the "doubtful nature" of many propositions about executive power in Yoo's memos.

72. *Public Committee Against Torture v. State of Israel,* HCJ No. 5100/94, July 15, 1999, 27, http://elyon1.court.gov.il/files_eng/94/000/051/a09/9405100.a09.pdf.

conclusion: is the threat of terrorism being overstated?

YES: The threat of terrorism is overblown and more manageable than suspected
John Mueller, *Ohio State University*

NO: The threat is profound and will remain so for some time
Walter Laqueur, *Center for Strategic and International Studies*

Most of the essays in this volume, though differing in important ways, operate under the assumption that terrorism poses a significant threat to nations and the international community, requiring thoughtful and assertive responses. This assumption was clear in Part I, which debates the nature of terrorist organizations; the root causes, motivations, and tactics of traditional and modern terrorism; and the possibility that terrorists might use weapons of mass destruction. And it has been a core component of Part II, which covers a range of issues related to counterterrorist responses—hard versus soft approaches; different international strategies; and how the rule of law fits in.

But is the underlying premise of the book correct, that terrorism is a high-priority issue, requiring a great deal of intellectual attention and policy action? In other words, are analysts and others accurately assessing the threat of terrorism? After all, as Graham Allison points out in the Foreword to this volume, misidentifying threats can lead to unfortunate policy outcomes.

In the book's final debate, John Mueller and Walter Laqueur review the terrorism and counterterrorism issues discussed and debated throughout the volume, and, with an eye toward the future, develop very different assessments of terrorist threats and the nature and necessity of government responses.

Mueller says the tendency in government is to overinflate national security threats, and there is no clearer example of this than the current take on terrorism. He believes any honest evaluation of today's terrorism, including that of al-Qaeda, leads to one conclusion: the threat is far less than meets the hype. Mueller points out that the probability of an American dying in a terrorist attack in his or her lifetime is about one in 75,000, while the chance of dying in an automobile accident is about one in eighty. Terrorism, then, is hardly the "existential threat" that is often portrayed. Indeed, for Mueller, the real threat comes not from terrorism, but from what he calls the "terrorism industry"—politicians, bureaucrats, journalists, and risk entrepreneurs who, for their own parochial reasons, stoke public fears by exaggerating the threat, leading to irrational government overreaction. He concludes that overwrought counterterrorism policies have proven far costlier than anything terrorists will likely ever be capable of doing.

Laqueur tackles the question from a very different vantage point. The issue, he says, is not the cost of overstating terrorist threats, but the risk of underestimating them. Reviewing the root causes, motivations, and global landscape of contemporary terrorism, Laqueur sees the threat as real, tangible, and, at least in the short to medium term, growing. Indeed, he believes the advent of "megaterrorism" (apocalyptic groups plus weapons of mass destruction) has not yet arrived. He agrees with Mueller that overreacting to terrorist threats is costly. But so is underreacting: nothing inspires violent global movements as much as perceptions of weakness in their enemies. Although democracies may be good at many things, Laqueur points out that dealing with violent asymmetric actors is, unfortunately, not one of them. Whereas terrorists abide by no laws and rules whatsoever, democratic states are bound by them. The tendency therefore, according to Laqueur, is to understate terrorist threats and the necessity of strong responses—that is, until the next major attack occurs.

These final essays bring home the point that terrorism, in one form or another, is destined to remain on the world scene. Like other age-old violent human phenomena—such as war and murder—there is no end in sight for terrorist violence. Yet the impact of terrorism now and into the future will depend on ever-shifting factors—the emergence and capacity of terror organizations; the lethality of specific acts of terrorism; threat perceptions and government responses. Understanding and addressing the complexities of terrorism will remain difficult, and imperfect. Continuing to research, analyze, disagree, and debate will remain the best tools for developing ways to meet the challenge.

The threat of terrorism is overblown and
YES: more manageable than suspected
John Mueller, *Ohio State University*

Fear and Overreaction: Terrorism's Most Damaging Effects

With the benefit of hindsight, it strongly appears that there has been a tendency to inflate national security threats and then, partly in consequence, to overreact to them.[1] For example, Americans have experienced anxieties over domestic and foreign communism, fears about the imminence of thermonuclear war, apprehensions over challenges posed by various "rogue states" or devils *du jour* (most of whom eventually faded into insignificance—remember Nasser, Sukarno, Qaddafi, Castro?), insecurities engendered by the Iran hostage crisis and the Japanese economic challenge of the 1980s, and worries about the "ethnic warfare" that was supposedly going to engulf the world in the 1990s. Not all concerns that could have been seized upon have evoked anxiety and overreaction, but it does appear that every threat to U.S. foreign policy in the last several decades that has come to be accepted as significant has then eventually been greatly inflated.

Americans seem to be at it again lately. The terrorism fear has led to policies that have often been unwise, costly, unnecessary, and sometimes massively counterproductive.

And the rhetoric of alarm continues at a high pitch. Thus in March 2008 Homeland Security czar Michael Chertoff proclaimed the "struggle" against terrorism to be a "significant existential" one—carefully differentiating it, apparently, from all those insignificant existential struggles Americans have waged in the past.[2] Meanwhile, the *New York Times* editorial board assured its readers in 2008 that "the fight against al-Qaeda is the central battle for this generation," and former Republican presidential nominee John McCain more expansively, and repeatedly, has labeled the struggle against radical Muslim extremism the "transcendental challenge of the 21st century," one that can affect "our very existence."[3] In a best-selling book, Michael Scheuer, formerly of the Central Intelligence Agency (CIA), repeatedly assures Americans that their "survival" is at stake and that they are engaged in a "war to the death."[4] Meanwhile, Democrats routinely insist that the terrorist menace has been energized and much heightened by the Republicans' misguided war in Iraq.

THE SCOPE OF THE THREAT

Like crime, terrorism can be carried out by a single individual or by a very small group and can never be completely expunged from the human experience. It is important, however, to assess the capacities of international terrorism to inflict damage. It is certainly true that it presents problems, but the "struggle" against it hardly seems existential or even transcendental, and the threat it presents appears to have been vastly overblown.

To evaluate the scope of the threat, it is sensible to focus primarily on al-Qaeda because it constitutes "the only Islamic terrorist organization that targets the U.S. homeland," as Glenn Carle stresses after twenty-three years of service with the CIA, including the post of deputy national intelligence officer for transnational threats.[5] Somewhat more broadly, Middle East specialist Fawaz Gerges points out that, over time, mainstream Islamists—the vast majority within the Islamist political movement—have given up on the use of force. In other words, the jihadists who are still willing to apply violence constitute a tiny minority. But he also notes that the vast majority even of this small group primarily focuses on various "infidel" Muslim regimes and consider those among them who carry out violence against the "far enemy"— mainly Europe and the United States—to be irresponsible and reckless adventurers who endanger the survival of the whole movement.[6]

It is possible, of course, that some other terrorist organization could generate designs to harm the United States directly, but for now, certainly, al-Qaeda stands essentially alone.

In evaluating al-Qaeda's general capacity to carry out its violent threats, a good place to start is with the analyses provided by Marc Sageman.[7] A former intelligence officer, Sageman has carefully and systematically combed through both open and classified data on jihadists and would-be jihadists around the world. In the process, he sorts the al-Qaeda enemy into three groups.

First, there is a cluster left over from the struggles in Afghanistan against the Soviets in the 1980s. Currently, they are huddled around and hiding out with Osama bin Laden somewhere in Afghanistan or Pakistan. This band, concludes Sageman, probably consists of a few dozen individuals. Joining them in the area are perhaps a hundred fighters left over from al-Qaeda's golden days in Afghanistan in the 1990s. These key portions of the enemy forces would total, then, less than 150 actual people. They may operate something resembling "training camps," but these appear to be quite minor affairs. They also assist with the Taliban's far larger and very troublesome insurgency in Afghanistan.

Beyond this tiny band, concludes Sageman, is the third group, which consists of thousands of sympathizers and would-be jihadists spread around the globe who mainly connect in Internet chat rooms, engage in radicalizing conversations, and variously dare each other to actually do something.

All of these rather hapless—perhaps even pathetic—people should, of course, be considered potentially dangerous. From time to time, they may be able to coalesce enough to carry out acts of terrorist violence, and policing efforts to stop them before they can do so are certainly justified. But the notion that they present an existential threat to just about anybody seems at least as fanciful as some of their schemes.

Moreover, the threat presented by these individuals is likely, concludes Sageman, to simply fade away with time—unless, of course, the United States overreacts and does something to enhance their numbers, prestige, and determination. And that something is, needless to say, entirely possible.

This decidedly unconventional evaluation of the threat resonates with other prominent experts who have spent years studying the issue. One of them is Gerges, who suggests that Sageman's third group may also include a small, but possibly growing, underclass of disaffected and hopeless young men in the Middle East, many of them scarcely literate, who, outraged at Israel and at America's war in Iraq, may provide cannon fodder for the jihad. However, these young men would mainly present problems in the Middle East (including in Iraq), not elsewhere.

Other estimates of al-Qaeda central's size generally are on the same order of magnitude as those suggested by Sageman. Egyptian intelligence, for example, puts the number at less than two hundred, while American intelligence estimates run from three hundred to upwards of five hundred.[8]

In a development that inflates al-Qaeda central's impact, there has been a tendency to conflate that organization with those fighting the American occupation in Iraq and with the destructive insurgency conducted by the Taliban in Afghanistan. But the force in Iraq, now in decline, was created independently and later linked itself up with al-Qaeda. For their part, the Taliban, who were distinctly uncomfortable as hosts to al-Qaeda in the past, are quick to point out that they are running their own war, thank you very much. They insist that al-Qaeda plays only a very small role in their efforts.

Another way to evaluate the al-Qaeda threat is to focus on the actual amount of violence perpetrated outside of war zones by Muslim extremists since the attacks of September 11, 2001. Included in the count would be terrorism of the much publicized and fear-inducing sort that occurred in Bali in 2002, in Saudi Arabia, Morocco, and Turkey in 2003, in the Philippines, Madrid, and Egypt in 2004, and in London and Jordan in 2005.

Three publications from think tanks have independently provided lists or tallies of violence committed by Muslim extremists outside of war zones such as Iraq, Israel, Chechnya, Sudan, Kashmir, and Afghanistan, whether that violence was perpetrated by domestic terrorists or by ones with substantial international connections.[9] The lists include not only attacks by al-Qaeda, but also those by its imitators, enthusiasts, look-alikes, and wannabes, as well as ones by groups with no apparent connection to it whatsoever.

Although these tallies make for grim reading, the total number of people killed in the years after 9/11 in such incidents comes to some two to three hundred per year. That, of course, is two to three hundred too many, but it hardly suggests that al-Qaeda's destructive capacities are monumental. By comparison, over the same period far more people have perished in the United States alone in bathtub drownings or in automobile accidents by people who have abandoned short-haul air flights because of the increased costs and waiting time imposed after 9/11 by the Transportation Security Administration.

Another assessment comes from astronomer Alan Harris. Using State Department figures, he estimates a worldwide death rate from international terrorism outside of war zones of one thousand per year—that is, he assumes in his estimate that there would be another 9/11-type attack somewhere in the world every several years. Over an eighty-year period under those conditions, some eighty thousand people would die, which would mean that the probability that a resident of the earth will die at the hands of international terrorists is about one in 75,000 (six billion divided by eighty thousand). By comparison, an American's chance of dying in an auto accident over the same time interval is about one in eighty. If there are no repeats of 9/11, the probability of being killed by an international terrorist over an eighty-year span becomes more like one in 120,000.

One reason for these remarkable numbers is that 9/11 proved to be substantially counterproductive from al-Qaeda's standpoint. In particular, it massively heightened concerns about terrorism around the world. And, no matter how much they might disagree on other issues (most notably on America's war on Iraq), there is a compelling incentive for states—including Arab and Muslim ones—to cooperate in dealing with any international terrorist threat emanating from groups and individuals connected to or sympathetic with al-Qaeda.

Given what seems to be the rather limited capacity of al-Qaeda and similar entities, these cooperative international policing efforts may not have prevented a large number of attacks, but more than three thousand "suspects" have been arrested around the world, and no doubt at least some of them were dangerous—although these multilateral efforts, particularly by Muslim states such as Sudan, Syria, Libya, and even Iran, have not received sufficient publicity. Overall, bin Laden and his gang seem mainly to have succeeded in uniting the world, including its huge Muslim portion, against their violent global jihad.

The main result among jihadists and religious nationalists has been a vehement rejection of al-Qaeda's strategy and methods. Moreover, even former jihadist associates now view that strategy as a loser and are reluctant to gamble on it.[10]

In addition, continuing, and perhaps accelerating, a long-range trend, state sponsorship of terrorism (at least against countries other than Israel) seems to be distinctly on the wane since 9/11, a phenomenon noted even by the Department of Homeland Security in a 2005 report.

The post-9/11 willingness of governments around the world to take on international terrorists has been much reinforced and amplified by subsequent, if sporadic, terrorist activity in places such as Pakistan, Saudi Arabia, Turkey, Indonesia, Egypt, Morocco, and Jordan. For example, the terrorist bombing in Bali in 2002 galvanized the Indonesian government into action. Extensive arrests and convictions—including of leaders who had previously enjoyed some degree of local fame and political popularity—seems to have severely degraded the capacity of the chief terrorist group, Jemaah Islamiyah. After terrorists attacked Saudis in Saudi Arabia in 2003, that country seemed, very much for self-interested reasons, to become considerably more serious about dealing with internal terrorism, including a clampdown on radical clerics and preachers. Some rather inept terrorist bombings in Casablanca in 2003 inspired a similar determined crackdown by Moroccan authorities.

Al-Qaeda–linked suicide terrorists killed sixty in simultaneous explosions in three hotels in Jordan in 2005. The most destructive of the bombs was set off in the midst of a group of Jordanians and Palestinians at a wedding party. It would be difficult to imagine a target likely to be stupider from the perspective of the terrorists. Not surprisingly, the main result of the attacks was to outrage Jordanians and other Arabs against the perpetrators. Massive protests were held in Jordan, and polls found that the percentage of respondents believing violence against civilian targets in order to defend Islam *never* to be justified jumped from 11 to 43, while the percentage expressing a lot of confidence in Osama bin Laden to "do the right thing" plunged from 25 to less than 1.

If this were not enough, al-Qaeda has continually expanded its enemies list in its declarations to the point that, analyst Peter Bergen notes, it has come to include "all Middle Eastern regimes; Muslims who do not share their views; most Western countries; Jews and Christians; the governments of India, Pakistan, Afghanistan, and Russia; most news organizations; the United Nations; and international NGOs."[11]

Meanwhile, after years of well-funded sleuthing the Federal Bureau of Investigation (FBI) and other investigative agencies have been unable to uncover a single true al-Qaeda sleeper cell or operative within the United States. (In an interesting similarity, that would be exactly the number of weapons of mass destruction uncovered by the U.S. military in Iraq over the same period.) Because some two billion foreigners have been admitted to the United States legally since 9/11 as well as many others illegally, the inability of the FBI to find any in the country suggests the terrorists are either far less diabolically clever than usually depicted or they are not trying very hard.

Any "threat" appears, then, to derive principally from Sageman's leaderless jihadists: self-selected people, often isolated from each other, who fantasize about performing dire deeds. From time to time, some of these characters may actually manage to do some harm, though in most cases their capacities and schemes—or alleged schemes—seem to be far less dangerous than initial press reports vividly, even hysterically, suggest. There is, for example, the diabolical would-be bomber of shopping malls in Rockford, Illinois, who exchanged two used stereo speakers (he could not afford the opening price of $100) for a bogus handgun and four equally bogus hand grenades supplied by an FBI informant.[12] Had the weapons been real, he might actually have managed to do some harm, but he clearly posed no threat that was existential (significant or otherwise) to the United States, to Illinois, to Rockford, or, indeed, to the shopping mall.

THE ATOMIC TERRORIST

For the number of terrorist casualties to change radically, terrorists would have to become *vastly* more capable of inflicting damage, and many (though not all) of those proclaiming the struggle against, and the threat presented by, al-Qaeda to be "existential" hinge their alarm on the prospect that the group could obtain weapons of mass destruction.

Actually, the terrorists would in fact pretty much have to acquire an atomic arsenal and the capacity to deploy and detonate it. Chemical arms do have the potential, under the appropriate circumstances, for panicking people; killing masses of people in open areas, however, is beyond their modest capabilities. It would take a ton of nerve gas or five tons of mustard gas to produce heavy casualties among unprotected people in an open area 1 kilometer square. Even for nerve gas, such casualties would require the concentrated delivery into a rather small area of about three hundred heavy artillery shells or seven 500-pound bombs. Biological weapons have greater destructive potential, but they are extremely difficult to deploy and to control. Explosive methods of dispersion may destroy the organisms, and, even if refrigerated, most of the organisms have a limited lifetime. "Dirty bombs" would spread potentially harmful radiation over a limited area, but would not kill anybody who walked away from the area.[13]

By contrast, nuclear weapons can inflict massive destruction, and an atomic bomb in the hands of a terrorist group could kill tens of thousands of people or even, in exceptional circumstances, more. Warnings about the possibility that small groups could fabricate nuclear weapons have been uttered repeatedly at least since 1946, and they escalated greatly after the September 11 attacks, even though the terrorists used weapons no more sophisticated than box-cutters on that terrible day.

However, these cries of alarm have obviously so far proven to be much off the mark. The issue is discussed in greater length elsewhere in this volume, but it may be useful to note here that making a nuclear weapon is an extraordinarily difficult task.[14] As the Gilmore Commission, a special advisory panel to the president and Congress, stresses, building a nuclear device capable of producing mass destruction presents "Herculean challenges." The process requires a lengthy sequence of steps, and if each is not fully met, the result is not simply a less powerful weapon, but one that cannot produce any significant nuclear yield at all or cannot be delivered. After assessing this issue in detail, physicists Christoph Wirz and Emmanuel Egger conclude that fabricating a nuclear weapon "could hardly be accomplished by a subnational group" because of "the difficulty of acquiring the necessary expertise, the technical requirements (which in several fields verge on the unfeasible), the lack of available materials and the lack of experience in working with these."[15]

A common concern envisions a newly nuclear country palming off a bomb or two to friendly terrorists for delivery abroad. However, this situation is exceedingly improbable because there would be too much risk, even for a country led by extremists, that the ultimate source of the weapon would be discovered before or after detonation, or that it would be exploded in a manner and on a target the donor would not approve—including on the donor itself. Nor is it likely that a working nuclear device could be stolen and detonated. "A theft," note Wirz and Egger, "would involve many risks and great efforts in terms of personnel, finances, and organization," while safety and security systems on the weapons "ensure that the successful use of a stolen weapon would be very unlikely."[16]

In testimony before the Senate Select Committee on Intelligence on January 11, 2007, FBI director Robert Mueller, who in previous testimony had been highly alarmist about the terrorist potential, stressed that his chief concern within the United States had become homegrown groups, and that, while remaining concerned that things could change in the future, "few if any terrorist groups" were likely to possess the required expertise to produce nuclear weapons—or, for that matter, biological or chemical ones.[17]

Moreover, alarmists never quite spell out how the atomic terrorist would actually go about causing a huge country like the United States to cease to exist—nor, disappointingly, are they ever closely queried on their dire declarations by journalists or others. A ground-burst atomic device of Hiroshima proportions could certainly devastate a few blocks of a city. If more than one were set off at the same time, the destruction would be, of course, even wider and would multiply the alarm severalfold. A massive calamity to be sure, but how does this lead to the extinguishment of the rest of the country? Do farmers in Iowa cease plowing because an atomic bomb went off in an eastern city? Do manufacturers close down their assembly lines? Do all churches, businesses, governmental structures, and community groups simply evaporate?

In 1999, two years before 9/11, the Gilmore Commission pressed a point it considered "self-evident," but one that nonetheless required "reiteration" because of the "rhetoric and hyperbole" surrounding the issue: although a terrorist attack with a weapon of mass destruction could be "serious and potentially catastrophic," it is "highly unlikely that it could ever completely undermine the national security, much less threaten the survival, of the United States." To hold otherwise "risks surrendering to the fear and intimidation that is precisely the terrorist's stock in trade."[18] The fact that terrorists subsequently managed to ram airplanes into three buildings on a sunny September morning does not render this point less sound.

Most important for present purposes, it seems likely that any notion that the actual al-Qaeda enemy could come up with nuclear weapons is far-fetched in the extreme. As Carle warns, "We must not take fright at the specter our leaders have exaggerated. In fact, we must see jihadists for the small, lethal, disjointed and miserable opponents that they are." Al-Qaeda "has only a handful of individuals capable of planning, organizing and leading a terrorist organization," and although they have threatened attacks with nuclear weapons, "its capabilities are far inferior to its desires."[19]

Indeed, despite the occasional huffing and puffing of its leaders and spokesmen over the years, one might wonder whether al-Qaeda even "desires" to set off an atomic explosion—or attack the United States at home at all. Although there have been plenty of terrorist attacks in the world since 2001, all (thus far, at least) have relied on conventional destructive methods. There has not even been the occasional gas bomb, not even in Iraq where the technology is hardly much of a secret—Saddam Hussein's government had extensively used chemical weapons in the past. It was in 1996 that one of the gurus in terrorism studies, Walter Laqueur, assured the world that some terrorist groups "almost certainly" will use weapons of mass destruction "in the foreseeable future."[20] Presumably, any future foreseeable in 1996 is now history, but in contrast to that confident assertion, terrorists in effect seem to be heeding the advice found in a memo on an al-Qaeda laptop seized in Pakistan in 2004: "Make use of that which is available . . . rather than waste valuable time becoming despondent over that which is not within your reach"—that is, keep it simple, stupid.[21]

And, in fact, it seems to be a general historical regularity that terrorists tend to prefer weapons that they know and understand, not new exotic ones. Indeed, the truly notable innovation for terrorists over the last few decades has not been in qualitative improvements in ordnance at all, but rather in a more effective method for delivering it: the suicide bomber.

REACTING TO THE THREAT

There are, then, several key facts for the American public to consider in evaluating how to respond to the terrorism challenge:

- There have been no al-Qaeda attacks whatsoever in the United States since 2001.

- No true al-Qaeda cell (nor scarcely anybody who might even be deemed to have a "connection" to the diabolical group) has been unearthed in the country.

- The homegrown "plotters" who have been apprehended, while perhaps potentially somewhat dangerous at least in a few cases, have mostly been flaky or almost absurdly incompetent.

- The total number of people killed worldwide by al-Qaeda types, maybes, and wannabes outside of war zones since 9/11 stands at some three hundred or fewer a year. Unless the terrorists are somehow able to massively increase their capacities—something that appears highly improbable—the likelihood a person living in the United States will perish at the hands of an international terrorist over an eighty-year period is about one in 75,000.

If dealing with enemies like that is this generation's (or century's) "central battle," it would seem it is likely to come out quite well.

However, the public apparently continues to remain unimpressed by this set of inconvenient observations. Polls suggest that people—or at any rate Americans—remain concerned about becoming the victims of terrorism, and the degree of worry does not seem to have changed all that much since 2001, even though no terrorism whatsoever has taken place in the country since that year.

In some respects, fear of terror may be something like playing the lottery except in reverse. The chances of winning the lottery or of dying from terrorism may be microscopic, but for monumental events that are, or seem, random, one can irrelevantly conclude that one's chances are just as good, or bad, as those of anyone else. Cass Sunstein labels the phenomenon "probability neglect." He argues, "When their emotions are intensely engaged, people's attention is focused on the bad outcome itself, and they are inattentive to the fact that it is unlikely to occur."[22]

The public appears to have chosen, then, to wallow in a false sense of insecurity (to apply a phrase suggested by the philosopher Leif Wenar), and it apparently plans to continue to do so. Accordingly, it will likely also presumably continue to demand that its leaders pay due deference to its insecurities and will uncritically approve as huge amounts of money are shelled out in a quixotic and mostly symbolic effort to assuage those insecurities.

In response to this apparent demand, something that might be called the "terrorism industry" has sprung up. This group consists of politicians, bureaucrats, journalists, and risk entrepreneurs who benefit in one way or another from exacerbating anxieties about terrorism.

Politicians and bureaucrats find it—or believe it—expedient to exaggerate and to inflate, desperate not to be thought soft on terrorism, and the interactive, if somewhat paradoxical, process is crisply described by Ian Lustick: the government "can never make enough progress toward 'protecting America' to reassure Americans against the fears it is helping to stoke."[23]

The media also play an important role. As has often been noted, the media appear to have a congenital incapacity for dealing with issues of risk and comparative probabilities—except, of course, in the sports and financial sections.

Risk entrepreneurs form the final layer of the terrorism industry. The monied response to 9/11 has swelled their ranks, and its members would be out of business if terrorism were to be back-burnered. Accordingly, they have every competitive incentive (and they are nothing if not competitive) to conclude it to be their civic duty to keep the pot boiling. As "a rising tide lifts all boats," suggests Lustick, "an intractable fear nourishes all schemes." And as it turns out, many of the agile risk entrepreneurs just happen to have stuff to sell, such as data mining software, antiradiation drugs, detention center bed space, and cargo inspection systems. Moreover, notes Jeffrey Rosen, dependent as they are on public acceptance for status and recognition, terrorism experts have an "incentive to exaggerate risks and pander to public fears."[24] Like other members of the terrorism industry, then, they are truly virtuosic at pouring out, and poring over, worst-case scenarios—or "worst-case fantasies," as military strategist Bernard Brodie once labeled them in a different context. The result of the process, as Bart Kosko points out, is a situation in which "government plays safe by overestimating the terrorist threat, while the terrorists oblige by overestimating their power."[25]

As the subtext (or sometimes the text) of the hysterical warnings persistently generated by the terrorism industry suggests, any "existential" threat comes not from what terrorists would do to us Americans, but what we would do to ourselves in response. The suggestion is that it is not only the most-feared terrorists who are suicidal.

Ultimately, then, the enemy, in fact, is us. Thus far at least, terrorism is a rather rare and, appropriately considered, not generally a terribly destructive phenomenon. But there is a danger that the terrorism industry's congenital (if self-serving and profitable) hysteria could become at least somewhat self-fulfilling should extensive further terrorism be visited upon the Home of the Brave. As military analyst William Arkin points out forcefully, although terrorists cannot destroy America, "every time we pretend we are fighting for our survival we not only confer greater power and importance to terrorists than they deserve but we also at the same time act as their main recruiting agent by suggesting that they have the slightest potential for success."[26]

Indeed, counterterrorism policies have been adopted that have been far more costly than anything the terrorists have done, or are likely ever to become capable of doing. Put differently, the physical, psychic, and economic costs of terrorism arise less from terrorist explosions than from the fear and from the hasty, ill-considered, expensive, and overwrought responses that terrorism too often inspires. The economic costs of the reaction to the 9/11 attacks have been much higher than those inflicted by the terrorists even in that record-shattering episode, and considerably more than three thousand Americans have died because, out of fear, they drove in cars rather than flew in airplanes, or because they were swept into wars made politically possible by the terrorist events. Moreover, as terrorist kingpin and devil *du jour* Osama bin Laden has gleefully noted, fear, alarmism, and overreaction suit the terrorists' agenda just fine because they create the damaging consequences the terrorists seek but are unable to perpetrate on their own.

All societies are "vulnerable" to tiny bands of suicidal fanatics in the sense that it is impossible to prevent every terrorist act. But the United States is hardly "vulnerable" in the sense that it can be toppled by dramatic acts of terrorist destruction, even extreme ones. A key element in a policy toward terrorism, therefore, should be to control, to deal with, or at least to productively worry about the fear and overreaction that terrorism so routinely inspires and that generally constitutes its most damaging effect.

NO:
The threat is profound and will remain so for some time
Walter Laqueur, *Center for Strategic and International Studies*

The Risks of Underestimating the Threat of Terrorism

More than eight years have passed since the twin towers fell in New York City and the United States declared its global "war on terrorism."[27] The president who spearheaded the initial phases of this endeavor has since left office, and a new president from another party is now in the White House.

Terrorism, nonetheless, remains high atop the national and international agenda and the subject of ceaseless comment and controversy. It also remains one of the most emotionally charged topics of public debate, though quite why this should be the case is not entirely clear, because the overwhelming majority of participants do not sympathize with terrorism.

Confusion prevails, but confusion alone does not explain the emotions. There is always confusion when a new international phenomenon appears on the scene. This was the case, for example, when communism first appeared, and also fascism. But terrorism is not an unprecedented phenomenon; it has been around since as far back as recorded history.

Sometimes, terrorism has wrought tremendous global tribulations, even sparking great wars such as World War I. At other times, it has receded into the background noise of world politics.

Something of a cottage industry has formed of late, mainly in academic departments, urging a wholesale reevaluation of terrorism; the thinking goes that the threat of terrorism is overblown and being overhyped. Some point out that death by lightning strike is far more likely than death by terrorism.

That may be true, but if a lightning strike was substituted with a devastating attack on a major Western city, perhaps with a weapon of mass destruction, the ramifications would be profound, likely altering the course of human history.

This is not to overstate the threat, merely to point out the costs of understatement.

In any event, it is quite fair to ask: what is the current state of the terrorist threat, and is it being assessed correctly? Misdiagnosing the threat almost certainly means misapplying the responses.

To best understand present and future challenges, one must first try to make sense of the traditional misunderstandings that have prevailed in the study of terrorism, a field as beholden to passion, emotion, and confusion as any other.

PASSIONATE MISCONCEPTIONS OVER ROOT CAUSES

Some of the misunderstandings about the nature of terrorism are rooted in ideology. In the 1970s, when terrorism was predominantly left wing in inspiration—or at least in rhetoric—it was probably not surprising that commentators belonging to the same political persuasion would produce explanations that were, at the very least, not unsympathetic as far as the terrorists were concerned. Thus it was argued that terrorism always occurred when there was intolerable oppression, social or national, and that the terrorists had genuine, legitimate grievances. Thus the conclusion was that if these grievances were eradicated, terrorism would also disappear.

Terrorism was seen as a revolutionary phenomenon; it was carried out by poor and desperate human beings and therefore had to be confronted with sympathetic understanding.

The argument stressing the left-wing character of terrorism is no longer widely heard except perhaps among members of certain sects trying to establish a popular front with Islamists in whom sect members see a powerful ally in the struggle against imperialism, even if they do not agree with the Islamists' fundamentalist doctrine, which they may find primitive and sometimes embarrassing. But the belief in a fatal link between poverty and violence has persisted. Whenever a major terrorist attack takes place, one hears appeals from high and low to provide financial help, to deal at long last with the "true causes of terrorism," the "roots" rather than their symptoms and outward manifestations. And these roots are believed to be poverty, unemployment, backwardness, and inequality.

As developed earlier in this volume, investigations have shown that poverty does not cause terrorism and prosperity does not cure it. Most terrorists are not poor and do not come from poor societies. In the Indian subcontinent, terrorism has occurred in the most prosperous (Punjab) and the most egalitarian (Kashmir) regions. By contrast, the poorest regions such as North Bihar have been relatively free of terrorism. In Arab countries such as Egypt and Saudi Arabia and also in North Africa, the terrorists have originated not in the poorest and most neglected districts, but from places with concentrations of radical preachers. The backwardness, if any, has been intellectual and cultural, not economic and social.

These findings have had only a limited impact on public opinion and politicians, and it is not difficult to see why there has been resistance to accepting them. There is the general feeling that poverty and backwardness are bad and that there is an urgent need to do more about them.

Reducing poverty in the developing world may be a moral as well as a political and economic imperative, but to expect decisive change from it in the foreseeable future as far as terrorism is concerned is unrealistic. Such an expectation ignores both the causes of backwardness and poverty and the motives for terrorism. Poverty combined with youth unemployment does create a social and psychological climate in which Islamism and various populists and religious sects flourish. That climate, in turn, provides some of the foot folk for violent groups in internal conflicts. According to some projections, the number of young unemployed in the Arab world and North Africa could reach fifty million in less than two decades.

Such a situation will not be conducive to political stability. It will increase the demographic pressure on Europe, because, according to polls, a majority of these young people want to emigrate there. Politically, the populist discontent will be directed against the rulers—the Islamists in Iran and the moderates in countries such as Egypt, Jordan, or Morocco. But how to help the failed economies of the Middle East and North Africa? What are the reasons for the backwardness and stagnation in that part of the world? The countries that have made substantial economic progress, such as China and India, South Korea and Taiwan, Malaysia and Turkey, did so without massive foreign assistance.

All of this points to a deep malaise and even an impending danger, but not to a direct link between the economic situation and international terrorism. There is a negative correlation: terrorists will not hesitate to bring about a further aggravation in the situation by, for example, causing great harm to the tourist industries in North Africa, Egypt, and Bali. Terrorism has spread to the Maldives in the Indian Ocean not because of poverty (it has the highest per capita gross national product in South East Asia thanks to its tourism industry), but because Islamic preachers of violence were permitted to act freely. One of the main targets of terrorism in Iraq has been the oil industry.

Sometimes it is argued that resolving religious, nationalist, and ethnic grievances would eradicate terrorism. If the issue at stake is the conflict over a certain territory or the demand for more autonomy, a compromise through negotiations seems a possibility. But recall that al-Qaeda was founded and 9/11 occurred not because of a territorial dispute or the feeling of national oppression but because of a religious commandment—the establishment of *sharia* through jihad.

As in the war against poverty, the initiatives to solve local conflicts are over-due and should be welcomed. Easing these conflicts would probably bring about a certain reduction in the incidence of terrorism. But the conflicts are many, and even if some of them have been defused in recent years, new ones have emerged. Nor are the issues usually clear-cut or the bones of contention easy to define—let alone solve.

And there should be no illusions about the wider effects of a peaceful solution of one conflict on another. To give but one obvious example: peace (or at least the absence of war) between Israel and the Palestinians would be a blessing for those concerned. However, the assumption that the solution of a local conflict (even one of great symbolic importance) would have a dramatic effect in other parts of the world is unfounded. Osama bin Laden did not go to war because of Gaza and Nablus; he did not send his warriors to fight in Palestine. Even the disappearance of the "Zionist entity" would not have a significant impact on his supporters, except perhaps to provide encouragement for further action.

Such a warning against illusions is called for because there is much wishful thinking and naïveté in this respect—a belief in quick fixes and miracle solutions. Some say, if only there could be peace between Israelis and Palestinians, all the other conflicts would become manageable. But the problems are as much in Europe, Asia, and Africa as in the Middle East; there is a great deal of free-floating aggression that could (and probably would) easily turn in other directions once one conflict has been defused.

Tackling these supposed sources of terrorism, even for the wrong reasons, will do no harm and may bring some good. But it will not bring analysts any closer to a comprehensive understanding of the sources of terrorism, let alone a capacity to respond effectively.

NATURE OF THE THREAT: NOW AND INTO THE FUTURE

It is always risky to make predictions about the future of terrorism, even more so than about political trends in general. It is certain, however, that terrorism will not disappear from the earth: at a time when full-scale war has become too dangerous and too expensive, terrorism has become the prevailing mode of conflict. As long as conflict persists among groups of human beings, so will terrorism.

Today, nearly all attention is focused on Islamic terrorism, but it is useful to remember from time to time that this has not always been the case—even less than thirty years ago—and that a great many conflicts, perceived oppressions, and other causes are calling for radical action in the world, which also may lead to terrorism in the years to come. These need not be even major conflicts in an era in which small groups will have access to weapons of mass destruction.

Islamic terrorism has certainly not yet run its full course, but it is unlikely that its present fanaticism will last forever; religious-nationalist fervor does not constantly burn with the same intensity. There is a phenomenon known in Egypt as "Salafi burnout," the mellowing of radical young people, the weakening of the original fanatical impetus. Like all other movements in history, messianic groups are subject to routinization, to the circulation of generations, to changing political circumstances, and to sudden or gradual changes in religious belief. This could happen as the result of either victory or defeat. One day it might be possible to appease militant Islamism—though hardly in a period of burning aggression when confidence and faith in global victory have not yet been broken.

The terrorist impetus is likely to decline as the result of setbacks. Attacks will continue, some will be crowned with success, perhaps spectacular success, but many will not. When Alfred Nobel invented dynamite many terrorists thought that it was the answer to their prayers. But theirs was a false hope. The trust put today in that invincible weapon suicide terrorism may in the end be equally misplaced. Even the use of weapons of mass destruction might not be the panacea some terrorists believe it will be. Perhaps the effect of such a weapon will be less deadly than anticipated, perhaps it will be so destructive as to be considered counterproductive. Statistics show that in the terrorist attacks over the past decade, considerably more Muslims were killed than infidels. Because terrorists do not operate in a vacuum, this situation is bound to lead to dissent among their followers and even among the fanatical preachers.

In brief, a united terrorist front, if ever established, may not last. It is unlikely that bin Laden and his close followers will be frontally challenged on theological or ideological grounds, but there has been criticism for political and tactical reasons such as the attacks against Muslim civilians, both Sunni and Shiite, and the failure to anticipate the massive retaliation of the West following the attacks of 9/11.

Some leading students of Islam have argued that radical Islamism reached its peak years ago and that its downfall and disappearance are only a question of time, perhaps not much time. Although some societies have been exposed to the rule of fundamentalist fanatics (such as Iran) or to radical Islamist attacks (such as Algeria), many Muslim countries have yet to undergo such first-hand experience; for them, *sharia* rule and the restoration of the caliphate are still brilliant dreams.

These, then, are the likely perspectives for the more distant future. But in a shorter-term perspective the danger remains acute and may, in fact, grow. Where and when are terrorist attacks most likely to occur? They will not necessarily be directed against the greatest and most dangerous enemy perceived by the terrorist leaders. Much depends on where the terrorists are strong and believe the enemy to be weak. That terrorist attacks are likely to continue in the Middle East goes without saying; other primary danger zones are central Asia, particularly Pakistan, and, more recently, nearly all of Western Europe.

Pakistan certainly remains at risk. Its madrassas continue to serve as breeding grounds for jihad fighters, and radical leaders can count on certain sympathies in the army and intelligence services. A failed Pakistan with nuclear weapons at its disposal would be a major nightmare.

Yet Europe is perhaps the most vulnerable battlefield, having become over the years the main base of terrorist support groups from the Middle East, North Africa, and Pakistan. This process has been facilitated by the growth of Muslim communities (and growing tensions with the local population), which have provided a reservoir of new recruits. The freedom of action for radicals to organize and indoctrinate in Western Europe is considerably greater than in the Arab and Muslim world. True, there were some arrests and closer controls after the events of 9/11 and the attacks in Madrid and London, but because of the legal and political restrictions under which European security services labor, effective counteraction remains exceedingly difficult.

For decades, Western European governments have been frequently criticized for not doing enough to integrate Muslim communities, but cultural and social integration are not what many immigrants want, and their preachers have constantly warned against it. Immigrants have wanted to preserve their political, cultural, and religious identities and their ways of life, and have resented interference by secular authorities. And yet the vast majority of first-generation immigrants simply wanted to live in peace and quiet and make a living for their families. But today they no longer have much control over their more radical offspring.

The radicalization of second-generation immigrants is a common phenomenon in general, and is certainly the case in Western Europe. This generation has been superficially acculturated, speaking fluently the language of the land, and yet feeling resentment and hostility more acutely. It is not necessarily the power of the fundamentalist message that inspires many of the younger radical activists or sympathizers; they are by no means the most pious believers when it comes to carrying out all the religious commandments. The British suicide bombers in 2005, for example, were not known for their religious orthodoxy; most of them did not pray regularly. Rather, it is the feeling of deep resentment because, unlike immigrants from other parts of the world, Muslim immigrants in Europe often find themselves unable to compete successfully in the classroom or the workplace. Feelings of being excluded, sexual repression (a taboo subject in this context), and other factors have led to free-floating aggression and higher rates of criminal behavior directed against the authorities and the neighbors.

As a result, non-Muslims in Europe have felt threatened in the streets they could once walk without fear. They have come to regard the new immigrants as antisocial elements who wanted to impose on non-Muslim Europeans their way of life. Pressure on the European governments has been growing from all sides, right and left, to stop immigration and restore law and order.

This, in brief, is the milieu in which Islamist terrorism and terrorist support groups in Western Europe have developed. There is little reason to assume that this trend will change fundamentally in the near future. On the contrary, the more the young generation of immigrants asserts itself, the more violence occurs in the streets, and the more terrorist attacks take place, the greater will be the anti-Muslim resentment of the rest of the population. The rapid demographic growth of the Muslim communities further strengthens the impression among original residents that they are being deprived of their rights in their own homeland, not even entitled to speak the truth about the prevailing situation (such as revealing how many prison inmates have Muslim backgrounds). Thus violent reactions to Muslims are on view in even the most liberal European countries such as the Netherlands, Belgium, and Denmark.

True, the number of extremists is still quite small. Among British Muslims, fewer than 20 percent have expressed sympathy and support for terrorist attacks. But this percentage still translates into several hundred thousand, far more than is needed for staging a terrorist campaign. Furthermore, such statistics do not take into account the growth of Muslim communities and Western Europe's continuing need for immigrants because of their low and declining birthrates. There is already great pressure on southern and western Europe to absorb the growing legions of unemployed in North Africa and the Middle East.

If acculturation and integration have been a failure in the short run, prospects are less hopeless from a long-term perspective. Young Muslims cannot be kept forever in hermetically sealed ghettos, even if their preachers make a valiant effort to do so. The young people are disgusted and repelled by alcohol, loose morals, general decadence, and all the other wickedness of the society surrounding them—as indoctrinated by their preachers—but at the same time they are fascinated and attracted by them. As one Berlin imam put it: the road to the mosque is long, and the temptations are many. This environment is bound to affect young people's activist fervor, and they will be exposed to not only the negative aspects of the society around them but also its values. Other religions had to face these temptations over the ages and often fought a losing battle.

It is frequently forgotten that only a relatively short period passed from the primitive beginnings of Islam in the Arabian Desert to the splendor and luxury (and learning and poetry) of Harun al-Rashid's Baghdad—from the austerity of the Qur'an to the not-so-austere Arabian Nights. The pulse of contemporary history is beating much faster, but is it beating fast enough? For it is a race against time. The advent of megaterrorism and the access to weapons of mass destruction are dangerous enough, but coupled with fanaticism they generate scenarios unpleasant even to contemplate.

RESPONDING TO THE THREAT

There can never be a final victory in the fight against terrorism, for terrorism (rather than full-scale war) is the contemporary manifestation of conflict, and conflict will not disappear from earth as far as one can look ahead.

But the history of counterterrorism does offer certain lessons, and it will be within the power of policymakers to make life for terrorists and potential terrorists much more difficult.

I have always felt uneasy about the term *war on terrorism*. Obviously, the military needs to play certain roles in this context, especially when dealing with countries that have failed to function and have become terrorist havens. The military may also be needed to deliver blows against terrorist concentrations. But these are not the most typical or frequent terrorist situations, and the military's role must remain limited.

As far as terrorism is concerned, there can be no overall military doctrine similar to the regular warfare philosophy developed by Clausewitz, Jomini, and others. An airplane or a battleship does not change its character wherever it operates, but the character of terrorism depends largely on the motivations of those engaging in it and the conditions under which it takes place. In this age of asymmetric warfare, the key response roles should be played by the intelligence and security services, which may sometimes only require the assistance of relatively small specialized military units.

The fact is, the use of massive force is frequently unpopular at home and, in any event, will be applied only in extreme cases when the core interests of the state are involved. To give but one example, the Russian government could deport the Chechens (or a significant proportion), thereby solving its problem with them in a Stalinist style. If the Chechens were to threaten Moscow or St. Petersburg or the fuel supply of the Russian state, there is little doubt but that such measures would be taken. But as long as the threat remains marginal and peripheral, the price to be paid for the application of massive force will be considered too high.

So what about softer power? Its utility ought to be maximized, and may be important in some cases, but it has its limitations as well. Joseph Nye has described soft power as based on culture and political ideas as influenced by the seductiveness of democracy, human rights, and individual opportunity. This is a powerful argument, and it is true that Washington has seldom used all its opportunities: the public diplomacy budget is about one-quarter of one percentage point of the defense budget.

But the question to be asked is: how seductive are Western values and ideas in the Muslim world? Cultural propaganda (public diplomacy) had an effect in Europe and even behind the Iron Curtain during the Cold War. But soft power will have no impact on radical Islamists who abhor democracy, who believe that human rights and tolerance are imperialist inventions, and who do not want any ideas circulating except those that appear in the Qur'an—as they interpret it.

At a minimum, Western radio and television would have to be beamed to an audience of which 70 percent firmly believes that the 9/11 attacks were carried out by the Israeli Mossad. Such an audience will not be impressed by exposure to Western pop culture or a truthful, matter-of-fact coverage of the news.

The why-do-they-hate-us question can be raised in this context, along with the question of what could be done about it. Disturbing figures have been published about the low (and falling) popularity of America abroad. Yet it is too often forgotten that international relations is not a popularity contest and that since the days of the Assyrians and the Roman Empire powerful countries have always been feared, resented, and envied; in short, they have not been loved. Neither the Ottoman nor the Spanish empires, neither the Chinese nor the Russian empires were ever popular. British sports were emulated in the colonies, and the French culture impressed the local elites in North Africa and Indochina, but the emulation did not lead to political support, let alone identification with the rulers. Had there been public opinion polls in the days of Alexander the Great (let alone Ghengis Khan), the results, one suspects, would have been quite negative.

Big powers will never be loved, but in the terrorist context it is essential that they be respected. As bin Laden's declarations prior to 9/11 show, it was lack of respect for America that made him launch his attacks. He felt certain that the risk he was running was small, for the United States was a paper tiger, lacking both the will and the capability to strike back. After all, after only a few attacks the Americans ran from Beirut in the 1980s and from Mogadishu in 1993, and there was every reason to believe that they would do so again.

ADAPTING TO THE RULES OF THE GAME: OPPORTUNITIES AND CHALLENGES

In contemplating a response to terrorism, it is most important to remember that terrorists abide by no doctrine other than that which they believe to be effective, whereas states largely adhere to the rules and laws of war that have been developed over centuries. Terrorists cannot possibly accept these rules. It would be suicidal from their point of view if, to give but one example, they were to wear uniforms or other distinguishing marks. The essence of their operations rests on hiding their identities. On the other hand, they and their well-wishers insist that when captured, they should enjoy all the rights and benefits accorded to belligerents, that they be humanely treated and released after the end of hostilities.

When regular soldiers do not stick to the rules of warfare, killing or maiming prisoners, carrying out massacres, taking hostages, or committing crimes against the civilian population, they will be treated as war criminals. If terrorists obeyed these norms, they would have little if any chance of success; the essence of today's terrorist operations is indiscriminate attacks against civilians. But governments defending themselves against terrorism are widely expected not to behave in a similar way but to adhere to international law as it developed in conditions quite different from those prevailing today.

Terrorism does not accept laws and rules, whereas governments are bound by them. This, in briefest outline, is asymmetric warfare. If any government were to behave in a similar way, not feeling bound by existing rules and laws such as those against the killing of prisoners, it would be bitterly denounced. When Syrian president Hafez Assad faced an insurgency (and an attempted assassination) by the Muslim Brotherhood in the city of Hama in 1980, his soldiers massacred some twenty thousand inhabitants. This put an end to all ideas of terrorism and guerrilla warfare in Syria.

Such behavior on the part of democratic governments would be denounced as barbaric, a relapse into the practices of long-gone precivilized days. But if governments accept the principle of asymmetric warfare, they will be severely, possibly fatally, handicapped. They cannot accept that terrorists are protected by the Geneva Conventions, which would mean, among other things, that they should be paid a salary while in captivity.

The problem will not arise if the terrorist group is small and not very dangerous. In this case, normal legal procedures will be sufficient to deal with the problem (but even this is not quite certain as weapons of mass destruction become more readily accessible). Nor will the issue of shedding legal restraint arise if the issues at stake are of marginal importance—if, in other words, no

core interests of the governments involved are concerned. But if the very survival of a society is at stake, it is most unlikely that governments will be
impeded in their defense by laws and norms belonging to a bygone (and more
humane) age.

Antiterrorist action in the West is an obstacle race, not so much because of
the ingenuity of the terrorists but because of the very nature of democratic
societies. Many terrorists or suspected terrorists have been detained in America
and in Europe, but only a handful have been put on trial and convicted because
inadmissible evidence was submitted or the authorities were reluctant to reveal
the sources of their information. As a result, many who were almost certainly
involved in terrorist operations were never arrested, while others were acquitted or released from detention.

As for those who are still detained, there have been loud protests against the
violation of their elementary human rights. Activists have argued that the real
danger is not terrorism (the extent and the consequences of which, they say,
have been greatly exaggerated) but the war against terrorism. Should free societies so easily give up their freedoms, which have been fought for and achieved
over many centuries?

Some scholars have foretold the coming of fascism in America (and to a
lesser extent in Europe); others have predicted an authoritarian regime gradually introduced by governments cleverly exploiting the present situation for
their own antidemocratic purposes. And it is quite likely indeed that among
those detained there have been and are innocent people and that some of the
controls introduced have interfered with human rights. However, there is
much reason to think that to combat terrorism effectively considerably more
stringent measures will be needed than those presently in force.

But these measures can be adopted only if there is overwhelming public support, and it would be unwise even to try to push them through until the learning process about the danger of terrorism in an age of weapons of mass
destruction has made further progress. Time will tell. If devastating attacks do
not occur, stringent antiterrorist measures will not be necessary. But if they do
happen, the demand for effective countermeasures will be overwhelming. One
could perhaps argue that further limitations of freedom are bound to be ineffective because terrorist groups are likely to be small or very small in the future
and therefore likely to slip through safety nets. This is indeed a danger—but
the advice to abstain from safety measures is a counsel of despair unlikely to be
accepted.

It could well be that, as far as the recent past is concerned, the danger of terrorism has been overstated. In World Wars I and II, more people were killed
and more material damage was sustained on certain days than through a

decade of terrorist attacks. I said as much in my *History of Terrorism* written in the 1970s, and it is certainly flattering to find this insight rediscovered three decades later. But I also noted that our societies are becoming more vulnerable and far more sensitive to the loss of life. The real issue at stake is not the attacks of the past but the coming dangers. Megaterrorism has not yet arrived; even 9/11 was a stage in between traditional terrorism and the shape of things to come: the use of weapons of mass destruction.

For the first time in human history, very small groups have, or will have, not just the motivation but also the potential to cause immense destruction. There will continue to be small groups of terrorists who will be interested in negotiated settlements, satisfied with less than the annihilation of the enemy. But there will be always more radical elements eager to continue the struggle. They are not necessarily rational actors, and their motivation may not be political but apocalyptic.

Perhaps this scenario is too pessimistic; perhaps the weapons of mass destruction, for whatever reason, will never be used. But it would be the first time in human history that such arms, once invented, had not been used.

In 1932, when Albert Einstein attempted to induce Sigmund Freud to support pacifism, Freud replied that there was no likelihood of suppressing humanity's aggressive tendencies. If there was any reason for hope, it was that people would turn away on rational grounds—that war had become too destructive, that it was no longer an endeavor of honor based on the old ideals.

Freud was partly correct: war (at least between great powers) has become far less likely for rational reasons. But his argument does not apply to terrorism motivated not mainly by political or economic interests, based not just on aggression but also on fanaticism with an admixture of madness.

Terrorism, therefore, will continue—not perhaps with the same intensity at all times, and some parts of the globe may be spared altogether. But there can be no victory, only an uphill struggle, sometimes successful, at other times not.

Notes

1. John Mueller, *Overblown* (New York: Free Press, 2006).
2. Jeffrey Rosen, "Man-Made Disaster," *New Republic,* December 24, 2008.
3. "All the Time He Needs," *New York Times,* April 16, 2008. For the McCain quotes, see, for example, "In Florida, Rivals Focus on Economy and Security," *New York Times,* January 28, 2008; and "Obama Leads McCain in Four Key Battleground States," *Washington Post,* June 26, 2008.
4. Michael Scheuer, *Imperial Hubris: Why the West Is Losing the War on Terror* (Dulles, Va.: Brassey's, 2004).

5. Glenn L. Carle, "Overstating Our Fears," *Washington Post,* July 13, 2008.

6. Fawaz A. Gerges, *The Far Enemy: Why Jihad Went Global* (New York: Cambridge University Press, 2005). Also see Gerges's essay in Chapter 4 of this volume.

7. Marc Sageman, *Leaderless Jihad* (Philadelphia: University of Pennsylvania Press, 2008). See also David Ignatius, "The Fading Jihadists," *Washington Post,* February 28, 2008.

8. Lawrence Wright, "The Rebellion Within," *New Yorker,* June 2, 2008.

9. Anthony H. Cordesman, *The Challenge of Biological Weapons* (Washington, D.C.: Center for Strategic and International Studies, 2005), 29–32; Brian Michael Jenkins, *Unconquerable Nation: Knowing Our Enemies and Strengthening Ourselves* (Santa Monica, Calif.: RAND, 2006), 179–184; IntelCenter, "Jihadi Attack Kill Statistics," Alexandria, Va., August 17, 2007, 11.

10. Gerges, *Far Enemy.*

11. Peter Bergen, "Where You Bin? The Return of Al Qaeda," *New Republic,* January 29, 2007.

12. Guy Lawson, "The Fear Factory," *Rolling Stone,* February 7, 2008.

13. On this issue, see Theodore Rockwell, "Radiation Chicken Little," *Washington Post,* September 16, 2003.

14. See also John Mueller, *Atomic Obsession: Nuclear Alarmism from Hiroshima to Al Qaeda* (New York: Oxford University Press, 2010).

15. Gilmore Commission (Advisory Panel to Assess Domestic Response Capabilities for Terrorism Involving Weapons of Mass Destruction), "First Annual Report: Assessing the Threat," RAND, Santa Monica, Calif., December 15, 1999; Christoph Wirz and Emmanuel Egger, "Use of Nuclear and Radiological Weapons by Terrorists?" *International Review of the Red Cross,* September 2005, www.icrc.org/Web/eng/siteeng0.nsf/htmlall/review-859-p497/$File/i rrc_859_Egger_Wirz.pdf.

16. Wirz and Egger, "Use of Nuclear and Radiological Weapons."

17. Robert Mueller, testimony before the Senate Select Committee on Intelligence, 110th Cong., 1st sess., January 11, 2007.

18. Gilmore Commission, "First Annual Report."

19. Carle, "Overstating Our Fears."

20. Walter Laqueur, "Postmodern Terrorism: New Rules for an Old Game," *Foreign Affairs* 75 (September/October 1996).

21. Craig Whitlock, "Homemade, Cheap and Dangerous," *Washington Post,* July 5, 2007.

22. Cass R. Sunstein, "Terrorism and Probability Neglect," *Journal of Risk and Uncertainty* (March–May 2003).

23. Ian S. Lustick, *Trapped in the War on Terror* (Philadelphia: University of Pennsylvania Press, 2006).

24. Jeffrey Rosen, *The Naked Crowd* (New York: Random House, 2004).

25. Bart Kosko, "Terror Threat May Be Mostly a Big Bluff," *Los Angeles Times,* September 13, 2004.

26. William Arkin, "Early Warning" blog, *Washington Post,* January 26, 2006.

27. This essay is adapted in part from Walter Laqueur, "The Terrorism to Come," *Policy Review* (August/September 2004): 49–64.

ABOUT THE AUTHOR

Stuart Gottlieb is director of policy studies at the MacMillan Center for International and Area Studies at Yale University, where he teaches advanced courses on American foreign policy and counterterrorism. He formerly served as a senior foreign policy advisor and speechwriter in the United States Senate (1999–2003), and continues to advise political and business leaders on issues relating to foreign policy and terrorism. Gottlieb received his Ph.D. in international relations from Columbia University, and is an Adjunct Professor at Columbia University's School of International and Public Affairs.